Thought
in
Prose

Thought

in

SECOND EDITION

Prose

edited by

RICHARD S. BEAL
Boston University

JACOB KORG
University of Washington

PRENTICE-HALL, INC.
Englewood Cliffs, N. J.

LIBRARY OF CONGRESS CATALOG CARD NO.:
62–9282

PRINTED IN THE UNITED STATES OF AMERICA
92001–C

First printing .... February, 1962
Second printing .... August, 1962
Third printing .... January, 1963
Fourth printing .... June, 1963
Fifth printing .... October, 1963

Preface

Although this second edition of *Thought in Prose* contains thirty new selections and makes some changes in the groupings of original selections, it follows the same principles which guided the first edition. That writing is the main business of freshman English seems to us beyond dispute. But we believe that learning to write well cannot be divorced from reading a variety of good prose or from developing an inquiring mind. The carefully planned selection which an anthology can provide continues to seem to us one of the best means of bringing before the student the kind of controlled variety which will encourage him to examine his own experience and ideas, to be receptive to the experience and ideas of others, and to be aware of the uses to which skilled writers put language.

We have kept to the organization of the first edition, moving in general from autobiographical, descriptive, and relatively simple expository selections to more complex expository problems and evaluations. In the early selections we have tried to provide readings which will encourage the student to examine and draw upon his own experience and observation, help him see something of the variety of language in the hands of skilled writers, and demonstrate the need for interpretation, organization, and unity in all writing. In those essays which deal substantively with language and thinking we have sought selections pointing up matters applicable to the student's own writing. Throughout, we have kept our original emphasis on closely related groups of selections which provide contexts for the individual essay, offering a total of seventeen such groups within the six major divisions of the whole. Such contexts, we believe, are provocative of a wide variety of both rhetorical and thematic comparisons, although we think of them as guiding suggestions only, realizing that to many instructors other patterns and lines of relationship will seem more apt to their intention.

In all selections we have tried to find expository prose of high quality, varied in style and difficulty, and representative of various rhetorical methods and aims, but consistently within the serious student's understanding. Except in a few instances we have preferred the experienced and skilled writer as writer—the artist, the historian, the critic, the philosopher addressing laymen—to the social scientist or other specialist. As in the first edition, we have emphasized selections ranging from two to four thousand words. Such a length offers the student something he can grasp as a whole at a single assignment and seems more likely to suggest usable writing techniques to him. It also makes practical the use of many of the selections for the study of types and rhetorical methods, if the instructor wishes to use them in this way. Finally, the length of the selections makes realistically possible the serious comparison of several pieces comparable or contrasting in form and theme. Pieces of this length continue to constitute about 60 per cent of the anthology, the remaining selections being about equally divided between longer and shorter pieces.

At the end of each selection are brief suggestions for discussion, rhetorical analysis, and writing. In the first appendix, we have included a discussion of methods and aims of prose, together with lists of selections particularly useful in teaching the several methods and aims. Thus, the instructor who prefers this approach or wishes to use it as an occasional supplement to other approaches may easily do so. Brief biographical notes are provided in the second appendix. Considerably more elaborate apparatus, noting various possible interrelations among selections, commenting upon individual selections, suggesting specific assignments, and offering full lists by rhetorical types is contained in the *Editors' Notes* available to instructors.

In compiling this edition, we have replaced selections or groups of selections which have proved less successful in the classroom, whatever their other merits may have been. We have particularly reviewed the grouping of selections, relocating some of the original pieces and choosing new ones to sharpen the thematic comparisons and contrasts. We have also added three annotated selections of varying degrees of difficulty to suggest at least the tactics of the annotated paper, if not to provide precise models.

To those who aided and abetted the first edition of this text with their good advice and suggestions, our debt continues. This second edition would not have been possible without the help of many of those who have used the text in their classes and have been kind enough to call our attention to the strengths and weaknesses they found. Without their guidance this edition would be something less than it is; had we time and skill to incorporate more of their suggestions, it would surely be better than it is. We should like particularly to acknowledge our special indebtedness to Professor Stanley Johnson of Portland State College and to Professor Justin M. Replogle of the University of Wisconsin who, having used the first edition, were kind enough to give us their very thorough and completely honest reviews of its shortcomings and their most useful advice for its improvement. Finally, we owe a genuine debt to our wives, Harriette Beal and Cynthia Korg, both for their patience and for their invaluable assistance in preparing the manuscript.

R.S.B.

J.K.

Contents

vii

2. THE UNCOMMON OBSERVER

3. THE SHAPE OF REALITY

PART TWO

Language, Thought, and Ideas

PART THREE

Man in
Society

1. THE AMERICAN SCENE

PART FOUR

Popular
Culture

PART FIVE

Knowledge
and Value

3. MORAL LAW AND THE CONDUCT OF LIFE

4. RELIGIOUS BELIEF IN OUR TIME

PART SIX

On
Literature

Thought
in
Prose

PART ONE

Interpreting
Experience

1. THE EYE OF MEMORY

The Vale and the Farm*

Herbert Read

When I went to school I learned that the Vale in which we lived had once been a lake, but long ago the sea had eaten through the hills in the east and so released the fresh waters, leaving a fertile plain. But such an idea would have seemed strange to my innocent mind, so remote was this menacing sea. Our farm was towards the western end of the Vale, and because all our land was as flat as once the surface of the lake had been, we could see around us the misty hills, the Moors to the north, the Wolds to the south, meeting dimly in the east where they were more distant. This rim of hills was nearest in the south, at least in effect; for as the sun sank in the west the windows of Stamper's farm in the south caught the blazing rays and cast them back at us, continually drawing our eyes in that direction. But we never traveled so far south as those hills; for the Church and the Market, the only outer places of pilgrimage, lay to the north, five or six miles away. By habit we faced north: the south was "behind."

I seemed to live, therefore, in a basin, wide and shallow like the milk-pans in the dairy; but the even bed of it was checkered with pastures and cornfields, and the rims were the soft blues and purples of the moorlands. This basin was my world, and I had no inkling of any larger world, for no strangers came to us out of it, and we never went into it. Very rarely my Father went to York or Northallerton, to buy a piece of machinery for the farm or to serve on a jury at the Assizes; but only our vague wonder accompanied him, and the toys he brought back with him might have

* From *The Innocent Eye*, by Herbert Read. Copyright, 1947, by Herbert Read. Reprinted by permission of Harold Over Associates Incorporated.

come, like sailors' curios, from Arabia or Cathay. The basin at times was very wide, especially in the clearness of a summer's day; but as dusk fell it would suddenly contract, the misty hills would draw near, and with night they had clasped us close: the center of the world had become a candle shining from the kitchen window. Inside, in the sitting-room where we spent most of our life, a lamp was lit, with a round glass shade like a full yellow moon. There we were bathed before the fire, said our prayers kneeling on the hearthrug, and then disappeared up the steep stairs lighted by a candle to bed; and once there, the world was finally blotted out. I think it returned with the same suddenness, at least in Summer; but the waking world was a new world, a hollow cube with light streaming in from one window across to a large bed holding, as the years went by, first one, then two, and finally three boys, overseen by two Apostles from one wall and adjured from another, above a chest of drawers, by a white pottery plaque within a pink-luster frame, printed with a vignette of an angel blowing a trumpet and the words:

PRAISE YE THE LORD.

Sometimes the child's mind went on living even during the darkness of night, listening to the velvet stillness of the fields. The stillness of a sleeping town, of a village, is nothing to the stillness of a remote farm; for the peace of day in such a place is so kindly that the ear is attuned to the subtlest sounds, and time is slow. If by chance a cow should low in the night it is like the abysmal cry of some hellish beast, bringing woe to the world. And who knows what hellish beasts might roam by night, for in the cave by the Church five miles away they once found the bones of many strange animals, wolves and hyenas, and even the tusks of mammoths. The night-sound that still echoes in my mind, however, is not of this kind: it is gentler and more musical—the distant sound of horse-hooves on the highroad, at first dim and uncertain, but growing louder until they more suddenly cease. To that distant sound, I realized later, I must have come into the world, for the Doctor arrived on horseback at four o'clock one December morning to find me uttering my first shriek.

I think I heard those hooves again the night my father died, but of this I am not certain; perhaps I shall remember when I come to relate that event, for now the memory of those years, which end shortly after my tenth birthday, comes fitfully, when the proper associations are aroused. If only I can recover the sense and uncertainty of those innocent years, years in which we seemed not so much to live as to be lived by forces outside us, by the wind and trees and moving clouds and all the mobile engines of our expanding world—then I am convinced I shall possess a key to much that has happened to me in this other world of conscious living. The echoes of my life which I find in my early childhood are too many to be dismissed as vain coincidences; but it is perhaps my conscious life which is the echo, the only real experiences in life being those lived with a virgin sensibility—so that we only hear a tone once, only see a color once, see, hear, touch, taste and smell everything but once, the first time. All life is an echo of our first sensations, and we build up our consciousness, our whole mental life, by variations and combinations of these elementary sensations. But it is more complicated than that, for the senses apprehended not only colors and tones and shapes, but also patterns and atmosphere, and our first discovery of these determines the larger patterns and subtler atmospheres of all our subsequent existence.

I have given the impression that the Farm was remote, but this is not strictly true. Not half a mile on each side of us was another farmhouse, and clustering near the one to the east were three or four cottages. We formed, therefore, a little community, remote as such; in Doomsday Book we had been described as a hamlet. The nearest village was two or three miles away, but to the south, so that it did not count for much until we began to go to school, which was not until towards the end of the period of which I write. Northwards our farm road ran through two fields and then joined the highroad running east and west; but eastward this road soon turned into a road running north and south, down which we turned northwards again, to the Church five miles away, and to Kirby, our real metropolis, six miles away.

The farmhouse was a square stone box with a roof of vivid red tiles; its front was to the south, and warm enough to shelter some apricot trees against the wall. But there was no traffic that way: all our exits and entrances were made on the north side, through the kitchen; and I think even our grandest visitors did not disdain that approach. Why should they? On the left as they entered direct into the kitchen was an old oak dresser; on the right a large open fireplace, with a great iron kettle hanging from the reckan, and an oven to the near side of it. A long deal table, glistening with a honey gold sheen from much scrubbing, filled the far side of the room; long benches ran down each side of it. The floor was flagged with stone, each stone neatly outlined with a border of some softer yellow stone, rubbed on after every washing. Sides of bacon and plum dusky hams hung from the beams of the wooden ceiling.

By day it was the scene of intense bustle. The kitchenmaid was down by five o'clock to light the fire; the laborers crept down in stockinged feet and drew on their heavy boots; they lit candles in their horn lanthorns and went out to the cattle. Breakfast was at seven, dinner at twelve, tea at five. Each morning of the week had its appropriate activity: Monday was washing day, Tuesday ironing, Wednesday and Saturday baking, Thursday 'turning out' upstairs and churning, Friday 'turning out' downstairs. Every day there was the milk to skim in the dairy—the dairy was to the left of the kitchen, and as big as any other room in the house. The milk was poured into large flat pans and allowed to settle; it was skimmed with horn scoops, like toothless combs.

At dinner, according to the time of the year, there would be from five to seven farm laborers, the two servant girls, and the family, with whom, for most of the time, there was a governess—a total of from ten to fifteen mouths to feed every day. The bustle reached its height about midday; the men would come in and sit on the dresser, swinging their legs impatiently; when the food was served, they sprang to the benches and ate in solid gusto, like animals. They disappeared as soon as the pudding had been served, some to smoke a pipe in the saddle room, others to do work which could not wait. Then all the clatter of washing up rose and subsided. More peaceful occupations filled the afternoon. The crickets began to sing in the hearth. The kettle boiled for tea. At nightfall a candle was lit, the foreman or the shepherd sat smoking in the armchair at the fireside end of the table. The latch clicked as the others came in one by one and went early to bed.

The kitchen was the scene of many events which afterwards flowed into my mind from the pages of books. Whenever in a tale a belated traveler saw a light and came through the darkness to ask for shelter, it was to this kitchen door. I can no longer identify the particular stories, but they do not belong to this period of childhood so much as to my later boyhood and youth, long after I had left the Farm; and even today my first memories easily usurp the function of the imagination, and clothe in familiar dimensions and patterns, exact and objective, the scenes which the romancer has purposely left vague. Perhaps the effect of all romance depends on this faculty we have of giving our own definition to the fancies of others. A mind without memories means a body without sensibility; our memories make our imaginative life, and it is only as we increase our memories, widening the imbricated shutters which divide our mind from the light, that we find with quick recognition those images of truth which the world is pleased to attribute to our creative gift.

STUDY QUESTIONS

1. Two of the notable qualities of this description are its restraint and essential simplicity. Read achieves this partly by his choice of details and partly by his orderly, controlled sentences. Pick out a paragraph and describe the kind of detail that Read uses. Describe his vocabulary and his sentence structure.

2. What does the author gain by giving exact information such as the direction in which certain things lie, the colors of the landscape, the reasons his father went to the city, and the mottoes on the plaque?

3. The author is concerned here not only with giving a vivid description but also in defining two reasons for the unusual importance of childhood experience. Summarize those two reasons.

4. How does the peculiar relation in the author's mind between the kitchen of the farm and scenes in books illustrate the theory of imaginative creation he expresses in the last sentence?

5. Nearly everyone retains a vivid memory of the place or places

where he spent his childhood. Write a description like this one of a childhood scene you remember, trying to create the general impression of the place through specific details. You may find it useful to follow the organization of Read's description of the farm kitchen.

6. Notice that these experiences from real life lead to an interesting general conclusion at the end of the description. Write a theme following this method. Tell some real experience you have had which has led you to some significant conclusion or general observation.

Reminiscences of Childhood*

Dylan Thomas

I like very much people telling me about their childhood, but they'll have to be quick or else I'll be telling them about mine.

I was born in a large Welsh town at the beginning of the Great War— an ugly, lovely town (or so it was and is to me), crawling, sprawling by a long and splendid curving shore where truant boys and sandfield boys and old men from nowhere, beachcombed, idled and paddled, watched the dockbound ships or the ships steaming away into wonder and India, magic and China, countries bright with oranges and loud with lions; threw stones into the sea for the barking outcast dogs; made castles and forts and harbours and race tracks in the sand; and on Saturday summer afternoons listened to the brass band, watched the Punch and Judy, or hung about on the fringes of the crowd to hear the fierce religious speakers who shouted at the sea, as though it were wicked and wrong to roll in and out like that, white-horsed and full of fishes.

One man, I remember, used to take off his hat and set fire to his hair every now and then, but I do not remember what it proved, if it proved anything at all, except that he was a very interesting man.

This sea-town was my world; outside a strange Wales, coal-pitted, mountained, river-run, full, so far as I knew, of choirs and football teams and sheep and storybook tall hats and red flannel petticoats, moved about its business which was none of mine.

Beyond that unknown Wales with its wild names like peals of bells in the darkness, and its mountain men clothed in the skins of animals perhaps and always singing, lay England which was London and the country called the Front, from which many of our neighbours never came back. It was a country to which only young men travelled.

* From *Quite Early One Morning,* by Dylan Thomas. Copyright, 1954, by New Directions. Reprinted by permission of New Directions and J. M. Dent Ltd.

At the beginning, the only "front" I knew was the little lobby before our front door. I could not understand how so many people never returned from there, but later I grew to know more, though still without understanding, and carried a wooden rifle in the park and shot down the invisible unknown enemy like a flock of wild birds. And the park itself was a world within the world of the sea-town. Quite near where I lived, so near that on summer evenings I could listen in my bed to the voices of older children playing ball on the sloping paper-littered bank, the park was full of terrors and treasures. Though it was only a little park, it held within its borders of old tall trees, notched with our names and shabby from our climbing, as many secret places, caverns and forests, prairies and deserts, as a country somewhere at the end of the sea.

And though we would explore it one day, armed and desperate, from end to end, from the robbers' den to the pirates' cabin, the highwayman's inn to the cattle ranch, or the hidden room in the undergrowth, where we held beetle races, and lit the wood fires and roasted potatoes and talked about Africa, and the makes of motor cars, yet still the next day, it remained as unexplored as the Poles—a country just born and always changing.

There were many secret societies but you could belong only to one; and in blood or red ink, and a rusty pocketknife, with, of course, an instrument to remove stones from horses' feet, you signed your name at the foot of a terrible document, swore death to all the other societies, crossed your heart that you would divulge no secret and that if you did, you would consent to torture by slow fire, and undertook to carry out by yourself a feat of either daring or endurance. You could take your choice: would you climb to the top of the tallest and most dangerous tree, and from there hurl stones and insults at grown-up passers-by, especially postmen, or any other men in uniform? Or would you ring every doorbell in the terrace, not forgetting the doorbell of the man with the red face who kept dogs and ran fast? Or would you swim in the reservoir, which was forbidden and had angry swans, or would you eat a whole old jam jar full of mud?

There were many more alternatives. I chose one of endurance and for half an hour, it may have been longer or shorter, held up off the ground a very heavy broken pram we had found in a bush. I thought my back would break and the half hour felt like a day, but I preferred it to braving the red face and the dogs, or to swallowing tadpoles.

We knew every inhabitant of the park, every regular visitor, every nursemaid, every gardener, every old man. We knew the hour when the alarming retired policeman came in to look at the dahlias and the hour when the old lady arrived in the Bath chair with six Pekinese, and a pale girl to read aloud to her. I think she read the newspaper, but we always said she read the *Wizard*. The face of the old man who sat summer and winter on the bench looking over the reservoir, I can see clearly now and I wrote a poem long long after I'd left the park and the sea-town called:

THE HUNCHBACK IN THE PARK

The hunchback in the park
A solitary mister
Propped between trees and water
From the opening of the garden lock
That lets the trees and water enter
Until the Sunday sombre ball at dark

Eating bread from a newspaper
Drinking water from the chained cup
That the children filled with gravel
In the fountain basin where I sailed my ship
Slept at night in a dog kennel
But nobody chained him up.

Like the park birds he came early
Like the water he sat down
And Mister they called Hey mister
The truant boys from the town
Running when he had heard them clearly
On out of sound

Past lake and rockery
Laughing when he shook his paper
Hunchbacked in mockery
Through the loud zoo of the willow groves
Dodging the park-keeper
With his stick that picked up leaves.

And the old dog sleeper
Alone between nurses and swans
While the boys among willows
Made the tigers jump out of their eyes
To roar on the rockery stones
And the groves were blue with sailors

Made all day until bell-time
A woman figure without fault
Straight as a young elm
Straight and tall from his crooked bones
That she might stand in the night
After the locks and the chains

All night in the unmade park
After the railings and shrubberies
The birds the grass the trees and the lake
And the wild boys innocent as strawberries
Had followed the hunchback
To his kennel in the dark.

And that park grew up with me; that small world widened as I learned
its secrets and boundaries, as I discovered new refuges and ambushes in its
woods and jungles; hidden homes and lairs for the multitudes of imagination, for cowboys and Indians, and the tall terrible half-people who rode

on nightmares through my bedroom. But it was not the only world—that world of rockery, gravel path, playbank, bowling green, bandstands, reservoir, dahlia garden, where an ancient keeper, known as Smoky, was the whiskered snake in the grass one must keep off. There was another world where with my friends I used to dawdle on half holidays along the bent and Devon-facing seashore, hoping for gold watches or the skull of a sheep or a message in a bottle to be washed up with the tide; and another where we used to wander whistling through the packed streets, stale as station sandwiches, round the impressive gasworks and the slaughter house, past by the blackened monuments and the museum that should have been in a museum. Or we scratched at a kind of cricket on the bald and cindery surface of the recreation ground, or we took a tram that shook like an iron jelly down to the gaunt pier, there to clamber under the pier, hanging perilously on to its skeleton legs or to run along to the end where patient men with the seaward eyes of the dockside unemployed capped and muffered, dangling from their mouths pipes that had long gone out, angled over the edge for unpleasant tasting fish.

Never was there such a town as ours, I thought, as we fought on the sandhills with rough boys or dared each other to climb up the scaffolding of half-built houses soon to be called Laburnum Beaches. Never was there such a town, I thought, for the smell of fish and chips on Saturday evenings; for the Saturday afternoon cinema matinees where we shouted and hissed our threepences away; for the crowds in the streets with leeks in their hats on international nights; for the park, the inexhaustible and mysterious, bushy red-Indian hiding park where the hunchback sat alone and the groves were blue with sailors. The memories of childhood have no order, and so I remember that never was there such a dame school as ours, so firm and kind and smelling of galoshes, with the sweet and fumbled music of the piano lessons drifting down from upstairs to the lonely schoolroom, where only the sometimes tearful wicked sat over undone sums, or to repeat a little crime—the pulling of a girl's hair during geography, the sly shin kick under the table during English literature. Behind the school was a narrow lane where only the oldest and boldest threw pebbles at windows, scuffled and boasted, fibbed about their relations—

"My father's got a chauffeur."

"What's he want a chauffeur for? He hasn't got a car."

"My father's the richest man in the town."

"My father's the richest man in Wales."

"My father owns the world."

And swapped gob-stoppers for slings, old knives for marbles, kite strings for foreign stamps.

The lane was always the place to tell your secrets; if you did not have any, you invented them. Occasionally now I dream that I am turning out of school into the lane of confidences when I say to the boys of my class, "At last, I have a real secret."

"What is it—what is it?"

"I can fly."

And when they do not believe me, I flap my arms and slowly leave the ground only a few inches at first, then gaining air until I fly waving my cap level with the upper windows of the school, peering in until the mistress at the piano screams and the metronome falls to the ground and stops, and there is no more time.

And I fly over the trees and chimneys of my town, over the dockyards skimming the masts and funnels, over Inkerman Street, Sebastopol Street, and the street where all the women wear men's caps, over the trees of the everlasting park, where a brass band shakes the leaves and sends them showering down on to the nurses and the children, the cripples and the idlers, and the gardeners, and the shouting boys: over the yellow seashore, and the stone-chasing dogs, and the old men, and the singing sea.

The memories of childhood have no order, and no end.

STUDY QUESTIONS

1. Notice that the child's world in this essay is not merely a series of sense impressions but that it also includes things he has heard about or read about, which he links, sometimes mistakenly, to the sights and sounds around him. Point out some places where Thomas combines firsthand experiences with information he has learned secondhand.

2. Obviously, this account mingles true experiences with imaginary ones, yet the author does not differentiate between them, describing both kinds of experience as though they were true. What does this demand from the reader? What effect does it create?

3. Show how the style and organization of the essay reflect Thomas' opinion that "the memories of childhood have no order. . . ." This does not mean that the essay is disorderly. Consider, for example, in the paragraph where this opinion is expressed, the repetition of the word "never."

4. Compare Thomas' writing with that of Read in the previous description. What differences do you find in vocabulary? In sentences? What effect does Thomas gain by frequent long sentences with parts loosely connected by "and" or "or"?

5. Everyone probably remembers very sharply many details of his childhood. Write an essay giving your impression of "the world" in which you first became aware of things and people around you.

6. It is also probably true of every child that he lives "in a world of his own" which has little or nothing to do with actuality. Describe some dream, imaginary activity, impossible ambition, or misunderstanding (like Thomas' "Front" or "secret society") from your own childhood.

A New England Boyhood*

Henry Adams

Boys are wild animals, rich in the treasures of sense, but the New England boy had a wider range of emotions than boys of more equable climates. He felt his nature crudely, as it was meant. To the boy Henry Adams, summer was drunken. Among senses, smell was the strongest—smell of hot pinewoods and sweet-fern in the scorching summer noon; of new-mown hay; of ploughed earth; of box hedges; of peaches, lilacs, syringas; of stables, barns, cow-yards; of salt water and low tide on the marshes; nothing came amiss. Next to smell came taste, and the children knew the taste of everything they saw or touched, from pennyroyal and flagroot to the shell of a pignut and the letters of a spelling-book—the taste of A-B, AB, suddenly revived on the boy's tongue sixty years afterwards. Light, line, and color as sensual pleasures, came later and were as crude as the rest. The New England light is glare, and the atmosphere harshens color. The boy was a full man before he ever knew what was meant by atmosphere; his idea of pleasure in light was the blaze of a New England sun. His idea of color was a peony, with the dew of early morning on its petals. The intense blue of the sea, as he saw it a mile or two away, from the Quincy hills; the cumuli in a June afternoon sky; the strong reds and greens and purples of colored prints and children's picture-books, as the American colors then ran; these were ideals. The opposites or antipathies were the cold grays of November evenings, and the thick, muddy thaws of Boston winter. With such standards, the Bostonian could not but develop a double nature. Life was a double thing. After a January blizzard, the boy who could look with pleasure into the violent snow-glare of the cold white sunshine, with its intense light and shade, scarcely knew what was meant by tone. He could reach it only by education.

Winter and summer, then, were two hostile lives, and bred two separate natures. Winter was always the effort to live; summer was tropical license. Whether the children rolled in the grass, or waded in the brook, or swam in the salt ocean, or sailed in the bay, or fished for smelts in the creeks, or netted minnows in the salt-marshes, or took to the pine-woods and the granite quarries, or chased muskrats and hunted snapping-turtles in the swamps, or mushrooms or nuts on the autumn hills, summer and country were always sensual living, while winter was always compulsory

*From *The Education of Henry Adams.* Copyright, 1918, by Houghton Mifflin Company. Reprinted by permission of the publishers.

learning. Summer was the multiplicity of nature; winter was school.

The bearing of the two seasons on the education of Henry Adams was no fancy; it was the most decisive force he ever knew; it ran through life, and made the division between its perplexing, warring, irreconcilable problems, irreducible opposites, with growing emphasis to the last year of study. From earliest childhood the boy was accustomed to feel that, for him, life was double. Winter and summer, town and country, law and liberty, were hostile, and the man who pretended they were not, was in his eyes a schoolmaster—that is, a man employed to tell lies to little boys. Though Quincy was but two hours' walk from Beacon Hill, it belonged in a different world. For two hundred years, every Adams, from father to son, had lived within sight of State Street, and sometimes had lived in it, yet none had ever taken kindly to the town, or been taken kindly by it. The boy inherited his double nature. He knew as yet nothing about his great-grandfather, who had died a dozen years before his own birth: he took for granted that any great-grandfather of his must have always been good, and his enemies wicked; but he divined his great-grandfather's character from his own. Never for a moment did he connect the two ideas of Boston and John Adams; they were separate and antagonistic; the idea of John Adams went with Quincy. He knew his grandfather John Quincy Adams only as an old man of seventy-five or eighty who was friendly and gentle with him, but except that he heard his grandfather always called "the President," and his grandmother "the Madam," he had no reason to suppose that his Adams grandfather differed in character from his Brooks grandfather who was equally kind and benevolent. He liked the Adams side best, but for no other reason than that it reminded him of the country, the summer, and the absence of restraint. Yet he felt also that Quincy was in a way inferior to Boston, and that socially Boston looked down on Quincy. The reason was clear enough even to a five-year-old child. Quincy had no Boston style. Little enough style had either; a simpler manner of life and thought could hardly exist, short of cave-dwelling. The flint-and-steel with which his grandfather Adams used to light his own fires in the early morning was still on the mantelpiece of his study. The idea of a livery or even a dress for servants, or of an evening toilette, was next to blasphemy. Bathrooms, water-supplies, lighting, heating, and the whole array of domestic comforts, were unknown at Quincy. Boston had already a bathroom, a water-supply, a furnace, and gas. The superiority of Boston was evident, but a child liked it no better for that.

The magnificence of his grandfather Brooks's house in Pearl Street or South Street has long ago disappeared, but perhaps his country house at Medford may still remain to show what impressed the mind of a boy in 1845 with the idea of city splendor. The President's place at Quincy was the larger and older and far the more interesting of the two; but a boy felt at once its inferiority in fashion. It showed plainly enough of its want of wealth. It smacked of colonial age, but not of Boston style or plush curtains. To the end of his life he never quite overcame the prejudice thus drawn in with his childish breath. He never could compel himself to care for nineteenth-century style. He was never able to adopt it, any more than his father or grandfather or great-grandfather had done. Not that he felt it as particularly hostile, for he reconciled himself to much that was worse; but because, for some remote reason, he was born an eighteenth-century child. The old house at Quincy was eighteenth century. What style it had was in its Queen Anne mahogany panels and its Louis Seize chairs and sofas. The panels belonged to an old colonial Vassall who built the house; the furniture had been brought back from Paris in 1789 or 1801 or 1817, along with porcelain and books and much else of old diplomatic remnants; and neither of the two eighteenth-century styles—neither English Queen Anne nor French Louis Seize—was comfortable for a boy, or for any one else. The dark mahogany had been painted white to suit daily life in winter gloom. Nothing seemed to favor, for a child's objects, the older forms. On the contrary, most boys, as well as grown-up people, preferred the new, with good reason, and the child felt himself distinctly at a disadvantage for the taste.

Nor had personal preference any share in his bias. The Brooks grandfather was as amiable and as sympathetic as the Adams grandfather. Both were born in 1767, and both died in 1848. Both were kind to children, and both belonged rather to the eighteenth than to the nineteenth centuries. The child knew no difference between them except that one was associated with winter and the other with summer, one with Boston, the other with Quincy. Even with Medford, the association was hardly easier. Once as a very young boy he was taken to pass a few days with his grandfather Brooks under charge of his aunt, but became so violently homesick that within twenty-four hours he was brought back in disgrace. Yet he could not remember ever being seriously homesick again.

The attachment to Quincy was not altogether sentimental or wholly sympathetic. Quincy was not a bed of thornless roses. Even there the curse of Cain set its mark. There as elsewhere a cruel universe combined to crush a child. As though three or four vigorous brothers and sisters, with the best will, were not enough to crush any child, every one else conspired towards an education which he hated. From cradle to grave this problem of running order through chaos, direction through space, discipline through freedom, unity through multiplicity, has always been, and must always be, the task of education, as it is the moral of religion, philosophy, science, art, politics, and economy; but a boy's will is his life, and he dies when it is broken, as the colt dies in harness, taking a new nature in becoming tame. Rarely has the boy felt kindly towards his tamers. Between him and his master has always been war. Henry Adams never knew a boy of his generation to like a master, and the task of remaining on friendly terms with one's own family, in such a relation, was never easy.

All the more singular it seemed afterwards to him that his first serious contact with the President should have been a struggle of will, in which the old man almost necessarily defeated the boy, but instead of leaving, as usual in such defeats, a lifelong sting, left rather an impression of as fair treatment as could be expected from a natural enemy. The boy met seldom with such restraint. He could not have been much more than six years old at the time—seven at the utmost—and his mother had taken him to Quincy for a long stay with the President during the summer. What became of the rest of the family he quite forgot; but he distinctly remembered standing at the house door one summer morning in a passionate outburst of rebellion against going to school. Naturally his mother was the immediate victim of his rage; that is what mothers are for, and boys also; but in this case the boy had his mother at unfair disadvantage, for she was a guest, and had no means of enforcing obedience. Henry showed a certain tactical ability by refusing to start, and he met all efforts at compulsion by successful, though too vehement protest. He was in a fair way to win, and was holding his own, with sufficient energy, at the bottom of the long staircase which led up to the door of the President's library, when the door opened, and the old man slowly came down. Putting on his hat, he took the boy's hand without a word, and walked with him, paralyzed by awe, up the road to the town. After the first moments of consternation at this interference in a domestic dispute, the boy reflected that an old gentleman close on eighty would never trouble himself to walk near a mile on a hot summer morning over a shadeless road to take a boy to school, and that it would be strange if a lad imbued with the passion of freedom could not find a corner to dodge around, somewhere before reaching the school door. Then and always, the boy insisted that this reasoning justified his apparent submission; but the old man did not stop, and the boy saw all his strategical points turned, one after another, until he found himself seated inside the school, and obviously the centre of curious if not malevolent criticism. Not till then did the President release his hand and depart.

The point was that this act, contrary to the inalienable rights of boys, and nullifying the social compact, ought to have made him dislike his grandfather for life. He could not recall that it had this effect even for a moment. With a certain maturity of mind, the child must have recognized that the President, though a tool of tyranny, had done his disreputable work with a certain intelligence. He had shown no temper, no irritation, no personal feeling, and had made no display of force. Above all, he had held his tongue. During their long walk he had said nothing; he had uttered no syllable of revolting cant about the duty of obedience and the wickedness of resistance to law; he had shown no concern in the matter; hardly even a consciousness of the boy's existence. Probably his mind at that moment was actually troubling itself little about his grandson's iniquities, and much about the iniquities of President Polk, but the boy could scarcely at that age feel the whole satisfaction of thinking that

President Polk was to be the vicarious victim of his own sins, and he gave his grandfather credit for intelligent silence. For this forbearance he felt instinctive respect. He admitted force as a form of right; he admitted even temper, under protest; but the seeds of a moral education would at that moment have fallen on the stoniest soil in Quincy, which is, as every one knows, the stoniest glacial and tidal drift known in any Puritan land.

STUDY QUESTIONS

1. This selection opens with a contrast. To what extent is this pattern of contrast carried through the whole selection?
2. Though it is about a child and a child's thoughts, this account tells about some reactions that are obviously those of an adult. Can you pick these out?
3. What is the purpose and effect of telling autobiography in the third person, as Henry Adams does?
4. What prevented Henry Adams from hating his grandfather as he hated everyone else who tried to discipline him?
5. Write a theme describing an incident of family life that made a profound impression on you when you were a child.
6. Do you detect any differences between the way of rearing children when Henry Adams was a boy and the present way? Write a theme contrasting and evaluating old-fashioned and modern concepts of child-raising and family life.

Steamboat Town*

Mark Twain

When I was a boy, there was but one permanent ambition among my comrades in our village on the west bank of the Mississippi River. That was, to be a steamboatman. We had transient ambitions of other sorts, but they were only transient. When a circus came and went, it left us all burning to become clowns; the first negro minstrel show that ever came to our section left us all suffering to try that kind of life; now and then we had a hope that, if we lived and were good, God would permit us to be pirates. These ambitions faded out, each in its turn; but the ambition to be a steamboatman always remained.

Once a day a cheap, gaudy packet arrived upward from St. Louis, and another downward from Keokuk. Before these events, the day was glorious with expectancy; after them, the day was a dead and empty thing.

* From *Life on the Mississippi*, by Mark Twain. Reprinted by permission of Harper & Brothers.

Not only the boys, but the whole village, felt this. After all these years I can picture that old time to myself now, just as it was then: the white town drowsing in the sunshine of a summer's morning; the streets empty, or pretty nearly so; one or two clerks sitting in front of the Water Street stores, with their splint-bottomed chairs tilted back against the walls, chins on breasts, hats slouched over their faces, asleep—with shingle-shavings enough around to show what broke them down; a sow and a litter of pigs loafing along the sidewalk, doing a good business in watermelon rinds and seeds; two or three lonely little freight piles scattered about the "levee"; a pile of "skids" on the slope of the stone-paved wharf, and the fragrant town drunkard asleep in the shadow of them; two or three wood flats at the head of the wharf, but nobody to listen to the peaceful lapping of the wavelets against them; the great Mississippi, the majestic, the magnificent Mississippi, rolling its mile-wide tide along, shining in the sun; the dense forest away on the other side; the "point" above the town, and the "point" below, bounding the river-glimpse and turning it into a sort of sea, and withal a very still and brilliant and lonely one. Presently a film of dark smoke appears above one of those remote "points"; instantly a negro drayman, famous for his quick eye and prodigious voice, lifts up the cry, "S-t-e-a-m-boat a-comin'!" and the scene changes! The town drunkard stirs, the clerks wake up, a furious clatter of drays follows, every house and store pours out a human contribution, and all in a twinkling the dead town is alive and moving. Drays, carts, men, boys, all go hurrying from many quarters to a common center, the wharf. Assembled there, the people fasten their eyes upon the coming boat as upon a wonder they are seeing for the first time. And the boat *is* rather a handsome sight, too. She is long and sharp and trim and pretty; she has two tall, fancy-topped chimneys, with a gilded device of some kind swung between them; a fanciful pilot-house, all glass and "gingerbread," perched on top of the "texas" deck behind them; the paddle-boxes are gorgeous with a picture or with gilded rays above the boat's name; the boiler-deck, the hurricane-deck, and the texas deck are fenced and ornamented with clean white railings; there is a flag gallantly flying from the jack-staff; the furnace doors are open and the fires glaring bravely; the upper decks are black with passengers; the captain stands by the big bell, calm, imposing, the envy of all; great volumes of the blackest smoke are rolling and tumbling out of the chimneys—a husbanded grandeur created with a bit of pitch-pine just before arriving at a town; the crew are grouped on the forecastle; the broad stage is run far out over the port bow, and an envied deck-hand stands picturesquely on the end of it with a coil of rope in his hand; the pent steam is screaming through the gaugecocks; the captain lifts his hand, a bell rings, the wheels stop; then they turn back, churning the water to foam, and the steamer is at rest. Then such a scramble as there is to get aboard, and to get ashore, and to take in freight and to discharge freight, all at one and the same time; and such a yelling and cursing as the mates facilitate it all with! Ten minutes later the steamer is under way again, with no flag on the jack-staff and no black smoke issuing from the chimneys. After ten more minutes the town is dead again, and the town drunkard asleep by the skids once more.

My father was a justice of the peace, and I supposed he possessed the power of life and death over all men, and could hang anybody that offended him. This was distinction enough for me as a general thing; but the desire to be a steamboatman kept intruding, nevertheless. I first wanted to be a cabin-boy, so that I could come out with a white apron on and shake a table-cloth over the side, where all my old comrades could see me: later I thought I would rather be the deck-hand who stood on the end of the stage-plank with the coil of rope in his hand, because he was particularly conspicuous. But these were only day-dreams—they were too heavenly to be contemplated as real possibilities. By and by one of our boys went away. He was not heard of for a long time. At last he turned up as an apprentice engineer or "striker" on a steamboat. This thing shook the bottom out of all my Sunday-school teachings. That boy had been notoriously worldly, and I just the reverse; yet he was exalted to this eminence, and I left in obscurity and misery. There was nothing generous about this fellow in his greatness. He would always manage to have a rusty bolt to scrub while his boat tarried at our town, and he would sit on the inside guard and scrub it, where we all could see him and envy him and loathe him. And whenever his boat was laid up he would come home and swell around the town in his blackest and greasiest clothes, so that nobody could help remembering that he was a steamboatman; and he used all sorts of steamboat technicalities in his talk, as if he were so used to them that he forgot common people could not understand them. He would speak of the "labboard" side of a horse in an easy, natural way that would make one wish he was dead. And he was always talking about "St. Looy" like an old citizen; he would refer casually to occasions when he was "coming down Fourth Street," or when he was "passing by the Planter's House," or when there was a fire and he took a turn on the brakes of "the old Big Missouri"; and then he would go on and lie about how many towns the size of ours were burned down there that day. Two or three of the boys had long been persons of consideration among us because they had been to St. Louis once and had a vague general knowledge of its wonders, but the day of their glory was over now. They lapsed into a humble silence, and learned to disappear when the ruthless "cub"-engineer approached. This fellow had money, too, and hair-oil. Also an ignorant silver watch and a showy brass watch-chain. He wore a leather belt and used no suspenders. If ever a youth was cordially admired and hated by his comrades, this one was. No girl could withstand his charms. He "cut out" every boy in the village. When his boat blew up at last, it diffused a tranquil contentment among us such as we had not known for months. But when he came home the next week, alive, renowned, and appeared in

church all battered up and bandaged, a shining hero, stared at and wondered over by everybody, it seemed to us that the partiality of Providence
for an undeserving reptile had reached a point where it was open to
criticism.

This creature's career could produce but one result, and it speedily followed. Boy after boy managed to get on the river. The minister's son
became an engineer. The doctor's and the postmaster's sons became "mud
clerks"; the wholesale liquor dealer's son became a barkeeper on a boat;
four sons of the chief merchant, and two sons of the county judge, became
pilots. Pilot was the grandest position of all. The pilot, even in those days
of trivial wages, had a princely salary—from a hundred and fifty to two
hundred and fifty dollars a month, and no board to pay. Two months of
his wages would pay a preacher's salary for a year. Now some of us were
left disconsolate. We could not get on the river—at least our parents
would not let us.

So, by and by, I ran away. I said I would never come home again till I
was a pilot and could come in glory. But somehow I could not manage it.
I went meekly aboard a few of the boats that lay packed together like
sardines at the long St. Louis wharf, and humbly inquired for the pilots,
but got only a cold shoulder and short words from mates and clerks. I
had to make the best of this sort of treatment for the time being, but I had
comforting day-dreams of a future when I should be a great and honored
pilot, with plenty of money, and could kill some of these mates and clerks
and pay for them.

STUDY QUESTIONS

1. This very concrete description provides excellent illustrations of
   some standard principles for the arrangement of details within a
   paragraph. What principle governs the arrangement of materials
   in the second paragraph, for example? Examine several paragraphs
   and explain the principle of organization in them.
2. Why is the description of the town at the arrival of the steamboat
   so successful?
3. Note that the description of the steamboat's arrival consists of two
   contrasting parts. Compare the verbs used in these two sections to
   see if they add to the contrasting effect.
4. In the description of the boy who succeeded in becoming a steamboatman, what double awareness operates to produce the humor?
5. What is Twain's attitude toward the town he describes?
6. Write a description of some place which, like the town in this description, has a very different appearance on different occasions.
   Possibilities are a gym when it is empty or when it is being used,
   a street on a sunny day or in the rain, a shop at a busy time or at
   a slack one.

Child's Time and Clock Time*

Jesse Stuart

When I was a boy, I knew what a clock was. My mother had one which sat on the mantel and ticked the time away. I was glad I didn't sleep in this room so I wouldn't have to hear it. I didn't like the ticking of a clock. In those days I slept upstairs alone in this very house where we live today.

We had an alarm clock which my father set on a chair by his bed to wake him at four. He would get up, build fires in the fireplace and kitchen stove, feed his hogs, horses, and cows, and then eat his own breakfast and be off before daylight (in winter) to the railroad section four miles away. Dad often walked to work by lantern light or by starlight. Sometimes he went by bright moonlight. But when his alarm clock went off, we could hear the noise all over this house. After this clock's strange mechanical sound, I found it difficult to go to sleep again. I learned at the age of eight that an alarm clock can be an extremely disturbing thing in one's life.

Then Dad had a watch, which kept almost perfect time. He used to have me sit on his lap and show me this timepiece. He told me about what a wonderful thing this watch was, and he taught me to tell time by it. I learned how man measured time before I knew exactly what time was. Time was something to me, when I was a child, like wind and water. Time was flowing and eternal, like an invisible river. We could divide it into seconds, minutes, hours, days, weeks, months, and years, but that didn't bring us any closer to it. There were yesterdays, and time was with us now, and there would be tomorrows.

I had my way of dividing time. I didn't use a watch or a clock. My day started in the early morning when the sun came up. Then there were the hours of light, which were not long enough, and finally nighttime, which I loved for its beauty but hated because it sent me to bed. And there were the four seasons. These were my simple measurements of time. I didn't remember the day of the week nor the hour of the day. These didn't matter.

When I was a boy and played on the W-Hollow hill slopes and down in the valleys by the little streams, when I waded up and down the main W-Hollow stream and pinhooked minnows and killed water snakes with

* Reprinted by permission from *The Year of My Rebirth,* by Jesse Stuart, published by McGraw-Hill Book Company, Inc. Copyright, 1956, Jesse Stuart.

sticks, the only ticking of the seconds I heard was the falling of water over the rocks. This was the soft rhythmical beating of time. This was the noise that time made. When I hunted at night and crept under rock cliffs to get out of a rainstorm, I would lie on dry leaves and listen to raindrops dripping from the rocks to the ground. This was another noise that time made. And when the winds blew, fast or slow, their rhythms recorded the passing of time. When the dark, ugly storm clouds raced across the sky, or when the white thunderheads floated out, lazylike, across the blue, it was the passing of time. All my work and all my play in those days were measured by this sort of time. This was the natural schedule that I grew up by.

The dripping of rain from the rock cliffs or the falling of leaves through the bright air never hurried me. I took my time. I had plenty of it for dreams. The warm winds of summer made me lazy and detached. The autumn winds made me sad. The winter winds shrill and cold, made me hustle. And the soft spring winds stirred me to awareness of life's reawakening. I didn't need a watch in those days. I never was a clock watcher.

In fact I never owned a watch until after I began teaching school. First I borrowed my father's watch. Later I forced myself to wear one until I got used to it. Gradually my watch became a natural part of my clothing which was hard for me to do without. Minutes and seconds began to count. I was on a tight man-made schedule. I couldn't escape it. I not only needed a watch, but I had to have an accurate one like Dad's "railroad" watch. It had to keep the exact time. For trains and planes were usually on schedule and wouldn't wait for me. And at the other end somebody was there to meet me. I had to lecture at a certain hour. I had to be out of the hotel at this or that time of day. That constant tension of man-made time gripped me in a vice.

This is the "tight schedule." It is one in which minutes are big things, hours are actually precious. The watch that keeps perfect time is on the wrist. A man flicks his arm up again and again to keep up with the flow of seconds and minutes.

And then there was my heart. I treated my heart like a clock, too. Not that I remembered it often. No, I never gave it a thought. But I wound it too tight.

Now these tight schedules are fast becoming memories for me, like the old clock that sat on the mantel, the alarm clock on the chair beside my father's bed, and his watch that was inspected by the railroad company so he would be to his work on time. I'm back now on nature's schedule. My timepieces are rain, wind, and the seasons. I can tell by the sun in the morning about what time of day it is. I know the hour certain species of birds get hungry and fly for their breakfast. I know the time of morning the ground squirrels make a noise about their feeding. I know the time the red-birds sing, for they waken me at four-thirty each morning. Happily, I listen to them and then go back to sleep. I would rather have them wake me with a song at four-thirty than leap up at an alarm clock's buzzing at seven.

I hear time dripping from the cliffs and bluffs to the leaves below. I've about lost the habit of throwing up my arm every few seconds to glance at my watch. I have other ways of telling time. I have the ways of my youth.

STUDY QUESTIONS

1. How do the different attitudes toward time divide the essay naturally into three sections?

2. What contrasts between the child's world and the adult's world are suggested by the different ways of measuring time?

3. All of the selections thus far have been describing childhood in some way. Stuart's tone, however, is perhaps most consciously nostalgic. How does he create this tone? How would you differentiate between Stuart's tone and that of Read? Of Twain? Does Stuart completely avoid sentimentality? Explain.

4. At the end of the essay, the grown invalid finds that he has begun to measure time by nature, as he did in his childhood. However, in what way is his way of telling time by nature different from the childhood way?

5. Note that at the end of the essay the author seems to feel that his childhood self was wiser about this subject than his adult self. Have you ever come to the conclusion that children are more perceptive or more realistic about some things than adults? Write a theme explaining this.

6. Would it be possible for you to keep track of time without a watch, by events in your environment? Write a theme arguing that watches are unnecessary, and that people might be better off without them.

I Discover "Huckleberry Finn"*

H. L. Mencken

If I undertook to tell you the effect it ["Huckleberry Finn"] had upon me my talk would sound frantic, and even delirious. Its impact was genuinely terrific. I had not gone further than the first incomparable chapter before I realized, child though I was, that I had entered a domain of new and gorgeous wonders, and thereafter I pressed on steadily to the last word. My gait, of course, was still slow, but it became steadily faster

* Reprinted from *Happy Days*, by H. L. Mencken, by permission of Alfred A. Knopf, Inc. Copyright, 1939, 1940, by Alfred A. Knopf, Inc.

as I proceeded. As the blurbs on the slip-covers of murder mysteries say, I simply couldn't put the book down. After dinner that evening, braving a possible uproar, I took it into the family sitting-room, and resumed it while my father searched the *Evening News* hopefully for reports of the arrest, clubbing and hanging of labor leaders. Anon, he noticed what I was at, and demanded to know the name of the book I was reading. When I held up the green volume his comment was "Well, I'll be durned!"

I sensed instantly that there was no reproof in this, but a kind of shy rejoicing. Then he told me that he had once been a great reader of Mark Twain himself—in his younger days. He had got hold of all the volumes as they came out—"The Innocents" in 1869, when he was still a boy himself; "Roughing It" in 1872, "The Gilded Age" in 1873, "Tom Sawyer" in 1876, "A Tramp Abroad" in 1880, the year of my birth, and so on down to date. (All these far from pristine firsts are still in the Biblioteca Menckeniana in Hollins street, minus a few that were lent to neighbor boys and never returned, and had to be replaced.) My father read them in the halcyon days before children, labor troubles and Grover Cleveland had begun to frazzle him, and he still got them down from the shelf on quiet evenings, after the first-named were packed off to bed. But a man of advancing years and cares had to consider also the sorrows of the world, and so he read in Mark less than aforetime.

As for me, I proceeded to take the whole canon at a gulp—and presently gagged distressfully. "Huckleberry Finn," of course, was as transparent to a boy of eight as to a man of eighty, and almost as pungent and exhilarating, but there were passages in "A Tramp Abroad" that baffled me, and many more in "The Innocents," and a whole swarm in "The Gilded Age." I well recall wrestling with the woodcut by W. F. Brown on page 113 of the "Tramp." It shows five little German girls swinging on a heavy chain stretched between two stone posts on a street in Heilbronn, and the legend under it is "Generations of Bare Feet." That legend is silly, for all the girls have shoes on, but what puzzled me about it was something quite different. It was a confusion between the word *generation* and the word *federation,* which latter was often in my father's speech in those days, for the American Federation of Labor had got under way only a few years before, and was just beginning in earnest to harass and alarm employers. Why I didn't consult the dictionary (or my mother, or my father himself) I simply can't tell you. At eight or nine, I suppose, intelligence is no more than a small spot of light on the floor of a large and murky room. So instead of seeking help I passed on, wondering idiotically what possible relation there could be between a gang of little girls in pigtails and the Haymarket anarchists, and it was six or seven years later before the "Tramp" became clear to me, and began to delight me.

It then had the curious effect of generating in me both a great interest in Germany and a vast contempt for the German language. I was already aware, of course, that the Mencken family was of German origin, for my

Grandfather Mencken, in his care for me as *Stammhalter*, did not neglect to describe eloquently its past glories at the German universities, and to expound its connections to the most remote degrees. But my father, who was only half German, had no apparent interest in either the German land or its people, and when he spoke of the latter at all, which was not often, it was usually in sniffish terms. He never visited Germany, and never signified any desire to do so, though I recall my mother suggesting, more than once, that a trip there would be swell. It was "A Tramp Abroad" that made me German-conscious, and I still believe that it is the best guide-book to Germany ever written. Today, of course, it is archaic, but it was still reliable down to 1910, when I made my own first trip. The uproarious essay on "The Awful German Language," which appears at the end of it as an appendix, worked the other way. That is to say, it confirmed my growing feeling, born of my struggles with the conjugations and declensions taught at F. Knapp's Institute, that German was an irrational and even insane tongue, and not worth the sufferings of a freeborn American. These diverse impressions have continued with me ever since. I am still convinced that Germany, in the intervals of peace, is the most pleasant country to travel in ever heard of, and I am still convinced that the German language is of a generally preposterous and malignant character.

"Huck," of course, was my favorite, and I read it over and over. In fact, I read it regularly not less than annually down to my forties, and only a few months ago I hauled it out and read it once more—and found it as magnificent as ever. Only one other book, down to the beginning of my teens, ever beset me with a force even remotely comparable to its smash, and that was a volume called "Boys' Useful Pastimes," by "Prof. Robert Griffith, A.M., principal of Newton High School." This was given to me by my Grandmother Mencken at Christmas, 1889, and it remained my constant companion for at least six years. The sub-title describes its contents: "Pleasant and profitable amusement for spare hours, comprising chapters on the use and care of tools, and detailed instructions by means of which boys can make with their own hands a large number of toys, household ornaments, scientific appliances, and many pretty, amusing and necessary articles for the playground, the house and out-of-doors." Manual training was still a novelty in those days, and I suspect that the professor was no master of it, for many of his plans and specifications were completely unintelligible to me, and also to all the neighborhood boys who dropped in to help and advise. I doubt, indeed, that any human being on earth, short of an astrophysicist, could have made anything of his directions for building boat models. But in other cases he was relatively explicit and understandable, and my brother Charlie and I, after long efforts, managed to make a steam-engine (or, more accurately, a steam-mill) according to his recipe. The boiler was a baking-powder tin, and the steam, issuing out of a small hole in the top, operated a sort of fan or mill-wheel. How we provided heat to make steam I forget, but I remember clearly that my mother considered the process dangerous, and ordered us to take the engine out of the cellar and keep it in the backyard.

I had no more mechanical skill than a cow, but I also managed to make various other things that the professor described, including a what-not for the parlor (my mother professed to admire it, but never put it into service), a rabbit-trap (set in the backyard, it never caught anything, not even a cat), and a fancy table ornamented with twigs from the pear tree arranged in more or less geometrical designs. "Boys' Useful Pastimes" was printed by A. L. Burt on stout paper, and remains extant to this day —a rather remarkable fact, for other boys often borrowed it, and sometimes they kept it on their work-benches for a long while, and thumbed it diligently. One of those boys was Johnnie Sponsler, whose father kept a store in the Frederick road, very near Hollins street. Johnnie was vastly interested in electricity, as indeed were most other boys of the time, for such things as electric lights, motors, telephones and doorbells were just coming in. He thus made hard use of Professor Griffith's Part VII, which was headed "Scientific Apparatus and Experiments," and included directions for making a static machine, and for electroplating door-keys. He later abandoned the sciences for the postal service, and is now, I believe, retired. "Boys' Useful Pastimes," and my apparent interest in it, may have been responsible for my father's decision to transfer me from F. Knapp's Institute to the Baltimore Polytechnic in 1892. If so, it did me an evil service in the end, for my native incapacity for mechanics made my studies at the Polytechnic a sheer waste of time, though I managed somehow to pass the examinations, even in such abysmal subjects as steam engineering.

The influence of "Huck Finn" was immensely more powerful and durable. It not only reinforced my native aversion to the common run of boys' books; it also set me upon a systematic exploration of all the volumes in the old secretary, and before I finished with them I had looked into every one of them, including even Brother Schultz's sombre history of Freemasonry in Maryland. How many were actually intelligible to a boy of eight, nine, ten? I should say about a fourth. I managed to get through most of Dickens, but only by dint of hard labor, and it was not until I discovered Thackeray, at fourteen, that the English novel really began to lift me. George Eliot floored me as effectively as a text in Hittite, and to the present day I have never read "Adam Bede" or "Daniel Deronda" or "The Mill on the Floss," or developed any desire to do so. So far as I am concerned, they will remain mere names to the end of the chapter, and as hollow and insignificant as the names of Gog and Magog.

But I plowed through Chambers' Encyclopedia relentlessly, beginning with the shortest articles and gradually working my way into the longer ones. The kitchen-midden of irrelevant and incredible information that still burdens me had its origins in those pages, and I almost wore them out acquiring it. I read, too, the whole of Lossing, nearly all of Charlotte M. Yonge, and even some of Duyckinck, perhaps the dullest historian ever catalogued by faunal naturalists on this or any other earth. My brother Charlie and I enjoyed "Our Living World" chiefly because of the colored pictures, but I also read long stretches of it, and astonished my father by calling off the names of nearly all the wild beasts when the circus visited Baltimore in 1889. Finally, I recall reading both "Life Among the Mormons" and "One Thousand Proofs That the Earth Is Not a Globe."

Thus launched upon the career of a bookworm, I presently began to reach out right and left for more fodder. When the Enoch Pratt Free Library of Baltimore opened a branch in Hollins street, in March, 1886, I was still a shade too young to be excited, but I had a card before I was nine, and began an almost daily harrying of the virgins at the delivery desk. In 1888 my father subscribed to *Once-a-Week,* the predecessor of *Collier's,* and a little while later there began to come with it a long series of cheap reprints of contemporary classics, running from Tennyson's poems to Justin M'Carthy's "History of Our Own Times"; and simultaneously there appeared from parts unknown a similar series of cheap reprints of scientific papers, including some of Herbert Spencer. I read them all, sometimes with shivers of puzzlement and sometimes with delight, but always calling for more. I began to inhabit a world that was two-thirds letterpress and only one-third trees, fields, streets and people. I acquired round shoulders, spindly shanks, and a despondent view of humanity. I read everything that I could find in English, taking in some of it but boggling most of it.

This madness ran on until I reached adolescence, and began to distinguish between one necktie and another, and to notice the curiously divergent shapes, dispositions and aromas of girls. Then, gradually, I began to let up.

But to this day I am still what might be called a reader, and have a high regard for authors.

STUDY QUESTIONS

1. What is notable or unusual about the vocabulary used by Mencken? Compare it to that of Greene in the following selection.
2. On what principle is this selection organized? Are discussions like those of the author's confusion between *generation* and *federation* irrelevant digressions?
3. To what extent is the random reading of Mencken like that described by Greene in the following selection? Is Mencken's attitude toward it the same? Explain.
4. Is any progress observable in the kind of reading Mencken did?

5. Does Mencken's choice of reading matter show any particular tastes? How do you account for his liking or disliking certain books?

6. Write a theme relating your experiences to a book which you read as a child and which you think has had a lasting influence on you.

*The Lost Childhood**

Graham Greene

Perhaps it is only in childhood that books have any deep influence on our lives. In later life we admire, we are entertained, we may modify some views we already hold, but we are more likely to find in books merely a confirmation of what is in our minds already: as in a love affair it is our own features that we see reflected flatteringly back.

But in childhood all books are books of divination, telling us about the future, and like the fortune teller who sees a long journey in the cards or death by water they influence the future. I suppose that is why books excited us so much. What do we ever get nowadays from reading to equal the excitement and the revelation in those first fourteen years? Of course I should be interested to hear that a new novel by Mr. E. M. Forster was going to appear this spring, but I could never compare that mild expectation of civilized pleasure with the missed heartbeat, the appalled glee I felt when I found on a library shelf a novel by Rider Haggard, Percy Westerman, Captain Brereton or Stanley Weyman which I had not read before. No, it is in those early years that I would look for the crisis, the moment when life took a new slant in its journey towards death.

I remember distinctly the suddenness with which a key turned in a lock and I found I could read—not just the sentences in a reading book with the syllables coupled like railway carriages, but a real book. It was paper-covered with the picture of a boy, bound and gagged, dangling at the end of a rope inside a well with the water rising above his waist—an adventure of Dixon Brett, detective. All a long summer holiday I kept my secret, as I believed: I did not want anybody to know that I could read. I suppose I half consciously realized even then that this was the dangerous moment. I was safe so long as I could not read—the wheels had not begun to turn, but now the future stood around on bookshelves everywhere waiting for the child to choose—the life of a chartered accountant perhaps, a colonial civil servant, a planter in China, a steady job in a bank,

* From *The Lost Childhood and Other Essays* by Graham Greene. Copyright, 1951, by Graham Greene. Reprinted by permission of the Viking Press, Inc., New York, and Eyre & Spottiswoode, Ltd.

happiness and misery, eventually one particular form of death, for surely we choose our death much as we choose our job. It grows out of our acts and our evasions, out of our fears and out of our moments of courage. I suppose my mother must have discovered my secret, for on the journey home I was presented for the train with another real book, a copy of Ballantyne's *Coral Island* with only a single picture to look at, a coloured frontispiece. But I would admit nothing. All the long journey I stared at the one picture and never opened the book.

But there on the shelves at home (so many shelves for we were a large family) the books waited—one book in particular, but before I reach that one down let me take a few others at random from the shelf. Each was a crystal in which the child dreamed that he saw life moving. Here in a cover stamped dramatically in several colours was Captain Gilson's *The Pirate Aeroplane.* I must have read that book six times at least—the story of a lost civilization in the Sahara and of a villainous Yankee pirate with an aeroplane like a box kite and bombs the size of tennis balls who held the golden city to ransom. It was saved by the hero, a young subaltern who crept up to the pirate camp to put the aeroplane out of action. He was captured and watched his enemies dig his grave. He was to be shot at dawn, and to pass the time and keep his mind from uncomfortable thoughts the amiable Yankee pirate played cards with him—the mild nursery game of Kuhn Kan. The memory of that nocturnal game on the edge of life haunted me for years, until I set it to rest at last in one of my own novels with a game of poker played in remotely similar circumstances.

And here is *Sophy of Kravonia* by Anthony Hope—the story of a kitchen-maid who became a queen. One of the first films I ever saw, about 1911, was made from that book, and I can still hear the rumble of the Queen's guns crossing the high Kravonian pass beaten hollowly out on a single piano. Then there was Stanley Weyman's *The Story of Francis Cludde,* and above all other books at that time of my life, *King Solomon's Mines.*

This book did not perhaps provide the crisis, but it certainly influenced the future. If it had not been for that romantic tale of Allan Quatermain, Sir Henry Curtis, Captain Good, and, above all, the ancient witch Gagool, would I at nineteen have studied the appointments list of the Colonial Office and very nearly picked on the Nigerian Navy for a career? And later, when surely I ought to have known better, the odd African fixation remained. In 1935 I found myself sick with fever on a camp bed in a Liberian native's hut with a candle going out in an empty whiskey bottle and a rat moving in the shadows. Wasn't it the incurable fascination of Gagool with her bare yellow skull, the wrinkled scalp that moved and contracted like the hood of a cobra, that led me to work all through 1942 in a little stuffy office in Freetown, Sierra Leone? There is not much in common between the land of the Kukuanas, behind the desert and the mountain range of Sheba's Breast, and a tin-roofed house on a bit of swamp where the vultures moved like domestic turkeys and the pi-dogs kept me awake on moonlight nights with their wailing, and the white women yellowed by atebrin drove by to the club; but the two belonged at any rate to the same continent, and, however distantly, to the same region of the imagination—the region of uncertainty, of not knowing the way about. Once I came a little nearer to Gagool and her witch-hunters, one night in Zigita on the Liberian side of the French Guinea border, when my servants sat in their shuttered hut with their hands over their eyes and someone beat a drum and a whole town stayed behind closed doors while the big bush devil—whom it would mean blindness to see—moved between the huts.

But *King Solomon's Mines* could not finally satisfy. It was not the right answer. The key did not quite fit. Gagool I could recognize—didn't she wait for me in dreams every night in the passage by the linen cupboard, near the nursery door? and she continues to wait, when the mind is sick or tired, though now she is dressed in the theological garments of Despair and speaks in Spenser's accents:

> The longer life, I wote the greater sin,
> The greater sin, the greater punishment.

Yes, Gagool has remained a permanent part of the imagination, but Quatermain and Curtis—weren't they, even when I was only ten years old, a little too good to be true? They were men of such unyielding integrity (they would only admit to a fault in order to show how it might be overcome) that the wavering personality of a child could not rest for long against those monumental shoulders. A child, after all, knows most of the game—it is only an attitude to it that he lacks. He is quite well aware of cowardice, shame, deception, disappointment. Sir Henry Curtis perched upon a rock bleeding from a dozen wounds but fighting on with the remnant of the Greys against the hordes of Twala was too heroic. These men were like Platonic ideas: they were not life as one had already begun to know it.

But when—perhaps I was fourteen by that time—I took Miss Marjorie Bowen's *The Viper of Milan* from the library shelf, the future for better or worse really struck. From that moment I began to write. All the other possible futures slid away: the potential civil servant, the don, the clerk had to look for other incarnations. Imitation after imitation of Miss Bowen's magnificent novel went into exercise books—stories of sixteenth-century Italy or twelfth-century England marked with enormous brutality and a despairing romanticism. It was as if I had been supplied once and for all with a subject.

Why? On the surface *The Viper of Milan* is only the story of a war between Gian Galeazzo Visconti, Duke of Milan, and Mastino della Scala, Duke of Verona, told with zest and cunning and an amazing pictorial sense. Why did it creep in and colour and explain the terrible living world of the stone stairs and the never quiet dormitory? It was no good in that real world to dream that one would ever be a Sir Henry Curtis, but della Scala who at last turned from an honesty that never paid and betrayed his friends and died dishonoured and a failure even at treachery—it was easier for a child to escape behind his mask. As for Visconti, with his beauty, his patience and his genius for evil, I had watched him pass by many a time in his black Sunday suit smelling of mothballs. His name was Carter. He exercised terror from a distance like a snowcloud over the young fields. Goodness has only once found a perfect incarnation in a human body and never will again, but evil can always find a home there. Human nature is not black and white but black and grey. I read all that in *The Viper of Milan* and I looked round and I saw that it was so.

There was another theme I found there. At the end of *The Viper of Milan*—you will remember if you have once read it—comes the great scene of complete success—della Scala is dead, Ferrara, Verona, Novara, Mantua have all fallen, the messengers pour in with news of fresh victories, the whole world outside is cracking up, and Visconti sits and jokes in the wine light. I was not on the classical side or I would have discovered, I suppose, in Greek literature instead of in Miss Bowen's novel the sense of doom that lies over success—the feeling that the pendulum is about to swing. That too made sense; one looked around and saw the doomed everywhere—the champion runner who one day would sag over the tape; the head of the school who would atone, poor devil, during forty dreary undistinguished years; the scholar . . . and when success began to touch oneself too, however mildly, one could only pray that failure would not be held off for too long.

One had lived for fourteen years in a wild jungle country without a map, but now the paths had been traced and naturally one had to follow them. But I think it was Miss Bowen's apparent zest that made me want to write. One could not read her without believing that to write was to live and to enjoy, and before one had discovered one's mistake it was too late—the first book one does enjoy. Anyway she had given me my pattern—religion might later explain it to me in other terms, but the pattern was already there—perfect evil walking the world where perfect good can never walk again, and only the pendulum ensures that after all in the end justice is done. Man is never satisfied, and often I have wished that my hand had not moved further than *King Solomon's Mines*, and that the future I had taken down from the nursery shelf had been a district office in Sierra Leone and twelve tours of malarial duty and a finishing dose of blackwater fever when the danger of retirement approached. What is the good of wishing? The books are always there, the moment of crisis waits, and now our children in their turn are taking down the future and opening the pages. In his poem "Germinal" A.E. wrote:

In ancient shadows and twilights
  Where childhood had stayed,
The world's great sorrows were born
  And its heroes were made.
In the lost boyhood of Judas
  Christ was betrayed.

STUDY QUESTIONS

1. What does Greene mean by saying that in childhood all books are "books of divination"?

2. In what way did his reading merge with the outside world he experienced, even when he was an adult?

3. What did *The Viper of Milan* supply that Greene did not find in *King Solomon's Mines?*

4. Is it fair to conclude, from Greene's report of his own experience, that "trash" can feed a child's imagination just as effectively as carefully-chosen reading matter?

5. Write a theme describing some of the books you read as a child and explaining why you think you remember them.

6. Can you attribute some of your present interests, as Greene does, to the influence of books or movies you encountered when you were very young? If so, write a theme describing this situation.

2. THE UNCOMMON OBSERVER

Visiting a Coal Mine*

George Orwell

When you go down a coal mine it is important to try and get to the coal face when the "fillers" are at work. This is not easy, because when the mine is working visitors are a nuisance and are not encouraged, but if you go at any other time, it is possible to come away with a totally wrong impression. On a Sunday, for instance, a mine seems almost peaceful. The time to go there is when the machines are roaring and the air is black with coal dust, and when you can actually see what the miners have to do. At those times the place is like hell, or at any rate like my own mental picture of hell. Most of the things one imagines in hell are there—

* From *The Orwell Reader,* "Fiction, Essays, and Reportage," by George Orwell, ©, 1956, by Harcourt, Brace and Company, Inc. Reprinted by permission of Harcourt, Brace and Company, Inc. and Martin Secker & Warburg, Ltd.

heat, noise, confusion, darkness, foul air, and, above all, unbearably cramped space. Everything except the fire, for there is no fire down there except the feeble beams of Davy lamps and electric torches which scarcely penetrate the clouds of coal dust.

When you have finally got there—and getting there is a job in itself: I will explain that in a moment—you crawl through the last line of pit props and see opposite you a shiny black wall three or four feet high. This is the coal face. Overhead is the smooth ceiling made by the rock from which the coal has been cut; underneath is the rock again, so that the gallery you are in is only as high as the ledge of coal itself, probably not much more than a yard. The first impression of all, overmastering everything else for a while, is the frightful, deafening din from the conveyor belt which carries the coal away. You cannot see very far, because the fog of coal dust throws back the beam of your lamp, but you can see on either side of you the line of half-naked kneeling men, one to every four or five yards, driving their shovels under the fallen coal and flinging it swiftly over their left shoulders. They are feeding it on to the conveyor belt, a moving rubber belt a couple of feet wide which runs a yard or two behind them. Down this belt a glittering river of coal races constantly. In a big mine it is carrying away several tons of coal every minute. It bears it off to some place in the main roads where it is shot into tubs holding half a ton, and thence dragged to the cages and hoisted to the outer air.

It is impossible to watch the "fillers" at work without feeling a pang of envy for their toughness. It is a dreadful job that they do, an almost superhuman job by the standards of an ordinary person. For they are not only shifting monstrous quantities of coal, they are also doing it in a position that doubles or trebles the work. They have got to remain kneeling all the while—they could hardly rise from their knees without hitting the ceiling—and you can easily see by trying it what a tremendous effort this means. Shoveling is comparatively easy when you are standing up, because you can use your knee and thigh to drive the shovel along; kneeling down, the whole of the strain is thrown upon your arm and belly muscles. And the other conditions do not exactly make things easier. There is the heat—it varies, but in some mines it is suffocating—and the coal dust that stuffs up your throat and nostrils and collects along your eyelids, and the unending rattle of the conveyor belt, which in that confined space is rather like the rattle of a machine gun. But the fillers look and work as though they were made of iron. They really do look like iron—hammered iron statues—under the smooth coat of coal dust which clings to them from head to foot. It is only when you see miners down the mine and naked that you realize what splendid men they are. Most of them are small (big men are at a disadvantage in that job) but nearly all of them have the most noble bodies: wide shoulders tapering to slender supple waists, and small pronounced buttocks and sinewy thighs, with not an ounce of waste flesh anywhere. In the hotter mines they wear only a pair of thin drawers, clogs and knee-pads; in the hottest mines of all, only the clogs and knee-pads. You can hardly tell by the look of them whether they are young or old. They may be any age up to sixty or even sixty-five, but when they are black and naked they all look alike. No one could do their work who had not a young man's body, and a figure fit for a guardsman at that; just a few pounds of extra flesh on the waistline, and the constant bending would be impossible. You can never forget that spectacle once you have seen it—the line of bowed, kneeling figures, sooty black all over, driving their huge shovels under the coal with stupendous force and speed. They are on the job for seven and a half hours, theoretically without a break, for there is no time "off." Actually they snatch a quarter of an hour or so at some time during the shift to eat the food they have brought with them, usually a hunk of bread and dripping and a bottle of cold tea. The first time I was watching the "fillers" at work I put my hand upon some dreadful slimy thing among the coal dust. It was a chewed quid of tobacco. Nearly all the miners chew tobacco, which is said to be good against thirst.

Probably you have to go down several coal mines before you can get much grasp of the processes that are going on round you. This is chiefly because the mere effort of getting from place to place makes it difficult to notice anything else. In some ways it is even disappointing, or at least is unlike what you have expected. You get into the cage, which is a steel box about as wide as a telephone box and two or three times as long. It holds ten men, but they pack it like pilchards in a tin, and a tall man cannot stand upright in it. The steel door shuts upon you, and somebody working the winding gear above drops you into the void. You have the usual momentary qualm in your belly and a bursting sensation in the ears, but not much sensation of movement till you get near the bottom, when the cage slows down so abruptly that you could swear it is going upward again. In the middle of the run the cage probably touches sixty miles an hour; in some of the deeper mines it touches even more. When you crawl out at the bottom you are perhaps four hundred yards under ground. That is to say you have a tolerable-sized mountain on top of you; hundreds of yards of solid rock, bones of extinct beasts, subsoil, flints, roots of growing things, green grass and cows grazing on it—all this suspended over your head and held back only by wooden props as thick as the calf of your leg. But because of the speed at which the cage has brought you down, and the complete blackness through which you have traveled, you hardly feel yourself deeper down than you would be at the bottom of the Piccadilly tube.

What *is* surprising, on the other hand, is the immense horizontal distances that have to be traveled under ground. Before I had been down a mine I had vaguely imagined the miner stepping out of the cage and getting to work on a ledge of coal a few yards away. I had not realized that before he even gets to his work he may have to creep through passages as long as from London Bridge to Oxford Circus. In the beginning, of course, a mine shaft is sunk somewhere near a seam of coal. But as that seam is worked out and fresh seams are followed up, the workings get farther and farther from the pit bottom. If it is a mile from the pit bottom to the coal face, that is probably an average distance; three miles is a fairly normal one; there are even said to be a few mines where it is as much as five miles. But these distances bear no relation to distances above ground. For in all that mile or three miles as it may be, there is hardly anywhere outside the main road, and not many places even there, where a man can stand upright.

You do not notice the effect of this till you have gone a few hundred yards. You start off, stooping slightly, down the dim-lit gallery, eight or ten feet wide and about five high, with the walls built up with slabs of shale, like the stone walls in Derbyshire. Every yard or two there are wooden props holding up the beams and girders; some of the girders have buckled into fantastic curves under which you have to duck. Usually it is bad going underfoot—thick dust or jagged chunks of shale, and in some mines where there is water it is as mucky as a farmyard. Also there is the track for the coal tubs, like a miniature railway track with sleepers a foot or two apart, which is tiresome to walk on. Everything is gray with shale dust; there is a dusty fiery smell which seems to be the same in all mines. You see mysterious machines of which you never learn the purpose, and bundles of tools slung together on wires, and sometimes mice darting away from the beam of the lamps. They are surprisingly common, especially in mines where there are or have been horses. It would be interesting to know how they got there in the first place; possibly by falling down the shaft—for they say a mouse can fall any distance uninjured, owing to its surface area being so large relative to its weight. You press yourself against the wall to make way for lines of tubs jolting slowly toward the shaft, drawn by an endless steel cable operated from the surface. You creep through sacking curtains and thick wooden doors which, when they are opened, let out fierce blasts of air. These doors are an important part of the ventilation system. The exhausted air is sucked out of one shaft by means of fans, and the fresh air enters the other of its own accord. But if left to itself the air will take the shortest way round, leaving the deeper workings unventilated; so all short-cuts have to be partitioned off.

At the start to walk stooping is rather a joke, but it is a joke that soon wears off. I am handicapped by being exceptionally tall, but when the roof falls to four feet or less it is a tough job for anybody except a dwarf or a child. You have not only got to bend double, you have also got to keep your head up all the while so as to see the beams and girders and dodge them when they come. You have, therefore, a constant crick in the neck, but this is nothing to the pain in your knees and thighs. After half a mile it becomes (I am not exaggerating) an unbearable agony. You begin to wonder whether you will ever get to the end—still more, how on earth you are going to get back. Your pace grows slower and slower. You come to a stretch of a couple of hundred yards where it is all exceptionally low and you have to work yourself along in a squatting position. Then suddenly the roof opens out to a mysterious height—scene of an old fall of rock, probably—and for twenty whole yards you can stand upright. The relief is overwhelming. But after this there is another low stretch of a hundred yards and then a succession of beams which you have to crawl under. You go down on all fours; even this is a relief after the squatting business. But when you come to the end of the beams and try to get up again, you find that your knees have temporarily struck work and refuse to lift you. You call a halt, ignominiously, and say that you would like to rest for a minute or two. Your guide (a miner) is sympathetic. He knows that your muscles are not the same as his. "Only another four hundred yards," he says encouragingly; you feel that he might as well say another four hundred miles. But finally you do somehow creep as far as the coal face. You have gone a mile and taken the best part of an hour; a miner would do it in not much more than twenty minutes. Having got there, you have to sprawl in the coal dust and get your strength back for several minutes before you can even watch the work in progress with any kind of intelligence.

Coming back is worse than going, not only because you are already tired out but because the journey back to the shaft is probably slightly uphill. You get through the low places at the speed of a tortoise, and you have no shame now about calling a halt when your knees give way. Even the lamp you are carrying becomes a nuisance and probably when you stumble you drop it; whereupon, if it is a Davy lamp, it goes out. Ducking the beams becomes more and more of an effort, and sometimes you forget to duck. You try walking head down as the miners do, and then you bang your backbone. Even the miners bang their backbones fairly often. This is the reason why in very hot mines, where it is necessary to go about half naked, most of the miners have what they call "buttons down the back"—that is, a permanent scab on each vertebra. When the track is downhill the miners sometimes fit their clogs, which are hollow underneath, on the trolley rails and slide down. In mines where the "traveling" is very bad all the miners carry sticks about two and a half feet long, hollowed out below the handle. In normal places you keep your hand on top of the stick and in the low places you slide your hand down into the hollow. These sticks are a great help, and the wooden crash-helmets—a comparatively recent invention—are a godsend. They look like a French or Italian steel helmet, but they are made of some kind of pith and very light, and so strong that you can take a violent blow on the head without feeling it. When finally you get back to the surface you have been perhaps three hours underground and traveled two miles, and you are more exhausted than you would be by a twenty-five-mile walk above ground. For a week afterward your thighs are so stiff that coming downstairs is quite a difficult feat; you have to work your way down in a peculiar sidelong manner, without bending the knees. Your miner friends notice the stiffness of your walk and chaff you about it. ("How'd ta like to work down pit, eh?" etc.). Yet even a miner who has been long away from work—from illness, for instance—when he comes back to the pit, suffers badly for the first few days.

STUDY QUESTIONS

1. Describe the order in which the elements of this description are arranged. Could they have been logically arranged otherwise? What are the advantages of Orwell's arrangement for his purpose?
2. What particularly effective and expressive comparisons does Orwell use?
3. What effect does Orwell gain by stressing the lowness of the ceiling in a mine, the kneeling position in which the miners work, the long "traveling" distance?
4. What would you say was Orwell's attitude toward his subject? Does it promote or interfere with a fair and objective description?
5. Write a theme describing some job or activity you are familiar with, being sure to give an outsider an accurate idea of the problems involved in it.
6. Write a theme describing some unusual place or scene you have visited. Plan your description by asking yourself what aspects of the subject the general reader is likely to be most curious about, and eliminate everything not peculiar to the subject.

Creole Carrier-Girl*

Lafcadio Hearn

Those who believe that great physical endurance and physical energy cannot exist in the tropics do not know the Creole carrier-girl. At a very early age—perhaps at five years—she learns to carry small articles upon her head—a bowl of rice—a dobanne, or red earthen decanter, full of water—even an orange on a plate; and before long she is able to balance these perfectly without using her hands to steady them. (I have often seen children actually run with cans of water upon their heads, and never spill a drop.) At nine or ten she is able to carry thus a tolerably heavy basket, or a trait (a wooden tray with deep outward sloping sides) containing a weight of from twenty to thirty pounds; and is able to accompany her mother, sister, or cousin on long peddling journeys

* From *Two Years in the French West Indies,* 1890.

—walking barefoot twelve and fifteen miles a day. At sixteen or seventeen she is a tall robust girl—lithe, vigorous, tough—all tendon and hard flesh; —she carries a tray or a basket of the largest size, and a burden of one hundred and twenty to one hundred and fifty pounds weight;—she can now earn about thirty francs (about six dollars) a month, *by walking fifty miles a day*, as an itinerant seller.

Among her class there are figures to make you dream of Atalanta;— and all, whether ugly or attractive as to feature, are finely shapen as to body and limb. Brought into existence by extraordinary necessities of environment, the type is a peculiarly local one—a type of human thoroughbred representing the true secret of grace: economy of force. There are no corpulent porteuses for the long interior routes; all are built lightly and firmly as racers. There are no old porteuses;—to do the work even at forty signifies a constitution of astounding solidity. After the full force of youth and health is spent, the poor carrier must seek lighter labor;—she can no longer compete with the girls. For in this calling the young body is taxed to its utmost capacity of strength, endurance, and rapid motion.

As a general rule, the weight is such that no well-freighted porteuse can, unassisted, either "load" or "unload" (châgé or déchâgé, in Creole phrase); the effort to do so would burst a blood vessel, wrench a nerve, rupture a muscle. She cannot even sit down under her burden without risk of breaking her neck; absolute perfection of the balance is necessary for self-preservation. A case came under my own observation of a woman rupturing a muscle in her arm through careless haste in the mere act of aiding another to unload.

And no one not a brute will ever refuse to aid a woman to lift or to relieve herself of her burden;—you may see the wealthiest merchant, the proudest planter, gladly do it;—the meanness of refusing, or of making any conditions for the performance of his little kindness has only been imagined in those strange Stories of Devils wherewith the oral and uncollected literature of the Creole abounds.

Preparing for her journey, the young màchanne (marchande) puts on the poorest and briefest chemise in her possession, and the most worn of her light calico robes. These are all she wears. The robe is drawn upward and forward, so as to reach a little below the knee, and is confined thus by a waist-string, or a long kerchief bound tightly round the loins. Instead of a Madras or painted turban-kerchief, she binds a plain mouchoir neatly and closely about her head; and if her hair be long, it is combed back and gathered into a loop behind. Then, with a second mouchoir of coarser quality she makes a pad, or, as she calls it, tòche, by winding the kerchief round her fingers as you would coil up a piece of string;—and the soft mass, flattened with a patting of the hand, is placed upon her head, over the coiffure. On this the great loaded trait is poised.

She wears no shoes! To wear shoes and do her work swiftly and well in such a land of mountains would be impossible. She must climb thou-

sands and descend thousands of feet every day—march up and down
slopes so steep that the horses of the country all break down after a few
years of similar journeying. The girl invariably outlasts the horse—
though carrying an equal weight. Shoes, unless extraordinarily well
made, would shift place a little with every change from ascent to descent,
or the reverse, during the march—would yield and loosen with the ever-
varying strain—would compress the toes—produce corns, bunions, raw
places by rubbing, and soon cripple the porteuse. Remember, she has to
walk perhaps fifty miles between dawn and dark, under a sun to which a
single hour's exposure, without the protection of an umbrella, is perilous
to any European or American—the terrible sun of the tropics! Sandals
are the only conceivable footgear suited to such a calling as hers; but she
needs no sandals: the soles of her feet are toughened so as to feel no
asperities, and present to sharp pebbles a surface at once yielding and resisting, like a cushion of solid caoutchouc.

Besides her load, she carries only a canvas purse tied to her girdle on
the right side, and on the left a very small bottle of rum, or white tafia—
usually the latter, because it is so cheap. . . . For she may not always find
the Gouyave Water to drink—the cold clear pure stream conveyed to the
fountains of Saint Pierre from the highest mountains by a beautiful and
marvelous plan of hydraulic engineering: she will have to drink betimes
the common spring-water of the bamboo-fountains on the remoter high-
roads; and this may cause dysentery if swallowed without a spoonful of
spirits. Therefore she never travels without a little liquor.

. . . So!—She is ready: "Châgé moin, souplè, chè!" She bends to lift the
end of the heavy trait: some one takes the other—yon!—dè!—toua!—it is
on her head. Perhaps she winces an instant;—the weight is not perfectly
balanced; she settles it with her hands—gets it in the exact place. Then,
all steady—lithe, light, half naked—away she moves with a long springy
step. So even her walk that the burden never sways; yet so rapid her motion that however good a walker you may fancy yourself to be you will
tire out after a sustained effort of fifteen minutes to follow her uphill.
Fifteen minutes!—and she can keep up that pace without slackening—
save for a minute to eat and drink at midday—for at least twelve hours
and fifty-six minutes, the extreme length of a West Indian day. She
starts before dawn; tries to reach her resting-place by sunset; after dark,
like all her people, she is afraid of meeting zombis.

Let me give you some idea of her average speed under an average
weight of one hundred and twenty-five pounds—estimates based partly
upon my own observations, partly upon the declarations of the trustworthy merchants who employ her, and partly on the assertion of habi-
tants of the burghs or cities named—all of which statements perfectly
agree. From Saint Pierre to Basse-Point, by the national road, the distance is a trifle less than twenty-seven kilometres and three quarters. She
makes the transit easily in three hours and a half; and returns in the

afternoon, after an absence of scarcely more than eight hours. From Saint Pierre to Morne Rouge—two thousand feet up in the mountains (an ascent so abrupt that no one able to pay carriage-fare dreams of attempting to walk it)—the distance is seven kilometres and three quarters. She makes it in little more than an hour. But this represents only the beginning of her journey. She passes on to Grande Anse, twenty-one and three-quarter kilometres away. But she does not rest there: she returns at the same pace, and reaches Saint Pierre before dark. From Saint Pierre to Gros-Morne the distance to be twice traversed by her is more than thirty-two kilometres. A journey of sixty-four kilometres—daily, perhaps—forty miles! And there are many màchannes who make yet longer trips—trips of three or four days' duration;—these rest at villages upon their route. . . .

Forty to fifty miles a day, always under a weight of more than a hundred pounds—for when the trait has been emptied she puts in stones for ballast;—carrying her employer's merchandise and money over the mountain ranges, beyond the peaks, across the ravines, through the tropical forest, sometimes through by-ways haunted by the fer-de-lance—and this in summer or winter, the season of rains or the season of heat, the time of fevers or the time of hurricanes, at a franc a day! . . . How does she live upon it?

There are twenty sous to the franc. The girl leaves Saint Pierre with her load at early morning. At the second village, Morne Rouge, she halts to buy one, two, or three biscuits at a sou apiece; and reaching Ajoupa-Bouillon later in the forenoon, she may buy another biscuit or two. Altogether she may be expected to eat five sous of biscuit or bread before reaching the Grande Anse, where she probably has a meal waiting for her. This ought to cost her ten sous—especially if there be meat in her ragoût: which represents a total expense of fifteen sous for eatables. Then there is the additional cost of the cheap liquor, which she must mix with her drinking water, as it would be more than dangerous to swallow pure cold water in her heated condition; two or three sous more. This almost makes the franc. But such a hasty and really erroneous estimate does not include expenses of lodging and clothing;—she may sleep on the bare floor sometimes, and twenty francs a year may keep her in clothes; but she must rent the floor and pay for the clothes out of that franc. As a matter of fact she not only does all this upon her twenty sous a day, but can even economize something which will enable her, when her youth and force decline, to start in business for herself. And her economy will not seem so wonderful when I assure you that thousands of men here—huge men muscled like bulls and lions—live upon an average expenditure of five sous a day. One sou of bread, two sous of manioc flour, one sou of dried codfish, one sou of tafia: such is their meal.

There are women carriers who earn more than a franc a day—women with a particular talent for selling, who are paid on commission—from ten to fifteen per cent. These eventually make themselves independent in many instances;—they continue to sell and bargain in person, but hire a young girl to carry the goods.

STUDY QUESTIONS

1. Writing in 1890, Hearn marvels in this selection at the beauty and accomplishment of the Creole carrier-girls, and seems to idealize their way of life. Compare this with Orwell's attitude toward the work of the coal miner. Would it have been possible for Orwell to describe his visit to the coal mine in such a way that the reader would have felt that the miners' life was good? Is one of these descriptions more "objective" than the other?

2. Examine the vocabulary of Hearn and that of Orwell. If you did not know the dates of these selections, could you place one as earlier than the other on the basis of vocabulary?

3. What is the logic of organization in this selection? What effect would be produced if the discussion of the girls' pay had been placed first? If the discussion of preparation for the journey had been placed first?

4. Analyze the description of the carrier-girl's preparation for the journey. What proportion of the detail given actually paints the picture of the girl, and what proportion provides explanation for her preparation and dress?

5. Observe some kind of worker closely and write a description of his preparation for his work or for his execution of the job. Consider, for example, a carpenter, bricklayer, bulldozer operator, or similar skilled workman.

6. Compare Orwell's description of the miners and Hearn's description of the carrier-girls in some detail and write an analysis of the differences in attitude of the two authors toward their subjects.

Dr. Skinner*

Samuel Butler

Dr. Skinner had been a burning and a shining light in every position he had filled from his boyhood upwards. He was a very great genius. Everyone knew this; they said, indeed, that he was one of the few people to whom the word genius could be applied without exaggeration. Had he not taken I don't know how many University Scholarships in his freshman's year? Had he not been afterwards Senior Wrangler, First

* From *The Way of All Flesh*, 1903, ch. xxvii. Reprinted by permission of E. P. Dutton, Inc. New York; Jonathan Cape, Ltd.; and the Executors of Samuel Butler.

Chancellor's Medallist and I do not know how many more things besides? And then, he was such a wonderful speaker; at the Union Debating Club he had been without a rival, and had, of course, been president; his moral character—a point on which so many geniuses were weak—was absolutely irreproachable; foremost of all, however, among his many great qualities, and perhaps more remarkable even than his genius was what biographers have called "the simple-minded and childlike earnestness of his character," an earnestness which might be perceived by the solemnity with which he spoke even about trifles. It is hardly necessary to say he was on the Liberal side in politics.

His personal appearance was not particularly prepossessing. He was about the middle height, portly, and had a couple of fierce grey eyes, that flashed fire from beneath a pair of great, bushy, beetling eyebrows and overawed all who came near him. It was in respect of his personal appearance, however, that, if he was vulnerable at all, his weak place was to be found. His hair when he was a young man was red, but after he had taken his degree he had a brain fever which caused him to have his head shaved; when he reappeared he did so wearing a wig, and one which was a good deal further off red than his own hair had been. He not only had never discarded his wig, but year by year it had edged itself a little more and a little more off red, till by the time he was forty, there was not a trace of red remaining, and his wig was brown.

When Dr. Skinner was a very young man, hardly more than five-and-twenty, the head-mastership of the Roughborough Grammar School had fallen vacant, and he had been unhesitatingly appointed. The result justified the selection. Dr. Skinner's pupils distinguished themselves at whichever University they went to. He moulded their minds after the model of his own, and stamped an impression upon them which was indelible in after-life; whatever else a Roughborough man might be, he was sure to make everyone feel that he was a God-fearing earnest Christian and a Liberal, if not a Radical, in politics. Some boys, of course, were incapable of appreciating the beauty and loftiness of Dr. Skinner's nature. Some such boys, alas! there will be in every school; upon them Dr. Skinner's hand was very properly a heavy one. His hand was against them, and theirs against him during the whole time of the connection between them. They not only disliked him, but they hated all that he more especially embodied, and throughout their lives disliked all that reminded them of him. Such boys, however, were in a minority, the spirit of the place being decidedly Skinnerian.

I once had the honour of playing a game of chess with this great man. It was during the Christmas holidays, and I had come down to Roughborough for a few days to see Alethea Pontifex (who was then living there) on business. It was very gracious of him to take notice of me, for if I was a light of literature at all it was of the very lightest kind.

It is true that in the intervals of business I had written a good deal, but my works had been almost exclusively for the stage, and for those theatres that devoted themselves to extravaganza and burlesque. I had written many pieces of this description, full of puns and comic songs, and they had had a fair success, but my best piece had been a treatment of English history during the Reformation period, in the course of which I had introduced Cranmer, Sir Thomas More, Henry the Eighth, Catherine of Arragon, and Thomas Cromwell (in his youth better known as the *Malleus Monachorum*), and had made them dance a breakdown. I had also dramatised "The Pilgrim's Progress" for a Christmas Pantomime, and made an important scene of Vanity Fair, with Mr. Greatheart, Apollyon, Christiana, Mercy, and Hopeful as the principal characters. The orchestra played music taken from Handel's best known works, but the time was a good deal altered, and altogether the tunes were not exactly as Handel left them. Mr. Greatheart was very stout and he had a red nose; he wore a capacious waistcoat, and a shirt with a huge frill down the middle of the front. Hopeful was up to as much mischief as I could give him; he wore the costume of a young swell of the period, and had a cigar in his mouth which was continually going out.

Christiana did not wear much of anything: indeed it was said that the dress which the Stage Manager had originally proposed for her had been considered inadequate even by the Lord Chamberlain, but this is not the case. With all these delinquencies upon my mind it was natural that I should feel convinced of sin while playing chess (which I hate) with the great Dr. Skinner of Roughborough—the historian of Athens and editor of Demosthenes. Dr. Skinner, moreover, was one of those who pride themselves on being able to set people at their ease at once, and I had been sitting on the edge of my chair all the evening. But I have always been very easily overawed by a schoolmaster.

The game had been a long one, and at half-past nine, when supper came in, we had each of us a few pieces remaining. "What will you take for supper, Dr. Skinner?" said Mrs. Skinner in a silvery voice.

He made no answer for some time, but at last in a tone of almost superhuman solemnity, he said, first, "Nothing," and then, "Nothing whatever."

By and by, however, I had a sense come over me as though I were nearer the consummation of all things than I had ever yet been. The room seemed to grow dark, as an expression came over Dr. Skinner's face, which showed that he was about to speak. The expression gathered force, the room grew darker and darker. "Stay," he at length added, and I felt that here at any rate was an end to a suspense which was rapidly becoming unbearable. "Stay—I may presently take a glass of cold water— and a small piece of bread and butter."

As he said the word "butter" his voice sank to a hardly audible whisper; then there was a sigh as though of relief when the sentence was concluded, and the universe this time was safe.

Another ten minutes of solemn silence finished the game. The Doctor rose briskly from his seat and placed himself at the supper table. "Mrs. Skinner," he exclaimed jauntily, "what are those mysterious-looking objects surrounded by potatoes?"

"Those are oysters, Dr. Skinner."

"Give me some, and give Overton some."

And so on till he had eaten a good plate of oysters, a scallop shell of minced veal nicely browned, some apple tart, and a hunk of bread and cheese. This was the small piece of bread and butter.

The cloth was now removed and tumblers with teaspoons in them, a lemon or two and a jug of boiling water were placed upon the table. Then the great man unbent. His face beamed.

"And what shall it be to drink?" he exclaimed persuasively. "Shall it be brandy and water? No. It shall be gin and water. Gin is the more wholesome liquor."

So gin it was, hot and stiff, too.

Who can wonder at him or do anything but pity him? Was he not headmaster of Roughborough School? To whom had he owed money at any time? Whose ox had he taken, whose ass had he taken, or whom had he defrauded? What whisper had ever been breathed against his moral character? If he had become rich it was by the most honourable of all means —his literary attainments; over and above his great works of scholarship, his "Meditations upon the Epistle and Character of St. Jude" had placed him among the most popular of English theologians; it was so exhaustive that no one who bought it need ever meditate upon the subject again— indeed it exhausted all who had anything to do with it. He had made £5000 by this work alone, and would very likely make another £5000 before he died. A man who had done all this and wanted a piece of bread and butter had a right to announce the fact with some pomp and circumstance. Nor should his words be taken without searching for what he used to call a "deeper and more hidden meaning." Those who searched for this even in his lightest utterances would not be without their reward. They would find that "bread and butter" was Skinnerese for oyster-patties and apple tart, and "gin hot" the true translation of water.

But independently of their money value, his works had made him a lasting name in literature. So probably Gallio was under the impression that his fame would rest upon the treatises on natural history which we gather from Seneca that he compiled, and which for aught we know may have contained a complete theory of evolution; but the treatises are all gone and Gallio has become immortal for the very last reason in the world that he expected, and for the very last reason that would have flattered his vanity. He has become immortal because he cared nothing about the most important movement with which he was ever brought into connection (I wish people who are in search of immortality would lay the lesson to heart and not make so much noise about important movements), and so, if Dr. Skinner becomes immortal, it will probably be for some reason very different from the one which he so fondly imagined.

Could it be expected to enter into the head of such a man as this that in reality he was making his money by corrupting youth; that it was his paid profession to make the worse appear the better reason in the eyes of those who were too young and inexperienced to be able to find him out; that he kept out of the sight of those whom he professed to teach material points of the argument, for the production of which they had a right to rely upon the honour of anyone who made professions of sincerity; that he was a passionate, half-turkey-cock, half-gander of a man whose sallow, bilious face and hobble-gobble voice could scare the timid, but who would take to his heels readily enough if he were met firmly; that his "Meditations on St. Jude," such as they were, were cribbed without acknowledgment, and would have been beneath contempt if so many people did not believe them to have been written honestly? Mrs. Skinner might have perhaps kept him a little more in his proper place if she had thought it worth while to try, but she had enough to attend to in looking after her household and seeing that the boys were well fed and, if they were ill, properly looked after—which she took good care they were.

STUDY QUESTIONS

1. Orwell and Hearn, in their descriptions, have been concerned with depicting types rather than individuals. To what extent is Butler picturing Dr. Skinner as an individual and to what extent is he using him as a type? What kinds of details are common to the three descriptions? What kinds are different?

2. In what way does Dr. Skinner's wig reflect something about his character in general?

3. Why do you think the narrator feels Dr. Skinner should be pitied?

4. What is the leading character trait stressed in this description?

5. How would you summarize Butler's attitude toward Dr. Skinner? In doing this, you will want to examine the tone of the selection, noting where it is ironic, matter-of-fact, or indignant.

6. Write a description of a person you know who has some marked character trait. Try to use Butler's method of projecting his character through his speech, actions, dress and other outward signs, instead of telling the reader directly what it is.

New York*

E. B. White

On any person who desires such queer prizes, New York will bestow the gift of loneliness and the gift of privacy. It is this largess that accounts for the presence within the city's walls of a considerable section of the population; for the residents of Manhattan are to a large extent strangers who have pulled up stakes somewhere and come to town, seeking sanctuary or fulfillment or some greater or lesser grail. The capacity to make such dubious gifts is a mysterious quality of New York. It can destroy an individual, or it can fulfill him, depending a good deal on luck. No one should come to New York to live unless he is willing to be lucky.

New York is the concentrate of art and commerce and sport and religion and entertainment and finance, bringing to a single compact arena the gladiator, the evangelist, the promoter, the actor, the trader and the merchant. It carries on its lapel the unexpungeable odor of the long past, so that no matter where you sit in New York you feel the vibrations of great times and tall deeds, of queer people and events and undertakings. I am sitting at the moment in a stifling hotel room in 90-degree heat, half-way down an air shaft, in midtown. No air moves in or out of the room, yet I am curiously affected by emanations from the immediate surroundings. I am twenty-two blocks from where Rudolph Valentino lay in state, eight blocks from where Nathan Hale was executed, five blocks from the publisher's office where Ernest Hemingway hit Max Eastman on the nose, four miles from where Walt Whitman sat sweating out editorials for the Brooklyn Eagle, thirty-four blocks from the street Willa Cather lived in when she came to New York to write books about Nebraska, one block from where Marceline used to clown on the boards of the Hippodrome, thirty-six blocks from the spot where the historian Joe Gould kicked a radio to pieces in full view of the public, thirteen blocks from where Harry Thaw shot Stanford White, five blocks from where I used to usher at the Metropolitan Opera and only a hundred and twelve blocks from the spot where Clarence Day the Elder was washed of his sins in the Church of the Epiphany (I could continue this list indefinitely); and for that matter I am probably occupying the very room that any number of exalted characters sat in, some of them on hot, breathless afternoons, lonely and private and full of their own sense of emanations from without.

When I went down to lunch a few minutes ago I noticed that the man sitting next to me (about eighteen inches away along the wall) was Fred Stone. The eighteen inches were both the connection and the separation that New York provides for its inhabitants. My only connection with Fred Stone was that I saw him in *The Wizard of Oz* around the beginning of the century. But our waiter felt the same stimulus from being close to a man from Oz, and after Mr. Stone left the room the waiter told me that when he (the waiter) was a young man just arrived in the country and before he could understand a word of English, he had taken his girl for their first theater date to *The Wizard of Oz*. It was a wonderful show, the waiter recalled—a man of straw, a man of tin. Wonderful! (And still only eighteen inches away.) "Mr. Stone is a very hearty eater," said the waiter thoughtfully, content with this fragile participation in destiny, this link with Oz.

New York blends the gift of privacy with the excitement of participation; and better than most dense communities it succeeds in insulating the individual (if he wants it, and almost everybody wants or needs it) against all enormous and violent and wonderful events that are taking place every minute. Since I have been sitting in this miasmic air shaft, a good many rather splashy events have occurred in town. A man shot and killed his wife in a fit of jealousy. It caused no stir outside his block and got only small mention in the papers. I did not attend. Since my arrival, the greatest air show ever staged in all the world took place in town. I didn't attend and neither did most of the eight million other inhabitants, although they say there was quite a crowd. I didn't even hear any planes except a couple of westbound commercial airliners that habitually use this air shaft to fly over. The biggest ocean-going ships on the North Atlantic arrived and departed. I didn't notice them and neither did most other New Yorkers. I am told this is the greatest seaport in the world, with six hundred and fifty miles of water front, and ships calling here from many exotic lands, but the only boat I've happened to notice since my arrival was a small sloop tacking out of the East River night before last on the ebb tide when I was walking across the Brooklyn Bridge. I heard the *Queen Mary* blow one midnight, though, and the sound carried the whole history of departure and longing and loss. The Lions have been in convention. I've seen not one Lion. A friend of mine saw one and told me about him. (He was lame, and was wearing a bolero.) At the ballgrounds and horse parks the greatest sporting spectacles have been enacted. I saw no ballplayer, no race horse. The governor came to town. I heard the siren scream, but that was all there was to that—an eighteen-inch margin again. A man was killed by a falling cornice. I was not a party to the tragedy, and again the inches counted heavily.

I mention these merely to show that New York is peculiarly constructed to absorb almost anything that comes along (whether a thousand-foot liner out of the East or a twenty-thousand-man convention out of the West) without inflicting the event on its inhabitants; so that every event is, in a sense, optional, and the inhabitant is in the happy position of being able to choose his spectacle and so conserve his soul. In most metropolises, small and large, the choice is often not with the individual at all. He is thrown to the Lions. The Lions are overwhelming; the event is unavoidable. A cornice falls, and it hits every citizen on the head, every last man in town. I sometimes think that the only event that hits every New Yorker on the head is the annual St. Patrick's Day parade, which is fairly penetrating—the Irish are a hard race to tune out, there are 500,000 of them in residence, and they have the police force right in the family.

The quality in New York that insulates its inhabitants from life may simply weaken them as individuals. Perhaps it is healthier to live in a community where, when a cornice falls, you feel the blow; where, when the governor passes, you see at any rate his hat.

I am not defending New York in this regard. Many of its settlers are probably here merely to escape, not face, reality. But whatever it means, it is a rather rare gift, and I believe it has a positive effect on the creative capacities of New Yorkers—for creation is in part merely the business of forgoing the great and small distractions.

Although New York often imparts a feeling of great forlornness or forsakenness, it seldom seems dead or unresourceful; and you always feel that either by shifting your location ten blocks or by reducing your fortune by five dollars you can experience rejuvenation. Many people who have no real independence of spirit depend on the city's tremendous variety and sources of excitement for spiritual sustenance and maintenance of morale. In the country there are a few chances of sudden rejuvenation—a shift in weather, perhaps, or something arriving in the mail. But in New York the chances are endless. I think that although many persons are here from some excess of spirit (which caused them to break away from their small town), some, too, are here from a deficiency of spirit, who find in New York a protection, or any easy substitution.

There are roughly three New Yorks. There is, first, the New York of the man or woman who was born here, who takes the city for granted and accepts its size and its turbulence as natural and inevitable. Second, there is the New York of the commuter—the city that is devoured by locusts each day and spat out at night. Third, there is the New York of the person who was born somewhere else and came to New York in quest of something. Of these three trembling cities the greatest is the last—the city of final destination, the city that is a goal. It is this third city that accounts for New York's high-strung disposition, its poetical deportment, its dedication to the arts, and its incomparable achievements. Commuters give the city its tidal restlessness; natives give it solidity and continuity; but the settlers give it passion. And whether it is a farmer arriving from Italy to set up a small grocery store in a slum, or a young girl arriving from a small town in Mississippi to escape the indignity of being observed by her neighbors, or a boy arriving from the Corn Belt with a manuscript in his suitcase and a pain in his heart, it makes no difference: each embraces New York with the intense excitement of first love, each absorbs New York with the fresh eyes of an adventurer, each generates heat and light to dwarf the Consolidated Edison Company.

The commuter is the queerest bird of all. The suburb he inhabits has no essential vitality of its own and is a mere roost where he comes at day's end to go to sleep. Except in rare cases, the man who lives in Mamaroneck or Little Neck or Teaneck, and works in New York, discovers nothing much about the city except the time of arrival and departure of trains and buses, and the path to a quick lunch. He is desk-bound, and has never, idly roaming in the gloaming, stumbled suddenly on Belvedere Tower in the Park, seen the ramparts rise sheer from the water of the pond, and the boys along the shore fishing for minnows, girls stretched out negligently on the shelves of the rocks; he has never come suddenly on anything at all in New York as a loiterer, because he has had no time between trains. He has fished in Manhattan's wallet and dug out coins, but has never listened to Manhattan's breathing, never awakened to its morning, never dropped off to sleep in its night.

STUDY QUESTIONS

1. E. B. White is one of the most successful writers of a particular kind of contemporary style. What specific things do you notice about his diction, sentence structure, choice of detail? Compare E. B. White's style with that of Orwell. How would you describe the tone of each? What accounts for the differences?

2. Would you describe this selection as an attack on New York or a defense of it? Explain your answer.

3. Both this and the following essay by Morris Freedman are evaluations of New York. Do they have any areas of agreement? What are their principal areas of disagreement?

4. What is the point of the paradoxical situations mentioned in the paragraph beginning "New York blends the gift of privacy . . . ?"

5. Take an environment with which you are very familiar and following White's method, give an objective account of it, telling how it might appear to different kinds of people.

6. Write a description of some place whose "atmosphere" you have found impressive, conveying as well as you can the feelings and emotions it evokes.

Wonderful Town?*

Morris Freedman

> New York, New York, it's a helluva town,
> The Bronx is up and the Battery's down,
> The People ride in a hole in the ground. . . .

The one thing even the most hardened New Yorker (Chicagoan, Philadelphian) cannot avoid is the sheer presence of the city, its physical bulk, its complexities of movement, its squashing crowds, its oppression and indifference. Where Sherwood Anderson was the chronicler of small town terrors, John Cheever today records metropolitan and suburban horrors. For cities exist by size, by forcing huge numbers of people through funnels into small areas, by neglecting utterly the eye's need and the body's need of nature, the mind's need for occasional separateness. Sooner or later, the plain difficulty of daily living—of getting from home to work and back again; of shopping; of going to the theatre, concert hall, or museum—makes anything the city may offer just not worth it. Only a whimsical, arch romanticist like E. B. White can after many years still address poems of adoration to the city, but then he has his Maine refuge.

Take New York. You can't get from any Long Island community into the city in much under an hour, and a quite uncomfortable one too, whether you drive through crowded traffic or bounce in a Long Island Railroad car or stand in the subway, lurching, elbows pinned, sweating, all the way to or from Jamaica or Flushing. I speak of Long Island, but it's the same for Westchester, Connecticut, New Jersey, Riverdale. That much publicized commuter's bus in Chicago with luxurious accommodations is just a desperate effort to do something about the problem; it would take a fleet of such buses, snarling traffic all the more, to take care of all Chicago commuters.

Return to the city? Before we left New York—never to return we hope —such a movement was growing. Defeated, frustrated suburbanites were giving up their daily two-to-three-hour battle of attrition. They sold their split-level and ranch homes, took apartments at huge rents in the city, enrolled their children in private schools, disposed of their cars (or else settled down with them to that peculiar game adults play in New York, like musical chairs, of periodic daily shifting of parked automo-

*From *The New Republic*, June 10, 1957. Reprinted by permission of *The New Republic* and of the author.

biles). They accepted the lack of space, of greenery, of views of sky; the presence of smoke, soot, dirt and noise.

But the worst thing these returning exiles accepted, I feel now, was a kind of living with the ever-present sense of the imminence of disaster. I am aware now, away from the city for nearly two years, of how casually one accepts sudden death in New York—the killing of a woman crossing Herald Square, her skull crumpled by a truck (I saw that); a plane hitting the Empire State Building (I worked across the street); the forcing of someone off a crowded subway platform into the path of a train (I used to look at daily headlines describing that; they said the person jumped or fell, but how could anyone ever know?); the falling of a flower pot or a wooden beam from the heights of a building, to hit an old Negro man or kill a chauffeur in a Rolls-Royce (I read about these); and the countless daily acts of mayhem, so commonplace they never got into the newspapers. I remember two great winter strikes in New York in recent years that threatened disaster, one resulting in a shortage of milk, the other, of fuel. I remember, too, the shudder that swept the city when international politics seemed to be getting out of control and everyone became a private, momentary volunteer for Civil Defense, watching the skies for the plane that carried the little bomb. There was that occasional comic feeling, too, not unmixed with panic, of being jammed on Manhattan Island as in a Marx Brothers' stateroom.

One accepts the nightmares of the city for the sake of culture, sophisticated society, jobs. As for the culture, during our last year in New York, my wife and I went to the theatre just once. That night cost us, with modest tickets, close to $20 and several hours of nervous harassment. Even the museums and art galleries get intolerably crowded. Perhaps one can work harried and exhausted; it is more difficult to respond to art in that condition. Metropolitan social life and metropolitan jobs, too, once the enchantment wears off, become thoughtlessly competitive. Social caste becomes determined by work caste, and that, in turn, all too often, by one-upmanship. Insiderism, snobbism, intrigue, become techniques of daily living. The most routine and essential services become marked by callousness; bus drivers ignore you in the rain; doctors and hospitals treat you as a moving cadaver on an assembly line. Anonymity is Everyman; as one must forget one's identity in the frantic motions at the beginning, middle, and end of the work day, so one forgets it in his office, at parties, with friends, even, at last, with his family and with himself.

Not everyone, of course, is lost, nor do all the lost lose themselves in the same way, but those that survive illustrate what it takes to stay alive and at what expense. I think of people I know who are not anonymous bodies in the big city. All are persons of the greatest self-understanding and independence of spirit and mind. But they, too, have clearly compromised with the demons; it is obvious that their work could be so much richer were they not required to spend so much of their resources countering the hazards of the city.

I know about the "cosmopolitanism" of New Yorkers. To me they are monstrous solipsists (as I was), with a built-in provincialism far narrower and more pernicious than anything found in the provinces. The urban area is their universe. In part, like any provincialism, this comes from innocence; in greater part, however, it is the result of the general competitive atmosphere: if one successfully bulls his way through the subway, through an office, through a cocktail shindig, through domestic difficulties, then the results *must* be worth it. If the game is worth the playing, it must be worth the winning. To some degree, every big city dweller must be afflicted with this notion, else why does he remain? Why else does he allow himself to live in tenements, in an outrageous climate (there isn't a big city in this country today with a decent climate), tied down to a job sometimes easily duplicated elsewhere?

The answer is that more and more he is breaking away. Sometimes reasons of health force him, against his will, to join the exodus; other times, retirement gives him an excuse for release; and sometimes, he flees in sudden awareness of the Kafka-esque bleakness. Relocation is becoming a national pastime, with more Americans living outside the state they were born in than ever before. It has become easier, even cheaper, to travel and to move one's household. The American family, as social workers and sociologists have been discovering with some surprise, has a built-in cohesiveness and stability it takes with it anywhere. The highways of the country are dotted with station wagons carrying families and pulling trailers. Cities and towns have become so much the same everywhere that one can pick up and leave home, school, church, shopping center, and a thousand miles away find everything duplicated. And if television has brought the glories of the big cities to the countryside at large, it has also brought that countryside into the big cities, one way or another. There is no longer a great unknown west of the Hudson or of the Mississippi.

The big city exodus is not unrelated to the growing sense of responsibility toward one's family. *Life* magazine recently reported on businessmen who retired young and moved their families away from the city to live in vacation territory, where they might spend more time with wives and children. There's a growing feeling that one just isn't doing right by one's offspring if the child isn't exposed to the countryside, some time, some way. Witness the boom in children's summer camps surrounding big cities. What makes more sense than to move the whole kit and caboodle to that countryside for all four seasons?

Artists, writers, free-floating intellectuals, who once made their way in droves to the big cities, are now finding small centers in congenial countryside which satisfy their longings. A Joseph Wood Krutch moves to Arizona; a Stanley Walker to Texas; a Leslie Fiedler to Montana. And one suddenly realizes that writers have long functioned well removed from the big city: William Faulkner and Eudora Welty in Mississippi; Oliver La Farge, Ramon Sender in New Mexico; Walter van Tilburg Clark, until his recent move to California, in Nevada and Montana.

American cultural life which used to be centripetally focused on big cities is now becoming centrifugal. Advertising and business administration college graduates may still head for New York or Chicago first, but scientists and engineers are spreading out. Young people interested in writing, painting, music, or just scholarship no longer find that they have to head for the metropolis. The state universities more and more are meeting local needs. One of the high-powered creative writing college programs in the country is in Iowa, the heart of the corn belt that used to send so many young writers to Greenwich Village. The state universities of Ohio, Michigan, Wisconsin, Illinois are now foremost centers for study in the humanities. The University of New Mexico, in Albuquerque, is planning to sponsor a young artist for a summer of creative work at the D. H. Lawrence ranch in Taos, given by Frieda Lawrence Ravagli to the University before her death. Frank Lloyd Wright has a major center for architectural thought and production in Arizona, at Taliesin West. Colonies of creative workers—of varying degrees of seriousness, to be sure—are to be found in the Carmel area of California, in Santa Fé and Taos in New Mexico, clustered about the many universities one finds in the climatically and scenically pleasing Far West and Southwest. Even persons who for one reason or another cannot break away completely from the big city try to reduce their dependence on it. Television and publishing personages in New York, for example, get out to the Connecticut woods or the Virginia hills and come to Manhattan only on business.

There is no real possibility, I suppose, of the big city's disappearing, or of its growing significantly smaller. But there is also no question, it seems to me, that the attractions once thought to be exclusive to the big city are now available in some form in the remotest areas of the country. Mencken has gone, and with him the definition of the hinterland as a cultural "Sahara." Artur Rubinstein, returning from a recent tour through that Sahara, commented: "Small towns throughout America are more receptive to fine music than old cities in France. . . ." Not only do small cities offer musical recitals of various sorts (I have just attended a concert of the Modern Jazz Quartet), symphony concerts, art exhibitions (including traveling displays from the big Eastern museums), theatre productions (unfortunately all too often imitative of Broadway box-office hits although I have just seen a first-rate presentation of *The Devil's Disciple* in Albuquerque), opportunities for study and thought, but also all sorts of things big cities no longer, and in some cases, never did offer— a relaxed pace of living, attractive physical setting, usually an authentic and as yet uncorrupted atmosphere, companions of the same stimulating type to be found in big cities and also of a type never to be found there. And you can *choose* among these offerings.

The small city abominations Anderson, Lewis, and Mencken catalogued have all but disappeared as the result of the greatly changed technology and sociology in American life since the twenties. Books and television are as ubiquitous as the latest enlightened theories of psychology, sociology, literature, history and politics, broadcast far and wide by *Life,* Murrow, and Anchor Books. Privacy, if one wants that, is as available as in New York or Chicago, in some ways more available, for small cities tend not to become fragmented like big ones into neighborhoods and tenement communities, or into social cliques centering around one's job, with everyone jostling one another. The campus of the University of New Mexico is a freer and more relaxed place, intellectually more curious and open, than many institutions of higher learning in the metropolitan centers of the Midwest and East. Rotarians, Kiwanians, and Lions are all now "enlightened," and kid themselves, not least, to be sure, because of what Anderson, Mencken and Lewis wrote. What many would consider the minimum essentials of civilization have spread everywhere: name a city of 100,000 or so, and it will surely have a first-rate restaurant offering a continental cuisine, a hi-fi shop, and a haberdashery discreetly advertising Ivy League suits and accessories. The big city is no longer the exclusive showplace for the signs of wealth and urbanity.

Nor is the widespread enlightenment I speak of merely a matter of mass consumption of culture; creativity, I submit, is flourishing widely and significantly outside the city. It is true that writers, artists, musicians, thinkers cannot meet for lunch or drinks in the country at large as regularly and endlessly as in the cafés of Greenwich Village or Morningside Heights. But then the work turned out today in the metropolitan centers alone is often of a rather special character and comes from a different impulse from the work produced elsewhere. There was a time when artists had to borrow strength and assurance from one another, and the Chicago and New York salons were indispensable hothouses for cultivating talent, but today the soil is fertile almost anywhere but in the city, where it has become, at best, almost used up, at worst, poisoned. There is a nervous, frenetic quality about art exclusively manufactured in the city, in subject, tone, and achievement; it is focused narrowly inward; it springs as much from a badgering jealousy as from serious intention. (A friend, I learn, is to have a play produced on Broadway next year. I applaud him now and share unreservedly in his good fortune; two years ago, in New York, my feelings would have been less generous, instinctively competitive.)

Creation must always be, even ultimately in the city, entirely personal and lonesome, indifferent to society. A Saul Bellow, a Bernard Malamud, a Herbert Gold, a Leslie Fiedler, a Flannery O'Connor, a John Steinbeck, a Tennessee Williams, all move through the world at large, quite alone, and write. As for that catalytic contact with personalities and ideas, always so important anywhere for productivity, one gets that at writers' conferences, with students (always stimulating and fresh in their responses and challenges), or with genuinely responsive people anywhere. Young writers used to complain to me that the togetherness of artists in the city had somehow crippled and sabotaged them; either they spent their time in interminable talk, evading their tasks; or the sirens of advertising, television, and publishing lured them away from their most serious purpose; or they fell into the easy and ready patterns established for them by dominant figures. The important idioms of our time have come from the lone artists, those geographically self-exiled from metropolis—Hemingway and Faulkner—or spiritually alienated from it—Cheever and Salinger.

Let me concede that the city always beckons, always lurks as the arena where the artist must submit himself to judgment. The city will always remain a place for occasional sojourn, where the artist can measure the response to his work and find out what is going on everywhere in his discipline. He carries on his routine business in the city and may even get himself recharged there, like a salesman attending a convention. But he does his solid work in the field, in the setting which provides an opportunity for a more authentic engagement with people, with ideas, and with oneself than most cities today can—in Jackson, Mississippi, on a Cuban island, in Santa Fé, in Majorca.

Subject, of course, to all sorts of exceptions and modifications, it seems easier to be eccentric, or to put it more happily, to be yourself, in a small city today amidst normal surroundings than in a big one. The most important thing smaller cities now almost alone offer in the United States is the one great thing it was thought in the twenties only the big city could offer (benighted metropolitan captives still think this)—a genuine chance to become most fully oneself, to carry out thought to serious conclusions, to develop meaningful relationships with family and friends, to work productively with one's best talents.

I was born, raised, and earned my living in New York, but the finest hour for me was when I picked up my hat and said, Farewell, my unlovely.

STUDY QUESTIONS

1. Into what two broad sections is this essay divided? Are the illustrations in each half appropriate to its subject?
2. What part, according to Freedman, does competitiveness play in the attitude of New Yorkers toward their city? What changes does the essay mention as having lessened the big city's importance to art and culture?
3. To what extent do the different impressions about New York conveyed by this essay and that of E. B. White depend upon differences in tone and attitude? Both essays dwell upon sudden

disasters that sometimes occur; but what differences in their attitudes toward these are apparent?

4. Which of Freedman's objections to the big city are fundamental and which are more or less incidental? Could some of them be met by undertaking certain reforms? Are there any which could not possibly be satisfied?

5. Do you agree that other environments may be more favorable to creative work than the big city? Write an essay on this subject, focusing on some particular environment with which you are familiar.

6. Has Freedman failed to mention any advantages or compensations offered by big city living? If you think he has, describe some of these in the form of an argument against his point of view.

The Old Pacific Capital*

Robert Louis Stevenson

The Bay of Monterey has been compared by no less a person than General Sherman to a bent fishing-hook; and the comparison, if less important than the march through Georgia, still shows the eye of a soldier for topography. Santa Cruz sits exposed at the shank; the mouth of the Salinas river is at the middle of the bend; and Monterey itself is cosily ensconced beside the barb. Thus the ancient capital of California faces across the bay, while the Pacific Ocean, though hidden by low hills and forests, bombards her left flank and rear with never-dying surf. In front of the town, the long line of seabeach trends north and north-west, and then westward to enclose the bay. The waves which lap so quietly about the jetties of Monterey grow louder and larger in the distance; you can see the breakers leaping high and white by day; at night, the outline of the shore is traced in transparent silver by the moonlight and the flying foam; and from all round, even in quiet weather, the low, distant, thrilling roar of the Pacific hangs over the coast and the adjacent country like smoke above a battle.

These long beaches are enticing to the idle man. It would be hard to find a walk more solitary and at the same time more exciting to the mind. Crowds of ducks and sea-gulls hover over the sea. Sandpipers trot in and out by troops after the retiring waves, trilling together in a chorus of infinitesimal song. Strange sea-tangles, new to the European eye, the bones of whales, or sometimes a whole whale's carcase, white with carrion-gulls and poisoning the wind, lie scattered here and there along the sands. The

---

* From "The Old Pacific Capital," first published in *Frazer's Magazine*, November, 1880.

waves come in slowly, vast and green, curve their translucent necks, and burst with a surprising uproar, that runs, waxing and waning, up and down the long key-board of the beach. The foam of these great ruins mounts in an instant to the ridge of the sand glacis, swiftly fleets back again, and is met and buried by the next breaker. The interest is perpetually fresh. On no other coast that I know shall you enjoy, in calm, sunny weather, such a spectacle of Ocean's greatness, such beauty of changing colour, or such degrees of thunder in the sound. The very air is more than usually salt by this Homeric deep.

Inshore, a tract of sand-hills borders on the beach. Here and there a lagoon, more or less brackish, attracts the birds and hunters. A rough, spotty undergrowth partially conceals the sand. The crouching, hardy live-oaks flourish singly or in thickets—the kind of wood for murderers to crawl among—and here and there the skirts of the forest extend downward from the hills with a floor of turf and aisles of pine-trees hung with Spaniard's Beard. Through this quaint desert the railway cars drew near to Monterey from the junction at Salina City—though that and so many other things are now for ever altered—and it was from here that you had the first view of the old township lying in the sands, its white windmills bickering in the chill, perpetual wind, and the first fogs of the evening drawing drearily around it from the sea.

The one common note of all this country is the haunting presence of the ocean. A great faint sound of breakers follows you high up into the inland cañons; the roar of water dwells in the clean, empty rooms of Monterey as in a shell upon the chimney; go where you will, you have but to pause and listen to hear the voice of the Pacific. You pass out of the town to the southwest, and mount the hill among pine woods. Glade, thicket, and grove surround you. You follow winding sandy tracks that lead nowhither. You see a deer; a multitude of quail arises. But the sound of the sea still follows you as you advance, like that of wind among the trees, only harsher and stranger to the ear; and when at length you gain the summit, out breaks on every hand and with freshened vigour, that same unending, distant, whispering rumble of the ocean; for now you are on the top of the Monterey peninsula, and the noise no longer only mounts to you from behind along the beach towards Santa Cruz, but from your right also, round by Chinatown and Pinos lighthouse, and from down before you to the mouth of the Carmello river. The whole woodland is begirt with thundering surges. The silence that immediately surrounds you where you stand is not so much broken as it is haunted by this distant, circling rumour. It sets your senses upon edge; you strain your attention; you are clearly and unusually conscious of small sounds near at hand; you walk listening like an Indian hunter; and that voice of the Pacific is a sort of disquieting company to you in your walk. . . .

The woods and the Pacific rule between them the climate of this seaboard region. On the streets of Monterey, when the air does not smell salt from the one, it will be blowing perfumed from the resinous treetops of the other. For days together a hot, dry air will overhang the town, close as from an oven, yet healthful and aromatic in the nostrils. The cause is not far to seek, for the woods are afire, and the hot wind is blowing from the hills. These fires are one of the great dangers in California. I have seen from Monterey as many as three at the same time, by day a cloud of smoke, by night a red coal of conflagration in the distance. A little thing will start them, and, if the wind be favourable, they gallop over miles of country faster than a horse. The inhabitants must turn out and work like demons, for it is not only the pleasant groves that are destroyed; the climate and the soil are equally at stake, and these fires prevent the rains of the next winter and dry up perennial fountains. California has been a land of promise in its time, like Palestine; but if the woods continue so swiftly to perish, it may become, like Palestine, a land of desolation.

To visit the woods while they are languidly burning is a strange piece of experience. The fire passes through the underbrush at a run. Every here and there a tree flares up instantaneously from root to summit, scattering tufts of flame, and is quenched, it seems, as quickly. But this last is only in semblance. For after this first squib-like conflagration of the dry moss and twigs, there remains behind a deep-rooted and consuming fire in the very entrails of the tree. The resin of the pitch-pine is principally condensed at the base of the bole and in the spreading roots. Thus, after the light, shadowy, skirmishing flames, which are only as the match to the explosion, have already scampered down the wind into the distance, the true harm is but beginning for this giant of the woods. You may approach the tree from one side, and see it, scorched indeed from top to bottom, but apparently survivor of the peril. Make the circuit, and there, on the other side of the column, is a clear mass of living coal, spreading like an ulcer; while underground, to their most extended fibre, the roots are being eaten out by fire, and the smoke is rising through the fissures to the surface. A little while, and, without a nod of warning, the huge pine-tree snaps off short across the ground and falls prostrate with a crash. Meanwhile the fire continues its silent business; the roots are reduced to a fine ash; and long afterwards, if you pass by, you will find the earth pierced with radiating galleries, and preserving the design of all these subterranean spurs, as though it were the mould for a new tree instead of the print of an old one. These pitch-pines of Monterey are, with the single exception of the Monterey cypress, the most fantastic of forest trees. No words can give an idea of the contortion of their growth; they might figure without change in a circle of the nether hell as Dante pictured it; and at the rate at which trees grow, and at which forest fires spring up and gallop through the hills of California, we may look forward to a time when there will not be one of them left standing in that land of their nativity. At least they have not so much to fear from the axe, but perish by what may be called a natural although violent death; while it is man in his short-sighted greed that robs the country of the nobler red-wood. Yet a little while and perhaps all the hills of sea-board California may be as bald as Tamalpais. . . .

But it is the Pacific that exercises the most direct and obvious power upon the climate. At sunset, for months together, vast, wet, melancholy fogs arise and come shoreward from the ocean. From the hill-top above Monterey the scene is often noble, although it is always sad. The upper air is still bright with sunlight; a glow still rests upon the Gabelano Peak; but the fogs are in possession of the lower levels; they crawl in scarves among the sandhills; they float, a little higher, in clouds of a gigantic size and often of a wild configuration; to the south, where they have struck the seaward shoulder of the mountains of Santa Lucia, they double back and spire up skyward like smoke. Where their shadow touches, colour dies out of the world. The air grows chill and deadly as they advance. The trade-wind freshens, the trees begin to sigh, and all the windmills in Monterey are whirling and creaking and filling their cisterns with the brackish water of the sands. It takes but a little while till the invasion is complete. The sea, in its lighter order, has submerged the earth. Monterey is curtained in for the night in thick, wet, salt, and frigid clouds, so to remain till day returns; and before the sun's rays they slowly disperse and retreat in broken squadrons to the bosom of the sea. And yet often when the fog is thickest and most chill, a few steps out of the town and up the slope, the night will be dry and warm and full of inland perfume.

STUDY QUESTIONS

1. What principle controls the order or arrangement of parts in this description? What are the unifying elements?

2. What kinds of verbs does Stevenson make use of? What verbs are particularly effective in the description of the sea and the fire?

3. This essay was written in the latter part of the nineteenth century. Compare the diction and sentence structure in it with that in the earlier selections by Orwell or E. B. White. What specific differences do you notice?

4. In the last paragraph, Stevenson seems to see Monterey as occupying an ambiguous or contradictory position. Exactly what feeling is delicately suggested by it?

5. Write a description of a city or town, or part of one, that you found interesting and remember well.

6. Make it a point to observe some place or area very carefully in order to write a clear and thorough description of it. Notice all the details about it that seem significant and decide what dominant impression the place makes upon an observer. Then write a description in which you try to make your reader able to visualize what you have seen and also convey the feeling or quality of the

place. Good subjects for this exercise are rooms in homes, streets, public places. Avoid subjects that seem to have no particular personality.

The Wind at Djémila*

Albert Camus

There are certain places that kill the spirit within a man so that a truth may be born, a truth that is its own denial. When I went to Djémila, there was wind and sun—but that comes later. First I should say that a deep, heavy, flawless silence hangs over the place, a silence balanced against the bird-cries, the felt-like sounds of a three-holed flute, the stamping of goats, the shuffle of movement that emphasizes the quiet desolation. Now and then, far away on the edge of the plateau, a dry clacking whirr marks the sudden flight of a bird bursting from its hiding place among the stones. Every road in the city, every path winding among the ruins, the wide streets paved with flagstones, the huge public square lying between the arch of triumph and the temple in the hill—all lead toward the ravines that close in on Djémila from all sides. Djémila, its buildings spread out like a card game under a limitless sky. In the old ruined city, confronted by nothing but dead stones and emptiness, as the day wanes and the mountains loom larger in the purple shadows of dusk, you find the essence of your soul. The wind blows on the plateau, and in the great confusion of wind and sun that mixes light with the ruins, something happens that brings you face to face with yourself, in the solitude and silence of the lifeless city.

It takes a long time to go to Djémila. It is not a place where the traveller stops to rest and then goes on. The road to Djémila leads nowhere, opens on no country; you go there so you can return. The dead city lies at the end of a long sinuous road which, because it promises to end around every curve, seems much the longer. Finally, on a high plateau splattered with color, sunk between the high mountains, the yellow skeleton of Djémila appears like a forest of bones. Among its scattered trees and dry grass, in the midst of the hills and dry stones, the city lies hopeless, ugly, negative.

Our group of visitors wandered through its arid splendor all day. Little by little the dry wind, hardly perceptible at the beginning of the after-

* From *Noces* by Albert Camus. Translation by Georges Joyaux and used by his permission. Reprinted by permission of Librairie Gallimard, Paris, and of Alfred A. Knopf, Inc., authorized publishers of Camus in American translation.

noon, grew stronger and stronger until it seemed to fill the landscape. It blew from an opening in the mountains far to the east, ran across the rim of the horizon, and cascaded into the city among the stones and sun, whistling through the ruins, swirling about the columns, spreading out with a shout into the square. I felt myself bending before it like the mast of a ship; it tore the flesh from the bones, burned the eyes, chapped the lips, shrivelled the skin. Rubbed smooth by the gale, stunned with the effort of resistance, I lost consciousness of my body—like a pebble polished by the tides I was polished by the wind, ground down to my soul. I seemed to be floating in an earth-force, until finally the pulse of the wind fused with the pulse of my blood and the beating of my heart merged with the great clangorous rhythm of nature around me. The wind carved me in the shape of the stripped, barren land; in its embrace I was a stone among stones, an impersonal thing, alone like a column or an olive tree in the wind and sky.

The violent bath of sun and wind wore down the feeling of life within me until there was only a weak flutter of wings beneath the surface, only a spark of protest, only a faint rebelliousness of spirit. Cut adrift, blown out to the four corners of the world, I was of the wind and in the wind, part of the broken columns and the arch, of the flagstones warm in the sun, of the pale mountains looming over the deserted city—apart, separate, alienated from the world and from myself.

I know that I exist, I am conscious of the present moment. I can be sure of nothing more. Like a man imprisoned for life in a bare cell, knowing that tomorrow will be the same as today, and all tomorrows after, I know only the present and the now—there is nothing to wait for, no future. This truth I found in the dry landscape and wind of Djémila, a truth that came from the land itself, a touch of solitude, detachment, and death common to us both. As I stood among the columns and their oblique shadows, problems of life and death plummeted out of my mind like wounded birds from the air. When night came, stifling the sounds and lights of the town under the ashy blackness falling from the sky, I was alone and abandoned, defenseless against an inner voice that whispered, No, there is nothing.

Few people realize that there is a refusal to accept things which has nothing to do with renouncing them. What do we mean when we say *future, improvement, progress?* I do not understand the words. I refuse obstinately to believe that there is a *later* in the world because I refuse to renounce the richness of the present moment. I can find no pleasure in believing, as some do, that death is a door that opens on another life; to me it is always closed. I cannot say, as some do, that death is a valley one must cross; to me it is a horrible, ignoble adventure. All that people say about death is simply an attempt to lighten the load of life they carry, but as I watch the heavy flight of the birds above Djémila, I realize that life is a burden that I do not want to lose. Nothing beyond the present concerns me, nothing beyond death. There is still too much youth in my blood for me to speak of death with assurance, but when the time comes to face its silence, I know what I shall say—that death is death, and nothing more, a step not toward something but away from something.

A man lives with a few familiar ideas, two or three at most, and here and there, in contact with the world and men, they are polished, shaped, changed. It takes years for a man to evolve an idea that he can call his own, one he can speak of with authority. A man in his youth looks the world in the face; as he grows older he steps aside to see it in profile. So it is with death. A young man has not yet had time to shape and polish his concept of death and nothingness, though he recognizes how horrible it is and fears it with the physical fear of an animal who does not want to lose the sun. But youth has no illusions, and has neither the time nor the sense of pity needed to construct them. I found the idea and meaning of death at Djémila, in the solemn, dismal cry of stone rising from the serrated land, in the gravelike dusk of the falling sun. From the winds of Djémila I learned that men must find how to look facts in the face, so that they can regain the lost innocence and shining certainty with which ancient men saw death. In recognizing and clasping death, man regains his youth. (But not through illness, a contemptible nostrum against death, an apprenticeship of self-pity to prepare man for death, a feeble attempt to shield him from the inevitability of death.) This I learned at Djémila, that the only way to live is with a real understanding of the meaning of death—that it is a separation from what you have in the here and now, that in dying you lose the world of the present moment, and that beyond that there is nothing.

It is surprising that we have opinions about so many things and yet so few about death. We say, "It is good," or "It is evil." We fear it, or we welcome it. Because it is a plain and simple thing we find it incomprehensible. We can no more discuss it or define it than we can discuss or define a color—what is *blue,* and what is *death?* I have seen dogs die, and a few people; all I remember is that I did not like to touch them. And though I may say to myself, "I must die," the words mean nothing. I cannot really believe it, and I have only the experience of seeing others die to give it any meaning. But when I think of flowers, smiles, young girls, the world around me, I do not want to die. I know then that I fear death because I am jealous of life. I envy those who will live after I am dead, those for whom flowers and smiles and desires will have full meaning in terms of flesh and blood and feeling. I enjoy life too much to be unselfish, and I care little about eternity. Yet I know that someday they will say to me as I lie there with fear in my guts and my life cupped in my hands, "You are brave and must know the truth—you are going to die. . . ." I do not know what death is, but the thought of its blankness brings angry blood beating in my head and the urge to smash the world into bits.

But men die, nevertheless. The doctor says, "When you are cured—" and then you die. I do not like to be lied to. There are times when the world lies, and times when it tells the truth—Djémila told the truth, a sad insistent truth. I prefer to see death clearly, to look at it plainly, in the full heat of my enjoyment of life and horror of death. I am afraid of death only because it will separate me from the world of the living, because I am attached to the here and now. To lose a fear of death, we must create in ourselves a consciousness of what death really is, we must feel an awareness of the life, the body, and the instant that we lose when we die. Beyond that there is nothing. The lonely song I heard in the wind on the hills of Djémila drove this bitter truth deeper into my mind.

In the evening we climbed the slopes leading toward the town, listening to the guide, "Here is the old pagan city—this section, lying outside, is where the Christians lived. Later we shall see—" Men and societies rose and fell in this land; conquering armies marked it with changing civilizations, measuring greatness by the boundaries of empire. Only the ruins survive. Djémila is a denial of all their aspirations, for this skeleton of a city, with the white pigeons wheeling above the square in the dusk, is a symbol of defeat. The great cry of stone that the city utters, among the hills and the silence, is a clear cry of poetry—of indifference, loneliness, despair—the true signs of a beauty that tightens the heart. As Djémila faded behind me—with its lonely sky, the birdsongs on the far plateau, the sudden scamperings of goats on the flanks of the hills—I knew that there in the relaxed and sonorous dusk I had looked at the live face of a God on his altar.

ŊTUDY QUESTIONS

1. Would you call this description prevailingly objective or subjective? Is it more or less objective than the description by Stevenson? Why?

2. Point out some of the striking comparisons that help to convey Camus' feeling about the town he is describing.

3. In what way does Djémila reflect for Camus the condition of human life in general? What was the "truth" that was born in the author as the result of his visit to Djémila?

4. What relations do you see between Camus' statement that "A man lives with a few familiar ideas, two or three at most, and here and there, in contact with the world and men, they are polished, shaped, changed," and the generalizations which Read and Thomas make in the first two selections of this anthology? As you read ahead in the selections under "The Shape of Reality," consider the extent to which these ideas are related to some of the ideas in those selections.

5. Do you think another person might have reacted to Djémila in a less pessimistic way? If you disagree with Camus' view, write a

theme explaining your disagreement and suggesting what other attitudes toward such a place as Djémila might be possible.

6. Write an "interpretation" of a place you have visited that seemed to you especially typical or meaningful.

The Role of the Mountain Men*

George F. Ruxton

The trappers of the Rocky Mountains belong to a "genus" more approximating to the primitive savage than perhaps any other class of civilised man. Their lives being spent in the remote wilderness of the mountains, with no other companion than Nature herself, their habits and character assume a most singular cast of simplicity mingled with ferocity, appearing to take their colouring from the scenes and objects which surround them. Knowing no wants save those of nature, their sole care is to procure sufficient food to support life, and the necessary clothing to protect them from the rigorous climate. This, with the assistance of their trusty rifles, they are generally able to effect, but sometimes at the expense of great peril and hardship. When engaged in their avocation, the natural instinct of primitive man is ever alive, for the purpose of guarding against danger and the provision of necessary food.

Keen observers of nature, they rival the beasts of prey in discovering the haunts and habits of game, and in their skill and cunning in capturing it. Constantly exposed to perils of all kinds, they become callous to any feeling of danger, and destroy human as well as animal life with as little scruple and as freely as they expose their own. Of laws, human or divine, they neither know nor care to know. Their wish is their law, and to attain it they do not scruple as to ways and means. Firm friends and bitter enemies, with them it is "a word and a blow," and the blow often first. They may have good qualities, but they are those of the animal; and people fond of giving hard names call them revengeful, bloodthirsty, drunkards (when the wherewithal is to be had), gamblers, regardless of the laws of *meum* and *tuum*—in fact, "White Indians." However, there are exceptions, and I *have* met honest mountain-men. Their animal qualities, however, are undeniable. Strong, active, hardy as bears, daring, expert in the use of their weapons, they are just what uncivilised white man might be supposed to be in a brute state, depending upon his instinct for the support of life. Not a hole or corner in the vast wilderness of the "Far West" but has been ransacked by these hardy men. From the Mississippi

* From *Adventures in Mexico and the Rocky Mountains* (London, 1849).

to the mouth of the Colorado of the West, from the frozen regions of the
North to the Gila in Mexico, the beaver-hunter has set his traps in every
creek and stream. All this vast country, but for the daring enterprise of
these men, would be even now a *terra incognita* to geographers, as indeed
a great portion still is; but there is not an acre that has not been passed
and repassed by the trappers in their perilous excursions. The mountains
and streams still retain the names assigned to them by the rude hunters; and these alone are the hardy pioneers who have paved the way for
the settlement of the western country.

Trappers are of two kinds, the "hired hand" and the "free trapper":
the former hired for the hunt by the fur companies; the latter, supplied
with animals and traps by the company, is paid a certain price for his furs
and peltries.

There is also the trapper "on his own hook"; but this class is very small.
He has his own animals and traps, hunts where he chooses, and sells his
peltries to whom he pleases.

On starting for a hunt, the trapper fits himself out with the necessary
equipment, either from the Indian trading-forts, or from some of the petty
traders—*coureurs des bois*—who frequent the western country. This
equipment consists usually of two or three horses or mules—one for saddle, the others for packs—and six traps, which are carried in a bag of
leather called a *trap-sack*. Ammunition, a few pounds of tobacco, dressed
deer-skins for moccasins, &c., are carried in a wallet of dressed buffalo-
skin, called a *possible-sack*. His "possibles" and "trap-sack" are generally carried on the saddle-mule when hunting, the others being packed
with the furs. The costume of the trapper is a hunting-shirt of dressed
buckskin, ornamented with long fringes; pantaloons of the same material,
and decorated with porcupine quills and long fringes down the outside of
the leg. A flexible felt hat and moccasins clothe his extremities. Over his
left shoulder and under his right arm hang his powder-horn and bullet-
pouch, in which he carries his balls, flint and steel, and odds and ends of
all kinds. Round the waist is a belt, in which is stuck a large butcher-
knife in a sheath of buffalo-hide, made fast to the belt by a chain or guard
of steel; which also supports a little buckskin case containing a whetstone.
A tomahawk is also often added; and, of course, a long heavy rifle is part
and parcel of his equipment. I had nearly forgotten the pipe-holder,
which hangs around his neck, and is generally a *gâge d'amour*, and a triumph of squaw workmanship, in shape of a heart, garnished with beads
and porcupine-quills.

Thus provided, and having determined the locality of his trapping-
ground, he starts to the mountains, sometimes alone, sometimes with three
or four in company, as soon as the breaking up of the ice allows him to
commence operations. Arrived on his hunting-grounds, he follows the
creeks and streams, keeping a sharp look-out for "sign." If he sees a prostrate cotton-wood tree, he examines it to discover if it be the work of

beaver—whether "thrown" for the purpose of food, or to dam the stream. The track of the beaver on the mud or sand under the bank is also examined; and if the "sign" be fresh, he sets his trap in the run of the animal, hiding it under water, and attaching it by a stout chain to a picket driven in the bank, or to a bush or tree. A "float-stick" is made fast to the trap by a cord a few feet long, which, if the animal carry away the trap, floats on the water and points out its position. The trap is baited with the "medicine," an oily substance obtained from a gland in the scrotum of the beaver, but distinct from the testes. A stick is dipped into this and planted over the trap; and the beaver, attracted by the smell, and wishing a close inspection, very foolishly puts his leg into the trap, and is a "gone beaver."

When a lodge is discovered, the trap is set at the edge of the dam, at the point where the animal passes from deep to shoal water, and always under water. Early in the morning the hunter mounts his mule and examines the traps. The captured animals are skinned, and the tails, which are a great dainty, carefully packed into camp. The skin is then stretched over a hoop or framework of osier-twigs, and is allowed to dry, the flesh and fatty substance being carefully scraped (grained). When dry, it is folded into a square sheet, the fur turned inwards, and the bundle, containing about ten to twenty skins, tightly pressed and corded, and is ready for transportation.

During the hunt, regardless of Indian vicinity, the fearless trapper wanders far and near in search of "sign." His nerves must ever be in a state of tension, and his mind ever present at his call. His eagle eye sweeps round the country, and in an instant detects any foreign appearance. A turned leaf, a blade of grass pressed down, the uneasiness of the wild animals, the flight of birds, are all paragraphs to him written in nature's legible hand and plainest language. All the wits of the subtle savage are called into play to gain an advantage over the wily woodsman; but with the natural instinct of primitive man, the white hunter has the advantages of a civilised mind, and, thus provided, seldom fails to outwit, under equal advantages, the cunning savage.

Sometimes, following on his trail, the Indian watches him set his traps on a shrub-belted stream, and, passing up the bed, like Bruce of old, so that he may leave no track, he lies in wait in the bushes until the hunter comes to examine his carefully-set traps. Then, waiting until he approaches his ambushment within a few feet, whiz flies the home-drawn arrow, never failing at such close quarters to bring the victim to the ground. For one white scalp, however, that dangles in the smoke of an Indian's lodge, a dozen black ones, at the end of the hunt, ornament the camp-fires of the "rendezvous."

At a certain time, when the hunt is over, or they have loaded their pack-animals, the trappers proceed to the "rendezvous," the locality of which has been previously agreed upon; and here the traders and agents of the fur companies await them, with such assortment of goods as their hardy customers may require, including generally a fair supply of alcohol. The trappers drop in singly and in small bands, bringing their packs of beaver to this mountain market, not unfrequently to the value of a thousand dollars each, the produce of one hunt. The dissipation of the "rendezvous," however, soon turns the trapper's pocket inside out. The goods brought by the traders, although of the most inferior quality, are sold at enormous prices:—Coffee, twenty and thirty shillings a pint-cup, which is the usual measure; tobacco fetches ten and fifteen shillings a plug; alcohol, from twenty to fifty shillings a pint; gunpowder, sixteen shillings a pint-cup; and all other articles at proportionately exorbitant prices.

The "beaver" is purchased at from two to eight dollars per pound; the Hudson's Bay Company alone buying it by the pluie, or "plew," that is, the whole skin, giving a certain price for skins, whether of old beaver or "kittens."

The "rendezvous" is one continued scene of drunkenness, gambling, and brawling and fighting, as long as the money and credit of the trappers last. Seated, Indian fashion, round the fires, with a blanket spread before them, groups are seen with their "decks" of cards, playing at "euker," "poker," and "seven-up," the regular mountain games. The stakes are "beaver," which here is current coin; and when the fur is gone, their horses, mules, rifles, and shirts, hunting-packs, and *breeches,* are staked. Daring gamblers make the rounds of the camp, challenging each other to play for the trapper's highest stake,—his horse, his squaw (if he have one), and, as once happened, his scalp. There goes "hos and beaver!" is the mountain expression when any great loss is sustained; and, sooner or later, "hos and beaver" invariably find their way into the insatiable pockets of the traders. A trapper often squanders the produce of his hunt, amounting to hundreds of dollars, in a couple of hours; and, supplied on credit with another equipment, leaves the "rendezvous" for another expedition, which has the same result time after time; although one tolerably successful hunt would enable him to return to the settlements and civilised life, with an ample sum to purchase and stock a farm, and enjoy himself in ease and comfort the remainder of his days.

An old trapper, a French Canadian, assured me that he had received fifteen thousand dollars for beaver during a sojourn of twenty years in the mountains. Every year he resolved in his mind to return to Canada, and, with this object, always converted his fur into cash; but a fortnight at the "rendezvous" always cleaned him out, and, at the end of twenty years, he had not even credit sufficient to buy a pound of powder.

These annual gatherings are often the scene of bloody duels, for over their cups and cards no men are more quarrelsome than your mountaineers. Rifles, at twenty paces, settle all differences, and, as may be imagined, the fall of one or other of the combination is certain, or, as sometimes happens, both fall to the word "fire."

STUDY QUESTIONS

1. In what ways do DeVoto's and Ruxton's accounts of the mountain men agree with each other? In what ways is Ruxton's description more complete?

2. Ruxton begins by saying that the mountain men are like savages or animals. Do they display any qualities characteristic of a more advanced state of civilization?

3. Show how the selection achieves balance by giving both the good and the bad qualities of the mountain men.

4. Note that in describing this specialized occupation the author finds it necessary to use—and sometimes to define—special terms. In some cases it is possible to guess the origins of these terms. Make a list of these together with their meanings and probable derivations.

5. What contrasts between the trappers' professional and their moral standards are evident from Ruxton's description? How can they be accounted for?

6. What qualities found in the mountain men remain typical of modern Americans? To what extent have these men supplied an ideal for Americans as the cowboys have?

The Value of Observation*

Bernard DeVoto

Skill develops from controlled, corrected repetitions of an act for which one has some knack. Skill is a product of experience and criticism and intelligence. Analysis cannot much transcend those truisms. Between the amateur and the professional, between the duffer and the expert, between the novice and the veteran there is a difference not only in degree but in kind. The skillful man is, within the function of his skill, a different integration, a different nervous and muscular and psychological organization. He has specialized responses of great intricacy. His associative faculties have patterns of screening, acceptance and rejection, analysis and sifting, evaluation and selective adjustment much too complex for conscious direction. Yet as the patterns of appraisal and adjustment exert their automatic and perhaps metabolic energy, they are accompanied by a conscious process fully as complex. A tennis player or a watchmaker or an airplane pilot is an automatism but he is also criticism and wisdom. It is hardly too much to say that a mountain man's life was skill. He

*From *Across the Wide Missouri* by Bernard DeVoto. Copyright, 1947, by Houghton Mifflin Company. Reprinted by permission of the publishers.

not only worked in the wilderness, he also lived there and he did so from sun to sun by the exercise of total skill. It was probably as intricate a skill as any ever developed by any way of working or living anywhere. Certainly it was the most complex of the wilderness crafts practiced on this continent. The mountains, the aridity, the distances, and the climates imposed severities far greater than those laid on forest-runners, rivermen, or any other of our symbolic pioneers. Mountain craft developed out of the crafts which earlier pioneers had acquired and, like its predecessors, incorporated Indian crafts, but it had a unique integration of its own. It had specific crafts, technologies, theorems and rationales and rules of thumb, codes of operating procedure—but it was a pattern of total behavior.

Treatises could be written on the specific details; we lack space even for generalizations. Why do you follow the ridges into or out of unfamiliar country? What do you do for a companion who has collapsed from want of water while crossing a desert? How do you get meat when you find yourself without gunpowder in a country barren of game? What tribe of Indians made this trail, how many were in the band, what errand were they on, were they going to or coming back from it, how far from home were they, were their horses laden, how many horses did they have and why, how many squaws accompanied them, what mood were they in? Also, how old is the trail, where are those Indians now, and what does the product of these answers require of you? Prodigies of such sign-reading are recorded by impressed greenhorns, travelers, and army men, and the exercise of critical reference and deduction which they exhibit would seem prodigious if it were not routine. But reading formal sign, however impressive to Doctor Watson or Captain Frémont, is less impressive than the interpretation of observed circumstances too minute to be called sign. A branch floats down a stream—is this natural, or the work of animals, or of Indians or trappers? Another branch or a bush or even a pebble is out of place—why? On the limits of the plain, blurred by heat mirage, or against the gloom of distant cottonwoods, or across an angle of sky between branches or where hill and mountain meet, there is a tenth of a second of what may have been movement—did men or animals make it, and, if animals, why? Buffalo are moving downwind, an elk is in an unlikely place or posture, too many magpies are hollering, a wolf's howl is off key—what does it mean?

Such minutiae could be extended indefinitely. As the trapper's mind is dealing with them, it is simultaneously performing a still more complex judgement on the countryside, the route across it, and the weather. It is recording the immediate details in relation to the remembered and the forecast. A ten-mile traverse is in relation to a goal a hundred miles, or five hundred miles away: there are economies of time, effort, comfort, and horseflesh on any of which success or even survival may depend. Modify the reading further, in relation to season, to Indians, to what has happened. Modify it again in relation to stream flow, storms past, storms indicated. Again in relation to the meat supply. To the state of the grass. To the equipment on hand. . . . You are two thousand miles from depots of supply and from help in time of trouble.

All this (with much more) is a continuous reference and checking along the margin or in the background of the trapper's consciousness while he practices his crafts as hunter, wrangler, furrier, freighter, tanner, cordwainer, smith, gunmaker, dowser, merchant. The result is a high-level integration of faculties. The mountain man had mastered his conditions—how well is apparent as soon as soldiers, goldseekers, or emigrants come into his country and suffer where he has lived comfortably and die where he has been in no danger. He had no faculties or intelligence that the soldier or the goldseeker lacked; he had none that you and I lack. He had only skill. A skill so effective that, living in an Indian country, he made a more successful adaptation to it than the Indian—and this without reference to his superior material equipment. There was no craft and no skill at which the mountain man did not come to excel the Indian. He saw, smelled, and heard just as far and no farther. But there is something after all in the laborious accretion that convolutes the forebrain and increases the cultural heritage, for he made more of it.

STUDY QUESTIONS

1. DeVoto undoubtedly read Ruxton as one of many sources while writing *Across the Wide Missouri,* from which this brief selection is taken. Do you find any details which suggest this? Is DeVoto more or less objective than Ruxton?

2. What is the difference, according to DeVoto, between "skill" and "a knack"? What qualities possessed by the mountain men would be useful in writing a description? Which would be useful to a detective? To a poker player?

3. What connection is there between the opinion expressed in DeVoto's last sentence and the theory of evolution?

4. What possible reason may be given for the fact that the mountaineers adapted to their environment even more successfully than the Indians, who grew up in it?

5. Describe some activity which requires what DeVoto calls "the exercise of critical reference and deduction." Examples would be playing a game like bridge or checkers, predicting the weather, finding out why a car won't start.

6. Tell how you made (or could have made) an elaborate deduction from a small clue.

The Mountain Man as Western Hero:
Kit Carson*

Henry Nash Smith

The first generation of fictional Wild Western heroes after Cooper—the sons of Leatherstocking—were primarily symbols of anarchic freedom. The notion that men who ranged the wilderness had fled from the restraints of civilization—for better or for worse, according to the social philosophy of the observer—had been greatly strengthened during the 1830's by the spectacular development of the Rocky Mountain fur trade. The fur trapper, or Mountain Man, was much more clearly uncivilized than Daniel Boone had been. The prime theater of his activities lay hundreds of miles distant from the frontier beyond the Great American Desert, and was not a region that invited agricultural settlement. He had adopted many more Indian ways than had the typical pioneers of the area east of the Mississippi. His costume, his speech, his outlook on life, often enough his Indian squaw, gave him a decidedly savage aspect. Yet the trappers dominated the exploration of the trans-Mississippi region, and the successor of Boone and Leatherstocking in the role of typical Wild Western hero was certain to be a mountain man. Cooper had acknowledged this fact in *The Prairie* by transporting Leatherstocking beyond the Mississippi and trying halfheartedly to make him over into a trapper. But Leatherstocking did not really belong in the Far West—a region about which his creator knew next to nothing. Besides, the old hunter considered the vocation of a trapper somewhat beneath his dignity.

This low opinion of the fur trade was shared by Timothy Flint, whose *The Shoshonee Valley,* published in 1830, is the first novel in which mountain men figure as characters. It is true that Flint divides his trappers into two classes. A few, potentially virtuous, experience in the presence of mountain landscapes "a certain half chill sensation of the awful and sublime" which will be recognized as evidence of at least rudimentary ethical nobility. But by far the greater number of the trappers are as insensitive as deer to the charms of the scenery, and therefore by implication vulgar or wicked.[1] These "strange, fearless, and adamantine men," Flint

* Henry Nash Smith, *Virgin Land: The American West as Symbol and Myth.* Cambridge, Mass.: Harvard University Press, Copyright, 1950, by The President and Fellows of Harvard College.
1 *The Shoshonee Valley; A Romance,* 2 vols. (Cincinnati, 1830), I, 21.— The substance of Chapters VIII, IX, and X appeared in the *Southwest Review* (XXVIII, 164-189, Winter, 1943; XXXIII, 276-284, 378-384, Summer, Autumn, 1948; XXXIV, 182-188, Spring, 1949). I wish to thank the editor of that magazine for permission to reprint the material here.

says,

renouncing society, casting off fear, and all the common impulses and affections of our nature . . . finding in their own ingenuity, their knife, gun and traps, all the Divinity, of which their stern nature and condition taught them the necessity . . . became almost as inaccessible to passions and wants, and as sufficient to themselves, as the trees, or the rocks with which they were conversant.[2]

Such an existence satisfies man's baser impulses. Few who have tasted its dangerous joys can return with pleasure to the tedious routine of the settlements. Life in the mountains is especially attractive because of its unrestricted love and licensed polygamy. All the trappers have

an instinctive fondness for the reckless savage life, alternately indolent and laborious, full and fasting, occupied in hunting, fighting, feasting, intriguing, and amours, interdicted by no laws, or difficult morals, or any restraints, but the invisible ones of Indian habit and opinion.[3]

Charles Sealsfield, although he was not committed to the essentially theocratic social theory of the New Englander Flint, was equally certain that the Western trapper was a monster, peculiar to America, produced by the absolute freedom of wilderness life. He asserts that the fur trade is carried on by men to whose intractable minds even the rational liberty of the settled portions of the United States seemed an intolerable retraint.[4] Having fled to the wilderness to escape the control of law, the trappers come to regard a wild freedom as the one absolute necessity of existence. In this situation, every man must rely upon his own physical prowess. Warlike skills, practical cunning, and sheer ferocity are developed to the highest degree. The true trapper hates mankind and kills any rival with "a real fiendish joy."[5]

The picture of the mountain man presented in David H. Coyner's fictionalized narrative *The Lost Trappers* (1847) is in substantial agreement with Sealsfield's, although it has less of his overstraining and love of hyperbole. Coyner asserts that the mountain man rejects civilized life deliberately because he despises its

dull uniformity and monotony . . . when compared in his mind with the stirring scenes of wild western adventure. The security and protection of the laws have no attraction for him; for he wants no other means of defence than his rifle,

---

[2] *Ibid.*, I, 20.
[3] *Ibid.*, I, 21-22.
[4] Charles Sealsfield (pseud. of Karl Anton Postl), *Life in the New World; or, Sketches of American Society,* first published in 1835-1837, in German; Eng. trans. Gustavus C. Hebbe and James Mackay (New York, 1844), p. 42.
[5] *Ibid.*, p. 43

which is his daily companion. He is impatient of the formalities and the galling restrictions of well organized society, and prefers the latitude and liberty of a life in the woods.[6]

Emerson Bennett, whose novel *The Prairie Flower* may have been based upon a narrative composed by an actual traveler on the Oregon Trail, introduces a few passages of remarkably accurate dialogue in the scenes dealing with the four trappers who figure in the story; one of them tells tall tales which belong to the authentic tradition of Davy Crockett.[7] But Bennett has nothing to contribute to the interpretation of the mountain man's character. He merely reshuffles the standard themes—the trapper's love of freedom, his indifference to hardship and danger, his hatred of the dull life of settled communities.[8] The novelist is noncommittal concerning the ethical character of the trapper, mingling hints of primitivistic approval with contradictory suggestions of moral condemnation, and concludes tamely that the mountain man is "a strange compound of odds and ends—of inexplicable incongruities—of good and evil." [9] As a straw in the wind pointing to the future development of the Wild Western hero we may note that Bennett's trappers, to the horror of the genteel hero Frank Leighton, delight in scalping Indians.[1] Leatherstocking, who always insisted that the white man and the Indian had different "gifts," had never condoned scalping by whites. As the literary Western hero moves beyond the Mississippi he is becoming more and more fully assimilated to the mores of the Indian.

At the same time, he is conceived as more and more completely autonomous, isolated, and self-contained. This is in accord with factual reporting by firsthand observers in the mountains. Lewis H. Garrard's autobiographical narrative *Wah-To-Yah*, for example, places great emphasis upon the mountain men's anarchic freedom and self-sufficiency. In the trappers' camps Garrard experienced "a grand sensation of liberty and a total absence of fear." There was no one to say what he should do; no "conventional rules of society constrained him to any particular form of dress, manner, or speech." It is true that Garrard was a youngster on his first vacation away from home, but he reports other attitudes than his own. He quotes the kindly advice of an old mountaineer:

6 David H. Coyner, *The Lost Trappers; A Collection of Interesting Scenes and Events in the Rocky Mountains* (New York, 1847), pp. xii-xiii.
7 *The Prairie Flower; or, Adventures in the Far West* (Cincinnati, 1849), p. 31. Harold A. Blaine has noted extensive plagiarism from George F. Ruxton's *Adventures in Mexico* and *Life in the Far West* in *The Prairie Flower* ("The Frontiersman in American Prose Fiction: 1800-1860," unpublished doctor's thesis, Western Reserve University, 1936, pp. 239-240).
8 *Ibid.*, p. 29; *Leni-Leoti; or, Adventures in the Far West* (Cincinnati, 1849), p. 38.
9 *The Prairie Flower*, p. 29.
1 *Idem.*

If you see a man's mule running off, do n't stop it—let it go to the devil; it is n't yourn. If his possible sack falls off, do n't tell him of it; he'll find it out. At camp, help cook—get wood an' water—make yourself active—get your pipe, an' smoke it—do n't ask too many questions, an' you'll pass! [2]

The dissolution of the bonds that tie man to man in society could hardly be carried farther than this.

The best known mountain man was Kit Carson, who owed his fame to Jessie Benton Frémont's skillful editing of her husband's reports on his exploring expeditions in the early 1840's.[3] Although these narratives had been widely read before 1846, the Mexican War created an even greater audience for them by bringing to bear on everything related to the winning of the West the yeasty nationalism aroused by the conflict. The momentary effect was to make of the fur trapper and mountain man just such a pioneer of empire as the glorifiers of Kentucky had tried to make of Boone in earlier decades. This in turn implied that Carson must be depicted according to canons of progress and civilization and even gentility that had not previously been invoked in discussion of the mountain man. Carson, like Boone, had now to be transformed into

one of the best of those noble and original characters that have from time to time sprung up on and beyond our frontier, retreating with it to the west, and drawing from association with uncultivated nature, not the rudeness and sensualism of the savage, but genuine simplicity and truthfulness of disposition, and generosity, bravery, and single heartedness to a degree rarely found in society.

Barbaric life in the wilderness held grave dangers for the ethical purity considered obligatory in national heroes. But if the typical Wild Westerner was, the contemporary journalist just quoted was forced to admit, "uncurbed," a prey to his own base passions, still an unassailable formula could be found for Carson: "In the school of men thus formed by hardships, exposure, peril, and temptation, our hero acquired all their virtues, and escaped their vices." [4] This almost exactly reproduces Timothy Flint's characterization of Boone and Cooper's characterization of Leatherstocking.

The pure and noble Carson was developed in later years by a series of

[2] Lewis H. Garrard, *Wah-To-Yah, and the Taos Trail; or, Prairie Travel and Scalp Dances, with a Look at Los Rancheros from Muleback and the Rocky Mountain Campfire* (Cincinnati, 1850), pp. 270-271.

[3] The publicizing of Carson through Frémont's reports is pointed out by James Madison Cutts, *The Conquest of California and New Mexico* (Philadelphia, 1847), pp. 166-167; and by Charles E. Averill, *Kit Carson, The Prince of the Gold Hunters; or, The Adventures of the Sacramento* (Boston, 1849), p. 58.

[4] Cutts, *Conquest of California*, pp. 165-167. This anonymous account of Carson was also reprinted in *The Rough and Ready Annual; or Military Souvenir* (New York, 1848), pp. 153-168.

biographers. The first of these, DeWitt C. Peters, was an army surgeon who had been stationed near the famous scout's home in New Mexico during the 1850's, and who made use of an autobiographical narrative dictated by the hero. The Peters biography appeared in 1858 before Kit's death and established the genteel interpretation of his character. Kit himself complained that Peters "laid it on a leetle too thick." [5] One instance will illustrate the doctor's method. Commenting upon the return of a trapping expedition under command of Ewing Young to Santa Fé in 1831, Peters confronts the fact that according to Carson's own account the mountain men went on a long spree. But this will never do. The biographer therefore commits the following extravaganza:

Young Kit, at this period of his life, imitated the example set by his elders, for he wished to be considered by them as an equal and a friend. He, however, passed through this terrible ordeal, which most frequently ruins its votary, and eventually came out brighter, clearer and more noble for the conscience-polish which he received. He contracted no bad habits, but learned the usefulness and happiness of resisting temptation, and became so well schooled that he was able, by the caution and advice of wisdom, founded on experience, to prevent many a promising and skillful hand from grasping ruin in the same vortex. [6]

Two subsequent biographies of Carson, one by an obscure novelist named Charles Burdett in 1862, and one by the famous popularizer of history, John S. C. Abbott, in 1873, are based on Peters and the Frémont reports, with various flourishes on the theme of the mountain man's spectacular refinement. Burdett implies that Carson never touched liquor, and emphasizes his extreme frugality amid men who loved to spend a year's earnings in a single splurge. [7] Abbott, accepting these positions as established, goes to the further extreme of maintaining that no oath ever passed Carson's lips. As Abbott remarks, "Even the rude and profane trappers around him could appreciate the superior dignity of such a character." [8] The historian also invoked the outworn theme of communion with nature (in this instance, in the Yellowstone country) as the source of his hero's virtue:

Men of little book culture, and with but slight acquaintance with the elegancies of polished life, have often a high appreciation of the beauties and the sublimities of nature. Think of such a man as Kit Carson, with his native delicacy of mind; a delicacy which never allowed him to use a profane word, to indulge in intoxicat-

---

[5] Edwin L. Sabin, *Kit Carson Days: 1809-1868* (Chicago, 1914), p. 506.
[6] DeWitt C. Peters, *The Life and Adventures of Kit Carson, the Nestor of the Rocky Mountains, from Facts Narrated by Himself* (New York, 1858), p. 50.
[7] Charles Burdett, *Life of Kit Carson: The Great Western Hunter and Guide* (Philadelphia, 1862), pp. 83-84, 367, 369.
[8] John S. C. Abbott, *Christopher Carson. Familiarly Known as Kit Carson* (New York, 1873), p. 70.

ing drinks, to be guilty of an impure action; a man who enjoyed, above all things else, the communings of his own spirit with the silence, the solitude, the grandeur, with which God has invested the illimitable wilderness; think of such a man in the midst of such scenes as we are now describing.[9]

This sort of thing could lead only to more and more acute distress in the reader. The future belonged to a different Kit Carson who had been developed entirely apart from the genteel conception—the Indian fighter, the daredevil horseman, the slayer of grizzly bears, the ancestor of the hundreds of two-gun men who came in later decades to people the Beadle dime novels. The rip-roaring Kit Carson made a brief appearance in Emerson Bennett's *The Prairie Flower* in 1849,[1] and came fully into his own in a thriller called *Kit Carson, The Prince of the Gold Hunters*, by one Charles Averill. This is probably the book dealing with his exploits that Kit found in October of that year amid the plunder taken by Apaches from a wagon train they had stampeded. He was decently embarrassed by it.[2]

Averill's novel was one of the consequences of a literary trend that had almost as much to do with Kit's rise to fame as did his association with Frémont. The subliterary story of adventure deliberately contrived for a mass audience, called "steam literature" because it was printed on the newly introduced rotary steam presses, was developed by editors of the weekly story papers established in imitation of the penny daily newspaper in the late 1830's and early 1840's. The earliest of these weeklies were the Boston *Notion* and *New World*, and *Brother Jonathan* of New York. At first the story papers relied heavily on pirated British fiction. Thus in 1842 both the *New World* and *Brother Jonathan* brought out Bulwer-Lytton's *Zanoni* at a "shilling," that is 12½¢.[3] In 1844 Maturin M. Ballou, then twenty-five years old, Boston-born son of the noted Universalist minister Hosea Ballou, joined forces with another young writer named Frederick Gleason in publishing three sea stories that Ballou had written under the pseudonym "Lieutenant Murray." The tales were highly successful—the first, *Fanny Campbell*, sold 80,000 copies within a few months —and the two young partners immediately expanded their publishing venture by hiring writers to grind out novelettes for them, including some, like Mrs. Ann S. Stephens and Justin B. Jones ("Harry Hazel"), who later found steady employment on Beadle's staff. This series, selling at a

[9] *Ibid.*, pp. 183-184.
[1] *The Prairie Flower*, pp. 58-60.
[2] *Kit Carson's Autobiography*, ed. Milo M. Quaife (Chicago, 1935), p. 135. Later Wild Western heroes sometimes took it for granted that they would be described in the newspapers and books down in the clearings (Oregon Sol in Edward S. Ellis, *Nathan Todd; or, The Fate of the Sioux' Captive*. Beadle's Dime Novels, No. 18, 1860, p. 64).
[3] Frederic Hudson, *Journalism in the United States, from 1690 to 1872* (New York, 1873), pp. 587-589.

shilling, was the ancestor of the many comparable series published during the second half of the century by Beadle and his competitors. Gleason and Ballou also pioneered the development of a national system of distribution by maintaining agents in nine cities, including Samuel French of New York.[4]

In 1846 Gleason and Ballou established a weekly story paper, *The Flag of Our Union,* which soon outstripped the *Boston Notion* and its other competitors to dominate the field. After holding the lead for five years it yielded in turn to the *New York Ledger,* which Robert Bonner bought in 1851 and publicized by the most sensational methods.[5] But Ballou had plenty of energy left. In 1854 he forced Gleason to sell out to him, and after various experiments, in 1857 inaugurated a series called *The Weekly Novelette,* selling for four cents. Each issue carried one-fifth of a story, so that the whole story cost twenty cents.[6] In that year Ballou's publications included *The Flag of Our Union,* a story weekly with a circulation of 80,000; *The Dollar Magazine,* a monthly with a circulation of 100,000; and *Ballou's Pictorial,* an illustrated weekly with a circulation of 140,000. To provide fiction for these various periodicals Ballou had enlarged his staff. Several of the newly added writers also went over to Beadle later, including Dr. John Hovey Robinson, A. J. H. Duganne, the veteran E. Z. C. Judson ("Ned Buntline"), and the most successful of all, Edward S. Ellis, who was still in his teens. Ballou himself was the author of at least two stories published later by Beadle. Under Ballou's guidance these writers, by the late 1850's, had developed the standard procedures of the popular adventure story.[7] They could turn with ease from pseudo-Gothic tales of knights in armor to yarns about pirates in the Caribbean; but popular demand brought most of them back in the end to the standard subjects of the American past: the Revolution, Kentucky, and, with increasing frequency, the Far West. Bennett's and Averill's stories belong to this class.[8]

The cast of characters in Averill's *Kit Carson* is substantially that standardized by Cooper—a genteel hero, a heroine, assorted villains, and the faithful guide—but the pattern has undergone a significant evolution.

[4] Ralph Admari, "Ballou, the Father of the Dime Novel," *American Book Collector,* IV, 121-122 (September-October, 1933).
[5] Ralph Admari, "Bonner and 'The Ledger,' " *ibid.,* VI, 176-181 (May-June, 1935).
[6] *Ibid.,* IV, 123; Hudson, *Journalism in the United States,* p. 647.
[7] Admari, "Ballou," *American Book Collector,* IV, 124.
[8] Bennett's early novels were published by various firms in Cincinnati (including J. A. & U. P. James) and subsequently by T. B. Peterson of Philadelphia: these publishing centers were feeling the same impulses that were motivating Ballou and Gleason in Boston, and Bonner in New York. In 1856 Bonner hired Bennett to write for the *New York Ledger,* and in 1867 Bennett became a contributor to Street & Smith's *New York Weekly* (with "Sol Slocum; or The Maid of the Juniata. A Tale of the Frontier," beginning on December 26 in Vol. XXIII, No. 6, p. 4).

The logic of the Far Western materials has begun to make itself felt. Although the upper-class Eastern hero is still present, he has sunk into insignificance, and is hardly more than a vestigial remnant beside the gigantic figure of Carson. Furthermore, Kit is presented without any mystical or genteel mummery; he is notable for his prowess and his courage alone. He is introduced to both the official hero and the reader by the device of a miniature, described with a quaint hagiological charm which is only increased by the contrast between subject and medium. The painting depicts

a man on horseback, in the dress of a western hunter, equipped like a trapper of the prairies; his tall and strongly knit frame drawn up, erect and lithe as the pine tree of his own forests; his broad, sun-burnt face developing a countenance, on which a life of danger and hardship had set its weather-beaten seal, and placed in boldest relief the unerring signs of a nature which for reckless daring and most indomitable hardihood, could know scarce a human superior.

Far in the background of the painting, rolled the waving grass of a boundless prairie; amid the silent wilderness of which, towered the noble figure of the hunter-horseman, half Indian, half whiteman in appearance, with rifle, horse and dog for his sole companions, in all that dreary waste; though to the right a yelling pack of wolves were seen upon his track, and on his left the thick, black smoke, in curling wreaths, proclaimed the prairie fire, while in the clear, gray eye that looked from the thrilling picture forth, there seemed to glance a look of proud indifference to all, and the conscious confidence of ennobling self-reliance! [9]

This figure, which the reader will recognize has little physical resemblance to the actual Kit Carson, is the Leatherstocking of *The Prairie,* made younger, mounted on a horse, and given an appreciably greater degree of self-assurance. Gone is the humility of the former servant, but gone also is the power to commune with nature. The Wild Western hero has been secularized—if the term may be employed in this connection—and magnified. He no longer looks to God through nature, for nature is no longer benign: its symbols are the wolves and the prairie fire. The scene has been shifted from the deep fertile forests east of the Mississippi to the barren plains. The landscape within which the Western hero operates has become, in Averill's words, a "dreary waste." It throws the hero back in upon himself and accentuates his terrible and sublime isolation. He is an anarchic and self-contained atom—hardly even a monad—alone in a hostile, or at best a neutral, universe.

This portrait of Kit Carson establishes the lines along which the Wild Western story was to develop for the next half century, until it should reach the seemingly indestructible state of petrification which it exhibits in our own day and is apparently destined to maintain through successive geological epochs while subtler and more ambitious literary forms come

[9] *Kit Carson, The Prince of the Gold Hunters,* pp. 57-58.

and go. In Averill's tale the stage is already set for the entrance of Erastus Beadle.[1]

STUDY QUESTIONS

1. Unlike the earlier essays of DeVoto and Ruxton, this selection surveys the fictional presentation of the backwoods hero. By comparing these essays, point out some clear differences between the actual historical figure and the one portrayed in books.

2. What qualities of the trappers seem to have been stressed by the earlier writers? How did this emphasis change? To what single factor does Smith attribute the major responsibility for this change?

3. This essay shows how biography and fiction can collaborate in developing a personal reputation. To what extent were the biographies fictional? To what extent was the fiction true to life?

4. How does Smith explain the "evolution" in the literary presentation of Kit Carson?

5. What changes in American life and thought are reflected in the developments that took place in this type of literature?

6. This selection is an example of a research paper whose subject is a type of literary hero. Notice that by grouping together books about the same sort of hero the author develops significant trends and contrasts. Similar results would emerge from any well-conducted survey of a literary type. Write a research paper describing the appearance of a type of character in fiction, the movies, TV plays or some other medium. Possibilities would be the American cowboy, the criminal, the young executive, the housewife, the college student, the soldier.

[1] Carson appears occasionally in the Beadle stories, as for example in James F. C. Adams's *The Fighting Trapper; or Kit Carson to the Rescue.* Beadle's New York Dime Library, No. 1045 (1901, reprint of original ed. 1879). The story contains an old trapper, Vic Vannoven, "rough but generous," toward whom the heroine feels as she would toward her father, so that we recognize him as a legitimate descendant of Leatherstocking. Kit Carson, young and agile, "the most renowned Indian fighter the world ever produced," appears briefly toward the end of the story to rescue the heroine and her party. He preserves the elusive, almost elfish quality he had had in Emerson Bennett's *The Prairie Flower.* Adams, incidentally, was not so violent a prohibitionist as the genteel biographers were. After the fight Kit offers brandy to the party, and he consumes "quiet draughts" during his turn on guard during the night (p. 26).

3. THE SHAPE OF REALITY

The Principle of Vision*

George Henry Lewes

Insight is the first condition of Art. Yet many a man who has never been beyond his village will be silent about that which he knows well, and will fancy himself called upon to speak of the tropics or the Andes—on the reports of others. Never having seen a greater man than the parson and the squire—and not having seen into them—he selects Cromwell, and Plato, Raphael and Napoleon, as his models, in the vain belief that these impressive personalities will make his work impressive. Of course, I am speaking figuratively. By "never having been beyond his village," I understand a mental no less than topographical limitation. The penetrating sympathy of genius will, even from a village, traverse the whole world. What I mean is, that unless by personal experience, no matter through what avenues, a man has gained clear insight into the facts of life, he cannot successfully place them before us; and whatever insight he *has* gained, be it of important or of unimportant facts, will be of value if truly reproduced. No sunset is precisely similar to another, no two souls are affected by it in a precisely similar way. Thus may the commonest phenomenon have a novelty. To the eye that can read aright there is an infinite variety even in the most ordinary human being. But to the careless, indiscriminating eye all individuality is merged in a misty generality. Nature and men yield nothing new to such a mind. Of what avail is it for a man to walk out into the tremulous mist of morning, to watch the slow sunset, and wait for the rising stars, if he can tell us nothing about these but what others have already told us—if he feels nothing but what others have already felt? Let a man look for himself and tell truly what he sees. We will listen to that. We must listen to it, for its very authenticity has the subtle power of compulsion. What others have seen and felt we can learn better from their own lips. . . .

Perception, as distinguished from sensation, is the presentation before consciousness of the details which once were present in conjunction with the object at this moment affecting sense. These details are inferred to be still in conjunction with the object, although not revealed to sense. Thus, when an apple is perceived by me, who merely see it, all that sense reports is of a certain coloured surface: the roundness, the firmness, the fragrance,

* From "The Principles of Success in Literature." first published in *Fortnightly Review*, 1865.

and taste of the apple are not present to sense, but are made present to consciousness by the act of perception. The eye sees a certain coloured surface; the mind sees at the same instant many other co-existent but unapparent facts—it reinstates in their due order these unapparent facts. Were it not for this mental vision supplying the deficiencies of ocular vision, the coloured surface would be an enigma. But the suggestion of sense rapidly recalls the experiences previously associated with the object. The apparent facts disclose the facts that are unapparent.

Inference is only a higher form of the same process. We look from the window, see the dripping leaves and the wet ground, and infer that rain has fallen. It is on inferences of this kind that all knowledge depends. The extension of the known to the unknown, of the apparent to the unapparent, gives us science. Except in the grandeur of its sweep, the mind pursues the same course in the interpretation of geological facts as in the interpretation of the ordinary incidents of daily experience. To read the pages of the great Stone Book, and to perceive from the wet streets that rain has fallen, are forms of the same intellectual process. In the one case the inference traverses immeasurable spaces of time, connecting the apparent facts with causes (unapparent facts) similar to those which have been associated in experience with such results; in the other case the inference connects wet streets and swollen gutters with causes which have been associated in experience with such results. Let the inference span with its mighty arch a myriad of years, or link together the events of a few minutes, in each case the arch rises from the ground of familiar facts, and reaches an antecedent which is known to be a cause capable of producing them. . . .

In general, men are passive under sense and the routine of habitual inferences. They are unable to free themselves from the importunities of the apparent facts and apparent relations which solicit their attention; and when they make room for unapparent facts, it is only for those which are familiar to their minds. Hence they can see little more than what they have been taught to see; they can only think what they have been taught to think. For independent vision, and original conception, we must go to children and men of genius. The spontaneity of the one is the power of the other. Ordinary men live among marvels and feel no wonder, grow familiar with objects and learn nothing new about them. Then comes an independent mind which *sees;* and it surprises us to find how servile we have been to habit and opinion, how blind to what we also might have seen, had we used our eyes. The link, so long hidden, has now been made visible to us. We hasten to make it visible to others. But the flash of light which revealed that obscured object does not help us to discover others. Darkness still conceals much that we do not even suspect. We continue our routine. We always think our views correct and complete; if we thought otherwise they would cease to be our views; and when the man of keener insight discloses our error, and reveals relations hitherto unsuspected, we learn to see with his eyes, and exclaim: "Now surely we have got the truth."

STUDY QUESTIONS

1. Lewes' insistence that art depends upon the uniqueness with which each man sees reality is frequently held to be one of the basic principles of good writing. To what extent have the writers in the section entitled "The Uncommon Observer," demonstrated "insight" in their writing? To what extent have they written about things within their own experience?

2. What is the difference, according to Lewes, between "sensation" and "perception"? Between "perception" and "inference"?

3. This short selection provides a convenient and useful example of simple definition of terms. What methods does Lewes use to define such terms as "sensation," "perception," and "inference"?

4. Why do we not ordinarily "perceive" as well as we might?

5. Write a description following Lewes' suggestion about "perception." Take some object or place that is familiar to you, and examine it as though you were seeing it for the first time, with the mind as well as the eye. Then organize your results into a written description.

6. Do you agree with Lewes that one must actually undergo a particular experience to write about it convincingly? If you do not, accept his challenge by writing an account of a place or experience of which you do not have firsthand knowledge, trying to make it as authentic as you can. If you do agree with Lewes, write an expository theme supported by examples, explaining the problems into which you think a writer will fall if he tries to write about experiences he has not had.

Observation and Interpretation*

John Steinbeck and Edward F. Ricketts

The design of a book is the pattern of a reality controlled and shaped by the mind of the writer. This is completely understood about poetry or fiction, but it is too seldom realized about books of fact. And yet the impulse which drives a man to poetry will send another man into the tide pools and force him to try to report what he finds there. Why is an expedition to Tibet undertaken, or a sea bottom dredged? Why do men, sitting at the microscope, examine the calcareous plates of a sea-cucumber, and, finding a new arrangement and number, feel an exaltation

*From *Log of the Sea of Cortez* by John Steinbeck and Edward F. Ricketts. Copyright, 1951, by John Steinbeck. Reprinted by permission of The Viking Press, Inc., New York.

and give the new species a name, and write about it possessively? It would be good to know the impulse truly, not to be confused by the "services to science" platitudes or the other little mazes into which we entice our minds so that they will not know what we are doing.

We have a book to write about the Gulf of California. We could do one of several things about its design. But we have decided to let it form itself: its boundaries a boat and a sea; its duration a six weeks' charter time; its subject everything we could see and think and even imagine; its limits—our own without reservation.

We made a trip into the Gulf; sometimes we dignified it by calling it an expedition. Once it was called the Sea of Cortez, and that is a better-sounding and a more exciting name. We stopped in many little harbors and near barren coasts to collect and preserve the marine invertebrates of the littoral. One of the reasons we gave ourselves this trip—and when we used this reason, we called the trip an expedition—was to observe the distribution of invertebrates, to see and record their kinds and numbers, how they lived together, what they ate, and how they reproduced. That plan was simple, straight-forward, and only a part of the truth. But we did tell the truth to ourselves. We were curious. Our curiosity was not limited, but was as wide and horizonless as that of Darwin or Agassiz or Linnaeus or Pliny. We wanted to see everything our eyes would accommodate, to think what we could, and, out of our seeing and thinking, to build some kind of structure in modeled imitation of the observed reality. We knew that what we would see and record and construct would be warped, as all knowledge patterns are warped, first, by the collective pleasure and stream of our time and race, second by the thrust of our individual personalities. But knowing this, we might not fall into too many holes—we might maintain some balance between our warp and the separate thing, the external reality. The oneness of these two might take its contribution from both. For example: the Mexican sierra has "XVII-15-IX" spines in the dorsal fin. These can easily be counted. But if the sierra strikes hard 'on the line so that our hands are burned, if the fish sounds and nearly escapes and finally comes in over the rail, his colors pulsing and his tail beating the air, a whole new relational externality has come into being—an entity which is more than the sum of the fish plus the fisherman. The only way to count the spines of the sierra unaffected by this second relational reality is to sit in a laboratory, open an evil-smelling jar, remove a stiff colorless fish from formalin solution, count the spines, and write the truth "D. XVII-15-IX." There you have recorded a reality which cannot be assailed—probably the least important reality concerning either the fish or yourself.

It is good to know what you are doing. The man with his pickled fish has set down one truth and has recorded in his experience many lies. The fish is not that color, that texture, that dead, nor does he smell that way.

Such things we had considered in the months of planning our expedition and we were determined not to let a passion for unassailable little truths draw in the horizons and crowd the sky down on us. We knew that what seemed to us true could be only relatively true anyway. There is no other kind of observation. The man with his pickled fish has sacrificed a great observation about himself, the fish, and the focal point, which is his thought on both the sierra and himself.

We suppose this was the mental provisioning of our expedition. We said, "Let's go wide open. Let's see what we see, record what we find, and not fool ourselves with conventional scientific structures. We could not observe a completely objective Sea of Cortez anyway, for in that lonely and uninhabited Gulf our boat and ourselves would change in the moment we entered. By going there, we would bring a new factor to the Gulf. Let us consider that factor and not be betrayed by this myth of permanent objective reality. If it exists at all, it is only available in pickled tatters or in distorted flashes. Let us go," we said, "into the Sea of Cortez, realizing that we become forever a part of it; that our rubber boots slogging through a flat of eelgrass, that the rocks we turn over in a tide pool, make us truly and permanently a factor in the ecology of the region. We shall take something away from it, but we shall leave something too." And if we seem a small factor in a huge pattern, nevertheless it is of relative importance. We take a tiny colony of soft corals from a rock in a little water world. And that isn't terribly important to the tide pool. Fifty miles away the Japanese shrimp boats are dredging with overlapping scoops, bringing up tons of shrimps, rapidly destroying the species so that it may never come back, and with the species destroying the ecological balance of the whole region. That isn't very important in the world. And six thousand miles away the great bombs are falling on London and the stars are not moved thereby. None of it is important or all of it is.

We determined to go doubly open so that in the end we could, if we wished, describe the sierra thus: "D. XVII-15-IX; A. II-15-IX," but also we could see the fish alive and swimming, feel it plunge against the lines, drag it threshing over the rail, and even finally eat it. And there is no reason why either approach should be inaccurate. Spine-count description need not suffer because another approach is also used. Perhaps out of the two approaches, we thought, there might emerge a picture more complete and even more accurate than either alone could produce. And so we went.

STUDY QUESTIONS

1. The opening generalization of this selection, that "the design of a book is the pattern of a reality controlled and shaped by the mind of the writer," is a thesis implicit in a number of selections in the whole first section of this anthology. Explain how it seems to be implied in the selections by Herbert Read, Graham Greene, George

Orwell, Lafcadio Hearn, or others. What implications does this generalization have for the problem of organizing a theme?

2. The authors state that "all knowledge patterns are warped." Does this mean that the scientist cannot provide us with an "objective" description of reality?

3. What different kinds of "truth" do the authors discuss in this selection?

4. Explain in your own words what you think the authors mean by "reality."

5. Observe some object or place, record the checkable truths about it, and then write two brief descriptions, one in which you try to present these truths with the greatest possible objectivity, and the other in which you present it in terms of your interpreted sense perceptions.

6. Select one of the descriptions from the group entitled "The Uncommon Observer," such as that of coal mines by Orwell, or of Monterey by Stevenson; read in an encyclopedia some equivalent account of it; and write a paper describing the relative degree of "objectivity" in the two accounts.

Getting at the Truth*

Marchette Chute

This is a rather presumptuous title for a biographer to use, since truth is a very large word. In the sense that it means the reality about a human being it is probably impossible for a biographer to achieve. In the sense that it means a reasonable presentation of all the available facts it is more nearly possible, but even this limited goal is harder to reach than it appears to be. A biographer needs to be both humble and cautious when he remembers the nature of the material he is working with, for a historical fact is rather like the flamingo that Alice in Wonderland tried to use as a croquet mallet. As soon as she got its neck nicely straightened out and was ready to hit the ball, it would turn and look at her with puzzled expression, and any biographer knows that what is called a "fact" has a way of doing the same.

Here is a small example. When I was writing my forthcoming biography, "Ben Jonson of Westminster," I wanted to give a paragraph or two to Sir Philip Sidney, who had a great influence on Jonson. No one thinks of Sidney without thinking of chivalry, and to underline the point I intended to use a story that Sir Fulke Greville told of him. Sidney died of gangrene, from a musket shot that shattered his thigh, and Greville says

* "Getting at the Truth" by Marchette Chute, from *The Saturday Review*, September 19, 1953. Reprinted by permission.

that Sidney failed to put on his leg armor while preparing for battle because the marshal of the camp was not wearing leg armor and Sidney was unwilling to do anything that would give him a special advantage.

The story is so characteristic both of Sidney himself and of the misplaced high-mindedness of late Renaissance chivalry that I wanted to use it, and since Sir Fulke Greville was one of Sidney's closest friends the information seemed to be reliable enough. But it is always well to check each piece of information as thoroughly as possible and so I consulted another account of Sidney written by a contemporary, this time a doctor who knew the family fairly well. The doctor, Thomas Moffet, mentioned the episode but he said that Sidney left off his leg armor because he was in a hurry.

The information was beginning to twist in my hand and could no longer be trusted. So I consulted still another contemporary who had mentioned the episode, to see which of the two he agreed with. This was Sir John Smythe, a military expert who brought out his book a few years after Sidney's death. Sir John was an old-fashioned conservative who advocated the use of heavy armor even on horseback, and he deplored the current craze for leaving off leg protection, "the imitating of which . . . cost that noble and worthy gentleman Sir Philip Sidney his life."

So here I was with three entirely different reasons why Sidney left off his leg armor, all advanced by careful writers who were contemporaries of his. The flamingo had a legitimate reason for looking around with a puzzled expression.

The only thing to do in a case like this is to examine the point of view of the three men who are supplying the conflicting evidence. Sir Fulke Greville was trying to prove a thesis: that his beloved friend had an extremely chivalric nature. Sir John Smythe also was trying to prove a thesis: that the advocates of light arming followed a theory that could lead to disaster. Only the doctor, Thomas Moffet, was not trying to prove a thesis. He was not using his own explanation to reinforce some point he wanted to make. He did not want anything except to set down on paper what he believed to be the facts; and since we do not have Sidney's own explanation of why he did not put on leg armor, the chances are that Dr. Moffet is the safest man to trust.

For Moffet was without desire. Nothing can so quickly blur and distort the facts as desire—the wish to use the facts for some purpose of your own —and nothing can so surely destroy the truth. As soon as the witness wants to prove something he is no longer impartial and his evidence is no longer to be trusted.

The only safe way to study contemporary testimony is to bear constantly in mind this possibility of prejudice and to put almost as much attention on the writer himself as on what he has written. For instance, Sir Anthony Weldon's description of the Court of King James is lively enough and often used as source material; but a note from the publisher admits that the pamphlet was issued as a warning to anyone who wished to "side with this bloody house" of Stuart. The publisher, at any rate, did not consider Weldon an impartial witness. At about the same time Arthur Wilson published his history of Great Britain, which contained an irresistibly vivid account of the agonized death of the Countess of Somerset. Wilson sounds reasonably impartial; but his patron was the Earl of Essex, who had good reason to hate that particular countess, and there is evidence that he invented the whole scene to gratify his patron.

Sometimes a writer will contradict what he has already written, and in that case the only thing to do is to investigate what has changed his point of view. For instance, in 1608 Captain John Smith issued a description of his capture by Powhatan, and he made it clear that the Indian chief had treated him with unwavering courtesy and hospitality. In 1624 the story was repeated in Smith's "General History of Virginia," but the writer's circumstances had changed. Smith needed money, "having a prince's mind imprisoned in a poor man's purse," and, he wanted the book to be profitable. Powhatan's daughter, the princess Pocahontas, had recently been in the news, for her visit to England had aroused a great deal of interest among the sort of people that Smith hoped would buy his book. So Smith supplied a new version of the story, in which the once-hospitable Powhatan would have permitted the hero's brains to be dashed out if Pocahontas had not saved his life. It was the second story that achieved fame, and of course it may have been true. But it is impossible to trust it because the desire of the writer is so obviously involved; as Smith said in his prospectus, he needed money and hoped that the book would give "satisfaction."

It might seem that there was an easy way for a biographer to avoid the use of this kind of prejudiced testimony. All he has to do is to construct his biography from evidence that cannot be tampered with—from parish records, legal documents, bills, accounts, court records, and so on. Out of these solid gray blocks of impersonal evidence it should surely be possible to construct a road that will lead straight to the truth and that will never bend itself to the misleading curve of personal desire.

This might be so if the only problem involved were the reliability of the material. But there is another kind of desire that is much more subtle, much more pervasive, and much more dangerous than the occasional distortions of fact that contemporary writers may have permitted themselves to make; and this kind of desire can destroy the truth of a biography even if every individual fact in it is as solid and as uncompromising as rock. Even if the road is built of the best and most reliable materials it can still curve away from the truth because of this other desire that threatens it: the desire of the biographer himself.

A biographer is not a court record or a legal document. He is a human being, writing about another human being, and his own temperament, his own point of view, and his own frame of reference are unconsciously imposed upon the man he is writing about. Even if the biographer is free from Captain Smith's temptation—the need for making money—and wants to write nothing but the literal truth, he is still handicapped by the fact that there is no such thing as a completely objective human being.

An illustration of what can happen if the point of view is sufficiently strong is the curious conclusion that the nineteenth-century biographers reached about William Shakespeare. Shakespeare joined a company of London actors in 1594, was listed as an actor in 1598 and 1603, and was still listed as one of the "men actors" in the company in 1609. Shortly before he joined this company Shakespeare dedicated two narrative poems to the Earl of Southampton, and several years after Shakespeare died his collected plays were dedicated to the Earl of Pembroke. This was his only relationship with either of the two noblemen, and there is nothing to connect him with them during the fifteen years in which he belonged to the same acting company and during which he wrote nearly all his plays.

But here the desire of the biographers entered in. They had been reared in the strict code of nineteenth-century gentility and they accepted two ideas without question. One was that there are few things more important than an English lord; the other was that there are few things less important than a mere actor. They already knew the undeniable fact that Shakespeare was one of the greatest men who ever lived; and while they could not go quite so far as to claim him as an actual member of the nobility, it was clear to them that he must have been the treasured friend of both the Earl of Southampton and the Earl of Pembroke and that he must have written his plays either while basking in their exalted company or while he was roaming the green countryside by the waters of the river Avon. (It is another basic conviction of the English gentleman that there is nothing so inspiring as nature.) The notion that Shakespeare had spent all these years as the working member of a company of London actors was so abhorrent that it was never seriously considered. It could not be so; therefore it was not.

These biographers did their work well. When New South Wales built its beautiful memorial library to Shakespeare, it was the coat of arms of the Earl of Southampton that alternated with that of royalty in dignified splendor over the bookshelves. Shakespeare had been re-created in the image of desire, and desire will always ignore whatever is not relevant to its purpose. Because the English gentlemen did not like Shakespeare's background it was explained away as though it had never existed, and Shakespeare ceased to be an actor because so lowly a trade was not suited to so great a man.

All this is not to say that a biography should be lacking in a point of view. If it does not have a point of view it will be nothing more than a kind of expanded article for an encyclopedia—a string of facts arranged in chronological order with no claim to being a real biography at all. A biography must have a point of view and it must have a frame of reference.

But it should be a point of view and a frame of reference implicit in the material itself and not imposed upon it.

It might seem that the ideal biographical system, if it could be achieved, would be to go through the years of research without feeling any kind of emotion. The biographer would be a kind of fact-finding machine and then suddenly, after his years of research, a kind of total vision would fall upon him and he would transcribe it in his best and most persuasive English for a waiting public. But research is fortunately not done by machinery, nor are visions likely to descend in that helpful manner. They are the product not only of many facts but also of much thinking, and it is only when the biographer begins to get emotional in his thinking that he ought to beware.

It is easy enough to make good resolutions in advance, but a biographer cannot altogether control his sense of excitement when the climax of his years of research draws near and he begins to see the pieces fall into place. Almost without his volition, A, B, and D fit together and start to form a pattern, and it is almost impossible for the biographer not to start searching for C. Something turns up that looks remarkably like C, and with a little trimming of the edges and the ignoring of one very slight discrepancy it will fill the place allotted for C magnificently.

It is at this point that the biographer ought to take a deep breath and sit on his hands until he has had time to calm down. He has no real, fundamental reason to believe that his discovery is C, except for the fact that he wants it to be. He is like a man looking for a missing piece in a difficult jigsaw puzzle, who has found one so nearly the right shape that he cannot resist the desire to jam it into place.

If the biographer had refused to be tempted by his supposed discovery of C and had gone on with his research, he might have found not only the connecting, illuminating fact he needed but much more besides. He is not going to look for it now. Desire has blocked the way. And by so much his biography will fall short of what might have been the truth.

It would not be accurate to say that a biographer should be wholly lacking in desire. Curiosity is a form of desire. So is the final wish to get the material down on paper in a form that will be fair to the reader's interest and worthy of the subject. But a subconscious desire to push the facts around is one of the most dangerous things a biographer can encounter, and all the more dangerous because it is so difficult to know when he is encountering it.

The reason Alice had so much trouble with her flamingo is that the average flamingo does not wish to be used as a croquet mallet. It has other purposes in view. The same thing is true of a fact, which can be just as self-willed as a flamingo and has its own kind of stubborn integrity. To try to force a series of facts into a previously desired arrangement is a form of misuse to which no self-respecting fact will willingly submit itself. The best and only way to treat it is to leave it alone and be willing to follow where it leads, rather than to press your own wishes upon it. To put the whole thing into a single sentence: you will never succeed in getting at the truth if you think you know, ahead of time, what the truth ought to be.

STUDY QUESTIONS

1. How do you suppose Miss Chute gathered the information that enabled her to evaluate the opinions about Sidney's leg-armor?
2. Notice how great a proportion of this essay is devoted to the rather complicated examples the author is compelled to use. What is the proportion? Could she have accomplished her purpose without these examples?
3. Compare Miss Chute's procedure in learning the facts with Dewey's account of "reflective thinking" in "What is Thinking?"
4. What evidence do you find in Henry Nash Smith's "Mountain Man as Western Hero" that he has or has not evaluated various opinions about his subject?
5. Have you ever had to resort to complicated and troublesome methods to learn some necessary facts—something in connection with registration, the time of a train or plane departure, the facts about a possible job, or about a person? If you have had an experience of this sort, write a theme describing your difficulties and the moral and emotional situation surrounding them.
6. One of the most common mistakes among readers is that of accepting a statement of fact or opinion just because it is in print. A good remedy for this is reading two biographical accounts of some person in whom you are interested and comparing the differences in attitude, interpretation, and even in facts that will emerge. Read accounts of some historical figure in two or three encyclopedias and write a report comparing the accounts.

The Literary Use of Language*

David Daiches

Life is a jungle of events whose meanings are at once too casual (and to that extent insignificant) and too full of possible implication (without offering us any guidance as to which implication or set of implications we should choose). The skilled storyteller makes those meanings at once more significant and less confused. He chooses or invents a tractable piece of life and proceeds both to define its meaning more

* From *A Study of Literature* by David Daiches. Reprinted by permission of the Cornell University Press.

precisely than the meaning of any event in real life can be known (Can we even talk of the "meaning" of events in real life, unless we mean simply their causes and effects?) and to enrich its meaning in a wholly unique manner. Is it possible simultaneously to define a meaning more precisely and to enrich it? We can see that this is possible if we consider what the skillful writer of fiction (and, indeed, of any kind of creative literature) actually does.

Let us take a very simple example. Consider that a journalist has been asked to stand for a while in a city street and then write up an account of the street and what took place there. As soon as he begins to write he will have to make his own definition of his subject. What in fact is meant by "the street and what took place there"? To define even the street requires a choice: is it simply the thoroughfare leading from one place to another, or are we to include the buildings which flank it, and if we include the buildings what aspects of them are we to include? A street, in fact, can be considered in an indefinite number of ways. As for defining "what took place there," we strike here immediately the problem of selection. Clearly, it would be physically impossible as well as wholly pointless for the writer to give an account of every single event which in fact occurred while he was there, or even of every single event which he observed. Our journalist would have to select from among the plethora of events—the actions and gestures of people, the movement of traffic, all the innumerable activities of city life—what he considered of importance or of interest on some standard or other. He would have to define "street" and "what took place there" before writing or in the process of writing. And he would have to make up his mind about his perspective. Should he try to get closer to some things than to others; should he vary the distance at which he stood from people and things, or maintain a simple gradation from foreground to background? These and other questions he will have to answer, consciously or unconsciously, in presenting us with a verbal picture of that street at that time. Having done so, he will have presented to us aspects of a situation which we can recognize as one which we either have known or might have known. If he can use the language with any ability at all, even if he can put together a number of sentences which say, however badly or crudely, what he saw (or rather, what he thought he saw) that he considered worth mentioning, we shall be able to recognize his account as corresponding to something of which we have had experience—assuming, of course, that we are products of the same civilization and are familiar with that kind of city street. That is to say, we should *recognize* the description as, in a general sort of way at least, true. The writer, without using any other skill than is required of a reasonably competent journalist, would have defined his subject intelligibly and recognizably. Out of the moving chaos of reality he will have isolated a static picture, which a certain class of readers would consent to, as reflecting in some sense an actual state of affairs.

Our journalist might do more than that. He might manage to convey to readers who have not had experience of that kind of city street at all a sense of the authenticity of his picture. He can do this by "style," by the selection and organization of his imagery, by using words in such a way that the reader is persuaded into recognizing not what he has seen but what he might have seen. The first stage is where we recognize what we know, the second is where we recognize what we might have known, and there is a third—where, while we recognize what we have known or might have known, we at the same time see, and know to be authentic, what we should never have seen for ourselves. The interesting fact is that where a writer succeeds in making authentic a picture of a kind that his readers might not have seen, he will very probably be doing more—he will be giving them at the same time a new insight which coexists with the feeling of recognition. This is because "style," that way of writing which makes convincing in its own right what would otherwise be merely recognizable, can rarely do this without going further. For such a style is the result of the ability to choose and order words in such a way that what is described becomes not merely something existing, something which happens to be in a particular place at a particular time, but something that is linked with man's wider fate, that suggests, and keeps on suggesting the more we read, ever wider categories of experiences until there is included something with which we can make contact, which touches what we, too, find recognizable. And then it becomes irrelevant whether what is described exists in fact in the real world or not. The mere journalist drops his words one by one, and there they lie, in the order in which he dropped them, specific but still, corresponding accurately enough to what the author intends to say, but having no further life of their own. But the true creative writer drops his words into our mind like stones in a pool, and the ever-widening circles of meaning eventually ring round and encompass the store of our own experience. And—to continue the metaphor—in doing so they provide a new context for familiar things, and what has been lying half dead in our mind and imagination takes on new life in virtue of its new context, so that we not only recognize what we feel we knew but see the familiar take on rich and exciting new meanings.

If, therefore, the journalist who described what went on in a particular city street during a given period of time had the literary skill (and the initial combination of feeling for life and feeling for language which alone can make such a skill *realizable*) to present his observations in such a way that when he wrote of businessmen entering and leaving the bank, children coming home from school, housewives out shopping, loiterers, barking dogs, lumbering busses, or whatever else he cared to note, he was able to convey to the reader something of the tragedy or the comedy of human affairs, wringing some human insight out of these multifarious incidents so that the reader not only sees what he already knew or even admits as authentic what he did not know, but sees simultaneously what he knew and what he never saw before, recognizes the picture in the light of his deepest, half-intuitive knowledge of what man's experience is and can be and at the same time sees it as a new illumination—if he can do this, then he has moved from journalism into art. He has shown that he can make the means of expression comment on what is expressed so as simultaneously to define and expand his subject matter: define it by using words that block off the wrong meanings, which show with complete compulsion that what is meant is *this* rather than *that,* and expand it by choosing and arranging words and larger units of expression so that they set going the appropriate overtones and suggestions which help to elevate a description of people's behavior to an account of man's fate.

STUDY QUESTIONS

1. What differences or similarities are there between Daiches' description of the functions of the storyteller, and Steinbeck and Ricketts' description of their intention in *The Sea of Cortez?*

2. What three decisions does the writer have to make in order to give an account of something from real life?

3. What, according to Daiches, is the difference between the subject matter of the journalist and the subject matter of the artist?

4. What are Daiches' three stages of the transcription of life?

5. Write a theme about a familiar subject or experience which you think will enable the reader to recognize what you are describing, and at the same time provide him with an insight into it which he probably could not have achieved himself. The subject should, naturally, be something you are familiar with. Your superior insight should depend, not on special information which you happen to possess, but on your special interest in or understanding of the subject.

6. Transcribe some actual experience, aiming to give your reader a fair and accurate impression of it by omitting irrelevancies and stressing the main features.

PART TWO

Language, Thought, and Ideas

1. THE WRITTEN WORD

Writing and Speech*

Harold Whitehall

All of us have a grammar. The fact that we use and understand English in daily affairs means that we use and understand, for the most part unconsciously, the major grammatical patterns of our language. Yet because of the effects of education, many of us have come to think of a relatively formal written English and its reflection among those who "speak by the book" as the only genuine English, and to consider its grammar as the only acceptable English grammar. That is by no means true. The basic form of present-day American English is the patterned, rhythmed, and segmented code of voice signals called *speech*—speech as used in everyday conversation by highly educated people (*cultivated speech*), by the general run of our population (*common speech*), or by some rural persons in such geographically isolated areas as the Ozark Plateau, the Appalachian Mountains, or the woodland areas of northern New England (*folk speech*). From the code of speech, the language of formal writing is something of an abstraction, differing in details of grammar and vocabulary and lacking clear indication of the bodily gestures and meaningful qualities of the voice which accompany ordinary conversation. Thus, serious written English may be regarded as a rather artificial dialect of our language. To acquire that dialect, the would-be writer needs to know a good deal about its structural details, and particularly about those in which it differs from the less formal varieties of speech.

---

* From *Structural Essentials of English*, copyright, 1951, by Harold Whitehall. Copyright, 1954, 1956, by Harcourt, Brace and Company, Inc. Reprinted by permission of Harcourt, Brace and Company, Inc.

Even a moment's reflection will show that the spoken American language is backed by expressive features lacking in the written language: the rise or fall of the voice at the ends of phrases and sentences; the application of vocal loudness to this or that word or part of a word; the use of gesture; the meaningful rasp or liquidity, shouting or muting, drawling or clipping, whining or breaking, melody or whispering imparted to the quality of the voice. Written English, lacking clear indication of such features, must be so managed that it compensates for what it lacks. It must be more carefully organized than speech in order to overcome its communicative deficiencies as compared with speech. In speech, we safeguard meaning by the use of intonation, stress, gesture, and voice qualities. In writing, we must deal with our medium in such a way that the meaning cannot possibly be misunderstood. In the absence of an actual hearer capable of interrupting and demanding further explanation, a clear writer is always conscious of "a reader over his shoulder." All this despite the fact that writing, being permanent, as compared with speech, which is evanescent, allows not only reading but also rereading.

Nor is this all. If written English is somewhat abstract, somewhat artificial, it is also generalized—national, not geographically or socially limited in scope. We must realize that comparatively few of us make use in our day-to-day affairs of a generalized spoken American English that is at all comparable with it. Such a language—a Received Standard Spoken English—exists, but not for the most part in this country where the practical need for it is slight. It exists in England, where the practical need for it is great. In England, many people still start their linguistic careers speaking one or another of the regional dialects, dialects so different from each other in vocabulary and grammar, so quilt-crazy in their distribution, that they form real barriers to generalized, national communication. Yet, in a modern, democratic country, general communication is a necessity. For that reason, Englishmen are willing to accept the notion both of a generalized spoken and a generalized written form of expression on a level above the dialects, and are willing to make the effort of learning them in school and elsewhere. We would be equally willing if our everyday speech happened to resemble this specimen from the English county of Lancaster:

"Nay! my heart misgi'es me! There's summat abeawt this neet's wark as is noan jannock. Look thee here! Yon chap's noan t' first sheep theaw's lifted tax-free fro't' mooar, an' aw've niver been one to worrit abeawt it, that aw hav'nt. But toneet, someheaw, it's noan t'same. There's summat beawn't 'appen—aw con feel it i' my booans. This een, an unconny wind wor burrin' i't'ling, an' not a cleawd i't' sky; an' whin aw went deawn to' t'well for watter, t'bats wor flyin' reawn it in a widdershins ring. Mark my words, there's mooar to coom."

In the United States, our language situation is quite different. Ours is probably the only country on earth in which three thousand miles of travel will bring no difficulty of spoken communication. We do have, of course, regional and social differences of language. The speech of Maine does not coincide in all points with that of Texas, nor the speech of Georgia with that of Minnesota. The speech of cultivated people in urban centers is not precisely that of the general mass of our citizens, nor that of rural residents of limited education in geographically secluded areas. Yet, unless we deliberately choose to emphasize disparities for social and other reasons, our regional and social speech differences create no great barriers to the free exchange of opinions and ideas. They consist of flavoring rather than substance.

Precisely for that reason, pressures for the adoption of a generalized national spoken American English comparable in acceptance and prestige with Received Standard Spoken British have proved largely unavailing. In American life, one may use cultivated or common speech Southern, cultivated or common speech Northeastern, or cultivated or common speech North Middle Western, without encountering any great practical disadvantage. Our standards of speech are mainly regional standards, and most of us, in actual fact, speak some kind of a patois in which one or another of the cultivated or common speech regional varieties of American English blends quite happily with elements absorbed from reading and the educational process. We are very fortunate in this—fortunate that American historical and sociological conditions have removed difficulties of spoken communication found in most other parts of the world.

In a lesser sense, however, our good fortune is something of a misfortune. Because an American can understand other Americans no matter what regional or social class they come from, he is apt to underestimate the necessity for a generalized and abstract written American English. Because he finds no pressing reason for standardizing his speech, he is likely to misunderstand the necessity for standardizing his writing. He would like to write as he speaks. Moreover, the differences between the various regional and social varieties of American speech, being slight, are often of so subtle a nature that he tends to find difficulty in discriminating them. Slight as they are, when transferred to writing they are sufficient to make a reader pause, to induce a momentary feeling of unfamiliarity, to interrupt his consideration of the *matter* of expression by unwittingly calling attention to the *manner* of expression. Outside frankly literary writing (particularly the writing of poetry), such pauses, such unfamiliarities, such interruptions will hinder rather than help the writer's communicative purpose. If writing must be generalized, it must be generalized with a good reason: to speak with a local accent is not disadvantageous; to write serious prose with a local accent definitely is.

The moral of all this is clear. To gain command of serious written English is to acquire, quite deliberately, an abstract and generalized variety of the language differing by nature and purpose from any social or regional variety whatsoever. It is to sacrifice the local for the general, the spontaneous for the permanent. It is to bring to the study of written American English something of the perspective we normally reserve for the study of foreign languages. It is to master a set of grammatical and vocabulary patterns not because they are "correct" but because experience has proved them efficient in the communicative activity of writing.

The word "correct" is deliberately introduced here. The clear distinctions between spoken and written language mentioned in the paragraphs above have been all too often masked by the pernicious doctrine of "correctness." Perhaps that is to be expected. Without the flexible medium of language, a human society in human terms would be impossible. Without language, there could be no continuous record of experience, no diversification of labor, no great social institutions—the humanity of man could never have been achieved. But social activities breed social rituals and social judgments. Because language is *the* basic social instrument, it has inevitably acquired social attitudes so complex and variegated that they have often been allowed to obscure its primary communicative function. For far too many of us, knowledge of language is confused with knowledge of judgments on language that are socially acceptable. Education in the English language has become, for the most part, education in linguistic niceties—a poor substitute for that real linguistic education which ought to show us the major and minor patterns of our language, the way in which they interlock in function, the ways in which they can be manipulated for effective expression. As a result, the instrument of communication which should be every man's servant has become most men's master. This need not be so. Our self-confidence is immediately bolstered, our attitudes towards the study of writing techniques tremendously improved, once we realize that the difficulties of writing English do not spring from faulty nurture, restricted intelligence, or beyond-the-tracks environment but from the necessary change-over from one kind of English to another—that they are neither unpardonable nor irremediable.

Such is the milieu of the written English with which this little book is concerned. No matter what irrationalities surround the details and the perspectives by which English is normally viewed, the fact that it has so admirably served and is still serving the needs of many fine writers guarantees that it is neither an impossible nor an unworthy instrument of human expression. Let us admit that all languages, spoken or written, are man-made things, that their weaknesses as well as their strengths are implicit in their human origin. Let us admit that the world has never known either a faultless language nor one constructed on what to us seems a strictly logical system. The proper approach to written English is first to understand what the medium is; then to concede its limitations and to use its strengths to the best possible effect. Every communicative medium has a set of resistances that the communicator must overcome. Marble is hard; paint relatively unmanageable; music barely descriptive. No small part of any kind of composition is contributed directly by tensions set up between the craftsman's demands on his medium on the one hand and its inherent resistances on the other. To this, the science, craft, and art of expression in written American English is no exception.

STUDY QUESTIONS

1. This brief introductory chapter from Harold Whitehall's *Structural Essentials of English* offers a good insight into some of the reasons for the difficulties we all experience in learning to write well. Can you point out some examples of "grammatical and vocabulary patterns" which seem to you to occur in writing but not in speech?

2. How does the dialect situation in England differ from that in the United States? What bearing does this have on the kind of standard English people learn in schools in the two countries?

3. What is the difference between "just talk" and responsible writing? Why can they not be the same?

4. In the next to the last paragraph of this selection, Whitehall opposes the doctrine of "correctness." Why, in his view, is this doctrine "pernicious"? Does Whitehall argue here that one need not learn what are usually referred to as "correct" patterns of writing and speech? If not, precisely what is his point?

5. Whitehall develops this selection largely by using comparisons and contrasts. Point out the various comparisons which he uses.

6. Note carefully the description of differences between speech and writing outlined in the second paragraph of this selection. Then study some simple piece of writing—this selection for example—and describe the means by which the writer has tried to be conscious of "a reader over his shoulder."

On the Differences Between Writing and Speaking

William Hazlitt

> Some minds are proportioned to that which may be dispatched at once, or within a short return of time; others to that which begins afar off and is to be won with length of pursuit. —BACON

It is a common observation that few persons can be found who speak and write equally well. Not only is it obvious that the two faculties do not always go together in the same proportions, but they are not unusually in direct opposition to each other. We find that the greatest authors often make the worst company in the world, and again some of the liveliest fellows imaginable in conversation or extempore speaking seem to lose all this vivacity and spirit the moment they set pen to paper. For this a greater degree of quickness or slowness of parts, education, habit, temper, turn of mind and a variety of collateral and predisposing causes are necessary to account. The subject is at least curious and worthy of an attempt to explain it. I shall endeavor to illustrate the difference by familiar examples rather than by analytical reasonings. The philosopher of old was not unwise who defined motion by getting up and walking.

The great leading distinction between writing and speaking is, that more time is allowed for the one than the other, and hence different faculties are required for, and different objects attained by each. He is properly the best speaker who can collect together the greatest number of apposite ideas at a moment's warning; he is properly the best writer who can give utterance to the greatest quantity of valuable knowledge in the course of his whole life. The chief requisite for the one, then, appears to be quickness and facility of perception—for the other, patience of soul and a power increasing with the difficulties it has to master. He cannot be denied to be an expert speaker, a lively companion, who is never at a loss for something to say on every occasion or subject that offers. He, by the same rule, will make a respectable writer who, by dint of study, can find out anything good to say upon any one point that has not been touched upon before, or who by asking for time, can give the most complete and comprehensive view of any question. The one must be done off-hand, at a single blow; the other can only be done by a repetition of blows, by having time to think and do better.

In speaking, less is required of you, if you only do it at once with grace and spirit; in writing, you stipulate for all that you are capable of, but you have the choice of your own time and subject.

We see persons of that standard or texture of mind that they can do nothing but on the spur of the occasion; if they have time to deliberate they are lost. There are others who have no resource, who cannot advance a step by any efforts or assistance beyond a successful arrangement of commonplaces; but these they have always at command, at everybody's service. Set the same person to write a common paragraph and he cannot get through it for very weariness; ask him a question, ever so little out of the common road and he stares you in the face. What does all this bustle, animation, plausibility and command of words amount to? A lively flow of animal spirits, a good deal of confidence, a communicative turn, and a tolerably tenacious memory with respect to floating opinions and current phrases. Beyond the routine of the daily newspapers and coffee-house criticism, such persons do not venture to think at all; or if they did it would be so much the worse for them, for they would only be perplexed in the attempt and would perform their part in the mechanism of society with so much the less alacrity and easy volubility.

The most dashing orator I ever heard is the flattest writer I ever read. In speaking, he was like a volcano vomiting out *lava;* in writing, he is like a volcano burnt out. Nothing but the dry cinders, the hard shell remains. The tongues of flame with which in haranguing a mixed assembly he used to illuminate his subject and almost scorched up the panting air, do not appear painted on the margin of his works. He was the model of a flashy, powerful demagogue—a madman blest with a fit audience.

It is not merely that the same individual cannot sit down quietly in his closet and produce the same or a correspondent effect but sit down yourself and read one of these very popular and electrical effusions (for they have been published), and you would not believe it to be the same! The thunder-and-lightning mixture of the orator turns out a mere drab-colored suit in the person of the prose writer. We wonder at the change and think there must be some mistake, some legerdemain trick played off upon us, by which what before appeared so fine now appears to be so worthless. The deception took place *before;* now it is removed. The orator's vehemence of gesture, the loudness of the voice, the speaking eye, the conscious attitude, the inexplicable dumb show and noise,—all "those brave sublunary things that made his raptures clear,"—are no longer there and without these he is nothing—his "fire and ire" turn to puddle and ditch-water, and the god of eloquence and of our idolatry sinks into a common mortal, or an image of lead, with a few labels, nicknames, and party watchwords stuck in his mouth. The truth is that these always made up the stock of his intellectual wealth, but a certain exaggeration and extravagance of *manner* covered the nakedness and swelled out the emptiness of the *matter.*

An orator can hardly get beyond *commonplaces;* if he does he gets beyond his hearers. The most successful speakers, even in the House of Commons, have not been the best scholars or the finest writers. Those speeches that in general told the best at the time are not now readable. What were the materials of which they were chiefly composed? An imposing detail of passing events, a formal display of official documents, an appeal to established maxims, an echo of popular clamor, some worn-out metaphor newly vamped up,—some hackneyed argument used for the hundredth, nay thousandth time, to fall in with the interests, the passions, or prejudices of listening and devoted admirers—some truth or falsehood repeated as the Shibboleth of party time out of mind, which gathers strength from sympathy as it spreads, because it is understood or assented to by the million, and finds in the increased action of the minds of numbers the weight and force of an instinct. A *commonplace* does not leave the mind "sceptical, puzzled, and undecided in the moment of action"; "it gives a body to opinion and a permanence to fugitive belief." It operates mechanically and opens an instantaneous and infallible communication between the hearer and the speaker. A set of cant phrases, arranged in sounding sentences, and pronounced "with good emphasis and discretion," keep the gross and irritable humors of an audience in constant fermentation, and levy no tax on the understanding. To give a reason for anything is to breed a doubt of it, which doubt you may not remove in the sequel, either because your reason may not be a good one or because the person to whom it is addressed may not be able to comprehend it or because *others* may not be able to comprehend it. He who offers to go into the grounds of an acknowledged axiom risks the unanimity of the company "by most admired disorder," as he who digs to the foundation of a building to show its solidity, risks its falling. But a commonplace is enshrined in its own unquestioned evidence, and constitutes its own immortal basis.

The writer must be original or he is nothing. He is not to take up with ready-made goods, for he has time allowed him to create his own materials, and to make novel combinations of thought and fancy, to contend with unforeseen difficulties of style and execution, while we look on and admire the growing work in secret and at leisure. There is a degree of finishing as well as of solid strength in writing which is not to be got at every day, and we can wait for perfection. The author owes a debt to truth and nature which he cannot satisfy at sight, but he has pawned his head on redeeming it. It is not a string of clap-traps to answer a temporary or party purpose—violent, vulgar, and illiberal—but general and lasting truth that we require at his hands. We go to him as pupils, not as partisans. We have a right to expect from him profounder views of things, finer observations, more ingenious illustrations, happier and bolder expressions. He is to give the choice and picked results of a whole life of study, what he has struck out in his most felicitous moods, has treasured up with most pride, has labored to bring to light with most anxiety and confidence of success. He can wait. He is not satisfied with a reason he has offered for something; let him wait till he finds a better reason. There is some word, some phrase, some idiom that expresses a particular idea better than any other, but he cannot for the life of him recollect it; let him wait till he does. Is it strange that among twenty thousand words in the English language the one of all others that he most needs should have escaped him? There are more things in nature than there are words in the English language, and he must not expect to lay rash hands on them all at once. You will allow a writer a year to think of a subject; he should not put you off with a truism at last. You allow him a year more to find out words for his thoughts; he should not give us an echo of all the fine things that have been said a hundred times. A person in habits of composition often hesitates in conversation for a particular word; it is because he is in search of the best word and *that* he cannot hit upon. In writing he would stop till it came. It is not true, however, that the scholar could avail himself of a more ordinary word if he chose, or readily acquire a command of ordinary language; for his associations are habitually intense, not vague and shallow, and words occur to him only as *tallies* to certain modifications of feeling. They are links in the chain of thought. His imagination is fastidious, and rejects all those that are "of no mark or likelihood."

To conclude this account with what perhaps I ought to have set out with

—a definition of the character of an author. There are persons who in society, in public intercourse, feel no excitement,

> Dull as the lake that slumbers in the storm,

but who, when left alone, can lash themselves into a foam. They are never less alone than when alone. Mount them on a dinner table, and they have nothing to say; shut them up in a room to themselves, and they are inspired. They are "made fierce with dark keeping." In revenge for being tongue-tied, a torrent of words flows from their pens, and the storm which was so long collecting comes down apace. It never rains but it pours. Is not this strange, unaccountable? Not at all so. They have a real interest, a real knowledge of the subject, and they cannot summon up all that interest, or bring all that knowledge to bear while they have anything else to attend to. Till they can do justice to the feeling they have, they can do nothing. For this they look into their own minds, not in the faces of a gaping multitude. What they would say (if they could) does not lie at the orifices of the mouth ready for delivery, but is wrapped in the folds of the heart and registered in the chambers of the brain. In the sacred cause of truth that stirs them they would put their whole strength, their whole being into requisition; and as it implies a greater effort to drag their words and ideas from their lurking places, so there is no end when they are once set in motion. The whole of a man's thoughts and feelings cannot lie on the surface, made up for use; but the whole must be a greater quantity, a mightier power, if they could be got at, layer upon layer, and brought into play by the levers of imagination and reflection. Such a person then sees farther and feels deeper than most others. He plucks up an argument by the roots, he tears out the very heart of his subject. He has more pride in conquering the difficulties of a question, than vanity in courting the favor of an audience. He wishes to satisfy himself before he pretends to enlighten the public.

STUDY QUESTIONS

1. Hazlitt says that the major difference between writing and speaking is the time available. But what other differences does this imply?
2. What part, according to Hazlitt, does personality play in determining excellence in speaking or writing?
3. For clarity or emphasis Hazlitt occasionally makes use of a metaphor or other figure of speech. Locate some of these and comment on their effectiveness.
4. On the basis of Hazlitt's account of the methods and responsibilities of the writer, formulate a short statement giving advice to writers.
5. Do you think Hazlitt's opinion that speaking does not require originality, logic or objectivity minimizes its value or importance? If

so, write an essay defending the public speech as an important and useful medium of communication.

6. Note that Hazlitt's discussion complements that of Whitehall in "Writing and Speech." Write a theme on this subject combining their views in order to arrive at a more complete account of the differences between writing and speaking.

A Speech Is Written*

Robert E. Sherwood

As I have said, Hopkins did not originate policy and then convince Roosevelt it was right. He had too much intelligence as well as respect for his Chief to attempt the role of mastermind. He made it his job to provide a sounding board for discussions of the best means of attaining the goals that the President set for himself. Roosevelt liked to think out loud, but his greatest difficulty was finding a listener who was both understanding and entirely trustworthy. That was Hopkins—and this was the process that Rosenman and I watched over and over again in the preparation of the speeches and messages in which Roosevelt made known his policies to the nation and to the world. The work that was put in on these speeches was prodigious, for Roosevelt with his acute sense of history knew that all of those words would constitute the bulk of the estate that he would leave to posterity and that his ultimate measurement would depend on the reconciliation of what he said with what he did. Therefore, utmost importance was attached to his public utterances and utmost care exercised in their preparation. In the previous chapter I have mentioned the Cleveland speech which took a night and a day to prepare, but such speed in preparation was unusual, even for a campaign speech, which was necessarily a creature of the moment. The important speeches sometimes required a week or more of hard labor, with a considerable amount of planning before the intensive work started. I don't know what was the record number of distinct drafts of a single speech but it must have been well over twelve, and in the final draft there might not be one sentence that had survived from the first draft. There were of course numerous routine speeches of a ceremonial nature which were not considered of major significance—but, in wartime, even in these Roosevelt was aware that he had a world audience and that everything he said might be material for the propaganda which flooded the air waves. If such a speech

* From *Roosevelt and Hopkins* by Robert E. Sherwood. Copyright, 1948, by Robert E. Sherwood. Reprinted by permission of Harper & Brothers, publishers.

were opening a Bond Drive, a first draft would be prepared by the Treasury Department; if it were launching a new campaign for funds for the Red Cross, the Community Chest, National Brotherhood Week, etc., the organization concerned would send in suggestions as to what it wanted the President to say. This submitted material was almost always so rhetorical, so studiously literary, that it did not sound at all like Roosevelt's normal style and it had to be subjected to the process of simplification or even oversimplification that he demanded. He was happiest when he could express himself in the homeliest, even tritest phrases, such as "common or garden," "clear as crystal," "rule of thumb," "neither here nor there," "armchair strategists," or "simple as ABC."

When he wanted to give a speech for some important purpose, whether it was connected with a special occasion or not, he would discuss it first at length with Hopkins, Rosenman and me, telling us what particular points he wanted to make, what sort of audience he wished primarily to reach and what the maximum word limit was to be (he generally put it far too low). He would dictate pages and pages, approaching his main topic, sometimes hitting it squarely on the nose with terrific impact, sometimes rambling so far away from it that he couldn't get back, in which case he would say, "Well—something along those lines—you boys can fix it up." I think he greatly enjoyed these sessions, when he felt free to say anything he pleased, uttering all kinds of personal insults, with the knowledge that none of it need appear in the final version. When he stopped dictating, because another appointment was due or it was time to go to bed, we would go to the Cabinet Room in the West Wing and start reading through all the assembled material. The President kept a special "Speech Folder" into which he put newspaper clippings that he had marked, indicating either his approval of some sentiment expressed or indignation that such falsehood should get into print (he could not always remember what the marking signified). There were also all sorts of letters from all sorts of people, known and unknown, containing suggestions as to what he should say, and there were random bits of his own dictation, thoughts that had suddenly occurred to him during the preceding days and weeks which might be useful sometime. All of this material was sifted, and added to the newly dictated material with the aid of scissors and paste and a few connecting clauses, until something resembling a coherent speech was put together and fair copies of it made. It was generally two or three times too long. When the President was free to see us again, we handed him this draft and he looked immediately at the last page to see its number, whereupon he announced that at least ninety-two per cent of it must be cut. He then started to read through it, pausing frequently to dictate "Insert A," "Insert G," etc. Each time he decided to dictate something he said, "Grace—take a law," a line he gladly borrowed from the Kaufman-Hart-Rodgers musical show, "I'd Rather Be Right," in which George M. Cohan played the part of Franklin D. Roosevelt.

The President himself had never seen this show but he enjoyed what he heard about it.

When he had finished dictating inserts, the speech was far longer than it had been and farther from any coherent form. We then returned to the Cabinet Room and started a second draft. This process went on day and night. Sometimes, while the work was in progress, events would intervene —for instance: on a Sunday evening in July, 1943, we were at Shangri-la finishing up a speech devoted primarily to home-front problems—price stabilization, rationing, manpower, etc.—when news came of the fall of Benito Mussolini, and the speech had to be started all over again; this however, was a pleasure for all.

Most of Roosevelt's work on speeches was done during the evening. We would gather for the standard cocktail ceremony in the Oval Study at 7:15. The President sat behind his desk, the tray before him. He mixed the ingredients with the deliberation of an alchemist but with what appeared to be a certain lack of precision since he carried on a steady conversation while doing it. His bourbon old-fashioneds were excellent, but I did not care for his Martinis, in which he used two kinds of vermouth (when he had them) and sometimes a dash of absinthe. Hopkins occasionally talked him into making Scotch whisky sours, although he didn't really like them. The usual canapés of cream cheese or fish paste on small circles of toast were served, also popcorn. Roosevelt was an extremely mild drinker—he did not have wine with meals except at large, formal dinners, and I don't recall ever having seen him drink brandy or other liqueurs or a highball; but he certainly loved the cocktail period and the stream of small talk that went with it.

After dinner he sat on the couch to the left of the fireplace, his feet up on the stool specially built for him, and started reading the latest speech draft. Grace Tully sat next to him, taking more dictation until Dorothy Brady or Toinette Bachelder came in to relieve her. Sometimes Roosevelt read the speech out loud, to see how it sounded, for every word was judged not by its appearance in print but by its effectiveness over the radio. About 10 o'clock, a tray with drinks was brought in. The President sometimes had a glass of beer but more often a horse's neck (ginger ale and lemon peel). He was by now yawning and losing interest in the speech and he usually went to bed before eleven. During these evening sessions, the telephone almost never rang. Now and then a dispatch might be brought in, which Roosevelt would read and pass on to Hopkins without a word or a change of expression, but otherwise one would have thought this house the most peaceful, remote retreat in a war-wracked world.

After leaving the Study, we would spend most of the night in the Cabinet Room producing another draft which would go to the President with his breakfast in the morning. Sometimes we would send a call for help to Archibald MacLeish, Librarian of Congress, who would come in late at night to help bring a diffuse speech into focus. More than once, before the

White House windows were blacked out after Pearl Harbor, Mrs. Roosevelt saw the lights burning in the Cabinet Room at 3:00 A.M. and telephoned down to tell us we were working too hard and should go to bed. Of course, the fact was that she herself was sitting up working at that hour.

We had to get up early in the morning to be ready for summons in case the President wanted to work on the speech before his first appointment. We generally had breakfast on trays in Hopkins' room and it was rarely a cheerful gathering. The draft that had been completed a few hours previously looked awful in the morning light and the judgment on it that we most often expressed was, "I only hope that the reputation of Franklin Delano Roosevelt does not depend on this terrible speech."

After the session in the President's bedroom, Rosenman and I went over to the Cabinet Room to await the summons. The signal bells announced the President's approach to his cffice and we stood by the French windows leading out to the colonnade and watched him go by in his armless, cushionless, uncomfortable wheelchair, pushed by his Negro valet, Chief Petty Officer Arthur Prettyman. Accompanying him was the detail of Secret Service men, some of them carrying the large, overflowing wire baskets of papers on which he had been working the night before and the dispatches that had come in that morning. When Fala came abreast of the wheelchair as it rolled along, Roosevelt would reach down and scratch his neck. This progress to the day's work by a crippled man was a sight to stir the most torpid imagination; for here was a clear glimpse of the Roosevelt that the people believed him to be—the chin up, the cigarette holder tilted at what was always described as "a jaunty angle" and the air of irrepressible confidence that whatever problems the day might bring, he would find a way to handle them. The fact that this confidence was not always justified made it none the less authentic and reassuring.

When I saw the President go by on these mornings, I felt that nobody who worked for him had a right to feel tired. That was not an unusual feeling: it went all through the wartime Administration in Washington, extending to all sorts of people, some of whom disagreed with him politically and most of whom never laid eyes on him. It was, I think, Henry Pringle who, when working in a government agency shortly after Pearl Harbor, suggested as a wall slogan for bureaucrats' offices: EXHAUSTION IS NOT ENOUGH!

The speeches had to be checked and counterchecked with various departments and agencies, most of all with the Army and Navy; many speeches that were sent over to the War Department came back with corrections and suggestions penciled in the handwriting of General Marshall. The work of the so-called "ghost writers" consisted largely of the painstaking, arduous verification of facts and figures. We felt, *"The New York Times* can make mistakes, the *World Almanac* can make mistakes—but the President of the United States must not make mistakes." This constant thought imposed a harrowing responsibility. After 1940, the White House had its resident statistician—Isador Lubin, the Commissioner of Labor Statistics, who was constantly available and incalculably valuable to Roosevelt and to Hopkins in checking every decimal point.

Although the speeches were usually seen in advance by the War and Navy Departments and sometimes (though not always) by the State Department, they were kept otherwise under close wraps of secrecy. There were always various eminent officials who wanted to know what the President was going to say. They were particularly anxious to make sure that he was going to include the several pages of material that they had submitted on their own particular departments. They knew they could get nowhere with Hopkins in their quest of inside information; so they concentrated on Rosenman, who would fob them off with the misstatement that, "The President is weighing that in his mind right now." We used to derive enjoyment from the thought of various important personages around Washington listening to the Presidential broadcasts and then, as the strains of "The Star Spangled Banner" broke out at the finish, cursing, "He didn't use a *word* of that stuff that I sent him." It was even more enjoyable to picture the amazed expression of some anonymous citizen in Council Bluffs who had written a letter to the President and then heard something from that letter incorporated in a Fireside Chat.

On the final two days of preparation of a speech Roosevelt would really buckle down to serious work and then what had seemed a formless, aimless mess of words would begin to assume tautness and sharpness. He studied every implication for its effect on various groups in the nation and on allies and enemies and neutrals. He paid a great deal of attention to the punctuation, not for its correctness but for its aid or hindrance to him in reading the speech aloud. Grace Tully liked to insert a great many commas, and the President loved to strike them out. He once said to her, "Grace! How many times do I have to tell you not to waste the taxpayers' commas?" He liked dashes, which were visual aids, and hated semicolons and parentheses. I don't think he ever used the sonorous phrase, "And I quote—" If he had to have quotation marks, he did not refer to them, knowing they would appear in the printed version.

In the final draft of a speech, every word was counted and Roosevelt finally decided the precise number that he would be able to crowd into thirty minutes. His sense of timing was phenomenal. His normal rate was 100 words a minute, but he would say, "There are some paragraphs in this speech that I can take quickly so I can handle a total of 3,150 words"— and that did not mean 3,162. At other times, he would feel that he had to be deliberate in his delivery and the words would have to be cut to 2,800. This cutting was the most difficult work of all because, by the time we had come to the ninth or tenth draft, we felt sure the speech had been boiled down to the ultimate monosyllable. Roosevelt's estimates were rarely off more than a split second on his broadcasts. Speeches before audiences were difficult to estimate, of course, because crowd responses are unpredictable, but he was generally accurate even on these. In the Teamsters' speech, the roars of laughter and applause were so frequent and prolonged that the speech ran some fifteen minutes overtime, but that did not upset Roosevelt at all despite the fact that, since it was a campaign speech, the Democratic National Committee had to pay the heavy excess charges.

When a speech was finally closed up, about six o'clock in the evening, the President was wheeled over to Dr. McIntire's office for the sinus treatments that were a regular part of his day. Then he went upstairs for cocktails and dinner, after which he chatted or worked on his correspondence or his stamp albums, without seeming to give much attention to the final reading copy of his speech which was typed on special limp paper, to avoid rustling noises as he turned the pages, and bound in a black leather looseleaf folder. But when he started to broadcast he seemed to know it by heart. When he looked down at his manuscript, he was usually not looking at the words he was then speaking but at the next paragraph to determine where he would put his pauses and which of his large assortment of inflections he would employ. As one who has had considerable experience in the theater, I marveled at the unfailing precision with which he made his points, his grace in reconciling the sublime with the ridiculous, as though he had been rehearsing these lines for weeks and delivering them before audiences for months. Those who worked with him on speeches were all too well aware that he was no slave to his prepared text. He could and did ad-lib at will, and that was something which always amused him greatly. During the days of preparation, Hopkins, Rosenman and I would sometimes unite in opposition to some line, usually of a jocose nature, which the President wanted to include. It was our duty to make every effort to avoid being yes men and so we kept at him until we had persuaded him that the line should be cut out but, if he really liked it well enough, he would keep it in mind and then ad-lib it, and later would be full of apologies to us for his "unfortunate slip of the tongue." He was almost always immensely good humored about the arguments we offered him—he liked to appear persecuted and complain that "They won't let me say anything of my own in my own speech." There were times, however, when he was worn out and angered by something else and then he would be cantankerous with us because we were the only convenient targets; we learned that on such occasions it was best to shut up and to revive our arguments later after he had had some rest and felt more amiable. Referring again to my experiences in the theater, I can testify that he was normally the most untemperamental genius I have ever encountered. That is one of the reasons why he was able to sleep so well at night.

STUDY QUESTIONS

1. Break down the process described here into its four most important steps. Does the complexity of this procedure mean that writing of this kind must be done by a staff or does it have any bearing on the problems of the individual writer?

2 Point out the passages that are devoted primarily to characterization rather than to the business of writing speeches. Are they merely digressive or do they have some connection with the main topic?

3. Can the time limit described by Sherwood be considered an advantage? Would these speeches have been better if there had been less time for their preparation? More time? If Roosevelt had done *all* the writing himself?

4. Did President Roosevelt's delegation of much of the writing task to subordinates mean that the final product was not *his?* In what way did his position as a writer differ from that of the average writer? In what other situations might a procedure like Roosevelt's be followed?

5. Sherwood observes elsewhere in the book from which this selection was taken that Roosevelt gave a good deal of attention to his speeches in a time of war, when he might have been expected to be concerned with such decisive events as battles and alliances. What conclusions about the role of language in history are suggested by the observation? What has the importance of language, communication and ideas been in history or in some historical situation you are familiar with?

6. Describe the steps in some fairly elaborate operation you have taken part in, such as a camping trip, the arranging of a social function, writing a long term report, running an experiment, or building or making something that took several days or weeks.

The Gettysburg Address*

Gilbert Highet

FOURSCORE and seven years ago ...

These five words stand at the entrance to the best-known monument of American prose, one of the finest utterances in the entire language, and surely one of the greatest speeches in all history. Greatness is like granite: it is molded in fire, and it lasts for many centuries.

Fourscore and seven years ago ... It is strange to think that President Lincoln was looking back to the 4th of July 1776, and that he and his speech are now further removed from us than he himself was from George

* From *A Clerk of Oxenford* by Gilbert Highet. Copyright 1954 by Gilbert Highet. Reprinted by permission of Oxford University Press.

Washington and the Declaration of Independence. Fourscore and seven years before the Gettysburg Address, a small group of patriots signed the Declaration. Fourscore and seven years after the Gettysburg Address, it was the year 1950 (in November 1950 the Chinese had just entered the war in Korea), and that date is already receding rapidly into our troubled, adventurous, and valiant past.

Inadequately prepared and at first scarcely realized in its full importance, the dedication of the graveyard at Gettysburg was one of the supreme moments of American history. The battle itself had been a turning point of the war. On the 4th of July 1863, General Meade repelled Lee's invasion of Pennsylvania. Although he did not follow up his victory, he had broken one of the most formidable aggressive enterprises of the Confederate armies. Losses were heavy on both sides. Thousands of dead were left on the field, and thousands of wounded died in the hot days following the battle. At first, their burial was more or less haphazard; but thoughtful men gradually came to feel that an adequate burying place and memorial were required. These were established by an interstate commission that autumn, and the finest speaker in the North was invited to dedicate them. This was the scholar and statesman Edward Everett of Harvard. He made a good speech—which is still extant: not at all academic, it is full of close strategic analysis and deep historical understanding.

Lincoln was not invited to speak, at first. Although people knew him as an effective debater, they were not sure whether he was capable of making a serious speech on such a solemn occasion. But one of the impressive things about Lincoln's career is that he constantly strove to *grow*. He was anxious to appear on that occasion and to say something worthy of it. (Also, it has been suggested, he was anxious to remove the impression that he did not know how to behave properly—an impression which had been strengthened by a shocking story about his clowning on the battlefield of Antietam the previous year.) Therefore when he was invited he took considerable care with his speech. He drafted rather more than half of it in the White House before leaving, finished it in the hotel at Gettysburg the night before the ceremony (not in the train, as sometimes reported), and wrote out a fair copy next morning.

There are many accounts of the day itself, 19 November 1863. There are many descriptions of Lincoln, all showing the same curious blend of grandeur and awkwardness, or lack of dignity, or—it would be best to call it humility. In the procession he rode horseback: a tall lean man in a high plug hat, straddling a short horse, with his feet too near the ground. He arrived before the chief speaker, and had to wait patiently for half an hour or more. His own speech came right at the end of a long and exhausting ceremony, lasted less than three minutes, and made little impression on the audience. In part this was because they were tired, in part because (as eyewitnesses said) he ended almost before they knew he had begun, and in part because he did not speak the Address, but read it, very slowly, in a thin high voice, with a marked Kentucky accent, pronouncing "to" as "toe" and dropping his final R's.

Some people of course were alert enough to be impressed. Everett congratulated him at once. But most of the newspapers paid little attention to the speech, and some sneered at it. The *Patriot and Union* of Harrisburg wrote, "We pass over the silly remarks of the President; for the credit of the nation we are willing . . . that they shall no more be repeated or thought of"; and the London *Times* said, "The ceremony was rendered ludicrous by some of the sallies of that poor President Lincoln," calling his remarks "dull and commonplace." The first commendation of the Address came in a single sentence of the Chicago *Tribune,* and the first discriminating and detailed praise of it appeared in the Springfield *Republican,* the Providence *Journal,* and the Philadelphia *Bulletin.* However, three weeks after the ceremony and then again the following spring, the editor of *Harper's Weekly* published a sincere and thorough eulogy of the Address, and soon it was attaining recognition as a masterpiece.

At the time, Lincoln could not care much about the reception of his words. He was exhausted and ill. In the train back to Washington, he lay down with a wet towel on his head. He had caught smallpox. At that moment he was incubating it, and he was stricken down soon after he re-entered the White House. Fortunately it was a mild attack, and it evoked one of his best jokes: he told his visitors, "At last I have something I can give to everybody."

He had more than that to give to everybody. He was a unique person, far greater than most people realize until they read his life with care. The wisdom of his policy, the sources of his statesmanship—these were things too complex to be discussed in a brief essay. But we can say something about the Gettysburg Address as a work of art.

A work of art. Yes: for Lincoln was a literary artist, trained both by others and by himself. The textbooks he used as a boy were full of difficult exercises and skillful devices in formal rhetoric, stressing the qualities he practiced in his own speaking: antithesis, parallelism, and verbal harmony. Then he read and reread many admirable models of thought and expression: the King James Bible, the essays of Bacon, the best plays of Shakespeare. His favorites were *Hamlet, Lear, Macbeth, Richard III,* and *Henry VIII,* which he had read dozens of times. He loved reading aloud, too, and spent hours reading poetry to his friends. (He told his partner Herndon that he preferred getting the sense of any document by reading it aloud.) Therefore his serious speeches are important parts of the long and noble classical tradition of oratory which begins in Greece, runs through Rome to the modern world, and is still capable (if we do not neglect it) of producing masterpieces.

The first proof of this is that the Gettysburg Address is full of quotations—or rather of adaptations—which give it strength. It is partly religious, partly (in the highest sense) political: therefore it is interwoven with memories of the Bible and memories of American history. The first and the last words are biblical cadences. Normally Lincoln did not say "fourscore" when he meant eighty; but on this solemn occasion he recalled the important dates in the Bible—such as the age of Abraham when his first son was born to him, and he was "fourscore and six years old" (Gen. 16:16; cf. Exod. 7:7). Similarly he did not say there was a chance that democracy might die out: he recalled the somber phrasing of the Book of Job—where Bildad speaks of the destruction of one who shall vanish without a trace, and says that "his branch shall be cut off; his remembrance shall perish from the earth" (Job 18:16-17; cf. Jer. 10:11, Micah 7:2). Then again, the famous description of our State as "government of the people, by the people, for the people" was adumbrated by Daniel Webster in 1830 (he spoke of "the people's government, made for the people, made by the people, and answerable to the people") and then elaborated in 1854 by the abolitionist Theodore Parker (as "government of all the people, by all the people, for all the people"). There is good reason to think that Lincoln took the important phrase "under God" (which he interpolated at the last moment) from Weems, the biographer of Washington; and we know that it had been used at least once by Washington himself.

Analyzing the Address further, we find that it is based on a highly imaginative theme, or group of themes. The subject is—how can we put it so as not to disfigure it?—the subject is the kinship of life and death, that mysterious linkage which we see sometimes as the physical succession of birth and death in our world, sometimes as the contrast, which is perhaps a unity, between death and immortality. The first sentence is concerned with birth:

Our *fathers brought forth a new* nation, *conceived* in l:berty.

The final phrase but one expresses the hope that

this nation, under God, shall have a *new birth* of freedom.

And the last phrase of all speaks of continuing life as the triumph over death. Again and again throughout the speech, this mystical contrast and kinship reappear: "those who *gave their lives* that that nation might *live,*" "the brave men *living* and *dead,*" and so in the central assertion that the dead have already consecrated their own burial place, while "it is for us, the *living,* rather to be dedicated . . . to the great task remaining." The Gettysburg Address is a prose poem; it belongs to the same world as the great elegies, and the adagios of Beethoven.

Its structure, however, is that of a skillfully contrived speech. The oratorical pattern is perfectly clear. Lincoln describes the occasion, dedicates the ground, and then draws a larger conclusion by calling on his hearers to dedicate themselves to the preservation of the Union. But within that, we can trace his constant use of at least two important rhetorical devices.

The first of these is *antithesis*: opposition, contrast. The speech is full of it. Listen:

The world will little *note*
            nor long *remember*   what *we say here*
    but   it can never *forget*   what *they did here.*

And so in nearly every sentence: "brave men, *living* and *dead*"; "to *add* or *detract.*" There is antithesis of the Founding Fathers and the men of Lincoln's own time:

Our *fathers brought forth* a new nation . . .
now *we* are testing whether that nation . . . can *long endure.*

And there is the more terrible antithesis of those who have already died and those who still live to do their duty. Now, antithesis is the figure of contrast and conflict. Lincoln was speaking in the midst of a great civil war.

The other important pattern is different. It is technically called *tricolon* —the division of an idea into three harmonious parts, usually of increasing power. The most famous phrase of the Address is a tricolon:

                government of the people
                        by the people
            and   for the people.

The most solemn sentence is a tricolon:

        we cannot dedicate
        we cannot consecrate
        we cannot hallow   this ground.

And above all, the last sentence (which has sometimes been criticized as too complex) is essentially two parallel phrases, with a tricolon growing out of the second and then producing another tricolon: a trunk, three branches, and a cluster of flowers. Lincoln says that it is for his hearers to be dedicated to the great task remaining before them. Then he goes on.

                that from these honored dead

—apparently he means "in such a way that from these honored dead"—

                we take increased devotion to that cause.

Next, he restates this more briefly:

                that we here highly resolve . . .

And now the actual resolution follows, in three parts of growing intensity:

that these dead shall not have died in vain
that this nation, under God, shall have a new birth of freedom

and that

    (one more tricolon)

government of the people
by the people
and   for the people
shall not perish from the earth.

Now, the tricolon is the figure which, through division, emphasizes basic harmony and unity. Lincoln used antithesis because he was speaking to a people at war. He used the tricolon because he was hoping, planning, praying for peace.

No one thinks that when he was drafting the Gettysburg Address, Lincoln deliberately looked up these quotations and consciously chose these particular patterns of thought. No, he chose the theme. From its development and from the emotional tone of the entire occasion, all the rest followed, or grew—by that marvelous process of choice and rejection which is essential to artistic creation. It does not spoil such a work of art to analyze it as closely as we have done; it is altogether fitting and proper that we should do this: for it helps us to penetrate more deeply into the rich meaning of the Gettysburg Address, and it allows us the very rare privilege of watching the workings of a great man's mind.

STUDY QUESTIONS

1. Why does the author tell some of the circumstances of the speech? What relation do they have to his purpose?
2. What is his purpose? What is he trying to show by this discussion and analysis?
3. In what ways does Highet find that the Address and its composition reflect Lincoln's character?
4. Does he satisfactorily show that Lincoln's literary training was a factor in the composition of the speech?
5. What other themes, not mentioned by Highet, can be found in the Gettysburg Address?
6. Using Highet's essay as a model, take another famous speech and analyze it to show its appropriateness, its relation to the character of the speaker, its underlying unity, or its exploitation of special rhetorical devices.

You Can't Write Writing*

Wendell Johnson

This discussion is not designed to take the place of a textbook for the teaching of effective communicative writings, but it is offered in the hope that a brief statement of a few simple principles upon which such writing is based might serve at least to raise the question as to why these principles are not more adequately taught by English instructors.

The first of these principles has already been given in the statement that clearness depends upon, and can be measured in terms of, the degree of agreement between the writer and his readers as to what the words of the writer represent. Simply by striving for a high degree of such agreement, the writer discovers, in some measure, his ingenuity in achieving it. He discovers the usefulness of conditional and quantifying terms, the confusion created by leaving out significantly differentiating details, the degree to which the meaning of a term varies from context to context, and the kinds of differences he must allow for among his readers' habits of interpreting words. He learns to rely less on the dictionary and more on the linguistic habits of the people for whom he writes. He discovers that literary posing, pleasurable as it may be, usually can be enjoyed only at the expense of effective communication—that Chesterton's paradoxes or Paul de Kruif's chronic astonishment are more titillating than informative. He discovers that there are various levels of abstraction, and that if he goes systematically from lower to higher levels he can use so-called abstract words and still be reasonably clear.

Above all, perhaps, he discovers the basic significance of order, or relations, or structure, or organization. This matter of structural relationships has wide ramifications, and no writer ever exhausts it, but the student quickly grasps some of its more obvious aspects, if he is striving for agreement between himself and his reader. It does not take him long to understand that the organization of what he writes should correspond to the organization of what he is writing about if the reader is to follow him readily. The graduate students with whom I work frequently have difficulty organizing their descriptions of experimental techniques or procedures, and I have found that it is more helpful to refer them to a cookbook than to a textbook on composition. By examining a cookbook they see at once that the organization of a description of procedure is determined simply by the order of the events that make up the procedure. First you do *a*, and then *b*, and then *c*, and you write it in that order because you do it in that order. This simple principle of order is fundamental in practically all descriptive, narrative, and expository writing, and it is obvious to anyone who is attempting to be considerate of the reader.

One might suppose that graduate students would know this, but in spite of the years they have spent in English courses most of them seem not to have learned much about it. The more significant fact is that, as a rule, they learn quite readily to apply this simple principle, once it is clearly explained and demonstrated to them. In this case, certainly, one can make a tree that either God or the English teachers forgot to make.

One aspect of organization that seems to have eluded practically all graduate students is that involved in the making of transitions. Even those who have been taught how to lay beads in a row have not been taught how to string them. Just as the order of what one writes is determined by the order of the parts or events involved in what one is writing about, so the ways in which transitions are made in the writing are determined by the ways in which the parts or events are related in the realities one is describing, narrating, or explaining. The ability to move from one sentence or paragraph or chapter to the next, in such a way as to blend them into a unified whole, is largely dependent upon an understanding of the reasons for going from one to the next, of why one statement should follow another instead of the reverse, of why one should say, "It follows, then," rather than "But." And these reasons are found in the character of the relations existing among the details of that about which the writing is being done. This becomes obvious to one who is not trying to write writing, but who is attempting, rather, to write-about-something-for-someone.

Another principle underlying communicative writing is that clarity is a prerequisite to validity. It is to be considered that statements that flow beautifully and are grammatically superb may be, also, utterly devoid of factual meaning, or meaningful but vague, or precise but invalid. For writing to be effective, in the sense in which I am using this term, it may or may not be grammatically correct, but it must be both clear and valid. It can be clear without having validity, but if it is unclear its validity cannot well be determined. It must, then, first of all, be clear; it must be that before the question of its validity can even be raised. We ask the writer, "What do you mean?" before we ask, "How do you know?" Until we reach agreement as to precisely what he is writing about, we cannot possibly reach agreement as to whether, or in what degree, his statements are true.

Only to the extent that the various readers of a statement agree as to the specific conditions or observations required for ascertaining its validity can the question of its validity have meaning. And the extent to which the readers of the statement agree on these conditions is, of course, indicative of the extent to which the statement is clear. If a statement is such

that its readers do not agree at all as to how it might be verified or refuted, the statement may be "beautiful" or "rich in meaning" or grammatically irreproachable, but it is also, from the point of view of scientific
courses such as I am teaching, nonsense. It cannot be demonstrated to be
valid or invalid, and is meaningful, therefore, to its author, possibly to his
English teacher, and perhaps to his psychiatrist.

My graduate students have not learned this, either. They show this in a
particularly disturbing manner when they first attempt to state the topics
or problems they propose to investigate in undertaking their theses. They
quite characteristically propose problems which preclude the possibility
of clear discussion. They propose questions for investigation, for which
they desire to obtain precise answers, but which are so stated as to be unanswerable. Apparently they have never been taught that one cannot get
a precise answer to a vague question—that the terminology of the question limits the clarity and thus the validity of the answer. Many students
are so befuddled on this point that they do not recognize any relation at
all between clarity and validity. They actually assume, for example, that
they can ask, "What causes personality maladjustments?" without speci-
fying what they mean by "causes," or by "personality," or by "maladjustments," or what observations one is to make in order to comply with
their definition of "what." Many of them appear to have been taught that
to eliminate the vagueness of a question or statement is to destroy its
"richness of meaning"—that for a statement to be "full of meaning" it
must not mean anything in particular!

Even though they have been so taught, and come, therefore, to the
graduate college quite untrained in the writing of valid statements, they
can be taught, to a considerable degree, to gauge the validity of what they
write. They can be trained to do this by being trained, first, to write
clearly. For when a statement is made clearly—when there is reasonable
agreement among its readers as to what it represents in the realm of fact—
its validity can be judged, or a procedure for determining its degree of
validity can be devised.

In summary, then, what graduate students, as I know them, have not
been well taught—and what, in my judgment, their English instructors
should have been able to teach them, because the students do learn readily
—is the ability to write a clear, organized, unified, and valid document.
They have been made familiar with grammar, for the most part, and they
have picked up a few tricks of literary flavoring. The grammar can be
used to advantage; most of the literary condiments have to be chucked. . . .

My own narrow concern with all this lies in the fact that the ineffective-
ness of the English instruction in our schools makes for a serious difficulty
in the graduate college in all its branches. But the problem has an importance far more vast than this fact could ever give to it. For the ability of
the individual, and of groups of individuals, to use language clearly and
with validity is basic to personal efficiency and general development—it

is basic to sanity itself—and it is fundamental to intelligent social organization and to the adequate management of national and international problems. The teachers of English in our schools and universities have been and are being entrusted with the heavy responsibility of training the members of our society in the effective communicative use of our language. It is not a responsibility that they can meet appropriately merely by teaching the formalism of grammar, or superciliously disclaim by asserting that effective writing is an art and cannot be taught.

Effective writing is a human necessity in anything resembling a democratic culture, and this becomes increasingly true as the culture becomes increasingly complex. If the effective use of language cannot be taught, or if it is not to be taught to a far greater extent than it has been, we may well have occasion to despair of the grand experiment dreamed by Voltaire, championed by Washington and Franklin, and cherished by the American people through many generations. And if we must despair of that, then truly, even if you do learn to speak correct English, it may well not seem to matter very much "who you talk it to." For when the people cannot adequately speak or write their language, there arise strong men to speak and write it for them—and "at" them.

The issues of which I write are by no means to be regarded as academic issues. We are a symbolic class of life. To say that we are human is to say, above all and with incalculable significance, that our problems, as individuals, as groups, and as a world culture, are symbolic problems. They are problems that center around the symbols of government, the symbols of finance and general economy, of social status, of power and prestige, of class and race. They are the problems involved in the great institutionalized symbol systems of the Church, the Law, the State. They are problems of meaning, of evaluation, of orientation, processes which, on human levels, are predominantly symbolic in character. It is not the vestige of some forebear's whim that the whole structure of our educational system is founded squarely on the three R's, for reading, writing, and the use of numbers are forms of behavior in the absence of which *human* society would disintegrate and vanish. The degree to which these forms of behavior are cultivated and made adequate determines, more than does anything else, the degree to which a symbolic class of life may escape the threat of self-destruction and achieve cultural maturity. Our maladjustment, no less than our genius, as individuals and as groups, lies in our way of responding to and with symbols.

The place of the teacher of English in the structure of a symbolic society is, thus and indeed, not one to be occupied by petulant little men engrossed in verbal "fancy work." It is not too much to say that our possibilities for progress are determined, and limited, by those who instruct us in the use of our language. This view is as disheartening, perhaps, as it is challenging, but the more challenging it is to some, the less disheartening it need be to others.

1. What are the three requirements Johnson makes of a good paper?
2. Johnson is speaking here of what might be called objective expository writing. To what extent are his demands and his criteria for good writing equally applicable to all kinds of writing?
3. Johnson thinks that a statement cannot communicate unless reader and author agree on the meaning of the terms in it. Is this necessarily true in every case? Consider, for example, some of the autobiographical and descriptive selections in Section I.
4. What, according to Johnson, is the relationship between clarity and validity?
5. Write a theme giving some examples and explaining more fully what Johnson means by his observation that the problems faced by men are "symbolic problems." Good examples for this would be problems of meaning, feeling or interpretation which have been important in history.
6. Do you think Johnson may be exaggerating when he says that our possibilities for progress depend upon teachers of language? Write a theme describing others who are, to some extent, responsible for progress, being sure that by "progress" you mean the same thing as Johnson.

On Style*

Arthur Schopenhauer

Style is the physiognomy of the mind, and a safer index to character than the face. To imitate another man's style is like wearing a mask, which, be it never so fine, is not long in arousing disgust and abhorrence, because it is lifeless; so that even the ugliest living face is better. Hence those who write in Latin and copy the manner of ancient authors, may be said to speak through a mask; the reader, it is true, hears what they say, but he cannot observe their physiognomy too; he cannot see their *style*. With the Latin works of writers who think for themselves, the case is different, and their style is visible; writers, I mean, who have not condescended to any sort of imitation, such as Scotus Erigena, Petrarch, Bacon, Descartes, Spinoza, and many others. And affectation in style is like making grimaces. Further, the language in which a man writes is the physiognomy of the nation to which he belongs; and here there are many hard and fast differences, beginning from the language of the Greeks, down to that of the Caribbean islanders.

*From *The Art of Literature,* selected and translated by T. Bailey Saunders, 1891.

To form a provisional estimate of the value of a writer's productions, it is not directly necessary to know the subject on which he has thought, or what it is that he has said about it; that would imply a perusal of all his works. It will be enough, in the main, to know *how* he has thought. This, which means the essential temper or general quality of his mind, may be precisely determined by his style. A man's style shows the *formal* nature of all his thoughts—the formal nature which can never change, be the subject or the character of his thoughts what it may: it is, as it were, the dough out of which all the contents of his mind are kneaded. When Eulenspiegel was asked how long it would take to walk to the next village, he gave the seemingly incongruous answer: *Walk.* He wanted to find out by the man's pace the distance he would cover in a given time. In the same way, when I have read a few pages of an author, I know fairly well how far he can bring me.

Every mediocre writer tries to mask his own natural style, because in his heart he knows the truth of what I am saying. He is thus forced, at the outset, to give up any attempt at being frank or naïve—a privilege which is thereby reserved for superior minds, conscious of their own worth, and therefore sure of themselves. What I mean is that these everyday writers are absolutely unable to resolve upon writing just as they think; because they have a notion that, were they to do so, their work might possibly look very childish and simple. For all that, it would not be without its value. If they would only go honestly to work, and say, quite simply, the things they have really thought, and just as they have thought them, these writers would be readable and, within their own proper sphere, even instructive.

But instead of that, they try to make the reader believe that their thoughts have gone much further and deeper than is really the case. They say what they have to say in long sentences that wind about in a forced and unnatural way; they coin new words and write prolix periods which go round and round the thought and wrap it up in a sort of disguise. They tremble between the two separate aims of communicating what they want to say and of concealing it. Their object is to dress it up so that it may look learned or deep, in order to give people the impression that there is very much more in it than for the moment meets the eye. They either jot down their thoughts bit by bit, in short, ambiguous, and paradoxical sentences, which apparently mean much more than they say,—of this kind of writing Schelling's treatises on natural philosophy are a splendid instance; or else they hold forth with a deluge of words and the most intolerable diffusiveness, as though no end of fuss were necessary to make the reader understand the deep meaning of their sentences, whereas it is some quite simple if not actually trivial idea,—examples of which may be found in plenty in the popular works of Fichte, and the philosophical manuals of a hundred other miserable dunces not worth mentioning; or, again, they try to write in some particular style which they have been pleased to take up and think very grand, a style, for example, *par excellence* profound and scientific, where the reader is tormented to death by the narcotic effect of long-spun periods without a single idea in them,—such as are furnished in a special measure by those most impudent of all mortals, the Hegelians; or it may be that it is an intellectual style they have striven after, where it seems as though their object were to go crazy altogether; and so on in many other cases. All these endeavours to put off the *nascetur ridiculus mus* [1]—to avoid showing the funny little creature that is born after such mighty throes—often make it difficult to know what it is that they really mean. And then, too, they write down words, nay, even whole sentences, without attaching any meaning to them themselves, but in the hope that some one else will get sense out of them.

And what is at the bottom of all this? Nothing but the untiring effort to sell words for thoughts; a mode of merchandise that is always trying to make fresh openings for itself, and by means of odd expressions, turns of phrase, and combinations of every sort, whether new or used in a new sense, to produce the appearance of intellect in order to make up for the very painfully felt lack of it.

.   .   .

As a matter of fact we find that every really great writer tries to express his thoughts as purely, clearly, definitely and shortly as possible. Simplicity has always been held to be a mark of truth; it is also a mark of genius. Style receives its beauty from the thought it expresses; but with sham-thinkers the thoughts are supposed to be fine because of the style. Style is nothing but the mere silhouette of thought; and an obscure or bad style means a dull or confused brain.

The first rule, then, for a good style is that *the author should have something to say;* nay, this is in itself almost all that is necessary. Ah, how much it means! The neglect of this rule is a fundamental trait in the philosophical writing, and, in fact, in all the reflective literature, of my country, more especially since Fichte. These writers all let it be seen that they want to appear as though they had something to say; whereas they have nothing to say. Writing of this kind was brought in by the pseudo-philosophers at the Universities, and now it is current everywhere, even among the first literary notabilities of the age. It is the mother of that strained and vague style, where there seem to be two or even more meanings in the sentence; also of that prolix and cumbrous manner of expression, called *le stile empesé;* again, of that mere waste of words which consists in pouring them out like a flood; finally, of that trick of concealing the direst poverty of thought under a farrago of never-ending chatter which clacks away like a windmill and quite stupefies one—stuff which a man may read for hours together without getting hold of a single clearly

---

[1] From Horace's line, *"Parturient montes, nascetur ridiculus mus"* (The lab'ring mountain scarce brings forth a mouse) .—Eds.

expressed and definite idea. However, people are easy-going, and they have formed the habit of reading page upon page of all sorts of such verbiage, without having any particular idea of what the author really means. They fancy it is all as it should be, and fail to discover that he is writing simply for writing's sake.

.   .   .

On the other hand, an intelligent author really speaks to us when he writes, and that is why he is able to rouse our interest and commune with us. It is the intelligent author alone who puts individual words together with a full consciousness of their meaning, and chooses them with deliberate design. Consequently, his discourse stands to that of the writer described above, much as a picture that has been really painted to one that has been produced by the use of a stencil. In the one case, every word, every touch of the brush, has a special purpose; in the other, all is done mechanically. The same distinction may be observed in music. For just as Lichtenberg says that Garrick's soul seemed to be in every muscle in his body, so it is the omnipresence of intellect that always and everywhere characterises the work of genius.

I have alluded to the tediousness which marks the works of these writers; and in this connection it is to be observed, generally, that tediousness is of two kinds: objective and subjective. A work is objectively tedious when it contains the defect in question; that is to say, when its author has no perfectly clear thought or knowledge to communicate. For if a man has any clear thought or knowledge in him, his aim will be to communicate it, and he will direct his energies to this end; so that the ideas he furnishes are everywhere clearly expressed. The result is that he is neither diffuse, nor unmeaning, nor confused, and consequently not tedious. In such a case, even though the author is at bottom in error, the error is at any rate clearly worked out and well thought over, so that it is at least formally correct; and thus some value always attaches to the work. But for the same reason a work that is objectively tedious is at all times devoid of any value whatever.

The other kind of tediousness is only relative: a reader may find a work dull because he has no interest in the question treated of in it, and this means that his intellect is restricted. The best work may, therefore, be tedious subjectively, tedious, I mean, to this or that particular person; just as, contrarily, the worst work may be subjectively engrossing to this or that particular person who has an interest in the question treated of, or in the writer of the book.

It would generally serve writers in good stead if they would see that, whilst a man should, if possible, think like a great genius, he should talk the same language as everyone else. Authors should use common words to say uncommon things. But they do just the opposite. We find them trying to wrap up trivial ideas in grand words, and to clothe their very ordinary thoughts in the most extraordinary phrases, the most far-fetched, unnatural, and out-of-the-way expressions. Their sentences perpetually stalk about on stilts. They take so much pleasure in bombast, and write in such a high-flown, bloated, affected, hyperbolical and acrobatic style that their prototype is Ancient Pistol, whom his friend Falstaff once impatiently told to say what he had to say *like a man of this world.*[2]

There is no expression in any other language exactly answering to the French *stile empesé;* but the thing itself exists all the more often. When associated with affectation, it is in literature what assumption of dignity, grand airs and primness are in society; and equally intolerable. Dulness of mind is fond of donning this dress; just as in ordinary life it is stupid people who like being demure and formal.

An author who writes in the prim style resembles a man who dresses himself up in order to avoid being confounded or put on the same level with the mob—a risk never run by the *gentleman,* even in his worst clothes. The plebian may be known by a certain showiness of attire and a wish to have everything spic and span; and, in the same way, the commonplace person is betrayed by his style.

Nevertheless, an author follows a false aim if he tries to write exactly as he speaks. There is no style of writing but should have a certain trace of kinship with the *epigraphic* or *monumental* style, which is, indeed, the ancestor of all styles. For an author to write as he speaks is just as reprehensible as the opposite fault, to speak as he writes; for this gives a pedantic effect to what he says, and at the same time makes him hardly intelligible.

An obscure and vague manner of expression is always and everywhere a very bad sign. In ninety-nine cases out of a hundred it comes from vagueness of thought; and this again almost always means that there is something radically wrong and incongruous about the thought itself—in a word, that it is incorrect. When a right thought springs up in the mind, it strives after expression and is not long in reaching it; for clear thought easily finds words to fit it. If a man is capable of thinking anything at all, he is also always able to express it in clear, intelligible, and unambiguous terms. Those writers who construct difficult, obscure, involved, and equivocal sentences, most certainly do not know aright what it is that they want to say: they have only a dull consciousness of it, which is still in the stage of struggle to shape itself as thought. Often, indeed, their desire is to conceal from themselves and others that they really have nothing at all to say. They wish to appear to know what they do not know, to think what they do not think, to say what they do not say. If a man has some real communication to make, which will he choose—an indistinct or a clear way of expressing himself?

2 *King Henry IV*, Part II. Act v. Sc. 3.

STUDY QUESTIONS

1. Schopenhauer's illustrations of bad style are drawn from his acquaintance with the writing of his nineteenth century German contemporaries; but the same abuses of style are committed in English by writers today. Find some illustrations in your reading of the bad styles described by Schopenhauer, such as the falsely profound, the long-winded and vague, the style specializing in short, ambiguous sentences, and the style that expresses a small idea in big words.

2. Does Schopenhauer's account of what the "mediocre writer" does to "improve" his writing explain some of the faults encountered in bad writing?

3. Wendell Johnson, in "You Can't Write Writing," puts the blame for the poor writing of his students on their English teachers. Does Schopenhauer's essay suggest that some other part of the faculty may also be responsible?

4. Does this essay express any emotion? If so, explain where and how it expresses it.

5. What does Schopenhauer mean by "subjective" and "objective" tediousness?

6. Do you think Schopenhauer's point that style of writing may be more revealing than subject matter applies to other activities? Write an essay showing how the manner of doing a thing may reveal personality in some activity such as talking, driving a car, behavior at a party, playing a game or doing a job.

Literature and the Schoolma'm*

H. L. Mencken

With precious few exceptions, all the books on style in English are by writers quite unable to write. The subject, indeed, seems to exercise a special and dreadful fascination over schoolma'ms, bucolic college professors, and other such pseudo-literates. One never hears of treatises on it by George Moore or James Branch Cabell, but the pedagogues, male and female, are at it all the time. In a thousand texts they set forth their depressing ideas about it, and millions of suffering high-school pupils have to study what they say. Their central aim, of course, is to reduce the whole thing to a series of simple rules—the over-mastering passion of their melancholy order, at all times and everywhere. They aspire to teach it as bridge whist, the American Legion flagdrill and double-entry book-

* Reprinted from *Prejudices: Fifth Series* by H. L. Mencken, by permission of Alfred A. Knopf, Inc. Copyright 1926 by Alfred A. Knopf, Inc.

keeping are taught. They fail as ignominiously as that Athenian of legend who essayed to train a regiment of grasshoppers in the goose-step.

For the essence of a sound style is that it cannot be reduced to rules—that it is a living and breathing thing, with something of the devilish in it—that it fits its proprietor tightly and yet ever so loosely, as his skin fits him. It is, in fact, quite as securely an integral part of him as that skin is. It hardens as his arteries harden. It has *Katzenjammer* on the days succeeding his indiscretions. It is gaudy when he is young and gathers decorum when he grows old. On the day after he makes a mash on a new girl it glows and glitters. If he has fed well, it is mellow. If he has gastritis it is bitter. In brief, a style is always the outward and visible symbol of a man, and it cannot be anything else. To attempt to teach it is as silly as to set up courses in making love. The man who makes love out of a book is not making love at all; he is simply imitating someone else making love. God help him if, in love or literary composition, his preceptor be a pedagogue!

The schoolma'm theory that the writing of English may be taught is based upon a faulty inference from a sound observation. The sound observation is that the great majority of American high-school pupils, when they attempt to put their thoughts upon paper, produce only a mass of confused and puerile nonsense—that they express themselves so clumsily that it is often quite impossible to understand them at all. The faulty inference is to the effect that what ails them is a defective technical equipment—that they can be trained to write clearly as a dog may be trained to walk on its hind legs. This is all wrong. What ails them is not a defective technical equipment but a defective natural equipment. They write badly simply because they cannot think clearly. They cannot think clearly because they lack the brains. Trying to teach them is as hopeless as trying to teach a dog with only one hind leg. Any human being who can speak English understandably has all the materials necessary to write English clearly, and even beautifully. There is nothing mysterious about the written language; it is precisely the same, in essence, as the spoken language. If a man can think in English at all, he can find words enough to express his ideas. The fact is proved abundantly by the excellent writing that often comes from so-called ignorant men. It is proved anew by the even better writing that is done on higher levels by persons of great simplicity, for example, Abraham Lincoln. Such writing commonly arouses little enthusiasm among pedagogues. Its transparency excites their professional disdain, and they are offended by its use of homely words and phrases. They prefer something more ornate and complex—something, as they would probably put it, demanding more thought. But the thought they yearn for is the kind, alas, that they secrete themselves—the muddled, high-falutin, vapid thought that one finds in their own text-books.

I do not denounce them because they write so badly; I merely record the fact in a sad, scientific spirit. Even in such twilight regions of the intellect the style remains the man. What is in the head infallibly oozes out of the nub of the pen. If it is sparkling Burgundy the writing is full of life and charm. If it is mush the writing is mush too. The late Dr. Harding, twenty-ninth President of the Federal Union, was a highly self-conscious stylist. He practiced prose composition assiduously, and was regarded by the pedagogues of Marion, Ohio, and vicinity as a very talented fellow. But when he sent a message to Congress it was so muddled in style that even the late Henry Cabot Lodge, a professional literary man, could not understand it. Why? Simply because Dr. Harding's thoughts, on the high and grave subjects he discussed, were so muddled that he couldn't understand them himself. But on matters within his range of customary meditation he was clear and even charming, as all of us are. I once heard him deliver a brief address upon the ideals of the Elks. It was a topic close to his heart, and he had thought about it at length and *con amore*. The result was an excellent speech—clear, logical, forceful, and with a touch of wild, romantic beauty. His sentences hung together. He employed simple words, and put them together with skill. But when, at a public meeting in Washington, he essayed to deliver an oration on the subject of the late Dante Alighieri, he quickly became so obscure and absurd that even the Diplomatic Corps began to snicker. The cause was plain: he knew no more about Dante than a Tennessee county judge knows about the Institutes of Justinian. Trying to formulate ideas upon the topic, he could get together only a few disjected fragments and ghosts of ideas—here an ear, there a section of tibia, beyond a puff of soul substance or other gas. The resultant speech was thus enigmatical, cacophonous and awful stuff. It sounded precisely like a lecture by a college professor on style.

A pedagogue, confronted by Dr. Harding in class, would have set him to the business of what is called improving his vocabulary—that is, to the business of making his writing even worse than it was. Dr. Harding, in point of fact, had all the vocabulary that he needed, and a great deal more. Any idea that he could formulate clearly he could convey clearly. Any idea that genuinely moved him he could invest with charm—which is to say, with what the pedagogues call style. I believe that this capacity is possessed by all literate persons above the age of fourteen. It is not acquired by studying textbooks; it is acquired by learning how to think. Children even younger often show it. I have a niece, now eleven years old, who already has an excellent style. When she writes to me about things that interest her—in other words, about the things she is capable of thinking about—she puts her thoughts into clear, dignified and admirable English. Her vocabulary, so far, is unspoiled by schoolma'ms. She doesn't try to knock me out by bombarding me with hard words, and phrases filched from Addison. She is unaffected, and hence her writing is charming. But if she essayed to send me a communication on the subject, say, of Balkan politics or government ownership, her style would descend instantly to the level of that of Dr. Harding's state papers.

To sum up, style cannot go beyond the ideas which lie at the heart of it. If they are clear, it too will be clear. If they are held passionately, it will be eloquent. Trying to teach it to persons who cannot think, especially when the business is attempted by persons who also cannot think, is a great waste of time, and an immoral imposition upon the taxpayers of the nation. It would be far more logical to devote all the energy to teaching, not writing, but logic—and probably just as useless. For I doubt that the art of thinking can be taught at all—at any rate, by school-teachers. It is not acquired, but congenital. Some persons are born with it. Their ideas flow in straight channels; they are capable of lucid reasoning; when they say anything it is instantly understandable; when they write anything it is clear and persuasive. They constitute, I should say, about one-eighth of one per cent. of the human race. The rest of God's children are just as incapable of logical thought as they are incapable of jumping over the moon. Trying to teach them to think is as vain an enterprise as trying to teach a streptococcus the principles of Americanism. The only thing to do with them is to make Ph.D.'s of them, and set them to writing handbooks on style.

STUDY QUESTIONS

1. On what two things, according to Mencken, does style depend?
2. What parts would Mencken assign to heredity and environment in influencing style?
3. Choose some words and expressions that determine the tone of the essay. How would you describe the tone?
4. Do Mencken's comments on the relation of thought and style imply a view of human nature? How would you describe this view?
5. Why should it be impossible to teach style while it is possible to teach writing itself? Does Mencken offer any ideas that help to solve this problem? Does the question imply that Mencken may be mistaken?
6. Do you think Mencken's view that "what is in the head finally oozes out of the nub" can be substantiated by the examples of famous writers? In order to discuss this question one has to deal with writers whose lives and opinions are well known to see if their styles correspond with "what is in the head."

2. WRITING AND THINKING

Language and Thought*

Susanne K. Langer

A symbol is not the same thing as a sign; that is a fact that psychologists and philosophers often overlook. All intelligent animals use signs; so do we. To them as well as to us sounds and smells and motions are signs of food, danger, the presence of other beings, or of rain or storm. Furthermore, some animals not only attend to signs but produce them for the benefit of others. Dogs bark at the door to be let in; rabbits thump to call each other; the cooing of doves and the growl of a wolf defending his kill are unequivocal signs of feelings and intentions to be reckoned with by other creatures.

We use signs just as animals do, though with considerably more elaboration. We stop at red lights and go on green; we answer calls and bells, watch the sky for coming storms, read trouble or promise or anger in each other's eyes. That is animal intelligence raised to the human level. Those of us who are dog lovers can probably all tell wonderful stories of how high our dogs have sometimes risen in the scale of clever sign interpretation and sign using.

A sign is anything that announces the existence or the imminence of some event, the presence of a thing or a person, or a change in a state of affairs. There are signs of the weather, signs of danger, signs of future good or evil, signs of what the past has been. In every case a sign is closely bound up with something to be noted or expected in experience. It is always a part of the situation to which it refers, though the reference may be remote in space and time. In so far as we are led to note or expect the signified event we are making correct use of a sign. This is the essence of rational behavior, which animals show in varying degrees. It is entirely realistic, being closely bound up with the actual objective course of history—learned by experience, and cashed in or voided by further experience.

If man had kept to the straight and narrow path of sign using, he would be like the other animals, though perhaps a little brighter. He would not talk, but grunt and gesticulate and point. He would make his wishes known, give warnings, perhaps develop a social system like that of bees and ants, with such a wonderful efficiency of communal enterprise that all men would have plenty to eat, warm apartments—all exactly alike and perfectly convenient—to live in, and everybody could and would sit in the sun or by the fire, as the climate demanded, not talking but just basking, with every want satisfied, most of his life. The young would romp and make love, the old would sleep, the middle-aged would do the routine work almost unconsciously and eat a great deal. But that would be the life of a social, superintelligent, purely sign-using animal.

To us who are human, it does not sound very glorious. We want to go places and do things, own all sorts of gadgets that we do not absolutely need, and when we sit down to take it easy we want to talk. Rights and property, social position, special talents and virtues, and above all our ideas, are what we live for. We have gone off on a tangent that takes us far away from the mere biological cycle that animal generations accomplish; and that is because we can use not only signs but symbols.

A symbol differs from a sign in that it does not announce the presence of the object, the being, condition, or whatnot, which is its meaning, but merely *brings this thing to mind*. It is not a mere "substitute sign" to which we react as though it were the object itself. The fact is that our reaction to hearing a person's name is quite different from our reaction to the person himself. There are certain rare cases where a symbol stands directly for its meaning: in religious experience, for instance, the Host is not only a symbol but a Presence. But symbols in the ordinary sense are not mystic. They are the same sort of thing that ordinary signs are; only they do not call our attention to something necessarily present or to be physically dealt with—they call up merely a conception of the thing they "mean."

The difference between a sign and a symbol is, in brief, that a sign causes us to think or act *in face of* the thing signified, whereas a symbol causes us to think *about* the thing symbolized. Therein lies the great importance of symbolism for human life, its power to make this life so different from any other animal biography that generations of men have found it incredible to suppose that they were of purely zoological origin. A sign is always embedded in reality, in a present that emerges from the actual past and stretches to the future; but a symbol may be divorced from reality altogether. It may refer to what is *not* the case, to a mere idea, a figment, a dream. It serves, therefore, to liberate thought from the immediate stimuli of a physically present world; and that liberation marks the essential difference between human and nonhuman mentality. Animals think, but they think *of* and *at* things; men think primarily *about* things. Words, pictures, and memory images are symbols that may be combined and varied in a thousand ways. The result is a symbolic structure whose meaning is a complex of all their respective meanings, and this kaleidoscope of *ideas* is the typical product of the human brain that we call the "stream of thought."

The process of transforming all direct experience into imagery or into that supreme mode of symbolic expression, language, has so completely taken possession of the human mind that it is not only a special talent but a dominant, organic need. All our sense impressions leave their traces in our memory not only as signs disposing our practical reactions in the future but also as symbols, images representing our *ideas* of things; and the tendency to manipulate ideas, to combine and abstract, mix and extend them by playing with symbols, is man's outstanding characteristic. It seems to be what his brain most naturally and spontaneously does. Therefore his primitive mental function is not judging reality, but *dreaming his desires*.

Dreaming is apparently a basic function of human brains, for it is free and unexhausting like our metabolism, heartbeat, and breath. It is easier to dream than not to dream, as it is easier to breathe than to refrain from breathing. The symbolic character of dreams is fairly well established. Symbol mongering, on this ineffectual, uncritical level, seems to be instinctive, the fulfillment of an elementary need rather than the purposeful exercise of a high and difficult talent.

The special power of man's mind rests on the evolution of this special activity, not on any transcendently high development of animal intelligence. We are not immeasurably higher than other animals; we are different. We have a biological need and with it a biological gift that they do not share.

Because man has not only the ability but the constant need of *conceiving* what has happened to him, what surrounds him, what is demanded of him—in short, of symbolizing nature, himself, and his hopes and fears—he has a constant and crying need of *expression*. What he cannot express, he cannot conceive; what he cannot conceive is chaos, and fills him with terror.

If we bear in mind this all-important craving for expression we get a new picture of man's behavior; for from this trait spring his powers and his weaknesses. The process of symbolic transformation that all our experiences undergo is nothing more nor less than the process of *conception*, which underlies the human faculties of abstraction and imagination.

When we are faced with a strange or difficult situation, we cannot react directly, as other creatures do, with flight, aggression, or any such simple instinctive pattern. Our whole reaction depends on how we manage to conceive the situation—whether we cast it in a definite dramatic form, whether we see it is a disaster, a challenge, a fulfillment of doom, or a fiat of the Divine Will. In words or dreamlike images, in artistic or religious or even in cynical form, we must *construe* the events of life. There is great virtue in the figure of speech, "I can *make* nothing of it," to express a failure to understand something. Thought and memory are processes of *making* the thought content and the memory image; the pattern of our ideas is given by the symbols through which we express them. And in the course of manipulating those symbols we inevitably distort the original experience, as we abstract certain features of it, embroider and reinforce those features with other ideas, until the conception we project on the screen of memory is quite different from anything in our real history.

Conception is a necessary and elementary process; what we do with our conceptions is another story. That is the entire history of human culture —of intelligence and morality, folly and superstition, ritual, language, and the arts—all the phenomena that set man apart from, and above, the rest of the animal kingdom. As the religious mind has to make all human history a drama of sin and salvation in order to define its own moral attitudes, so a scientist wrestles with the mere presentation of "the facts" before he can reason about them. The process of *envisaging* facts, values, hopes, and fears underlies our whole behavior pattern; and this process is reflected in the evolution of an extraordinary phenomenon found always, and only, in human societies—the phenomenon of language.

Language is the highest and most amazing achievement of the symbolistic human mind. The power it bestows is almost inestimable, for without it anything properly called "thought" is impossible. The birth of language is the dawn of humanity. The line between man and beast— between the highest ape and the lowest savage—is the language line. Whether the primitive Neanderthal man was anthropoid or human depends less on his cranial capacity, his upright posture, or even his use of tools and fire, than on one issue we shall probably never be able to settle —whether or not he spoke.

In all physical traits and practical responses, such as skills and visual judgments, we can find a certain continuity between animal and human mentality. Sign using is an ever evolving, ever improving function throughout the whole animal kingdom, from the lowly worm that shrinks into his hole at the sound of an approaching foot, to the dog obeying his master's command, and even to the learned scientist who watches the movements of an index needle.

This continuity of the sign-using talent has led psychologists to the belief that language is evolved from the vocal expressions, grunts and coos and cries, whereby animals vent their feelings or signal their fellows; that man has elaborated this sort of communion to the point where it makes a perfect exchange of ideas possible.

I do not believe that this doctrine of the origin of language is correct. The essence of language is symbolic, not signific; we use it first and most vitally to formulate and hold ideas in our own minds. Conception, not social control, is its first and foremost benefit.

Watch a young child that is just learning to speak play with a toy; he says the name of the object, e.g.: "Horsey! horsey! horsey!" over and over again, looks at the object, moves it, always saying the name to himself or to the world at large. It is quite a time before he talks to anyone in particular; he talks first of all to himself. This is his way of forming and fixing the *conception* of the object in his mind, and around this conception all his knowledge of it grows. *Names* are the essence of language; for the *name* is what abstracts the conception of the horse from the horse itself, and lets the mere idea recur at the speaking of the name. This permits the conception gathered from one horse experience to be exemplified again by another instance of a horse, so that the notion embodied in the name is a general notion.

To this end, the baby uses a word long before he *asks for* the object; when he wants his horsey he is likely to cry and fret, because he is reacting to an actual environment, not forming ideas. He uses the animal language of *signs* for his wants; talking is still a purely symbolic process—its practical value has not really impressed him yet.

Language need not be vocal; it may be purely visual, like written language, or even tactual, like the deaf-mute system of speech; but it *must be denotative.* The sounds, intended or unintended, whereby animals communicate do not constitute a language, because they are signs, not names. They never fall into an organic pattern, a meaningful syntax of even the most rudimentary sort, as all language seems to do with a sort of driving necessity. That is because signs refer to actual situations, in which things have obvious relations to each other that require only to be noted; but symbols refer to ideas, which are not physically there for inspection, so their connections and features have to be represented. This gives all true language a natural tendency toward growth and development, which seems almost like a life of its own. Languages are not invented; they grow with our need for expression.

In contrast, animal "speech" never has a structure. It is merely an emotional response. Apes may greet their ration of yams with a shout of "Nga!" But they do not say "Nga" between meals. If they could *talk about* their yams instead of just saluting them, they would be the most primitive men instead of the most anthropoid of beasts. They would have ideas, and tell each other things true or false, rational or irrational; they would make plans and invent laws and sing their own praises, as men do.

STUDY QUESTIONS

1. What is the essential difference, according to this essay, between the mental processes of animals and men? How does this difference affect man's reactions to his problems?
2. Why is the comfortable and uneventful life described in the fourth paragraph impossible for man? What does it have to do with his power of conceiving ideas?
3. The author contends that expression is one of man's basic needs. Can you supply any evidence from experience to support this view?
4. How do the theories about language offered here help to explain language irregularities and idioms?

5. Though the ability to symbolize gives man a great advantage, it is clear from this essay that it involves some disadvantages and special responsibilities as well. Write a theme on this topic, mentioning some of the problems and dangers inherent in the use of language. The essays by Monroe Beardsley and Max Black may provide further information about this subject.

6. The author bases her argument in part on the "stream of consciousness" with which the mind seems constantly occupied. Drawing on your own experience, write a theme describing the peculiarities of the stream of thought. Does it have direction? Can it be interrupted? What changes it? Does it arouse emotions? What relation does it have to language and other forms of expression? Can you recall any experiences that illustrate the peculiarities of the "stream of consciousness," such as irrational recollections?

On Contexts and Vagueness*

Monroe Beardsley

MEANING AND CONTEXT

One of the fundamental facts about words is that the most useful ones in our language have many meanings. That is partly why they are so useful: they work overtime (but, as we shall see, not for nothing). Think of all the various things we mean by the word "foot" on different occasions: one of the lower extremities of the human body, a measure of verse, the ground about a tree, twelve inches, the floor in front of the stairs. The same is true of nearly every common noun or verb. The editors of *The American College Dictionary,* in their preliminary investigation of words most frequently used, found 55 distinct senses of the word "point" in 1,100 occurrences of the word, and they distinguished 109 different senses of the word "run."

Considering the number of ways of taking a particular word, the task of speaking clearly and being understood would seem pretty hopeless if it were not for another very important fact about language. Though a word may have many senses, these senses can be controlled, up to a point, by the *context* in which the word is used. When we find the word in a particular verbal setting—that is, take it with the words that come before and after it in a discourse—we can usually decide quite definitely which of the many senses of the word is relevant. If a poet says his verse has three feet, it doesn't occur to you that he could mean it's a yard long or is three-legged (unless perhaps you are a critic planning to puncture the

* Reprinted by permission from *Thinking Straight,* 2nd Ed., pp. 153-159; 167-173. Copyright, 1956, by Prentice-Hall, Inc., Englewood Cliffs, N. J.

poet with a pun about his "limping verse"). The context rules out these maverick senses quite decisively.

We might be puzzled if we read in a newspaper that "in the suicide's pocket the police found a large envelope full of bills." In this sentence, as it stands, the word "bills" can easily be taken in two very different senses. But if the context were expanded so as to read, "The police were surprised to find in the suicide's pocket a large envelope full of bills of various denominations," we should understand that "bills" meant *paper money,* and we might wonder whether it was indeed suicide or accident. Or if the context were expanded differently, so as to read, "The police were surprised to find in the suicide's pocket a large envelope full of unpaid bills," we should understand that "bills" meant *requests for payment of a debt,* and we might wonder whether that explains the suicide.

This is a rather simple illustration of the way in which the context of a word helps to pick out one of its senses and fix that sense. But of course "context" is used broadly here: it may be the rest of a sentence (the *immediate* context), a page, a whole book, or a newspaper file. A "shady street" is one thing; a "shady neighborhood" is something else. The word "strike" means one action on the front page of a paper and another action on the sports page; the words "liberal" and "patriotic" mean certain attitudes in *The New York Times* and mostly different ones in *The Chicago Tribune.* When some time ago a British physicist announced with pleasure that the hydrogen bomb is "safe," his statement caused gasps of surprise; in the technical talk of atomic scientists, "safe" apparently means that it couldn't set off a chain reaction that might destroy the earth itself. This is not the way the man in the street uses the word.

Many common words like "line," "pipe," "base," "stock," and "head," have acquired many serviceable meanings in different occupational contexts—say, in the shoptalk of plumbers, pitchers, or plastic engineers. Think of what the word "wing" means to a birdwatcher, an airman, a stagehand, a general, or an architect. But just because these meanings are so completely distinct—no one can confuse the wing of an airplane with the wing of a house—it is easy to control them by very light contextual pressure. A word or two makes it clear that it is the airman's wing rather than the architect's that is referred to. But when the differences between the senses of a word are slighter and subtler (they may be even more important, however), the most careful management of the context may be required to get and keep one sense in focus. The exact meaning of a word like "middle class" or "evolution" or "justice" may depend upon the whole book in which it appears.

That is why it is often easy to misrepresent what someone has said by quoting some of his remarks out of their context. The words may not, strictly speaking, be *mis*quoted, but their meaning has been changed. The political candidate's promise to obtain peace or balance the budget is echoed and attacked by his opponent—who is careful to leave out the conditions and qualifications that originally surrounded it. Even if a writer is scrupulous enough to put in dots to indicate that something has been left out, he may not be *quite* scrupulous enough to stick to the original meaning. You have seen advertisements of a new play, with a few words from a review. The phrase ". . . emotional subtlety . . . (Bridgeport *Post*)" may be from a sentence that goes: "It has all the emotional subtlety of a barroom brawl." The phrase ". . . great drama . . . (New Haven *Register*)" may be from a sentence that goes: "No doubt it was considered a great drama when it first appeared in 1927, but . . ." And this is nothing to what a professional wiretapper can do if he records a telephone conversation and picks out words to rerecord on a new tape.

Representative Wayne L. Hays, a member of the Special House Committee set up by the 83rd Congress to investigate tax-exempt foundations, frequently argued during the committee's hearings that the "research directors" of the committee were willing to make judgments on passages torn out of contexts that might change their meaning considerably. He finally made a dramatic demonstration of this by producing three paragraphs which the associate research director testified were "closely comparable" with, and parallel to, Communist literature that he had read. They were excerpts from two papal encyclicals.

A loose and sloppy writer lays himself open particularly to accidental misquotation, but any writer would find it very hard to write a paragraph that is proof against a deliberate and skillful excerpt-lifter. Dean Sturges of the Yale Law School perhaps came as close as anyone can when, in 1949, the Harvard Law School *Record* asked him for an appropriate comment on the Harvard Law School's decision to admit women students for the first time. Dean Sturges is reported to have sent the following telegram:

YALE LAW FACULTY AND STUDENT BODY DEEPLY MOVED. FEEL IT QUITE POSSIBLE HARVARD MAY MAKE CONTRIBUTION TO WOMANHOOD. DOUBT MANY ADVERSE CONSEQUENCES HARVARD FACULTY OR STUDENT BODY. WE HAVE ALWAYS FOLLOWED WITH GENUINE INTEREST LONG STRUGGLE HARVARD LIBERALS IN THIS MATTER. OUR MANY GENERATIONS OF WOMEN GRADUATES ARE OF COURSE A PRIDE AND JOY. BEST WISHES.

Try digging a quotable compliment out of that.

The importance of context in the interpretation of meaning varies from one discourse to another. In a technical article on mathematics or physics, most sentences can stand pretty much on their own feet and be well understood apart from their context. Scientific terms are designed to resist the influence of context so that they can pass from one context to another without changing their meaning. But sentences in ordinary discourse that contain pronouns often lean on other sentences that contain the antecedents of those pronouns. Moreover, some words in our language—and they are among the most useful, but the trickiest, ones—are so adaptable to their context, like chameleons, that they take most of their character from it, and when they are considered apart from any context, they have only the most indefinite meaning. Words like "efficient," "dangerous," "internal," "successful," "free," tell us very little unless we are told, for example, the *purpose* for which it is efficient, or the *standards* in terms of which the success is judged. Contexts like "freehanded," "free lunch," "free love," "free will," "freeborn," "free association," help to limit the word "free" to a somewhat more definite range of meaning, but even in such cases we often feel that we don't know exactly what the word "free" means unless the context provides answers to the questions: "Free *from* what?" "Free *for* what?" "Free *to do* what?"

Another thing that shows the importance of context is the fact that when people use the wrong word we sometimes know what word should have been used. When Mrs. Malaprop says, "I would by no means wish a daughter of mine to be a progeny of learning . . . I would have her instructed in geometry, that she might know something of the contagious countries," we understand what she thought she was saying because the context so clearly tells us what words are called for if the sentences are to make sense. A malapropism is a word that is wrongly used in a sentence in place of another word that sounds somewhat like it. And if we couldn't tell from the context what the appropriate word would be, we could never recognize a malapropism.

But of course it would be a mistake to overemphasize contextual influence and say that a word *never* has the same meaning in two different contexts. If this were true, language would be even more difficult to manage than it is now. A person who says, "I believe in the dictionary" and later "I believe in the Bible" is presumably using the word "believe" in the same sense in both contexts. Perhaps sometimes when we say that a word is used twice in the same sense we ignore slight differences that could be important for one purpose or another. It is a good idea to keep in mind that a change in context *may* make a change in the sense, but it doesn't seem that it *must*. In the present paragraph the word "context" has, up to this point, been used three times, in three slightly different (immediate) contexts; but it has about the same meaning each time.

It is only when the context is considerably different that the meaning is likely to change. A person who says, "I believe in the dictionary," and, later, "I don't believe in ghosts," is using the word "believe" in two very different senses. But in each of these contexts it can have only one possible meaning, and when the whole context is taken into account there *may* be no question what that meaning is. "I believe in a federal world government" means about the same as "I believe *there should be* a federal world government." "I believe in extrasensory perception," means about the same as "I believe *there is such a thing as* extrasensory perception." "I believe in woman's intuition" means about the same as "I believe *that some of the things that* women intuit *are true*."

When a word can have different meanings in different kinds of context, we can say that it has variable meaning. Its meaning *varies,* and it therefore has a variety of senses when it appears in the dictionary. Some words are more variable than others. But the variable meaning of words doesn't ordinarily give us any trouble so long as there is enough contextual control. The trouble arises when the context is not complete enough to rule out all but one possible meaning. If I say, "Henry rents the house," there is no way for you to tell from the sentence itself whether Henry rents the house *from* someone or *to* someone. When a word can have one (but not both) of two (or more) meanings in a certain context, we shall say that the word is ambiguous *in that context.*

The ambiguity of a word is always relative to a context: no word is ambiguous *in itself.* Some words like "freedom," "religion," "democracy," are ambiguous in quite a few contexts, and that is why you have to be careful in interpreting and in using them. Sometimes such words are said to be "meaningless," but the trouble with them is just the opposite: they have so many subtly different meanings that it takes a good deal of skill —more than most writers command—to keep their meanings well under control. And when the writer fails in this task, it is up to the reader. Other words, such as the common nouns, are variable in meaning but are hardly ever ambiguous. It takes a good deal of ingenuity to write a medium-sized sentence in which the word "foot" is ambiguous.

A case of ambiguity, as we have defined it, is a case where there is some *doubt* about the way a discourse is to be interpreted, and you have to choose between alternative readings. Unfortunately, this is not the way the word "ambiguity" is always used. When A. E. Housman, in his poem "To an Athlete Dying Young," writes,

> Home they brought him, shoulder high,
> Townsman of a stiller town,

the word "town" has at least two meanings: the young man's village is quieter for the funeral than it was on the day everyone cheered his victory, and also he is now among the noiseless dead. But "town" is not ambiguous here. It has *both* meanings at once, and there is no uncertainty about them at all.

This sort of double meaning, or multiple meaning as it may be called, is also characteristic of one type of pun. There is the old pun, for example, about the two women leaning out of their windows across an alley and shouting at each other angrily: they can never come to an agreement because they are arguing from different premises. Another type of pun is built on *homonyms,* that is, words that have the same sound but different senses ("boy," "buoy"; "recede," "reseed"; "bier," "beer"; "air," "heir"). If you want to call homonyms the same word because they have the same sound, you would then have to say that such words have an even more variable meaning than we supposed. On the whole, we may as well call them different words if they are spelt differently, and then we shall not need to say any more about homonyms, except to note that they can give rise to the sort of pun made by Macbeth when he says he will plant circumstantial evidence on the grooms:

> "If he do bleed,
> I'll *gild* the faces of the grooms withal,
> For it must seem their *guilt*."

This sort of double entendre, whether in pun or poem, is sometimes called "ambiguity," but it is a very different thing from ambiguity in the sense in which we are using the term. The distinction can be clarified by means of some terms that come up later (in Chapter 6). The important thing at the moment is to note that there is a difference. The high-pressure context of a poem can squeeze many senses, all at once, out of some of its words; this is the multiple meaning of poetic discourse. But we have ambiguity, in the strict sense, when the context is too loose and flabby to hold the words steadily to *any* definite sense. The poet has managed to say several things at once; the ambiguous writer has not quite succeeded in saying anything.

VAGUENESS

A statement is either true or false; it can't be half-and-half. (A "half-truth" is false.) And an object is either an airplane or it is not; it can't be more or less an airplane. "True" and "airplane" are *either-or* words, but many other words in our language are not either-or words, but *more-or-less* words. A piece of bread can be more or less stale, an argument more or less convincing, a person more or less rich, tired, or bald. These words refer to qualities that vary in degree or amount. They are terms of comparison, or *comparative terms*. Under this label we shall include all words about which it makes sense to ask: How much? or How many? You can ask, "How rich is the Aga Khan?" or "How stale is the bread?" You can't ask, "How airplane is this object?" and when people ask, as they occasionally do, "How true is this statement?" this seems to be a loose colloquial way of asking, not how *true* it is, but how much *evidence* there is for it—which is quite a different thing.

Most of our common comparative terms are also used to classify things. We speak of bread as being more or less stale; but also, in terms of its degree of staleness, we divide bread into *stale* bread and *fresh* bread. If a person is rich enough, we call him "rich," and make a threefold division here between the rich, the poor, and the ones who are neither. If a person loses enough hair, we call him "bald"; if a tire loses enough air, we call it "flat"; and if a driver has enough accidents, we call him "unsafe."

The word "enough" is a key word here, for it leads us to ask questions like this: Exactly *how* dry must bread be in order to be stale? How much money must a man have in order to be rich? How many hairs must a man lose in order to be bald? How many accidents must a driver have, and how serious must they be, if he is to be considered unsafe?

These are all natural questions, and the important point about language that we want to be clear about here is just that *they have no answers*. We have never come to any agreement, tacit or explicit, about these words; there is simply no general rule according to which anyone with less than 196 hairs is bald, or anyone with more than $17,412.35 is rich. How old is middle-aged? Where does red leave off and orange begin? How cold is a cold shoulder? We have never drawn a line at any particular place, and so there is no definite line: this is what we mean when we say that a word is *vague*.

A vague word refers to a certain range of variation in intensity or quantity. Think of a sort of scale, ranging, say, from people with no money to the person who has the most, or from people with no hair to people with bushy tresses, or from bread right out of the oven to bread that has been around for months. In the case of a vague word, there is always a certain part of the scale to which the word definitely, and by universal agreement, applies: anyone who has twenty millions is surely rich, anyone with nothing but a slight fringe of hair is bald, and bread that has begun to mold is definitely stale. Moreover, there is always a certain part of the scale to which the word definitely does *not* apply: a person with only forty-five dollars is *not* rich; a person with hair covering the top of his head is certainly *not* bald; and bread that is only an hour old is *not* stale.

But in between these two parts of the scale there is a *doubtful area* where we have not decided whether to apply the word or not. There will be borderline savings accounts, heads of hair, and loaves of bread that you can describe either way, just as there are people you don't know whether to call "middle-aged" or not. If the word were *precise*, it would be defined so as to draw a sharp line. It is just the nature of a vague word that the line it draws is fuzzy.

As you can see, vagueness is a very different sort of thing from ambiguity. In ambiguity you have a choice between two distinct senses of a word, which may be as unrelated as plane geometry and marital disorders (as in two senses of "triangle"), only there is no way to decide how to choose. In vagueness, you know what the sense is all right, but you don't know *how much* there is of the quality referred to. Thus a word that has several meanings may be vague in some senses but not in others (compare "cold war" and "cold shoulder," "hot jazz" and "hot air"). And even when there is no question about the sense of a word, its doubtful area may shift from context to context. A large child is not the same as a large elephant; in both of these contexts the word is vague, but the doubtful area for children would be in pounds, and for elephants in hundreds of pounds. Compare "hot day," "hot bath," "hot oven" and "hot star." In each of these contexts "hot" means a different degree of temperature, and some of these "hot's" are fuzzier than others: "It's a hot day" is very loosely used, but when the cook book advises a "hot oven" for popovers, this has a pretty definite agreed-upon meaning.

So far, we have defined the word "vague" in such a way that only comparative terms are vague. But it is useful to broaden this a little further. Some words that are not comparative words themselves are defined in terms of other words that *are* comparative words. "Explosion" means "a rapid combustion"; thus, so long as there is no general rule that specifies *how* rapid a combustion must be before it is to be called an explosion, the word "explosion" is vague in *one* respect. Similarly, "democracy," in some of its senses, is vague in some respects. When you want to know whether a given word is vague, then, ask yourself, first, whether there is any question of *degree* involved in applying the word, and second, whether the degree involved is anywhere precisely specified.

It is important to realize that vague words can be very useful. In fact, some of them are useful *because* they are vague: it is handy to be able to report that the room was "crowded," without having to calculate the number of people per square foot; it is equally handy for us to be able to speak of the "context" of a word, without having to specify exactly and for all cases exactly how many words before and after a given word we shall include in its context. As for most other vague words, if we haven't bothered to make them precise it may be simply that we haven't needed to do so. A vague word is useful so long as it marks *some* distinction: that is, as long as we can point out something to which the word surely applies (the New England town meeting is definitely a democracy, in one sense of this word) and something to which the word surely does not apply (the Franco government in Spain is definitely *not* a democracy, in the same sense of this word).

Or take another example. The words "good taste" and "bad taste" are vague: how bad does taste have to be before it is "bad"? When the Senate Judiciary Subcommittee on Juvenile Delinquency was investigating comic books, in the spring of 1954, it was struck by a comic book whose cover showed a man with a bloody axe in one hand, holding up a severed woman's head in the other. The publisher of this comic book, who was testifying, cited it as an example of "good taste." Senator Kefauver, somewhat taken aback, asked the logically correct question to discover whether the publisher really meant anything by this description: how would the cover have to look if it were in *bad* taste? "It would be in bad taste," replied the publisher, "if the head were held a little higher, with the blood dripping out." This showed that he was drawing *some* line, though perhaps a rather odd one, and hence that "good taste" at least meant *something* to him.

Vague words get us into trouble only when we don't notice that they are vague. We expect too much of them, and they let us down. We think there must be a sharp line between "neutrality" and "involvement," when in fact there is just a blurry no man's land. Sheep and goats, chairs and tables, males and females can be separated from each other in a way that will satisfy nearly everyone, for these words have highly determinate meanings. Moreover, nature and human workmanship have provided us with easily distinguishable things instead of borderline cases. But two heads of hair may differ by a single hair, two bank accounts by less than a dollar, and the ages of two people by a few minutes. In such cases, there will be heads of hair, bank accounts, and people's ages that we won't have any generally agreed upon way of describing.

And this is why it is essential for words to be reasonably precise when questions of truth and falsity arise. The main counts of the Government's indictment of Professor Owen Lattimore accused him of "following the Communist line" and being a "promoter of Communist interests." These counts were thrown out by the Court of Appeals on the ground of vagueness, in keeping with the Sixth Amendment, which specifies that a person has a right to know what crime he is accused of before he can be tried. If the words used to describe the crime are not clear, how can he know what he is being tried for, and how can he defend himself? And how can the jury be expected to decide objectively whether he is guilty of it or not?

But of course, no matter how vague a word may be, we can always make it as precise as we wish for particular purposes and in particular contexts. We *can* draw a sharp line when we want to. A herring is a large sardine; that is a vague way of talking. For its convenience, however, the Food and Drug Administration calls a sardine a "herring" only when it is at least nine inches long. That is fairly precise. In common speech, the words "urban" and "rural" are vague. But the United States Census makes a sharper distinction: if a town has a population of 2,500 or more it is "urban," if not, it is "rural." "High-income group" is vague, but Congress, in a particular act, may arbitrarily draw the line at $25,000. This is a perfectly sensible procedure. Of course, it will always sound odd to say that a person making $25,000 a year is in a "high-income group," whereas a person making $24,999.99 is not. But you have to draw the line *somewhere* if you draw it at all. Where the scale is in terms of pennies, any particular place to draw the line will seem arbitrary.

Sometimes the line drawn may, in fact, be *too* arbitrary for the purpose at hand. If a great deal hinges on the distinction, it may be more than such a slight difference will bear. It doesn't seem fair to pass a student who gets 60 and fail a student who gets 59; we don't feel sure enough about the accuracy of tests and grades to make such an important result depend upon such a minute difference. This is why some educators prefer to use a vaguer scale, such as A, B, C, or Pass, High Pass, Honors, for grading students. Precision is always relative to what we want to do with it. Unnecessary precision is pedantic and fussy, like honing a razor to cut butter. Still, to develop skill in careful thinking, it is sometimes useful to practice a little pedantry. If you know how to make precise distinctions, you are free to decide, in a given case, just how far you ought to go. Each case is different, and only by studying it carefully can you determine what degree of vagueness is probably safe and perhaps desirable.

We would have little trouble in handling vague words, once we understood their habits, if it were not for one ingenious way of misusing them that may impose upon our thinking when we are off guard. It consists in arguing that there is no difference, or no important difference, between two things because the apparent difference is made up of a whole series of small differences. It doesn't matter much whether you smoke ten cigarettes a day or eleven, it doesn't matter much whether you smoke eleven or twelve, and so on. Someone might argue that therefore it doesn't matter whether you smoke ten or forty: there is no difference between heavy smoking and light smoking because any attempt to draw the line, say between thirteen and fourteen, is arbitrary. The amount of freedom you enjoy in one country only differs in degree from the amount of freedom you enjoy in another country; sometimes people argue that since it is only a difference of degree, it is therefore not much of a difference at all: "they are both about the same."

This sort of argument commits the black-or-white fallacy. It is a subtle attempt to paralyze choice by belittling an important difference. It is especially plausible when the distinctions are vague. The prefix "crypto-" has in recent years been used to great advantage in muddling people's thinking about political attitudes. As it is sometimes loosely used, a man can apparently be a disguised, or "crypto-" Communist without knowing it, or, indeed, without doing anything about it. According to this line of thought, a Democrat is a "crypto-liberal," a liberal is a "crypto-socialist," a socialist is a "crypto-communist," and a communist is a traitor; therefore Democrats are traitors, or practically traitors. When put in such a bare form, without any fancy trimmings, this argument doesn't look as though it would fool anyone. But it has been a staple commodity with some rabble rousers, who have done their best to make it appear that there is no important difference between both ends of their equation.

The same method of reasoning sometimes turns up in discussions of the degree of economic difficulty the United States economy may be undergoing at a certain time. There is "inventory correction," "rolling adjustment," "recession," and "depression," and (because the black-or-white fallacy works both ways) there may be an attempt to play down the differences by those who want to show that current troubles are *worse* than they really are (hardly distinguishable from a small depression) and at the same time by those who want to show that current troubles are *not as bad* as they really are (merely a sizeable inventory correction). The only way to get a proper perspective on the situation, and escape both fallacious arguments, is to insist on some definite distinctions between these various ills. For example, let's not call it a depression unless it involves a downward movement on the part of nearly every economic index, and unemployment of at least five million over a period of at least two years. If that seems *too* fine a line, it is easy enough to relax it. But at least we can keep the discussion from bogging down in a mushy terminology like "crypto-depression."

The black-or-white argument is a favorite with extremists, who are blind to the differences between shades of gray because to them the only "real" difference is between black and white. On a scale of cigarette smoking or civil liberty the *big* differences are made up of many *small* differences, but that doesn't make the big difference any less big. There are differences in *kind* and there are differences in *degree*, but some differences in degree are, from a practical point of view, just as crucial as differences in kind. We succeed only in drugging our thinking when we allow these differences to be smudged over by verbal trickery.

STUDY   QUESTIONS

1. What is meant by context? Is the context of a particular word always language or can other media act as contexts? How many other kinds of context that would have some effect on the meaning of words can you name?

2. Beardsley points out that in most cases the meaning of a word depends to a considerable extent on factors outside itself. Is this a desirable state of affairs? Would it not be better to have a language in which each word was assigned a definite and unchanging meaning? Are there any such languages?

3. What is the difference between *vagueness* and *ambiguity* of language?

4. Students of writing are often told that they must seek the *exact* word for the meaning they have in mind. Beardsley's discussion shows that this may be a complicated task involving a number of responsibilities in controlling language. What are those responsibilities?

5. From the point of view of the writer, are the problems of words discussed by Beardsley more important in some uses of language than in others? Or are they equally important but somewhat different in the various kinds? Explain.

6. Among the following words, which would you call vague and which would you call definite: immoral, civilization, homicidal, criminal (adjective), benefactor, contributor, subscriber, alteration, destruction, improvement. Write a short theme on any group of these explaining why some of them are vaguer in meaning than others.

Emotive Language*

Max Black

Personal and impersonal aspects of utterance. We have already said that any utterance normally gives some information about the speaker himself, as well as other matters. Let us, therefore, refer to the personal and impersonal aspects of an utterance. By the first term we shall mean the information given about the speaker, and more especially about the attitudes, feelings, and wishes that caused him to make the utterance; by the second, whatever other information may be conveyed by the utterance. The personal aspects may be further divided into expressive and dynamic aspects. The utterance is expressive insofar as it is caused by the speaker's feelings or attitudes, *without any desired effect on a hearer*. An involuntary cry of pain or joy is markedly expressive in this sense. The utterance is dynamic insofar as it is caused by the speaker's desire to produce actions or other effects in a hearer; a command or a question is markedly dynamic in this sense. Actual utterances vary widely in the relative importance of their expressive, dynamic, and impersonal aspects.

Statement and suggestion. No human speaker explicitly symbolizes all that he conveys to the hearer; we must constantly "read between the lines." One important consequence of this has already been mentioned. A speaker very rarely says: "I want you to feel that I am a thoroughly likable person of the sort you can trust; I am not much interested in tariffs (or whatever it may be) except insofar as some knowledge of this subject is necessary to persuade you to trust me." Such devastating frankness would be self-defeating, but many a speaker talks in such a way as to convey the same impression. Intelligent understanding of the utterance requires an awareness of much more than is "said in so many words." The *general setting* of the utterance (whether it is predominantly "scientific" or "poetic," intended to produce approval, result in actions, and so on) is not usually symbolized explicitly.

Let us examine a striking instance of "reading between the lines." In answering a letter not long ago, a certain Senator began his reply with the words "My dear Wop"—an action that led to considerable indignation on the part of his correspondent and many of the lady's sympathizers. Furious letters were written to Congress and the newspapers, and the Sen-

* Reprinted by permission from *Critical Thinking,* 2nd Ed., by Max Black, pp. 166-176. Copyright, 1952, by Prentice-Hall, Inc., Englewood Cliffs, N. J.

ator's action was denounced at meetings of protest as "undemocratic" and "un-American."

Why all this fuss about three words? A foreigner, not thoroughly familiar with the subtleties of the American language, would find on enquiry, that "Wop" means about the same as "Italian" or "person of Italian origin." "Well, well," he might wonder, in his naive way, "is it so insulting to an American to be accused of having Italian ancestors?" The answer, of course, is that "Wop" is a term of powerful *abuse*, conventionally used as a way of expressing a high degree of contempt for the person addressed. The three words might be expanded in some such way as this: "Madam, the usual rules of politeness require me to use the words 'My dear so-and-so.' I show my contempt for you and your opinions by refusing even to call you by your name. I am pretty sure that you can't be an American; I suspect that you are of Italian origin; and I regard Italians in general as inferior and degenerate."

Yet the abusive Senator did not *say* all this "in so many words"—even though much of it is quite clearly understood by his readers. Offense is properly taken at the insulting suggestions of the utterance, rather than at its explicitly formulated content.

The unformulated implications and suggestions of an utterance are not always abusive. Often we convey feelings of approval, enjoyment, or appreciation by gesture, tone of voice, and choice of words. The means employed are so flexible and variable that usually we are hardly aware of them, even while constantly responding to their influence. A large part of the information conveyed by utterance is *suggested, not stated*.

When a purported fact, a wish, a judgment of value, and so forth, are conveyed by means of a symbol conventionally used for that purpose we shall say the fact, wish, and so on, has been stated; when information is conveyed by means not conventionally reserved for that purpose we shall say that that information has been suggested. Thus, a statement is an explicitly formulated assertion, command, desire, judgment, and so forth, while a suggestion is conveyed, though not explicitly formulated. (It is, however, hard to draw a sharp line between suggestion and statement, as here defined. Sometimes, of course, there can be no doubt at all that an important part of a given utterance has been suggested, though not explicitly symbolized. The man who asks "When did you start smoking so heavily?" has not *actually* said "You are smoking heavily.")

All human languages rely, to an astonishing degree, on what is understood, though not said "in so many words." It has been reported of the Eskimos that "Their phrases are as sober as their faces. A gleam in an Eskimo's eye tells you more than half a dozen of our sentences concerning desire, repugnance, or another emotion. Each Eskimo's word is like that gleam: it suggests at once what has happened and what is to come. . . ." (Gontran de Poncins, *Kabloona*, page 247.) The more articulate languages of Western civilization, though not as suggestive as those of the Eskimo, still retain enormous suggestive power.

Emotive and neutral language. Among the most effective suggestions conveyed in human utterance are those expressive of the speaker's *feelings* (and especially feelings of approval or disapproval). Not only *feelings* are conveyed by suggestion: Any statement about "impersonal" matters of fact makes use of tacit assumptions, which are suggested, not stated. Nevertheless, the uses of suggestion to communicate the nature of a speaker's feelings are particularly important, for the following reasons:

1. Suggested feelings concerning a person or object can powerfully influence people's opinions. To call a man a "Red" is already to turn an audience against him; to call him a "dirty Red," in certain contexts, is practically to condemn him outright. Such "name calling" is usually more successful than explicit statement or reasoned argument.

2. Feelings, especially strong feelings, concerning a person or object spontaneously find expression in the use of "satisfying" symbols. (All praise and abuse tends to become poetic.) An angry man tends to *show* his anger rather than talk *about* it: thus the means by which he expresses his feelings will be a suggestion, not a statement. In general, suggestion is a very "natural" way of conveying a feeling.

Much attention has accordingly been given, in recent times, to the use of those signs that particularly lend themselves to the expression and communication of feelings. Such symbols are termed emotive, and are contrasted with neutral symbols. An emotive word, then, is one expressive of strong feelings (especially of approval or disapproval) on the part of the speaker. The use of emotive words has a tendency to produce similar feelings in the hearer.

The English language has a few words reserved for the expression of feeling and used for no other purpose—exclamations like "Shame!" "Hurrah!" "Encore!" While these words are highly emotive according to our definition, they express very generalized feelings. For this reason (and because they are so seldom used in discourse) they have negligible influence in determining people's views concerning *specific* topics.

If an advertiser wants to predispose the man in the street in favor of his product, he will probably adopt more subtle means to recommend it. Suppose he is selling a dentifrice consisting of powdered beef bone (an actual case): the slogan "Hurrah for powdered beef bone!" is unlikely to enlist many customers for the new product, even though repeated thousands of times in newspaper advertisements and on the radio. For the words "powdered beef bone" have suggestions that are unfavorable to the advertiser's purpose: we have all seen raw bones, and we are led to think of an unappetizing mess of blood-stained splinters, not at all the sort of stuff we would choose for cleaning the teeth. How much better then from the advertiser's standpoint to label the product "Numin" (the name actually chosen). Instead of the *negative* emotive force of "powdered beef bone," we have a *positive* emotive appeal of the substitute term, "Numin." For the latter has a scientific flavor, as of some new vitamin, and can therefore be relied upon to attract the man in the street.

The device used in this instance to stimulate a favorable reaction to a certain object (the dentifrice) consists in *the choice of a name having agreeable associations.* The English language is very rich in words approximately equivalent in *explicit* meaning, while markedly divergent in their emotive associations and suggestions.

The terms "government official," "bureaucrat," and "public servant" have much the same explicit meaning, yet the first is neutral, the second abusive, and the last honorific. "Liquidation of the opposition" sounds a great deal more agreeable than "torture and murder of the minority." A man may "talk eloquently" or "jabber"; a statesman may "have the gift of compromise" or be a "slippery trimmer"; a friend is "understandably confused," an enemy "has gone a bit off his noodle"; all these examples were in a single newspaper editorial.

The list of examples could be indefinitely extended, for nearly all the words we use are colored with some shade of respect or contempt, and every notion can be so worded as to make its subject seem either admirable or ridiculous.

The expression and influence of attitudes by means of such highly emotive words as those we have cited should be too obvious to escape notice. *But these cases are not exceptional.* The view that only in "propaganda" and abuse is language used emotively is none the less profoundly mistaken for being widely held. We must insist, to the contrary, that language is *normally* used to express attitudes and exert influence as well as to convey explicit statement; it is as much of an exception for language to be "uncolored" or neutral as for matter to be without odor.

Since the emotive and suggestive influence of language is so strong, we must take account of it in our general program of establishing principles and standards of right thinking. (If, on the other hand, we were to neglect these aspects of language, and pay attention only to what is explicitly stated in neutral terms, we should be behaving like a pilot who refused to take account of any part of an iceberg that was not visible above the water.) By discussing a concrete example in detail, we shall now illustrate the types of critical procedure that are appropriate.

ANALYSIS OF A SPECIMEN OF HIGHLY EMOTIVE WRITING.

A recent newspaper editorial opened with this sentence:

(A) "A fabulously rich playboy, who got tired of his ponies, got the idea that he would like to repudiate the free enterprise that privileged his grandfather to endow him with so many million dollars he could never hope to count them."

This passage tells us a good deal more about the editorial writer (or his employer) than about the millionaire who is the target of his abuse. Yet the passage does contain a little *impersonal* information (true or false), and the first step in analysis is to make this context explicit. An experienced journalist who happened to read (A) would immediately "discount" much of what was said. What this probably means, he might comment, is:

(B) "The rich man in question is supporting federal control of industry."

After the invective of (A), this partial translation appears insipid. Clearly the writer had little interest in conveying the information expressed by (B).

We proceed, therefore, to identify the *emotive suggestions* of the original passage. A convenient way of doing this is to begin by picking out (say by underlining) all the words and phrases that make a notable contribution to the total impression intended. After this has been done, we try to state explicitly the nature of the suggestion conveyed in each case. Proceeding in this fashion, we get the following analysis:

Language used	*Suggestion conveyed*
"*playboy*," "*ponies*"	X (the man in question) is an idler and gambler
"*fabulously rich*"	X is excessively wealthy
"*so many million dollars he could never hope to count them*"	
"*got tired of*"	X is irresponsible—makes decisions for no good reason
"*got the idea*"	
"*would like to repudiate*"	
"*privileged*"	X has received special and unearned favors
"*endow*"	

It will be seen that these suggestions reinforce each other in painting the picture of a most unattractive character. The malice of the writer's intention is obvious when the various suggestions are combined in a single explicit statement, in some such fashion as this:

(C) The man in question is an idle gambler, who has far more money than he deserves, and is now irresponsibly using the vast financial power that he did nothing to earn.

This last statement, if made explicitly, might well be libellous and expose its author to a legal suit for damages. Yet even so it would probably be less effective than the hints and innuendoes of the original passage (A). In all such cases the rule holds that the outspoken accusation is less dangerous than the whispered calumny.

A good way of neutralizing the suggestive power of the original passage is to replace the crucial emotive terms and phrases by others having *opposite emotive tendency* (but approximately the same explicit content). In this way we get the following substitute for (A):

(D) A very wealthy American sportsman has decided to oppose the system of unregulated commercial trading that enabled his grandfather to leave him his large fortune.

(You would do well to compare versions A and D very carefully, in order to decide for yourself whether the latter can be regarded as a "fair translation" of the former.)

It still remains for us to determine whether the suggestions contained in the original passage (and explicitly formulated in C) are to be regarded as justified. *We must guard carefully against assuming that the implicit suggestions of an utterance can be automatically rejected without further examination, just because they are suggested and not explicitly stated.* Such an assumption would be grossly mistaken, for there are many occasions on which the expression of our feelings is perfectly justified.

We take as a second instance of highly emotive language a passage from one of Garrison's addresses to the public:

I am aware that many object to the severity of my language; but is there not cause for severity? I will be as harsh as truth, and as uncompromising as justice. On this subject, I do not wish to think, or speak, or write, with moderation; No! no! Tell a man whose house is on fire to give a moderate alarm; tell him to moderately rescue his wife from the hands of the ravisher; tell the mother to gradually extricate her babe from the fire into which it has fallen; But urge me not to use moderation in a cause like the present. I am in earnest—I will not equivocate—I will not retreat a single inch,—AND I WILL BE HEARD.

This is the language of a man laboring under strong emotions, conveyed in words well fitted to communicate indignation. Shall we say he is wrong to have the feelings or to attempt to communicate them? Or that he ought to resort to the pallid and ineffective use of "neutral" language? Surely not. But to grant the right of Garrison or anybody else to express feelings and attitudes towards a subject by the most effective means he can find at hand is a very different thing from admitting without further examination that the specific emotion or attitude is justified. The suggestions of eloquence, rhetoric or poetry, insofar as they consist of claims that might be true or false, must submit to enquiries into their evidence, general credibility, consistency; if their moving appeals to our feelings are justified, they should survive such examination without detriment or loss of eloquence.

Returning to our original example, then, we must ask *what evidence* is provided for the claim formulated in (C). In this particular instance, the answer is quickly given: for *no reasons at all* are brought forward in support of the scurrilous accusation. Even while we admit the editorial writer's general privilege of accusing his subject of idleness, irresponsibility, and so forth, in the manner he has chosen, we must object strenuously that in the case at issue his accusation is presented as a bare assertion, destitute of any supporting evidence in its favor. Our summing up of the value of passage (A) might take some such form as this: "The passage is intended to arouse prejudice against its subject, by representing him as idle, irresponsible, and undeservedly wealthy. It appeals successfully to the reader's presumed dislike of these qualities. But it offers no particle of evidence in support of its hostile contention."

SUGGESTED RULES OF PROCEDURE FOR THE CRITICISM OF EMOTIVELY TONED UTTERANCE.

The painstaking analysis illustrated in the last section will be too elaborate for everyday use—life is too short for us to be always ferreting out the full emotive implications of what we read and hear. It is nevertheless of much value as a training in critical awareness of the suggestive overtones of human utterance to perform a few such exercises in great detail. When this is done, the following suggestions for procedure may be helpful:

1. Begin by reading the passage slowly, carefully, and calmly several times, noting any points in the utterance that seem to deserve further examination. (The reader will pardon this insistence on so elementary and obvious a point. Experience shows that once the excitement of the chase has been aroused, there is a tendency to "discover" sinister or profound implications in a passage, before even reading it with any degree of attention!)

2. State the general intention and context of the utterance. [E.g., "This is a report of a new scientific discovery made to an audience thoroughly familiar with the general background, and made by a man who is trying to suppress all that is personal in the circumstances he is describing." Or "This is an advertisement whose main object is to arouse curiosity concerning a mysteriously labelled new product; it is designed to appeal especially to women to make them more receptive to later 'follow-ups.'" It is useful also to try to determine the evidence used in arriving at this verdict concerning the general nature of the symbolic situation.]

3. Extract the words and phrases in the passage that are particularly effective in conveying the desired suggestion. [Crude instances of this, such as those discussed in the last section, are easily detected. More subtle suggestions, e.g., those due to the general style of a passage, may easily escape notice. It is an excellent practice here, as throughout this training, to compare one's results with those of others working independently on the same passage. Hunting down the reasons for disagreement will often bring to light unsuspected resources of the language used.]

4. Make the suggestions of each word explicit, and combine the partial suggestions in a single statement. [This has been illustrated by the analysis preceding version (C) above. You will soon find, on trial, that the suggestions of a word or phrase can be made explicit only in a rough and approximate way. Paraphras-

ing the implicit content largely neutralizes its emotive influence. Instead of extracting the implicit content in this way, a useful variation is to rewrite the original passage reversing the emotive effect of the critical terms, as illustrated in statement (D) above.]

5. Formulate, in neutral language, the impersonal content of the original passage. [The products of steps 4 and 5 should together approximate in informative content to the original passage.]

6. Determine the evidence in favor of the original passage, as now elaborated.

STUDY QUESTIONS

1. How does the fact that language has suggested meaning as well as explicit meaning make the task of using it more complicated than that of using chemical or mathematical symbols?

2. What does Black's observation about such synonyms as "government official," "bureaucrat" and "public servant" suggest about synonyms in general? Consider also these pairs of synonyms: thrift, stinginess; proud, vain; speed, haste; clever, intelligent; joy, happiness; sleep, slumber; new, novel.

3. What subjects and occasions justify the use of emotive language? Consider, for example, a legislature discussing a tax rise, an address by a candidate for election, a salesman describing his product to a prospect, a paper describing the results of a scientific experiment, a speech at a college commencement ceremony; a doctor describing a patient's condition to him. Specify what sort of feeling would be evoked (if any) in each case.

4. Apply Black's six rules for criticism of emotionally toned utterances to the following:
   Trespassers Will Be Prosecuted
   Trust in God and keep your powder dry.
   Men are born free, but everywhere they are in chains.
   "It is a pleasure for me to address the Ladies' Luncheon Club this afternoon."
   "Good morning, Bill. How's the family?"
   His parents were poor but honest.
   In which of these is the suggested meaning nearly the opposite of the explicit meaning?

5. Describe a use of language—advertising, poetry, Biblical texts such as the Sermon on the Mount, or political oratory—in which suggested meaning is more important than explicit meaning.

6. Examine the writing in a newspaper or magazine you often read to see how important suggestion is in it. Write a theme describing the use of suggestive language in periodicals, telling where it generally appears, where it is appropriate, and giving examples of it from your reading.

Words and Things: Cultural Change and Meaning Change*

Robert M. Estrich and Hans Sperber

Every American understands the meaning of *stump* in sentences like "he was unrivalled by any stump orator of the day" [1] and "this year things were not going very well for him on the stump." [2] But the majority —at least if our students are representative—do not know how the word acquired the meaning of political speaking. The peculiar exigencies of public life in early America developed, even before the Revolution, certain recognized forms of public address. Things which would now be discussed in a hall were then discussed in open-air meetings. The speaker, who had to compete not only with the noise of a more or less undisciplined crowd but also with the sounds of what we wrongly call silent nature, would naturally try to find a vantage point where he could be seen and heard. In some places a rock might be handy or a barrel brought up, but almost everywhere in the clearings a tree stump would offer itself as a primitive platform. As early as 1775 such a scene is described in a Tory ballad:

> When Congress sent great Washington
> All clothed in power and breeches,
> To meet old Britain's warlike sons
> And make some rebel speeches;
>
> . . .
>
> Upon a stump, he placed himself,
> Great Washington did he,
> And through the nose of lawyer Close
> Proclaimed great Liberty. [3]

Wirt's *Life of Patrick Henry* provides an even earlier example: an anecdote from the French and Indian wars describes the stump as "the common *rostrum*, you know, of the field-orator of Virginia." [4] In the

---

* *Three Keys to Language* by Robert Estrich and Hans Sperber, New York, 1952, Holt, Rinehart and Winston, Inc. By permission.
[1] James A. Farley, *Behind the Ballots* (New York: Harcourt, Brace and Company, 1939), p. 25.
[2] Wilbur L. Cross, *Connecticut Yankee* (New Haven: Yale University Press, 1943), p. 235.
[3] Frank Moore, ed., *Songs and Ballads of the American Revolution* (New York: D. Appleton & Company, 1856), pp. 99-101.
[4] William Wirt, *The Life and Character of Patrick Henry* (Philadelphia: Porter & Coates, n.d.), p. 21.

1820's when the Eastern cities like Boston and New York had their indoor
meeting places and even rural communities had reached the point at which
the erection of a platform added dignity to the occasion, the stump was
still in common use in the South. David Crockett's campaigns were carried on in the old fashion. His autobiography records a story of his first
campaign for Congress in 1827 when, at a political gathering in a crossroads clearing, he "mounted the stump that had been cut down for the
occasion, and began to bushwhack in the most approved style." [5]

The linguist has now to ask why, when the stump rostrum disappeared
even in the remote parts of the country, did not the word *stump* disappear from the political vocabulary? The answer is that by this time the
word had acquired connotations which suggested not so much the actual
presence of a stump as a certain style ("bushwhacking") favored by those
who had used the stump as a platform. The process—and its symptomatic value as an indication of the lowering of the tone of political
address in the second quarter of the nineteenth century—is clearly illustrated in Garnett Andrews' *Reminiscences of an Old Georgia Lawyer:*

> The lawyers of that day differed from those of the present in not practicing
> popular oratory "from the stump." I do not remember to have heard or to have
> heard of, any one canvassing from that forum prior to the advent of nullification.
> With that doctrine came popular oratory as a means of winning the "sweet voices"
> of the people. Though I recollect the barbecue, the grocery-treats and such like
> convivial entertainments, at which candidates "most did congregate," and in
> which they participated, I have no recollection of "the gift of the gab" being called
> into requisition. It was not thought a necessary accomplishment for our early
> Presidents and Governors, nor important, even, for members of Congress, to be
> "gifted" in that way. Our people did not then, as now, graduate a man's talents
> by his tongue only. Men of worth, learning and station had a fair chance for
> office, though not winning of speech. Now, if Washington were living, with all
> his prestige, I don't know but he might be turned down, by the popular vote of a
> county, where all the voters could be addressed by a second-rate lawyer who
> might "get the grin against him from the stump." [6]

What the stump style was like can be gathered from anecdotes like the
following successful impertinence of Crockett's. He was being completely
ignored by one of his competitors, General William Arnold, at an open-air
political rally. Arnold

> had been speaking for a considerable time, when a large flock of guinea-fowls
> came very near to where he was, and set up the most unmerciful chattering that
> ever was heard. They so confused the general that he made a stop, and requested

[5] *Life of David Crockett . . . an Autobiography* (New York: Perkins Book
Co., 1903), p. 240.
[6] Garnett Andrews, *Reminiscences of an Old Georgia Lawyer* (Atlanta,
Georgia: Franklin Steam Printing House, 1870), p. 22.

that they might be driven away. I let him finish his speech, and then walking up to him, said aloud, "Well, colonel, you are the first man I ever saw that understood the language of fowls." I told him that he had not had the politeness to name me in his speech, and that when my little friends, the guinea-fowls, had come up and began to holler, "Crockett, Crockett, Crockett," he had been ungenerous enough to stop, and drive *them* all away. This raised a universal shout among the people for me, and the general seemed mighty bad plagued.[7]

Perhaps even more revealing is this one vouched for by Garnett Andrews:

Now, the Democratic orator, coming from the literary and wealthy town of Athens, was dressed as became a gentleman from such a place—from such a city, I should say, for there are neither towns nor villages now. And our Colonel, the Whig, coming from the back-woods, was dressed like a back-woodsman. The Democrat happening to speak of himself as one of the "wool-hat boys," his adversary replied to that part of his speech, after the following manner:

"The gentleman spoke of himself as one of the 'wool-hat boys.' Now, look at this picture and then look on that. Here I am with my short homespun-jacket, cotton-shirt, copperas-pants, red-shoes, tanned and made by my old friend, Dick Spooner, and there lies my wool-hat, made by my other neighbor, Tom Hasklet. And there sits your 'wool-hat boy' with his broad-cloth coat, linen-shirt, white-vest, so fine that I don't know what to call it, cassimere-pants, shining, polished boots, and there lies his fine beaver, too stuck-up and proud to come near my old wool-hat."

Here the Democrat rose and said, "If I do wear fine clothes they are not paid for." [8]

Before attempting to draw our conclusions, we cannot resist quoting one more of Andrews' anecdotes about this same orator. We can justify including it here because in a book which tries to illustrate the social point of view about language, this story is necessary to make complete the picture of the milieu from which came "stump speaking." And we should also like to pass on to our reader some of the fun we have had in collecting our material.

Delivering a fourth of July speech, after the usual denunciations of the mother country and laudations of the United States, he led off in this style:

"Whose afeared? whose scared, though she does call herself mistress of the seas? for if she is mistress we will be masters. And, my fellow citizens, by rights they are our seas anyhow, for if there had been no Mississippi they would have had no seas no how. And if we were to turn that river into the lakes or the big cave of Kentucky, we would leave her ships in a puddle-hole at the bottom, surrounded by fluttering fish, turtles, snakes and alligators." Great applause.[9]

---

[7] Crockett, *op. cit.*, p. 159.
[8] Andrews, *op. cit.*, pp. 82-83.
[9] *Ibid.*, p. 82.

Such examples of chauvinism and of how "to get the grin" against an opponent make us see how effective this stump style was in winning an unsophisticated audience. But to make permanent the place of the word in American political life the disapproval of the upper classes of the mode it characterized was also important, probably in exact proportion to its popular appeal. Pejorative connotations can entrench a word as firmly as any other. And the upper classes did disapprove of stump speaking. By 1880 Justin McCarthy could speak of "a series of enterprises which in the homely and undignified language of American politics would probably be called 'stumping the country.' " [10] The fact that McCarthy was British had something to do, of course, with the harshness of his remark, but it is certainly not the whole explanation. Few American authors have given more convincing evidence of their sympathetic understanding of popular American points of view and customs than James Russell Lowell. Still even to him the use of stump language meant bad taste, and, if resorted to by a President of the United States, it was more than offensive—it was unforgivable. As the first point in his essay, "The President on the Stump," he declared that "Mr. Johnson is the first of our Presidents who has descended to the stump, and spoken to the people as if they were a mob."

To try now to state in linguistic terms the problem we have been tracing, evidently *stump* and the many phrases containing the word have undergone a change of meaning. But, at least in one respect, the process is different from the processes analyzed in the last chapter. Semantic changes based on metaphor and similar devices are regularly achieved by the conscious and purposeful action of transferring a word from its original sphere to some area of meaning—say from the race track into politics. Nothing of such an aimed action can be the cause of the change of meaning in *stump*—at any rate, as far as these earlier uses are concerned. Here the change of meaning is evidently caused by facts outside language. Tree stumps were used by public speakers. This custom became more or less obsolete. But before the stump had disappeared as the political stage, the word *stump* had acquired a usefulness not limited to situations where speaking from a real stump was alluded to. The word could therefore survive even after its origin was no longer evident in the thing it described. When Lowell said that the President *descended* to the stump, instead of *mounted*, the original meaning was not present in his mind. Thus a change of meaning was completed that cannot be explained by any conscious action on the part of the speakers, but resulted from the natural wear and tear of an often used word.

The validity of our sketch in general cannot be weakened by pointing to cases where an occasional use of *stump* indicates deliberate metaphor.

[10] Justin McCarthy, *History of Our Own Times* (New York: Harper & Brothers, n.d.), I, 48.

The editorial writer of the Richmond *Whig* may have had a feeling of deliberate metaphor when he spoke of

. . . an innovation in New York electioneering, which we hail with the greatest satisfaction, as promising auspicious results to the American character and institutions. We mean the introduction of the good old Virginia mode of taking the stump—of going before the People, and discussing in their presence the great affairs of State. . . .[11]

The general change, nevertheless, was clearly the combined result of the action of a large number of individual speakers. It would be absurd to assume that each individual contributing to the result acted from the same motive or with the same understanding, either in shifting meaning or in shifting the grammatical function of the word from noun to verb or adjective. What most people are unaware of may appear to others a slight and unessential inaccuracy, and to the few others whose linguistic awareness is constantly alert, a metaphor.

What we learn from the history of *stump* is that many word problems cannot be fully understood unless we know something of the history of the thing which the words designate. This seems a self-evident truism, but to the great damage of etymology and word history its importance was not realized until the late 1890's, when Rudolf Meringer and Hugo Schuchardt launched their *Wörter-und-Sachen* investigations—studies combining word history with culture history.[12]

The type of semantic change that *stump* represents is by no means rare. In modern use there exists a large number of words whose meanings cannot be explained on the basis of modern conditions but become clear if we study the history of the things involved. A *ring* in general is something round, and therefore the place where a boxing contest is fought could never have been called a *ring* if from the very beginning it had been what it is today, a roped-in square. But before boxing became a well-regulated sport, the battleground was not limited by ropes but by the spectators themselves, who formed a circle around the contestants. This is the situation implied by the earliest (1659) quotation in the *Oxford English Dictionary:* "The soldyers generally say they will not fight, but will make a ring for their officers to fight in." It takes very little knowledge of human nature to see that as soon as a fistic brawl was in the offing the cry, "Form a ring," would call spectators. Here are the natural-sounding preliminaries to a ruckus in Cincinnati in 1856:

"What!" exclaimed Hoss Head, drawing himself out to his full length and giving the diminutives before him rather a scornful look. "What! you want to fight, do you? Just clar a ring, boys, and stan' back, if you want to see me eat

[11] Richmond *Whig*, September, 1840.
[12] The magazine *Wörter und Sachen* was not founded until 1909.

them two critters in half a minit. I can do it by any watch in this crowd. Just clar the ring." [13]

We do not know at what date a staked, roped, square ring became mandatory. The earliest rules of prize fighting, Jack Broughton's in 1743, do not mention it but do refer to "being parted from the rails," which suggests that the stage in his amphitheater was somehow enclosed. But not until the London Prize-Ring Rules of 1838 do we find a defined square required—in contests where rules could be enforced: "The ring shall be made on the turf, and shall be four-and-twenty feet square, formed of eight stakes and ropes. . . ." [14] However, Wignall reproduces a print of Richard Humphries, a popular fighter of the 1780's, on the turf in a staked and roped "ring." Probably more important than the dates of the introduction of the square ring is the fact that its use was of slow growth. A distinction between a match and a brawl was for a long time very hard to make. What surprises the modern reader of a book like Wignall's is that down past the middle of the nineteenth century in both England and America the bruisers who fought even championship matches fought as many of their contests outside the ring as in it. The curious can find in Wignall, for instance, dozens of stories of more or less official matches fought with bare knuckles wherever it was handy in streets, in alleys, in fields, on docks, and in innyards. If the ring was used at all, it was likely to be a hastily staked-up affair, ready for moving at a moment's notice of the arrival of the police, and often broken down by the spectators, eager to see better or to aid in the mayhem if the fighter on whom the big money was placed was in danger of losing.

To take only one example, here is a characteristic fight in the career of the man who was from 1852 to 1858 the recognized champion of America, John Morrissey. Morrissey apparently fought only three of his fights under the formal conditions of the London Prize-Ring Rules. The rest were brawls, mostly the inevitable concomitant of gang warfare. This one was at least not casual, for a formal challenge had been made and accepted and a place and date set "to fight to a finish for a side bet of $100 and the glory of being the kingpin bruiser of New York:"

Numerous admirers . . . had cleared a place for the fight. . . . There was no ring, but by general consent the throng had kept a space open for the combat. . . . The fight began with some light sparring. . . . Then Morrissey made a rush. . . .
Clutching each other in grips of steel they butted and pounded their heads together, tearing at each other's face with their teeth and gouging for the eyes with talon-like fingers. . . . They never changed positions while the struggle went on, for the minute they were down the crowd closed in on them and the surging bodies

---

[13] *Green Peas, Picked from the Patch of Invisible Green, Esq.,* (Cincinnati: Moore, Wilstach, Keys & Overend, 1856), p. 23.
[14] Quoted in Trevor C. Wignall, *The Story of Boxing* (London: Hutchinson & Co., 1923), p. 312.

of the combatants pressed against the feet and legs of the surrounding on lookers. The wonder is that the two on the ground were saved from being trampled to death.[15]

The most easily available picture of a typical early ring is the Currier and Ives print of 1860 showing *The Great Fight for the Championship between John C. Heenan "The Benicia Boy," & Tom Sayers "Champion of England."* It places the boxers in this, the most memorable boxing match of the nineteenth century, in a roped-off square similar to that in use today, save that it is not on a platform in an arena but staked into the ground outdoors.[16] Even here, however, in a great international match, carefully organized and well refereed, reported by journalists as famous as William Makepeace Thackeray, the distinguished audience before the end rushed the ring and

scarcely left the combatants six square feet to fight in. Umpires, referees, and all were overwhelmed, and the whole thing became a mere close mob round the two fighting men. After this, four other rounds were fought, in the midst of this dense mass of partisans of either side, who, however, allowed the men to fight in the fairest way they could, consistent with their having hardly any room to fight at all.[17]

Obviously prize fighting in 1860 was not yet so far removed from the primitive that the ring was necessarily more than a mob of spectators encircling the boxers.

Pictures and antiques are of inestimable value to the linguist in this kind of research. But language itself can often supply the necessary detail. Even without pictures of a square ring, we should know what had occurred to the boxing place as soon as we read in any writer of the past that a boxer retires to his corner.

The changes which turned a ring into a square were gradual, as is natural enough when a fight can be anything from a brawl to a duel or an exhibition, and when, as was true of John Morrissey, the same man could engage in all three in pursuit of his professional career. But frequently the word which depends on a thing or a situation for its meaning can have that meaning changed almost overnight. In 1931 Frederick Lewis Allen found it necessary in *Only Yesterday* to explain that the New York Curb Market had been in 1919 literally what its name implies, an open air exchange in the street:

[15] This eyewitness account appeared in *The Police Gazette* in 1880, but we have excerpted a few lines from the quotations used by Herbert Asbury in *Sucker's Progress* (New York: Dodd, Mead & Company, 1938), pp. 366-367.

[16] Harry T. Peters, *Currier and Ives* (New York: Doubleday, Doran & Company, 1942), plate 55.

[17] From the report of the London *Times*, quoted by Wignall, *op. cit.*, p. 184.

The Curb Market record referred to trading on a real curb—to that extraordinary outdoor market in Broad Street, New York, where boys with telephone receivers clamped to their heads hung out of windows high above the street and grimaced and wigwagged through the din to traders clustered on the pavement below.[18]

The Curb was housed in its present building on Trinity Place in 1921. Immediately thereupon the word, following the pattern of *stump*, was left with a meaning which referred only to the nature of its selling activities and its method of listing securities, not to its physical place of operation. With its change of place a change of meaning had been made complete, and a skilled journalist only a few years later found it wise to remind his readers of the facts.

The word *knot* as used in determining the progress of a ship has given rise to amateurish suggestions. It has even been explained as a wrong spelling of the abbreviation *naut.* for *nautical (mile)*. It is nothing more, however, than the common word *knot*, and its technical meaning becomes clear from passages like the following early description of the method of logging a ship's progress:

The English have another invention. They have a sandglass, which runs only a half a minute or the one hundred twentieth part of an hour in order to measure the way as exactly as possible. Furthermore they also have, around a revolving wheel or axis, a long line, which is divided into certain parts by several knots. To the end of this line they tie a little boat about one foot long and half as wide, to the back end of which they attach a plate of lead so that it may sink deeper than the front and so that the wind cannot carry it away. . . . It must remain steadily at the place where it is thrown in, while the ship sails on. It unwinds continuously as the ship progresses. Then how many knots are unreeled while the sand glass runs must be observed. If six appear within half a minute, one concludes that the ship is sailing two miles an hour. If more or fewer appear, one establishes the proportion.[19]

The knotted line is only part of a measuring apparatus consisting of a reel, the line itself, and a piece of wood (the "little boat"), which in English has the name *log*. The earliest form of the *log* which we have been able to find is the one pictured in the *Encyclopedia Britannica* and there described as "a wooden quadrant about $\frac{1}{2}$ in. thick with a radius of about 5 or 6 in., its circumference being weighted with lead to keep it upright in the sea and to retard its passage through the water." Primitive as this looks compared to the developed modern patent or continuous log, it is probably a highly refined form of something still more primitive. The conjecture seems likely that the first log was only a sizable piece of wood

---

[18] Frederick Lewis Allen, *Only Yesterday* (New York: Harper & Brothers, 1931), p. 9.
[19] Translated from *"Fortsetzung des Geöffneten See-Hafens,"* pp. 74-75, *Der Geöffnete Ritter-Platz* (Hamburg; 1715).

attached to a measurable line; hence the name. "But some derive the naut. *log* from Arab. *lauh,* plank, tablet. Hence *log-book,* originally for recording rate of progress, and verb to *log,* enter in book." [20] We cannot now prove either etymology, but clearly the problem is to be settled by a study of the history of the thing as well as of the word.

These samples should have convinced the reader of how important it is in any philological investigation to be acquainted with cultural history and especially with its most commonplace facts—the history of tools, the habits of sportsmen, sailors, businessmen, and what not. But it is no less important to be familiar with the ideas of the past, including its errors and superstitions.

STUDY QUESTIONS

1. What generalization is offered to explain the survival of words such as "stump," which is derived from something which has disappeared?

2. What is the effect of giving several quotations, instead of one or two, to illustrate the older uses of the words under discussion?

3. What reasons do the authors give for believing that the survival of "stump" did not depend on a metaphoric usage?

4. What general relation between language and culture does the essay refer to?

5. Can you think of any other examples of words like "stump," which have survived their origins? Write a brief history of such a word, explaining the conditions under which it originated.

6. This essay makes the point that it is often necessary to examine cultural conditions in order to understand the origin of a word, but the reverse is equally true. Word histories often reveal significant cultural or historical facts. Write a theme showing how some word's etymology does this. Possibilities are: paper, book, alcohol, county, donnybrook, ostracize, boycott, khaki. Useful reference books for this project are an unabridged dictionary or the New English Dictionary.

[20] Ernest Weekley, *Concise Etymological Dictionary of Modern English* (New York: E. P. Dutton & Co., 1924), s.v. *log.*

What Is Thinking?*

John Dewey

I. DIFFERENT MEANINGS OF THOUGHT

No one can tell another person in any definite way how he *should* think, any more than how he ought to breathe or to have his blood circulate. But the various ways in which men *do* think can be told and can be described in their general features. Some of these ways are better than others; the reasons why they are better can be set forth. The person who understands what the better ways of thinking are and why they are better can, if he will, change his own personal ways until they become more effective; until, that is to say, they do better the work that thinking can do and that other mental operations cannot do so well. The better way of thinking that is to be considered in this book is called reflective thinking: the kind of thinking that consists in turning a subject over in the mind and giving it serious and consecutive consideration. Before we take up this main theme, we shall, however, first take note briefly of some other mental processes to which the name *thought* is sometimes given.

All the time we are awake and sometimes when we are asleep, something is, as we say, going through our heads. When we are asleep we call that kind of sequence "dreaming." We also have daydreams, reveries, castles built in the air, and mental streams that are even more idle and chaotic. To this uncontrolled coursing of ideas through our heads the name of "thinking" is sometimes given. It is automatic and unregulated. Many a child has attempted to see whether he could not "stop thinking" —that is, stop this procession of mental states through his mind—and in vain. More of our waking life than most of us would care to admit is whiled away in this inconsequential trifling with mental pictures, random recollections, pleasant but unfounded hopes, flitting, half-developed impressions. Hence it is that he who offers "a penny for your thoughts" does not expect to drive any great bargain if his offer is taken; he will only find out what happens to be "going through the mind" and what "goes" in this fashion rarely leaves much that is worth while behind.

In this sense, silly folk and dullards *think*. The story is told of a man in slight repute for intelligence, who, desiring to be chosen selectman in his New England town, addressed a knot of neighbors in this wise: "I hear you don't believe I know enough to hold office. I wish you to under-

---

* From *How We Think*, 1933, by John Dewey. Reprinted by special permission of D. C. Heath and Company.

stand that I am thinking about something or other most of the time."
Now, reflective thought is like this random coursing of things through the
mind in that it consists of a succession of things thought of, but it is unlike in that the mere chance occurrence of any chance "something or
other" in an irregular sequence does not suffice. Reflection involves not
simply a sequence of ideas, but a *con*-sequence—a consecutive ordering
in such a way that each determines the next as its proper outcome, while
each outcome in turn leans back on, or refers to, its predecessors. The
successive portions of a reflective thought grow out of one another and
support one another; they do not come and go in a medley. Each phase is
a step from something to something—technically speaking, it is a *term* of
thought. Each term leaves a deposit that is utilized in the next term.
The stream or flow becomes a train or chain. There are in any reflective
thought definite units that are linked together so that there is a sustained
movement to a common end.

The second meaning of thinking limits it to things not sensed or directly
perceived, to things *not* seen, heard, touched, smelt, or tasted. We ask the
man telling a story if he saw a certain incident happen, and his reply may
be, "No, I only thought of it." A note of invention, as distinct from faithful record of observation, is present. Most important in this class are
successions of imaginative incidents and episodes that have a certain co-
herence, hang together on a continuous thread, and thus lie between
kaleidoscopic flights of fancy and considerations deliberately employed
to establish a conclusion. The imaginative stories poured forth by children possess all degrees of internal congruity; some are disjointed, some
are articulated. When connected, they simulate reflective thought: indeed,
they usually occur in minds of logical capacity. These imaginative enterprises often precede thinking of the close-knit type and prepare the way
for it. In this sense, a thought or idea is a mental picture of something
not actually present, and thinking is the succession of such pictures.

In contrast, reflective thinking has a purpose beyond the entertainment
afforded by the train of agreeable mental inventions and pictures. The
train must lead somewhere; it must tend to a conclusion that can be
substantiated outside the course of the images. A story of a giant may
satisfy merely because of the story itself; a reflective conclusion that a
giant lived at a certain date and place on the earth would have to have
some justification outside of the chain of ideas in order to be a valid or
sound conclusion. This contrasting element is probably best conveyed in
the ordinary saying: "Think it *out*." The phrase suggests an entangle-
ment to be straightened out, something obscure to be cleared up through
the application of thought. There is a goal to be reachd, and this end sets
a task that controls the sequence of ideas.

A third meaning of thought is practically synonymous with *belief*. "I
think it is going to be colder tomorrow," or "I think Hungary is larger
than Jugo-Slavia" is equivalent to "I believe so-and-so." When we say,

"Men used to think the world was flat," we obviously refer to a belief that was held by our ancestors. This meaning of thought is narrower than those previously mentioned. A belief refers to something beyond itself by which its value is tested; it makes an assertion about some matter of fact or some principle or law. It means that a specified state of fact or law is accepted or rejected, that it is something proper to be affirmed or at least acquiesced in. It is hardly necessary to lay stress upon the importance of belief. It covers all the matters of which we have no sure knowledge and yet which we are sufficiently confident of to act upon and also the matters that we now accept as certainly true, as knowledge, but which nevertheless may be questioned in the future—just as much that passed as knowledge in the past has now passed into the limbo of mere opinion or of error.

There is nothing in the mere fact of thought as identical with belief that reveals whether the belief is well founded or not. Two different men say, "I believe the world is spherical." One man, if challenged, could produce little or no evidence for thinking as he does. It is an idea that he has picked up from others and that he accepts because the idea is generally current, not because he has examined into the matter and not because his own mind has taken any active part in reaching and framing the belief.

Such "thoughts" grow up unconsciously. They are picked up—we know not how. From obscure sources and by unnoticed channels they insinuate themselves into the mind and become unconsciously a part of our mental furniture. Tradition, instruction, imitation—all of which depend upon authority in some form, or appeal to our own advantage, or fall in with a strong passion—are responsible for them. Such thoughts are prejudices; that is, prejudgments, not conclusions reached as the result of personal mental activity, such as observing, collecting, and examining evidence. Even when they happen to be correct, their correctness is a matter of accident as far as the person who entertains them is concerned.

Thus we are brought again, by way of contrast, to the particular kind of thinking that we are to study in this volume, *reflective thinking.* Thought, in the two first senses mentioned, may be harmful to the mind because it distracts from the real world, and because it may be a waste of time. On the other hand, if indulged in judiciously these thoughts may afford genuine enjoyment and also be a source of needed recreation. But in either case they can make no claim to truth; they cannot hold themselves up as something that the mind should accept, assert, and be willing to act upon. They may involve a kind of emotional commitment, but not intellectual and practical commitment. Beliefs, on the other hand, do involve precisely this commitment and consequently sooner or later they demand our investigation to find out upon what grounds they rest. To think of a cloud as a whale or a camel—in the sense of to "fancy"—does not commit one to the conclusion that the person having the idea would ride the camel or extract oil from the whale. But when Columbus "thought" the world was round, in the sense of "believed it to be so," he and his followers were thereby committed to a series of other beliefs and actions: to beliefs about routes to India, about what would happen if ships traveled far westward on the Atlantic, etc., precisely as thinking that the world was flat had committed those who held it to belief in the impossibility of circumnavigation, and in the limitation of the earth to regions in the small civilized part of it Europeans were already acquainted with, etc.

The earlier thought, belief in the flatness of the earth, had some foundation in evidence; it rested upon what men could see easily within the limits of their vision. But this evidence was not further looked into; it was not checked by considering other evidence; there was no search for new evidence. Ultimately the belief rested on laziness, inertia, custom, absence of courage and energy in investigation. The later belief rests upon careful and extensive study, upon purposeful widening of the area of observation, upon reasoning out the conclusions of alternative conceptions to see what would follow in case one or the other were adopted for belief. As distinct from the first kind of thinking there was an orderly chain of ideas; as distinct from the second, there was a controlling purpose and end; as distinct from the third, there was personal examination, scrutiny, inquiry.

Because Columbus did not accept unhesitatingly the current traditional theory, because he doubted and inquired, he arrived at his thought. Skeptical of what, from long habit, seemed most certain, and credulous of what seemed impossible, he went on thinking until he could produce evidence for both his confidence and his disbelief. Even if his conclusion had finally turned out wrong, it would have been a different sort of belief from those it antagonized, because it was reached by a different method. *Active, persistent, and careful consideration of any belief or supposed form of knowledge in the light of the grounds that support it and the further conclusions to which it tends* constitutes reflective thought. Any one of the first three kinds of thought may elicit this type; but once begun, it includes a conscious and voluntary effort to establish belief upon a firm basis of evidence and rationality.

II. THE CENTRAL FACTOR IN THINKING

There are, however, no sharp lines of demarcation between the various operations just outlined. The problem of attaining correct habits of reflection would be much easier than it is, did not the different modes of thinking blend insensibly into one another. So far, we have considered rather extreme instances of each kind in order to get the field clearly before us. Let us now reverse this operation; let us consider a rudimentary case of thinking, lying between careful examination of evidence and a mere irresponsible stream of fancies. A man is walking on a warm day. The sky was clear the last time he observed it; but presently he notes, while occupied primarily with other things, that the air is cooler. It occurs to him that it is probably going to rain; looking up, he sees a dark cloud between him and the sun, and he then quickens his steps. What, if anything, in such a situation can be called thought? Neither the act of walking nor the noting of the cold is a thought. Walking is one direction of activity; looking and noting are other modes of activity. The likelihood that it will rain is, however, something *suggested*. The pedestrian *feels* the cold; first he *thinks* of clouds, then he looks and perceives them, and then he thinks of something he does not see: a storm. This *suggested possibility* is the idea, the thought. If it is believed in as a genuine possibility which may occur, it is the kind of thought whch falls within the scope of knowledge and which requires reflective consideration.

Up to a certain point there is the same sort of situation as when one who looks at a cloud is reminded of a human figure and face. Thinking in both of these cases (the cases of belief and of fancy) involves noting or perceiving a fact, followed by something else that is not observed but that is brought to mind, suggested by the thing seen. One thing reminds us, as we say, of the other. Side by side, however, with this factor of agreement in the two cases of suggestion is a factor of marked disagreement. We do not *believe* in the face suggested by the cloud; we do not consider at all the probability of its being a fact. There is no *reflective* thought. The danger of rain, on the contrary, presents itself to us as a genuine possibility—a fact of the same nature as the observed coolness. Put differently, we do not regard the cloud as meaning or indicating a face, but merely as suggesting it, while we do consider that the coolness may *mean* rain. In the first case, on seeing an object, we just happen, as we say, to think of something else; in the second, we consider the *possibility and nature of the connection between the object seen and the object suggested*. The seen thing is regarded as in some way *the ground or basis of belief* in the suggested thing; it possesses the quality of *evidence*.

This function whereby one thing signifies or indicates another, thus leading us to consider how far the one may be regarded as warrant for belief in the other, is, then, the central factor in all reflective or distinctively intellectual thinking. By calling up various situations to which such terms as *signifies* and *indicates* apply, the student will realize for himself the actual facts denoted. Synonyms for these terms are: points to, tells of, betokens, prognosticates, represents, stands for, implies.[1] We also say one thing portends another, is ominous of another, or a symptom of it, or a key to it, or (if the connection is quite obscure) that it gives a hint, clue, or intimation. Reflection is not identical with the mere fact that one thing indicates, means, another thing. It commences when we

---

[1] *Implies* is more often used when a principle or general truth brings about belief in some other truth; the other phrases are more frequently used to denote the cases in which a fact or event leads us to believe in some other fact or in a law.

begin to inquire into the reliability, the worth, of any particular indication; when we try to test its value and see what guarantee there is that
the existing data *really* point to the idea that is suggested in such a way
as to *justify* acceptance of the latter.

Reflection thus implies that something is believed in (or disbelieved in),
not on its own direct account, but through something else which stands as
witness, evidence, proof, voucher, warrant; that is, as *ground of belief*.
At one time, rain is actually felt or directly experienced; at another time,
we *infer* that it has rained from the appearance of the grass and trees, or
that it is going to rain because of the condition of the air or the state of
the barometer. At one time, we see a man (or suppose we do) without any
intermediary fact; at another time, we are not quite sure what we see, and
hunt for accompanying facts that will serve as signs, indications, tokens
of what we are to believe.

Thinking, for the purposes of this inquiry, is accordingly defined as *that
operation in which present facts suggest other facts (or truths) in such a
way as to induce belief in what is suggested on the ground of real relation
in the things themselves*, a relation between what suggests and what is
suggested. A cloud *suggests* a weasel or a whale; it does not *mean* the
latter, because there is no tie, or bond, in the things themselves between
what is seen and what is suggested. Ashes not merely suggest a previous
fire, but they signify there has been a fire, because ashes are produced by
combustion and, if they are genuine ashes, only by combustion. It is an
objective connection, the link in actual things, that makes one thing the
ground, warrant, evidence, for believing in something else.

III. PHASES OF REFLECTIVE THINKING

We may carry our account further by noting that *reflective* thinking, in
distinction from other operations to which we apply the name of thought,
involves (1) a state of doubt, hesitation, perplexity, mental difficulty, in
which thinking originates, and (2) an act of searching, hunting, inquiring,
to find material that will resolve the doubt, settle and dispose of the
perplexity.

In our illustration, the shock of coolness generated confusion and suspended belief, at least momentarily. Because it was unexpected, it was a
shock or an interruption needing to be accounted for, identified, or placed.
To say that the abrupt occurrence of the change of temperature constitutes a problem may sound forced and artificial; but if we are willing to
extend the meaning of the word *problem* to whatever—no matter how
slight and commonplace in character—perplexes and challenges the mind
so that it makes belief at all uncertain, there is a genuine problem, or
question, involved in an experience of sudden change.

The turning of the head, the lifting of the eyes, the scanning of the
heavens, are activities adapted to bring to recognition facts that will

answer the question presented by the sudden coolness. The facts as they first presented themselves were perplexing; they suggested, however, clouds. The act of looking was an act to discover whether this suggested explanation held good. It may again seem forced to speak of this looking, almost automatic, as an act of research, or inquiry. But once more, if we are willing to generalize our conceptions of our mental operations to include the trivial and ordinary as well as the technical and recondite, there is no good reason for refusing to give this title to the act of looking. For the result of the act is to bring facts before the mind that enable a person to reach a conclusion on the basis of evidence. In so far, then, as the act of looking was deliberate, was performed with the intention of getting an external basis on which to rest a belief, it exemplifies in an elementary way the operation of hunting, searching, inquiring, involved in any reflective operation.

Another instance, commonplace also, yet not quite so trivial, may enforce this lesson. A man traveling in an unfamiliar region comes to a branching of the road. Having no sure knowledge to fall back upon, he is brought to a standstill of hesitation and suspense. Which road is right? And how shall his perplexity be resolved? There are but two alternatives: he must either blindly and arbitrarily take his course, trusting to luck for the outcome, or he must discover grounds for the conclusion that a given road is right. Any attempt to decide the matter by thinking will involve inquiring into other facts, whether brought to mind by memory, or by further observation, or by both. The perplexed wayfarer must carefully scrutinize what is before him and he must cudgel his memory. He looks for evidence that will support belief in favor of either of the roads—for evidence that will weight down one suggestion. He may climb a tree; he may go first in this direction, then in that, looking, in either case, for signs, clues, indications. He wants something in the nature of a signboard or a map, and *his reflection is aimed at the discovery of facts that will serve this purpose.*

The foregoing illustration may be generalized. Thinking begins in what may fairly enough be called a *forked-road* situation, a situation that is ambiguous, that presents a dilemma, that proposes alternatives. As long as our activity glides smoothly along from one thing to another, or as long as we permit our imagination to entertain fancies at pleasure, there is no call for reflection. Difficulty or obstruction in the way of reaching a belief brings us, however, to a pause. In the suspense of uncertainty, we metaphorically climb a tree; we try to find some standpoint from which we may survey additional facts and, getting a more commanding view of the situation, decide how the facts stand related to one another.

Demand for the solution of a perplexity is the steadying and guiding factor in the entire process of reflection. Where there is no question of a problem to be solved or a difficulty to be surmounted, the course of suggestions flows on at random; we have the first type of thought described.

If the stream of suggestions is controlled simply by their emotional congruity, their fitting agreeably into a single picture or story, we have the second type. But a question to be answered, an ambiguity to be resolved, sets up an end and holds the current of ideas to a definite channel. Every suggested conclusion is tested by its reference to this regulating end, by its pertinence to the problem in hand. This need of straightening out a perplexity also controls the kind of inquiry undertaken. A traveler whose end is the most beautiful path will look for other signs and will test suggestions on another basis than if he wishes to discover the way to a given city. *The nature of the problem fixes the end of thought,* and *the end controls the process of thinking.*

IV. SUMMARY

We may recapitulate by saying that the origin of thinking is some perplexity, confusion, or doubt. Thinking is not a case of spontaneous combustion; it does not occur just on "general principles." There is something that occasions and evokes it. General appeals to a child (or a grown-up) to think, irrespective of the existence in his own experience of some difficulty that troubles him and disturbs his equilibrium, are as futile as advice to lift himself by his bootstraps.

Given a difficulty, the next step is suggestion of some way out—the formation of some tentative plan or project, the entertaining of some theory that will account for the peculiarities in question, the consideration of some solution for the problem. The data at hand cannot supply the solution; they can only suggest it. What, then, are the sources of the suggestion? Clearly, past experience and a fund of relevant knowledge at one's command. If the person has had some acquaintance with similar situations, if he has dealt with material of the same sort before, suggestions more or less apt and helpful will arise. But unless there has been some analogous experience, confusion remains mere confusion. Even when a child (or a grown-up) has a problem, it is wholly futile to urge him to think when he has no prior experiences that involve some of the same conditions.

There may, however, be a state of perplexity and also previous experience out of which suggestions emerge, and yet thinking need not be reflective. For the person may not be sufficiently *critical* about the ideas that occur to him. He may jump at a conclusion without weighing the grounds on which it rests; he may forego or unduly shorten the act of hunting, inquiring; he may take the first "answer," or solution, that comes to him because of mental sloth, torpor, impatience to get something settled. One can think reflectively only when one is willing to endure suspense and to undergo the trouble of searching. To many persons both suspense of judgement and intellectual search are disagreeable; they want to get them ended as soon as possible. They cultivate an over-positive and dogmatic habit of mind, or feel perhaps that a condition of doubt will be regarded as evidence of mental inferiority. It is at the point where examination and test enter into investigation that the difference between reflective thought and bad thinking comes in. To be genuinely thoughtful, we must be willing to sustain and protract that state of doubt which is the stimulus to thorough inquiry, so as not to accept an idea or make positive assertion of a belief until justifying reasons have been found.

STUDY QUESTIONS

1. What is the difference between mere "thinking" in the ordinary use of the term and "reflection"? What is the role of doubt in thinking?

2. Why would Columbus' opinion about the shape of the earth have been different in value from earlier opinions, even if it had turned out to be wrong?

3. What part does memory seem to play in the examples given by Dewey?

4. This selection provides an example both of definition and of process. Outline the steps Dewey takes in defining "thinking" and explain the methods he uses. Discuss the factors which make Dewey's explanation of the "phases of reflective thinking" a clear explanation of process.

5. Describe some case in which you found yourself in what Dewey calls a "forked-road situation," and tell how you resolved the problem.

6. Tell how you examined or tested an opinion you had and were forced to change your mind about it. Be sure to take some relatively simple and concrete example, and to tell exactly what facts or ideas led you to your new opinion.

Persuasion by Logical Argument*

Newman and Genevieve Birk

The closely organized logical argument usually follows a basic plan of this kind: (1) The writer or speaker states the question clearly and fairly, defining any terms that might be ambiguous, and limiting the argument to the specific issues which he regards as important; he may in this preliminary step of his argument consider the history of the question and its present significance. (2) He states his position and supports that position by citing facts and authorities, and by reasoning from the evi-

* From *Understanding and Using English* by Newman P. Birk and Genevieve Birk, revised edition, 1958. Copyright, 1958, by The Odyssey Press, Inc. Reprinted by the kind permission of the authors and the publishers.

dence he presents. (3) He recognizes and refutes any outstanding arguments against his ideas. (4) He summarizes his argument and emphasizes the merits of his position or his proposal. Less formal arguments are likely to include these four steps too, but to follow a more personal, less orderly plan.

The writer of convincing argument must have studied his subject thoroughly. He must know exactly what the major issues are, so that he will not waste words in arguing trivial side issues or points on which there is general agreement. He must have not merely facts and authorities to support his position, but trustworthy, representative, up-to-date facts and reputable authorities. He must know his subject well enough to know more than one side of it. Argument, unlike some other kinds of persuasion, assumes opposition; understanding that opposition, being able to concede its strength on some points, but also to demonstrate its weakness on vital points, may be a large part of successful argumentation. In order to see weaknesses in the opposition, and in order to evaluate his own evidence and to arrive at sound conclusions, the writer needs, in addition to knowledge, skill in logical reasoning.

The reader of argument also needs this skill. If he is a critical reader, he will ask two questions about a piece of argumentative prose: Is the evidence good? Is the reasoning sound? In answering the first question he will be helped immeasurably, of course, if he has read and thought about the subject, if he himself has some command of the facts and some acquaintance with the recognized authorities in the field. But without this knowledge he still can make valid judgments about the evidence on which the writer's conclusions are based. He can see how well the writer's statements are substantiated. Some of them may be unsubstantiated, or practically so: "leading scientists agree," or "as psychologists tell us," or "the facts are well known," or "experiments have proved" is not equivalent to quoting scientists, psychologists, facts, or results of specific experiments. Some statements may have unreliable substantiation because the sources are unauthoritative or prejudiced: "the Podunk *Post-Examiner* of April 10, 1958, says . . ."; "the last issue of *Popular Reading* contains an article which settles this issue for all time"; "John Smith's authoritative study [written in 1935] says the last word on college football"; "the *Democratic Digest* gives an impartial account of the political situation." The reader can also recognize the citing of irrelevant authority—Thomas Jefferson, for example, quoted to support an argument against national health insurance; or a famous chemist quoted on old age pensions, or a prominent businessman on modern art. Persons competent in one field are not necessarily authorities in another. Finally, a reader can make some judgment of the evidence by asking himself how much of it there is, and whether the writer seems to have minimized or ignored evidence on the other side.

In answering the second question—Is the reasoning sound?—the reader is aided by a knowledge of logic. Frequently, while reading or listening to argument, one has an elusive sense of illogic in the thinking, a feeling of something's-wrong-but-I-can't-put-my-finger-on-it. A knowledge of the two kinds of logical thinking called *induction* and *deduction,* and of the common errors in logic, called *fallacies,* makes it easier to detect weaknesses in reasoning and also to recognize and to practice sound reasoning.

A. INDUCTION

Induction is the kind of reasoning by which we examine a number of particulars or specific instances and on the basis of them arrive at a conclusion. The scientific method is inductive when the scientist observes a recurrent phenomenon and arrives at the conclusion or hypothesis that under certain conditions this phenomenon will always take place; if in the course of time further observation supports his hypothesis and if no exceptions are observed, his conclusion is generally accepted as truth and is sometimes called a law. In everyday living, too, we arrive at conclusions by induction. Every cat we encounter has claws; we conclude that all cats have claws. Every rose we smell is fragrant; we conclude that all roses are fragrant. An acquaintance has, on various occasions, paid back money he has borrowed; we conclude that he is frequently out of funds but that he pays his debts. Every Saturday morning for six weeks the new paper boy is late in delivering the paper; we conclude that he sleeps on Saturday mornings and we no longer look for the paper before nine o'clock. In each case we have reasoned inductively from a number of instances; we have moved from an observation of some things to a generalization about all things in the same category.

Occasionally, in restricted situations, it is possible to examine every instance. For example, a teacher may note that student A is present in class today, student B is present, C is present, and so on through the whole class list; by simple counting, the teacher can conclude that all members of the class are present today. Ordinarily, though, it is impossible to examine every instance—the claws of every cat, for example, or the nervous system of every cockroach, or every case of diphtheria, or every ruptured appendix, or the opinion of every voter. One must make an inductive jump from the instances he can know to a conclusion embracing things of the same sort that he cannot know. Inductive reasoning arrives, therefore, not at "truth" or "law," but at probability. The probability grows stronger and the induction becomes sounder when a substantial number of instances are examined, when the instances examined are typical, and when the exceptions, if any, are infrequent and explainable.

A conclusion based on too few instances or on untypical instances is called a *hasty generalization.* It is the most common fallacy in inductive reasoning, and is responsible for much misinformation and prejudice: "Negroes are lazy." "Why do you say that?" "Well we had a Negro cook who was the laziest mortal I ever saw, and look at Bob Jones—he doesn't even try to get a job." The speaker is, of course, generalizing on the basis of only two examples, assuming that these examples are typical, and ignoring the countless exceptions. The hasty generalization may also occur in scientific research; further research may reveal exceptions which modify or invalidate the earlier conclusion.

Cause-effect induction is reasoning about why things happen and about the relationship between them. We observe effects and arrive at a conclusion about their cause; or we observe a set of circumstances (causes) and draw a conclusion about their effects; or we observe some effects and reason from them that there will be other effects. A doctor examines a patient, learns his symptoms, and from the data makes a diagnosis; he has started with the effects of the illness and reasoned to the cause of them. In cause-to-effect thinking the process is reversed because we can see the causes and, usually with the help of past inductions, can predict the effects. A student visits football practice two days before the opening game; he observes that two players are fighting on the field, that the captain and the coach are on bad terms, that the team's best passer is on the bench with a broken arm, and that the backfield is slow; seeing these causes, he predicts that this will not be a successful team. Effect-to-effect thinking is chain reasoning which also usually relies on past inductions: "That little accident [cause] smashed the right front fender [observed effect]; Father will be angry and will make me pay for a new fender [further effect reasoned on the basis of past instances]; I won't be able to take Jane to the prom [ultimate effect]."

A great deal of scientific investigation deals with causal relationships; that is, with observing and describing those orderly connections between elements and events in the universe, on the basis of which causes can be assigned and effects predicted with accuracy. In our daily thinking, too, we make numerous cause-effect inductions, many of which, however, lack scientific exactitude; they need to be verified before they can be held as logical conclusions. The following effect-to-cause inductions are fairly typical of the kind of reasoning we hear and perhaps do every day. During a storm, the back door slams with such force that the glass breaks; we assume that the wind blew the door. A friend is obviously depressed on the day grades come out; we say that he is badly disappointed in his grades. An engagement is broken a month after the engaged girl's family loses its money; we conclude that the engagement was broken for that reason. All these inductions need further verification, for the cause in each case may well be different from the one assigned; the door may have been slammed by a member of the family who is happy to have the storm blamed for it; the friend may be depressed and the engagement may have been broken for any number of reasons.

These examples illustrate two common fallacies in cause-effect induction. The first fallacy is oversimplifying, and attributing to a single cause effects which actually have complex causes. "I failed the course because the teacher was unreasonably hard" is sometimes an example of this over-simplification. Other familiar examples are: "The atomic bomb won World War II"; "The Hoover administration was responsible for the de-pression of the nineteen thirties"; "The reason for the high cost of living is the high wages paid to labor."

Often closely related to oversimplification of the cause is the logical fal-lacy of seeing a cause-effect relationship between events which have only an accidental time relationship. This fallacy is called *post hoc ergo prop-ter hoc*, Latin for "after that therefore because of that." A common in-stance of this reasoning is a statement like "I won't vote for the Demo-crats again. Six months after they got into office the city taxes went up two dollars." It is possible, of course, that the Democrats were responsible for the tax increase; but it is also possible that any administration would have found higher taxes necessary. Asserting without proof a cause-effect relationship simply because one event follows another is as illogical as as-serting that breakfast causes lunch. Many superstitions are maintained by this *post hoc ergo propter hoc* thinking. A superstitious person walks under a ladder, and an hour later, for reasons entirely unrelated to that incident, has a quarrel with a good friend; he forgets or ignores the real causes of the quarrel, falls into the logical confusion of after-I-walked-under-the-ladder-therefore-because-I-walked-under-the-ladder, and is confirmed in his original faulty induction that walking under ladders brings bad luck.

Induction by analogy occurs when one observes that two things are sim-ilar in some ways, and then reasons, from the observed likenesses, that they are also similar in other ways. For example, Sir Isaac Newton ob-served that certain combustible substances—oils, turpentine, camphor, etc. —had refractive powers two or three times greater than might be expected from their densities. He reasoned by analogy that the diamond, with its very high refractive powers, was also combustible. This inference was correct.

Reasoning from analogy is dangerous, however, and argument by analogy alone is seldom convincing, because analogous situations or ob-jects have differences as well as similarities and the differences may out-weigh the similarities. Sir David Brewster, a nineteenth-century physicist and biographer of Sir Isaac Newton, pointed out that if Newton had rea-soned from analogy the combustibility of greenockite and octahedrite, which also have high refractive powers, he would have been wrong. His reasoning about the diamond simply happened to be right. Long observa-tion of Mars has given astronomers a body of data from which they have arrived inductively at a number of conclusions about that planet. Some people have reasoned by analogy that since Mars has atmosphere, tem-peratures, and seasonal changes comparable to earth's, it must also have life like ours. This conclusion is questionable; it disregards the observed differences between the two planets.

Analogy is not logical proof. In informative writing it is, as we have said earlier, a useful method of clarifying a difficult subject. Skillful analogy also has great persuasive power. But it should be used in conjunction with, not as a substitute for, more strictly logical reasoning; and it is effective only when the similarities are striking and the differences slight between the things being compared. The following induction by analogy is weak because the comparison is far-fetched and the differences are glaring:

Even the most durable machines break down if they are worked constantly for long periods of time. Their parts wear out; they become inefficient. Are students supposed to be stronger than machines? Do they deserve less attention and care? We should have shorter assignments and longer vacations.

The following famous passage illustrates effective analogy. The comparison is used not to prove, but to describe and to persuade:

In the field of world policy I would dedicate this Nation to the policy of the good neighbor—the neighbor who resolutely respects himself and because he does so, respects the rights of others—the neighbor who respects his obligations and respects the sanctity of his agreements in and with a world of neighbors.—Franklin D. Roosevelt, *First Inaugural Address.*

B. DEDUCTION

Inductive reasoning, as we have seen, moves from individual circumstances or instances to a conclusion; this conclusion, unless every possible instance has been examined, expresses probability; the probability is as strong as the weight of evidence which supports it. Deduction is reasoning from stated propositions or premises to a conclusion. If the conclusion follows logically from the premises and if the premises are true, deduction arrives at proof or certainty.

All men are mortal.
John is a man.
Therefore John is mortal.

The statement above is a *syllogism*, the pattern in which, in formal logic, a deductive argument is expressed. The syllogism consists of three statements—two premises and a conclusion. It contains three and only three main terms, each of which appears twice, but not twice in the same statement. The terms are given these names: the *major term* is the predicate of the conclusion; the *minor term* is the subject of the conclusion; and the *middle term* appears in both premises. The major term in the syllogism above is "mortal," and the premise in which it appears is called the *major premise*. The minor term is "John," and the premise in which it appears is called the *minor premise*. The middle term, "man/men," appears in both premises.

Diagramming the syllogism sometimes makes the relationship of statements clearer:

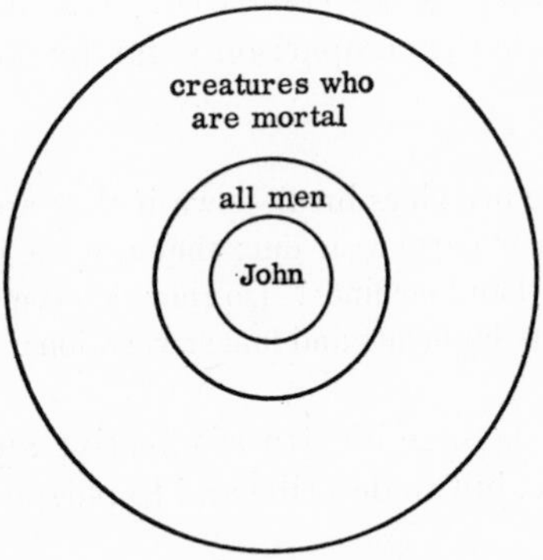

If all men are included in the larger group of mortal things (major premise), and if John is included in the group of all men (minor premise), then John is inevitably included in the group of those who are mortal (conclusion).

There are four patterns of the syllogism, in which the terms have different positions. In the following examples, the middle term (the term which appears in both premises) is printed in capital letters to show its position in the four patterns or "figures" of the syllogism:

Figure 1:   All DOGS are carnivorous.
           My cocker is a DOG.
           Therefore my cocker is carnivorous.

Figure 2:   No thief CAN BE TRUSTED.
           All good men CAN BE TRUSTED.
           Therefore no good men are thieves.

Figure 3:   Every COLLEGE STUDENT has great opportunities.
           Some COLLEGE STUDENTS are poor.
           Therefore some poor people have great opportunities.

Figure 4:   Most people devote themselves to MATERIAL GAIN.
           MATERIAL GAIN is not a worthy goal in life.
           Therefore most people do not devote themselves to a worthy goal in life.

When a syllogism has any of these four relationships between terms and between premises and conclusion, its argument is said to be *valid*. It is worth noting here that a "valid" argument is not necessarily *factually true.* For example, for some readers, the conclusions in the second and fourth syllogism above will seem untrue because one or both of the two premises seem untrue. Perhaps the point will be clearer if we look at more obvious examples:

Major premise: All Irishmen have hot tempers.
Minor premise: He is Irish.
Conclusion: Therefore he is hot tempered.

Major premise: Poisonous snakes should be killed.
Minor premise: Garter snakes are poisonous.
Conclusion: Therefore garter snakes should be killed.

These two arguments are "valid" because they have the logical form of Figure 1 of the syllogism. However, the conclusions are unreliable because the major premise of the first syllogism is a hasty generalization, and the minor premise of the second syllogism is a misstatement of fact. In judging the truth or reliability of a deductive argument, one must ask two questions: Are the premises true? Is the argument valid? If the answer to both questions is "yes," the deduction can be accepted as true.[1]

C. FALLACIES

We have mentioned earlier the common fallacies in inductive reasoning: hasty generalization, oversimplification of complex causes, *post hoc ergo propter hoc* argument, and faulty analogy. The most common fallacies in deductive argument come from the faulty relationship of parts of the syllogism. Such fallacies sometimes produce a slippery illogic in the reasoning, difficult to detect. For example, in the first figure of the syllogism illustrated on page 154, the subject of the major premise is the predicate of the minor premise; the form of the syllogism is *All X is Y; Z is X; therefore Z is Y.* In the following syllogism of the same pattern, the terms are shifted:

All tigers are felines. (*X is Y*)
My cat is a feline. (*Z is Y*)
Therefore my cat is a tiger. (∴ *Z is X*)

The illogic here is made apparent by the absurdity of the conclusion; but it may not be so apparent in a similarly constructed syllogism:

[1] True premises and a valid argument can produce only a true conclusion. Untrue premises, as we have seen, can produce questionable or untrue conclusions. But it may be worth noting that a conclusion may happen to be true even though it is drawn from false premises: All cats are birds; all pigeons are cats; therefore all pigeons are birds. The conclusion here is true for reasons other than those stated in the premises.

All communists say Russia doesn't want war.
He says Russia doesn't want war.
Therefore he is a communist.

Diagramming such arguments is a good way of seeing why they are invalid:

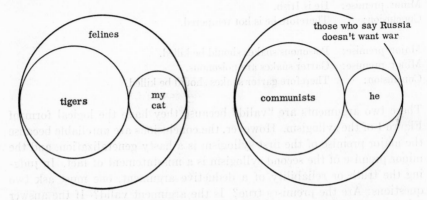

My cat and *he* are in the large circles of *felines* and *those who say Russia doesn't want war*, but not necessarily in the smaller circles of *tigers* and *communists*. There is no established relationship between the terms (tigers and my cat; communists and he) except the fact that they are both members of a larger group.

Another fallacy is in conclusions drawn from negative premises. If one premise is negative, the conclusion must be negative in a valid argument; if both premises are negative, no conclusion can be drawn.

Valid: All those attending the meeting are freshmen.
          John is not a freshman.
          Therefore John is not attending the meeting.

Invalid: No freshmen are attending the meeting.
          John is not a freshman.
          Therefore John is attending the meeting.

No conclusion can be drawn from the last two negative premises; John may or may not be attending the meeting.

In a valid argument, the conclusion follows inevitably from the premises. *Non-sequitur* (Latin for "it does not follow") is the fallacy of leaping to a conclusion not warranted by the premises. Drawing a conclusion from negative premises is one form of *non-sequitur*. Other examples are:

Anyone who works hard deserves a vacation now and then.
I work hard.
Therefore my parents should give me a trip to Bermuda.

Men who have made sacrifices for their country should be honored.
I have made sacrifices for my country.
Therefore I should be President.

The faults in the two preceding syllogisms are closely related to another fallacy of logical relationship—*the shifting of the meaning of terms between the major and the minor premise.* The shifted meaning is equivalent to a fourth term in the syllogism. For example:

Man is the only creature capable of reason.
Mary is not a man.
Therefore Mary is incapable of reason.

The meaning of *man* has been shifted from *mankind* in the major premise to *male* in the minor premise. Other examples of shifted meanings are:

Men who have devoted themselves to the service of the community should hold public office.
I have devoted myself to the service of the community by running a bakery for fifteen years.
Therefore I should hold public office.

Government employees who are sympathetic with Russian policy should be discharged.
This government employee belonged in 1943 to an organization which was friendly toward Russia.
Therefore he should be discharged.

We seldom encounter the complete syllogism except in discussions of logic and in very formal argument. More usual is a reduced form of the syllogism in which one or two of the three parts, though implied, are not stated. The reduced syllogism is called an *enthymeme.* Sometimes in the enthymeme the conclusion of the syllogism is omitted because it is obvious: *Students who are found cheating on examinations fail the course; Clarence has been found cheating on an examination;* [the obvious omitted conclusion: therefore Clarence will fail the course]. Sometimes the minor premise is omitted for the same reason: *I like candidates who speak their minds; I'm going to vote for you* [omitted premise: you speak your mind]; Sometimes both the minor premise and the conclusion are omitted because the major premise adequately communicates them: *I date only men who have cars;* [omitted: you don't have a car; therefore I won't have a date with you]. Most frequently the major premise is omitted because the communicator assumes (often wrongly) that it is universally accepted and so does not require proof or even statement. One of the most useful skills of the hearer or reader of argument, therefore, is the ability to supply the omitted major premise. By recognizing that premise and examining it critically, he can better judge the reliability of the argument. The enthymemes below are familiar informal arguments; the major premise on which each one is based is put in brackets.

Jim must have been in a fight; he has a black eye. [Major premise: All black eyes are the result of fights.]

So he forgot he made the appointment. What can you expect? He's a college professor. [Major premise: College professors usually forget appointments. *Or,* College professors are absent-minded.]

He must be a grind! He got all A's last semester. [Students who get A records are grinds.]

He can't be a good doctor. He's in favor of socialized medicine. [No good doctor is in favor of socialized medicine.]

You're crazy, saying the meat tastes spoiled. I got it at the store just an hour ago. [Meat is always fresh when it is bought at stores.]

What a coward. He's a conscientious objector, you know. [All conscientious objectors are cowards.]

Naturally he's a delinquent. He reads ten comic books a week. [Reading comics always produces delinquency.]

Of course it's true; I read it in the paper. [Everything printed in the newspapers is true.]

They won't be happy together; he's two years younger than she. [Marriages are always unhappy if the man is younger than the woman.]

I think they'll be very nice neighbors. They have a new Cadillac. [People are nice neighbors if tney have a new Cadillac.]

We're not talking about the same girl. The one I knew last summer had blond hair. [Once a blonde always a blonde.]

His mother has trained him to be neat around the house; he'll make a wonderful husband. [Any man who is neat around the house is a wonderful husband; also, a man trained by his mother to be neat around the house will continue to be neat when he is married.]

Two other logical fallacies, not peculiar to induction or to deduction, but involving the quality of the whole argument, are *begging the question* and *ignoring the question*.

Begging the question is assuming, without proof, the truth of a proposition which actually needs proof. If an arguer says, "This senseless language requirement should be abolished," he is, with the word *senseless*, begging the question; the question is whether or not the language requirement is senseless; if it is, it should of course be abolished; simply calling it senseless is not a logical argument in its disfavor. "This corrupt political machine should be replaced by good government" is another example of begging the question. No proof is offered that the government under attack is a "corrupt political machine," or that the government supported by the speaker will be "good." Both propositions are simply assumed. *Arguing in a circle* is one form of begging the question:

People who are poor lack ambition because if they didn't lack ambition they wouldn't be poor.

The study of literature is worthwhile because literature is a worthwhile subject.

Such argument in a circle is sometimes baffling, particularly when the argument is long and the circular motion is therefore difficult to detect. What the arguer in a circle does, technically, is offer as proof of his first proposition a second proposition which can be proved only by proving the first.

Ignoring the question is diverting attention from the real issues, or shifting the argument to some other ground. It has many forms. Name-calling, introducing irrelevant facts, and using other devices of charged language may be means of ignoring the real question. Sometimes a new argument is introduced in an effort to obscure the original issue: "I told you, Dorothy, I can't afford to buy you a coat this winter." "I don't see why not. Susan Jones has a new coat. I should think you'd want me to be well dressed. It's a good thing someone in this family takes some pride in appearance. You haven't even shaved today." Arguing that an accused murderess should be acquitted because she is the mother of three children, and that a candidate should be mayor because he is a veteran of two wars are examples of ignoring the question by shifting from the central issues; the questions here are "Did she commit the murder?" and "Will he make a good mayor?" What is called argument *ad hominem* (to the man) is a way of ignoring the question by a shift from reasonable consideration of a measure to an attack on the character of the opponent; his ancestry, his religion, the fact that his first wife divorced him, that his son was arrested for speeding, etc. may be introduced to appeal to prejudice while the real question—the merits and defects of the measure itself— is ignored.

D. THE TEXTURE OF LOGICAL THOUGHT

Although we have separated induction and deduction for purposes of discussion, the two processes work together in most acts of reasoning. A simple illustration of the interplay between them is this: A friend asks you one afternoon to go with him to a movie at the neighborhood theatre. You say, "No; it's Saturday." Behind your refusal lies an induction, based on instances in your own experience, that on Saturday afternoons many school children attend this theatre and are very noisy. You make a quick deduction: Every Saturday afternoon this theatre is full of noisy school children; this is Saturday; therefore the theatre will be full of noisy school children. Another inductive-deductive process also takes place. You have arrived at the generalization that you do not enjoy a movie if you cannot hear all of it. You reason: I do not want to go to a movie if I cannot hear all of it; I will not be able to hear all of it today (because of the noise of the children); therefore I do not want to go to this movie on this day. Still another reasoning process about your relationship with the friend who has asked you to go to the movie may occur. From your past experience with him you may have induced: Jack is not offended if for some good reason I refuse his invitations. Now you may deduce: I am refusing this invitation for a good reason; therefore Jack will not be offended. In this kind of thinking, the inductions and deductions are almost automatic. In more complex reasoning they are formulated only after conscious and disciplined thought.

We have said earlier that induction is important in scientific thinking: it enables human beings to arrive at generalizations and hypotheses about the world they live in, to see cause-effect relationships, and, on the basis of established probabilities, to make predictions and produce effects by controlling causes. As a science advances and its inductive hypotheses are further substantiated, the substantiated hypotheses supply premises from which deductive conclusions are drawn. One kind of reasoning leads to, supports, and leads back to the other. In the same way, in a logical argument, observed instances have perhaps led the speaker or writer inductively to the position he takes in the argument. From his inductions he may reason deductively about what should be done in a particular situation.

Closely interwoven though the two kinds of reasoning are, it is useful to have some knowledge of their differences, of the different kinds of reliability they can arrive at, and of the common fallacies in each kind of thinking. Being able to reduce a confusing argument to syllogistic form will enable one to see more clearly its premises and its validity. Being alert to hasty generalization, to faulty cause-effect reasoning, to conclusions which do not follow the premises, to question-begging and to ignoring the question will help one judge the soundness of an argument. A knowledge of the processes of reasoning, in short, provides instruments of analysis with which one can better examine the texture of his own argument and the arguments of others.

E. TONE

In persuasion by logical argument, the writer may be formal or informal in his attitude toward his audience; but he is usually less concerned with getting their liking than with winning their respect. For this respect, he depends largely on the quality of the argument itself. If he presents the issues fairly; if he is reasonable in considering opposing points of view; if his evidence is good and his thinking clear and sound; if he respects the intelligence of his audience and assumes that they will not be convinced by slippery illogic and devices like arguments *ad hominem*, he will almost certainly gain a respectful hearing for what he has to say.

As a rule, the most skillful argument is reasonable in tone as well as in thought; it gives the impression of trying to arrive at truth, not merely to win a case; it is good tempered, and free from dogmatism and conceit. Fighting-mad arguments and dogmatic statements do sometimes affect already-sympathetic or prejudiced audiences; but they are likely to alienate and offend an impartial audience. Benjamin Franklin, wise in argument and diplomacy, wrote in his autobiography:

I made it a rule to forbear all direct contradiction to the sentiments of others, and all positive assertion of my own. I even forbade myself . . . the use of every word or expression in the language that imported a fix'd opinion, such as *certainly, undoubtedly*, etc., and I adopted, instead of them, *I conceive, I apprehend*, or *I imagine* a thing to be so or so; or it *so appears to me at present*. When another asserted something that I thought an error, I deny'd myself the pleasure of contradicting him abruptly, and of showing immediately some absurdity in his proposition; and in answering I began by observing that in certain cases of circumstances his opinion would be right, but in the present case there *appear'd* or *seem'd* to me some difference, etc. I soon found the advantage of this change in my manner; the conversations I engag'd in went on more pleasantly. The modest way in which I propos'd my opinions procur'd them a readier reception and less contradiction; I had less mortification when I was found to be in the wrong, and I more easily prevail'd with others to give up their mistakes and join with me when I happened to be in the right.

And this mode, which I at first put on with some violence to natural inclination, became at length so easy, and so habitual to me, that perhaps for these fifty years past no one has ever heard a dogmatical expression escape me. And to this habit (after my character of integrity) I think it principally owing that I had early so much weight with my fellow-citizens when I proposed new institutions, or alterations in the old, and so much influence in public councils when I became a member; for I was but a bad speaker, never eloquent, subject to much hesitation in my choice of words, hardly correct in language, and yet I generally carried my points.

STUDY QUESTIONS

1. What, according to the authors, are the steps in formal logical argument? How does such argument differ from other kinds of persuasion? What questions will the critical reader of argument ask himself?

2. Define "induction" and "deduction." What are the strengths and weaknesses of each of these? How often will you find one or the other used exclusively? In what kinds of writing will you find the heaviest reliance upon induction? Upon deduction?

3. What four factors determine the validity of deductive reasoning? Define and give two or three examples of the enthymeme other than those examples in the text.

4. List the fallacies of reasoning which the authors define and be prepared to cite an example of each from your reading or from arguments in which you have engaged with your friends.

5. Set down in outline form the steps of an argument on some controversial issue. Then write a paper, filling in this outline with the necessary details or explanations to make it an effective piece of writing.

6. Examine one or more editorials in a newspaper or magazine, being on the watch for the kinds of fallacies which the Birks have discussed. Write a paper defining and illustrating the fallacies which appear, and evaluating the editorials in the light of your findings.

Of Matters of Taste and Opinion*

Lionel Ruby

We have been engaged in analyzing matters of logic and science. In science, we all agree, statements must be proved by evidence. In physics and chemistry, certainly, scientific laws are not just "matters of opinion." A successful laboratory test is something quite definite and convincing. The law court, too, requires proof. In a criminal trial the evidence must prove a man guilty "beyond a reasonable doubt." There may be differences of opinion concerning some verdicts—miscarriages of justice occurring in acquittals as well as in convictions—but the rule is that it is the evidence that counts. Most cases would be decided in the same way by the ultimate criterion of the law court: the judgment of the "reasonable man." In the social sciences, too, we try to get beyond matters of mere opinion. Carefully tabulated statistics tell us what per-

* From *The Art of Making Sense* by Lionel Ruby. Copyright 1954 by Lionel Ruby. Published by J. B. Lippincott Company.

centage of paroled convicts will probably "go straight" thereafter, within a given "margin of error."

We agree that logic is relevant in questions concerning facts, for these questions involve evidence and proof. There is an important class of statements, however, which we have not yet examined. These are "value judgments," which many people regard as exempt from the requirement of proof. Examples: "Shakespeare was a great poet." "It is morally wrong for a judge to take a bribe." A value judgment asserts that something is either good or bad in an *aesthetic* or a *moral* sense. This restriction means that we shall not refer to the purely technical sense of good (or bad) in this discussion, as when we speak of "a good automobile tire" (one that will run a long distance), or "a good repair job." Value judgments, then, are statements such as "X is beautiful" (possessing aesthetic excellence) or "X is morally right." Value judgments obviously refer also to statements that things are ugly or that actions are morally wrong.

Value judgments are usually contrasted with "factual statements," which make assertions about events that can be observed in the world of space and time. By a factual statement we do not necessarily mean a true statement. A factual statement, in the sense in which we use this term, refers to one that is *about* facts. Factual statements are true or false, for they may describe the facts correctly or incorrectly. "The Tribune Tower in Chicago is higher than the Leaning Tower of Pisa" is a factual type of statement. So also is "The Leaning Tower is higher than the Tribune Tower." "The Tribune Tower is more beautiful than the Leaning Tower," on the other hand, is a value judgment.

Now, there is general agreement that it is possible to specify the kind of evidence which would prove factual statements true or false, but many people think that value judgments are incapable of proof. Value judgments, it is said, are "mere matters of opinion." It is important to note the precise sense in which this ambiguous phrase is meant. An "opinion" sometimes means a judgment that has a certain measure of probability, but not certainty, as when a man says that lower tariffs will make us more prosperous. When the evidence is conflicting, as in a case of this kind, we may speak of "legitimate differences of opinion." Some opinions in this sense may be true, and others false. When people say that value judgments are *mere* matters of opinion, on the other hand, they usually mean "a matter of personal feeling or preference," or a "matter of taste." When we qualify the word "opinion" by *mere* in this discussion, this is the view to which we refer. According to this view, value judgments are incapable of proof and outside the realm of logical or scientific criticism.

If the "mere opinion" point of view is correct, then one value judgment is "as good as another" and proof is not only impossible but irrelevant. (We use the word "proof" here to include the presentation of evidence which might show that one judgment was at least nearer the truth than another.) If one value judgment is as incapable of justification as another, then reason and intelligence are irrelevant in the discussion of such matters. In this chapter we shall endeavor to show that logic *is* relevant in the discussion of value judgments as well as in the realm of scientific or "factual" statements. We shall first discuss the theory which holds that value judgments are incapable of logical or scientific justification. We shall then discuss the sense in which logic is relevant.

There is an ancient adage which tells us that "of matters of taste there is no disputing." This is sensible advice. If you prefer the light meat of turkey and I prefer the dark, this establishes a basis for harmony such as prevailed in the famous Spratt family, and it would seem fruitless to argue the question as to which *really* tastes better. We may grant that it is impossible to prove that the taste of black caviar is superior to that of red, even though most "epicures" prefer the former. Some people would even argue that it is a fact, not a "matter of taste," that French cuisine is superior to English cooking, but mankind has wisely decided that these are matters that *ought* not to be disputed. But how far, and to what kinds of things, can this principle be applied? "Matter of taste" is frequently used for things other than gustatory flavors. It often covers individual preferences and likes or dislikes in the arts as well, and it is sometimes held that ethical judgments are matters of taste. Let us examine the "taste theory" as applied in the fields of aesthetics and ethics.

No logical problem arises when one says that he prefers the sound of a piano to that of a violin, or when he says *"I prefer* Tchaikovsky to Brahms." He is merely describing his personal taste. The interesting problem for logic arises when he says, "Tchaikovsky is a better composer than Brahms," or "Tchaikovsky's symphonies are more beautiful than those of Brahms." Some literary critics regard *Gone With the Wind* as a second-rate novel, despite its phenomenal popularity all over the world, and there are professors of English literature who say that Joyce Kilmer's "Trees" is bad poetry. Are these judgments true, or false, or *neither?* The "taste" theory holds that they are neither. When we assert value judgments of this kind, the taste theory tells us, we mean nothing more than "this is my preference," so the matter is not an arguable one. "X is beautiful," this theory tells us, means nothing more than "I like X," and "X is better than Y" means only "I prefer X to Y." If we grant that the speaker is telling the truth, and not lying about his actual preference, that is an end of the matter.

Is there no disputing "matters of taste" in the arts? In practice, of course, we do dispute such matters. The word "taste" is often used in a sense other than "personal preference": for "keenness of discernment, or insight." Immanuel Kant, in one of his rare flashes of humor, once played on the double meaning of "taste" when he said: "Art is a matter of taste, but there is no point in arguing matters of taste with the tasteless." Even when a person says that he prefers Tchaikovsky to Brahms, a Brahmsian is apt to accuse him of having a perverse taste. The Brahmsian believes that a person of "genuine" taste will prefer Brahms to Tchaikovsky. But most of us believe that *some* value judgments involve facts, rather than matters of mere opinion. We may agree that it is impossible to prove that Brahms is a better composer than Tchaikovsky, or vice versa—that such judgments are matters of mere opinion. But suppose I say that Ezio Pinza sings more beautifully than at least one man who lives in the state of South Dakota, or that Pinza is not the worst singer of all time. These last judgments, we may say, are facts. This indicates that we believe that there are standards of merit in the arts and that *some* value judgments are not mere matters of personal opinion or preference. In at least some cases, then, most of us would reject the view that "X is beautiful" can be translated into "I like X." Semantically, it appears, this translation does not satisfy what we *mean* by "beauty."

Similar considerations apply to the taste theory in the field of ethics. Let us first contrast a factual statement with a value judgment in ethics. "It is illegal to serve liquor to women at bars in the State of Indiana" is a statement of fact, which happens to be true. We can verify this statement by looking up the law. "Women ought not to sit at bars" is a value judgment which asserts that such conduct is morally wrong. The taste theory holds that this value judgment cannot be proved true (or false); that it means nothing more than "I don't like to see women sitting at bars." But again, this seems to be an inadequate translation of our meaning. When we say, "It would be wrong to abolish freedom of speech" we usually mean that we wouldn't like it, but we also mean much more than that. Consciously or unconsciously we carry in our minds a definition of "wrong"—a standard of what is right and wrong—and when we say that it would be wrong to abolish freedom of speech we mean that such an action has characteristics and consequences which permit its classification under our conception of "wrongful actions." The semantic translation of "wrong" into "I dislike it" seems to be an inadequate translation of our *meaning*. We dislike all sorts of things we don't consider morally wrong: inappropriate color combinations, for example. When we say "evil" we usually dislike the thing referred to, but we may also dislike a righteous man. Before we discuss further what we do mean, however, let us consider a second kind of translation of value judgments.

This second theory, which holds that value judgments cannot be logically supported or justified, is the "approval theory." This theory tells us that judgments concerning right and wrong can be translated into, "My group approves or disapproves." This view is usually associated with the doctrine of "ethical relativism." * The relativist holds that nothing is always right or wrong, but that these terms are relative to time, place, and

* "Relativism" is a vague word. We may mean "relative to the individual," "to a social group," or "to the human race as a whole." In this discussion we refer to the most common type of the doctrine: group relativism.

circumstance. The relativist is impressed by the great variety of contrary customs in different parts of the world. Monogamy is customary in western countries; polygyny in Arab countries; and in some places polyandry is the custom. Polygyny, the relativist says, is morally wrong in the United States but right in Saudi Arabia. What one country considers right, another considers wrong. What a single nation considers right at one time it considers wrong at another time. The relativist quotes Pascal:

> Three degrees of latitude reverse all jurisprudence; a meridian decides the truth. Fundamental laws change after a few years of possession; right has its epochs. . . . A strange justice that is bounded by a river! Truth on this side of the Pyrenees, error on the other side.

When we say that polygyny is morally right in Arabia, the group-approval theory says, we mean that the Arabians *approve* of this matrimonial system; when we say it is morally wrong here, we mean that the Americans disapprove. When we say they approve, we say it is morally right for them; when we say we disapprove we mean it is morally wrong for us. "Right" and "wrong," then, depend on local customs.

This theory has an appealing plausibility when we consider the variable customs throughout the world. It appears presumptuous for one nation to tell another that its customs are "immoral." It would be too easy to return the compliment. But the group-approval theory also seems quite inadequate as a reflection of what we *mean* by right and wrong. If group approval *makes* an action right then it would be nonsensical, if not meaningless, to say: "I think this action is wrong, but I am in a minority." For "wrong" can have no meaning in this remark if the approval of the majority *makes* the action right. But does anyone seriously believe that the majority can never be mistaken in its judgment about right and wrong?

Let us sum up our discussion thus far. Our problem: Are all value judgments unprovable matters of opinion? We have discussed two "translations" of aesthetic and moral judgments. We noted that genuine expressions of preference are not disputable, in the sense that a statement of personal preference requires no further evidence to support it. If value judgments were no more than expressions of likes and dislikes then they too would not be disputable. An interesting consequence confronts the follower of the taste theory: He must admit that there never has been and that there never will be a genuine dispute over morality, but only "verbal" disputes. For if one man asserts that the police are justified in using "third degree" methods to extort confessions (meaning: he likes it), and another says that such methods are morally wrong (meaning: he dislikes it), there is really no dispute between them. When one man means "I like it," and another means "I don't like it," there isn't any real disagreement, any more than there is when I say I like whipped cream in coffee and you say you don't.

The approval theory also makes moral discussion impossible. All we can say is: Take a "Gallup poll"; find out who has the votes. If fifty-one per cent vote "wrong" then it *is* wrong. But "This has the vote of the majority" seems quite different from saying, "This is morally right." We must obey the laws, of course, but we may consider a law morally wrong and seek to change it by legal procedures. Legality is not necessarily the same thing as morality.

If the approval theory were correct, furthermore, then the following consequences would have to be accepted: A country behind the Iron Curtain denies freedom and minority rights to its citizens, it enslaves millions, puts political dissenters to the torture rack, and decrees that the children's children of these dissenters shall be denied political and civil rights. If the majority of the people in that country should approve of these actions, the approval theory tells us, then these things become morally right in that country. But is the only relevant question here: Do the majority approve? Would the abolition of the freedom of religious worship in the United States be right if fifty-one percent approved? Is the morality of such a matter determined by making an accurate count of the votes?

The taste and approval theories, then, make logical discussion irrelevant in value judgments. We have seen that these theories are inadequate translations of our meanings. Nevertheless, these theories do contain real insights into the nature of value judgments, for there *is* a sense in which logic is irrelevant in such judgments. But—and this is the basic weakness of these theories—they ignore the sense in which logic is relevant. The senses in which logic is relevant and irrelevant in value judgments are harmonized by the "value-standard theory."

Let us consider a problem in ethics. Ought we to legalize gambling? My first reaction may be, "Yes, I don't see why not. Let people gamble if they wish to," or "No, gambling is wrong." But there is a counterpart of the "law of rationality" in the field of values. The law of rationality tells us that we ought to justify our beliefs by evidence and reasons, instead of asserting them dogmatically. Similarly, if I am a reflective person, I will seek to justify my value judgments. I will think about my reasons for approving or disapproving of gambling, instead of saying, "I like (or dislike) gambling," or "The community approves (or disapproves) of gambling." I ought to consider the logical consequences of my choice. My thinking may proceed along the following lines: "It is impossible to suppress the human desire to gamble. If this desire is denied a legal outlet it will find an illegal one. Illegal gambling funnels vast sums of money into the hands of undesirable elements in the community, and gives these elements great power. They corrupt the police force and may even control the political machines in our great cities." These considerations make me lean toward legalization. Now I consider the other side: "If gambling is legalized it may become respectable to gamble, and many more people may take to this vice. It is also possible that undesirable elements may manage to obtain control of legalized gambling."

Implicit in my thinking about this problem is the notion that the "public good" ought to be served. If I finally decide that, considering all the consequences, we ought to legalize gambling, I may justify my decision in some such fashion as this: "We ought to promote the general welfare. This duty requires us to choose the greater of two possible goods, or the lesser of two evils. The consequences that will follow from the legalization of gambling will, on the whole, diminish the general welfare less than the alternatives. Therefore we ought to legalize gambling." This is a "logical proof" of a value judgment. My major premise is a value standard which I *assume* as a basis for value decisions. My minor premise is a factual assertion to the effect that legalized gambling will diminish the general welfare least. ("General welfare," of course, is a term whose minimal meaning connotes freedom *and* respect for law, and I must define it in any actual discussion.) I then arrive at my conclusion.

Similarly, if I say that "government regulation of newspapers is wrong," I ought to define what I mean by "wrong" in terms of a value standard. I should make my value standard explicit—whatever that value standard may be. I should then show how my standard applies to the matter of government regulation. If by "wrong" I mean "that which diminishes the general welfare," I must show how regulation will have that effect.

The value-standard analysis of value judgments makes logical discussion possible. A discussion of the legalization of gambling is not only a legitimate procedure but very useful when each disputant accepts the same value standard. Public discussion of such questions helps to clarify the consequences that follow from one or another course of action and thus leads to a thoughtful decision. Most value disputes, actually, involve disagreements concerning the appropriate means to mutually accepted ends. This is of course not necessarily the case: Some may have standards other than that of the general good, and not everyone who says that he seeks the general good actually does. Some may pay lip service to this standard, but belie their acceptance by their actual behavior. "Hypocrisy," as La Rochefoucauld said, "is the homage which vice pays to virtue."

Value judgments, then, can be justified in terms of standards. But the question may now be raised: Can the *standards* be justified by logical reasoning? The answer is Yes—up to a point. If I say that the compulsory arbitration of labor-management disputes is wrong because "this would violate the principle of free enterprise," I have used the principle of free-enterprise (a standard) to justify a value judgment. I may be able to justify the standard of free enterprise in terms of a more basic standard, such as the "general welfare." But I may not be able to justify this basic standard. Basic standards may not themselves be capable of justification. Every value judgment finally rests on premises, or reasons,

or assumptions that we cannot prove, but which we simply accept—
though we may not ourselves be aware of the assumptions we are making.
This is the insight of the taste theory, that *basic standards* cannot be provided by logic. Our differences with the taste theory, however, are many.
The taste theory ignores the use of standards; it ignores the fact that
most differences of opinion presuppose mutually accepted standards and
that discussion may thus turn disagreement into agreement; and "liking"
is hardly the word for our acceptance of our basic standards. The basic
standards are in the nature of personal commitments to a way of life,
rather than likings or dislikings. And one more word concerning our basic
standards. We ought never to consider these standards exempt from discussion, for no standard is absolutely final. As an individual develops in
maturity he may see beyond his present "ultimates."

We have noted a basic insight of the taste theory. Similarly, the relativistic approval theory has the insight that time, place, and circumstance
alter cases; that different customs may be equally right, depending on
the histories, traditions, and circumstances of life in different countries,
and that we ought not to judge other countries by a blind application of
the standards that happen to prevail in our own. These insights are accepted by the value standard theory. The difference between the two
theories may best be brought out by an example.

The "untouchable" taboo in India is probably approved by the majority of the Indian people. According to the approval theory, if the
people of a foreign country approve of a custom then that custom must
be right *for them*. It is thus not only improper for us to criticize the Indians for their caste system, but it must also be wrong for *Indians* to
criticize, for the mere fact of approval makes the system morally right in
India. The present government in India, however, seeks to abolish this
system. The Nehru government obviously does not accept the approval
theory. It believes that the system is wrong *in India* because it believes
that the outcast system diminishes the general welfare of the Indians, or
because it violates the principle that every human being should be treated
as an end-in-himself, and never as a mere means to an end.

To many, it would seem outrageous to condemn the Nehru government
for seeking to abolish untouchability. If we believe that the Nehru government is right, then we do not accept the approval theory. And if Indian critics of untouchability are at least logically justified in their
criticism of the system, then it is logically permissible for Americans to
join in these criticisms, at least on the same grounds as those used by
Nehru. It is of course an extremely complex and difficult problem to
decide whether a given custom is right or wrong. In judging untouchability we must consider the history of India, its traditions, religion and
customs of life, and we should also consider the adequacy of the standard
we employ in making our value judgment. But these are matters open
to logical discussion.

Approval theorists are of course seldom consistent in applying their theory. This inconsistency indicates that most approval theorists do not themselves really believe that it is approval alone that makes an action right. They, too, assume that there are reasons for value judgments. They may say that polygyny must be right in a particular community "because the people approve of this custom." But if we ask them: *"Why* do the people approve?" we may get an answer something like this: "Large numbers of men were killed off in constant wars, or in dangerous occupations like seal-hunting, and this resulted in a 'surplus' of women." A reason of this kind, however, indicates that this community judged polygyny right because it was thought desirable for the general good, and this is the use of a standard. Anthropologists, indeed, tell us that most customs are based on the necessity (or the presumed necessity) for particular kinds of behavior. If a group is to cope successfully with its environment it must of course adapt its customs to that environment. Obviously approval has its basis in reasons, and the *reasons* are conceived as those which make the action right.

A similar type of value standard analysis may be applied to aesthetic judgments. When I say that a novel is "good"—not merely that I like it —I must justify my judgment. I should define what I mean by "good," and I thus presuppose an aesthetic or critical standard of excellence in fiction. Perhaps my standard is that a good novel should have characters who are "real people," a significant human situation properly developed, etc. One may quarrel with my standard, or with its application to a particular work, but such questions are not entirely outside the realm of rational discussion, as the taste theory presupposes. Our *ultimate* criteria may of course be "matters of taste," but an ultimate criterion accepted after thoughtful consideration is quite different from a snap-judgment made on the basis of surface liking or disliking, such as, "This is a good novel, because I like stories about artists."

We have been seeking to justify the value standard theory in ethical and aesthetic value judgments. Reflection, we believe, will reveal that most of us do apply standards even though we may not be conscious of doing so. Let us consider an example.

In the following scene from Shaw's *Pygmalion*, Alfred Doolittle, the dustman, has asked Higgins for a five-pound note if he is to allow his daughter Liza to remain with Higgins for the linguistic experiments.

PICKERING: I think you ought to know, Doolittle, that Mr. Higgins' intentions are entirely honorable.

DOOLITTLE: Course they are, Governor. If I thought they wasn't I'd ask fifty.

HIGGINS [revolted]: Do you mean to say that you would sell your daughter for fifty pounds?

DOOLITTLE: Not in a general way I wouldn't; but to oblige a gentleman like you I'd do a good deal, I do assure you.

PICKERING: Have you no morals, man?

DOOLITTLE [unabashed]: Can't afford them, Governor. Neither could you if you was as poor as me. Not that I mean any harm, you know. But if Liza is going to have a bit out of this, why not me too?

HIGGINS [troubled]: I don't know what to do, Pickering. There can be no question that as a matter of morals it's a positive crime to give this chap a farthing. And yet I feel a rough sort of justice in his claim.

DOOLITTLE: That's it, Governor. That's all I say. A father's heart, as it were.

The reader may regard this selection as a witty presentation of the relativistic point of view. "Morals" seem to depend on one's situation in life. Circumstances alter cases. But implicit in Shaw's satire is the assumption that Doolittle's "honesty" is somehow praiseworthy, and that hypocrisy is the great sin. These standards we may regard as "absolutes." And most relativists justify their position by the argument that this position leads to tolerance of other people's ways. Tolerance, once more, is accepted as an unquestioned good, in other words, as a standard.

We have argued that logic is relevant in value judgments. We shall now sum up the different ways in which logic helps us to clarify our standards in the field of ethics.

1. Logic clarifies what we *mean* by right and wrong, in terms of our moral standards.

2. Logic helps us to determine whether a particular judgment makes sense in terms of these standards. We ought to work out the consequences that follow from our choices. We may find that we are defeating our own ends. Many people have supported the mandatory death penalty for kidnapping on the ground that it will effectively discourage the commission of this crime. But one should consider some other consequences. The death penalty—for kidnapping as such—eliminates any inducement to the kidnapper to bring his victim back alive, and juries will be reluctant to render a verdict of guilty in cases not involving murder, for a guilty verdict will mean the death penalty. If we want victims brought back alive, and if we want juries to do their duty, we may wish to revise our approval of the mandatory death penalty for kidnapping.

3. Logical analysis may also show that we are striving for the wrong ends, as many Socialists discovered when they saw that the abolition of private property in Russia did not bring about the elimination of cruelty and oppression. They also discovered that the State can be a harsh exploiter of the working man.

4. Logical analysis may also reveal self-inconsistencies in our own thinking. Few of us, perhaps, are as inconsistent as was the Mexican Society for the Prevention of Cruelty to Animals when it raised a considerable sum of money in a benefit performance at the bull ring. But we are sometimes as inconsistent as was King David—though in other contexts —when he condemned the rich man (in Nathan's parable) for taking away

the poor man's little ewe lamb. David himself had sent Uriah to his death in order to possess the beautiful Bathsheba.

We see, then, that logic is relevant in all human problems: in problems of values as well as those of a scientific nature. To dismiss judgments of value as mere matters of opinion, and not subject to discussion, is to invite an irrationalist attitude, an attitude which dismisses the criteria of logical analysis, rational deliberation, and the testing of our opinions by experience.

Reason is opposed to dogmatism, fanaticism, and obscurantism. The rational way of life offers no panaceas: the rational individual recognizes the complexities of human problems, and the difficulties in proving one side or the other in controversial issues. But there is no human problem that is inherently insoluble, and if we try hard enough, using the best methods that the human race has so far devised for thinking about these problems, we are justified in the faith that we shall solve them, one by one. The best methods, as we have seen, require working out the probable consequences of our ideas, and testing them in experience.

Many years ago Socrates taught that "the unexamined life is not worth living": the life that is not scrutinized by intelligence is a life not fit for a human being. Reason—or intelligence—is not all, but it is our greatest asset. The rational path leads to the enlightment of the human mind and brings us illumination in place of darkness.

STUDY QUESTIONS

1. Ruby begins by pointing out that value judgments are not as different from factual statements as they are often thought to be. But, as the end of the essay shows, the two are far from identical in their relation to logic. Discuss the differences between the two that the essay does not eliminate.

2. What is required if two debaters are to argue a question of value judgment effectively?

3. What limit is there to the effectiveness of logic in the consideration of value judgments? Does this limit also apply to the consideration of questions of fact?

4. Note that Ruby uses illustrations in an interesting manner. He often introduces them as a way of exposing the inadequacy of some view he disagrees with. Point out some examples of this.

5. Ruby says that one's preference for a work of art can be supported logically by reference to a basic standard of value. Write a theme carrying out this exercise. Describe your opinion of some book, movie, painting or other work of art which you favor or dislike, and justify your opinion by supporting it with some standard of value which is generally accepted.

6. Do you agree that "logic is relevant in all human problems"? Can you think of any in which it is irrelevant or only incidentally relevant? Explain why.

3. EXAMINING IDEAS

What Every Yale Freshman Should Know*

Edmund S. Morgan

The world does not much like curiosity. The world says that curiosity killed the cat. The world dismisses curiosity by calling it idle, or *mere* idle, curiosity—even though curious persons are seldom idle. Parents do their best to extinguish curiosity in their children, because it makes life difficult to be faced every day with a string of unanswerable questions about what makes fire hot or why grass grows, or to have to halt junior's investigations before they end in explosion and sudden death. Children whose curiosity survives parental discipline and who manage to grow up before they blow up are invited to join the Yale faculty. Within the university they go on asking their questions and trying to find the answers. In the eyes of a scholar, that is mainly what a university is for. It is a place where the world's hostility to curiosity can be defied.

Some of the questions that scholars ask seem to the world to be scarcely worth asking, let alone answering. They ask about the behavior of protons, the dating of a Roman coin, the structure of a poem. They ask questions too minute and specialized for you and me to understand without years of explanation.

If the world inquires of one of them why he wants to know the answer to a particular question, he may say, especially if he is a scientist, that the answer will in some obscure way make possible a new machine or weapon or gadget. He talks that way because he knows that the world understands and respects utility and that it does not understand much else. But to his colleagues and to you he will probably not speak this language. You are now part of the university, and he will expect you to understand that he wants to know the answer simply because he does not know it, the way a mountain climber wants to climb a mountain simply because it is there.

Similarly a historian, when asked by outsiders why he studies history, may come out with a line of talk that he has learned to repeat on such occasions, something about knowledge of the past making it possible to understand the present and mold the future. I am sure you have all heard it at one time or another. But if you really want to know why a historian studies the past, the answer is much simpler: he wants to know about it

---

* From the *Saturday Review,* Jan. 23, 1960. Reprinted by permission of the *Saturday Review* and of the author.

because it is there. Something happened, and he would like to know what.

All this does not mean that the answers which scholars find to their questions have no consequences. They may have enormous consequences: they may completely alter the character of human life. But the consequences seldom form the reason for asking the questions or pursuing the answers. It is true that scholars can be put to work answering questions for the sake of the consequences, as thousands are working now, for example, in search of a cure for cancer. But this is not the primary function of the scholar. For the scholar the consequences are usually incidental to the satisfaction of curiosity. Even for the medical scholar, the desire to stamp out a dreaded disease may be a less powerful motive than the desire to find out about the nature of living matter. Similarly Einstein did not wish to create an atomic bomb or to harness atomic energy. He simply wanted to find out about energy and matter.

I said that curiosity was a dangerous quality. It is dangerous not only because of incidental effects like the atomic bomb but also because it is really nothing more or less than a desire for truth. For some reason this phrase sounds less dangerous than curiosity. In fact, the desire for truth sounds rather respectable. Since so many respectable people assure us that they have found the truth, it does not sound like a dangerous thing to look for. But it is. The search for it has again and again overturned institutions and beliefs of long standing, in science, in religion, and in politics. It is easy enough to see today that these past revolutions brought great benefits to mankind. It was less easy to see the benefits while the revolutions were taking place, especially if you happened to be quite satisfied with the way things were before. Similarly it is not always easy today to see that the satisfaction of a scholar's curiosity is worth the disruption of society that may result from it. The search for truth is, and always has been, a subversive activity. And scholars have learned that they cannot engage in it without an occasional fight.

You may therefore find them rather belligerent toward any threat to the free pursuit of curiosity. They are wary of committing themselves to institutions or beliefs that might impose limitations on them or deliver ready-made answers to their questions. You will find them suspicious of loyalty oaths, religious creeds, or affiliations with political parties. In particular they will try to preserve their university as a sanctuary within whose walls *any* question can be asked.

This wariness of commitment can sometimes degenerate into a scholarly vice, a vice that paralyzes curiosity instead of preserving it. A scholar at his worst sometimes seems to be simply a man who cannot make up his mind. Every classroom from here to Melbourne has echoed with the feeble phrases of academic indecision: "There are two schools of thought on this question, and the truth probably lies halfway between them." When you hear this sentence repeated, or when you are tempted to repeat it yourself, remember that the truth may lie between two extremes, but it assuredly does not lie halfway between right and wrong. Don't short-circuit your curiosity by assuming you have found the answer when you have only made a tidy list of possible answers.

Dedication to curiosity should not end in indecision. It should, in fact, mean willingness to follow the mind into difficult decisions.

A second quality that makes a scholar has no apparent relation to the first and yet is inseparably connected to it. It is a compulsion to communicate. A scholar is driven by a force as strong as his curiosity, that compels him to tell the world the things he has learned. He cannot rest with learning something: he has to tell about it. Scholarship begins in curiosity, but it ends in communication. And though scholars may in a university take refuge from the world, they also acknowledge responsibility to the world, the responsibility to communicate freely and fully everything that they discover within the walls of their sanctuary. The search for truth needs no justification, and when a man thinks he has found any part of it, he cannot and ought not to be silent. The world may sometimes not care to listen, but the scholar must keep telling it until he has succeeded in communicating.

Now, there are only two methods of communication for scholars, writing and speaking. The scholar publishes his discoveries in books and articles and he teaches them in the classroom. Sometimes one or the other method will satisfy him, but most of us feel the need for both. The scholar who merely writes books falls into the habit of speaking only to the experts. If he works at his subject long enough, he reaches the position where there is no one else quite expert enough to understand him, and he winds up writing to himself. On the other hand, if he writes not at all, he may become so enamored of his own voice that he ceases to be a scholar and becomes a mere showman.

Communication is not merely the desire and the responsibility of the scholar; it is his discipline, the proving ground where he tests his findings against criticism. Without communication his pursuit of truth withers into eccentricity. He necessarily spends much of his time alone, in the library or the laboratory, looking for the answers to his questions. But he needs to be rubbing constantly against other minds. He needs to be tested, probed, and pushed around. He needs to be made to explain himself. Only when he has expressed himself, only when he has communicated his thoughts, can he be sure that he is thinking clearly.

The scholar, in other words, needs company to keep him making sense. And in particular he needs the company of fresh minds, to whom he must explain things from the beginning. He needs people who will challenge him at every step, who will take nothing for granted. He needs, in short, you.

You may have various purposes in coming here, and you may fulfill them: you may play football or tennis or the trombone; you may sing in the glee club, act in plays, and act up on college weekends. But what the faculty expects of you is four years of scholarship, and they will be satisfied with nothing less. For four years we expect you to join us in the pursuit of truth, and we will demand of you the same things we demand of ourselves: curiosity and communication.

Curiosity, of course, is not something you get simply by wishing for it. But it is surprisingly contagious. The curiosity we expect is more than a passing interest. We will not be satisfied by your ability to ask an occasional bright question, nor yet by your assimilation of a lot of predigested information. The accumulation of information is a necessary part of scholarship, and unfortunately the part most likely to be tested on examinations, especially those wretched ones called "objective examinations" where the truth is always supposed to lie in answer space A, B, C, D, or E, but never apparently in X, Y, or Z. But the curiosity we expect of you cannot be satisfied by passing examinations or by memorizing other people's answers to other people's questions. We do not wish to put you through a mere course of mental gymnastics. We want you to be content with nothing less than the whole truth about the subject that interests you. Which means that we want you to be forever discontent with how little you know about it and how little we know about it. We want you to back us into corners, show us up, make us confess we don't know. Does this sound formidable? It is not. We may tell you what we know with great assurance, but push us and you will find the gaps.

Follow your own minds into the gaps. Follow your minds where curiosity takes them. You will not get the whole truth, not about protons, not about the structure of a poem, not even about a Roman coin. Nobody does. But if you learn anything, it ought to change your minds, and hopefully it will change ours too. It will be a sign that we have both wasted four years if you leave here thinking pretty much the same way that you do now or if you leave us thinking the same way *we* do now.

We expect of you, then, that you will be curious for the truth. We also expect that you communicate whatever truth you find, and that you do it both in speech and in writing. Many people suppose that they know something if they can stammer out an approximation of what they mean in speech. They are mistaken. It is extremely unlikely that you have thought clearly if you cannot express yourself clearly, especially in writing. Writing is more than an instrument of communication. It is an instrument of thought. You should have acquired some competence in its use by now. I suspect from past experience that you have not. But even if you have, you have a great deal more to learn about it. And if you do not know much more about it four years from now, it will again be a sign that we have failed in part of our job, the job of making you communicate clearly.

Communication is a two-way process, and a university is a community of scholars, where questions are asked and the answers communicated, your answers to us, ours to you. For the next four years we will be engaged as scholars together in this community. After the four years are over, most of you will leave Yale, but if our community is a successful one, if we really do communicate with each other, I believe that you will continue to be in some sense scholars, asking new questions, looking for new answers, and communicating them to the world.

STUDY QUESTIONS

1. How do the university and the world outside it differ in their attitudes toward knowledge? Does this explain why misunderstandings often arise?

2. How can the search for truth be called "subversive"?

3. How convincing is Morgan's description of the place of the process of question and answer and give and take that is supposed to go on between student and professor? Does it correspond to your experience?

4. In what ways does Morgan agree with the views in "The Educational Value of Doubt" by Martin? What relations do you see between Morgan's notion of "curiosity" and Dewey's "reflective thinking" as it is described in "What Is Thinking?"

5. Morgan says that the search for truth has "again and again overturned institutions and beliefs of long standing in science, in religion, and in politics." Write a theme describing an example of this in some detail.

6. Do you agree with Morgan's idea of the function of education? Has he neglected to point out the importance of education in communicating truths already known, in keeping society going, in preserving and extending established gains? Write a theme pointing out the incompleteness or unsoundness of his views, if you think they are incomplete or unsound.

*The Educational Value of Doubt**

Everett Dean Martin

Professor Dewey somewhere speaks of education as freeing the mind of "bunk." It is a large task. No one wholly succeeds. I never saw a completely "debunked" individual. Strive as we may to eradicate it, there is always in our thinking an amount of error, of wish-fancy accepted as objective fact, of exaggeration, special pleading, self-justification. Many of our beliefs are not founded in reason at all, but are demanded by

* Reprinted from *The Meaning of a Liberal Education* by Everett Dean Martin. By permission of W. W. Norton and Company, Inc. Copyright, 1954, by Mrs. Daphne Mason.

some unconscious and repressed impulse in our nature. Men make a virtue of their faith when in fact they are *victims* of it; they can no more help believing certain things than a neurotic can stop a compulsive habit.

It is said that it is easy to doubt and that to believe is an accomplishment. It is not so. It is easier to believe than to doubt. The things we must train ourselves to doubt are as a rule just the things we wish to believe. It is children and savages and the illiterate who have the most implicit faith. It is said that unbelief is sin. This is not so; it is nobler to doubt than to believe, for to doubt is often to take sides with fact against oneself. Nietzsche said that this trait is characteristic of "higher men." It was Huxley, as I remember it, who considered that man could in nothing fall so low as when he deliberately took refuge in the absurd. Even with a rationalist like Huxley doubt is not merely a function of the intellect. Under certain circumstances it is a moral necessity.

The pursuit of knowledge is not the same, however, as scrupulous avoidance of error. He who strives to do his own thinking must accept responsibility for himself. He must expect that he will make mistakes. He may end in total failure. He must take his chances and be willing to pay the cost of his adventure. I know professional scholars who are so afraid they may write or say something which their colleagues will show to be wrong that they never express an opinion of their own or commit themselves to any down-right statement. Such equivocation and qualifying—playing safe—is not what I mean by doubt. I do not mean merely that one should be always on guard against the possibility of error, but that one should learn to hold all one's beliefs with a half-amused lightheartedness. Most minds are loaded down with the seriousness of their convictions. Solemnity in the presence of our eternal verities is awkwardness, and makes us always a little ridiculous, giving us the appearance of one about to shake hands with the President. Why not enjoy the humor of the situation? Our great truths may all the while be "spoofing" us. It will do no harm to give them a sly wink now and then.

Crowd men have no sense of humor. It is very difficult to educate solemn and opinionated people. Like Omar, they always come out by that same door wherein they went. I have known students to complete a course of study having learned nothing, because of their disinclination to consider any fact which might cause them to surrender some belief about religion or economic theory with which they entered. Whoever leaves an institution of learning with the same general outlook on life that he had when he first came might better have employed his time otherwise. He is not a student; he is a church-member. . . .

The significant thing is not the particular belief which a man gives up or retains but the manner in which he believes what he does believe. Change the latter and you change a basic habit pattern; you change the man.

Not all scepticism has educational value. There is a kind of doubting which is merely the negative response of the unteachable, the suspiciousness of the wilfully ignorant, the refusal of the incurious to examine disturbing and challenging evidence. There are, as an eighteenth century philosopher said, minds that are moulded to the form of one idea. Many people, after they have accepted one idea, tame it and keep it as a sort of watch-dog to frighten all other ideas away. This refusal to be convinced may appear to be scepticism; it is only stubbornness. The late Mr. Bryan and his followers were very sceptical of evolution. But this hostile attitude is very different from the scepticism of those scientists who hold that the theory is a mere working hypothesis which is yet to be confirmed. The scepticism of ignorance is motivated by the desire to save an old faith. Savages have been known to exhibit this incredulity toward certain aspects of our more advanced knowledge. If you were to tell the natives of Borneo that there is no dragon in the sky which eats up the moon during an eclipse, that there are no spirits and no magic, I imagine they would laugh in your face and think you a fool. Many a discovery and invention has been greeted by a grinning and incredulous public even in civilized society. The scepticism which has value is that which leads one on to further study and investigation. And it is characterized by intellectual modesty.

Philosophic doubt is not the pitiable condition of the soul that timid spirits imagine. It is not pessimism or cynicism, but a healthy and cheerful habit. It gives peace of mind. Men who stop pretending can sleep o' nights. There is a certain scepticism which is in no sense the spirit that denies. It is a frank recognition of the things as they come. It is almost a test of a man's honesty, among those who have stopped to think about the nature and limitations of our knowledge. Certainly cultivated people do not exhibit the same degree of cock-sureness as do the ignorant. People think the old saying about "doubting the intelligence that doubts" is funny. Popular audiences will always laugh at it. But why not? It is a platitude that the more a man learns the more he realizes how little he knows. Existence is filled with inscrutable mystery. To none of the profound questions that we ask of it is there any final answer. We must be satisfied ultimately with surmise, with symbol and poetic fancy. Speculations about the soul, God, the ultimate nature of reality and the course of destiny, and as to whether existence has any meaning or purpose beyond our own, or whether our life itself is worthwhile—all these speculations and many others of similar nature lead to no conclusions in fact, and we return always to the point from which we started. The very terms in which we put such questions are often meaningless when closely examined by the intellect, and the answer to them is determined by our own moods.

There is a general belief that science can answer the riddle. But science is only one possible view of things, the one best adapted to the needs of creatures like ourselves. It cannot deal with questions of value. It can tell us how things operate, their relative mass and positions in space and time, but it cannot tell us what they are in themselves, nor why they exist nor anything about their goodness or beauty. The more exact scientific knowledge becomes, the more closely it approaches mathematics. Pure mathematics deals only with abstractions and logical relations and can dismiss the whole world of objects. Science presupposes the data of experience and the validity of its own logical principles. It substitutes its mechanized order of things for things as we experience them.

Human reasoning is partial in all its processes. We think successfully about things when we ignore all the aspects or qualities of them except those which are relevant to the purpose at hand. The H_2O-ness of water is no more the ultimate nature of water than is its wetness, or its thirst quenching quality. That it is H_2O is only one of the things that may be said about water. Now if we add together bits of onesided and partial scientific knowledge, we do not thereby gain a sum total which is the equivalent of reality as a whole. We have a useful instrument for dealing with our environment, because in thought we have greatly simplified it by ignoring in each instance all that is irrelevant. But what we now have is a universe of discourse, a human construction which is what it is because we are always more interested in some aspects of things than in others.

All our ideas are views—they have been likened to snapshots. The world of which we are part is in flux. It comes to us as process, and our intellect does not grasp the movement any more than we can restore the movement of a man running by adding together a series of photographs. The movement always takes place between the pictures. Intellect is an instrument, not a mirror. Our world is not reducible to a form of thought, and when men speak of truth, reality, cause, substance, they are really only saying what they mean by certain words. The world, as James said, has its meanings for us because we are interested spectators, and so far as we can see none of these meanings are final. Whitehead and others have shown that some of the basic concepts of physical science which have held sway since the seventeenth century are now subject to revision. Santayana says that knowledge is faith—animal faith. It would be strange if it were otherwise, if hairy little creatures such as we are, whose ancestors lived in trees and made queer guttural noises, should so organize human discourse as to be able to say the last word about reality as a whole. It is well that we should marvel at our achievements of knowledge, for they are man's noblest work; but let us remember that human reason, itself a phase and part of the process of nature, can only view the whole process from its own partial standpoint, and that is enough unless we aspire to infallibility.

Man is a disputatious animal who loves to speak like Sir Oracle. Uneducated people, ashamed of their ignorance, commit themselves hastily and cling to their commitments, for to change one's mind is an admission that one was mistaken. We wish to be vindicated as having all along been in the right. Hence, it is more natural to contend for a principle than to test a hypothesis. The ego becomes identified with certain convictions. We feel ourselves personally injured if our convictions are subjected to criticism. We are not ordinarily grateful to the person who points out our errors and sets us right. But if our education is to proceed, we must get over our delusion of infallibility.

This fiction of infallibility is very common, and those who have not learned to doubt this fiction, who are sure that they have the truth and are on the side of the right are as a rule the more ignorant and provincial elements of the population. It is no accident that Fundamentalism, prohibition, and other forms of moral regulation exist in inverse ratio to urbanity and have their strongholds in rural communities. People to whom it never occurs to ask how they know so clearly they are right when better informed people have doubts on the subject, are the ones who naturally strive to coerce their neighbors. To many minds there are no social or moral problems. The answer is always known by the crusader. It is very simple. To him there can be no two opinions. The standards which prevail in his own parish, the self-expression of his own type, are the will of God. Principles of right and wrong are known immediately without reflection or regard to the situations where they are to be applied; they are revealed to conscience. "Right is right and wrong is wrong everywhere and forever the same!" ...

I am not asserting dogmatically that we cannot know truth or the nature of reality. I am not suggesting that we cannot be educated without ending in universal scepticism or agnostic negation. It seems to me that we have, or can have, such knowledge as will make our intellects fairly adequate instruments in the performance of their proper functions. But I do not see what such functioning has to do with ascribing finality to our beliefs or trying to legislate for all possible worlds. I am not suggesting an attitude of despair in the pursuit of truth, but am trying to state the very reason for any learning at all, for what is the use of it if we know it all before we start?

Education may not end in doubt, but it ends when a man stops doubting. But why speak of the end of a process that should continue through life? As I see it, the process is more often discontinued at the point of some fictitious certainty than in any moment of doubt. Doubt, the willingness to admit that conjecture is subject to revision, is a spur to learning. The recognition that our truths are not copies of eternal realities but are human creations designed to meet human needs, puts one in a teachable frame of mind. And the discovery that thinking may be creative makes intellectual activity interesting. ...

If it is true that men can only be made to act under the lash of blind faith and enthusiasm, then the estate of man is a sorry one indeed. For most of the things done will end in tragic failure. It is only the conceit of ignorance to believe that the world can be straightened once for all by people who do not know what they are doing. Moreover, to say that ignorance is necessary to the accomplishment of good is to say, that ignorance is desirable and better for man than knowledge. There have been those who held such a view. Obscurantists always hold it. It is the philosophy of pessimism, and it is interesting to note that it is the believer and the devotee, the man of action and not the gentle doubter who finally ends in pessimism.

For want of intelligence the devotees of causes have been the mischief makers in all times. We cannot always know who does the most good in the world, but the evil that men do lives after them and it is sometimes possible to estimate the amount of harm done. Who has done the most harm in human history, the sceptics or the believers, the devotees of causes or the devotees of culture and urbanity? St. Bernard with his crusade, or Abelard with his doubts? The men who conducted the Inquisition, or the men who doubted the doctrine of the Trinity? Calvin and the obscurantists on both sides of the Reformation, or Erasmus and the Humanists? Cromwell and his Puritans or Voltaire and the Deists? Robespierre or Goethe?

The devotees to causes have kept human life in turmoil. If the immorality they would cure has slain its thousands, their "morality" has slain its tens of thousands. In most cases the strife has been useless and for causes that might have been won in other ways, really won. The devotee of a cause requires little provocation to practice persecution, and only the opportunity to play the tyrant.

Doubt not only has educational value: it preserves social sanity. I would suggest as part of everyone's education the reading of such authors as Lucian, Epicurus, Abelard, Hobbes, Montaigne, Rabelais, Erasmus, Lessing, Voltaire, Hume and Anatole France. There is no blood on these men's hands. They have quietly smiled in the face of bigotry and superstition. In their words there is laughter and there is light. Perhaps no one of them ever intended to be a liberator of mankind. They merely thought and spoke as free spirits, and their very presence puts sham and cant and unction and coercion and mistaken zeal to shame. They have done more for freedom and truth than all the armies of crusading devotees.

STUDY QUESTIONS

1. Explain Martin's paradoxical opinions that doubt is the way to knowledge and modesty the way to power.
2. Explain what is meant by Martin's statement, "All our ideas are views. . . ."
3. Is it fair to conclude that, if Martin is right, and nothing can finally be known, education is largely a waste of time?
4. To what extent do Martin and John Stuart Mill agree on the value of doubt?
5. Do you agree with Martin that the "gentle doubters" of the world

have done more good than the "devotees of causes"? Write a theme explaining and defending your point of view.

6. Write a theme about some important question about which you are still in doubt, explaining the issue, and telling why you have not reached a definite decision. Or, if you disagree with Martin, describe a question which you have definitely decided in your own mind, and explain why you feel you are better off for having settled your doubts.

The Teaching Process*

Jacques Barzun

It is over a quarter of a century since I first obeyed the summons to teach and I can only hope the habit has not become a compulsion. "Oh to sit next a man who has spent his life in trying to educate others!" groaned Oscar Wilde. My belief is that the last thing a good teacher wants to do is to teach outside the classroom; certainly my own vision of bliss halfway through a term is solitary confinement in a soundproof cell. But feeling this way, I often wonder what originally made the impulse to teach take root. In the lives of so many good men one reads that they "drifted into teaching." They drift out again. It is clear that teachers are born, not made, and circumstances usually permit rather than compel. It is impossible to think of William James *not* teaching or of his brother Henry consenting to give a simple explanation. For many people, doing is far easier than talking about it.

From which I conclude that the teaching impulse goes something like this: a fellow human being is puzzled or stymied. He wants to open a door or spell "accommodate." The would-be helper has two choices. He can open the door, spell the word; or he can show his pupil how to do it for himself. The second way is harder and takes more time, but a strong instinct in the born teacher makes him prefer it. It seems somehow to turn an accident into an opportunity for permanent creation. The raw material is what the learner can do, and upon this the teacher-artist builds by the familiar process of taking apart and putting together. He must break down the new and puzzling situation into simpler bits and lead the beginner in the right order from one bit to the next. What the simpler bits and the right order are no one can know ahead of time. They vary for each individual and the teacher must grope around until he finds a "first step" that the particular pupil can manage. In any school subject, of course,

* From *Teacher in America* by Jacques Barzun, by permission of Little, Brown & Company, and Atlantic Monthly Press. Copyright, 1944, 1945, by Jacques Barzun.

this technique does not stop with the opening of a door. The need for it goes on and on—as it seems, forever—and it takes the stubbornness of a saint coupled with the imagination of a demon for a teacher to pursue his art of improvisation gracefully, unwearyingly, endlessly.

Nor is this a purely mental task. All the while, the teacher must keep his charge's feelings in good order. A rattled student can do nothing and a muddled teacher will rattle or dishearten almost any student. The teacher must not talk too much or too fast, must not trip over his own tongue, must not think out loud, must not forget, in short, that he is handling a pair of runaway horses—the pupil and a dramatic situation.

Patience is a quality proverbially required for good teaching, but it is not surprising that many good teachers turn out to be impatient people—though not with their students. Their stock of forbearance gives out before they get home. What sustains them in class is that the situation is always changing. Three successive failures to do one thing may all seem identical to the bystander, but the good teacher will notice a change, a progression, or else the clear sign that the attempt must be postponed until some other preliminary progress has been made.

It is obvious that the relation of teacher to pupil is an emotional one and most complex and unstable besides. To begin with, the motives, the forces that make teaching "go," are different on both sides of the desk. The pupil has some curiosity and he wants to know what grownups know. The master has curiosity also, but it is chiefly about the way the pupil's mind—or hand—works. Remembering his own efforts and the pleasure of discovery, the master finds a satisfaction which I have called artistic in seeing how a new human being will meet and make his own some part of our culture—our ways, our thoughts, even our errors and superstitions. This interest, however, does not last forever. As the master grows away from his own learning period, he also finds that mankind repeats itself. Fewer and fewer students appear new and original. They make the same mistakes at the same places and never seem to go very far into a subject which, for him, is still an expanding universe. Hence young teachers are best; they are the most energetic, most intuitive, and the least resented.

For side by side with his eagerness, the pupil feels resentment arising from the fact that the grownup who teaches him appears to know it all. There is, incidentally, no worse professional disease for the teacher than the habit of putting questions with a half-smile that says "I know that one, and I will tell it you: come along, my pretty." Telling and questioning must not be put-up jobs designed to make the teacher feel good about himself. It is as bad as the Jehovah complex among doctors. Even under the best conditions of fair play and deliberate spontaneity, the pupil, while needing and wanting knowledge, will hate and resist it. This resistance often makes one feel that the human mind is made of some wonderfully tough rubber, which you can stretch a little by pulling hard, but which snaps back into shape the moment you let go.

It is exasperating, but consider how the student feels, subjected to daily and hourly stretching. "Here am I," he thinks, "with my brains nicely organized—with everything, if not in its place, at least in a place where I can find it—and you come along with a new and strange item that you want to force into my previous arrangement. Naturally I resist. You persist. I begin to dislike you. But at the same time, you show me aspects of this new fact or idea which in spite of myself mesh in with my existing desires. You seem to know the contents of my mind. You show me the proper place for your contribution to my stock of knowledge. Finally, there is brooding over us a vague threat of disgrace for me if I do not accept your offering and keep it and show you that I still have it when you—dreadful thought!—*examine* me. So I give in, I shut my eyes and swallow. I write little notes about it to myself, and with luck the burr sticks: I have learned something. Thanks to you? Well, not exactly. Thanks to you and thanks to me. I shall always be grateful for your efforts, but do not expect me to love you, at least not for a long, long time. When I am fully formed and somewhat battered by the world and yet not too displeased with myself, I shall generously believe that I owe it all to you. It will be an exaggeration on the other side, just as my present dislike is an injustice. Strike an average between the two and that will be a fair measure of my debt."

At any stage in learning, this inner dialogue between opposite feelings goes on. It should go on. Teaching is possible only because there is a dialogue and one part of the mind can be used to rearrange the other. The whole secret of teaching—and it is no secret—consists in splitting the opposition, downing the conservatives by making an alliance with the radicals. It goes without saying that I am not using these words here in their workaday sense. My meaning applies to the multiplication table as well as to anything else. The conservative part of the pupil's mind is passive, stubborn, mute; but his radical minority, that is, his curiosity and his desire to grow up, may be aroused to action. The move forward is generally short; then the conservatives return to power; they preserve, they feel pride of ownership in the new acquisition and begin to think they had it as a birthright. This rhythmical action is one reason why teaching and learning must not go on all the time, nor at an accelerated pace: time and rest are needed for absorption. Psychologists confirm the fact when they tell us that it is really in summer that our muscles learn how to skate, and in winter how to swim.

If I have dwelt on the emotions of teaching and being taught, it is because many people believe that schooling only engages the mind—and only temporarily at that. "I've forgotten," says the average man, "all I ever learned at school." And he mentally contrasts this happy oblivion with the fact that he still knows how to open oysters and ride a bicycle. But my description of teaching applies equally to physical things and to metaphysical. We may forget the substance of American History but we are probably scarred for life by the form and feeling of it as imparted by book and teacher. Why is it that the businessman's economics and the well-bred woman's taste in art are normally twenty-five years behind the times? It is that one's lifelong opinions are those picked up before maturity—at school and college.

This is why a "teacher's influence," if he does exert one, is not so big a joke as it seems. Notice in the lives of distinguished men how invariably there is a Mr. Bowles or a Dr. Tompkins or a Professor Clunk—whom no one ever heard of, but who is "remembered" for inspiring, guiding, and teaching decisively at the critical time. We can all see the mark left by a teacher in physical arts like tennis or music. The pupils of Leopold Auer or Tobias Matthay can be recognized at forty paces by their posture and even in a dark room by the sound they make. For in these disciplines the teacher usually falls back on direct imitation: "Hold your hand like this," or more simply, "Watch me." Well, much good teaching is of the "watch me" order, but the more abstract the knowledge, the less easy it is to imitate the teacher, and the genuine student wants to do the real thing in a real way *by himself.*

Consequently, the whole aim of good teaching is to turn the young learner, by nature a little copycat, into an independent, self-propelling creature, who cannot merely learn but study—that is, work as his own boss to the limit of his powers. This is to turn pupils into students, and it can be done on any rung of the ladder of learning. When I was a child, the multiplication table was taught from a printed sheet which had to be memorized one "square" at a time—the one's and the two's and so on up to nine. It never occurred to the teacher to show us how the answers could be arrived at also by addition, which we already knew. No one said, "Look: if four times four is sixteen, you ought to be able to figure out, without aid from memory, what five times four is, because that amounts to four more one's added to the sixteen." This would at first have been puzzling, *more* complicated and difficult than memory work, but once explained and grasped, it would have been an instrument for learning and checking the whole business of multiplication. We could temporarily have dispensed with the teacher and cut loose from the printed table.[1]

This is another way of saying that the only thing worth teaching anybody is a principle. Naturally principles involve facts and some facts must be learned "bare" because they do not rest on any principle. The capital of Alaska is Juneau and, so far as I know, that is all there is to it; but a European child ought not to learn that Washington is the capital of the United States without fixing firmly in his mind the relation between

[1] I find that General Grant complained of the same thing: "Both winters were spent in going over the same old arithmetic which I knew every word of before and repeating 'A noun is the name of a thing,' which I had also heard my Georgetown teachers repeat until I had come to believe it." (*Memoirs*, New York, 1894, p. 20.)

the city and the man who led his countrymen to freedom. That would be missing an association, which is the germ of a principle. And just as a complex athletic feat is made possible by rapid and accurate co-ordination, so all valuable learning hangs together and *works* by associations which make sense.

Since associations are rooted in habit and habits in feelings, we can see that anything which makes school seem a nightmare or a joke, which brands the teacher as a fool, or a fraud, is the archenemy of all learning. It so happens that there is one professional disease, or rather vice, which generates precisely this feeling and whose consequences are therefore fatal. I refer to Hokum and I hasten to explain what I mean. Hokum is the counterfeit of true intellectual currency. It is words without meaning, verbal filler, artificial apples of knowledge. From the necessities of the case, nine tenths of all teaching is done with words, whence the ever-present temptation of hokum.

Words should point to things, seen or unseen. But they can also be used to wrap up emptiness of heart and lack of thought. The student accepts some pompous, false, meaningless formula, and passes it back on demand, to be rewarded with—appropriately enough—a passing grade. All the dull second-rate opinions, all the definitions that don't define, all the moral platitudes that "sound good," all the conventional adjectives ("gentle Shakespeare"), all the pretenses that a teacher makes about the feelings of his students towards him and vice versa, all the intimations that something must be learned because it has somehow got lodged among learnable things (like the Binomial Theorem or the date of Magna Carta)—all this in all its forms gives off the atmosphere of hokum, which healthy people everywhere find absolutely unbreathable.

In a modern play, I think by A. A. Milne, this schoolmarm vice has been caught and set down in a brief dialogue which goes something like this:—

GOVERNESS. Recite.
PUPIL. "The Battle of Blenheim." (*Long pause*)
GOVERNESS. By?
PUPIL. (*silence*).
GOVERNESS. By Robert Southey.
PUPIL. By Robert Southey.
GOVERNESS. Who was Robert Southey?
PUPIL. (*pause*). I don't know.
GOVERNESS. One of our greatest poets. Begin again.
PUPIL. The Battle of Blenheim by Robert Southey one of our greatest poets.

As this example shows, hokum is subtle and I will forbear to analyze it. It hides in the porous part of solid learning and vitiates it by making it stupid and ridiculous. I remember once giving a short quiz to a class of young women who had been reading about the Renaissance. I asked for some "identification" of names and put Petrarch in the list. One girl, who had evidently read a textbook, wrote down: "Petrarch—the vanguard of the new emphasis." I spent a good hour trying to explain why this parroting of opinion was not only not "correct" but blind hokum, hokum absolute. It was not an easy job because so many teachers and books deal exclusively in that cheap commodity. The child's instinct is first to believe the Word, spoken or printed; then with growing good sense to disbelieve it, but to trust to its hokum value for getting through by "satisfying" the teacher. Great heavens, what satisfactions!

To carry my anecdote one step further, I believe I made a lifelong friend and a convert to decent learning by persuading my student that almost any honest mistake would have been truer than the absurdity she was palming off. She might better have been trivial: "Petrarch was an Italian"; or flippant: "Wrote poems to a girl named Laura"; or downright mistaken: "Also spelled Plutarch," rather than do what she did. My difficulty—and this is the important point—was in convincing her that I meant what I said, in breaking down the strongest superstition of the young, which is that everybody but themselves prefers make-believe and lives by it.

STUDY QUESTIONS

1. Explain why Barzun conceives teaching to be not "a purely mental task." In what way is good teaching a "permanent creation"?

2. According to Barzun, what is the natural emotional relationship between student and teacher? Do you agree with him that this attitude is natural?

3. What, according to Barzun's clearly implied distinction, is the difference between a "pupil" and a "student"?

4. Barzun has had considerable success in writing for laymen on a variety of humane subjects. Examine this selection and be prepared to point out qualities of style which may have contributed to the success of his writing.

5. Write a theme describing a relationship you have had with a teacher and telling whether or not you felt the relationship promoted the learning process.

6. Write a theme filling the gap deliberately left by Barzun at the place where he feels it is best not to explain what he means by "hokum." Tell what you think he means by this word, analyzing the characteristics and purposes of hokum, and giving any examples you have noted in your own experience.

Knowledge and Learning*

John Henry Newman

I suppose the *primâ-facie* view which the public at large would take of a University, considering it as a place of Education, is nothing more or less than a place for acquiring a great deal of knowledge on a great many subjects. Memory is one of the first developed of mental faculties; a boy's business when he goes to school is to learn, that is, to store up things in his memory. For some years his intellect is little more than an instrument for taking in facts, or a receptacle for storing them; he welcomes them as fast as they come to him; he lives on what is without; he has his eyes ever about him; he has a lively susceptibility of impressions; he imbibes information of every kind; and little does he make his own in a true sense of the word, living rather upon his neighbors all around him. He has opinions, religious, political, and literary, and, for a boy, is very positive in them and sure about them; but he gets them from his schoolfellows, or his masters, or his parents, as the case may be. Such as he is in his other relations, such also is he in his school exercises; his mind is observant, sharp, ready, retentive; he is almost passive in the acquisition of knowledge. I say this in no disparagement of the idea of a clever boy. Geography, chronology, history, language, natural history, he heaps up the matter of these studies as treasures for a future day. It is the seven years of plenty with him; he gathers in by handfuls, like the Egyptians, without counting; and though, as time goes on, there is exercise for his argumentative powers in the Elements of Mathematics, and for his taste in the Poets and Orators, still, while at school, or at least, till quite the last years of his time, he acquires, and little more; and when he is leaving for the University, he is mainly the creature of foreign influences and circumstances, and made up of accidents, homogeneous or not, as the case may be. Moreover, the moral habits, which are a boy's praise, encourage and assist this result; that is, diligence, assiduity, regularity, despatch, persevering application; for these are the direct conditions of acquisition, and naturally lead to it. Acquirements, again, are emphatically producible, and at a moment; they are a something to show, both for master and scholar; an audience, even though ignorant themselves of the subjects of an examination, can comprehend when questions are answered and when they are not. Here again is a reason why mental culture is in the minds of men identified with the acquisition of knowledge.

The same notion possesses the public mind, when it passes on from the

* From *The Idea of a University*, 1852.

thought of a school to that of a University: and with the best of reasons so far as this, that there is no true culture without acquirements, and that philosophy presupposes knowledge. It requires a great deal of reading, or a wide range of information, to warrant us in putting forth our opinions on any serious subject; and without such learning the most original mind may be able indeed to dazzle, to amuse, to refute, to perplex, but not to come to any useful result or any trustworthy conclusion. There are indeed persons who profess a different view of the matter, and even act upon it. Every now and then you will find a person of vigorous or fertile mind, who relies upon his own resources, despises all former authors, and gives the world, with the utmost fearlessness, his views upon religion, or history, or any other popular subject. And his works may sell for a while; he may get a name in his day; but this will be all. His readers are sure to find on the long run that his doctrines are mere theories, and not the expression of facts, that they are chaff instead of bread, and then his popularity drops as suddenly as it rose.

Knowledge then is the indispensable condition of expansion of mind, and the instrument of attaining to it; this cannot be denied, it is ever to be insisted on; I begin with it as a first principle; however, the very truth of it carries men too far, and confirms to them the notion that it is the whole of the matter. A narrow mind is thought to be that which contains little knowledge; and an enlarged mind, that which holds a great deal; and what seems to put the matter beyond dispute is, the fact of the great number of studies which are pursued in a University, by its very profession. Lectures are given on every kind of subject; examinations are held; prizes awarded. There are moral, metaphysical, physical Professors; Professors of languages, of history, of mathematics, of experimental science. Lists of questions are published, wonderful for their range and depth, variety and difficulty; treatises are written, which carry upon their very face the evidence of extensive reading or multifarious information; what then is wanting for mental culture to a person of large reading and scientific attainments? what is grasp of mind but acquirement? where shall philosophical repose be found, but in the consciousness and enjoyment of large intellectual possessions?

And yet this notion is, I conceive, a mistake, and my present business is to show that it is one, and that the end of a Liberal Education is not mere knowledge, or knowledge considered in its *matter;* and I shall best attain my object, by actually setting down some cases, which will be generally granted to be instances of the process of enlightenment or enlargement of mind, and others which are not, and thus, by the comparison, you will be able to judge for yourselves, Gentlemen, whether Knowledge, that is, acquirement, is after all the real principle of the enlargement, or whether that principle is not rather something beyond it.

For instance, let a person, whose experience has hitherto been confined to the more calm and unpretending scenery of these islands, . . . go for the first time into parts where physical nature puts on her wilder and more awful forms, whether at home or abroad, as into mountainous districts; or let one, who has ever lived in a quiet village, go for the first time to a great metropolis,—then I suppose he will have a sensation which perhaps he never had before. He has a feeling not in addition or increase of former feelings, but of something different in its nature. He will perhaps be borne forward, and find for a time that he has lost his bearings. He has made a certain progress, and he has a consciousness of mental enlargement; he does not stand where he did, he has a new centre, and a range of thoughts to which he was before a stranger.

Again, the view of the heavens which the telescope opens upon us, if allowed to fill and possess the mind, may almost whirl it round and make it dizzy. It brings in a flood of ideas, and is rightly called an intellectual enlargement, whatever is meant by the term.

And so again, the sight of beasts of prey and other foreign animals, their strangeness, the originality (if I may use the term) of their forms and gestures and habits and their variety and independence of each other, throw us out of ourselves into another creation, and as if under another Creator, if I may so express the temptation which may come on the mind. We seem to have new faculties, or a new exercise for our faculties, by this addition to our knowledge; like a prisoner, who, having been accustomed to wear manacles or fetters, suddenly finds his arms and legs free.

Hence Physical Science generally, in all its departments, as bringing before us the exuberant riches and resources, yet the orderly course of the Universe, elevates and excites the student, and at first, I may say, almost takes away his breath, while in time it exercises a tranquilizing influence upon him.

Again, the study of history is said to enlarge and enlighten the mind, and why? because, as I conceive, it gives it a power of judging of passing events, and of all events, and a conscious superiority over them, which before it did not possess.

And in like manner, what is called seeing the world, entering into active life, going into society, travelling, gaining acquaintance with the various classes of the community, coming into contact with the principles and modes of thought of various parties, interests, and races, their views, aims, habits and manners, their religious creeds and forms of worship,—gaining experience how various yet how alike men are, how low-minded, how bad, how opposed, yet how confident in their opinions; all this exerts a perceptible influence upon the mind, which it is impossible to mistake, be it good or be it bad, and is popularly called its enlargement.

And then again, the first time the mind comes across the arguments and speculations of unbelievers, and feels what a novel light they cast upon what he has hitherto accounted sacred; and still more, if it gives into them and embraces them, and throws off as so much prejudice what it has hitherto held, and, as if waking from a dream, begins to realize to its imagination that there is now no such thing as law and the transgression of law, that sin is a phantom, and punishment a bugbear, that it is free to sin, free to enjoy the world and the flesh; and still further, when it does enjoy them, and reflects that it may think and hold just what it will, that "the world is all before it where to choose," and what system to build up as its own private persuasion; when this torrent of wilful thoughts rushes over and inundates it, who will deny that the fruit of the tree of knowledge, or what the mind takes for knowledge, has made it one of the gods, with a sense of expansion and elevation,—an intoxication in reality, still, so far as the subjective state of the mind goes, an illumination? Hence the fanaticism of individuals or nations, who suddenly cast off their Maker. Their eyes are opened; and, like the judgment-stricken king in the Tragedy, they see two suns, and a magic universe, out of which they look back upon their former state of faith and innocence with a sort of contempt and indignation, as if they were then but fools, and the dupes of imposture.

On the other hand, Religion has its own enlargement, and an enlargement, not of tumult, but of peace. It is often remarked of uneducated persons, who have hitherto thought little of the unseen world, that, on their turning to God, looking into themselves, regulating their hearts, reforming their conduct, and meditating on death and judgment, heaven and hell, they seem to become, in point of intellect, different beings from what they were. Before, they took things as they came, and thought no more of one thing than another. But now every event has a meaning; they have their own estimate of whatever happens to them; they are mindful of times and seasons, and compare the present with the past; and the world, no longer dull, monotonous, unprofitable, and hopeless, is a various and complicated drama, with parts and an object, and an awful moral.

Now from these instances, to which many more might be added, it is plain, first, that the communication of knowledge certainly is either a condition or the means of that sense of enlargement or enlightenment, of which at this day we hear so much in certain quarters: this cannot be denied; but next, it is equally plain, that such communication is not the whole of the process. The enlargement consists, not merely in the passive reception into the mind of a number of ideas hitherto unknown to it, but in the mind's energetic and simultaneous action upon and towards and among those new ideas, which are rushing in upon it. It is the action of a formative power, reducing to order and meaning the matter of our acquirements; it is a making the objects of our knowledge subjectively our own, or, to use a familiar word, it is a digestion of what we receive, into the substance of our previous state of thought; and without this no enlargement is said to follow. There is no enlargement, unless there be a comparison of ideas one with another, as they come before the mind, and a systematizing of them. We feel our minds to be growing and expanding *then,* when we not only learn, but refer what we learn to what we know already. It is not the mere addition to our knowledge that is the illumination; but the locomotion, the movement onwards, of that mental centre, to which both what we know, and what we are learning, the accumulating mass of our acquirements, gravitates. And therefore a truly great intellect, and recognized to be such by the common opinion of mankind, such as the intellect of Aristotle, or of St. Thomas, or of Newton, or of Goethe, . . . is one which takes a connected view of old and new, past and present, far and near, and which has an insight into the influence of all these one on another; without which there is no whole, and no centre. It possesses the knowledge, not only of things, but also of their mutual true relations; knowledge, not merely considered as acquirement but as philosophy.

Accordingly, when this analytical, distributive, harmonizing process is away, the mind experiences no enlargement, and is not reckoned as enlightened or comprehensive, whatever it may add to its knowledge. For instance, a great memory, as I have already said, does not make a philosopher, any more than a dictionary can be called a grammar. There are men who embrace in their minds a vast multitude of ideas, but with little sensibility about their real relations towards each other. These may be antiquarians, annalists, naturalists; they may be learned in the law; they may be versed in statistics; they are most useful in their own place; I should shrink from speaking disrespectfully of them; still, there is nothing in such attainments to guarantee the absence of narrowness of mind. If they are nothing more than well-read men, or men of information, they have not what specially deserves the name of culture of mind, or fulfills the type of Liberal Education.

In like manner, we sometimes fall in with persons who have seen much of the world, and of the men who, in their day, have played a conspicuous part in it, but who generalize nothing, and have no observation, in the true sense of the word. They abound in information in detail, curious and entertaining, about men and things; and, having lived under the influence of no very clear or settled principles, religious or political, they speak of every one and every thing, only as so many phenomena, which are complete in themselves, and lead to nothing, not discussing them, or teaching any truth, or instructing the hearer, but simply talking. No one would say that these persons, well informed as they are, had attained to any great culture of intellect or to philosophy.

The case is the same still more strikingly where the persons in question are beyond dispute men of inferior powers and deficient education. Perhaps they have been much in foreign countries, and they receive, in a passive, otiose, unfruitful way, the various facts which are forced upon them there. Seafaring men, for example, range from one end of the earth to the other; but the multiplicity of external objects, which they have encountered, forms no symmetrical and consistent picture upon their imagination; they see the tapestry of human life, as it were on the wrong side, and it tells no story. They sleep, and they rise up, and they find themselves, now in Europe, now in Asia; they see visions of great cities and wild regions; they are in the marts of commerce, or amid the islands of the South; they gaze on Pompey's Pillar, or on the Andes; and nothing which meets them carries them forward or backward, to any idea beyond itself. Nothing has a drift or relation; nothing has a history or a promise. Every thing stands by itself, and comes and goes in its turn, like the shifting scenes of a show, which leave the spectator where he was. Perhaps you are near such a man on a particular occasion, and expect him to be shocked or perplexed at something which occurs; but one thing is much the same to him as another, or, if he is perplexed, it is as not knowing what to say, whether it is right to admire, or to ridicule, or to disapprove, while conscious that some expression of opinion is expected from him; for in fact he has no standard of judgment at all, and no landmarks to guide him to a conclusion. Such is mere acquisition, and, I repeat, no one would dream of calling it philosophy.

Instances, such as these, confirm, by the contrast, the conclusion I have already drawn from those which preceded them. That only is true enlargement of mind which is the power of viewing many things at once as one whole, of referring them severally to their true place in the universal system, of understanding their respective values, and determining their mutual dependence. Thus is that form of Universal Knowledge, of which I have on a former occasion spoken, set up in the individual intellect, and constitutes its perfection. Possessed of this real illumination, the mind never views any part of the extended subject-matter of Knowledge without recollecting that it is but a part, or without the associations which spring from this recollection. It makes every thing in some sort lead to every thing else; it would communicate the image of the whole to every separate portion, till that whole becomes in imagination like a spirit, every where pervading and penetrating its component parts, and giving them one definite meaning. Just as our bodily organs, when mentioned, recall their function in the body, as the word "creation" suggests the Creator, and "subjects" a sovereign, so, in the mind of the Philosopher, as we are abstractedly conceiving of him, the elements of the physical and moral world, sciences, arts, pursuits, ranks, offices, events, opinions, individualities, are all viewed as one, with correlative functions, and as gradually by successive combinations converging, one and all, to the true centre.

To have even a portion of this illuminative reason and true philosophy is the highest state to which nature can aspire, in the way of intellect; it puts the mind above the influences of chance and necessity, above anxiety, suspense, unsettlement, and superstition, which is the lot of the many. Men, whose minds are possessed with some one object, take exaggerated views of its importance, are feverish in the pursuit of it, make it the measure of things which are utterly foreign to it, and are startled and despond if it happens to fail them. They are ever in alarm or in transport. Those on the other hand who have no object or principle whatever to hold by, lose their way, every step they take. They are thrown out, and do not know what to think or say, at every fresh juncture; they have no view of persons, or occurrences, or facts, which come suddenly upon them, and they hang upon the opinion of others, for want of internal resources. But the intellect, which has been disciplined to the perfection of its powers, which knows, and thinks while it knows, which has learned to leaven the dense mass of facts and events with the elastic force of reason, such an intellect cannot be partial, cannot be exclusive, cannot be impetuous, cannot be at a loss, cannot but be patient, collected, and majestically calm, because it discerns the end in every beginning, the origin in every end, the law in every interruption, the limit in each delay; because it ever knows where its stands, and how its path lies from one point to another. It is the τετράγωνος of the Peripatetic,[1] and has the "nil admirari"[2] of the Stoic,—

> Felix qui potuit rerum cognoscere causas,
> Atque metus omnes, et inexorabile fatum
> Subjecit pedibus, strepitumque Acherontis avari.[3]

There are men who, when in difficulties, originate at the moment vast ideas or dazzling projects; who, under the influence of excitement, are able to cast a light, almost as if from inspiration, on a subject or course of action which comes before them; who have a sudden presence of mind equal to any emergency, rising with the occasion, and an undaunted magnanimous bearing, and an energy and keenness which is but made intense by opposition. This is genius, this is heroism; it is the exhibition of a natural gift, which no culture can teach, at which no Institution can aim; here, on the contrary, we are concerned, not with mere nature, but with training and teaching. That perfection of the Intellect, which is the result of Education, and its *beau ideal,* to be imparted to individuals in their respective measures, is the clear, calm, accurate vision and comprehension of all things, as far as the finite mind can embrace them, each in its place, and with its own characteristics upon it. It is almost prophetic from its knowledge of history; it is almost heart-searching from its knowledge of human nature; it has almost supernatural charity from its freedom from littleness and prejudice; it has almost the repose of faith, because nothing can startle it; it has almost the beauty and harmony of heavenly contemplation, so intimate is it with the eternal order of things and the music of the spheres.

[1] An allusion to Aristotle's *Ethics*—the good and *foursquare* man.
[2] To be amazed at nothing.
[3] Happy the man who can understand nature's causes, and thus spurn all fear and inexorable fate and the roar of greedy Acheron.

STUDY QUESTIONS

1. Exactly what does Newman mean by the phrase "enlargement of the mind"? How does a man whose mind has undergone this process differ from others?

2. How does Newman help to explain why the mere accumulation of facts or information is not education? Newman's discussion is very closely related to the ideas of Martin. In what way does he add depth and complexity to those ideas?

3. Newman's discussion suggests that a man who undertakes education must have certain capacities to begin with. What are they? How does Newman rank them in value?

4. What was Newman's objection to the popular education of his day? Exactly what advantage does he see in the kind of education that requires residence as compared with the kind that requires the passing of examinations? To what extent would Barzun agree with Newman?

5. Write a theme explaining your own educational aims.

6. Much of contemporary education is based on a point of view directly opposed to Newman's. Write a theme criticizing his opinions, showing why they are impractical or unrealistic.

*Education and Higher Learning**

Etienne Gilson

The aim and purpose of this address will be to describe the proper relationship that obtains, or should obtain, between education and higher learning. By the word "education" I intend to signify the system of schools now existing in most American and European countries, from primary schools up to universities, together with the programs and the general spirit that inspire their teaching methods. Naturally, since there is a great deal of variety within this system, my remarks will be of a general nature. They will deal with tendencies rather than with concrete facts. If and where exceptions are to be found, it should be understood beforehand that my remarks simply do not apply. If there is any truth in what I am about to say, it can be a global truth only. As to "higher learning," it will always signify that part of any complete school system that deals with liberal learning and, in consequence, with creative learning. We may have to use one or two concrete examples; yet, thus considered in its entire abstraction and generality, our problem will not be

* This selection was given as a lecture in Convocation Hall at the University of Toronto as part of the centennial celebration of St. Michael's College in 1952. Reprinted by permission of St. Michael's College.

discussed in terms of any local, national, or continental situation. Even the political notions it may have to touch upon will not be borrowed from practical politics, but from political philosophy. I trust, however, that the main consequences of these reflections will not appear irrelevant to practical life. For education is a field of human activity in which it is most necessary that speculation go before action.

Let us first consider teaching as it is commonly understood in European as well as in American public schools, or even high schools, below the university level. Its object is an immediately practical one. A civilized country is made up of citizens who can read and write, perform elementary arithmetical operations, say something about the place of their own country in both space and time; last, not the least, it is made up of citizens who know enough in order to discharge one of the many functions necessary to the welfare of the community. Incidentally, this is what justifies the right of intervention by the State in matters of education, and this right extends much farther than some of us would feel willing to concede. In his encyclical letter *Repraesentanti in terra,* December 31, 1929, Pope Pius XI expressly says: "The State can demand, and therefore see to it, that all citizens be endowed with the necessary knowledge of their civic and national duties, nay, with a certain amount of intellectual, moral, and physical culture which, given the conditions prevailing in our own times, is necessarily required for the common good." Education, then, has become a public service to the full extent to which it has become a public necessity. At the same time, and to the same extent, education is tending to become more and more practical in nature, because, for the State, the common good of the body politic is a practical end. Such is the reason why our schools are progressively tending either to become vocational schools or, at least, to prepare children in view of such schools, wherein they will ultimately qualify for some specialized job.

The same remark applies even to colleges and universities. From a mere glance at their programs, it appears that their proper function is to turn out, year in, year out, the right number of trained engineers, physicians, lawyers, farmers, and businessmen necessary to the welfare of a civilized country. Professors and teachers of all types are no exceptions to the rule. Our students express themselves correctly when they say that they are looking for a teaching *job.* To teach is not to speculate, an avocation for which nobody ever was paid. To teach is to act. What do we require from future teachers at all levels? Simply that they know what they will have to teach. In many cases we content ourselves with making sure that they will be able to learn it a week ahead of their pupils. Indeed, there would be no sense in protesting against the generalized tendency that now prevails to assign useful ends to our modern system of education.

Here, however, a distinction should be made between the two notions of "practicality" and of "usefulness." Were these identical, there would be for us no problem to discuss. We could then quote with unqualified approval the forceful remarks of A. N. Whitehead on the subject.[1] "Pedants," Whitehead says, "sneer at an education which is useful. But if education is not useful, what is it? Is it a talent, to be hidden away in a napkin? Of course education should be useful, whatever your aim in life. It was useful to St. Augustine and it was useful to Napoleon. It is useful, because understanding is useful." To this, which is undoubtedly true, we nevertheless beg to add that understanding is not always useful in the same way. What Napoleon learned at the artillery school of Brienne was the art of handling guns; a useful art in its own way, to be sure, but a very practically useful one. As to what St. Augustine had learned from St. Ambrose and from Plotinus, it was infinitely more useful still, since it was the way to achieve salvation, than which nothing can be more useful to man; yet, at the same time, he had also learned that salvation was beatitude; that is, the love of truth for its own sake, than which nothing less practical and more speculative can possibly be conceived. Understanding is always useful indeed, but when he himself wrote about the "divine beauty" of Lagrange's equations, Whitehead would have been much better understood by St. Augustine than by Napoleon. *Gaudium de veritate,* the joy born in us from the mere sight of truth: is it useful? Of course it is. But because it is an end in itself, not a means to any other end, it is not at all practical.

Seen from this precise point of view, the practical trend now prevailing in modern education raises a difficult problem. Does it provide boys and girls, students in all fields, with the proper feeling for the supreme importance of that type of knowledge which, precisely because it is not practical, might well be the most useful of all? In protesting against those who believe in the possibility of useless knowledge, Whitehead probably had in mind the distinction drawn by Cardinal Newman, whose works he knew so well, between a "liberal" education and a "useful" education. But a more careful examination of his text clearly shows that where he was writing "useful," what the Cardinal had in mind was "practical." In his Fifth Discourse, *On the Scope and Nature of University Education,* Newman has lovingly described what he used to call "liberal knowledge" as a knowledge "sufficient for itself, apart from every external and ulterior object." [2] To which he added that to educate for such knowledge is the true scope of a university. Even after granting to Whitehead that this

[1] A. N. Whitehead, *The Aims of Education* (Mentor Books, 1949), p. 14.
[2] Newman was well aware of this derivation as well as of its ideological implications. Speaking of the word "liberal," Newman says: "Now, first, in its grammatical sense it is opposed to *servile;* and by 'servile work' is understood, as our catechisms inform us, bodily labour, mechanical employment, and the like, in which the mind has little or no part." (*The Idea of a University,* London: Longman's, Green and Co., 1912, p. 106.) Liberal knowledge, Newman has just observed, is "the especial property of a University and a gentleman" (p. 106). When such expressions are used in their literal meaning, "we contrast a liberal education with a commercial education or a professional" (p. 107).

knowledge is eminently useful, the fact remains that its own type of usefulness has nothing to do with practicality. How is it, then, that instead of keeping faith with Newman's ideal, the general trend of our modern school system is to stress the kind of knowledge that is not sufficient for itself, but always aims at some external and ulterior object?

Let us honestly face the difficulty. "Liberal knowledge" is not a new formula. Originally it pointed out the knowledge of the so-called "liberal arts"; that is to say, according to Cicero's own commentary, the knowledge of those arts which it is befitting for a free man to know: *artes libero dignae.* As to the other arts—namely, the mechanical ones—they were good for hand workers or, to say it more bluntly, for slaves. Of course legal slaves have long ceased to exist, yet, unless I am mistaken, more than a shade of this ancient meaning is still hovering over the language of Cardinal Newman [3] especially where he identifies "liberal knowledge" with "a gentleman's knowledge." [4] Not being myself an Englishman, I cannot pretend to know what it is to be a "gentleman." Yet I will make bold to say that, in Cardinal Newman's own mind, to study in view of becoming a skilled carpenter, a bricklayer, or even a trained mechanic would not have answered his definition of a gentleman's knowledge. When, to his own dismay, a true gentleman finds himself afflicted with a natural gift for such mechanical avocations, to resort to the British category of "hobby" is for him the only way to indulge his taste without losing his social dignity. Whatever else he may have been, the student described by Newman as a gentleman could certainly afford a university training free from immediate professional preoccupations. A truly Oxonian ideal indeed, at least as Oxford used to be in the good old times, but one which, in most parts of the world today, looks more like a dream than a reality. This gentlemanly type of education presupposes a measure of those worldly possessions which only wealthy men can afford to despise. Without in the least denying that modern universities are still successfully engaged in the task of turning out gentlemen, one may at least observe that the meaning of the word no longer is exactly what it used to be. In our own day, just as all women are ladies, all men are gentlemen.

The reason for this change is a political one. A democratic type of society has progressively replaced the aristocratic social order of Newman's England. This is not a question of political regimes, but rather a change in social structures, coming in the wake of political revolutions. There is no other choice than between aristocracy, which stands for inequality, and democracy, which stands for equality. Whether it calls itself a kingdom, an empire, a republic, or even a democratic republic, a society remains an aristocracy to the full extent that it maintains a privileged class, be it only that of those who "have" as against those who "have not." In modern democracies, this measure is steadily becoming

[3] Newman, *The Idea of a University,* pp. 107-108.
[4] Newman, *The Idea of a University,* p. 111.

an always smaller and smaller one, and this fact is not without deeply affecting the nature and the spirit of their systems of education, especially with respect to their attitude toward liberal knowledge and higher learning.

From the time of its very origins, which, for Western civilization, is that of ancient Greece, free and liberal speculation has always been made possible by the existence of a leisured class whose members, if they felt so inclined, could dedicate themselves to speculative research and to contemplation. For this reason, Aristotle says, the first men to philosophize were priests. The remark clearly applies to the middle ages, when nobody could become a scholar unless he was a cleric.[5] When both in Greece and in modern societies laymen became interested in learning, the existence of lay philosophers, scientists, and scholars of any sort was made possible either because they themselves belonged to the aristocracy of their time, which was the case for Francis Bacon and for Descartes, or else because some enlightened members of that aristocracy provided them with the intellectual leisure necessary for disinterested speculation. The Florence of the Medici, Elizabethan England, the France of Louis XIV, where writers, artists, and scientists of all countries stood a fair chance of being supported by the King or by the nobility, are so many outstanding examples of what aristocratic societies can do for liberal knowledge. This type of culture was truly liberal, because it was not expected to bring about any practical results either for those who paid for it or for those who were being paid to produce it. Princes would then find it natural to favor the development of the arts and the sciences simply because they knew that beauty and truth were good things to be enjoyed for their own sake. Artists and scientists had no idea of making a fortune out of their work. So long as their protectors gave them enough to live, they considered themselves highly privileged, as indeed they were, since they were free to live a wholly unpractical life, the only one in which they were interested.

The kind of education that befits such a type of aristocratic culture is easy to define: it is the education of the elite, by an elite, and for an elite. In such circumstances, education is the received method whereby an aristocracy recruits its future members or, at least, the competent body of citizens who, sharing in the benefits of the prevailing social system, are interested in insuring its survival. No wonder, then, that at the very times when it gave birth to a Dante, a Shakespeare, or a Descartes, Eu-

---

[5] One of the most revolutionary effects of Christianity was to call *all men*, slaves or not, ignorant or learned, to the most liberal type of knowledge, which is that of truth embraced for its own sake. Faith made it accessible to all. This is the deep-seated reason why the Catholic Church has always favored liberal studies. In as much as they are truly liberal, studies aim to lead human minds to truth enjoyed for its own sake; that is, to contemplation. And what is eternal life, if not the eternal enjoyment of absolute Truth?

rope had practically no system of public schools; so much so, that by far the larger number of its inhabitants were illiterate. Aristocracy is a great producer of higher learning and of liberal knowledge, only it keeps it to itself; it is a spring rather than a stream.

Not so in democratic societies, whose systems of education naturally follow the rule of their political life. What they want is an education of the whole people, given by men who themselves belong among the people and, consequently, intended for the greater benefit of the people in its entirety. This time we find ourselves confronted with a powerful system of intellectual irrigation whose streams are visible everywhere; the only questions are: Where is the spring? Where are the sources? Can there still be sources in a society whose natural tendency is to universalize education and, consequently, to equalize it?

This is a genuine issue, which we must have the courage to face, not in any spirit of criticism, and still less of hostility, toward democracy, but with the sincere desire to understand its educational problems and thus throw some light on its difficulties. There are several interrelated reasons why, whereas aristocracies were more interested in creating intellectual culture than in spreading it, democracies seem to be more eager to distribute higher learning than to create it. Among these reasons there is a particularly obvious one. If our school system exists, not in view of a chosen minority, but in view of all, its average level should answer the average level of the population as a whole. Hence the unavoidable consequence that the best gifted among the pupils will be discriminated against. Nor should we imagine that creative minds will multiply in direct proportion to the growth of the school population. The reverse is much more likely to happen. In aristocratic societies, genius has often found access to higher culture, even under adverse circumstances; in democratic societies, it will have no higher culture to which to gain access. Since equality in ignorance is easier to achieve than equality in learning, each and every teacher will have to equalize his class at the bottom level rather than at the top one, and the whole school system will spontaneously obey the same law. It is anti-democratic to teach all children what only some of them are able to learn. Nay, it is anti-democratic to teach what all children can learn by means of methods which only a minority of pupils are able to follow. Since, as has been said, democracy stands for equality, democratic societies have a duty to teach only what is accessible to all and to see to it that it be made accessible to all. The overwhelming weight of their school population is therefore bound to lower the center of gravity in their school systems. The first peril for democracies, therefore, is to consider it their duty, in order to educate all citizens, to teach each of them less and less and in a less and less intelligent way.

It is not easy to say such things without sounding satirical, which I have no intention of being. I myself am an old teacher, and I would not let it be thought either that I am pining for a return of our countries to some aristocratic type of society, or that, when I remember what schools used to be around 1890, I see things deteriorating from bad to worse. Much progress has been achieved; the only point I am stressing is: Has there been progress all along the line? We are teaching more and more, but are we teaching better and better? And, if not, is it not because, confronted as they are with the legitimate task of providing learning for all their citizens, modern democracies have to cope with entirely new problems for which they are not prepared? The task of turning learning into a commodity and education into a public service is something both necessary and unheard of, for which there is no historical precedent. We should not feel too surprised to see the democratic State handling education like coal, hydroelectric power, or public means of transportation. The State must control everything in order to insure the equal distribution of all necessary goods among all citizens, including even education. We do not want this progress to stop, we simply do not want it to defeat its own purpose; and this is what the democratic State is going to do if it does not handle learning according to its own nature, which, because it is born of the mind, is wholly unlike any other kind of commodity.

We have reached such a pass that pedagogical authorities are beginning to think that learning is there in view of the schools, not the schools in view of learning.[6] This very year some schoolteachers made once more the time-honored discovery that the spelling of their mother tongue stood in need of being simplified. I need not quote the name of the country, because there is not a single language in the world whose spelling could not be made simpler than it is. The only trouble is that, in order to be perfectly simple, spelling has to be purely phonetic, in which case nobody can understand what he reads. This, however, is not my point. What I am interested in is the main rule set up by the committee on the simplification of spelling in that country. According to the school inspector who wrote the report, the committee decided either to accept, or else to reject, all suggested changes "according as they could, or could not, facilitate the teaching of the language." This curious pedagogical imperialism implies that the proper function of spelling is to be taught. Such teachers do not consider themselves the servants of learning, but its owners; so they have a full right to change it in order to facilitate their work. And indeed, why not? If all citizens have an equal right to know spelling, spelling should

---

[6] A striking symptom of this disease, and one that deserves special study, is the present tendency of pedagogy to become an independent discipline. There are pedagogues whose ambition it is to teach how to teach. As often as not, such teachers undertake to teach disciplines which they themselves do not know, or know imperfectly, to those who know them. Their attitude implies that the divorce of teaching from learning is now complete. Moreover, this also turns teaching itself into a "servile work." What is more, the divorce of teaching from learning threatens our whole educational system with failure; for the only effective pedagogical methods are those that proceed from learning itself, through the person of the teacher, to the person of the pupil.

be made foolproof and equally available to all citizens. I am sorry to say, without any trace of irony, that this is the principle which we now apply to practically all disciplines, from spelling to metaphysics. We do not impart learning such as it is, but such as it ought to be in order to be teachable to the millions. From time to time, some simple-minded professor attempts to make his pupils understand, not himself, but that which he teaches. The rumor soon begins to spread that the poor man cannot make himself understood. So he is a bad teacher, and we turn *him* out of his class, not the pupils.

Besides the general lowering of its level, another consequence follows from this democratic treatment of education at the hands of the State; namely, its predominately practical character. Nothing is more logical; and this time, since all citizens are part and parcel of the democratic State, all we have to do is to consult ourselves in order to know its will. Time and again, we have heard fathers say with solemn gravity: "I want my son to have an education." In point of fact, we all have said it ourselves, but what we really have meant is: "I want my son to get a job." A perfectly legitimate desire indeed. At the end of their studies, good students should get jobs that will turn them into citizens equally useful to themselves, to their future families, and to their country. Since such is the wish of the vast majority of its citizens, the democratic State will naturally tend to give them what they want; that is, a sound, practical education with no frills. This is what all teaching States are now doing, and they do it pretty well. Once more, I am not criticizing; I am merely trying to observe facts, and the outstanding fact, in this case, is that what we agreed to call "liberal knowledge," precisely because it has no practical usefulness, is bound to be eliminated together with the frills. The steady decline of classical studies, in Europe as well as in America, is a clear instance of what I have in mind. Even their strongest supporters cannot pretend that classical humanities are practically useful in everyday life; those among us who try to defend them on this ground are simply betraying their cause. Even if classical humanities may be put to practical use, this cannot be the reason why they should be taught. Such an aristocratic type of education simply cannot be universalized. As a consequence, no room can be made for it in the programs of schools which must cater to all citizens. So we teach them too little, or too late, which is little better than not to teach them at all. Why complain? Liberal knowledge, Newman says, is to itself its own end; in our industrial age, contemplation is a luxury which very few States can afford to subsidize. The cold truth is that the practical uselessness which recommended liberal education to Cardinal Newman's mind today justifies its exclusion from the curriculum of our democratic schools. Even societies cannot have their cake and eat it.

Yet there should be somebody to make the cake, and it is to be feared that, unless they re-examine their own educational problem, democracies will soon find themselves with nothing to eat. First of all, democratic education rests upon the principle of equality applied to the human understanding. But this application is a fallacy of the well-known type, which consists in applying to two different orders what is true of only one of them. The notion of democracy is a social one; it expresses the common will of a people to deal with its own members as if all men were born free and equal. On the contrary, human understanding is a fact of nature, and whether we like it or not, facts of nature are not equal. Nature is not democratic. Physical and intellectual inequalities can be corrected, or compensated; the democratic State can see to it that even the less gifted among its citizens be given a fair chance to learn and to know something; it can narrow the gap that separates creative genius from merely normal intellects, and even from abnormally backward ones; above all, democracy can prevent natural inequalities from begetting social privileges sometimes worse than the natural ones; yet, when all is said and done, nature can be corrected, not suppressed. Understanding is not equal in men. Intellectual life is just what it is, not what society would like it to be. Unless democracies accept its laws just as they are, they may well turn out an always larger number of teachers, they will have less and less to teach.

We are simply forgetting that intellectual superiority and fitness for speculative knowledge are one and the same thing. In this sense, liberal knowledge is the only source of all practically useful knowledge, without any exception. Classical humanities are not the only relevant example. As a token of the general nature of the problem, I beg to quote the growing misconception of what science itself actually is. On June 16, 1952, the continental edition of the British *Daily Mail* announced to its readers that the United States had their first atom submarine "nearly ready." To this the same newspaper added the following personal comment of the President of the United States: "The day that the propellers of this new submarine first bite into the water will be the most momentous day in the field of atomic science, since the first flash of light down in the desert seven years ago." A typically democratic statement indeed, in which "science" merely means "engineering." The first flash of light in the field of atomic science did not shine in any desert seven years ago, but in the minds of Einstein and of other scientists who were speculating about the structure of matter and not looking for atom bombs or for atom submarines. True science is liberal knowledge; scientists seek after it for its own sake; engineers put it to practical use; they do not want to know in order to know, but in order to make. Yet it is a positive and well-established fact that the more speculative and liberal it is, the more fruitful scientific knowledge proves to be in its practical applications. Pasteur saved millions of human lives although he himself was not a physician. Nearer home, I do not think that Dr. Banting, who was a physician, ever intended to find a specific for diabetes; yet when he first isolated insulin, the specific was found. Science found it; medicine applied it.

If this be true, our democratic system of education now finds itself at a crossroad. It has done wonders in the past and we do not want it to undo them. There must be an education for the millions; the learning included in this type of mass education should be both practical and simple, that is to say, adapted to the general needs and to the average intellectual aptitudes of its pupils; yet, at the same time, even a thoroughly democratic system of education should not allow its ceaselessly growing body to lead its head. Unless they themselves provide, not a new aristocratic social class, but their own intellectual elite, which is something different, the social and technical progress of which our modern democratic States are so justly proud will soon come to to end. In peace and war, the powerful industrial equipment of the greatest among modern nations can be rendered obsolete at any time by the abstract speculation of some unknown scientist using a few sheets of paper and a pencil in the solitude of his own study. Nor should we forget that the times of the greatest national perils are also those when foreign scientists are no longer an available commodity.[7] This is not for democracies a matter of choice. None of them can hope indefinitely to consume the products of natural aristocracy without adding its own contribution to the common good. What we now need, within our present system of universal education, is another system, this time of selection, whose proper object will be not to thwart the best gifted intellects which it is our task to educate. Unless it follows such a policy, no nation can hope to prosper for a very long time. True democracy in education certainly consists in insuring the intellectual survival of even the unfit; it cannot possibly consist in preventing the natural superiority of the fittest from bearing their fruits to the greater benefit of all.

This obvious truth should not be so hard to understand. There is nothing less democratic, in the usual sense of the word, than sports and games. Championship is the triumph of carefully cultivated natural inequalities. There is no point in pretending that, in a democracy, every citizen should be able to beat Olympic records. We simply could not do it, however hard we might try, but we do not resent the fact. We do not ask our directors

---

[7] Even this very practical point is not always understood. In the Toronto *Globe and Mail,* Sept. 12, 1952, Sir Eric Rideal, a distinguished British scientist then visiting Ottawa, issued the timely warning: "You cannot trade on the originality of another country forever." If there is an obvious truth, this is one. Yet the next issue of the same paper (Sept. 13) summed up the consensus of a group of leading Canadian industrialists in this terse sentence: "Sir Eric is all wet." Their main objection was that, to carry out his suggestion "would definitely not be good for the Canadian pocketbook," the more so as "the importation of ideas is easy and there is no tax on them." This statement deserves to endure as an outstanding specimen in the history of mental parasitology. At any rate, the complete failure of Sir Eric to convey an exceedingly simple idea is enough to show that the task of importing them is not as easy as it might seem.

of athletics to prevent some students from running as fast as they can because if they did they would run faster than the others. We do not consider it democratic to set athletic standards as low as possible. On the contrary, we fully realize the fact that the exceptional performances of a few world champions act as a fruitful challenge whose effects are actually felt in all stadiums and on all athletic fields. What is democratic, here as everywhere else, is to keep both competition and selection as widely open as possible, and then to set up the highest conceivable standard as a standing invitation to all. In short, the only sound policy for any democracy is to raise the average level of its people by cultivating the excellency of the best among its citizens.[8]

What we understand so well concerning the education of the body, could we not understand it concerning the education of the mind? Unless we do, we shall go on drifting along the same way which has already led us to make pedagogy the judge of learning. It can be concisely described in Shakespeare's terse words: "My foot my tutor." High school programs adapted to the kind of pupils they receive; university programs adapted to the kind of pupils that high schools are permitted by law to provide; and no provision made for the free development of liberal knowledge under all its forms, whose creative activity is the life and blood of any system of education! Things have gone so far that I might cite several countries in which, despairing as it were of saving higher learning, their governments have erected, outside universities, new institutions specialized in research work, where scholars seek but do not teach, while university professors teach but do not seek. I beg to say that, in so far as public education is concerned, wholly to surrender to this new tendency would be nothing less than the beginning of the end. The remedy we need should not consist in killing the patient. Since it is the course of nature that education derives its substance from the creative activity of a few speculative minds, let us rather help nature to follow its course. Where there is no higher learning, the presence of creative minds becomes less probable,

---

[8] Many professors and college presidents bitterly complain about the fact that students exhibit a much more marked taste for athletics than for academic studies. I beg to suggest that the students are right on this point. To the extent that they are not "professional," sports and athletics are enjoyed for their own sake and are to themselves their own end. From this point of view, which has not escaped the perspicacity of Cardinal Newman (*op. cit.*, pp. 107-108), "manly games, or games of skill, or military prowess, though bodily, are, it seems, accounted liberal." And rightly so. But if this is true, then athletics is now the only part of our school programs which is, officially and unrestrictedly, animated by a liberal spirit. Instead of asking for less athletics, we should rather bring back to the classroom the liberal spirit which once inspired it and still inspires athletics. Our only choice, therefore, is either to eliminate from our programs everything whose practical usefulness is not perceptible to students themselves, or else to say to them frankly that practical usefulness should not be the end of their education. Where the liberal spirit still prevails, students derive as much pleasure from the classroom as from the athletic field.

intellectual light ceases to shine, routine and pedantry set in, and living truths shrivel into desiccated formulas. Then we begin complaining about the general decay of studies, as if students could still take an interest in matters which, even for those who teach them, have already lost their meaning. The situation needs attention, but it is not desperate. All we have to do in order to mend it is to refuse to allow our educational body to grow too big for its soul, and to remember that its soul is liberal knowledge, itself the source of higher learning.

STUDY QUESTIONS

1. Recapitulate the changes in education described by Gilson. To what historical causes does he attribute them?

2. Gilson refers to Cardinal Newman's observation that liberal knowledge is its own end. How does he show that this characteristic once was an advantage and is now a disadvantage?

3. Compare the views of Morgan and Gilson on the potential usefulness of purely speculative thinking and research.

4. Why does Gilson disapprove of the separation of teaching and research which he describes as being effected in some countries?

5. What dangers to education are presented by democracy? Do you agree with his opinions about this? If not, write a theme opposing them.

6. Do you agree that "democratic education rests upon the principle of equality applied to the human understanding"? If you are dissatisfied with this formulation of the democratic view of education, write a theme describing democratic principles as they should be applied to education.

PART THREE

Man

in Society

1. THE AMERICAN SCENE

The New American*

D. W. Brogan

What is this new man, the new American? Here we move into deep waters of sociological theory in which I can hardly keep afloat, much less swim. Is the new American society producing a new American or a new myth about the new American? Maybe a new American; but some of the reasons advanced are not totally convincing. The new American may be conformist, but was the old often nonconformist? I wrote in the first edition of this book that "any well-established village in New England or the northern Middle West could afford a town drunkard, a town atheist and a few Democrats." It can now afford more than one town drunkard (called "alcoholics," of course), being a Democrat is less bold today than it was; some of the nicest people are Democrats; but a town atheist? "There are no atheists in the foxholes," and America is now in a foxhole that she may have to inhabit for a generation. The consequence of this predicament is that refusal to give lip service, at least, to the American religion is a kind of treason and is punished as it was in the America of a century ago.

It is not the social coercion of the real dissenter, the man who by his action or inaction condemns the faith of his neighbors, that is the new thing. (All that need be said on democratic conformity was said by Tocqueville.) What is new is the increasing condemnation of the man who conforms *too* vigorously, who pursues happiness in indisputably American terms, but pursues it with too little regard for his neighbor's comfort. Of course he *is* in competition with them, but he mustn't rub that fact in or

* From *The American Character* by D. W. Brogan, by permission of Alfred A. Knopf, Inc. Copyright, 1956, by Denis W. Brogan.

rejoice too much in victory. He must win without showing it and, to be able to win, he must not antagonize the other runners, who will gang up on him if he does. The race is still to the swift but mere swiftness is not enough if its too ostentatious display leads to some other competitor's bumping or spiking, with the approval of the other competitors—and the spectators. So far this new-found consideration may be only skin deep; it may be only a tactic, but it is interesting that it is a tactic.[1]

It is, on the surface, a long way from the traditional pioneer; it may be more than a change of methods; it may be a change of spirit. And yet, and yet! By European standards, what is still notable about American life is that competition, even by the new, softer, more formally amiable methods, is the accepted way of life. So is the lavishness of the prizes; so is the acceptance of the fact that not everybody can answer the $64,000 question —and the absence of jealousy of the winners. This absence of jealousy, this conviction that the game is worth playing and the results not cooked, is one of the chief sources of American wealth, well-being, and political stability. No one (hardly anyone, Negroes excepted) feels automatically excluded from the pursuit of happiness. Even the Negroes feel less excluded than they did. There is consequently a universal acceptance of the legitimacy of the political authority of "We, the People of the United States," that startles and impresses European visitors like Père Bruckberger. In this very important sense, a more perfect union has been attained than is known in any country in Europe and which pleases or angers European visitors in accordance with their personal temperaments and doctrines.

There is, of course, a danger or a promise that the formal good manners of the American acquisitive society will in fact weaken the acquisitive motive and habit. Not only can no one be rich on the old scale (taxes see to that), but achievement in the field of production is not admired as it was in the older, simpler, cruder American society. No great business magnate will ever know the free command of wealth that Rockefeller and Carnegie knew; the admiration, just short of worship, that Edison and Henry Ford I knew. Whether the lessened rewards will begin to eat into the will to "succeed" of the young American we do not yet know. The old battle of the strong had the attractions of battle. The modern business career is more like the peace-time career of the professional soldier than the bloody campaigns that brought the Robber Barons to the top. It is not insignifi-

---

[1] How far the new spirit has gone is illustrated by the innocent remark of an Irish-American contractor, specializing in pulling down buildings and excavating foundations, traditionally tough trades. Mr. Howard Collins notes the change. " 'When I started in this business, everybody was a roughneck. Talked dirty, dressed dirty, lived dirty. Now the men come to work in nice clothes, drive nice cars, live in nice houses, have nice families. Funny thing that's happened in this country—nobody *has* to be tough any more.' " *The New Yorker*, December 31, 1955.

cant that the services of the Robber Barons are now better appreciated when (outside Texas) they are, as a breed, almost extinct.

In discussing this question we are all at school to Mr. David Riesman, and if the "inner directed" are indeed in retreat, are becoming un-American, the United States may be moving nearer the Soviet Union than it realizes, for Communism, too, professes to create a new man as unlike the conscience-driven heroes of Dostoievsky as the modern dweller in the executive suite, in gray flannel, is unlike such flamboyant pirates as Jim Fisk. If it is no longer a matter of "keeping up with the Joneses," but of everybody keeping up with everybody else, it is possible that the American people will end up going round, in happy harmony, a mulberry bush that isn't there. And against such a danger a great deal of modern American religiosity is less than no safeguard.

It is not only a matter of adjusting to the great, anonymous, self-governing, mass-owned corporations to whose service and promises so many young Americans gladly give themselves. It is a matter of adjusting to a world in which mass organizations are the normal centers of life for more and more millions of human beings. It can be asserted that the United States must adjust or perish. And one aspect of that adjustment is the immense growth of the armed forces and of the economic units serving them. Millions of Americans in 1939 had little or nothing to do with the government of the United States. Millions of Americans in 1944 looked forward to a near and victorious future in which they would have nothing to do with that government. They were disillusioned. From that disillusion has come much of what has most disturbed the outside world in contemporary America, McCarthyism, "sounding-off" by cabinet officers, senators, generals, columnists, threats of atomic war, brisk denunciation of allies and the like. The Americans are forced to live not only in a world they have not made, but in a world that they definitely thought they had killed in its cradle. No wonder the average American is uneasy, ready to believe that the cause of all his discontents is treason or folly in his rulers, unwilling to accept the fact that the world was not made exclusively by or for Americans. Great wonder that, with all these natural grounds for resentment of the human situation, he has *not* revolted against prudence or duty, that he has accepted leadership every time that it has been offered, has, in such different activities as the Marshall Plan and the Korean War, given the world a lead and an example, has, with a readiness totally unforeseen in 1939 and only barely hoped for in 1944, risen to his duty. Those who expected much from the American people have not been disappointed.

There are other ways in which they have not been disappointed. Despite setbacks like the revival of lynching in Mississippi, the frenzies provoked by the threat of desegregation in southern schools, the revival of the most farcical and odious doctrines of race supremacy, in no field of human relations has the United States made more progress than in its dealing with Negro Americans. The churches, laggard enough in 1939, have in many cases been pioneers—above all, the Catholic Church, where bishops have shown that there is something to be said for a church in which authority does not come from the grass roots; grass roots are sometimes poisoned.

American trade unions are not led by or composed of angels. But they have proved a great stabilizing force and if the American economic system, called, a little naïvely, the "free-enterprise system," has secured such universal acceptance, it is in part due to the integration of the American worker in American industrial society by the trade unions.

In the same way, the social services, so bitterly opposed, open as some are to grave and increasing abuse, have made the government of the United States something less remote, less merely demanding than it was. The woes of the farmer may be real, but it is significant that he turns, simply and candidly, to the government to keep him in the state to which he thinks he is entitled. This is a change from the days of "root, hog, or die," but it represents less a change in attitude than an acceptance of the fact that the urbanization of the American society makes certain proud old agricultural attitudes very expensive. The American farmer, in his rugged way, would rather have money without control, and he may get it. But he is not yet ready to join a kolkhoz to get a living.

There are other changes whose consequences no one, at any rate not I, can foresee. What is to become of the equality between the sexes in an economy that both imposes the draft and pours the horn of plenty of veterans' benefits solely on the male part of the population? What is to become of the school system when its task changes from that of adjusting the young to a new society to giving them intellectual tools to run it? What is to become of a society that can afford leisure on an unprecedented scale and may have to find uses for free men and citizens, deprived of their social utility by automation? No one knows and, final blessing, no one in America really thinks that he knows. Free from ideological baggage, the hopeful American plunges rather than strides forward. After all, said Cromwell, no man goes as far as the man who does not know where he is going. The American may be going to hell in a wheelbarrow or in a flying saucer. If he is, we'll all go with him. But I suspect that, humanly speaking, heaven's his destination. He won't quite get there, but he'll go far and fare better than if he doubted the general wisdom of his course. When ex-President Jackson was being buried, a visitor asked one of his slaves if he thought that General Jackson (like many soldier Presidents, a belated convert to formal Christianity) would go to heaven. "He will if he wants to." General Jackson was and is a symbol of the American.

STUDY QUESTIONS

1. The degree to which the portrayal of such an abstraction as "the new American" is convincing will depend largely upon the skill with which the writer draws concrete details to the support of his generalizations. How skillful has Brogan been in this? Do you accept his generalizations about "the new American"? What concrete details can you think of that seem to contradict his generalizations? Do these make his portrayal an "inaccurate" one? How accurate can such portrayals be?

2. What is the great change in the acquisitive drive of Americans that Brogan sees as a future possibility? What signs does Brogan see which indicate that Americans are genuinely united?

3. What is the post-war development in America that seems particularly significant to Brogan?

4. What relation do you find between Brogan's observation that overt competition is taboo in America, and Ortega y Gasset's view that the mass man loves comfort and the feeling that he is the equal of everyone?

5. Can you give further examples of the increasing participation of Americans in mass organizations and enterprises, such as Federal housing and power, social security, and military service? Do you think that individuality is compromised by this sort of activity?

6. Write a paper describing some type or kind of person—the college Freshman, the science instructor, the small town store-owner—in which you draw a series of generalizations about the type and support them with carefully selected detail.

White-Collar People*

C. Wright Mills

The white-collar people slipped quietly into modern society. Whatever history they have had is a history without events; whatever common interests they have do not lead to unity; whatever future they have will not be of their own making. If they aspire at all it is to a middle course, at a time when no middle course is available, and hence to an illusory course in an imaginary society. Internally, they are split, fragmented; externally, they are dependent on larger forces. Even if they gained the will to act, their actions, being unorganized, would be less a movement than a tangle of unconnected contests. As a group, they do not threaten anyone; as individuals, they do not practice an independent

* From *White Collar* by C. Wright Mills. © 1951, by Oxford University Press, Inc. Reprinted by permission.

way of life. So before an adequate idea of them could be formed, they have been taken for granted as familiar actors of the urban mass.

Yet it is to this white-collar world that one must look for much that is characteristic of twentieth-century existence. By their rise to numerical importance, the white-collar people have upset the nineteenth-century expectation that society would be divided between entrepreneurs and wage workers. By their mass way of life, they have transformed the tang and feel of the American experience. They carry, in a most revealing way, many of those psychological themes that characterize our epoch, and, in one way or another, every general theory of the main drift has had to take account of them. For above all else they are a new cast of actors, performing the major routines of twentieth-century society:

At the top of the white-collar world, the old captain of industry hands over his tasks to the manager of the corporation. Alongside the politician, with his string tie and ready tongue, the salaried bureaucrat, with brief case and slide rule, rises into political view. These top managers now command hierarchies of anonymous middle managers, floorwalkers, salaried foremen, county agents, federal inspectors, and police investigators trained in the law.

In the established professions, the doctor, lawyer, engineer, once was free and named on his own shingle; in the new white-collar world, the salaried specialists of the clinic, the junior partners in the law factory, the captive engineers of the corporation have begun to challenge free professional leadership. The old professions of medicine and law are still at the top of the professional world, but now all around them are men and women of new skills. There are a dozen kinds of social engineers and mechanical technicians, a multitude of girl Fridays, laboratory assistants, registered and unregistered nurses, draftsmen, statisticians, social workers.

In the salesrooms, which sometimes seem to coincide with the new society as a whole, are the stationary salesgirls in the department store, the mobile salesmen of insurance, the absentee salesmen—ad-men helping others sell from a distance. At the top are the prima donnas, the vice presidents who say that they are "merely salesmen, although perhaps a little more creative than others," and at the bottom, the five-and-dime clerks, selling commodities at a fixed price, hoping soon to leave the job for marriage.

In the enormous file of the office, in all the calculating rooms, accountants and purchasing agents replace the man who did his own figuring. And in the lower reaches of the white-collar world, office operatives grind along, loading and emptying the filing system; there are private secretaries and typists, entry clerks, billing clerks, corresponding clerks—a thousand kinds of clerks; the operators of light machinery, comptometers, dictaphones, addressographs; and the receptionists to let you in or keep you out. . . .

The nineteenth-century farmer and businessman were generally thought to be stalwart individuals—their own men, men who could quickly grow to be almost as big as anyone else. The twentieth-century white-collar man has never been independent as the farmer used to be, nor as hopeful of the main chance as the businessman. He is always somebody's man, the corporation's, the government's, the army's; and he is seen as the man who does not rise. The decline of the free entrepreneur and the rise of the dependent employee on the American scene has paralleled the decline of the independent individual and the rise of the little man in the American mind.

In a world crowded with big ugly forces, the white-collar man is readily assumed to possess all the supposed virtues of the small creature. He may be at the bottom of the social world, but he is, at the same time, gratifyingly middle class. It is easy as well as safe to sympathize with his troubles; he can do little or nothing about them. Other social actors threaten to become big and aggressive, to act out of selfish interests and deal in politics. The big businessman continues his big-business-as-usual through the normal rhythm of slump and war and boom; the big labor man, lifting his shaggy eyebrows, holds up the nation until his demands are met; the big farmer cultivates the Senate to see that big farmers get theirs. But not the white-collar man. He is more often pitiful than tragic, as he is seen collectively, fighting impersonal inflation, living out in slow misery his yearning for the quick American climb. He is pushed by forces beyond his control, pulled into movements he does not understand; he gets into situations in which his is the most helpless position. The white-collar man is the hero as victim, the small creature who is acted upon but who does not act, who works along unnoticed in somebody's office or store, never talking loud, never talking back, never taking a stand.

When the focus shifts from the generalized Little Man to specific white-collar types whom the public encounters, the images become diverse and often unsympathetic. Sympathy itself often carries a sharp patronizing edge; the word "clerk," for example, is likely to be preceded by "merely." Who talks willingly to the insurance agent, opens the door to the bill collector? "Everybody knows how rude and nasty salesgirls can be." Schoolteachers are standard subjects for businessmen's jokes. The housewife's opinion of private secretaries is not often friendly—indeed, much of white-collar fiction capitalizes on her hostility to "the office wife."

These are images of specific white-collar types seen from above. But from below, for two generations sons and daughters of the poor have looked forward eagerly to becoming even "mere" clerks. Parents have sacrificed to have even one child finish high school, business school, or college so that he could be the assistant to the executive, do the filing, type the letter, teach school, work in the government office, do something requiring technical skills: hold a white-collar job. In serious literature white-collar images are often subjects for lamentation; in popular writing they are often targets of aspiration.

Images of American types have not been built carefully by piecing together live experience. Here, as elsewhere, they have been made up out of tradition and schoolbook and the early, easy drift of the unalerted mind. And they have been reinforced and even created, especially in white-collar times, by the editorial machinery of popular amusement and mass communications.

Manipulations by professional image-makers are effective because their audiences do not or cannot know personally all the people they want to talk about or be like, and because they have an unconscious need to believe in certain types. In their need and inexperience, such audiences snatch and hold to the glimpses of types that are frozen into the language with which they see the world. Even when they meet the people behind the types face to face, previous images, linked deeply with feeling, blind them to what stands before them. Experience is trapped by false images, even as reality itself sometimes seems to imitate the soap opera and the publicity release.

Perhaps the most cherished national images are sentimental versions of historical types that no longer exist, if indeed they ever did. Underpinning many standard images of The American is the myth, in the words of the eminent historian, A. M. Schlesinger, Sr., of the "long tutelage to the soil" which, as "the chief formative influence," results in "courage, creative energy and resourcefulness. . . ." According to this idea, which clearly bears a nineteenth-century trademark, The American possesses magical independence, homely ingenuity, great capacity for work, all of which virtues he attained while struggling to subdue the vast continent.

One hundred years ago, when three-fourths of the people were farmers, there may have been some justification for engraving such an image and calling it The American. But since then, farmers have declined to scarcely more than one-tenth of the occupied populace, and new classes of salaried employees and wage-workers have risen. Deep-going historic changes resulting in wide diversities have long challenged the nationalistic historian who would cling to The American as a single type of ingenious farmer-artisan. In so far as universals can be found in life and character in America, they are due less to any common tutelage of the soil than to the leveling influences of urban civilization, and above all, to the standardization of the big technology and of the media of mass communication.

America is neither the nation of horse-traders and master builders of economic theory, nor the nation of go-getting, claim-jumping, cattle-rustling pioneers of frontier mythology. Nor have the traits rightly or wrongly associated with such historic types carried over into the contemporary population to any noticeable degree. Only a fraction of this population consists of free private enterprisers in any economic sense; there are now four times as many wage-workers and salary workers as independent entrepreneurs. "The struggle for life," William Dean Howells wrote in the 'nineties, "has changed from a free fight to an encounter of disciplined forces, and the free fighters that are left get ground to pieces. . . ."

If it is assumed that white-collar employees represent some sort of continuity with the old middle class of entrepreneurs, then it may be said that for the last hundred years the middle classes have been facing the slow expropriation of their holdings, and that for the last twenty years they have faced the spectre of unemployment. Both assertions rest on facts, but the facts have not been experienced by the middle class as a *double* crisis. The property question is not an issue to the new middle class of the present generation. That was fought out, and lost, before World War I, by the old middle class. The centralization of small properties is a development that has affected each generation back to our great-grandfathers, reaching its climax in the Progressive Era. It has been a secular trend of too slow a tempo to be felt as a continuing crisis by middle-class men and women, who often seem to have become more commodity-minded than property-minded. Yet history is not always enacted consciously; if expropriation is not felt as crisis, still it is a basic fact in the ways of life and the aspirations of the new middle class; and the facts of unemployment *are* felt as fears, hanging over the white-collar world.

By examining white-collar life, it is possible to learn something about what is becoming more typically "American" than the frontier character probably ever was. What must be grasped is the picture of society as a great salesroom, an enormous file, an incorporated brain, a new universe of management and manipulation. By understanding these diverse white-collar worlds, one can also understand better the shape and meaning of modern society as a whole, as well as the simple hopes and complex anxieties that grip all the people who are sweating it out in the middle of the twentieth century.

The troubles that confront the white-collar people are the troubles of all men and women living in the twentieth century. If these troubles seem particularly bitter to the new middle strata, perhaps that is because for a brief time these people felt themselves immune to troubles.

Before the First World War there were fewer little men, and in their brief monopoly of high-school education they were in fact protected from many of the sharper edges of the workings of capitalist progress. They were free to entertain deep illusions about their individual abilities and about the collective trustworthiness of the system. As their number has grown, however, they have become increasingly subject to wage-worker conditions. Especially since the Great Depression have white-collar people come up against all the old problems of capitalist society. They have been racked by slump and war and even by boom. They have learned about impersonal unemployment in depressions and about impersonal death by technological violence in war. And in good times, as prices rose faster than salaries, the money they thought they were making was silently taken away from them.

The material hardship of nineteenth-century industrial workers finds its parallel on the psychological level among twentieth-century white-collar employees. The new Little Man seems to have no firm roots, no sure loyalties to sustain his life and give it a center. He is not aware of having any history, his past being as brief as it is unheroic; he has lived through no golden age he can recall in time of trouble. Perhaps because he does not know where he is going, he is in a frantic hurry; perhaps because he does not know what frightens him, he is paralyzed with fear. This is especially a feature of his political life, where the paralysis results in the most profound apathy of modern times.

The uneasiness, the malaise of our time, is due to this root fact: in our politics and economy, in family life and religion—in practically every sphere of our existence—the certainties of the eighteenth and nineteenth centuries have disintegrated or been destroyed and, at the same time, no new sanctions or justifications for the new routines we live, and must live, have taken hold. So there is no acceptance and there is no rejection, no sweeping hope and no sweeping rebellion. There is no plan of life. Among white-collar people, the malaise is deep-rooted; for the absence of any order of belief has left them morally defenseless as individuals and politically impotent as a group. Newly created in a harsh time of creation, white-collar man has no culture to lean upon except the contents of a mass society that has shaped him and seeks to manipulate him to its alien ends. For security's sake, he must strain to attach himself somewhere, but no communities or organizations seem to be thoroughly his. This isolated position makes him excellent material for synthetic molding at the hands of popular culture—print, film, radio, and television. As a metropolitan dweller, he is especially open to the focused onslaught of all the manufactured loyalties and distractions that are contrived and urgently pressed upon those who live in worlds they never made.

In the case of the white-collar man, the alienation of the wage-worker from the products of his work is carried one step nearer to its Kafka-like completion. The salaried employee does not make anything, although he may handle much that he greatly desires but cannot have. No product of craftsmanship can be his to contemplate with pleasure as it is being created and after it is made. Being alienated from any product of his labor, and going year after year through the same paper routine, he turns his leisure all the more frenziedly to the *ersatz* diversion that is sold him, and partakes of the synthetic excitement that neither eases nor releases. He is bored at work and restless at play, and this terrible alternation wears him out.

In his work he often clashes with customer and superior, and must almost always be the standardized loser: he must smile and be personable, standing behind the counter, or waiting in the outer office. In many strata of white-collar employment, such traits as courtesy, helpfulness, and kindness, once intimate, are now part of the impersonal means of livelihood. Self-alienation is thus an accompaniment of his alienated labor.

When white-collar people get jobs, they sell not only their time and energy but their personalities as well. They sell by the week or month their smiles and their kindly gestures, and they must practice the prompt repression of resentment and aggression. For these intimate traits are of commercial relevance and required for the more efficient and profitable distribution of goods and services. Here are the new little Machiavellians, practicing their personal crafts for hire and for the profit of others, according to rules laid down by those above them.

In the eighteenth and nineteenth centuries, rationality was identified with freedom. The ideas of Freud about the individual, and of Marx about society, were strengthened by the assumption of the coincidence of freedom and rationality. Now rationality seems to have taken on a new form, to have its seat not in individual men, but in social institutions which by their bureaucratic planning and mathematical foresight usurp both freedom and rationality from the little individual men caught in them. The calculating hierarchies of department store and industrial corporation, of rationalized office and governmental bureau, lay out the gray ways of work and stereotype the permitted initiatives. And in all this bureaucratic usurpation of freedom and of rationality, the white-collar people are the interchangeable parts of the big chains of authority that bind the society together.

White-collar people, always visible but rarely seen, are politically voiceless. Stray politicians wandering in the political arena without party may put "white collar" people alongside businessmen, farmers, and wage-workers in their broadside appeals, but no platform of either major party has yet referred to them directly. Who fears the clerk? Neither *Alice Adams* nor *Kitty Foyle* could be a *Grapes of Wrath* for the "share-croppers in the dust bowl of business."

But while practical politicians, still living in the ideological air of the nineteenth century, have paid little attention to the new middle class, theoreticians of the left have vigorously claimed the salaried employee as a potential proletarian, and theoreticians of the right and center have hailed him as a sign of the continuing bulk and vigor of the middle class. Stray heretics from both camps have even thought, from time to time, that the higher-ups of the white-collar world might form a center of initiative for new political beginnings. In Germany, the "black-coated worker" was one of the harps that Hitler played on his way to power. In England, the party of labor is thought to have won electoral socialism by capturing the votes of the suburban salaried workers.

To the question, what political direction will the white-collar people take, there are as many answers as there are theorists. Yet to the observer of American materials, the political problem posed by these people is not so much what the direction may be as whether they will take any political direction at all.

Between the little man's consciousness and the issues of our epoch there seems to be a veil of indifference. His will seems numbed, his spirit meager. Other men of other strata are also politically indifferent, but electoral victories are imputed to them; they do have tireless pressure groups and excited captains who work in and around the hubs of power, to whom, it may be imagined, they have delegated their enthusiasms for public affairs. But white-collar people are scattered along the rims of all the wheels of power; no one is enthusiastic about them and, like political eunuchs, they themselves are without potency and without enthusiasm for the urgent political clash.

Estranged from community and society in a context of distrust and manipulation; alienated from work and, on the personality market, from self; expropriated of individual rationality, and politically apathetic—these are the new little people, the unwilling vanguard of modern society. These are some of the circumstances for the acceptance of which their hopeful training has quite unprepared them.

STUDY QUESTIONS

1. What historical developments (some of them not mentioned here by Mills) produced the large class of white-collar workers? Why is the white-collar worker at a disadvantage in the social and economic arena?

2. Is the white-collar worker more like an entrepreneur or a factory worker? How useful are appearances in deciding this question?

3. What does Mills feel to be the main cause of the unfortunate position of the white-collar class as opposed to other classes?

4. Compare Mills' analysis of "white-collar people" in this selection with Brogan's analysis of the "new American." To what extent do they contradict each other? Agree with each other? Is one more "objective" or "accurate" than the other? To what extent are all authors writing on such subjects controlling and shaping reality in the fashion which Steinbeck describes in "Observation and Writing"?

5. Do you think Mills' picture of the life of the white-collar worker is unduly pessimistic? If so, write a theme telling the other side, and showing how he is better off than workers at other times or in other classes.

6. In what ways are white-collar people characteristic of their time and representative of the "psychological themes" of our age?

A Generation of Bureaucrats*

William H. Whyte, Jr.

When I was a college senior in 1939, we used to sing a plaintive song about going out into the "cold, cold world." It wasn't really so very cold then, but we did enjoy meditating on the fraughtness of it all. It was a big break we were facing, we told ourselves, and those of us who were going to try our luck in the commercial world could be patronizing toward those who were going on to graduate work or to academic life. We were taking the leap.

Seniors still sing the song, but somehow the old note of portent is gone. There is no leap left to take. The union between the world of organization and the college has been so cemented that today's seniors can see a continuity between the college and the life thereafter that we never did. Come graduation, they do not go outside to a hostile world; they transfer.

For the senior who is headed for the corporation it is almost as if it were part of one master scheme. The locale shifts; the training continues, for at the same time that the colleges have been changing their curriculum to suit the corporation, the corporation has responded by setting up its own campuses and classrooms. By now the two have been so well molded that it's difficult to tell where one leaves off and the other begins.

The descent, every spring, of the corporations' recruiters has now become a built-in feature of campus life. If the college is large and its placement director efficient, the processing operation is visibly impressive. I have never been able to erase from my mind the memory of an ordinary day at Purdue's placement center. It is probably the largest and most effective placement operation in the country, yet, much as in a well-run group clinic, there seemed hardly any activity. In the main room some students were quietly studying company literature arranged on the tables for them; others were checking the interview timetables to find what recruiter they would see and to which cubicle he was assigned; at the central filing desk college employees were sorting the hundreds of names of men who had registered for placement. Except for a murmur from the row of cubicles there was little to indicate that scores of young men were, every hour on the half hour, making the decisions that would determine their whole future life.

Someone from a less organized era might conclude that the standardiza-

* From *The Organization Man* by William H. Whyte, Jr. Copyright © 1956, by William H. Whyte, Jr. Reprinted by permission of Simon and Schuster, Inc.

tion of this machinery—and the standardized future it portends—would repel students. It does not. For the median senior this is the optimum future; it meshes so closely with his own aspirations that it is almost as if the corporation was planned in response to an attitude poll.

Because they are the largest single group, the corporation-bound seniors are the most visible manifestation of their generation's values. But in essentials their contemporaries headed for other occupations respond to the same urges. The lawyers, the doctors, the scientists—their occupations are also subject to the same centralization, the same trend to group work and to bureaucratization. And so are the young men who will enter them. Whatever their many differences, in one great respect they are all of a piece: more than any generation in memory, theirs will be a generation of bureaucrats.

They are, above all, conservative. Their inclination to accept the status quo does not necessarily mean that in the historic sweep of ideas they are conservative—in the more classical sense of conservatism, it could be argued that the seniors will be, in effect if not by design, agents of revolution. But this is a matter we must leave to later historians. For the immediate present, at any rate, what ideological ferment college men exhibit is not in the direction of basic change.

This shows most clearly in their attitude toward politics. It used to be axiomatic that young men moved to the left end of the spectrum in revolt against their fathers and then, as the years went on, moved slowly to the right. A lot of people still believe this is true, and many businessmen fear that twenty years of the New Deal hopelessly corrupted our youth into radicalism. After the election of 1952 businessmen become somewhat more cheerful, but many are still apprehensive, and whenever a poll indicates that students don't realize that business makes only about 6 per cent profit, there is a flurry of demands for some new crusade to rescue our youth from socialistic tendencies.

If the seniors do any moving, however, it will be from dead center. Liberal groups have almost disappeared from the campus, and what few remain are anemic. There has been no noticeable activity at the other end of the spectrum either. When William Buckley, Jr., produced *God and Man at Yale*, some people thought this signaled the emergence of a strong right-wing movement among the young men. The militancy, however, has not proved particularly contagious; when the McCarthy issue roused and divided their elders, undergraduates seemed somewhat bored with it all.

Their conservatism is passive. No cause seizes them, and nothing so exuberant or willfully iconoclastic as the Veterans of Future Wars has reappeared. There are Democrats and Republicans, and at election time there is the usual flurry of rallies, but in comparison with the agitation of the thirties no one seems to care too much one way or the other. There has been personal unrest—the suspense over the prospect of military service assures this—but it rarely gets resolved into a thought-out protest.

Come spring and students may start whacking each other over the head or roughing up the townees and thereby cause a rush of concern over the wild younger generation. But there is no real revolution in them, and the next day they likely as not will be found with their feet firmly on the ground in the recruiters' cubicles.

Some observers attribute the disinterest to fear. I heard one instructor tell his colleagues that in his politics classes he warned students to keep their noses clean. "I tell them," he said, "that they'd better realize that what they say might be held against them, especially when we get to the part about Marx and Engels. Someday in the future they might find their comments bounced back at them in an investigation."

The advice, as his colleagues retorted, was outrageously unnecessary. The last thing students can be accused of now is dangerous discussion; they are not interested in the kind of big questions that stimulate heresy and whatever the subject—the corporation, government, religion—students grow restive if the talk tarries on the philosophical. Most are interested in the philosophical only to the extent of finding out what the accepted view is in order that they may accept it and get on to the practical matters. This spares the bystander from the lofty bulling and the elaborate pose of unorthodoxy that my contemporaries often used to affect, but it does make for a rather stringent utilitarianism.

Even in theological seminaries, this impatience to be on with the job has been evident. Writes Norman Pittenger, professor at General Theological Seminary:

It is a kind of authoritarianism in reverse. Theological students today, in contrast to their fellows of twenty years ago, want "to be told." I have gone out of my way to ask friends who teach in seminaries of other denominations whether they have recognized the new tendency. Without exception they have told me that they find the present generation of students less inquiring of mind, more ready to accept an authority, and indeed most anxious to have it "laid on the line."

In the seminary this means that the lecturer or teacher must be unusually careful lest his opinion, or what "the Bible says" or "the church teaches," shall be taken as the last word. . . . What troubles many of us is that students today are not willing enough to think things through for themselves. If this is what the Bible says, then how does it say it and why, and how do we know that this is indeed the teaching of Scripture? If this is what the church teaches, why does it teach it, what evidence can be given for the teaching and what right has the church to teach at all? Or if a professor says that such-and-such a view is correct, why does he say it and what real evidence can he produce that his statement is true? It would be better and healthier if the new respect for authority were more frequently found in combination with a spirit of inquiry, a ready willingness to think through what is authoritatively declared, and a refusal ever to accept anything simply because some reputable expert makes the statement.

In judging a college generation, one usually bases his judgment on how much it varies from one's own, and presumably superior, class, and I must confess that I find myself tempted to do so. Yet I do not think my generation has any license to damn the acquiescence of seniors as a weakening of intellectual fiber. It is easy for us to forget that if earlier generations were less content with society, there was a great deal less to be contented about. In the intervening years the economy has changed enormously, and even in retrospect the senior can hardly be expected to share former discontents. Society is not out of joint for him, and if he acquiesces it is not out of fear that he does so. He does not want to rebel against the status quo because he really likes it—and his elders, it might be added, are not suggesting anything bold and new to rebel *for*.

Perhaps contemporaryism would be a better word than conservatism to describe their posture. The present, more than the past, is their model; while they share the characteristic American faith in the future also, they see it as more of same. As they paraphrase what they are now reading about America, they argue that at last we have got it. The big questions are all settled; we know the direction, and while many minor details remain to be cleared up, we can be pretty sure of enjoying a wonderful upward rise.

While the degree of their optimism is peculiarly American, the spirit of acquiescence, it should be noted, is by no means confined to the youth of this country. In an Oxford magazine, called, aptly enough, *Couth,* one student writes this of his generation:

It is true that over the last thirty years it has been elementary good manners to be depressed. . . . But . . . we are not, really, in the least worried by our impending, and other people's present, disasters. This is not the Age of Anxiety. What distinguishes the comfortable young men of today from the uncomfortable young men of the last hundred years . . . is that for once the younger generation is not in revolt against anything. . . . We don't want to rebel against our elders. They are much too nice to be rebellable-against. Old revolutionaries as they are, they get rather cross with us and tell us we are stuffy and prudish, but even this can't provoke us into hostility. . . . Our fathers . . . brought us up to see them not as the representatives of ancient authority and unalterable law but as rebels against our grandfathers. So naturally we have grown up to be on their side, even if we feel on occasion that they were a wee bit hard on their fathers, or even a little naïve.[1]

More than before, there is a tremendous interest in techniques. Having no quarrel with society, they prefer to table the subject of ends and concentrate instead on means. Not what or why but *how* interests them, and any evangelical strain they have they can sublimate; once they have

[1] Similar tendencies have been noticed among German youth. In *Der Junge Arbeiter von Heute,* Karl Bednarik, a former leader in the socialist youth movement, has commented on the "bourgeoisification" of younger workers as a response to the postwar situation.

equated the common weal with organization—a task the curriculum makes easy—they will let the organization worry about goals. "These men do not question the system," an economics professor says of them, approvingly. "They want to get in there and lubricate and make them run better. They will be technicians of the society, not innovators."

The attitude of men majoring in social science is particularly revealing on this score. Not so very long ago, the younger social scientist was apt to see his discipline as a vehicle for protest about society as well as the study of it. The seniors that set the fashion for him were frequently angry men, and many of the big studies of the twenties and thirties—Robert and Helen Lynd's *Middletown*, for example—did not conceal strong opinions about the inequities in the social structure. But this is now old hat: it is the "bleeding-heart" school to the younger men (and to some not so young, too), for they do not wish to protest; they wish to collaborate. Reflecting the growing reconciliation with middle-class values that has affected all types of intellectuals, they are turning more and more to an interest in methodology, particularly the techniques of measurement. Older social scientists who have done studies on broad social problems find that the younger men are comparatively uninterested in the problems themselves. When the discussion period comes, the questions the younger men ask are on the technical points; not the what, or why, but the how.

The urge to be a technician, a collaborator, shows most markedly in the kind of jobs seniors prefer. They want to work for somebody else. Paradoxically, the old dream of independence through a business of one's own is held almost exclusively by factory workers—the one group, as a number of sociologists have reported, least able to fulfill it. Even at the bull-session level college seniors do not affect it, and when recruiting time comes around they make the preference clear. Consistently, placement officers find that of the men who intend to go into business—roughly one half of the class—less than 5 per cent express any desire to be an entrepreneur. About 15 to 20 per cent plan to go into their fathers' business. Of the rest, most have one simple goal: the big corporation.

And not just as a stopgap either. When I was a senior many of us liked to rationalize that we were simply playing it smart; we were going with big companies merely to learn the ropes the better to strike out on our own later. Today, seniors do not bother with this sort of talk; once the tie has been established with the big company, they believe, they will not switch to a small one, or, for that matter, to another big one. The relationship is to be for keeps.[2]

[2] One reason why seniors prefer big business is that the big companies go after them and the small ones don't. Of the 450,000 incorporated firms in the U.S., only about 1,000 actually recruit on the campuses, and it is these active 1,000 firms—generally the biggest—that get the cream. Sometimes college placement directors do line up the small company position, but even then they find the students apathetic. "Frankly," says one place-

It is not simply for security that they take the vows. Far more than their predecessors they understand bigness. My contemporaries, fearful of anonymity, used to talk of "being lost" in a big corporation. This did not prevent us from joining corporations, to be sure, but verbally, at least, it was fashionable to view the organization way with misgivings. Today this would show a want of sophistication. With many of the liberals who fifteen years ago helped stimulate the undergraduate distrust of bigness now busy writing tracts in praise of bigness, the ideological underpinnings for the debate have crumbled.

The fact that a majority of seniors headed for business shy from the idea of being entrepreneurs is only in part due to fear of economic risk. Seniors can put the choice in moral terms also, and the portrait of the entrepreneur as a young man detailed in postwar fiction preaches a sermon that seniors are predisposed to accept. What price bitch goddess Success? The entrepreneur, as many see him, is a selfish type motivated by greed, and he is, furthermore, unhappy. The big-time operator as sketched in fiction eventually so loses stomach for enterprise that he finds happiness only when he stops being an entrepreneur, forsakes "21," El Morocco, and the boss's wife and heads for the country. Citing such fiction, the student can moralize on his aversion to entrepreneurship. His heel quotient, he explains, is simply not big enough.

Not that he is afraid of risk, the senior can argue. Far from being afraid of taking chances, he is simply looking for the *best* place to take them in.[3] Small business is small because of nepotism and the roll-top desk outlook, the argument goes; big business, by contrast, has borrowed the tools of science and made them pay off. It has its great laboratories, its market-research departments, and the time and patience to use them. The odds, then, favor the man who joins big business. "We wouldn't hesitate to risk adopting new industrial techniques and products," explains a proponent of this calculated-risk theory, "but we would do it only after we had subjected it to tests of engineers, pre-testing in the market and that kind of thing." With big business, in short, risk-taking would be a cinch.

In turning their back on the Protestant Ethic they are consistent; if they do not cherish venture, neither do they cherish what in our lore was its historic reward. They are without avarice. Reflecting on the difference between the postwar classes and his own class of 1928, an erstwhile Yale

---

ment director, echoing many another, "the only kind I can interest in the small company job is the dynamic sort—the one type that is least likely to get lost in a big company. I would sooner interest the other kind; I point out to the shy, diffident fellows that in a small outfit they'd be something of a jack-of-all-trades, that they'd get a better chance to express themselves, to grow out of their shell. They still don't want it."

[3] A Youth Institute Survey of 4,660 young men indicated that only 20 per cent felt that they could not achieve all their economic desires by working for someone else.

history professor confessed that the former were so unmercenary he was almost a little homesick for his own. "We were a terrible class. It was the days of the roasted lark, Hell's entries, of the white-shoe boys. Everyone was playing the stock market—they even had a ticker down at the Hotel Taft—and I wound up for a while in a bucket shop down in Wall Street. But today you don't hear that kind of talk. They don't want a million. They are much more serious, much more worth while." He shook his head nostalgically.

Others have been similarly impressed. One recruiter went through three hundred interviews without one senior's mentioning salary, and the experience is not unusual. Indeed, sometimes seniors react as if a large income and security were antithetical. As some small companies have found to their amazement, the offer of a sales job netting $15,000 at the end of two years is often turned down in favor of an equivalent one with a large company netting $8,000. Along with the $8,000 job, the senior says in justification, goes a pension plan and other benefits. He could, of course, buy himself some rather handsome annuities with the extra $7,000 the small company offers, but this alternative does not suggest itself readily.

When seniors are put to speculating how much money they would like to make twenty or thirty years hence, they cite what they feel are modest figures. Back in forty-nine it was $10,000. Since then the rising cost of living has taken it up higher, but the median doesn't usually surpass $15,000.[4] For the most part seniors do not like to talk of the future in terms of the dollar—on several occasions I have been politely lectured by someone for so much as bringing the point up.

In popular fiction, as I will take up later, heroes aren't any less materialistic than they used to be, but they are decidedly more sanctimonious about it. So with seniors. While they talk little about money, they talk a great deal about the good life. This life is, first of all, calm and ordered. Many a senior confesses that he's thought of a career in teaching, but as he talks it appears that it is not so much that he likes teaching itself as the sort of life he associates with it—there is a touch of elms and quiet streets in the picture. For the good life is equable; it is a nice place out in the suburbs, a wife and three children, one, maybe two cars (you know, a little knock-about for the wife to run down to the station in), and a summer place up at the lake or out on the Cape, and, later, a good college education for the children. It is not, seniors explain, the money that counts.

[4] The figures depend a great deal on the college. In the study done by the Youth Research Institute on a cross section of college seniors the median figure is about $8,000. At Princeton and Williams, by contrast, the figure is almost double.

STUDY QUESTIONS

1. What are the implications of the phrase "they transfer," which Whyte uses to describe the emergence of seniors into the business world?

2. What are the elements of the new attitude Whyte finds among college students? To what causes and motives does he attribute the new attitude?

3. Does Whyte approve of the attitudes he is describing? What evidence can you cite to support your answer to this question?

4. What standard of judgment does Whyte admit he is using? Does this seem to be the best or most useful standard? What other approach might he have used in evaluating the behavior he is describing?

5. Whyte has described the college student's attitude toward the business world. Using his methods, write a theme describing the college student's attitude toward college and education. If these attitudes are subject to changes, be sure to describe them.

6. Are you satisfied with Whyte's profile of today's student and his attitude toward his future? If not, write a theme describing the attitudes of students you have known.

American Culture*

H. L. Mencken

The capital defect in the culture of These States is the lack of a civilized aristocracy, secure in its position, animated by an intelligent curiosity, skeptical of all facile generalizations, superior to the sentimentality of the mob, and delighting in the battle of ideas for its own sake. The word I use, despite the qualifying adjective, has got itself meanings, of course, that I by no means intend to convey. Any mention of an aristocracy, to a public fed upon democratic fustian, is bound to bring up images of stockbrokers' wives lolling obscenely in opera boxes, or of haughty Englishmen slaughtering whole generations of grouse in an inordinate and incomprehensible manner, or of bogus counts coming over to work their magic upon the daughters of breakfast-food and bathtub kings. This misconception belongs to the general American tradition. Its depth and extent are constantly revealed by the naïve assumption that the so-called fashionable folk of the large cities—chiefly wealthy industrials in the interior-decorator and country-club stage of culture—constitute an aristocracy, and by the scarcely less remarkable assumption that the peerage

*From *A Mencken Chrestomathy* by H. L. Mencken, by permission of Alfred A. Knopf, Inc. Copyright, 1920, 1949, by Alfred A. Knopf, Inc.

of England is identical with the gentry—that is, that such men as Lord Northcliffe, Lord Riddel and even Lord Reading were English gentlemen.

Here, as always, the worshiper is the father of the gods, and no less when they are evil than when they are benign. The inferior man must find himself superiors, that he may marvel at his political equality with them, and in the absence of recognizable superiors *de facto* he creates superiors *de jure*. The sublime principle of one man, one vote must be translated into terms of dollars, diamonds, fashionable intelligence; the equality of all men before the law must have clear and dramatic proofs. Sometimes, perhaps, the thing goes further and is more subtle. The inferior man needs an aristocracy to demonstate, not only his mere equality, but also his actual superiority. The society columns in the newspapers may have some such origin. They may visualize once more the accomplished journalist's understanding of the mob mind that he plays upon so skillfully, as upon some immense and cacophonous organ, always going *fortissimo*. What the inferior man and his wife see in the sinister revels of those brummagem first families, I suspect, is often a massive witness to their own higher rectitude—in brief, to their firmer grasp upon the immutable axioms of Christian virtue, the one sound boast of the nether nine-tenths of humanity in every land under the cross.

But this bugaboo aristocracy is actually bogus, and the evidence of its bogusness lies in the fact that it is insecure. One gets into it only onerously, but out of it very easily. Entrance is effected by dint of a long and bitter struggle, and the chief incidents of that struggle are almost intolerable humiliations. The aspirant must school and steel himself to sniffs and sneers; he must see the door slammed upon him a hundred times before ever it is thrown open to him. To get in at all he must show a talent for abasement—and abasement makes him timorous. Worse, that timorousness is not cured when he succeeds at last. On the contrary, it is made even more tremulous, for what he faces within the gates is a scheme of things made up almost wholly of harsh and often unintelligible taboos, and the penalty for violating even the least of them is swift and disastrous. He must exhibit exactly the right social habits, appetites and prejudices, public and private. He must harbor exactly the right enthusiasms and indignations. He must have a hearty taste for exactly the right sports and games. His attitude toward the fine arts must be properly tolerant and yet not a shade too eager. He must read and like exactly the right books, pamphlets and public journals. He must put up at the right hotels when he travels. His wife must patronize the right milliners. He himself must stick to the right haberdashery. He must live in the right neighborhood. He must even embrace the right doctrines of religion. It would ruin him, for all society column purposes, to move to Union Hill, N. J., or to drink coffee from his saucer, or to marry a chambermaid with a gold tooth, or to join the Seventh Day Adventists. Within the boundaries of his curious order he is worse fettered than a monk in a cell. Its obscure conception of propriety, its nebulous notion that this or that is honorable, hampers him in every direction, and very narrowly. What he resigns when he enters, even when he makes his first deprecating knock at the door, is every right to attack the ideas that happen to prevail within. Such as they are, he must accept them without question. And as they shift and change he must shift and change with them, silently and quickly.

Obviously, that order cannot constitute a genuine aristocracy, in any rational sense. A genuine aristocracy is grounded upon very much different principles. Its first and most salient character is its interior security, and the chief visible evidence of that security is the freedom that goes with it—not only freedom in act, the divine right of the aristocrat to do what he damn well pleases, so long as he does not violate the primary guarantees and obligations of his class, but also and more importantly freedom in thought, the liberty to try and err, the right to be his own man. It is the instinct of a true aristocracy, not to punish eccentricity by expulsion, but to throw a mantle of protection about it—to safeguard it from the suspicions and resentments of the lower orders. Those lower orders are inert, timid, inhospitable to ideas, hostile to changes, faithful to a few maudlin superstitions. All progress goes on on the higher levels. It is there that salient personalities, made secure by artificial immunities, may oscillate most widely from the normal track. It is within that entrenched fold, out of reach of the immemorial certainties of the mob, that extraordinary men of the lower orders may find their city of refuge, and breathe a clear air. This, indeed, is at once the hall-mark and the justification of a genuine aristocracy—that it is beyond responsibility to the general masses of men, and hence superior to both their degraded longings and their no less degraded aversions. It is nothing if it is not autonomous, curious, venturesome, courageous, and everything if it is. It is the custodian of the qualities that make for change and experiment; it is the class that organizes danger to the service of the race; it pays for its high prerogatives by standing in the forefront of the fray.

No such aristocracy, it must be plain, is now on view in the United States. The makings of one were visible in the Virginia of the Eighteenth Century, but with Jefferson and Washington the promise died. In New England, it seems to me, there was never anything of the sort, either in being or in nascency: there was only a theocracy that degenerated very quickly into a plutocracy on the one hand and a caste of sterile pedants on the other—the passion for God splitting into a lust for dollars and a weakness for mere words. Despite the common notion to the contrary—a notion generated by confusing literacy with intelligence—the New England of the great days never showed any genuine enthusiasm for ideas. It began its history as a slaughterhouse of ideas, and it is today not easily distinguishable from a cold-storage plant. Its celebrated adventures in mysticism, once apparently so bold and significant, are now seen to have been little more than an elaborate hocus-pocus—respectable Unitarians shocking the peasantry and scaring the horned cattle in the fields by masquerading in the robes of Rosicrucians. The notions that it embraced in those austere and far-off days were stale, and when it had finished with them they were dead. So in politics. Since the Civil War it has produced fewer political ideas, as political ideas run in the Republic, than any average county in Kansas or Nebraska. Appomattox seemed to be a victory for New England idealism. It was actually a victory for the New England plutocracy, and that plutocracy has dominated thought above the Housatonic ever since. The sect of professional idealists has so far dwindled that it has ceased to be of any importance, even as an opposition. When the plutocracy is challenged now, it is challenged by the proletariat.

Well, what is on view in New England is on view in all other parts of the nation, sometimes with ameliorations, but usually with the colors merely exaggerated. What one beholds, sweeping the eye over the land, is a culture that, like the national literature, is in three layers—the plutocracy on top, a vast mass of undifferentiated human blanks bossed by demagogues at the bottom, and a forlorn *intelligentsia* gasping out a precarious life between. I need not set out at any length, I hope, the intellectual deficiencies of the plutocracy—its utter failure to show anything even remotely resembling the makings of an aristocracy. It is badly educated, it is stupid, it is full of low-caste superstitions and indignations, it is without decent traditions or informing vision; above all, it is extraordinarily lacking in the most elemental independence and courage. Out of this class comes the grotesque fashionable society of our big towns, already described. It shows all the stigmata of inferiority—moral certainty, cruelty, suspicion of ideas, fear. Never does it function more revealingly than in the recurrent *pogroms* against radicalism, *i.e.*, against humorless persons who, like Andrew Jackson, take the platitudes of democracy seriously. And what is the theory at the bottom of all these proceedings? So far as it can be reduced to comprehensible terms it is much less a theory than a fear—a shivering, idiotic, discreditable fear of a mere banshee—an overpowering, paralyzing dread that some extra-eloquent Red, permitted to emit his balderdash unwhipped, may eventually convert a couple of courageous men, and that the courageous men, filled with indignation against the plutocracy, may take to the highroad, burn down a nail-factory or two, and slit the throat of some virtuous profiteer.

Obviously, it is out of reason to look for any hospitality to ideas in a class so extravagantly fearful of even the most palpably absurd of them. Its philosophy is firmly grounded upon the thesis that the existing order must stand forever free from attack, and not only from attack, but also from mere academic criticism, and its ethics are as firmly grounded upon the thesis that every attempt at any such criticism is a proof of moral turpitude. Within its own ranks, protected by what may be regarded as the privilege of the order, there is nothing to take the place of this criticism. In other countries the plutocracy has often produced men of reflective and analytical habit, eager to rationalize its instincts and to bring it into some sort of relationship to the main streams of human thought. The case of David Ricardo at once comes to mind, and there have been many others: John Bright, Richard Cobden, George Grote. But in the United States no such phenomenon has been visible. Nor has the plutocracy ever fostered an inquiring spirit among its intellectual valets and footmen, which is to say, among the gentlemen who compose headlines and leading articles for its newspapers. What chiefly distinguishes the daily press of the United States from the press of all other countries pretending to culture is not its lack of truthfulness or even its lack of dignity and honor, for these deficiencies are common to newspapers everywhere, but its incurable fear of ideas, its constant effort to evade the discussion of fundamentals by translating all issues into a few elemental fears, its incessant reduction of all reflection to mere emotion. It is, in the true sense, never well-informed. It is seldom intelligent, save in the arts of the mob-master. It is never courageously honest. Held harshly to a rigid correctness of opinion, it sinks rapidly into formalism and feebleness. Its yellow section is perhaps its best section, for there the only vestige of the old free journalist survives. In the more respectable papers one finds only a timid and petulant animosity to all questioning of the existing order, however urbane and sincere—a pervasive and ill-concealed dread that the mob now heated up against the orthdox hobgoblins may suddenly begin to unearth hobgoblins of its own, and so run amok.

For it is upon the emotions of the mob, of course, that the whole comedy is played. Theoretically, the mob is the repository of all political wisdom and virtue; actually, it is the ultimate source of all political power. Even the plutocracy cannot make war upon it openly, or forget the least of its weaknesses. The business of keeping it in order must be done discreetly, warily, with delicate technique. In the main that business consists in keeping alive its deep-seated fears—of strange faces, of unfamiliar ideas, of unhackneyed gestures, of untested liberties and responsibilities. The one permanent emotion of the inferior man, as of all the simpler mammals, is fear—fear of the unknown, the complex, the inexplicable. What he wants beyond everything else is security. His instincts incline him toward a society so organized that it will protect him at all hazards, and not only against perils to his hide but also against assaults upon his mind —against the need to grapple with unaccustomed problems, to weigh ideas, to think things out for himself, to scrutinize the platitudes upon which his everyday thinking is based.

STUDY QUESTIONS

1. Why, according to Mencken, does not the class that is the subject of newspaper society columns constitute a genuine aristocracy? What standards does Mencken set for a genuine aristocracy?

2. What is the basis of Mencken's criticism of the press? Do you think his criticism is valid? Explain your reasons.

3. Compare Mencken's vocabulary and his general approach to his subject with those of Brogan, Mills and Whyte. Are there significant differences? If so what are they?

4. To what extent does Mencken agree with Rossiter?

5. This essay of Mencken's was written in 1920. How well does it apply to the contemporary scene? Give some current examples of the conditions described here, or, if you feel that America has changed considerably since 1920, explain the differences.

6. Do you agree with Mencken that the lack of an aristocracy is a serious deficiency?

*Americans and Kwakiutls**

David Riesman

Moralists are constantly complaining that the ruling vice of the present time is pride. This is true in one sense, for indeed everybody thinks that he is better than his neighbor or refuses to obey his superior; but it is extremely false in another, for the same man who cannot endure subordination or equality has so contemptible an opinion of himself that he thinks he is born only to indulge in vulgar pleasures. He willingly takes up with low desires without daring to embark on lofty enterprises, of which he scarcely dreams.

Thus, far from thinking that humility ought to be preached to our contemporaries, I would have endeavors made to give them a more enlarged idea of themselves and of their kind. Humility is unwholesome to them; what they most want is, in my opinion, pride.

Tocqueville, *Democracy in America*

Ruth Benedict's book, *Patterns of Culture*, describes in vivid detail three primitive societies: the Pueblo (Zuñi) Indians of the southwest, the people of the Island of Dobu in the Pacific, and the Kwakiutl Indians of the northwest coast of America.[1]

The Pueblo Indians are pictured as a peaceable, cooperative society, in which no one wishes to be thought a great man and everyone wishes to be thought a good fellow. Sexual relations evoke little jealousy or other vio-

* From *The Lonely Crowd, A Study of the Changing American Character* by David Riesman, with Nathan Glazer and Reuel Denny. Reprinted by permission of Yale University Press. Copyright, 1950, 1953, by Yale University Press.
[1] *Patterns of Culture* (Boston, Houghton Mifflin, 1934; reprinted New York, Pelican Books, 1946).

lent response; infidelity is not severely punished. Death, too, is taken in stride, with little violent emotion; in general, emotion is subdued. While there are considerable variations in economic status, there is little display of economic power and even less of political power; there is a spirit of cooperation with family and community.

The Dobu, by contrast, are portrayed as virtually a society of paranoids in which each man's hand is against his neighbor's in sorcery, theft, and abuse; in which husband and wife alternate as captives of the spouse's kin; and in which infidelity is deeply resented. Dobuan economic life is built on sharp practice in inter-island trading, on an intense feeling for property rights, and on a hope of getting something for nothing through theft, magic, and fraud.

The third society, the Kwakiutl, is also intensely rivalrous. But the rivalry consists primarily in conspicuous consumption, typified by feasts called "potlatches," at which chiefs outdo each other in providing food and in burning up the blankets and sheets of copper which are the main counters of wealth in the society; sometimes even a house or a canoe is sent up in flames in a final bid for glory. Indeed, the society is a caricature of Veblen's conspicuous consumption; certainly, the potlatches of the Kwakiutl chiefs serve "as the legitimate channel by which the community's surplus product has been drained off and consumed, to the greater spiritual comfort of all parties concerned." Veblen was, in fact, familiar with these northwest-coast "coming-out parties."

I have asked students who have read Ruth Benedict's book which of these three cultures in their opinion most closely resembles the obviously more complex culture of the United States. The great majority see Americans as Kwakiutls. They emphasize American business rivalry, sex and status jealousy, and power drive. They see Americans as individualists, primarily interested in the display of wealth and station.

A minority of students, usually the more politically radical, say that America is more like Dobu. They emphasize the sharp practice of American business life, point to great jealousy and bitterness in family relations, and see American politics, domestic and international, as hardly less aggressive than Hobbes's state of nature.

No students I have talked with have argued that there are significant resemblances between the culture of the Hopi and Zuñi Pueblos and American culture—they wish that there were.

Yet when we turn then to examine the culture patterns of these very students, we see little evidence either of Dobu or Kwakiutl ways. The wealthy students go to great lengths not to be conspicuous—things are very different from the coon-coated days of the 20's. The proper uniform is one of purposeful shabbiness. In fact, none among the students except a very rare Lucullus dares to be thought uppity. Just as no modern Vanderbilt says "the public be damned," so no modern parent would say:

"Where Vanderbilt sits, there is the head of the table. I teach my son to be rich." [2]

It is, moreover, not only in the virtual disappearance of conspicuous consumption that the students have abandoned Kwakiutl-like modes of life. Other displays of gifts, native or acquired, have also become more subdued. A leading college swimming star told me: "I get sore at the guys I'm competing against. Something's wrong with me. I wish I could be like X who really cooperates with the other fellows. He doesn't care so much about winning."

There seems to be a discrepancy between the America that students make for themselves as students and the America they think they will move into when they leave the campus. Their image of the latter is based to a large extent on legends about America that are preserved in our literature. For example, many of our novelists and critics still believe that America, as compared with other cultures, is a materialistic nation of would-be Kwakiutl chiefs. There may have been some truth in this picture in the Gilded Age, though Henry James saw how ambiguous the issue of "materialism" was between America and Europe even then.

The materialism of these older cultures has been hidden by their status systems and by the fact that they had inherited many values from the era dependent on tradition-direction. The European masses simply have not had the money and leisure, until recent years, to duplicate American consumership patterns; when they do, they are, if anything, sometimes more vulgar, more materialistic.

The Europeans, nevertheless, have been only too glad to tell Americans that they were materialistic; and the Americans, feeling themselves *nouveaux riches* during the last century, paid to be told. They still pay: it is not only my students who fail to see that it is the turn of the rest of the world to be *nouveaux riches*, to be excited over the gadgets of an industrial age, while millions of Americans have turned away in boredom from attaching much emotional significance to the consumer-goods frontier.[3]

When, however, I try to point these things out to students who compare Americans with Kwakiutls, they answer that the advertisements show how much emotion is attached to goods consumption. But, when I ask them if they believe the ads themselves, they say scornfully that they do not. And when I ask if they know people who do, they find it hard to give examples, at least in the middle class. (If the advertisements powerfully affected people in the impoverished lower class who had small hope of mobility, there would surely be a revolution!) Yet the advertisements

[2] The remark is quoted by Justice Oliver Wendell Holmes, Jr., in "The Soldier's Faith," 1895, reprinted in *Speeches* (Boston, Little, Brown, 1934), p. 56.

[3] Mary McCarthy's fine article, "America the Beautiful," *Commentary,* IV (1947), 201 takes much the same attitude as the text.

must be reaching somebody, the students insist. Why, I ask, why isn't it possible that advertising as a whole is a fantastic fraud, presenting an image of America taken seriously by no one, least of all by the advertising men who create it? Just as the mass media persuade people that other people think politics is important, so they persuade people that everyone else cannot wait for his new refrigerator or car of suit of clothes. In neither case can people believe that "the others" are as apathetic as they feel themselves to be. And, while their indifference to politics may make people feel on the defensive, their indifference to advertising may allow them to feel superior. In fact, I think that a study of American advertising during the last quarter century would show that the advertising men themselves at least implicitly realize the consumer's loss of emotional enthusiasm. Where once car and refrigerator advertisements showed the housewife or husband exulting in the new possessions, today it is often only children in the ads who exult over the new Nash their father has just bought. In many contemporary ads the possession itself recedes into the background or is handled abstractly, surrealistically; it no longer throws off sparks or exclamation points; copy itself has become subtler or more matter of fact.

Of course many old-fashioned enthusiasts of consumption remain in America who have not yet been affected by the spread of other-directed consumer sophistication and repression of emotional response. A wonderful example is the small-town Irish mother in the movie, *A Letter to Three Wives,* whose greatest pride and joy in her dingy railroadside home is the big, shiny, new, not yet paid-for refrigerator. And it may be argued that even middle-class Americans have only covered over their materialism with a veneer of "good taste," without altering their fundamental drives. Nevertheless, the other-directed person, oriented as he is toward people, is simply unable to be as materialistic as many inner-directed people were. For genuine inner-directed materialism—real acquisitive attachment to things—one must go to the Dutch bourgeois or French peasant or others for whom older ways endure.

It is the other-directedness of Americans that has prevented their realizing this; between the advertisers on the one hand and the novelists and intellectuals on the other, they have assumed that *other* Americans were materialistic, while not giving sufficient credence to their own feelings. Indeed, the paradoxical situation in a stratum which is other-oriented is that people constantly make grave misjudgments as to what others, at least those with whom they are not in peer-group contact, but often also those with whom they spend much time, feel and think.

To be sure, the businessmen themselves often try to act as if it were still possible to be a Kwakiutl chief in the United States. When they write articles or make speeches, they like to talk about free enterprise, about tough competition, about risk-taking. These businessmen, of course, are like World War I Legionnaires, talking about the glorious days of yore.

Students and many others believe what the businessmen say on these occasions, but then have little opportunity to watch what they do. Perhaps the businessmen themselves are as much the victims of their own chants and rituals as the Kwakiutls.

Those few students who urge that America resembles Dobu can find little in student life to sustain their view, except perhaps a bit of cheating in love or on examinations. It is rather that they see the "capitalistic system" as a jungle of sharp practice, as if nothing had changed since the days of Mark Twain, Jack London, and Frank Norris. America is to them a land of lynchings, gangsterism, and deception by little foxes and big foxes. Yet, today, only small businessmen (car dealers or furnace repairmen, for instance) have many opportunities for the "wabu-wabu" trading, that is, the sharply manipulative property-pyramiding of the Dobuan canoeists.

If, however, these students turn to social science for their images of power in America, they will very frequently find their own view supported. The scattered remarks on the United States in *Patterns of Culture* are themselves an illustration. My students also read Robert Lynd's chapter on "The Pattern of American Culture" in *Knowledge for What?* [4] While noting contradictory exhortations to amity and brotherhood, Lynd emphasizes business as highly individualistic and politically ruthless; elsewhere he stresses the masterful ambition and conspicuous consumption typified by the older generation of the "X family" of Middletown. Ironically, the outlook of these and other sociological critics of business is confirmed and reflected by those neoclassical economists who construct models for the rational conduct of the firm—wittingly or unwittingly presenting businessmen as dismally "economic men."

Partly as a result of this image of the businessman, many students at privately endowed universities have become reluctant to consider business careers, and, as more and more young people are drawn into the colleges, these attitudes become increasingly widespread. The abler ones want something "higher" and look down their noses at the boys at Wharton or even at the Harvard Business School. Business is thought to be dull and disagreeable as well as morally suspect, and the genuine moral problem involved in career choice—namely, how best to develop one's potentialities for a full existence—is obfuscated by the false, over-dramatized choice of making money (and losing one's soul) in business versus penury (and saving one's soul) in government service or teaching. The notion that business today, especially big business, presents challenging intellectual problems and opportunities and is no more noticeably engaged in Dobuan sharp practice and Kwakiutl rivalry than any other career, seems not to exist even in the minds of students whose fathers are (perhaps woefully inarticulate) businessmen.

[4] Robert S. Lynd, *Knowledge for What?* (Princeton, Princeton University Press, 1939), pp. 54-113.

It is likely, then, that the students' image of business, and of American life generally, will have some self-confirming effects. Business will be forced to recruit from the less gifted and sensitive, who will not be able to take advantage of the opportunities for personal development business could offer and who, therefore, will not become models for younger men. Moreover, people who expect to meet hostility and calculation in others will justify an anticipatory hostility and calculation in themselves.

To be sure, there are plenty of unlovely, vicious, and mean Americans, in and out of business life; plenty of frightening southern mobs, northern hoodlums, dead-end kids with and without tuxedoes. There are many cultural islands in the United States where Dobu ways abound, just as there are survivals of late nineteenth-century Kwakiutl patterns. But these islands and survivals do not make a system of power, nor are they linked by any conspiracy, fascist or otherwise.

Now, of course, to show that Americans are neither like Kwakiutls nor Dobuans does not prove they are like Zuñi and Hopi Indians. Obviously, in any case, the comparisons must be very rough; from the standpoint of my character types all three tribes, as long as they are in the phase of high population growth potential, would be more or less dependent on tradition-direction. My purpose is to present a parable, not a description. There is evidence, though it is perhaps somewhat understressed by Ruth Benedict, that the Pueblo Indians are actually not so bland and amiable as they seem, that they are, to a degree, antagonistic cooperators, with a good deal of repressed hostility and envy that crops up in dreams and malicious gossip. But this only strengthens the analogy with the middle-class Americans, whose other-directed cooperativeness is also not completely mild but contains repressed antagonistic elements.

Indeed the whole emotional tone of life in the Pueblos reminds me strongly of the American peer-group, with its insulting "You think you're big." While the Kwakiutls pride themselves on their passions that lead them to commit murder, arson, and suicide, the Pueblos frown on any violent emotion.

Ruth Benedict writes:

A good man has . . . "a pleasing address, a yielding disposition, and a generous heart." . . . He should "talk lots, as they say—that is, he should always set people at their ease—and he should without fail co-operate easily with others either in the field or in ritual, never betraying a suspicion of arrogance or a strong emotion."

The quotation brings to mind one of the most striking patterns from our interviews with young people. When we ask them their best trait they are hard pressed for an answer, though they sometimes mention an ability to "get along well with everybody." When we ask them, "What is your worst trait?" the most frequent single answer is "temper." And when we go on to ask, "Is your temper, then, so bad?" it usually turns out that the interviewee has not got much of a temper. If we ask whether his temper has gotten him into much trouble, he can cite little evidence that it has. What may these answers—of course no proper sample—mean? My impression is that temper is considered the worst trait in the society of the glad hand. It is felt as an internal menace to one's cooperative attitude. Moreover, the peer-group regards rage and temper as faintly ridiculous: one must be able to take it with a smile or be charged with something even worse than temper, something no one will accuse himself of even in an interview—a lack of a sense of humor. The inner-directed man may also worry about temper, for instance, if he is religious, but his conscience-stricken inhibitions and reaction-formations leave the emotion still alive, volcano-like, within him—often ready to erupt in political indignation—whereas the other-directed man allows or compels his emotions to heal, though not without leaving scars, in an atmosphere of enforced good fellowship and tolerance.

Many young people today also set themselves an ideal in their sex lives not too different from the Zuñi norm. They feel they ought to take sex with little interpersonal emotion and certainly without jealousy. The word of the wise to the young—"Don't get involved"—has changed its meaning in a generation. Once it meant: don't get, or get someone, pregnant; don't run afoul of the law; don't get in the newspapers. Today the injunction seeks to control the personal experiencing of emotion that might disrupt the camaraderie of the peer-group.

The chief worry of the Pueblo Indians is directed not to each other's behavior but to the weather, and their religious ceremonies are primarily directed toward rain-making. To quiet their anxiety the Indians go through rituals that must be letter perfect. American young people have no such single ritual to assure personal or tribal success. However, one can see a similarity in the tendency to create rituals of a sort in all spheres of life. People make a ritual out of going to school, out of work, out of having fun, out of political participation as inside-dopesters or as indignants, as well as out of countless private compulsions. But the rituals, whether private or public, have usually to be rationalized as necessary; and since this is not self-evident and since the sign of success is not so explicit as a downpour of rain, the American young people can hardly get as much comfort from their rituals as the Pueblo Indians do from theirs.

The young people who express the views I have described have begun to pass out of the adolescent peer-groups; they have not yet taken their places in the adult patterning of American life. What will be the effect of the discrepancy between their picture of the United States as a place led by Kwakiutl chiefs, leading Kwakiutl-style followers, and the reality of their progress along the "Hopi Way"? Will they seek to bring about changes, through social and political action, that will make America more comfortable for the tolerant, other-directed types? Or will they seek to adopt more ruthless, Kwakiutl-like behavior as supposedly more compati ble with real life? Or, perchance, will they admit that they, too, are Americans, after all not so unique, which might require a revision of their images of power, their images of what Americans in general are like?

Doubtless, all these things can occur, and many more. But there is perhaps one additional factor which will shape both changing ideology and changing character. The students, aware of their own repressed competitiveness and envy, think that others may try to do to them what they themselves would not dare to do to others. The society *feels* to them like Kwakiutl or even Dobu, not only because that is the ideology about America they have learned but also because their own cooperativeness is tinged with an antagonism they have not yet completely silenced. And perhaps this gives us an answer to a puzzle about other-directed tolerance: why, if the other-directed person is tolerant, is he himself so afraid of getting out of line? Can he not depend on the tolerance of others? It may be that he feels his own tolerance precarious, his dreadful temper ready to let fly when given permission; if he feels so irritable himself, no matter how mild his behavior, he must fear the others, no matter how amiable they, too, many appear.

These students would prefer to live in the Pueblo culture, if they had to choose among the three described by Ruth Benedict. And, while this choice is in itself not to be quarreled with, the important fact is that they do not know that they already are living in such a culture. They want social security, not great achievements. They want approval, not fame. They are not eager to develop talents that might bring them into conflict, whereas the inner-directed young person tended to push himself to the limit of his talents and beyond. Few of them suffer, like youth in the earlier age, because they are "twenty, and so little accomplished." Whereas the inner-directed middle-class boy had to learn after twenty to adjust, to surrender his adolescent dreams and accept a burgher's modest lot, the other-directed boy never had such dreams. Learning to conform to the group almost as soon as he learns anything, he does not face, at adolescence, the need to choose between his family's world and that of his own generation or between his dreams and a world he never made.

Since, moreover, his adjustment to this group reality begins earlier, it becomes more a matter of conforming character and less a matter of conforming behavior. The popular song, "I don't want to set the world on fire," expresses a typical theme. The Kwakiutl wanted to do just that, literally to set the world on fire. The other-directed person prefers "love" to "glory." As Tocqueville saw, or foresaw: "He willingly takes up with low desires without daring to embark on lofty enterprises, of which he scarcely dreams."

There is a connection between the feeling these students and other young people have about their own fates and the contemporary notions of who runs the country. We have seen that the students feel themselves to be powerless, safe only when performing a ritual in approving company. Though they may seek to preserve emotional independence by not getting involved, this requirement is itself a peer-group mandate. How, then, as they look about them in America, do they explain their powerlessness? Somebody must have what they have not got: their powerlessness must be matched by power somewhere else. They see America as composed of Kwakiutls, not only because of their own residual and repressed Kwakiutl tendencies but even more because of their coerced cooperativeness. Some big chiefs must be doing this to them, they feel. They do not see that, to a great extent, it is they themselves who are doing it, through their own character.

The chiefs have lost the power, but the followers have not gained it. The savage believes that he will secure more power by drinking the blood or shrinking the head of his enemy. But the other-directed person, far from gaining, only becomes weaker from the weakness of his fellows.

STUDY QUESTIONS

1. How does the author explain the fact that the America the students criticized apparently does not exist?

2. Is any strong evidence offered to show that Americans are not as consumption-minded as they believe themselves to be?

3. Did the students think of themselves as generally like or generally unlike everyone else? Does this tend to support or contradict Riesman's conclusion?

4. What attitude toward power did the students take? Is it a simple or a complicated one?

5. To what extent do the attitudes and feelings described seem to you to be authentic? Write a theme examining Riesman's generalizations in the light of your knowledge of actual students and their opinions.

6. Write a theme describing the prevalent attitude among a group you know well on some fundamental question such as wealth, sex, honesty, dating, parental control, or family life.

2. DEMOCRACY AND LIBERTY

The Ideal Democracy*

Carl L. Becker

Democracy, like liberty or science or progress, is a word with which we are all so familiar that we rarely take the trouble to ask what we mean by it. It is a term, as the devotees of semantics say, which has no "referent"—there is no precise or palpable thing or object which we all think of when the word is pronounced. On the contrary, it is a word which connotes different things to different people, a kind of conceptual Gladstone bag which, with a little manipulation, can be made to accommodate almost any collection of social facts we may wish to carry about in it. In it we can as easily pack a dictatorship as any other form of government. We have only to stretch the concept to include any form of government supported by a majority of the people, for whatever reasons and by whatever means of expressing assent, and before we know it the empire of Napoleon, the Soviet regime of Stalin, and the Fascist systems of Mussolini and Hitler are all safely in the bag. But if this is what we mean by democracy, then virtually all forms of government are democratic, since virtually all governments, except in times of revolution, rest upon the explicit or implicit consent of the people. In order to discuss democracy intelligently it will be necessary, therefore, to define it, to attach to the word a sufficiently precise meaning to avoid the confusion which is not infrequently the chief result of such discussions.

All human institutions, we are told, have their ideal forms laid away in heaven, and we do not need to be told that the actual institutions conform but indifferently to these ideal counterparts. It would be possible then to define democracy either in terms of the ideal or in terms of the real form— to define it as government of the people, by the people, for the people; or to define it as government of the people, by the politicians, for whatever pressure groups can get their interests taken care of. But as a historian, I am naturally disposed to be satisfied with the meaning which, in the history of politics, men have commonly attributed to the word—a meaning, needless to say, which derives partly from the experience and partly from the aspirations of mankind. So regarded, the term democracy refers primarily to a form of government, and it has always meant government by the many as opposed to government by the one—government by the peo-

* From *Modern Democracy* by Carl Becker. Reprinted by permission of Yale University Press. Copyright, 1941, by Yale University Press.

ple as opposed to government by a tyrant, a dictator, or an absolute monarch. This is the most general meaning of the word as men have commonly understood it.

In this antithesis there are, however, certain implications, always tacitly understood, which give a more precise meaning to the term. Peisistratus, for example, was supported by a majority of the people, but his government was never regarded as a democracy for all that. Caesar's power derived from a popular mandate, conveyed through established republican forms, but that did not make his government any less a dictatorship. Napoleon called his government a democratic empire, but no one, least of all Napoleon himself, doubted that he had destroyed the last vestiges of the democratic republic. Since the Greeks first used the term, the essential test of democratic government has always been this: the source of political authority must be and remain in the people and not in the ruler. A democratic government has always meant one in which the citizens, or a sufficient number of them to represent more or less effectively the common will, freely act from time to time, and according to established forms, to appoint or recall the magistrates and to enact or revoke the laws by which the community is governed. This I take to be the meaning which history has impressed upon the term democracy as a form of government. It is, therefore, the meaning which I attach to it in these lectures.

The most obvious political fact of our time is that democracy as thus defined has suffered an astounding decline in prestige. Fifty years ago it was not impossible to regard democratic government, and the liberties that went with it, as a permanent conquest of the human spirit. In 1886 Andrew Carnegie published a book entitled *Triumphant Democracy*. Written without fear and without research, the book was not an achievement of the highest intellectual distinction perhaps; but the title at least expressed well enough the prevailing conviction—the conviction that democracy had fought the good fight, had won the decisive battles, and would inevitably, through its inherent merits, presently banish from the world the most flagrant political and social evils which from time immemorial had afflicted mankind. This conviction could no doubt be most easily entertained in the United States, where even the tradition of other forms of government was too remote and alien to color our native optimism. But even in Europe the downright skeptics, such as Lecky, were thought to be perverse, and so hardheaded a historian as J. B. Bury could proclaim with confidence that the long struggle for freedom of thought had finally been won.

I do not need to tell you that within a brief twenty years the prevailing optimism of that time has been quite dispelled. One European country after another has, willingly enough it seems, abandoned whatever democratic institutions it formerly enjoyed for some form of dictatorship. The spokesmen of Fascism and Communism announce with confidence that democracy, a sentimental aberration which the world has outgrown, is done for; and even the friends of democracy support it with declining conviction. They tell us that democracy, so far from being triumphant, is "at the crossroads" or "in retreat," and that its future is by no means assured. What are we to think of this sudden reversal in fortune and prestige? How explain it? What to do about it?

II

One of the presuppositions of modern thought is that institutions, in order to be understood, must be seen in relation to the conditions of time and place in which they appear. It is a little difficult for us to look at democracy in this way. We are so immersed in its present fortunes that we commonly see it only as a "close-up," filling the screen to the exclusion of other things to which it is in fact related. In order to form an objective judgment of its nature and significance, we must therefore first of all get it in proper perspective. Let us then, in imagination, remove from the immediate present scene to some cool high place where we can survey at a glance five or six thousand years of history, and note the part which democracy has played in human civilization. The view, if we have been accustomed to take democratic institutions for granted, is a bit bleak and disheartening. For we see at once that in all this long time, over the habitable globe, the great majority of the human race has neither known nor apparently much cared for our favorite institutions.

Civilization was already old when democracy made its first notable appearance among the small city states of ancient Greece, where it flourished brilliantly for a brief century or two and then disappeared. At about the same time something that might be called democracy appeared in Rome and other Italian cities, but even in Rome it did not survive the conquest of the world by the Roman Republic, except as a form of local administration in the cities of the empire. In the twelfth and thirteenth centuries certain favorably placed medieval cities enjoyed a measure of self-government, but in most instances it was soon replaced by the dictatorship of military conquerors, the oligarchic control of a few families, or the encroaching power of autocratic kings. The oldest democracy of modern times is the Swiss Confederation, the next oldest is the Dutch Republic. Parliamentary government in England does not antedate the late seventeenth century, the great American experiment is scarcely older. Not until the nineteenth century did democratic government make its way in any considerable part of the world—in the great states of continental Europe, in South America, in Canada and Australia, in South Africa and Japan.

From this brief survey it is obvious that, taking the experience of mankind as a test, democracy has as yet had but a limited and temporary success. There must be a reason for this significant fact. The reason is that democratic government is a species of social luxury, at best a delicate and precarious adventure which depends for success upon the validity of certain assumptions about the capacities and virtues of men, and upon the presence of certain material and intellectual conditions favorable to the exercise of these capacities and virtues. Let us take the material conditions first.

It is a striking fact that until recently democracy never flourished except in very small states—for the most part in cities. It is true that in both the Persian and the Roman empires a measure of self-government was accorded to local communities, but only in respect to purely local affairs; in no large state as a whole was democratic government found to be practicable. One essential reason is that until recently the means of communication were too slow and uncertain to create the necessary solidarity of interest and similarity of information over large areas. The principle of representation was well enough known to the Greeks, but in practice it proved impracticable except in limited areas and for special occasions. As late as the eighteenth century it was still the common opinion that the republican form of government, although the best ideally, was unsuited to large countries, even to a country no larger than France. This was the view of Montesquieu, and even of Rousseau. The view persisted into the nineteenth century, and English conservatives, who were opposed to the extension of the suffrage in England, consoled themselves with the notion that the America Civil War would confirm it—would demonstrate that government by and for the people would perish, if not from off the earth at least from large countries. If their hopes were confounded the reason is that the means of communication, figuratively speaking, were making large countries small. It is not altogether fanciful to suppose that, but for the railroad and the telegraph, the United States would today be divided into many small republics maneuvering for advantage and employing war and diplomacy for maintaining an unstable balance of power.

If one of the conditions essential to the success of democratic government is mobility, ease of communication, another is a certain measure of economic security. Democracy does not flourish in communities on the verge of destitution. In ancient and medieval times democratic government appeared for the most part in cities, the centers of prosperity. Farmers in the early Roman Republic and in the Swiss Cantons were not wealthy to be sure, but equality of possessions and of opportunity gave them a certain economic security. In medieval cities political privilege was confined to the prosperous merchants and craftsmen, and in Athens and the later Roman Republic democratic government was found to be workable only on condition that the poor citizens were subsidized by the government or paid for attending the assemblies and the law courts.

In modern times democratic institutions have, generally speaking, been most successful in new countries, such as the United States, Canada, and Australia, where the conditions of life have been easy for the people; and in European countries more or less in proportion to their industrial prosperity. In European countries, indeed, there has been a close correlation between the development of the industrial revolution and the emergence of democratic institutions. Holland and England, the first countries to experience the industrial revolution, were the first also (apart from Switzerland, where certain peculiar conditions obtained) to adopt democratic institutions; and as the industrial revolution spread to France, Belgium, Germany, and Italy, these countries in turn adopted at least a measure of democratic government. Democracy is in some sense an economic luxury, and it may be said that in modern times it has been a function of the development of new and potentially rich countries, or of the industrial revolution which suddenly dowered Europe with unaccustomed wealth. Now that prosperity is disappearing round every next corner, democracy works less well than it did.

So much for the material conditions essential for the success of democratic government. Supposing these conditions to exist, democratic government implies in addition the presence of certain capacities and virtues in its citizens. These capacities and virtues are bound up with the assumptions on which democracy rests, and are available only in so far as the assumptions are valid. The primary assumption of democratic government is that its citizens are capable of managing their own affairs. But life in any community involves a conflict of individual and class interests, and a corresponding divergence of opinion as to the measures to be adopted for the common good. The divergent opinions must be somehow reconciled, the conflict of interests somehow compromised. It must then be an assumption of democratic government that its citizens are rational creatures, sufficiently so at least to understand the interests in conflict; and it must be an assumption that they are men of good will, sufficiently so toward each other at least to make those concessions of individual and class interest required for effecting workable compromises. The citizens of a democracy should be, as Pericles said the citizens of Athens were, if not all originators at least all sound judges of good policy.

These are what may be called the minimum assumptions and the necessary conditions of democratic government anywhere and at any time. They may be noted to best advantage, not in any state, but in small groups within the state—in clubs and similar private associations of congenial and like-minded people united for a specific purpose. In such associations the membership is limited and select. The members are, or may easily become, all acquainted with each other. Everyone knows, or may easily find out, what is being done and who is doing it. There will of course be differences of opinion, and there may be disintegrating squabbles and intrigues. But on the whole, ends and means being specific and well understood, the problems of government are few and superficial; there is plenty of time for discussion; and since intelligence and good will can generally be taken for granted there is the disposition to make reasonable concessions and compromises. The analogy must be taken for what it is worth. States may not be the mystical blind Molochs of German philosophy, but any state is far more complex and intangible than a private association, and there is little resemblance between such associations and the democracies of modern times. Other things equal, the resemblance is closest in very small states, and it is in connection with the small city states of ancient Greece that the resemblance can best be noted.

The Greek states were limited in size, not as is often thought solely or even chiefly by the physiography of the country, but by some instinctive feeling of the Greek mind that a state is necessarily a natural association of people bound together by ties of kinship and a common tradition of rights and obligations. There must then, as Aristotle said, be a limit:

> For if the citizens of a state are to judge and distribute offices according to merit, they must know each other's characters; where they do not possess this knowledge, both the elections to offices and the decisions in the law courts will go wrong. Where the population is very large they are manifestly settled by haphazard, which clearly ought not to be. Besides, in overpopulous states foreigners and metics will readily acquire citizenship, for who will find them out?

It obviously did not occur to Aristotle that metics and foreigners should be free to acquire citizenship. It did not occur to him, or to any Greek of his time, or to the merchants of the self-governing medieval city, that a state should be composed of all the people inhabiting a given territory. A state was rather an incorporated body of people within, but distinct from, the population of the community.

Ancient and medieval democracies had thus something of the character of a private association. They were, so to speak, purely pragmatic phenomena, arising under very special conditions, and regarded as the most convenient way of managing the affairs of people bound together by community of interest and for the achievement of specific ends. There is no suggestion in Aristotle that democracy (polity) is intrinsically a superior form of government, no suggestion that it derives from a special ideology of its own. If it rests upon any superiority other than convenience, it is the superiority which it shares with any Greek state, that is to say, the superiority of Greek over barbarian civilization. In Aristotle's philosophy it is indeed difficult to find any clear-cut distinction between the democratic form of government and the state itself; the state, if it be worthy of the name, is always, whatever the form of government, "the government of freemen and equals," and in any state it is always necessary that "the freemen who compose the bulk of the people should have absolute power in some things." In Aristotle's philosophy the distinction between good and bad in politics is not between good and bad types of government, but between the good and the bad form of each type. Any type of government —monarchy, aristocracy, polity—is good provided the rulers aim at the good of all rather than at the good of the class to which they belong. From Aristotle's point of view neither democracy nor dictatorship is good or bad in itself, but only in the measure that it achieves, or fails to achieve, the aim of every good state, which is that "the inhabitants of it should be happy." It did not occur to Aristotle that democracy (polity), being in some special sense in harmony with the nature of man, was everywhere applicable, and therefore destined by fate or the gods to carry throughout the world a superior form of civilization.

It is in this respect chiefly that modern democracy differs from earlier forms. It rests upon something more than the minimum assumptions. It is reinforced by a full-blown ideology which, by endowing the individual with natural and imprescriptible rights, sets the democratic form of government off from all others as the one which alone can achieve the good life. What then are the essential tenets of the modern democratic faith?

III

The liberal democratic faith, as expressed in the works of eighteenth- and early nineteenth-century writers, is one of the formulations of the modern doctrine of progress. It will be well, therefore, to note briefly the historical antecedents of that doctrine.

In the long history of man on earth there comes a time when he remembers something of what has been, anticipates something that will be, knows the country he has traversed, wonders what lies beyond—the moment when he becomes aware of himself as a lonely, differentiated item in the world. Sooner or later there emerges for him the most devastating of all facts, namely, that in an indifferent universe which alone endures, he alone aspires, endeavors to attain, and attains only to be defeated in the end. From that moment his immediate experience ceases to be adequate, and he endeavors to project himself beyond it by creating ideal worlds of semblance, Utopias of other time or place in which all has been, may be, or will be well.

In ancient times Utopia was most easily projected into the unknown past, pushed back to the beginning of things—to the time of P'an Ku and the celestial emperors, to the Garden of Eden, or the reign of King Chronos when men lived like gods free from toil and grief. From this happy state of first created things there had obviously been a decline and fall, occasioned by disobedience and human frailty, and decreed as punishment by fate or the angry gods. The mind of man was therefore afflicted with pessimism, a sense of guilt for having betrayed the divine purpose, a feeling of inadequacy for bringing the world back to its original state of innocence and purity. To men who felt insecure in a changing world, and helpless in a world always changing for the worse, the future had little to offer. It could be regarded for the most part only with resignation, mitigated by individual penance or well-doing, or the hope of some miraculous intervention by the gods, or the return of the god-like kings, to set things right again, yet with little hope that from this setting right there would not be another falling away.

This pervasive pessimism was gradually dispelled in the Western world, partly by the Christian religion, chiefly by the secular intellectual revolution occurring roughly between the fifteenth and the eighteenth centuries. The Christian religion gave assurance that the lost golden age of the past would be restored for the virtuous in the future, and by proclaiming the supreme worth of the individual in the eyes of God enabled men to look forward with hope to the good life after death in the Heavenly City. Meantime, the secular intellectual revolution, centering in the matter-of-fact study of history and science, gradually emancipated the minds of men from resignation to fate and the angry gods. Accumulated knowledge of history, filling in time past with a continuous succession of credible events, banished all lost golden ages to the realm of myth, and enabled men to live without distress in a changing world since it could be regarded as not necessarily changing for the worse. At the same time, a more competent observation and measurement of the action of material things disclosed an outer world of nature, indifferent to man indeed, yet behaving, not as the unpredictable sport of the gods, but in ways understandable to human reason and therefore ultimately subject to man's control.

Thus the conditions were fulfilled which made it possible for men to conceive of Utopia, neither as a lost golden age of the past nor as a Heavenly City after death prepared by the gods for the virtuous, but as a future state on earth of man's own devising. In a world of nature that could be regarded as amenable to man's control, and in a world of changing social relations that need not be regarded as an inevitable decline and fall from original perfection, it was possible to formulate the modern doctrine of progress: the idea that, by deliberate intention and rational direction, men can set the terms and indefinitely improve the conditions of their mundane existence.

The eighteenth century was the moment in history when men first fully realized the engaging implications of this resplendent idea, the moment when, not yet having been brought to the harsh appraisal of experience, it could be accepted with unclouded optimism. Never had the universe seemed less mysterious, more open and visible, more eager to yield its secrets to common-sense questions. Never had the nature of man seemed less perverse, or the mind of man more pliable to the pressure of rational persuasion. The essential reason for this confident optimism is that the marvels of scientific discovery closed to the men of that time a God who still functioned but was no longer angry. God the Father could be conceived as a beneficent First Cause who, having performed his essential task of creation, had withdrawn from the affairs of men, leaving them competently prepared and fully instructed for the task of achieving their own salvation. In one tremendous sentence Rousseau expressed the eighteenth-century world view of the universe and man's place in it. "Is it simple," he exclaimed, "is it natural that God should have gone in search of Moses in order to speak to Jean Jacques Rousseau?"

God had indeed spoken to Rousseau, he had spoken to all men, but his revelation was contained, not in Holy Writ interpreted by Holy Church, but in the great Book of Nature which was open for all men to read. To this open book of nature men would go when they wanted to know what God had said to them. Here they would find recorded the laws of nature and of nature's God, disclosing a universe constructed according to a rational plan; and that men might read these laws aright they had been endowed with reason, a bit of the universal intelligence placed within the individual to make manifest to him the universal reason implicit in things and events. "Natural law," as Volney so clearly and confidently put it, "is the regular and constant order of facts by which God rules the universe; the order which his wisdom presents to the sense and reason of men, to serve them as an equal and common rule of conduct, and to guide them, without distinction of race or sect, toward perfection and happiness." Thus God had devised a planned economy, and had endowed men with the capacity for managing it: to bring his ideas, his conduct, and his institutions into harmony with the universal laws of nature was man's simple allotted task.

At all times political theory must accommodate itself in some fashion to the prevailing world view, and liberal-democratic political theory was no exception to this rule. From time immemorial authority and obedience had been the cardinal concepts both of the prevailing world view and of political and social theory. From time immemorial men had been regarded as subject to overruling authority—the authority of the gods, and the authority of kings who were themselves gods, or descended from gods, or endowed with divine authority to rule in place of gods; and from time immemorial obedience to such divine authority was thought to be the primary obligation of men. Even the Greeks, who were so little afraid of their gods that they could hob-nob with them in the most friendly and engaging way, regarded mortals as subject to them; and when they lost faith in the gods they deified the state as the highest good and subordinated the individual to it. But the eighteenth-century world view, making man the measure of all things, mitigated if it did not destroy this sharp contrast between authority and obedience. God still reigned but he did not govern. He had, so to speak, granted his subjects a constitution and authorized them to interpret it as they would in the supreme court of reason. Men were still subject to an overruling authority, but the subjection could be regarded as voluntary because self-imposed, and self-imposed because obedience was exacted by nothing more oppressive than their own rational intelligence.

Liberal-democratic political theory readily accommodated itself to this change in the world view. The voice of the people was now identified with the voice of God, and all authority was derived from it. The individual instead of the state or the prince was now deified and endowed with imprescriptible rights; and since ignorance or neglect of the rights of man was the chief cause of social evils, the first task of political science was to define these rights, the second to devise a form of government suited to guarantee them. The imprescriptible rights of man were easily defined, since they were self-evident: "All men are created equal, [and] are endowed by their Creator with certain inalienable rights, among which are life, liberty, and the pursuit of happiness." From this it followed that all just governments would remove those artificial restraints which impaired these rights, thereby liberating those natural impulses with which God had endowed the individual as a guide to thought and conduct. In the intellectual realm, freedom of thought and the competition of diverse opinion would disclose the truth, which all men, being rational creatures, would progressively recognize and willingly follow. In the economic realm, freedom of enterprise would disclose the natural aptitudes of each individual, and the ensuing competition of interests would stimulate effort, and thereby result in the maximum of material advantage for all. Liberty of the individual from social constraint thus turned out to be not only an inherent natural right but also a preordained natural mechanism for bringing about the material and moral progress of mankind. Men had only to follow reason and self-interest: something not themselves, God and Nature, would do whatever else was necessary for righteousness.

The modern liberal-democracy is associated with an ideology which rests upon something more than the minimum assumptions essential to any democratic government. It rests upon a philosophy of universally valid ends and means. Its fundamental assumption is the worth and dignity and creative capacity of the individual, so that the chief aim of government is the maximum of individual self-direction, the chief means to that end the minimum of compulsion by the state. Ideally considered, means and ends are conjoined in the concept of freedom: freedom of thought, so that the truth may prevail; freedom of occupation, so that careers may be open to talent; freedom of self-government, so that no one may be compelled against his will.

STUDY QUESTIONS

1. In this, a part of the first chapter of his *Modern Democracy*, Becker is concerned primarily to define the ideal democracy. In the later chapters of his book he defines "the reality," and describes what he conceives to be the "dilemma" of modern democracy. What devices does he use to define the ideal democracy in this selection? To what extent does he evaluate as well as define?
2. Study the skillful organization of this essay. Select one section and examine the paragraphs, noting transitions between paragraphs and sections, and the use of initial and final sentences in paragraphs.

3. What aspect of his general subject does Becker consider in each of the three major sections of this selection?

4. What material conditions does Becker think necessary for democracy? What assumptions does it make about its citizens? What does Becker mean when he says that modern democracy is "one of the formulations of the modern doctrine of progress"?

5. Becker's style has been often praised as a model of clarity and precision. Examine this selection, considering vocabulary and sentence structure as well as paragraphing, and be prepared to explain what characteristics contribute to its clarity.

3. Write a paper defining the ideal concept of something, say a college, government by town meeting, capitalism or some similiar abstraction.

From Individualism to Mass Democracy*

Edward Hallett Carr

The problem of political organization in the new society is to adapt to the mass civilization of the twentieth century conceptions of democracy formed in earlier and highly individualistic periods of history. The proclamation by the French revolution of popular sovereignty was a serious challenge to institutions which had grown up under quite different auspices and influences. It is no accident that Athenian democracy, which has been commonly regarded as the source and exemplar of democratic institutions, was the creation and prerogative of a limited and privileged group of the population. It is no accident that Locke, the founder of the modern democratic tradition, was the chosen philosopher and prophet of the eighteenth-century English Whig oligarchy. It is no accident that the magnificent structure of British nineteenth-century liberal democracy was built up on a highly restrictive property franchise. History points unmistakably to the the fact that political democracy, in the forms in which it has hitherto been known, flourishes best where some of the people, but not all of the people, are free and equal; and, since this conclusion is incompatible with the conditions of the new society and repugnant to the contemporary conscience, the task of saving democracy in our time is the task of reconciling it with the postulate of popular sovereignty and mass civilization.

Modern democracy, as it grew up and spread from its focus in western Europe over the past three centuries, rested on three main propositions: first, that the individual conscience is the ultimate source of decisions

* From *The New Society* by Edward Hallett Carr, by permission of Macmillan & Co. Ltd. and of St. Martin's Press, copyright 1951.

about what is right and wrong; second, that there exists between different individuals a fundamental harmony of interests strong enough to enable them to live peacefully together in society; third, that where action has to be taken in the name of society, rational discussion between individuals is the best method of reaching a decision on that action. Modern democracy is, in virtue of its origins, individualist, optimistic and rational. The three main propositions on which it is based have all been seriously challenged in the contemporary world. . . .

The prominent rôle assigned to reason in the original democratic scheme provides perhaps the most convincing explanation why democracy has hitherto always seemed to flourish best with a restrictive franchise. Much has been written in recent years of the decline of reason, and of respect for reason, in human affairs, when sometimes what has really happened has been the abandonment of the highly simplified eighteenth-century view of reason in favour of a subtler and more sophisticated analysis. But it is none the less true that the epoch-making changes in our attitude towards reason provide a key to some of the profoundest problems of contemporary democracy.

First of all, the notion that men of intelligence and good will were likely by process of rational discussion to reach a correct opinion on controversial political questions could be valid only in an age when such questions were comparatively few and simple enough to be accessible to the educated layman. It implicitly denied that any specialized knowledge was required to solve political problems. This hypothesis was perhaps tenable so long as the state was not required to intervene in economic issues, and the questions on which decisions had to be taken turned on matters of practical detail or general political principles. In the first half of the twentieth century these conditions had everywhere ceased to exist. In Great Britain major issues of a highly controversial character like the return to the gold standard in 1925 or the acceptance of the American loan in 1946 were of a kind in which no opinion seriously counted except that of the trained expert in possession of a vast array of facts and figures, some of them probably not available to the public. In such matters the ordinary citizen could not even have an intelligent opinion on the question who were the best experts to consult. The only rôle he could hope to play was to exercise his hunch at the election by choosing the right leader to consult the right experts about vital, though probably still unformulated, issues of policy which would ultimately affect his daily life.

At this initial stage of the argument reason itself is not dethroned from its supreme rôle in the decision of political issues. The citizen is merely asked to surrender his right of decision to the superior reason of the expert. At the second stage of the argument reason itself is used to dethrone reason. The social psychologist, employing rational methods of investigation, discovers that men in the mass are often most effectively moved by non-rational emotions such as admiration, envy, hatred, and can be most effectively reached not by rational argument, but by emotional appeals to eye and ear, or by sheer repetition. Propaganda is as essential a function of mass democracy as advertising of mass production. The political organizer takes a leaf out of the book of the commercial advertiser and sells the leader or the candidate to the voter by the same methods used to sell patent medicines or refrigerators. The appeal is no longer to the reason of the citizen, but to his gullibility. A more recent phenomenon has been the emergence of what Max Weber called the "charismatic leader" as the expression of the general will. The retreat from individualism seemed to issue at last—and not alone in the so-called totalitarian countries—in the exaltation of a single individual leader who personified and resumed within himself the qualities and aspirations of the "little man," of the ordinary individual lost and bewildered in the new mass society. But the principal qualification of the leader is no longer his capacity to reason correctly on political or economic issues, or even his capacity to choose the best experts to reason for him, but a good public face, a convincing voice, a sympathetic fireside manner on the radio; and these qualities are deliberately built up for him by his publicity agents. In this picture of the techniques of contemporary democracy, the party headquarters, the directing brain at the centre, still operates rationally, but uses irrational rather than rational means to achieve its ends—means which are, moreover, not merely irrational but largely irrelevant to the purposes to be pursued or to the decisions to be taken.

The third stage of the argument reaches deeper levels. Hegel, drawing out the philosophical implications of Rousseau's doctrine, had identified the course of history with universal reason, to which the individual reason stood in the same relation as the individual will to Rousseau's general will. Individual reason had been the corner-stone of individualist democracy. Marx took Hegel's collective reason to make it the corner-stone of the new mass democracy. Marx purported to reject the metaphysical character of Hegel's thought. But, equally with Hegel, he conceived of history pursuing a rational course, which could be analysed and even predicted in terms of reason. Hegel had spoken of the cunning of reason in history, using individuals to achieve purposes of which they themselves were unconscious. Marx would have rejected the turn of phrase as metaphysical. But his conception of history as a continuous process of class struggle contained elements of determinism which revealed its Hegelian ancestry, at any rate on one side. Marx remained a thorough-going rationalist. But the reason whose validity he accepted was collective rather than individual.

Marx played, however, a far more important part in what has been called "the flight from reason" than by the mere exaltation of the collective over the individual. By his vigorous assertion that "being determines consciousness, not consciousness being," that thinking is conditioned by the social environment of the thinker, and that ideas are the superstructure of a totality whose foundation is formed by the material conditions of life, Marx presented a clear challenge to what had hitherto been regarded as the sovereign or autonomous human reason. The actors who played significant parts in the historical drama were playing parts already written for them: this indeed was what made them significant. The function of individual reason was to identify itself with the universal reason which determined the course of history and to make itself the agent and executor of this universal reason. Some such view is indeed involved in any attempt to trace back historical events to underlying social causes; and Marx—and still more Engels—hedged a little in later years about the rôle of the individual in history. But the extraordinary vigour and conviction with which he drove home his main argument, and the political theory which he founded on it, give him a leading place among those nineteenth-century thinkers who shattered the comfortable belief of the Age of Enlightenment in the decisive power of individual reason in shaping the course of history.

Marx's keenest polemics were those directed to prove the "conditioned" character of the thinking of his opponents and particularly of the capitalist ruling class of the most advanced countries of his day. If they thought as they did it was because, as members of a class, "being" determined their "consciousness," and their ideas necessarily lacked any independent objectivity and validity. Hegel, as a good conservative, had exempted the current reality of the Prussian from the operation of the dialectic which had destroyed successively so many earlier historical forms. Marx, as a revolutionary, admitted no such absolute in the present, but only in the future. The proletariat, whose victory would automatically abolish classes, was alone the basis of absolute value; and collective proletarian thinking had thus an objectivity which was denied to the thinking of other classes. Marx's willingness, like that of Hegel, to admit an absolute as the culminating point of his dialectical process was, however, an element of inconsistency in his system; and, just as Marx was far more concerned to dissect capitalism than to provide a blueprint for socialism, so his use of the dialectic to lay bare the conditioned thinking of his opponents lay far nearer to his heart, and was far more effective, than his enunciation of the objective and absolute values of the proletariat. Marx's writings gave a powerful impetus to all forms of relativism. It seemed less important, at a time when the proletarian revolution was as yet nowhere in sight, to note his admission of absolute truth as a prerogative of the proletariat. The proletariat was for Marx the collective repository of Rousseau's infallible general will.

Another thinker of the later nineteenth century also helped to mould the climate of political opinion. Like Darwin, Freud was a scientist without pretensions to be a philosopher or, still less, a political thinker. But in the flight from reason at the end of the nineteenth century, he played the same popular rôle as Darwin had played a generation earlier in the philosophy of *laissez-faire*. Freud demonstrated that the fundamental attitudes of human beings in action and thought are largely determined at levels beneath that of consciousness, and that the supposedly rational explanations of those attitudes which we offer to ourselves and others are artificial and erroneous "rationalizations" of processes which we have failed to understand. Reason is given to us, Freud seems to say, not to direct our thought and action, but to camouflage the hidden forces which do direct it. This is a still more devastating version of the Marxist thesis of substructure and superstructure. The substructure of reality resides in the unconscious: what appears above the surface is no more than the reflexion, seen in a distorting ideological mirror, of what goes on underneath. The political conclusion from all this—Freud himself drew none —is that any attempt to appeal to the reason of the ordinary man is waste of time, or is useful merely as camouflage to conceal the real nature of the process of persuasion; the appeal must be made to those subconscious strata which are decisive for thought and action. The debunking of ideology undertaken by the political science of Marx is repeated in a far more drastic and far-reaching way by the psychological science of Freud and his successors.

By the middle of the nineteenth century, therefore, the propositions of Locke on which the theory of liberal democracy were founded had all been subjected to fundamental attack, and the attack broadened and deepened as the century went on. Individualism began to give way to collectivism both in economic organization and in the forms and practice of mass democracy: the age of mass civilization had begun. The alleged harmony of interests between individuals was replaced by the naked struggle between powerful classes and organized interest groups. The belief in the settlement of issues by rational discussion was undermined, first, by recognition of the complex and technical character of the issues involved, later and more seriously, by recognition that rational arguments were merely the conditioned reflection of the class interests of those who put them forward, and, last and most seriously of all, by the discovery that the democratic voter, like other human beings, is most effectively reached not by arguments directed to his reason, but by appeals directed to his irrational, subconscious prejudices. The picture of democracy which emerged from these criticisms was the picture of an arena where powerful interest-groups struggled for the mastery. The leaders themselves were often the spokesmen and instruments of historical processes which they did not fully understand; their followers consisted of voters recruited and marshalled for purposes of which they were wholly unconscious by all the subtle techniques of modern psychological science and modern commercial advertising.

The picture is overdrawn. But we shall not begin to understand the problems of mass democracy unless we recognize the serious elements of truth in it, unless we recognize how far we have moved away from the conceptions and from the conditions out of which the democratic tradition was born. From the conception of democracy as a select society of free individuals, enjoying equal rights and periodically electing to manage the affairs of the society, a small number of their peers, who deliberate together and decide by rational argument on the course to pursue (the assumption being that the course which appeals to the majority is likely to be the most rational), we have passed to the current reality of mass democracy. The typical mass democracy of today is a vast society of individuals, stratified by widely different social and economic backgrounds into a series of groups of classes, enjoying equal political rights the exercise of which is organized through two or more closely integrated political machines called parties. Between the parties and individual citizens stand an indeterminate number of entities variously known as unions, associations, lobbies or pressure-groups devoted to the promotion of some economic interest, or of some social or humanitarian cause in which keen critics usually detect a latent and perhaps unconscious interest. At the first stage of the democratic process, these associations and groups form a sort of exchange and mart where votes are traded for support of particular policies; the more votes such a group controls the better its chance of having its views incorporated in the party platform. At the second stage, when these bargains have been made, the party as a united entity "goes to the country" and endeavors by every form of political propaganda to win the support of the unattached voter. At the third stage, when the election has been decided, the parties once more dispute or bargain together, in the light of the votes cast, on the policies to be put into effect; the details of procedure at this third stage differ considerably in different democratic countries in accordance with varying constitutional requirements and party structures. What is important to note is that the first and third stages are fierce matters of bargaining. At the second stage, where the mass persuasion of the electorate is at issue, the methods employed now commonly approximate more and more closely to those of commercial advertisers, who, on the advice of modern psychologists, find the appeal to fear, envy or self-aggrandizement more effective than the appeal to reason. Certainly in the United States, where contemporary large-scale democracy has worked most successfully and where the strongest confidence is felt in its survival, experienced practitioners of politics would give little encouragement to the idea that rational argument exercises a major influence on the democratic process. We have returned to a barely disguised struggle of interest-groups in which the arguments used are for the most part no more than a rationalization of the interests concerned, and the rôle of persuasion is played by carefully calculated appeals to the irrational subconscious.

This discussion is intended to show not that mass democracy is more corrupt or less efficient than other forms of government (this I do not believe), but that mass democracy is a new phenomenon—a creation of the last half-century—which it is inappropriate and misleading to consider in terms of the philosophy of Locke or of the liberal democracy of the nineteenth century. It is new, because the new democratic society consists no longer of a homogeneous closed society of equal and economically secure individuals mutually recognizing one another's rights, but of ill co-ordinated, highly stratified masses of people of whom a large majority are primarily occupied with the daily struggle for existence. It is new, because the new democratic state can no longer be content to hold the ring in the strife of private economic interests, but must enter the arena at every moment and take the initiative in urgent issues of economic policy which affect the daily life of all the citizens, and especially of the least secure. It is new, because the old rationalist assumptions of Locke and of liberal democracy have broken down under the weight both of changed material conditions and of new scientific insights and inventions, and the leaders of the new democracy are concerned no longer primarily with the reflexion of opinion, but with the moulding and manipulation of opinion. To speak today of the defence of democracy as if we were defending something which we knew and had possessed for many decades or many centuries is self-deception and sham. . . .

STUDY QUESTIONS

1. How well do Carr and Becker agree as to the fundamental nature of democracy?

2. Explain what is meant by the term "universal reason" as it is used in this selection. What are the relative roles of reason and emotion in the history of democracy given by Carr?

3. How is present-day democracy different from what democracy was originally supposed to be, according to Carr's account?

4. Is Carr's writing as lucid as Becker's? How is it organized? Are there significant differences in organization, paragraphing, sentences, or vocabulary? Does the fact that Carr is advancing an explanation of a contemporary situation rather than explaining an ideal make his job more complex?

5. If Carr is right about the changes in democracy, what bearing do these changes have upon the traditional element of democracy? To what extent are the principles of the American Revolution, the French Revolution, the democratic state of Athens, and of such Documents as the Constitution and the Declaration of Independence relevant to present-day mass democracy?

6. Is Carr correct in contending that underground and irrational forces are the real moving powers of today's democracy? Write a theme which examines this point of view, using some contemporary political development as an example.

The Hero and Democracy*

Sidney Hook

If the hero is defined as an event-making individual who rede-termines the course of history, it follows at once that a democratic com-munity must be eternally on guard against him.

This simple, and to some unwelcome, conclusion is involved in the very conception of a democratic society. For in such a society leadership can-not arrogate to itself heroic power. At legally determined intervals gov-ernment must draw its sanction from the *freely given consent* of the governed. And so long as that consent is *freely* given, that is, after the opposition has been heard, the policy or action agreed upon becomes the one for which the community is responsible even though the leadership may have initiated it.[1]

The problem of leadership in a democracy is highly complex. Its im-portance warrants further clarification. Our reflections in this chapter, as distinct from the others, will be normative. They will involve judg-ments of value concerning democracy and democracy's good.

An old Chinese proverb tells us "the great man is a public misfortune." The sentiment aptly expresses the experience and wisdom of a peace-loving race. Were the victims of great men's glory to speak, not only in China but almost anywhere, they would echo this homely judgment with sighs and tears and curses. For on the whole, heroes in history have carved out their paths of greatness by wars, conquests, revolutions, and holy crusades.

And yet this Chinese proverb epitomizes only past history, and not all of that. A great man may sometimes be a public fortune. His absence is far from being a sign that we shall be spared great misfortunes. Indeed, in face of calamity the people pray for a deliverer. Among the calamities they pray to be delivered from may be the rule of an earlier deliverer. If we were to conclude from the evil things great men have done that their greatness is the source of their evil, we should have to condemn all talent and capacity because they are often abused.

Great men, then, may be good men. And still a democracy must be suspicious of them! For essential to democracy is the participation of the

* From *Hero in History* by Sidney Hook, by permission of The Humani-ties Press, Inc. Copyright, 1943, by Sidney Hook.
[1] For further amplification of the meaning of "freely given consent," see Chapter thirteen of my *Reason, Social Myths and Democracy,* New York, 1941; also "The Philosophical Presuppositions of Democracy," *Ethics,* April 1942.

governed in determining their own welfare. This participation is coupled with the *hope* that the governed will select and elect their governors wisely, that is, in such a way as to gratify as many of their needs and wants as the situation permits. But more important than this hope, which is sometimes sadly at variance with the facts, is the belief that it is more worthy of men to decide their own fate than to let others decide it for them.

The hero in a democratic community—the potentially event-making man—may sincerely believe that he accepts its underlying philosophy. But sooner or later he finds himself straining against two features of the democratic process. The first is the principle of majority rule, especially when he is convinced that the majority is wrong on a matter of great import. The second is the slowness of its operation even when he believes the majority is right.

No one believes in majority rule as a reasonable principle of decision in a family of small children, a prison, or an institution for the feeble-minded. To the extent that we accept majority rule as an essential feature of democracy, we are committed to the well-grounded belief that, on the whole, men are not infants, cretins, or criminals. But although men are capable of rationality, reason in human affairs is so much a matter of weighing interests, and interests so often are at variance with each other, that the majority's reason may be the minority's disaster. This proves that the principle of majority rule is not sufficient for democracy, not that it is unnecessary. Nor does it prove that certain rights are inalienable and absolute, for not one such right can be mentioned which under certain circumstances may not need to be abridged in the interest of other rights.

What is necessary in addition to the principle of majority rule is the recognition by every group interest in society of the legitimacy of any group interest, provided the group in question accepts the methods of *free* inquiry and democratic decision as principles of negotiating conflicts of interest. Even so the majority may be mistaken and unjust, even as the man who follows the lead of evidence may sometimes be mistaken while the man who acts blindly may be right. But the majority that provides a minority with the possibility of becoming a majority through the education of citizens by public opposition has gone as far as it can politically to meet legitimate grievance. Under the conditions indicated, the democrat who enjoys freedom of agitation must abide by the decision of the majority even when he believes it to be wrong.

This does not *in principle* justify toleration of a minority whose actual program calls for the overthrow of democratic political institutions by force of arms. Any particular minority may be tolerated on grounds of prudence or expediency, for example, where it is opposed to another minority, more dangerous at the moment, or where its suppression is likely to establish a precedent that may be extended to other minorities who are genuinely devoted to democratic processes.

The "potential hero" in a democracy sees what others do not. His will to action is stronger. His knowledge of what must be done to realize what he sees is surer. For these reasons, he finds himself, more likely than not, in a minority. His sense of his vocation impels him to fight for his insight. His loyalty to the democratic ideal compels him to make this insight the common faith of the majority. If the latter remain stubbornly intractable, his chances of heroic action, as a democrat, are lost. The hero fades into history as a "village Hampden."

Superior talent and strong vision, however, press for expression. So far as the hero does not renounce politics as a sphere of activity, his task becomes to get himself accepted by a majority. For, as a democrat, he does not dare to admit to himself or to others that he wants to make himself independent of the majority. In pursuit of a majority, he may seek to win it, broadly speaking, by the patient methods of education, relying upon the inherent reasonableness of his vision to make its way.

Insofar as he does this, and only so far, democracy is safe from the hero. This means that he courts failure. But the hero may master the arts of the demagogue and use the very instruments of democracy to debase its quality. Yet as long as democratic controls are not abolished, the hero as demagogue must still build up, cajole, and cater to the majority. He acquires a contempt for the group he leads by virtue of the methods by which he corrupts them. In the process, if his own will and insight grow uncertain and cloudy, he becomes just another politician. He is a hero who has missed his chance. But where his will and insight remain firm, the hero as demagogue must "fool" his following into accepting them. He must develop a public platform, on the basis of which he solicits confidence, and a secret program in whose behalf he uses the confidence so won. He becomes a threat to democracy. The greater his faith in himself, the more disinterested his intentions, the more fateful the issue to which his heroic vision drives him, the more insidious is the menace to the whole rationale of democracy. Particularly so if the hero or potential event-making character believes himself to be the indispensable instrument of his vision.

Until now we have assumed that the standpoint of the hero is one that cannot recommend itself to the majority in the light of free discussion and intelligent inquiry and that if it is adopted it is only in virtue of chicanery and demagogic fraud. Let us now assume that the majority is properly persuaded that the hero is right. The latter may still regard the processes of democracy as a fetter upon his calling. For these processes grind too slowly, and many things will not wait. If he is confident that he knows the community's good, and convinced that it hangs in the balance, the hero is tempted to confront it with a *fait accompli*. Well-intentioned opposition that delays and obstructs appears to him as objective betrayal, and can easily be pilloried as such. And he knows that, if he succeeds, a great deal will be forgiven him.

But need a democracy move slowly? No, for its pace can be accelerated by delegation of power to the leader or hero. Yet in the best of situations, this only mitigates the dangers of delay; it does not eliminate them. For a democracy cannot in advance delegate all its powers and remain a democracy. And the crucial situation is always one that involves the undelegated powers. Since power cannot in a democracy be delegated in perpetuity, the crucial situation may arise just when the delegation of power is up for *renewal*. Again, the delegation of power is always requested in a moment of crisis or emergency. But who is to determine when the moment is here?

The hero always presses for greater powers. It is natural to his vocation that he should do so. He is as eager to accept new powers as he is reluctant to surrender them after they are granted. And it is true that, in a troubled world, no democratic community can survive for long unless it entrusts its leaders with great powers. At the same time, what it gives with reluctance, it must take back with eagerness. The timing is all—and it is not likely that the hero and the community will agree on what time it is.

There cannot be any guarantee that a leader will not usurp delegated power to carry out a heroic event-making task. But a democracy would be foolish to refuse delegation of power for this reason if the situation is so crucial that decisive action must be taken at once. On the other hand, there may be no evidence that delegated powers will be abused. Nonetheless, a democracy would be foolish not to withdraw them promptly when the emergency is over, for they are a standing temptation to abuse and usurpation.

A democracy is imperiled not alone by its heroes, necessary as they may sometimes be for survival. It is imperiled by any group of its citizens who are more attached to the advantages or privileges they enjoy under democracy, or hope it will bring, than they are to the democratic process of bringing them about. For these groups, which set greater store on peace or prosperity or social status than they do on the methods of democracy to preserve (or modify) them, are the ones which feel justified in calling in the hero to cherish their "goods" even at the cost of democracy. An instructive example is furnished by conservative classes in western Europe who, convinced that democratic legislation had unjustly abridged the privileges of property, opened the gates to Mussolini and Hitler. True, their profession of democratic allegiance was merely lip service to begin with. But not so for the large numbers of the middle classes and even workers who constituted the mass base of Fascism. Security, fixed prices, employment meant more to them than democracy. They were to learn that when democracy goes, the goods for which it is sacrificed, without becoming more certain, are degraded in quality.

If we were to list as heroes the event-making men of the past, we should find few of them in the histories of democratic societies. It is in conformity with the genius of democratic society that this should be so.

There is great wisdom in the notorious political ingratitude of democratic communities. They usually refuse to glorify their leaders until they are dead. And the best reason for honoring these leaders is that they did not yield to the temptations of power, or that they were prepared to step down from positions of power even when they were convinced that they were right and the majority wrong.

Great men do not ask permission to be born. Nor do they ask permission of democracies to lead them. They find their own way to the tasks they feel called to fulfill, unless crushed by a hostile environment or isolated by the tide of events. Democracies do not have to seek these heroes when it seeks leaders. For if they exist, they will make themselves heard. A democracy must always be girded to protect itself against them even as it uses them, relying not on *their* intentions, which are always honorable but not infrequently messianic, but on the mechanisms of its own democratic institutions, on the plurality of centers of power and interest, and on the spirit of its education and morale.

In a democratic community education must pitch the ideal of the hero in a different key from that of the event-making man. The heroes in a democracy should be the great figures in the Pantheon of thought, the men of ideas, of social vision, of scientific achievement and artistic power. For it is these men who mould the intellectual ideals and social attitudes of the citizens, who without knowledge, quickened perception, and educated taste cannot realize the promise of democracy. If we are earnest in our belief in democracy, we must recognize that it is those who are affected by a basic policy who must pass upon it, either directly or indirectly. And if they are to pass upon it intelligently, know when to delegate power or withdraw it, and enhance the quality of political life by their participation, they must develop a sensitiveness to what is significant and what is trivial, an indifference to rhetorical bombast but a keen interest in what it conceals, an ability to isolate relevant issues and to weigh the available evidence.

The statesman in a democracy exercises his leadership by *proposing* a policy. But whether it is adopted and why depends upon the representatives of the democratic community who are chosen by individuals themselves potentially representatives. A successful democracy, therefore, may honor its statesmen; but it must honor its teachers more—whether they be prophets, scientists, poets, jurists, or philosophers. The true hero of democracy, then, should be not the soldier or the political leader, great as their services may be, but the teacher—the Jeffersons, Holmes, Deweys, Whitmans, and all others who have given the people vision, method, and knowledge.

It is the task of a democratic society to break down the invidious distinctions reflected in current linguistic usage between the hero and the masses or the average man. This can be accomplished in part by reinterpreting the meaning of the word "hero," and by recognizing that "heroes" can be made by fitting social opportunities more skillfully to specific talents. What we call "the average man" is not a biological but a social phenomenon. Human capacities are much more diversified than our social arrangements take note of.

Where we restrict social opportunities, so that only a few types of excellence are recognized, in respect to them the great mass of individuals, despite their differences, will appear as the dull, gray average. If, however, we extend social opportunities so that each person's specific talents have a stimulus to development and expression, we increase the range of possibility of distinctively significant work. From this point of view, a hero is any individual who does his work well and makes a unique contribution to the public good. It is sheer prejudice to believe that the grandeur and nobility associated with the heroic life can be found only in careers that reck little of human blood and suffering. Daily toil on any level has its own occasions of struggle, victory, and quiet death. A democracy should contrive its affairs, not to give one or a few the chance to reach heroic stature, but rather to take as a regulative ideal the slogan, "every man a hero."

We call this a "regulative ideal" because it would be Utopian to imagine that it could ever be literally embodied. As a regulative ideal it gives direction to policies that enable society to make the best of whatever powers are available to men.

What are the powers available to men? They are theoretically limited but practically indefinite. In the absence of an environment that encourages their expression, no one can speak with dogmatism about their nature and specific form. Nor can we be certain of the precise limit of human power without allowing for the willed effort that enables the runner to clear a hurdle that until then had been an insuperable obstacle.

A democracy should encourage the belief that all are called and all may be chosen. All may be chosen because a wisely contrived society will take as a point of departure the rich possibilities that nature herself gives through the spontaneous variations in the powers and capacities of men. These variations are the source and promise of new shoots of personality and value. The belief that all may be chosen, acted upon in a co-operating environment, may inspire the added increment of effort that often transforms promise into achievement.

Our conception of a democracy without event-making figures runs counter to a plausible but fundamentally mistaken critique of democracy developed by a notable school of Italian theorists—Mosca, Pareto, and Michels.[2] These men in different ways seek to establish the impossibility

[2] I have previously expounded and criticized the doctrines of this school from a somewhat different point of view in my *Reason, Social Myths and Democracy*, pp. 119 ff., New York, 1940.

of democracy. Their chief argument is that all political rule involves organization and that all organization, no matter how democratic its mythology, sooner or later comes under the effective control of a minority élite. The history of societies, despite the succession of different political *forms,* is in substance nothing but the succession of different political élites. Democracy is a political form that conceals both the conflicts of interest between the governing élite and the governed and the fact that these conflicts are always undemocratically resolved in favor of the former. To the extent that these élites make history, their outstanding leaders are heroes or event-making figures even in a democracy.

The whole force of this argument rests upon a failure to understand the nature of ideals, including political ideals. In addition, the critique overlooks the fact that the problems of political power are always *specific* and that they allow choices between courses of conduct that strengthen or weaken, extend or diminish particular political ideals. Finally, it underestimates the tremendous differences between societies, all of which fall short in varying degrees of the defined ideal of democracy, and the crucial importance of institutions in the never-ending process of realizing ideals.

In virtue of the nature of things and men, no ideal can be perfectly embodied. There is no such thing as absolute health, absolute wisdom, absolute democracy, an absolutely honest man—or an absolutely fat one. Yet when we employ these ideals intelligently we can order a series of flesh and blood men in such a way as to distinguish between them in respect to their being healthier, wiser, or fatter. And so with states. There is no absolutely democratic state, but we can tell when states are more democratic or less democratic. Ideals, in short, are functional. They are principles of organization and reorganization but cannot be identified with any particular organization as it exists at any place and time.

If we define a democratic society as one in which the government rests upon the freely given consent of the governed [3] it is obvious that no society is a perfect democracy, even one in which the members are so few that they can all meet in one place without delegating power to representatives. For we never can be sure that consent is freely given, that is, not in bondage to ignorance, rhetoric, or passion. Further, the division of labor requires that decisions be carried out by individuals and not by the assembly. There can be no guarantee that these decisions as well as the discretionary powers they entail will be carried out in the same spirit as that in which they were authorized.

What follows? That democracy is impossible? No more so than that a man cannot be healthy because he cannot enjoy perfect health. The defects when recognized become problems to be remedied by actions, institutions, checks, and restraints that are themselves informed by the principle or ideal of democracy. The remedies are of course imperfect,

---

[3] For a detailed analysis of this definition, see *ibid.,* p. 285.

fallible, and unguaranteed. But we do not therefore reject them. We continue to improve them—if we are democrats. And we test by the fruits of the process the validity of the unrealizable democratic principle that serves as our functional guide.

Mosca, Pareto, and Michels make much of the fact that when power is delegated in a democracy and when political organizations arise, as they must in a society sufficiently complex, the decisions of the government may reflect the interests of the governors more than the interests of the governed. This is indisputably true.

What follows? Not that democracy is impossible but that it is difficult. It is more difficult under certain social and historical conditions than under others. But as long as we hold to democratic principles, again the remedies consist in thinking up of specific mechanisms, devices, and checks which (1) increase the *participation* of the governed in the processes of government, (2) decrease the *concentrations* of powers—educational, religious, economic, political—in the hands of the governors, and (3) provide for the renewal or withdrawal of the mandates of power by the governed. Again, the remedies may be defective. But if we believe that those whose interests are affected by the policies of government should have a voice in determining those policies, either directly, or indirectly by controlling the makers of policy, the *direction* which the never-ending task of democratizing the social process must take is clear. Whether it does take that direction depends greatly upon us.

That there will always be a governing élite to administer government is true. There will also always be a medical élite to minister to our health. The governing élite will always have more power for good or evil than the medical élite. But it need not be more permanent or even as permanent as the medical élite. So long as the governing élite operates within a framework of a democracy, we have a choice between élites. Where élites must contend with out-élites, the victor must pay a price to the governed for victory. How high the price is depends in part at least on how much the governed ask.[4]

The great limitation of the thought of Mosca, Pareto, and Michels is their failure to appreciate the differential advantages of the specific institutions available in a democracy that enable us both to select élites and to curb them. They overlook the concrete ways in which the governed through pressure groups, strikes, public debates, committee hearings, radio discussion, letters and telegrams to newspapers and their representatives, petitions, mass meetings, primaries, and elections actually

---

[4] "For the working masses every 'final victory' proclaimed by their victorious leaders, even if it is a real step forward, can be only another starting point in their endless struggle *for more and always more*." Max Nomad, in his "Masters—Old and New," *The Making of Society,* edited by V. F. Calverton, p. 892.

contribute to moulding the basic policies and decisions of the government in a democracy.[5]

The crux of the issue raised by the contention that democracy is impossible because power is exercised by an organized minority may best be met by asking the following questions: Can a democracy get rid of its ruling élite? Can a democracy rid itself of a governing élite more easily or at a lesser cost than a nondemocratic society? There can hardly be any doubt about the answers. The evidence of politics and history shows that democracy can and has rid itself of governing élites, and that it can do so more easily than is generally possible in nondemocratic societies. That in consequence one élite is replaced by another is a feature of the political process in a complex society, not an indictment of democracy or a proof of its impossibility. Sufficient unto the day is the problem thereof!

Behind the facade of logical argument in the writings of Mosca, Pareto, and Michels are two significant assumptions. The first is that human nature has a fixed and unalterable character from which it can be predicted that democracy in action must fail, not in the innocent sense that a perfect democracy cannot be realized, but in the sense that a working democracy *cannot be bettered* from the standpoint of its own ideal. The second assumption is that the amount of freedom and democracy in a society is determined by a *law already known*. Both assumptions are false.

So far as the position of these social philosophers is based upon the constancy of human nature, their entire political wisdom consists in framing a simple alternative to man—rule or be ruled! But one does not have to be a Utopian to maintain that nothing in human nature limits us to this simple alternative. For other alternatives must be taken together with it. Who is to rule? Over what? For how long? Under what conditions and restrictions? Here is the place for intelligence, experiment, critical adaptation, and political discovery.

The amount and quality of freedom and democracy in a society are determined by many things—economic organization, education, tradition, religion, to name only a few. *But they depend just as much upon our willingness to fight for them as upon any other thing.*

Democracy is difficult, and it is made more difficult because many who call themselves democrats are totalitarians in disguise. The moral is not to call off the struggle but to struggle all the more.

STUDY QUESTIONS

1. In what ways are the impulses of the "hero" and the principles of democracy opposed to each other?

[5] *Cf.* the brief but excellent discussion of Glenn Morrow in *Ethics*, April 1942, pp. 299 *ff.*; also Arthur Bentley's important but neglected study, *The Process of Government*, Chicago, 1908.

2. At what point does Hook set the limits of liberty for minorities in a democracy? Are these limits different from those set by Mill in "On Liberty"?

3. How is the "governing élite" in a democracy different from that in other forms of government?

4. How does Hook counter the argument that even when a government is elected, as in a democracy, its actions may reflect its own interests rather than those of the people it governs?

5. Do you agree with Hook that the relationship between the leader and the led is essentially the same in a democracy and other forms of government?

6. Examine Hook's generalizations about the methods and temptations of the democratic hero in the light of the career of some democratic leader.

*The Decline of Heroes**

Arthur M. Schlesinger, Jr.

Ours is an age without heroes—and, when we say this, we suddenly realize how spectacularly the world has changed in a generation. Most of us grew up in a time of towering personalities. For better or for worse, great men seemed to dominate our lives and shape our destiny. In the United States we had Theodore Roosevelt, Woodrow Wilson, Franklin Roosevelt. In Great Britain, there were Lloyd George and Winston Churchill. In other lands, there were Lenin, Stalin, Hitler, Mussolini, Clemenceau, Gandhi, Kemal, Sun Yat-sen. Outside of politics there were Einstein, Freud, Keynes. Some of these great men influenced the world for good, others for evil; but, whether for good or for evil, the fact that each had not died at birth made a difference, one believed, to everyone who lived after them.

Today no one bestrides our narrow world like a colossus; we have no giants who play roles which one can imagine no one else playing in their stead. There are a few figures on the margin of uniqueness, perhaps: Adenauer, Nehru, Tito, De Gaulle, Chiang Kai-shek, Mao Tse-tung. But there seem to be none in the epic style of those mighty figures of our recent past who seized history with both hands and gave it an imprint, even a direction, which it otherwise might not have had. As De Gaulle himself remarked on hearing of Stalin's death, "The age of giants is over." Whatever one thought, whether one admired or detested Roosevelt or Churchill, Stalin or Hitler, one nevertheless felt the sheer weight of such personalities on one's own existence. We feel no comparable pressures today. Our own President, with all his pleasant qualities, has more or less

* © 1958, The Curtis Publishing Company. By permission of the author.

explicitly renounced any desire to impress his own views on history. The Macmillans, Khrushchevs and Gronchis have measurably less specific gravity than their predecessors. Other men could be in their places as leaders of America or Britain or Russia or Italy without any change in the course of history. Why ours should thus be an age without heroes, and whether this condition is good or bad for us and for civilization, are topics worthy of investigation.

Why have giants vanished from our midst? One must never neglect the role of accident in history; and accident no doubt plays a part here. But too many accidents of the same sort cease to be wholly accidental. One must inquire further. Why should our age not only be without great men but even seem actively hostile to them? Surely one reason we have so few heroes now is precisely that we had so many a generation ago. Greatness is hard for common humanity to bear. As Emerson said, "Heroism means difficulty, postponement of praise, postponement of ease, introduction of the world into the private apartment, introduction of eternity into the hours measured by the sitting-room clock." A world of heroes keeps people from living their own private lives.

Moreover, great men live dangerously. They introduce extremes into existence—extremes of good, extremes of evil—and ordinary men after a time flinch from the ultimates and yearn for undemanding security. The Second World War was the climax of an epoch of living dangerously. It is no surprise that it precipitated a universal revulsion against greatness. The war itself destroyed Hitler and Mussolini. And the architects of victory were hardly longer-lived. After the war, the British repudiated Churchill, and the Americans (with the adoption of the 22nd Amendment), Roosevelt. In due course, the French repudiated De Gaulle (they later repented, but it took the threat of civil war to bring him back); the Chinese, Chiang Kai-shek; and the Russians, Stalin. Khrushchev, in toppling Stalin from his pedestal, pronounced the general verdict against the uncommon man: the modern world, he said, had no use for the "cult of the individual." And, indeed, carried to the excesses to which the worshipers of Hitler and Stalin carried it, even to the much milder degree to which admirers of Roosevelt and Churchill sometimes carried it, the cult of the individual was dangerous. No man is infallible, and every man needs to be reminded of this on occasion. Still, our age has gone further than this—it objects not just to hero worship but to heroes. The century of the common man has come into its own.

This term, "common man," suggests the deeper problem. There is more involved than simply a dismissal of those colossi whom the world identified with a season of blood and agony. The common man has always regarded the great man with mixed feelings—resentment as well as admiration, hatred as well as love. The Athenian who refused to vote for Aristides because he was so tired of hearing him called "the Just" expressed a natural reaction. Great men make small men aware of their smallness. Rancor is one of the unavowed but potent emotions of politics; and one must never forget that the envy of the have-nots can be quite as consuming when the haves have character or intelligence as it is when they have merely material possessions.

Modern democracy inadvertently gave envy new scope. While the purpose of democracy was to give everyone a fair chance to rise, its method enabled rancorous men to invoke "equality" as an excuse for keeping all down to their own level. "I attribute the small number of distinguished men in political life," wrote Alexis de Tocqueville after visiting the United States in the 1830's, "to the ever-increasing despotism of the majority. . . . The power of the majority is so absolute and irresistible that one must give up one's rights as a citizen and almost abjure one's qualities as a human being, if one intends to stray from the track which it prescribes." James Bryce even titled a chapter in his American Commonwealth, Why Great Men Are Not Chosen President.

History has shown these prophets unduly pessimistic. Distinguished men do enter American politics; great men have been chosen President. Democracy demonstrates a capability for heroic leadership quite as much as it does a tendency toward mediocrity. Yet Tocqueville and the others were correct enough in detecting the dislike of great men as a permanent potentiality in a democracy. And the evolution of industrial society appears to have given this sentiment new force. More and more of us live and work within great organizations; an influential book has already singled out the organization man as the American of the future. The bureaucratization of American life, the decline of the working class, the growth of the white-collar class, the rise of suburbia—all this has meant the increasing homogeneity of American society. Though we continue to speak of ourselves as rugged individualists, our actual life has grown more and more collective and anonymous. As a Monsanto Chemical film put it, showing a group of technicians at work in a laboratory: "No geniuses here; just a bunch of average Americans working together." Our ideal is increasingly smooth absorption into the group rather than self-realization in the old-fashioned, strong-minded, don't-give-a-damn sense. Where does the great man fit into our homogenized society?

"The greatness of England is now all collective," John Stuart Mill wrote a century ago: "individually small, we only appear capable of anything great by our habit of combining." He might have been writing about contemporary America; but where we Americans are inclined to rejoice over the superiority of the "team," Mill added somberly, "It was men of another stamp than this that made England what it has been; and men of another stamp will be needed to prevent its decline."

But was Mill right? Do individuals really have impact on history? A powerful school of philosophers has denied any importance at all to great men. Such thinkers reject heroes as a childish hangover from the days when men ascribed everything to the action of gods. History, they assert, is not made by men, but by inexorable forces or irrevocable laws: if these forces or laws do not manifest themselves through one individual, they will do so through another. What has happened already has comprehensively and absolutely decided what will happen in the future. "If there is a single human action due to free will," wrote Tolstoi, "no historical law exists, and no conception of historical events can be formed." If all this is so, obviously the presence or absence of any particular "hero" at any particular time cannot make the slightest difference.

This view of history is a form of fatalistic determinism; and Tolstoi's *War and Peace* offers one of its most eloquent statements. Why, Tolstoi asked, did millions of men in the time of Napoleon, repudiating their common sense and their human feelings, move from west to east, slaughtering their fellows? The answers provided by historians seemed to him hopelessly superficial. His own answer was: "The war was bound to happen simply because it was bound to happen"; all previous history predetermined it. Where did this leave the great men? In Tolstoi's view, they were the most deluded figures of all. Great men, he said, "are but the labels that serve to give a name to an event and, like labels, they have the least possible connection with the event itself." The greater the man, "the more conspicuous is the inevitability and predestination of every act he commits." The hero, said Tolstoi, "is the slave of history."

There are many forms of historical fatalism. Toynbee and Spengler, with their theory of the inexorable growth and decay of civilizations, represent one form. The Marxists, with their theory that changes in the modes of production control the course of history, represent another. When Khrushchev denounced the practice of making "a hero" out of "a particular leader" and condemned the cult of the individual as "alien to the spirit of Marxism-Leninism," he was speaking the true spirit of his faith. And Marxism is not the only form of economic determinism; there are also, for example, economic determinists of the laissez-faire school who believe that all civilization is dependent on rigid adherence to a certain theory of the sacredness of private property.

Fatalists differ greatly among themselves. But, however much they differ, they unite in the conclusion that the individual plays no role of his own in history. If they are right, then nothing could matter less whether or not this is an age without heroes.

But they are not right. The philosophy of historical fatalism rests on serious fallacies. For one thing, it supposes that, because a thing happens, it had to happen. But causation is one matter; predestination another. The construction of a causal explanation after an event merely renders that event in some sense intelligible. It does not in the least show that this particular event, and no other, had to take place; that nothing else could possibly have occurred in its stead. The serious test of the fatalist case must be applied before the event. The only conclusive proof of fatalism would lie in the accurate prediction of events that have not yet happened. And to say, with Tolstoi, that all prior history predetermines everything that follows is to say nothing at all. It is to produce an explanation which applies equally to everything—and thus becomes so vague and limitless as to explain nothing.

Fatalism raises other difficulties. Thus it imputes reality to mystical historical "forces"—class, race, nation, the will of the people, the spirit of the times, history itself. But there are no such forces. They are merely abstractions or metaphors with no existence except in the mind of the beholder. The only evidence for them is deduction from the behavior of individuals. It is therefore the individual who constitutes the basic unit of history. And, while no individual can be wholly free—and, indeed, recent discoveries of the manifold ways in which we are unconsciously conditioned should constitute a salutary check on human vanity—one must assume the reality of an area of free choice until that assumption is challenged, not by metaphysical affirmation, but by verifiable proof— that is, consistently accurate prediction of the future.

Fatalism, moreover, is incompatible with human psychology and human morality. Anyone who rigorously accepted a deterministic view of life, for example, would have to abandon all notions of human responsibility, since it is manifestly unfair to praise or punish people for acts which are by definition beyond their control. But such fatalism is belied by the assumption of free choice which underlies every move we make, every word we utter, every thought we think. As Sir Isaiah Berlin observes of determinism, "If we begin to take it seriously, then, indeed, the changes in our language, our moral notions, our attitudes toward one another, our views of history, of society and of everything else will be too profound to be even adumbrated." We can no more imagine what the universe of the consistent determinist would be like than we can imagine what it would be like to live in a world without time or one with seventeen-dimensional space.

For the historian concerned with concrete interpretation of actual events, he can easily demonstrate the futility of fatalism by trying to apply it to specific historical episodes. According to the extreme determinist view, no particular individual can make the slightest difference. As slaves of history, all individuals are, so to speak, interchangeable parts. If Napoleon had not led his armies across Europe, Tolstoi implies, someone else would have. William James, combating this philosophic fatalism, once asked the determinists whether they really believed "the convergence of sociological pressures to have so impinged on Stratford on Avon about April 23, 1564, that a W. Shakespeare, with all his mental peculiarities, had to be born there." And did they further believe, James continued, that "if the aforesaid W. Shakespeare had died of cholera infantum, another mother at Stratford on Avon would needs have engendered a duplicate copy of him to restore the sociologic equilibrium?" Who could believe such stuff? Yet, if the determinists do not mean exactly this, how can they read the individual out of history?

In December, 1931, a British politician, crossing Fifth Avenue in New York between 76th and 77th streets around ten-thirty at night, was knocked down and gravely injured by an automobile. Fourteen months later an American politician, sitting in an open car in Miami, Florida, was fired on by an assassin; a man standing beside him was killed. Would the next two decades of history have been the same had Contasini's car killed Winston Churchill in 1931 and Zangara's bullets killed Franklin Roosevelt in 1933? Suppose, in addition, that Adolf Hitler had been killed in the street fighting during the Munich *Putsch* of 1923, and Lenin and Mussolini had died at birth. Where would our century be now?

Individuals, of course, must operate within limits. They cannot do everything. They cannot, for example, propel history into directions for which the environment and the human material are not prepared: no genius, however heroic, could have brought television to ancient Troy. Yet, as Sidney Hook has convincingly argued in his thoughtful book, *The Hero in History*, great men can count decisively "where the historical situation permits of major alternative paths of development."

This argument between fatalism and heroism is not one in which there is a lot to be said on both sides. The issue is far too sharp to be straddled. Either history is rigidly determined and foreordained, in which case individual striving does not matter; or it is not, in which case there is an essential role for the hero. Analysis of concrete episodes suggests that history is, within limits, open and unfinished; that men have lived who did what no substitute could ever have done; that their intervention set history on one path rather than another. If this is so, the old maxim, "There are no indispensable men," would seem another amiable fallacy. There is, then, a case for heroes.

To say that there is a case for heroes is not to say that there is a case for hero worship. The surrender of decision, the unquestioning submission to leadership, the prostration of the average man before the Great Man—these are the diseases of heroism, and they are fatal to human dignity. But, if carried too far, hero worship generates its own antidote. "Every hero," said Emerson, "becomes a bore at last." And we need not go too far. History amply shows that it is possible to have heroes without turning them into gods.

And history shows, too, that, when a society, in flight from hero worship, decides to do without great men at all, it gets into troubles of its own. Our contemporary American society, for example, has little use for the individualist. Individualism implies dissent from the group; dissent implies conflict; and conflict suddenly seems divisive, un-American and generally unbearable. Our greatest new industry is evidently the production of techniques to eliminate conflict, from positive thoughts through public relations to psychoanalysis, applied everywhere from the couch to the pulpit. Our national aspiration has become peace of mind, peace of soul. The symptomatic drug of our age is the tranquilizer. "Togetherness" is the banner under which we march into the brave new world.

Obviously society has had to evolve collective institutions to cope with problems that have grown increasingly complex and concentrated. But the collective approach can be overdone. If Khrushchev worried because his collectivist society developed a cult of the individual, maybe we Americans should start worrying as our so-called individualist society develops a cult of the group. We instinctively suppose that the tough questions will be solved by an interfaith conference or an interdisciplinary research team or an interdepartmental committee or an assembly of wise men meeting at Arden House. But are not these group tactics essentially means by which individuals hedge their bets and distribute their responsibilities? And do they not nearly always result in the dilution of insight and the triumph of mish-mash? If we are to survive, we must have ideas, vision, courage. These things are rarely produced by committees. Everything that matters in our intellectual and moral life begins with an individual confronting his own mind and conscience in a room by himself.

A bland society will never be creative. "The amount of eccentricity in a society," said John Stuart Mill, "has generally been proportional to the amount of genius, mental vigor and moral courage it contained. That so few now dare to be eccentric marks the chief danger of the time." If this condition frightened Mill in Victorian England, it should frighten us much more. For our national apotheosis of the group means that we systematically lop off the eccentrics, the originals, the proud, imaginative, lonely people from whom new ideas come. What began as a recoil from hero worship ends as a conspiracy against creativity. If worship of great men brings us to perdition by one path, flight from great men brings us there just as surely by another. When we do not admire great men, then our instinct for admiration is likely to end by settling on ourselves. The one thing worse for democracy than hero worship is self-worship.

A free society cannot get along without heroes, because they are the most vivid means of exhibiting the power of free men. The hero exposes to all mankind unsuspected possibilities of conception, unimagined resources of strength. "The appearance of a great man," wrote Emerson, "draws a new circle outside of our largest orbit and surprises and commands us." Carlyle likened ordinary, lethargic times, with their unbelief and perplexity, to dry, dead fuel, waiting for the lightning out of heaven to kindle it. "The great man, with his free force direct out of God's own hand, is the lightning. . . . The rest of men waited for him like fuel, and then they too would flame."

Great men enable us to rise to our own highest potentialities. They nerve lesser men to disregard the world and trust to their own deepest instinct. "In picking out from history our heroes," said William James, "each one of us may best fortify and inspire what creative energy may lie in his own soul. This is the last justification of hero worship." Which one of us has not gained fortitude and faith from the incarnation of ideals in men, from the wisdom of Socrates, from the wondrous creativity of Shakespeare, from the strength of Washington, from the compassion of Lincoln, and above all, perhaps, from the life and the death of Jesus? "We feed on genius," said Emerson. "Great men exist that there may be greater men."

Yet this may be only the smaller part of their service. Great men have another and larger role—to affirm human freedom against the supposed inevitabilities of history. The first hero was Prometheus, who defied the gods and thus asserted the independence and autonomy of man against all determinism. Zeus punished Prometheus, chaining him to a rock and encouraging a vulture to pluck at his vitals.

Ever since, man, like Prometheus, has warred against history. It has always been a bitter and remorseless fight; for the heavy weight of human inertia lies with fatalism. It takes a man of exceptional vision and strength and will—it takes, in short, a hero—to try to wrench history from what lesser men consider its preconceived path. And often history tortures the hero in the process, chains him to a rock and exposes him to the vulture. Yet, in the model of Prometheus, man can still hold his own against the gods. Brave men earn the right to shape their own destiny.

An age without great men is one which acquiesces in the drift of history. Such acquiescence is easy and seductive; the great appeal of fatalism, indeed, is as a refuge from the terror of responsibility. Where a belief in great men insistently reminds us that individuals can make a difference, fatalism reassures us that they can't. It thereby blesses our weakness and extenuates our failure. Fatalism, in Berlin's phrase, is "one of the great alibis" of history.

Let us not be complacent about our supposed capacity to get along without great men. If our society has lost its wish for heroes and its ability to produce them, it may well turn out to have lost everything else as well.

STUDY QUESTIONS

1. Note that Schlesinger refers to the book from which Hook's "The Hero and Democracy" was drawn. How well do the two agree as to the value of heroes?

2. How well do they agree on the position of a hero in a democracy? Where do they disagree?

3. Do you agree with Schlesinger that there are no heroes today? Can you give some reasons in addition to his own for this?

4. Unlike Hook, Schlesinger fails to give a definition of the hero. Can such a definition be inferred from what he says?

5. Do you agree that American society is unfavorable to the development of heroes? Do any favorable conditions exist in it?

6. Write a theme explaining the disagreement about the value of heroes shown by Hook and Schlesinger and drawing some conclusions from this disagreement.

From *Areopagitica**

John Milton

I deny not, but that it is of greatest concernment in the Church and Commonwealth, to have a vigilant eye how books demean themselves as well as men; and thereafter to confine, imprison, and do sharpest justice on them as malefactors. For books are not absolutely dead things, but do contain a potency of life in them to be as active as that soul was whose progeny they are; nay, they do preserve as in a vial the purest efficacy and extraction of that living intellect that bred them. I know they are as lively, and as vigorously productive, as those fabulous dragon's teeth; and being sown up and down, may chance to spring up armed men. And yet, on the other hand, unless wariness be used, as good almost kill a man as kill a good book. Who kills a man kills a reasonable creature, God's image; but he who destroys a good book, kills reason itself, kills the image of God, as it were in the eye. Many a man lives a burden to the earth; but a good book is the precious life-blood of a master spirit, embalmed and treasured up on purpose to a life beyond life. 'Tis true, no age can restore a life, whereof perhaps there is no great loss; and revolutions of ages do not oft recover the loss of a rejected truth, for the want of which whole nations fare the worse.

We should be wary therefore what persecution we raise against the living labours of public men, how we spill that seasoned life of man, preserved and stored up in books; since we see a kind of homicide may be thus committed, sometimes a martyrdom, and if it extend to the whole impression, a kind of massacre; whereof the execution ends not in the slaying of an elemental life, but strikes at that ethereal and fifth essence, the breath of reason itself, slays an immortality rather than a life. . . .

Good and evil we know in the field of this world grow up together almost inseparably; and the knowledge of good is so involved and interwoven with the knowledge of evil, and in so many cunning resemblances hardly to be discerned, that those confused seeds which were imposed upon Psyche as an incessant labour to cull out, and sort asunder, were not more intermixed. It was from out the rind of one apple tasted, that the

* First published in 1644.

knowledge of good and evil, as two twins cleaving together, leaped forth into the world. And perhaps this is that doom which Adam fell into of knowing good and evil, that is to say of knowing good by evil. As therefore the state of man now is; what wisdom can there be to choose, what continence to forbear without the knowledge of evil? He that can apprehend and consider vice with all her baits and seeming pleasures, and yet abstain, and yet distinguish, and yet prefer that which is truly better, he is the true warfaring Christian.

I cannot praise a fugitive and cloistered virtue, unexercised and unbreathed, that never sallies out and sees her adversary, but slinks out of the race, where that immortal garland is to be run for, not without dust and heat. Assuredly we bring not innocence into the world, we bring impurity much rather; that which purifies us is trial, and trial is by what is contrary. That virtue therefore which is but a youngling in the contemplation of evil, and knows not the utmost that vice promises to her followers, and rejects it, is but a blank virtue, not a pure; her whiteness is but an excremental whiteness. Which was the reason why our sage and serious poet Spenser, whom I dare be known to think a better teacher than Scotus or Aquinas, describing true temperance under the person of Guion, brings him in with his palmer through the cave of Mammon, and the bower of earthly bliss, that he might see and know, and yet abstain. Since therefore the knowledge and survey of vice is in this world so necessary to the constituting of human virtue, and the scanning of error to the confirmation of truth, how can we more safely, and with less danger, scout into the regions of sin and falsity than by reading all manner of tractates and hearing all manner of reason? And this is the benefit which may be had of books promiscuously read. . . .

Seeing, therefore, that those books, and those in great abundance, which are likeliest to taint both life and doctrine, cannot be suppressed without the fall of learning and of all ability in disputation, and that these books of either sort are most and soonest catching to the learned, from whom to the common people whatever is heretical or dissolute may quickly be conveyed, and that evil manners are as perfectly learnt without books a thousand other ways which cannot be stopped, and evil doctrine not with books can propagate, except a teacher guide, which he might also do without writing, and so beyond prohibiting, I am not able to unfold, how this cautelous enterprise of licensing can be exempted from the number of vain and impossible attempts. And he who were pleasantly disposed could not well avoid to liken it to the exploit of that gallant man who thought to pound up the crows by shutting his park gate.

Besides another inconvenience, if learned men be the first receivers out of books and dispreaders both of vice and error, how shall the licensers themselves be confided in, unless we can confer upon them, or they assume to themselves above all others in the land, the grace of infallibility and uncorruptedness? And again, if it be true that a wise man, like a good refiner, can gather gold out of the drossiest volume, and that a fool will be a fool with the best book, yea or without book; there is no reason that we should deprive a wise man of any advantage to his wisdom, while we seek to restrain from a fool, that which being restrained will be no hindrance to his folly. For if there should be so much exactness always used to keep that from him which is unfit for his reading, we should in the judgment of Aristotle not only, but of Solomon and of our Saviour, not vouchsafe him good precepts, and by consequence not willingly admit him to good books; as being certain that a wise man will make better use of an idle pamphlet, than a fool will do of sacred Scripture. . . .

If we think to regulate printing, thereby to rectify manners, we must regulate all recreations and pastimes, all that is delightful to man. No music must be heard, no song be set or sung, but what is grave and Doric. There must be licensing dancers, that no gesture, motion, or deportment be taught our youth but what by their allowance shall be thought honest; for such Plato was provided of. It will ask more than the work of twenty licensers to examine all the lutes, the violins, and the guitars in every house; they must not be suffered to prattle as they do, but must be licensed what they may say. And who shall silence all the airs and madrigals that whisper softness in chambers? The windows also, and the balconies must be thought on; there are shrewd books, with dangerous frontispieces, set to sale; who shall prohibit them, shall twenty licensers? The villages also must have their visitors to inquire what lectures the bagpipe and the re-beck reads, even to the ballatry and the gamut of every municipal fiddler, for these are the countryman's Arcadias, and his Monte Mayors.

Next, what more national corruption, for which England hears ill abroad, than household gluttony: who shall be the rectors of our daily rioting? And what shall be done to inhibit the multitudes that frequent those houses where drunkenness is sold and harboured? Our garments also should be referred to the licensing of some more sober workmasters to see them cut into a less wanton garb. Who shall regulate all the mixed conversation of our youth, male and female together, as is the fashion of this country? Who shall still appoint what shall be discoursed, what presumed, and no further? Lastly, who shall forbid and separate all idle resort, all evil company? These things will be, and must be; but how they shall be least hurtful, how least enticing, herein consists the grave and governing wisdom of a state.

To sequester out of the world into Atlantic and Utopian politics, which never can be drawn into use, will not mend our condition; but to ordain wisely as in this world of evil, in the midst whereof God hath placed us unavoidably. Nor is it Plato's licensing of books will do this, which necessarily pulls along with it so many other kinds of licensing, as will make us all both ridiculous and weary, and yet frustrate; but those unwritten, or at least unconstraining, laws of virtuous education, religious and civil nurture, which Plato there mentions as the bonds and ligaments of the commonwealth, the pillars and the sustainers of every written statute; these they be which will bear chief sway in such matters as these, when all licensing will be easily eluded. Impunity and remissness, for certain, are the bane of a commonwealth; but here the great art lies, to discern in what the law is to bid restraint and punishment, and in what things persuasion only is to work.

If every action, which is good or evil in man at ripe years, were to be under pittance and prescription and compulsion, what were virtue but a name, what praise could be then due to well-doing, what gramercy to be sober, just, or continent? Many there be that complain of divine Providence for suffering Adam to transgress; foolish tongues! When God gave him reason, he gave him freedom to choose, for reason is but choosing; he had been else a mere artificial Adam, such an Adam as he is in the motions. We ourselves esteem not of that obedience, or love, or gift, which is of force: God therefore left him free, set before him a provoking object, ever almost in his eyes; herein consisted his merit, herein the right of his reward, the praise of his abstinence. Wherefore did he create passions within us, pleasures round about us, but that these rightly tempered are the very ingredients of virtue?

They are not skillful considerers of human beings, who imagine to remove sin by removing the matter of sin; for, besides that it is a huge heap increasing under the very act of diminishing, though some part of it may for a time be withdrawn from some persons, it cannot from all, in such a universal thing as books are; and when this is done, yet the sin remains entire. Though ye take from a covetous man all his treasure, he has yet one jewel left, ye cannot bereave him of his covetousness. Banish all objects of lust, shut up all youth in the severest discipline that can be exercised in any hermitage, ye cannot make them chaste, that came not thither so; such great care and wisdom is required to the right managing of this point. Suppose we could expel sin by this means; look how much we thus expel of sin, so much we expel of virtue: for the matter of them both is the same; remove that, and ye remove them both alike.

This justifies the high providence of God, who, though he command us temperance, justice, continence, yet pours out before us, even to a profuseness, all desirable things, and gives us minds that can wander beyond all limit and satiety. Why should we then affect a rigour contrary to the manner of God and of nature, by abridging or scanting those means, which books freely permitted are, both to the trial of virtue and the exercise of truth? It would be better done, to learn that the law must needs be frivolous, which goes to restrain things, uncertainly and yet equally working to good and to evil. And were I the chooser, a dram of well-doing should be preferred before many times as much the forcible hindrance of evildoing. For God sure esteems the growth and completing of one virtuous person more than the restraint of ten vicious.

STUDY QUESTIONS

1. This is a brief selection from Milton's famous prose pamphlet written in 1644 as an argument against the restriction of freedom of the press. It is a powerfully persuasive argument by one of the masters of English prose, but it clearly belongs to an earlier period. What stylistic characteristics—vocabulary, sentence patterns, figures of speech—mark it off from the prose of such writers as Mill in the 19th century or Becker in our own century?

2. Why does Milton say that it is a worse crime to "kill" a book by suppressing or destroying it than to kill a man?

3. What is the logic of Milton's argument that it is important to read books that are wrong and evil as well as others?

4. What reasons does Milton give for arguing that censorship is impractical? What is the view of human nature which is the basis of Milton's point of view?

5. Do you agree with Milton that an extreme degree of freedom of the press is desirable? If you believe that certain kinds of censorship are justified, write a theme explaining your opinion.

6. Are you acquainted with any incidents or institutions involving censorship that existed or exist in the United States? Write a theme describing one of them and evaluating it against Milton's principles.

On Liberty*

John Stuart Mill

The subject of this Essay is not the so-called Liberty of the Will, so unfortunately opposed to the misnamed doctrine of Philosophical Necessity; but Civil, or Social Liberty: the nature and limits of the power which can be legitimately exercised by society over the individual. A question seldom stated, and hardly ever discussed, in general terms, but which profoundly influences the practical controversies of the age by its latent presence, and is likely soon to make itself recognized as the vital question of the future. It is so far from being new, that, in a certain sense, it has divided mankind, almost from the remotest ages; but in the stage of progress into which the more civilized portions of the species have now entered, it presents itself under new conditions, and requires a different and more fundamental treatment.

The struggle between Liberty and Authority is the most conspicuous feature in the portions of history with which we are earliest familiar, par-

* First published in 1859.

ticularly in that of Greece, Rome, and England. But in old times this contest was between subjects, or some classes of subjects, and the government. By liberty, was meant protection against the tyranny of the political rulers. The rulers were conceived (except in some of the popular governments of Greece) as in a necessarily antagonistic position to the people whom they ruled. They consisted of a governing One, or a governing tribe or caste, who derived their authority from inheritance or conquest; who, at all events, did not hold it at the pleasure of the governed, and whose supremacy men did not venture, perhaps did not desire, to contest, whatever precautions might be taken against its oppressive exercise. Their power was regarded as necessary, but also as highly dangerous; as a weapon which they would attempt to use against their subjects, no less than against external enemies. To prevent the weaker members of the community from being preyed upon by innumerable vultures, it was needful that there should be an animal of prey stronger than the rest, commissioned to keep them down. But as the king of vultures would be no less bent upon preying on the flock than any of the minor harpies, it was indispensable to be in a perpetual attitude of defence against his beak and claws. The aim, therefore, of patriots, was to set limits to the power which the ruler should be suffered to exercise over the community; and this limitation was what they meant by liberty. It was attempted in two ways. First, by obtaining a recognition of certain immunities, called political liberties or rights, which it was to be regarded as a breach of duty in the ruler to infringe, and which, if he did infringe, specific resistance, or general rebellion, was held to be justifiable. A second, and generally a later expedient, was the establishment of constitutional checks; by which the consent of the community, or a body of some sort supposed to represent its interests, was made a necessary condition to some of the more important acts of the governing power. To the first of these modes of limitation, the ruling power, in most European countries, was compelled, more or less, to submit. It was not so with the second; and to attain this, or when already in some degree possessed, to attain it more completely, became everywhere the principal object of the lovers of liberty. And so long as mankind were content to combat one enemy by another, and to be ruled by a master, on condition of being guaranteed more or less efficaciously against his tyranny, they did not carry their aspirations beyond this point.

A time, however, came, in the progress of human affairs, when men ceased to think it a necessity of nature that their governors should be an independent power, opposed in interest to themselves. It appeared to them much better than the various magistrates of the State should be their tenants or delegates, revocable at their pleasure. In that way alone, it seemed, could they have complete security that the powers of government would never be abused to their disadvantage. By degrees, this new demand for elective and temporary rulers became the prominent object of the exertions of the popular party, wherever any such party existed; and superseded, to a considerable extent, the previous efforts to limit the power of rulers. As the struggle proceeded for making the ruling power emanate from the periodical choice of the ruled, some persons began to think that too much importance had been attached to the limitation of the power itself. *That* (it might seem) was a resource against rulers whose interests were habitually opposed to those of the people. What was now wanted was, that the rulers should be identified with the people; that their interest and will should be the interest and will of the nation. The nation did not need to be protected against its own will. There was no fear of its tyrannizing over itself. Let the rulers be effectually responsible to it, promptly removable by it, and it could afford to trust them with power of which it could itself dictate the use to be made. Their power was but the nation's own power, concentrated, and in a form convenient for exercise. This mode of thought, or rather perhaps of feeling, was common among the last generation of European liberalism, in the Continental section of which, it still apparently predominates. Those who admit any limit to what a government may do, except in the case of such governments as they think ought not to exist, stand out as brilliant exceptions among the political thinkers of the Continent. A similar tone of sentiment might by this time have been prevalent in our own country, if the circumstances which for a time encouraged it had continued unaltered.

But, in political and philosophical theories, as well as in persons, success discloses faults and infirmities which failure might have concealed from observation. The notion, that the people have no need to limit their power over themselves, might seem axiomatic, when popular government was a thing only dreamed about, or read of as having existed at some distant period of the past. Neither was that notion necessarily disturbed by such temporary aberrations as those of the French Revolution, the worst of which were the work of an usurping few, and which, in any case, belonged, not to the permanent working of popular institutions, but to a sudden and convulsive outbreak against monarchical and aristocratic despotism. In time, however, a democratic republic came to occupy a large portion of the earth's surface, and made itself felt as one of the most powerful members of the community of nations; and elective and responsible government became subject to the observations and criticisms which wait upon a great existing fact. It was now perceived that such phrases as "self-government," and "the power of the people over themselves," do not express the true state of the case. The "people" who exercise the power, are not always the same people with those over whom it is exercised; and the self-government spoken of, is not the government of each by himself, but of each by all the rest. The will of the people, moreover, practically means, the will of the most numerous or the most active *part* of the people; the majority, or those who succeed in making themselves accepted as the majority: the people, consequently, *may* desire to oppress a part of their number; and precautions are as much needed against this, as against any other abuse of power. The limitation, therefore, of the power of government over individuals, loses none of its importance when the holders of powers are regularly accountable to the community, that is, to the strongest party therein. This view of things, recommending itself equally to the intelligence of thinkers and to the inclination of those important classes in European society to whose real or supposed interests democracy is adverse, has had no difficulty in establishing itself; and in political speculations "the tyranny of the majority" is now generally included among the evils against which society requires to be on its guard.

Like other tyrannies, the tyranny of the majority was at first, and is still vulgarly, held in dread, chiefly as operating through the acts of the public authorities. But reflecting persons perceived that when society is itself the tyrant—society collectively, over the separate individuals who compose it—its means of tyrannizing are not restricted to the acts which it may do by the hands of its political functionaries. Society can and does execute its own mandates: and if it issues wrong mandates instead of right, or any mandates at all in things with which it ought not to meddle, it practises a social tyranny more formidable than many kinds of political oppression, since, though not usually upheld by such extreme penalties, it leaves fewer means of escape, penetrating much more deeply into the details of life, and enslaving the soul itself. Protection, therefore, against the tyranny of the magistrate is not enough; there needs protection also against the tyranny of the prevailing opinion and feeling; against the tendency of society to impose, by other means than civil penalties, its own ideas and practices as rules of conduct on those who dissent from them; to fetter the development, and, if possible, prevent the formation, of any individuality not in harmony with its ways, and compel all characters to fashion themselves upon the model of its own. There is a limit to the legitimate interference of collective opinion with individual independence; and to find that limit, and maintain it against encroachment, is as indispensable to a good condition of human affairs, as protection against political despotism.

But though this proposition is not likely to be contested in general terms, the practical question, where to place the limit—how to make the fitting adjustment between individual independence and social control— is a subject on which nearly everything remains to be done. All that makes existence valuable to any one, depends on the enforcement of restraints upon the actions of other people. Some rules of conduct, therefore, must be imposed, by law in the first place, and by opinion on many things which are not fit subjects for the operation of law. What these rules should be, is the principal question in human affairs; but if we except a few of the most obvious cases, it is one of those which least progress has been made in resolving. No two ages, and scarcely any two countries, have decided it alike; and the decision of one age or country is a wonder to another. Yet the people of any given age and country no more suspect any difficulty in it, than if it were a subject on which mankind had always been agreed. The rules which obtain among themselvs appear to them self-evident and self-justifying. This all but universal illusion is one of the examples of the magical influence of custom, which is not only, as the proverb says, a second nature, but is continually mistaken for the first. The effect of custom, in preventing any misgiving respecting the rules of conduct which mankind impose on one another, is all the more complete because the subject is one on which it is not generally considered necessary that reasons should be given, either by one person to others, or by each to himself. People are accustomed to believe, and have been encouraged in the belief by some who aspire to the character of philosophers, that their feelings, on subjects of this nature, are better than reasons, and render reasons unnecessary. The practical principle which guides them to their opinions on the regulation of human conduct, is the feeling in each person's mind that everybody should be required to act as he, and those with whom he sympathizes, would like them to act. No one, indeed, acknowledges to himself that his standard of judgment is his own liking; but an opinion on a point of conduct, not supported by reasons, can only count as one person's preference; and if the reasons, when given, are a mere appeal to a similar preference felt by other people, it is still only many people's liking instead of one. To an ordinary man, however, his own preference, thus supported, is not only a perfectly satisfactory reason, but the only one he generally has for any of his notions of morality, taste, or propriety, which are not expressly written in his religious creed; and his chief guide in the interpretation even of that. Men's opinions, accordingly, on what is laudable or blameable, are affected by all the multifarious causes which influence their wishes in regard to the conduct of others, and which are as numerous as those which determine their wishes on any other subject. Sometimes their reason—at other times their prejudices or superstitions: often their social affections, not seldom their antisocial ones, their envy or jealousy, their arrogance or contemptuousness: but most commonly, their desires or fears for themselves—their legitimate or illegitimate self-interest. Wherever there is an ascendant class, a large portion of the morality of the country emanates from its class interests, and its feelings of class superiority. The morality between Spartans and Helots, between planters and negroes, between princes and subjects, between nobles and roturiers, between men and women, has been for the most part the creation of these class interests and feelings: and the sentiments thus generated, react in turn upon the moral feelings of the members of the ascendant class, in their relations among themselves. Where, on the other hand, a class, formerly ascendant, has lost its ascendancy, or where its ascendancy is unpopular, the prevailing moral sentiments frequently bear the impress of an impatient dislike of superiority. Another grand determining principle of the rules of conduct, both in act and forbearance, which have been enforced by law or opinion, has been the servility of mankind towards the supposed preferences or aversions of their temporal masters, or of their gods. This servility, though essentially selfish, is not hypocrisy; it gives rise to perfectly genuine sentiments of abhorrence; it made men burn magicians and heretics. Among so many baser influences, the general and obvious interests of society have of course had a share, and a large one, in the direction of the moral sentiments: less, however, as a matter of reason, and on their own account, than as a consequence of the sympathies and antipathies which grew out of them: and sympathies and antipathies which had little or nothing to do with the interests of society, have made themselves felt in the establishment of moralities with quite as great force.

The likings and dislikings of society, or of some powerful portion of it, are thus the main thing which has practically determined the rules laid down for general observance, under the penalties of law or opinion. And in general, those who have been in advance of society in thought and feeling, have left this condition of things unassailed in principle, however they may have come into conflict with it in some of its details. They have occupied themselves rather in inquiring what things society ought to like or dislike, than in questioning whether its likings or dislikings should be a law to individuals. They preferred endeavoring to alter the feelings of mankind on the particular points on which they were themselves heretical, rather than make common cause in defence of freedom, with heretics generally. The only case in which the higher ground has been taken on principle and maintained with consistency, by any but an individual here and there, is that of religious belief: a case instructive in many ways, and not least so as forming a most striking instance of the fallibility of what is called the moral sense: for the *odium theologicum*,[1] in a sincere bigot, is one of the most unequivocal cases of moral feeling. Those who first broke the yoke of what called itself the Universal Church, were in general as little willing to permit difference of religious opinion as that church itself. But when the heat of the conflict was over, without giving a complete victory to any party, and each church or sect was reduced to limit its hopes to retaining possession of the ground it already occupied; minorities, seeing that they had no chance of becoming majorities, were under the necessity of pleading to those whom they could not convert, for permission to differ. It is accordingly on this battle-field, almost solely, that the rights of the individual against society have been asserted on broad grounds of principle, and the claim of society to exercise authority over dissentients openly controverted. The great writers to whom the world owes what religious liberty it possesses, have mostly asserted freedom of conscience as an indefeasible right, and denied absolutely that a human being is accountable to others for his religious belief. Yet so natural to mankind is intolerance in whatever they really care about, that

[1] Detestation felt by one theologian or sect for another.

religious freedom has hardly anywhere been practically realized, except where religious indifference, which dislikes to have its peace disturbed by theological quarrels, has added its weight to the scale. In the minds of almost all religious persons, even in the most tolerant countries, the duty of toleration is admitted with tacit reserves. One person will bear with dissent in matters of church government, but not of dogma; another can tolerate everybody, short of a Papist or an Unitarian; another, every one who believes in revealed religion; a few extend their charity a little further, but stop at the belief in a God and in a future state. Wherever the sentiment of the majority is still genuine and intense, it is found to have abated little of its claim to be obeyed.

In England, from the peculiar circumstances of our political history, though the yoke of opinion is perhaps heavier, that of law is lighter, than in most other countries of Europe; and there is considerable jealousy of direct interference, by the legislative or the executive power, with private conduct; not so much from any just regard for the independence of the individual, as from the still subsisting habit of looking on the government as representing an opposite interest to the public. The majority have not yet learnt to feel the power of the government their power, or its opinions their opinions. When they do so, individual liberty will probably be as much exposed to invasion from the government, as it already is from public opinion. But, as yet, there is a considerable amount of feeling ready to be called forth against any attempt of the law to control individuals in things in which they have not hitherto been accustomed to be controlled by it; and this with very little discrimination as to whether the matter is, or is not, within the legitimate sphere of legal control; insomuch that the feeling, highly salutary on the whole, is perhaps quite as often misplaced as well grounded in the particular instances of its application. There is, in fact, no recognized principle by which the propriety or impropriety of government interference is customarily tested. People decide according to their personal preferences. Some, whenever they see any good to be done, or evil to be remedied, would willingly instigate the government to undertake the business; while others prefer to bear almost any amount of social evil, rather than add one to the departments of human interests amenable to governmental control. And men range themselves on one or the other side in any particular case, according to this general direction of their sentiments; or according to the degree of interest which they feel in the particular thing it is proposed that the government should do; or according to the belief they entertain that the government would, or would not, do it in the manner they prefer; but very rarely on account of any opinion to which they consistently adhere, as to what things are fit to be done by a government. And it seems to me that, in consequence of this absence of rule or principle, one side is at present as often wrong as the other; the interference of government is, with about equal frequency, improperly invoked and improperly condemned.

The object of this Essay is to assert one very simple principle, as entitled to govern absolutely the dealings of society with the individual in the way of compulsion and control, whether the means used be physical force in the form of legal penalties, or the moral coercion of public opinion. That principle is, that the sole end for which mankind are warranted, individually or collectively, in interfering with the liberty of action of any of their number, is self-protection. That the only purpose for which power can be rightfully exercised over any member of a civilized community, against his will, is to prevent harm to others. His own good, either physical or moral, is not a sufficient warrant. He cannot rightfully be compelled to do or forbear because it will be better for him to do so, because it will make him happier, because, in the opinions of others, to do so would be wise, or even right. These are good reasons for remonstrating with him, or reasoning with him, or persuading him, or entreating him, but not for compelling him, or visiting him with any evil, in case he do otherwise. To justify that, the conduct from which it is desired to deter him must be calculated to produce evil to some one else. The only part of the conduct of any one, for which he is amenable to society, is that which concerns others. In the part which merely concerns himself, his independence is, of right, absolute. Over himself, over his own body and mind, the individual is sovereign.

It is, perhaps, hardly necessary to say that this doctrine is meant to apply only to human beings in the maturity of their faculties. We are not speaking of children, or of young persons below the age which the law may fix as that of manhood or womanhood. Those who are still in a state to require being taken care of by others, must be protected against their own actions as well as against external injury. For the same reason, we may leave out of consideration those backward states of society in which the race itself may be considered as in its nonage. The early difficulties in the way of spontaneous progress are so great, that there is seldom any choice of means for overcoming them; and a ruler full of the spirit of improvement is warranted in the use of any expedients that will attain an end, perhaps otherwise unattainable. Despotism is a legitimate mode of government in dealing with barbarians, provided the end be their improvement, and the means justified by actually effecting that end. Liberty, as a principle, has no application to any state of things anterior to the time when mankind have become capable of being improved by free and equal discussion. Until then, there is nothing for them but implicit obedience to an Akbar or a Charlemagne, if they are so fortunate as to find one. But as soon as mankind have attained the capacity of being guided to their own improvement by conviction or persuasion (a period long since reached in all nations with whom we need here concern ourselves), compulsion, either in the direct form or in that of pains and penalties for non-compliance, is no longer admissible as a means to their own good, and justifiable only for the security of others.

It is proper to state that I forego any advantage which could be derived to my argument from the idea of abstract right, as a thing independent of utility. I regard utility as the ultimate appeal on all ethical questions; but it must be utility in the largest sense, grounded on the permanent interests of man as a progressive being. Those interests, I contend, authorize the subjection of individual spontaneity to external control, only in respect to those actions of each, which concern the interest of other people. If any one does an act hurtful to others there is a *primâ facie* case for punishing him, by law, or, where legal penalties are not safely applicable, by general disapprobation. There are also many positive acts for the benefit of others, which he may rightfully be compelled to perform; such as, to give evidence in a court of justice; to bear his fair share in the common defence, or in any other joint work necessary to the interest of the society of which he enjoys the protection; and to perform certain acts of individual beneficence, such as saving a fellow creature's life, or interposing to protect the defenceless against ill-usage, things which whenever it is obviously a man's duty to do, he may rightfully be made responsible to society for not doing. A person may cause evil to others not only by his actions but by his inaction, and in either case he is justly accountable to them for the injury. The latter case, it is true, requires a much more cautious exercise of compulsion than the former. To make any one answerable for doing evil to others, is the rule; to make him answerable for not preventing evil, is, comparatively speaking, the exception. Yet there are many cases clear enough and grave enough to justify that exception. In all things which regard the external relations of the individual, he is *de jure* amenable to those whose interests are concerned, and if need be, to society as their protector. There are often good reasons for not holding him to the responsibility; but these reasons must arise from the special expediences of the case: either because it is a kind of case in which he is on the whole likely to act better, when left to his own discretion, than when controlled in any way in which society have it in their power to control him; or because the attempt to exercise control would produce other evils, greater than those which it would prevent. When such reasons as these preclude the enforcement of responsibility, the conscience of the agent himself should step into the vacant judgment-seat, and protect those interests of others which have no external protection; judging himself all the more rigidly, because the case does not admit of his being made accountable to the judgment of his fellow-creatures.

But there is a sphere of action in which society, as distinguished from the individual, has, if any, only an indirect interest; comprehending all that portion of a person's life and conduct which affects only himself, or, if it also affects others, only with their free, voluntary, and undeceived consent and participation. When I say only himself, I mean directly, and in the first instance: for whatever affects himself, may affect others *through* himself; and the objection which may be grounded on this contingency, will receive consideration in the sequel. This, then, is the appropriate region of human liberty. It comprises, first, the inward domain of consciousness; demanding liberty of conscience, in the most comprehensive sense; liberty of thought and feeling; absolute freedom of opinion and sentiment on all subjects, practical or speculative, scientific, moral, or theological. The liberty of expressing and publishing opinions may seem to fall under a different principle, since it belongs to that part of the conduct of an individual which concerns other people; but, being almost of as much importance as the liberty of thought itself, and resting in great part on the same reasons, is practically inseparable from it. Secondly, the principle requires liberty of tastes and pursuits; of framing the plan of our life to suit our own character; of doing as we like, subject to such consequences as may follow; without impediment from our fellow-creatures, so long as what we do does not harm them, even though they should think our conduct foolish, perverse, or wrong. Thirdly, from this liberty of each individual, follows the liberty, within the same limits, of combination among individuals; freedom to unite, for any purpose not involving harm to others: the persons combining being supposed to be of full age, and not forced or deceived.

No society in which these liberties are not, on the whole, respected, is free, whatever may be its form of government; and none is completely free in which they do not exist absolute and unqualified. The only freedom which deserves the name, is that of pursuing our own good in our own way, so long as we do not attempt to deprive others of theirs, or impede their efforts to obtain it. Each is the proper guardian of his own health, whether bodily, or mental and spiritual. Mankind are greater gainers by suffering each other to live as seems good to themselves, than by compelling each to live as seems good to the rest.

Though this doctrine is anything but new, and, to some persons, may have the air of a truism, there is no doctrine which stands more directly opposed to the general tendency of existing opinion and practice. Society has expended fully as much effort in the attempt (according to its lights) to compel people to conform to its notions of personal, as of social excellence. The ancient commonwealths thought themselves entitled to practise, and the ancient philosophers countenanced, the regulation of every part of private conduct by public authority, on the ground that the State had a deep interest in the whole bodily and mental discipline of every one of its citizens; a mode of thinking which may have been admissible in small republics surrounded by powerful enemies, in constant peril of being subverted by foreign attack or internal commotion, and to which even a short interval of relaxed energy and self-command might so easily be fatal, that they could not afford to wait for the salutary permanent effects of freedom. In the modern world, the greater size of political communities, and above all, the separation between the spiritual and temporal authority (which placed the direction of men's consciences in other hands than those which controlled their worldly affairs), prevented so great an interference by law in the details of private life; but the engines of moral repression have been wielded more strenuously against divergence from the reigning opinion in self-regarding, than even in social matters; religion, the most powerful of the elements which have entered into the formation of moral feeling, having almost always been governed either by the ambition of a hierarchy, seeking control over every department of human conduct, or by the spirit of Puritanism. And some of those modern reformers who have placed themselves in strongest opposition to the religions of the past, have been noway behind either churches or sects in their assertion of the right of spiritual domination: M. Comte, in particular, whose social system, as unfolded in his *Traité de Politique Positive*, aims at establishing (though by moral more than by legal appliances) a despotism of society over the individual, surpassing anything contemplated in the political ideal of the most rigid disciplinarian among the ancient philosophers.

Apart from the peculiar tenets of individual thinkers, there is also in the world at large an increasing inclination to stretch unduly the powers of society over the individual, both by the force of opinion and even by that of legislation: and as the tendency of all the changes taking place in the world is to strengthen society, and diminish the power of the individual, this encroachment is not one of the evils which tend spontaneously to disappear, but, on the contrary, to grow more and more formidable. The disposition of mankind, whether as rulers or as fellow-citizens, to impose their own opinions and inclinations as a rule of conduct on others, is so energetically supported by some of the best and by some of the worst feelings incident to human nature, that it is hardly ever kept under restraint by anything but want of power; and as the power is not declining, but growing, unless a strong barrier of moral conviction can be raised against the mischief, we must expect, in the present circumstances of the world, to see it increase. . . .

STUDY QUESTIONS

1. What does Mill mean by "the tyranny of the majority"?
2. What two central principles here does Mill fail to support by logic or evidence? Why has Mill failed to support them in this way? Is it possible for them to be denied? If so, under what conditions?
3. Do you believe Mill should have included "property" together with "mind and body" among the things over which the individual has sovereignty? Why?
4. Mill says that the usual way of judging the rival claims of collective welfare and individual liberty has been by "likings and dislikings," but he does not say why he thinks this method is a poor

one. Why is it subject to criticism? Can anything be said in its defence?

5. Write a theme showing how some particular historical event reflected the issues Mills deals with here. Possibilities would be the trial of Socrates, the migration of colonists to America, the Scopes trial, or any case in which individual and collective wills clashed with each other.

6. Write a theme discussing the validity of one of the following in the light of Mill's principle that the individual should be sovereign over his own mind and body: compulsory schooling; compulsory military service; the pledge of allegiance to the flag in schools; the requirement that government workers take loyalty oaths; routine vaccination of school children.

From *On the Duty of Civil Disobedience**

Henry David Thoreau

I heartily accept the motto,—"That government is best which governs least"; and I should like to see it acted up to more rapidly and systematically. Carried out, it finally amounts to this, which also I believe,—"That government is best which governs not at all"; and when men are prepared for it, that will be the kind of government which they will have. Government is at best but an expedient; but most governments are usually, and all governments are sometimes, inexpedient. The objections which have been brought against a standing army, and they are many and weighty, and deserve to prevail, may also at last be brought against a standing government. The standing army is only an arm of the standing government. The government itself, which is only the mode which the people have chosen to execute their will, is equally liable to be abused and perverted before the people can act through it. Witness the present Mexican war, the work of comparatively a few individuals using the standing government as their tool; for, in the outset, the people would not have consented to this measure.

This American government,—what is it but a tradition, though a recent one, endeavoring to transmit itself unimpaired to posterity, but each instant losing some of its integrity? It has not the vitality and force of a single living man; for a single man can bend it to his will. It is a sort of wooden gun to the people themselves. But it is not the less necessary for this; for the people must have some complicated machinery or other, and hear its din, to satisfy that idea of government which they have. Governments show us how successfully men can be imposed on, even impose on

* First published in 1849.

themselves, for their own advantage. It is excellent, we must all allow. Yet this government never of itself furthered any enterprise, but by the alacrity with which it got out of its way. *It* does not keep the country free. *It* does not settle the West. *It* does not educate. The character inherent in the American people has done all that has been accomplished; and it would have done somewhat more, if the government had not sometimes got in its way. For government is an expedient by which men would fain succeed in letting one another alone; and, as has been said, when it is most expedient, the governed are most let alone by it. Trade and commerce, if they were not made of India-rubber, would never manage to bounce over the obstacles which legislators are continually putting in their way; and, if one were to judge these men wholly by the effects of their actions and not partly by their intentions, they would deserve to be classed and punished with those mischievous persons who put obstructions on the railroads.

But, to speak practically and as a citizen, unlike those who call themselves no-government men, I ask for, not at once no government, but *at once* a better government. Let every man make known what kind of government would command his respect, and that will be one step toward obtaining it.

After all, the practical reason why, when the power is once in the hands of the people, a majority are permitted, and for a long period continue, to rule is not because they are most likely to be in the right, nor because this seems fairest to the minority, but because they are physically the strongest. But a government in which the majority rule in all cases cannot be based on justice, even as far as men understand it. Can there not be a government in which majorities do not virtually decide right and wrong, but conscience?—in which majorities decide only those questions to which the rule of expediency is applicable? Must the citizen ever for a moment, or in the least degree, resign his conscience to the legislator? Why has every man a conscience, then? I think that we should be men first, and subjects afterward. It is not desirable to cultivate a respect for the law, so much as for the right. The only obligation which I have a right to assume is to do at any time what I think right. It is truly enough said, that a corporation has no conscience; but a corporation of conscientious men is a corporation *with* a conscience. Law never made men a whit more just; and, by means of their respect for it, even the well-disposed are daily made the agents of injustice. A common and natural result of an undue respect for law, is that you may see a file of soldiers, colonel, captain, corporal, privates, powder-monkeys, and all, marching in admirable order over hill and dale to the wars, against their wills, ay, against their common sense and consciences, which makes it very steep marching indeed, and produces a palpitation of the heart. They have no doubt that it is a damnable business in which they are concerned; they are all peaceably inclined. Now, what are they? Men at all? or small movable forts and magazines, at the service of some unscrupulous man in power? Visit the Navy-Yard, and behold a marine, such a man as an American government can make, or such as it can make a man with its black arts,—a mere shadow and reminiscence of humanity, a man laid out alive and standing, and already, as one may say, buried under arms with funeral accompaniments, . . .

The mass of men serve the state thus, not as men mainly, but as machines, with their bodies. They are the standing army, and the militia, jailors, constables, posse comitatus, etc. In most cases there is no free exercise whatever of the judgment or of the moral sense; but they put themselves on a level with wood and earth and stones; and wooden men can perhaps be manufactured that will serve the purpose as well. Such command no more respect than men of straw or a lump of dirt. They have the same sort of worth only as horses and dogs. Yet such as these even are commonly esteemed good citizens. Others—as most legislators, politicians, lawyers, ministers, and office-holders—serve the state chiefly with their heads; and, as they rarely make any moral distinctions, they are as likely to serve the Devil, without *intending* it, as God. A very few, as heroes, patriots, martyrs, reformers in the great sense, and *men*, serve the state with their consciences also, and so necessarily resist it for the most part; and they are commonly treated as enemies by it. . . .

How does it become a man to behave toward this American government to-day? I answer, that he cannot without disgrace be associated with it. I cannot for an instant recognize that political organization as *my* government which is the *slave's* government also.

All men recognize the right of revolution; that is, the right to refuse allegiance to, and to resist, the government, when its tyranny or its inefficiency are great and unendurable. But almost all say that such is not the case now. But such was the case, they think in the Revolution of '75. If one were to tell me that this was a bad government because it taxed certain foreign commodities brought to its ports, it is most probable that I should not make an ado about it, for I can do without them. All machines have their friction . . . But when the friction comes to have its machine, and oppression and robbery are organized, I say, let us not have such a machine any longer. In other words, when a sixth of the population of a nation which has undertaken to be the refuge of liberty are slaves, and a whole country is unjustly overrun and conquered by a foreign army, and subjected to military law, I think that it is not too soon for honest men to rebel and revolutionize. What makes this duty the more urgent is the fact that the country so overrun is not our own, but ours is the invading army. . . .

Practically speaking, the opponents to a reform in Massachusetts are not a hundred thousand politicians at the South, but a hundred thousand merchants and farmers here, who are more interested in commerce and agriculture than they are in humanity, and are not prepared to do justice to the slave and to Mexico, *cost what it may.* I quarrel not with far-off foes, but with those who, near at home, coöperate with, and do the bidding of, those far away, and without whom the latter would be harmless. We are accustomed to say, that the mass of men are unprepared; but improvement is slow, because the few are not materially wiser or better than the many. It is not so important that many should be as good as you, as that there be some absolute goodness somewhere; for that will leaven the whole lump. There are thousands who are *in opinion* opposed to slavery and to the war, who yet in effect do nothing to put an end to them; who, esteeming themselves children of Washington and Franklin, sit down with their hands in their pockets, and say that they know not what to do, and do nothing; who even postpone the question of freedom to the question of free-trade, and quietly read the prices-current along with the latest advices from Mexico, after dinner, and, it may be, fall asleep over them both. What is the price-current of an honest man and patriot to-day? They hesitate, and they regret, and sometimes they petition; but they do nothing in earnest and with effect. They will wait, well disposed, for others to remedy the evil, that they may no longer have it to regret. At most, they give only a cheap vote, and a feeble countenance and God-speed, to the right, as it goes by them. There are nine hundred and ninety-nine patrons of virtue to one virtuous man. But it is easier to deal with the real possessor of a thing than with the temporary guardian of it. . . .

Unjust laws exist: shall we be content to obey them, or shall we endeavor to amend them, and obey them until we have succeeded, or shall we transgress them at once? Men generally, under such a government as this, think that they ought to wait until they have persuaded the majority to alter them. They think that, if they should resist, the remedy would be worse than the evil. But it is the fault of the government iself that the remedy *is* worse than the evil. *It* makes it worse. Why is it not more apt to anticipate and provide for reform? Why does it not cherish its wise minority? Why does it cry and resist before it is hurt? Why does it not encourage its citizens to be on the alert to point out its faults, and *do* better than it would have them? Why does it always crucify Christ, and excommunicate Copernicus and Luther, and pronounce Washington and Franklin rebels? . . .

I do not hesitate to say, that those who call themselves Abolitionists should at once effectually withdraw their support, both in person and property, from the government of Massachusetts and not wait till they constitute a majority of one, before they suffer the right to prevail through them. I think that it is enough if they have God on their side, without waiting for that other one. Moreover, any man more right than his neighbors constitutes a majority of one already.

I meet this American government, or its representative, the state government, directly, and face to face, once a year—no more—in the person of its tax-gatherer; this is the only mode in which a man situated as I am necessarily meets it; and it then says distinctly, Recognize me; and the simplest, most effectual, and, in the present posture of affairs, the indispensablest mode of treating with it on this head, of expressing your little satisfaction with and love for it, is to deny it then. My civil neighbor, the tax-gatherer, is the very man I have to deal with,—for it is, after all, with men and not with parchment that I quarrel,—and he has voluntarily chosen to be an agent of the government. How shall he ever know well what he is and does as an officer of the government, or as a man, until he is obliged to consider whether he shall treat me, his neighbor, for whom he has respect, as a neighbor and well-disposed man, or as a maniac and disturber of the peace, and see if he can get over this obstruction to his neighborliness without a ruder and more impetuous thought of speech corresponding with his action. I know this well, and if one thousand, if one hundred, if ten men whom I could name,—if ten *honest* men only,—ay if *one* HONEST man, in this State of Massachusetts, *ceasing to hold slaves,* were actually to withdraw from this copartnership, and be locked up in the county jail therefor, it would be the abolition of slavery in America. For it matters not how small the beginning may seem to be: what is once well done is done forever. . . .

Under a government which imprisons any unjustly, the true place for a just man is also a prison. The proper place to-day, the only place which Massachusetts has provided for her freer and less desponding spirits, is in her prisons, to be put out and locked out of the State by her own act, as they have already put themselves out by their principles. It is there that the fugitive slave, and the Mexican prisoner on parole, and the Indian come to plead the wrongs of his race should find them; on that separate, but more free and honorable ground, where the State places those who are not *with* her, but *against* her,—the only house in a slave State in which a free man can abide with honor. If any think that their influence would be lost there, and their voices no longer afflict the ear of the State, that they would not be as an enemy within its walls, they do not know by how much truth is stronger than error, nor how much more eloquently and effectively he can combat injustice who has experienced a little in his own person. Cast your whole vote, not a strip of paper merely, but your whole influence. A minority is powerless while it conforms to the majority; it is not even a minority then; but it is irresistible when it clogs by its whole weight. If the alternative is to keep all just men in prison, or give up war and slavery, the State will not hesitate which to choose. If a thousand men were not to pay their tax-bills this year, that would not be a violent and bloody measure, as it would be to pay them, and enable the State to commit violence and shed innocent blood. This is, in fact, the definition of a peaceable revolution, if any such is possible. If the tax-gatherer, or any other public officer, asks me, as one has done, "But what shall I do?" my answer is, "If you really wish to do anything, resign your office." When the subject has refused allegiance, and the officer has resigned his office, then the revolution is accomplished. But even suppose blood should flow. Is there not a sort of blood shed when the conscience is wounded? Through this wound a man's real manhood and immortality flow out, and he bleeds to an everlasting death. I see this blood flowing now. . . .

The authority of government, even such as I am willing to submit to,— for I will cheerfully obey those who know and can do better than I, and in many things even those who neither know nor can do so well,—is still an impure one: to be strictly just, it must have the sanction and consent of the governed. It can have no pure right over my person and property but what I concede to it. The progress from an absolute to a limited monarchy, from a limited monarchy to a democracy, is a progress toward a true respect for the individual. Even the Chinese philosopher was wise enough to regard the individual as the basis of the empire. Is a democracy, such as we know it, the last improvement possible in government? Is it not possible to take a step further towards recognizing and organizing the rights of man? There will never be a really free and enlightened State until the State comes to recognize the individual as a higher and independent power, from which all its own power and authority are derived, and treats him accordingly. I please myself with imagining a State at last which can afford to be just to all men, and to treat the individual with respect as a neighbor; which even would not think it inconsistent with its own repose if a few were to live aloof from it, not meddling with it, nor embraced by it, who fulfilled all the duties of neighbors and fellow-men. A State which bore this kind of fruit, and suffered it to drop off as fast as it ripened, would prepare the way for a still more perfect and glorious State, which also I have imagined, but not yet anywhere seen.

STUDY QUESTIONS

1. This is an edited version of Thoreau's famous essay, but his essential thesis and reasoning are preserved. What is his view of the relation between the people and the government? How pertinent to contemporary issues is his view?

2. What is the fundamental principle underlying Thoreau's objection to slavery and to obedience to a government which condones it?

3. What method does Thoreau suggest for reforming the government? What does this method assume about the nature of the government that is to be reformed? Would the method work against a government that made use of violence and suppression?

4. Thoreau is, of course, dealing with a serious question here, but there are places where he uses satire and mockery to make his point. Locate some of these passages and discuss their effectiveness.

5. Is Thoreau's idea that liberty is found in anarchy a sound one? Is he right in believing that "that government is best which governs not at all"?

6. Are there any dangers in Thoreau's method of civil disobedience? Or do you believe that it is, on the whole, a sound one for the citizens of a democracy to use in reforming their government?

Fear of Public Opinion*

Bertrand Russell

Very few people can be happy unless on the whole their way of life and their outlook on the world is approved by those with whom they have social relations, and more especially by those with whom they live. It is a peculiarity of modern communities that they are divided into sets which differ profoundly in their morals and in their beliefs. This state of affairs began with the Reformation, or perhaps one should say with the Renaissance, and has grown more pronounced ever since. There were Protestants and Catholics, who differed not only in theology but on many more practical matters. There were aristocrats who permitted various kinds of action that were not tolerated among the bourgeoisie. Then there came to be latitudinarians and freethinkers who did not recognize the duties of religious observance. In our own day throughout the Continent of Europe there is a profound division between socialists and others, which covers not only politics but almost every department of life. In English-speaking countries the divisions are very numerous. In some sets art is admired while in others it is thought to be of the devil, at any rate if it is modern. In some sets devotion to the Empire is the supreme virtue, in others it is considered a vice, and in yet others a form of stupidity. Conventional people consider adultery one of the worst of crimes, but large sections of the population regard it as excusable if not positively laudable. Among Catholics divorce is totally forbidden, while most non-Catholics accept it as a necessary alleviation of matrimony.

Owing to these differences of outlook a person of given tastes and convictions may find himself practically an outcast while he lives in one set, although in another set he would be accepted as an entirely ordinary human being. A very great deal of unhappiness, especially among the young, arises in this way. A young man or young woman somehow catches ideas that are in the air, but finds that these ideas are anathema in the particular milieu in which he or she lives. It easily seems to the young as if the only milieu with which they are acquainted were representative of the whole world. They can scarcely believe that in another place or another set the views which they dare not avow for fear of being thought utterly perverse would be accepted as the ordinary commonplaces of the age.

* From *The Conquest of Happiness* by Bertrand Russell. By permission of Liveright, Publishers, N. Y. Copyright 1958, by Bertrand Russell.

Thus through ignorance of the world a great deal of unnecessary misery
is endured, sometimes only in youth, but not infrequently throughout life.
This isolation is not only a source of pain; it also causes a great dissipation of energy in the unnecessary task of maintaining mental independence against hostile surroundings, and in ninety-nine cases out of a
hundred produces a certain timidity in following out ideas to their logical
conclusions. The Brontë sisters never met any congenial people until after
their books had been published. This did not affect Emily, who was heroic
and in the grand manner, but it certainly did affect Charlotte, whose outlook, in spite of her talents, remained always to a large extent that of a
governess. Blake, like Emily Brontë, lived in extreme mental isolation,
but like her was great enough to overcome its bad effects, since he never
doubted that he was right and his critics wrong. His attitude toward
public opinion is expressed in the lines:

> *The only man that e'er I knew*
> *Who did not make me almost spew*
> *Was Fuseli: he was both Turk and Jew.*
> *And so, dear Christian friends, how do you do?*

But there are not many who have this degree of force in their inner life.
To almost everybody sympathetic surroundings are necessary to happiness. To the majority, of course, the surroundings in which they happen
to find themselves are sympathetic. They imbibe current prejudices in
youth, and instinctively adapt themselves to the beliefs and customs
which they find in existence around them. But to a large minority, which
includes practically all who have any intellectual or artistic merit, this attitude of acquiescence is impossible. A person born, let us say, in some
small country town finds himself from early youth surrounded by hostility
to everything that is necessary for mental excellence. If he wishes to read
serious books, other boys despise him and teachers tell him that such
works are unsettling. If he cares for art, his contemporaries think him
unmanly and his elders think him immoral. If he desires any career, however respectable, which has not been common in the circle to which he
belongs, he is told that he is setting himself up, and that what was good
enough for his father ought to be good enough for him. If he shows any
tendency to criticize his parents' religious tenets or political affiliations he
is likely to find himself in serious trouble. For all these reasons to most
young men and young women of exceptional merit adolescence is a time
of great unhappiness. To their more ordinary companions it may be a
time of gayety and enjoyment, but for themselves they want something
more serious, which they can find neither among their elders nor among
their contemporaries in the particular social setting in which chance has
caused them to be born.

When such young people go to a university they probably discover

congenial souls and enjoy a few years of great happiness. If they are
fortunate, they may succeed, on leaving the university, in obtaining some
kind of work that gives them still the possibility of choosing congenial
companions; an intelligent man who lives in a city as large as London or
New York can generally find some congenial set in which it is not necessary to practice any constraint or hypocrisy. But if his work compels him
to live in some smaller place, and more particularly if it necessitates
retention of the respect of ordinary people, as is the case for example with
a doctor or a lawyer, he may find himself throughout his whole life practically compelled to conceal his real tastes and convictions from most of
the people that he meets in the course of his day. This is especially true
in America because of the vastness of the country. In the most unlikely
places, north, south, east and west, one finds lonely individuals who know
from books that there are places where they would not be lonely, but who
have no chance to live in such places, and only the rarest opportunity of
congenial conversations. Real happiness in such circumstances is impossible to those who are built on a less magnificent scale than Blake and
Emily Brontë. If it is to become possible, some way must be found by
which the tyranny of public opinion can be either lessened or evaded, and
by which members of the intelligent minority can come to know each
other and enjoy each other's society.

In a good many cases unnecessary timidity makes the trouble worse
than it need be. Public opinion is always more tyrannical towards those
who obviously fear it than towards those who feel indifferent to it. A dog
will bark more loudly and bite more readily when people are afraid of
him than when they treat him with contempt, and the human herd has
something of this same characteristic. If you show that you are afraid of
them, you give promise of good hunting, whereas if you show indifference,
they begin to doubt their own power and therefore tend to let you alone.
I am not of course thinking of extreme forms of defiance. If you hold in
California the views that are conventional in Russia, or in Russia the
views that are conventional in California, you must accept the consequences. I am thinking, not of such extremes, but of much milder lapses
from conventionality, such as failure to dress correctly or to belong to
some church or to abstain from reading intelligent books. Such lapses,
if they are done with gayety and insouciance, not defiantly but spontaneously, will come to be tolerated even in the most conventional society.
Gradually it may become possible to acquire the position of licensed
lunatic, to whom things are permitted which in another man would be
thought unforgivable. This is largely a matter of a certain kind of good
nature and friendliness. Conventional people are roused to fury by departures from convention, largely because they regard such departures as
a criticism of themselves. They will pardon much unconventionality in a
man who has enough jollity and friendliness to make it clear, even to the
stupidest, that he is not engaged in criticizing them.

This method of escaping censure is, however, impossible to many of those whose tastes or opinions cause them to be out of sympathy with the herd. Their lack of sympathy makes them uncomfortable and causes them to have a pugnacious attitude, even if outwardly they conform or manage to avoid any sharp issue. People who are not in harmony with the conventions of their own set tend therefore to be prickly and uncomfortable and lacking in expansive good humor. These same people transported into another set, where their outlook is not thought strange, will seem to change their character entirely. From being serious, shy and retiring they may become gay and self-confident; from being angular they may become smooth and easy; from being self-centered they may become sociable and extrovert.

Wherever possible, therefore, young people who find themselves out of harmony with their surroundings should endeavor in the choice of a profession to select some career which will give them a chance of congenial companionship, even if this should entail a considerable loss of income. Often they hardly know that this is possible, since their knowledge of the world is very limited, and they may easily imagine that the prejudices to which they have become accustomed at home are world-wide. This is a matter in which older men should be able to give much assistance to the young, since a considerable experience of mankind is essential.

It is customary in these days of psychoanalysis to assume that, when any young person is out of harmony with his environment, the cause must lie in some psychological disorder. This is to my mind a complete mistake. Suppose, for example, that a young person has parents who believe the doctrine of evolution to be wicked. Nothing except intelligence is required in such a case to cause him to be out of sympathy with them. To be out of harmony with one's surroundings is of course a misfortune, but it is not always a misfortune to be avoided at all costs. Where the environment is stupid or prejudiced or cruel, it is a sign of merit to be out of harmony with it. And to some degree these characteristics exist in almost every environment. Galileo and Kepler had "dangerous thought" (as they are called in Japan), and so have the most intelligent men of our own day. It is not desirable that the social sense should be so strongly developed as to cause such men to fear the social hostility which their opinions may provoke. What is desirable is to find ways of making this hostility as slight and as ineffective as possible.

In the modern world the most important part of this problem arises in youth. If a man is once launched upon the right career and in the right surroundings, he can in most cases escape social persecution, but while he is young and his merits are still untested, he is liable to be at the mercy of ignorant people who consider themselves capable of judging in matters about which they know nothing, and who are outraged at the suggestion that so young a person may know better than they do with all their experience of the world. Many people who have ultimately escaped from the tyranny of ignorance have had so hard a fight and so long a time of repression that in the end they are embittered and their energy is impaired. There is a comfortable doctrine that genius will always make its way, and on the strength of this doctrine many people consider that the persecution of youthful talent cannot do much harm. But there is no ground whatever for accepting this doctrine. It is like the theory that murder will out. Obviously all the murders we know of have been discovered, but who knows how many there may be which have never been heard of? In like manner all the men of genius that we have ever heard of have triumphed over adverse circumstances, but that is no reason for supposing that there were not innumerable others who succumbed in youth. Moreover it is not a question only of genius, but also of talent, which is just as necessary to the community. And it is not only a question of emerging somehow, but also of emerging unembittered and with unimpaired energy. For all these reasons the way of youth should not be made too hard.

While it is desirable that the old should treat with respect the wishes of the young, it is not desirable that the young should treat with respect the wishes of the old. The reason is simple: namely, that in either case it is the lives of the young that are concerned, not the lives of the old. When the young attempt to regulate the lives of the old as, for example, by objecting to the remarriage of a widowed parent, they are quite as much in the wrong as are the old who attempt to regulate the lives of the young. Old and young alike, as soon as years of discretion have been reached, have a right to their own choices and if necessary to their own mistakes. Young people are ill-advised if they yield to the pressure of the old in any vital matter. Suppose, for example, that you are a young person who wishes to go on the stage, and that your parents oppose your wish, either on the ground that the stage is immoral or on the ground that it is socially inferior. They may bring every kind of pressure to bear; they may tell you that they will cast you off if you ignore their commands, they may say that you will certainly repent within a few years, they may mention whole strings of horrid examples of young persons who have been rash enough to do what you contemplate doing and came to a bad end in consequence. They may of course be right in thinking that the stage is not the career for you, it may be that you have no talent for acting, or that you have a bad voice. If this is the case, however, you will soon discover it from theatrical people, and there will still be plenty of time to adopt a different career. The arguments of parents should not be a sufficient reason for relinquishing the attempt. If, in spite of all they say, you carry out your intention, they will soon come round, much sooner in fact than either you or they suppose. If on the other hand you find professional opinion discouraging, that is another matter, for professional opinion must always be treated with respect by beginners.

I think that in general, apart from expert opinion, there is too much respect paid to the opinions of others, both in great matters and in small ones. One should respect public opinion in so far as is necessary to avoid starvation and to keep out of prison, but anything that goes beyond this is voluntary submission to an unnecessary tyranny, and is likely to interfere with happiness in all kinds of ways. Take, for example, the matter of expenditure. Very many people spend money in ways quite different from those that their natural tastes would enjoin, merely because they feel that the respect of their neighbors depends upon their possession of a good car and their ability to give good dinners. As a matter of fact, any man who can obviously afford a car but genuinely prefers travel or a good library will in the end be much more respected than if he behaved exactly like every one else. There is of course no point in deliberately flouting public opinion; this is still to be under its domination, though in a topsy-turvy way. But to be genuinely indifferent to it is both a strength and a source of happiness. And a society composed of men and women who do not bow too much to the conventions is a far more interesting society than one in which all behave alike. Where each person's character is developed individually, differences of type are preserved, and it is worth while to meet new people, because they are not mere replicas of those whom one has met already. This has been one of the advantages of aristocracy, since where status depended upon birth behavior was allowed to be erratic. In the modern world we are losing this source of social freedom, and therefore a more deliberate realization of the dangers of uniformity has become desirable. I do not mean that people should be intentionally eccentric, which is just as uninteresting as being conventional. I mean only that people should be natural, and should follow their spontaneous tastes in so far as these are not definitely antisocial.

In the modern world, owing to the swiftness of locomotion, people are less dependent than they used to be upon their geographically nearest neighbors. Those who have cars can regard as a neighbor any person living within twenty miles. They have therefore a much greater power than was formerly the case of choosing their companions. In any populous neighborhood a man must be very unfortunate if he cannot find congenial souls within twenty miles. The idea that one should know one's immediate neighbors has died out in large centers of population, but still lingers in small towns and in the country. It has become a foolish idea, since there is no need to be dependent upon immediate neighbors for society. More and more it becomes possible to choose our companions on account of congeniality rather than on account of mere propinquity. Happiness is promoted by associations of persons with similar tastes and similar opinions. Social intercourse may be expected to develop more and more along these lines, and it may be hoped that by these means the loneliness that now afflicts so many unconventional people will be gradually diminished almost to the vanishing point. This will undoubtedly increase their happiness, but it will of course diminish the sadistic pleasure which the conventional at present derive from having the unconventional at their mercy. I do not think, however, that this is a pleasure which we need be greatly concerned to preserve.

Fear of public opinion, like every other form of fear, is aggressive and stunts growth. It is difficult to achieve any kind of greatness while a fear of this kind remains strong, and it is impossible to acquire that freedom of spirit in which true happiness consists, for it is essential to happiness that our way of living should spring from our own deep impulses and not from the accidental tastes and desires of those who happen to be our neighbors, or even our relations. Fear of immediate neighbors is no doubt less than it was, but there is a new kind of fear, namely, the fear of what newspapers may say. This is quite as terrifying as anything connected with medieval witch hunts. When the newspaper chooses to make a scapegoat of some perhaps quite harmless person, the results may be very terrible. Fortunately, as yet this is a fate which most people escape through their obscurity; but as publicity gets more and more perfect in its methods, there will be an increasing danger in this novel form of social persecution. This is too grave a matter to be treated with disdain by the individual who is its victim, and whatever may be thought of the great principle of the freedom of the press, I think the line will have to be drawn more sharply than it is by the existing libel laws, and anything will have to be forbidden that makes life intolerable for innocent individuals, even if they should happen to have done or said things which, published maliciously, can cause them to become unpopular. The only ultimate cure for this evil is, however, an increase of toleration on the part of the public. The best way to increase toleration is to multiply the number of individuals who enjoy real happiness and do not therefore find their chief pleasure in the infliction of pain upon their fellow men.

STUDY QUESTIONS

1. What attitude toward public opinion does Russell recommend? Indifference? Obedience? Evasion? Or what?
2. How does the author explain the unhappiness which exceptionally intelligent young people sometimes experience?
3. In what way is this selection related to Mill's "On Liberty"?
4. Enumerate the practical suggestions Russell offers for dealing with public opinion.
5. Do you agree that in general "there is too much respect paid to the opinions of others"? Would not society be more unified and harmonious if more rather than less attention were paid to public opinion?
6. What is the difference between public and private opinion? How do private opinions, as distinguished from public ones, originate? To what extent is one entitled to hold a private opinion disapproved by his community? Write a theme exploring these and other questions which such proponents of personal liberty as Mill, Thoreau, and Russell have not considered.

3. THE LONG VIEW

The Conservative View of Man and Society*

Clinton Rossiter

The Conservative holds definite opinions about man's nature, his capacity for self-government, his relations with other men, the kind of life he should lead, and the rights he may properly claim. On these opinions rests the whole Conservative tradition.

Man, says the Conservative, is a composite of good and evil, a blend of ennobling excellencies and degrading imperfections. He is not perfect; he is not perfectible. If educated properly, placed in a favorable environment, and held in restraint by tradition and authority, he may display innate qualities of rationality, sociability, industry, decency, and love of liberty. Never, no matter how he is educated or situated or restrained, will he throw off completely his other innate qualities of irrationality, selfishness, laziness, depravity, and corruptibility. Man's nature is essentially immutable, and the immutable strain is one of deep-seated wickedness. Although some Conservatives find support for their skeptical view of man in recent experiments in psychology, most continue to rely on religious teaching and the study of history. Those who are Christians, and most Conservatives are, prefer to call the motivation for iniquitous and irrational behavior by its proper name: Original Sin.

The Conservative is often accused of putting too much stress on man's wickedness and irrationality and of overlooking his many good qualities, especially his capacity for reason. The Conservative's answer is candid enough. He is well aware of man's potentialities, but he must counter the optimism of the liberal and radical with certain cheerless reminders that are no less true for telling only half the truth: that evil exists independently of social or economic maladjustments; that we must search for the source of our discontents in defective human nature rather than in a defective social order; and that man, far from being malleable, is subject to cultural alteration only slowly and to a limited degree. The Conservative therefore considers it his stern duty to call attention, as did John Adams, to "the general frailty and depravity of human nature."

This view of human nature is saved from churlish cynicism by two splendid beliefs. First, man is touched with eternity. He has a precious soul; he is a religious entity. His urges toward sin are matched, and with

* Reprinted from *Conservatism in America* by Clinton Rossiter, by permission of Alfred A. Knopf, Inc. Copyright, 1955, by Clinton Rossiter.

God's grace are over-matched if never finally beaten down, by his aspiration for good. For this reason, the Conservative asserts, man is an object of reverence, and a recognition of man's heaven-ordained shortcomings serves only to deepen this reverence. Second, to quote from Burke, the father of all Conservatives, "The nature of man is intricate." The confession of an eminent psychologist, Gardner Murphy, "Not much, I believe, is known about man," is applauded by the Conservative, who then adds: "Not much, I believe, will ever be known about him." Man is a mysterious and complex being, and no amount of psychological research will ever solve the mystery or unravel the complexity.

No truth about human nature and capabilities is more important than this: man can govern himself, but there is no certainty that he will; free government is possible but far from inevitable. Man will need all the help he can get from education, religion, tradition, and institutions if he is to enjoy even a limited success in his experiments in self-government. He must be counseled, encouraged, informed, and checked. Above all, he must realize that the collective wisdom of the community, itself the union of countless partial and imperfect wisdoms like his own, is alone equal to this mightiest of social tasks. A clear recognition of man's conditional capacity for ruling himself and others is the first requisite of constitution-making.

Conservatism holds out obstinately against two popular beliefs about human relations in modern society: individualism and equality. Putting off a discussion of the Conservative and individualism for a few pages, let us hear what he has to say about the explosive question of equality.

Each man is equal to every other man in only one meaningful sense: he is a man, a physical and spiritual entity, and is thus entitled by God and nature to be treated as end rather than means. From the basic fact of moral equality come several secondary equalities that the modern Conservative recognizes, more eloquently in public than in private: equality of opportunity, the right of each individual to exploit his own talents up to their natural limits; equality before the law, the right to justice on the same terms as other men; and political equality, which takes the form of universal suffrage. Beyond this the Conservative is unwilling to go. Recognizing the infinite variety among men in talent, taste, appearance, intelligence, and virtue, he is candid enough to assert that this variety extends vertically as well as horizontally. Men are grossly unequal—and, what is more, can never be made equal—in all qualities of mind, body, and spirit.

The good society rests solidly on this great truth. The social order is organized in such a way as to take advantage of ineradicable natural distinctions among men. It exhibits a class structure in which there are several quite distinct levels, most men find their level early and stay in it without rancor, and equality of opportunity keeps the way at least partially open to ascent and decline. At the same time, the social order aims to temper those distinctions that are not natural. It recognizes the inevitability and indeed the necessity of orders and classes, but it insists that all privileges, ranks, and other visible signs of inequality be as natural and functional as possible. The Conservative, of course—and this point is of decisive importance—is much more inclined than other men to consider artificial distinctions as natural. Equity rather than equality is the mark of his society; the reconciliation rather than the abolition of classes is his constant aim. When he is forced to choose between liberty and equality, he throws his support unhesitatingly to liberty. Indeed, the preference for liberty over equality lies at the root of the Conservative tradition.

While Conservatism has retreated some distance from Burke and Adams under the pressures of modern democracy, it has refused to yield one salient: the belief in a ruling and serving aristocracy. "If there is any one point," Gertrude Himmelfarb writes, "any single empirical test, by which conservatism can be distinguished from liberalism, it is a respect for aristocracy and aristocratic institutions. Every tenet of liberalism repudiates the idea of a fixed aristocracy; every tenet of conservatism affirms it." If it is no longer good form to use the word *aristocracy* in political debate, nor good sense to expect that an aristocracy can be "fixed" to the extent that it was one hundred and fifty years ago, the Conservative is still moved powerfully by the urge to seek out the best men and place them in positions of authority. He continues to assert the beneficence of an aristocracy of talent and virtue, one that is trained for special service and thus entitled to special consideration. He continues to believe that it takes more than one generation to make a genuine aristocrat.

The world being what it is today, the Conservative spends a good deal of his time in the pulpit exhorting his fellow men to live godly, righteous, and sober lives. He does not do this gladly, for he is not by nature a Puritan, but the times seem to have made him our leading "moral athlete."

Man, the Conservative asserts, is stamped with sin and carnality, but he is also blessed with higher aspirations. If human nature in general can never be much improved, each individual may nevertheless bring his own savage and selfish impulses under control. It is his duty to himself, his fellows, and God to do just this—to shun vice, cultivate virtue, and submit to the guidance of what Lincoln called "the better angels of our nature." Only thus, through the moral striving of many men, can free government be secured and society be made stable.

What virtues must the individual cultivate? The Conservative of the tower, the Conservative of the field, the Conservative of the market place, and the Conservative of the assembly each give a somewhat different answer to this question, yet all agree to this catalogue of primary virtues: wisdom, justice, temperance, and courage; industry, frugality, piety, and honesty; contentment, obedience, compassion, and good manners. The good man is peaceful but not resigned and is conservative through habit and choice rather than sloth and cowardice. He assumes that duty comes before pleasure, self-sacrifice before self-indulgence. Believing that the test of life is accomplishment rather than enjoyment, he takes pride in doing a good job in the station to which he has been called. He is alert to the identity and malignity of the vices he must shun: ignorance, injustice, intemperance, and cowardice; laziness, luxury, selfishness, and dishonesty; envy, disobedience, violence, and bad manners. And he is aware, too, of the larger implications of his own life of virtue: self-government is for moral men; those who would be free must be virtuous.

Education starts a man on the road that leads through virtue to freedom. Only through education—in family, church, and school—can children be shaped into civilized men. Only through education can man's vices, which are tough, be brought under control and his virtues, which are frail, be nourished into robust health. The instruments of education should teach a man to think, survive, ply a trade, and enjoy his leisure. Their great mission, however, is to act as a conserving, civilizing force: to convey to each man his share of the inherited wisdom of the race, to train him to lead a moral, self-disciplined life, and to foster a love of order and respect for authority.

The Conservative's understanding of the mission of education explains his profound mistrust of modern theories, most of which, he feels, are grounded in a clear misreading of the nature and needs of children. The school has always been a conservative force in society, and the Conservative means to keep it that way. He admits that there is a stage in the education of some individuals—those who are to go on to leadership—when self-development and self-expression should get prime consideration. First things must come first, however, and before this stage is reached, the individual must be taught his community's values and be integrated into its structure.

Before we can describe the Conservative consensus on freedom and responsibility, we must learn more of the circumstances in which men can enjoy the one because they accept the other.

THE CONSERVATIVE VIEW OF SOCIETY

The Conservative's best thoughts are directed to society and the social process. The key points of his social theory appear to be these:

Society is a living organism with roots deep in the past. The true community, the Conservative likes to say, is a tree, not a machine. It rose to its present strength and glory through centuries of growth, and men must forbear to think of it as a mechanical contrivance that can be dismantled and reassembled in one generation. Prescription, not fiat, is the chief creative force in the social process.

Society is cellular. It is not an agglomeration of lonely individuals, but a grand, complex union of functional groups. Man is a social animal whose best interests are served by co-operating with other men. Indeed, he has no real meaning except as contributing member of one or more of these intrinsic groups: family, church, local community, and, at certain stages of historical development, occupational association. The group is important not only because it gives life, work, comfort, and spiritual support to the individual, but because it joins with thousands of other groups to form the one really stubborn roadblock against the march of the all-powerful state. The Conservative is careful not to ride the cellular analogy too hard, for he is aware that it can lead to a social theory in which man loses all dignity and personality.

In addition to the intrinsic groups, a healthy society will display a balanced combination of "institutions": constitution, common law, monarchy or presidency, legislature, courts, civil service, armed services and sub-divisions, colleges, schools, forms of property, corporations, co-operatives, trade unions, guilds, fraternal orders, and dozens of other instrumentalities and understandings that mold the lives of men. Such symbols of national unity and continuity as anthems, flags, rituals, battlefields, monuments, and pantheons of heroes are equally dear to the Conservative heart. All men are stanch defenders of the institutions that meet their practical and spiritual needs, but the Conservative places special trust in them. "Individuals may form communities," Disraeli warned, "but it is institutions alone that can create a nation."

Society is a unity. In the healthy community all these groups and institutions fit together into a harmonious unity, and attempts to reshape one part of society must inevitably disturb other parts. The Conservative, though something of a pluralist, never loses sight of the ultimate unity into which all groups and institutions must merge. He sees the social structure not as a series of neat strata laid one on top of another, but, in Coleridge's phrase, as "an indissoluble blending and interfusion of persons from top to bottom."

Society cannot be static. Change is the rule of life, for societies as for men. A community cannot stand still; it must develop or decline. "Society must alter," Russell Kirk acknowledges in *The Conservative Mind,* "for slow change is the means of its conservation, like the human body's perpetual renewal." In recognizing this great truth, the Conservative shows himself to be neither a reactionary nor stand-patter. Yet he is just as emphatically not a liberal or radical, and he therefore sets severe conditions upon social change, especially if it is to be worked by active reform. Change, he insists, must never be taken for its own sake; must have preservation, if possible even restoration, as its central object; be severely limited in scope and purpose; be a response to an undoubted social need— for example, the renovation or elimination of an institution that is plainly obsolete; be worked out by slow and careful stages; represent progress, "a change for the better"; be brought off under Conservative auspices, or with Conservatives intervening at the decisive moment; and finally, in

Disraeli's words, "be carried out in deference to the manners, the customs, the laws, the traditions of the people." The essence of Conservatism is the feeling for the possibilities and limits of natural, organic change. In the eloquent phrases of R. J. White, of Cambridge:

To discover the order which inheres in things rather than to impose an order upon them; to strengthen and perpetuate that order rather than to dispose things anew according to some formula which may be nothing more than a fashion; to legislate along the grain of human nature rather than against it; to pursue limited objectives with a watchful eye; to amend here, to prune there; in short, to preserve the method of nature in the conduct of the state . . . this is Conservatism.

Society must be stable. Although men can never hope to see their community completely stable, they can create an endurable condition of peace and order. To achieve this end, they must work unceasingly for a society that has this ideal appearance:

Common agreement on fundamentals exists among men of all ranks and stations. Loyalty, good will, fraternal sympathy, and a feeling for compromise pervade the political and social scene.

Institutions and groups are in functional adjustment. Political, economic, social, and cultural power is widely diffused among persons, groups, and other instruments; these are held by law, custom, and constitution in a state of operating equilibrium. For every show of power there is corresponding responsibility. A minimum of friction and maximum of accommodation exist between government and group, government and individual, group and individual.

The authority of each group, and especially of the government, is legitimate. The laws honor the traditions of the nation, are adjusted to the capacities of the citizenry, meet the requirements of abstract justice, and satisfy the needs of society. Men obey the laws cheerfully and readily, and they know why they obey them. They know, too, the difference between authority and authoritarianism.

Men are secure; they have a sense of being, belonging, and creating. Their labors are rewarded, their sorrows comforted, their needs satisfied. They have the deep feeling of serenity that arises not merely from material well-being, but from confidence in the future, from daily contact with decent and trustworthy men, and from participation in an even-handed system of justice. Predictability, morality, and equity are important ingredients of their security. Most important, however, is ordered liberty, which makes it possible for men to pursue their talents and tastes within a sheltering order.

Change and reform are sure-footed, discriminating, and respectful of the past. "Men breathe freely," as F. E. Dessauer puts it, "because change is limited. . . . The changes which are taking place do not frighten the affected." The currents of change are channeled into the stream of progress by institutions and values that have stood the tests of time and service.

Unity, balance, authority, security, continuity—these are the key elements of social stability. In longing for a society in which peace and order reign, the Conservative comes closest to the utopianism that he ridicules in others.

STUDY QUESTIONS

1. How do Rossiter's views contrast with those of Mill on: (a) the nature of man; (b) social equality; (c) social institutions; (d) the past?

2. Would you say, judging from Rossiter's ideas, that the liberal or the conservative lays a greater stress on moral qualities in social and political questions?

3. In what way, according to Rossiter, are principles of liberty and equality opposed to each other?

4. To what extent do Rossiter's views seem to harmonize with democratic ideals?

5. Analyze the organization and aims of this selection. To what extent do you think it is Rossiter's intention to define the conservative view? To evaluate it? To persuade his reader to accept it? Explain the grounds upon which you base your answer.

6. Do you find Rossiter's description of the conservative society attractive? Write a theme evaluating it, and explaining whether or not you would like to live in such a society.

The Mass Man*

José Ortega y Gasset

What is he like, this mass-man who to-day dominates public life, political and non-political, and why is he like it, that is, how has he been produced?

It will be well to answer both questions together, for they throw light on one another. The man who to-day is attempting to take the lead in European existence is very different from the man who directed the XIXth Century, but he was produced and prepared by the XIXth Century. Any keen mind of the years 1820, 1850, and 1880 could by simple *a priori* reasoning, foresee the gravity of the present historical situation, and in fact nothing is happening now which was not foreseen a hundred years ago.

"The masses are advancing," said Hegel in apocalyptic fashion. "Without some new spiritual influence, our age, which is a revolutionary age, will produce a catastrophe," was the pronouncement of Comte. "I see the flood-tide of nihilism rising," shrieked Nietzsche from a crag of the Engadine. It is false to say that history cannot be foretold. Numberless times this has been done. If the future offered no opening to prophecy, it could not be understood when fulfilled in the present and on the point of falling back into the past. The idea that the historian is on the reverse side a prophet, sums up the whole philosophy of history. It is true that it is only possible to anticipate the general structure of the future, but that is all that we in truth understand of the past or of the present. Accordingly, if you want a good view of your own age, look at it from far off. From what distance? The answer is simple. Just far enough to prevent you seeing Cleopatra's nose.

What appearance did life present to that multitudinous man who in ever-increasing abundance the XIXth Century kept producing? To start with, an appearance of universal material ease. Never had the average man been able to solve his economic problem with greater facility. Whilst there was a proportionate decrease of great fortunes and life became harder for the individual worker, the middle classes found their economic horizon widened every day. Every day added a new luxury to their standard of life. Every day their position was more secure and more independent of another's will. What before would have been considered one of fortune's gifts, inspiring humble gratitude toward destiny, was converted into a right, not to be grateful for, but to be insisted on.

From 1900 on, the worker likewise begins to extend and assure his existence. Nevertheless, he has to struggle to obtain his end. He does not, like the middle class, find the benefit attentively served up to him by a society and a state which are a marvel of organization. To this ease and security of economic conditions are to be added the physical ones, comfort and public order. Life runs on smooth rails, and there is no likelihood of anything violent or dangerous breaking in on it. Such a free, untrammelled situation was bound to instil into the depths of such souls an idea of existence which might be expressed in the witty and penetrating phrase of an old country like ours: "Wide is Castile." That is to say, in all its primary and decisive aspects, life presented itself to the new man as *exempt from restrictions*. The realisation of this fact and of its importance becomes immediate when we remember that such a freedom of existence was entirely lacking to the common men of the past. On the contrary, for them life was burdensome destiny, economically and physically. From birth, existence meant to them an accumulation of impediments which they were obliged to suffer, without possible solution other than to adapt themselves to them, to settle down in the narrow space they left available.

But still more evident is the contrast of situations, if we pass from the material to the civil and moral. The average man, from the second half of the XIXth Century on, finds no social barriers raised against him. That is to say, that as regards the forms of public life he no longer finds himself from birth confronted with obstacles and limitations. There is nothing to force him to limit his existence. Here again, "Wide is Castile." There are no "estates" or "castes." There are no civil privileges. The ordinary man learns that all men are equal before the law.

Never in the course of history had man been placed in vital surroundings even remotely familiar to those set up by the conditions just mentioned. We are, in fact, confronted with a radical innovation in human destiny, implanted by the XIXth Century. A new stage has been mounted for human existence, new both in the physical and the social aspects. Three principles have made possible this new world: liberal democracy, scientific experiment, and industrialism. The two latter may be summed-up in one word: technicism. Not one of those principles was invented by the XIXth Century; they proceed from the two previous centuries. The glory of the XIXth Century lies not in their discovery, but in their implantation. No one but recognises that fact. But it is not sufficient to recognise it in the abstract, it is necessary to realise its inevitable consequences.

The XIXth Century was of its essence revolutionary. This aspect is not to be looked for in the scenes of the barricades, which are mere incidents, but in the fact that it placed the average man—the great social mass—in conditions of life radically opposed to those by which he had always been surrounded. It turned his public existence upside down. Revolution is not the uprising against pre-existing order, but the setting up of a new order contradictory to the traditional one. Hence there is no exaggeration in saying that the man who is the product of the XIXth Century is, for the effects of public life, a man apart from all other men. The XVIIIth-Century man differs, of course, from the XVIIth-Century man, and this one in turn from his fellow of the XVIth Century, but they are all related, similar, even identical in essentials when confronted with this new man. For the "common" man of all periods "life" had principally meant limitation, obligation, dependence; in a word, pressure. Say oppression, if you like, provided it be understood not only in the juridical and social sense, but also in the cosmic. For it is this latter which has never been lacking up to a hundred years ago, the date at which starts the practically limitless expansion of scientific technique—physical and administrative. Previously, even for the rich and powerful, the world was a place of poverty, difficulty and danger.[1]

---

[1] However rich an individual might be in relation to his fellows, as the world in its totality was poor, the sphere of conveniences and commodities with which his wealth furnished him was very limited. The life of the average man to-day is easier, more convenient and softer than that of the most powerful of another age. What difference does it make to him not to be richer than others if the world is richer and furnishes him with magnificent roads, railways, telegraphs, hotels, personal safety and aspirin?

The world which surrounds the new man from his birth does not compel him to limit himself in any fashion, it sets up no veto in opposition to him; on the contrary, it incites his appetite, which in principle can increase indefinitely. Now it turns out—and this is most important—that this world of the XIXth and early XXth Centuries not only has the perfections and the completeness which it actually possesses, but furthermore suggests to those who dwell in it the radical assurance that to-morrow it will be still richer, ampler, more perfect, as if it enjoyed a spontaneous, inexhaustible power of increase. Even to-day, in spite of some signs which are making a tiny breach in that sturdy faith, even to-day, there are few men who doubt that motorcars will in five years' time be more comfortable and cheaper than to-day. They believe in this as they believe that the sun will rise in the morning. The metaphor is an exact one. For, in fact, the common man, finding himself in a world so excellent, technically and socially, believes that it has been produced by nature, and never thinks of the personal efforts of highly-endowed individuals which the creation of this new world presupposed. Still less will he admit the notion that all these facilities still require the support of certain difficult human virtues, the least failure of which would cause the rapid disappearance of the whole magnificent edifice.

This leads us to note down in our psychological chart of the mass-man of to-day two fundamental traits: the free expansion of his vital desires, and therefore, of his personality; and his radical ingratitude towards all that has made possible the ease of his existence. These traits together make up the well-known psychology of the spoilt child. And in fact it would entail no error to use this psychology as a "sight" through which to observe the soul of the masses of to-day. Heir to an ample and generous past—generous both in ideals and in activities—the new commonalty has been spoiled by the world around it. To spoil means to put no limit on caprice, to give one the impression that everything is permitted to him and that he has no obligations. The young child exposed to this regime has no experience of its own limits. By reason of the removal of all external restraint, all clashing with other things, he comes actually to believe that he is the only one that exists, and gets used to not considering others, especially not considering them as superior to himself. This feeling of another's superiority could only be instilled into him by someone who, being stronger than he is, should force him to give up some desire, to restrict himself, to restrain himself. He would then have learned this fundamental discipline: "Here I end and here begins another more powerful than I am. In the world, apparently, there are two people: I myself and another superior to me." The ordinary man of past times was daily taught this elemental wisdom by the world about him, because it was a world so rudely organised, that catastrophes were frequent, and there was nothing in it certain, abundant, stable. But the new masses find themselves in the presence of a prospect full of possibilities, and furthermore, quite secure with everything ready to their hands, independent of any previous efforts on their part, just as we find the sun in the heavens without our hoisting it up on our shoulders. No human being thanks another for the air he breathes, for no one has produced the air for him; it belongs to the sum-total of what "is there," of which we say "it is natural," because it never fails. And these spoiled masses are unintelligent enough to believe that the material and social organisation, placed at their disposition like the air, is of the same origin, since apparently it never fails them, and is al-most as perfect as the natural scheme of things.

My thesis, therefore, is this: the very perfection with which the XIXth Century gave an organisation to certain orders of existence has caused the masses benefited thereby to consider it, not as an organised, but as a natural system. Thus is explained and defined the absurd state of mind revealed by these masses; they are only concerned with their own well-being, and at the same time they remain alien to the cause of that well-being. As they do not see, beyond the benefits of civilisation, marvels of invention and construction which can only be maintained by great effort and foresight, they imagine that their role is limited to demanding these benefits peremptorily, as if they were natural rights. In the disturbances caused by scarcity of food, the mob goes in search of bread, and the means it employs is generally to wreck the bakeries. This may serve as a symbol of the attitude adopted, on a greater and more complicated scale, by the masses of to-day towards the civilisation by which they are supported.

NOBLE LIFE AND COMMON LIFE, OR EFFORT AND INERTIA

To start with, we are what our world invites us to be, and the basic fea-tures of our soul are impressed upon it by the form of its surroundings as in a mould. Naturally, for our life is no other than our relations with the world around. The general aspect which it presents to us will form the general aspect of our own life. It is for this reason that I stress so much the observation that the world into which the masses of to-day have been born displays features radically new to history. Whereas in past times life for the average man meant finding all around him difficulties, dangers, want, limitations of his destiny, dependence, the new world appears as a sphere of practically limitless possibilities, safe, and independent of anyone. Based on this primary and lasting impression, the mind of every contemporary man will be formed, just as previous minds were formed on the opposite impression. For that basic impression becomes an interior voice which ceaselessly utters certain words in the depths of each indi-vidual, and tenaciously suggests to him a definition of life which is, at the same time, a moral imperative. And if the traditional sentiment whis-pered: "To live is to feel oneself limited, and therefore to have to count with that which limits us," the newest voice shouts: "To live is to meet with no limitation whatever and, consequently, to abandon oneself calmly to one's self. Practically nothing is impossible, nothing is dangerous, and, in principle, nobody is superior to anybody." This basic experience completely modifies the traditional, persistent structure of the mass-man. For the latter always felt himself, by his nature, confronted with material limitations and higher social powers. Such, in his eyes, was life. If he succeeded in improving his situation, if he climbed the social ladder, he attributed this to a piece of fortune which was favourable to him in particular. And if not to this, then to an enormous effort, of which he knew well what it had cost him. In both cases it was a question of an exception to the general character of life and the world; an exception which, as such, was due to some very special cause.

But the modern mass finds complete freedom as its natural, established condition, without any special cause for it. Nothing from outside incites it to recognise limits to itself, and consequently, to refer at all times to other authorities higher than itself. Until lately, the Chinese peasant believed that the welfare of his existence depended on the private virtues which the Emperor was pleased to possess. Therefore, his life was constantly related to this supreme authority on which it depended. *But the man we are now analysing accustoms himself not to appeal from his own to any authority outside him.* He is satisfied with himself exactly as he is. Ingenuously, without any need of being vain, as the most natural thing in the world, he will tend to consider and affirm as good everything he finds within himself: opinions, appetities, preferences, tastes. Why not, if, as we have seen, nothing and nobody force him to realise that he is a second-class man, subject to many limitations, incapable of creating or conserving that very organisation which gives his life the fullness and contentedness on which he bases this assertion of his personality?

The mass-man would never have accepted authority external to himself had not his surroundings violently forced him to do so. As to-day, his surroundings do not so force him, the everlasting mass-man, true to his character, ceases to appeal to other authority and feels himself lord of his own existence. On the contrary the select man, the excellent man is urged, by interior necessity, to appeal from himself to some standard beyond himself, superior to himself, whose service he freely accepts. Let us recall that at the start we distinguished the excellent man from the common man by saying that the former is the one who makes great demands on himself, and the latter the one who makes no demands on himself, but contents himself with what he is, and is delighted with himself. Contrary to what is usually thought, it is the man of excellence, and not the common man who lives in essential servitude. Life has no savour for him unless he makes it consist in service to something transcendental. Hence he does not look upon the necessity of serving as an oppression. When, by chance, such necessity is lacking, he grows restless and invents some new standard, more difficult, more exigent, with which to coerce himself. This is life lived as a discipline—the noble life. Nobility is defined by the demands it makes on us—by obligations, not by rights. *Noblesse oblige.* "To live as one likes is plebeian; the noble man aspires to order and law" (Goethe). The privileges of nobility are not in their origin concessions or favours; on the contrary, they are conquests. And their maintenance supposes, in principle, that the privileged individual is capable of reconquering them, at any moment, if it were necessary, and anyone were to dispute them. Private rights or *privileges* are not, then, passive possession and mere enjoyment, but they represent the standard attained by personal effort. On the other hand, common rights, such as those "of the man and the citizen," are passive property, pure usufruct and benefit, the generous gift of fate which every man finds before him, and which answers to no effort whatever, unless it be that of breathing and avoiding insanity. I would say, then, that an impersonal right is held, a personal one is upheld.

STUDY QUESTIONS

1. Is there a parallel between Brogan's observation that overt competition is taboo in America and Ortega y Gasset's view that the mass-man loves comfort and the feeling that he is the equal of anyone? What relationships do you find between Ortega y Gasset's views and C. Wright Mills' description of the white-collar class?

2. Can you find any evidence in popular magazines or newspapers to support Ortega y Gasset's description of "the mass-man"?

3. In what way, according to the author, is the nineteenth century man different from those of previous centuries? What are the consequences of the mass-man's failure to understand the past?

4. To what extent does Ortega y Gasset agree with Rossiter? Is there any difference in their views of human nature?

5. Do you think that Ortega's description of the mass-man's attitude is fair or unfair? Write a theme evaluating his opinions.

6. Can it be argued that the conditions of modern life have improved character, instead of causing it to deteriorate, as Ortega believes?

The Future of American Liberalism*

Morris R. Cohen

We are now entering the world arena, and the question is no longer that of the special type of liberal civilization which once existed in the United States, but whether any type of liberal civilization can exist in our America. Liberal civilization has existed in many forms in many nations. What is its essence? Here again it is safer to indicate realities and let the result coin its own definition.

* From *The Faith of a Liberal.* Reprinted by permission of the Administrator of the Estate of Morris R. Cohen.

Liberal civilization came to the fore in Europe in the middle of the eighteenth century. It was a movement which banished the Inquisition, abolished the despotic power of kings, and broke up the system of censorship and of political and economic privilege in relation to taxation, trade, and obedience to oppressive laws. It was necessary to wage a long fight before monopoly privileges were taken away from the old aristocracy. The movement to extend education to everybody came to full force only in the nineteenth century. It was the nineteenth century that saw the removal of limitations on the suffrage as well as those on holding public office: property qualifications, religious affiliations, and the like. The liberal movement was directed to the wiping out of such restraints. The emancipation of women and their final admission to the privilege of the suffrage has occurred within our own day.

If a formula is necessary for all this, I would suggest that liberalism means a pride in human achievement, a faith in human effort, a conviction that the proper function of government is to remove the restraints upon human activity. The philosophy back of that is summed up in two great faiths or beliefs: the belief in progress, and the belief in toleration. I think those are the two fundamental ideas of liberalism.

The idea of progress can hardly be understood unless we have in mind the ideas against which the idea of progress was a reaction. The people who were in favor of progress had some definite objective. They were opposed to the old attitude which we associate with Calvinism, but which existed even in large sections of the Catholic Church, as well as in non-Christian groups. This was the view that human nature is profoundly and radically sinful and corrupt. Therefore human beings cannot be trusted to fulfill their natural inclination. Nature is sin. To indulge our natural impulses is sinful. That is an idea which is easily recognized; it has not yet died.

As a consequence of the idea that the human flesh is corrupt and our nature sinful, there was the necessity of relying upon authorities and magistrates, rules and blue laws. The excessive regulation of life by governments, such as we had in some of the Puritan colonies, was a natural consequence of that belief.

The belief in progress was a reaction against such a point of view. The believers in progress said: "No, human flesh is not originally corrupt. To be sure, man commits sins and crimes. You cannot deny that. But that is due to the bad institutions under which we live. If you could only wipe out the evil institutions under which man has lived, human nature would assert itself." This is the idea that underlies almost all of Shelley's writings—an idea that he got from Godwin.

There is something very beautiful and noble about that idea. There are, to my knowledge, few parallels in human history to the nobility of Condorcet in the shadow of the guillotine. He was hiding in a garret in Paris;

his life was hanging on a thread; and yet he was writing a marvelously enthusiastic sketch of the progress of the human race, anticipating for the human race an indefinite advance towards perfection.

The only fit parallel that I can find to the nobility of that act is Socrates discussing the immortality of the soul, just before drinking the hemlock, or Jesus saying, "Father, forgive them, for they know not what they do," during the crucifixion.

The idea of progress took root as a creed of hope and a fighting faith. In the course of time, however, progress came to be a shibboleth for a fatalistic optimism or meliorism. The notion that man inevitably progresses through the centuries came to claim the support of science under the name of evolution. But there is no evidence in science or history for the assumption that human nature is bound to become perfect as it develops in time.

There is no proof that human history is a simple straight line upward and onward, and there can be no such proof. For one thing, there are no clear meanings that can be assigned to the terms "upward" and "onward." Upward, of course, was a very definite idea under the old Ptolemaic astronomy. But under modern conditions one has to define "upward" with regard to standards. Unfortunately, people who talk glibly about progress and evolution generally have no very definite conception of any final goal or standard, or even of any definite direction.

Let us, however, go on to some of the more concrete expressions of this idea of progress. One of the ways in which the doctrine of progress is justified is by pointing to the history of mechanical inventions and to the growth of science. It is undoubtedly true that science has made rapid strides, but it is not true that all people today are more scientific than people were a hundred and fifty years ago, or three hundred years ago, or one thousand years ago: and on that point, I think, reflection will show that there is a very great deal of loose talk. Is it true, for instance, that a man who believes that the earth goes around the sun is more scientific than one who believes that the sun goes around the earth? If he has no reason, I fail to see that one belief or the other is scientific. How many college graduates are there who can prove that the earth does go around the sun? Having taught college students for many years, I venture to say that there are no more than two in a hundred who can offer a logical proof. And any such proofs are bound to be inadequate. This can be affirmed without any hesitation because it is a matter of mathematical demonstration. Motion is relative, and therefore there can be inherently no such thing as proof of the fact that the earth goes around the sun. All you can prove is that a certain system of equations will explain planetary motions and other physical phenomena better than other systems do. And that, of course, is a matter that can be proved to all who know mathematics. Obviously that applies to a very small portion of the educated public.

For that matter, most of popular science is just a new form of super-stition. What evidence is there that, because a man has read something about the romance of the atom, he really understands the world better; that he has attained a more scientific turn of mind? What evidence is there that because a man talks freely about psychology, or psychoanalysis and complexes and libidos and things of that sort, he really has scientific detachment and a sense of scientific evidence and scientific method? I should say that changes of lingo and various exercises of technical vocab-ulary do not indicate any growth of science—though the body of knowl-edge available today is larger than it was. People who want to use the material of science certainly have a better chance. But that does not mean that the great body of people today are more scientific than they were before.

Belief in gradual and inevitable progress becomes more and more diffi-cult to maintain, in the face of the carnage and destruction of two world wars and the failure of two victories to achieve the high objectives upon which so many wartime hopes were pinned. The kind of liberalism that was associated with this faith in progress through piecemeal cumulative reform has little appeal today and may well have less tomorrow. But is the liberal attitude necessarily dependent upon confidence in the inevita-ble success of our efforts? Many stout champions of the liberal cause have been frank to admit their inability to predict the future. Why can we not risk our lives in struggles of uncertain outcome? I am inclined to think that the faith in progress which is essential to the liberal attitude is not a faith in the inevitability of progress but rather a faith in its possibility.

That faith requires us to admit that we do not already possess the abso-lute truth. Such an admission runs counter to the religious, political, or economic convictions of many men and women. But it may be that the same catastrophes and failures which are destroying the faith in inevitable and gradual progress may also undermine the absolutisms that block the development of a liberalism fitted to the problems of our American future.

Today as in the time of Jesus those who seek the truth are the lovers of freedom. Conservatives and Communists generally do not seek the truth in social questions, because they already have it, or think they do. The peddlers of various brands of racial and national hatred do not seek the truth, because they fear it. Many more people do not seek the truth be-cause they do not know how or lack the energy or time or skill demanded by the quest for knowledge. And, of course, there are many scholars and pedants who seek the truth only in narrower and narrower fields. But the man who can strive, with Ulysses, "to follow knowledge like a sinking star, beyond the utmost bound of human thought," who accepts no limitations on what he may study or question, to whom every endeavor of the human spirit is deserving of critical consideration, is the true liberal.

Liberalism can move forward, like science, because it embraces self-correcting principles which permit the correction of error and partial truth without an overthrow of the system that makes such correction possible. Like science, liberalism is based on the faith that other human beings can carry forward, by rational methods, the gains that we have won in human understanding. The faith of the liberal, as of the scientist, grows out of a deep humility which recognizes the limitations of mortal finitude and acknowledges the impossibility of any individual's attaining correct answers to all the problems that he faces. But this humility is combined with a hope that, through rational communication and collaboration among individuals, a living body of common thought may be created which will more adequately answer the problems of an age or society than can any individual, whether he be a scientist or a dictator. In the long run, liberal democracy may outlast any form of dictatorship because the strength of a liberal democracy is not bounded by the prowess of any one man or party. The strength of liberalism lies in the fact that it enables each of us to rise above the limitations of our hereditary class prejudices and to contribute toward a body of *ideas and aspirations in action* that may incorporate more understanding than is vouchsafed to any single mortal. In the end, there is no way in which people can live together decently unless each individual or group realizes that the whole truth and virtue is not exclusively in its possession. This is a hard lesson to learn, but without it there can be no humane civilization.

Let us take the other great belief of liberalism: the belief in tolerance. This is very closely connected with scientific method. Unless one has a certain amount of skepticism in one's system, one cannot possibly believe in tolerance. What does tolerance mean? Tolerance means that we shall give our enemies a chance. If we are secure and we know that our enemies cannot hurt us, we may be willing to give them a chance. But suppose that we believe in a certain sacred truth—say the truth of the Messiah, or the truth of a certain economic order, or the truth of certain constitutional doctrines—and some scalawag preaches that these are not true. Shall we be tolerant to untruth? That seems to me to be the crux of the whole question of liberalism. The true liberal has a certain amount of skepticism. The true liberal, being impressed with scientific method, says: "Certainly we should, for, although I am convinced that what I believe to be the truth is the truth, the other man may have something to say which I haven't heard yet, or the other man may have a point of view which is worth investigating. On the whole, in the conflict of opinions, more truth will thus come out than if there is suppression."

This attitude involves a number of things which are generally not recognized. It involves not only a certain amount of skepticism in our own fundamental conviction, but a certain amount of detachment which very few people have. It is a rare gift to be able to be tolerant in that sense, because if we are pressed, if the enemy has the sword at our throats, we are not tempted to play fair and play according to the rules. We will do anything in our power to kill our assailant—or, at any rate, to get the sword away. And in general, people are not tolerant under stress, in periods of great passion, in periods of compulsion. Tolerance is a virtue that seems to thrive only in a certain leisure, in a certain cultivation. The people who show it best are the philosophers, because they thrive on diversity; or scientists, who also thrive upon the skepticism that is inherent in scientific method: "Come on with your doubts, everybody; the more the merrier." The scientific method is largely a method that consists in the development of the consequences of different hypotheses. It seems self-evident that from a point outside of a straight line only one parallel can be drawn. Along comes the Russian, Lobachevsky, and says: "I can conceive a point outside of a straight line through which more than one parallel can be drawn." Or the German, Riemann, who says: "No such line can be drawn through any point."

What is the attitude of the scientist? His business is primarily to develop the consequences of every one of these possible hypotheses. It is only because of that, because he is interested first of all in the play of ideas according to the rules of the game, that he can afford to be tolerant —to be hospitable to all sorts of denials and doubts.

In matters of religion we cannot so easily be tolerant. Suppose I know on the authority of the Koran that certain things are true, and somebody comes along and doubts it. I cannot listen to his doubts forever. Heretics generally talk too much anyway. The most important thing is that the true faith shall be maintained. Tolerance appears to be a sin under those conditions.

So it is with other matters of great importance, e.g., economic interest. Where the pressure is strong upon us, tolerance is not an easy thing to practice. And so what you have is that, in the course of various civilizations which have appeared in history, the fine flower of tolerance has appeared only rarely, and I do not think it is likely ever to become a permanent acquisition of human nature. Tolerance is the result of unusually favorable circumstances and training. Where a man can afford to care more for the rules of the game than for any particular result, he can be tolerant. The chivalrous knight and the genuine scientist show how this attitude is conditioned.

Can such a thing become universal? I do not think so. Consider, for example, the scientists as a body of citizens. Could it be said, for instance, that a group of scientists are politically more liberal than other men? I think on the whole they divide like the rest of us. Are the scientists as a body more liberal on the subject of religion? Perhaps a little, but not very much. After all, even a scientist devoted to the search for truth is tolerant only in those particular scientific lines in which he happens to be an expert. He knows the difficulty of being certain about the complex facts he has studied, and therefore he has a certain amount of skepticism; but outside of his own field he is as dogmatic as anybody else, because he is likely to know as little.

So it seems to me that since a generous stock of ignorance is one of the fundamental equipments with which the Creator has endowed all human beings, tolerance will always be a very rare phenomenon. Therefore, a civilization that depends upon tolerance is always in a very precarious condition. It may thrive for a hundred years or more, but it is inherently frail like the bloom of a flower.

The enemy of tolerance is fanaticism, the opposite of liberalism. The root of fanaticism is impatience with contradiction, and that impatience goes very deep into the roots of human nature. Watch boys in New York, for instance, on the 16th of September and their attitude towards the man who persists in wearing a straw hat. Or suppose somebody were to appear in the streets of Washington wearing clothes such as respectable senators wore in ancient Rome: irritation would soon express itself. It is to be seen when somebody pronounces words in an unaccustomed way. In our elemental reactions we are irritated by the unfamiliar, the uncouth, the unknown. We do not feel at home and are thrown out of gear by departures from the usual order of things. Such irritations may accumulate and lead to an explosion, especially if someone comes along and capitalizes —or certain widespread experiences capitalize—them.

Once, as I was sitting in a car, a young man back of me—a very tall and handsome man—was talking to a girl, and he was complaining very bitterly that there was no chance for anybody who was not a Jew to get along in New York City. I sympathized with him very much because he really felt deeply distressed. He had to explain to this lady why he was not so successful as she would like him to be. Here was an occasion in which all the irritations of his daily life were capitalized and accumulated, and the explosion was noticeable and voluminous. This seems to me to be the kind of stuff out of which race or group conflicts are made. Such irritations become organized as economic conflict, or religious conflict, or something of that sort. They form the substance which explodes if some one issue arises to touch off the fuse.

That is, in general, why I believe that civilization of the type that I have called liberal has no assurance of survival.

STUDY QUESTIONS

1. This essay should be contrasted with Rossiter's statement on the basic beliefs of conservatism. How do Cohen and Rossiter differ in their views of the nature of man, the role of the state, the desirable virtues, the values most deserving of protection and encouragement?

2. Rossiter and Cohen agree that provision must be made for social change. However, they do display some disagreement in this area. What is it?

3. According to Cohen, how do liberals and conservatives differ in their attitudes toward knowledge?

4. In spite of his belief in human achievement, Cohen admits that humanity in general is characterized by certain failings. What are they?

5. Cohen does not believe that liberal civilizations are likely to survive. If you disagree with him, write a theme expressing your opinion and supporting it with arguments based on the nature of liberal civilizations.

6. Cohen says comparatively little about the liberal attitude toward social organization and government. Write a theme stating the liberal philosophy of society. Rossiter's essay on conservatism may supply some useful approaches to the subject.

The Nature of Man*

Herbert J. Muller

The power to choose and carry out his own purposes may be held the essential condition of man's claim to peculiar dignity and worth. This is a disputable claim, especially in view of the use he has made of this power in recent times. It raises further questions. Is man actually free to choose his own purposes? If so, is he fit for freedom? Does he really want to be independent? Such questions in turn force a broader, more fundamental one: What is the essential nature of man? Implicit in all ethical and political theory, as in all the higher religions, is some conception of human nature. Any serious thought about what is good for man logically requires some idea of what he is good for. And here is the beginning of a deeper confusion.

In our own tradition the oldest, most persistent definition of man—older than Plato—has split him in two, conceiving him as an immortal soul somehow imprisoned in flesh. Christian thought intensified this dualism, magnifying both the beast and the angel in man. He was a fallen creature, a cesspool of natural depravity; and he was nevertheless potentially fit for an eternity of bliss with his Heavenly Father, in whose image he had been created. Secular thinkers then seized upon either of his dual aspects as the fundamental truth about him. To Hobbes he was incorrigibly selfish and aggressive, always lusting after power, and could be made obedient only by fear. To the philosophers of the Enlightenment he was naturally good and potentially still better, perfectible by virtue of being a rational animal, and therefore deserving of freedom. In the last century he was studied much more intensively as history became a major interest and the new sciences of man got under way—psychology, sociology, anthropology. As a result we now have an immense body of knowledge, and a profounder confusion than ever before. Having gone through the mill of Darwin, Nietzsche, Marx, Freud, Pareto, and Dewey, looked into the mirror of Zola, Dostoyevsky, D. H. Lawrence, Joyce, Kafka, and Sartre, modern man may be forgiven some uncertainty about his being. And these radically different conceptions of human nature not only have as different theoretical consequences for the good life and the good society, but make some difference in man's actual behavior. Although the ordinary man has a certain toughness of spirit that enables him to resist his mentors, he wants to be "natural," and his common sense is a tissue of more or less unconscious theory about his nature. He may violently resent criticism of his self-image.

The confusion is not hopeless, however. Much of it is due to an insistence on strictly undemonstrable assumptions, such as man's possession of an immortal soul, and more especially to an arbitrary selection of some one potentiality of human nature as its "essence." The fact remains that we do have an immense body of reliable knowledge, in particular the advantage of historical and anthropological perspectives that make it fairly easy to discount the many oversimplified definitions of man. It is possible, I think, to reach an agreement upon some broad generalizations —not broad enough to include all the ideal possibilities cherished by many men, but adequate as premises for a study of human freedom, and even surprisingly helpful in avoiding common confusion. I am accordingly stating as objective truths, not mere hypotheses or articles of faith, the premises that man is a social animal, an animal with unique powers of mind, and therefore a culture-building animal. Through the development of culture, which long tended to obscure the individual, he eventually realized that he was also an animal with a distinctive capacity for individuality, or personality.

That he is an animal I take it is unquestioned. This is the body, the flesh, the beast in him that believers in his immortal destiny are the first to emphasize. With other animals he shares such basic drives as hunger and sex, such basic emotions as fear and rage, and all the physical limits on freedom. He can also enjoy sensations of physical well-being, take pleasure in his kinship with other forms of life, feel at home in the natural world. Everyone knows these elemental pleasures and pains of the flesh, the beginnings of good and evil, but lofty thinkers tend to slight them. They have often sought a freedom from all bodily desire, under the aegis of disembodied reason or spirit. Gratified by the thought that man cannot live on bread alone, they may forget that man cannot live without it, that untold millions have died for want of it, and that today most of the world's population still have to live without enough of it. They may see nothing very bad in bodily suffering, or even view health with some suspicion.

That man is a social animal should be as plain. In this respect he is still akin to the many other animals who live in flocks, herds, swarms, and schools, not to mention the highly developed insect societies. The "state of nature" is for man a social state if only because of the prolonged helplessness of the human infant. As far back as we can see him, in prehistoric caves, we find him living in groups; and as he emerges more clearly we see him differing from other animals in that he takes care not only of his young but his old, even his dead. Nowhere do we see the anarchic individualism, the endless war of all against all, that Hobbes pictured as his natural state, and Schopenhauer assumed was his most natural tendency. Looking to the unformed child—the little savage in our midst—we see him eager to learn all kinds of rules, and indeed to make them up.

Even so, many "realists" still assume that man is essentially an anti-social animal, an egotist whose oldest, deepest instincts are hostile to law and order. Such assumptions grew out of the traditional emphasis on the natural depravity of man, and grew more plausible in a highly competitive society devoted to the pursuit of wealth and power. They took on the appearance of scientific authority from evolutionary thought, with its early emphasis on the constant struggle for survival. They were confirmed by Freud, who saw a blind self-seeking and mutual antagonism as the primal drive in the unconscious, described conscience as "merely the dread of society," and regarded civilization as a ceaseless struggle against the state of nature. And there is plainly some truth in such views, which in complacent periods may be the truth that most needs to be said. Any parent knows that the human child is not a born angel, trailing clouds of glory, and that he likes to break rules too. The best friends of man have always known that he has selfish, egotistical, unsocial tendencies. From their different point of view champions of individual freedom have likewise assumed a basic hostility between the individual and society.

Yet the historical evidence overwhelmingly confirms the natural sociality of man. Almost all societies, from the most primitive to the most civilized, have emphasized duties much more than rights or liberties, and almost all their members have accepted these duties without protest. The inconstant creature feared by political philosophers has generally been constant in obedience, often submitting to what may strike us as wholly arbitrary, unnecessary constraints on his selfish interests. From the evolutionary point of view, the struggle for survival has been primarily a struggle between species, not individuals, and man has succeeded primarily by co-operating, not fighting with his fellows. Today we overlook the extraordinary extent of his co-operative behavior—co-operation required by organized competition—because it is less conspicuous and dramatic than competitive, aggressive behavior, or simply because we have come to take it for granted. If men are naturally antagonistic, as Freud believed, they have none the less succeeded so well in living together that the "abnormal" individual is the one who does not accept the constraints of the group. As for the champions of individual freedom, they are a rare type historically, and have rarely been popular. Their ardor testifies that the impulse to accept and obey is much stronger than the impulse to rebel.

To define man as a social animal is therefore no more idealistic than to call a bee a social insect. His sociality does indeed provide a natural basis for idealism, in that his "selfish" interests always include the interests of some other selves, the need of warmth and affection. It involves a natural sympathy and natural piety, as in the care of his dead, which may flower in ideals of our common humanity, or of "natural rights"; it is not based primarily on anything so uncertain as enlightened self-interest. But this is also to say that it is generally unreasoned. Another word for man's constancy is inertia, another word for sociality is herd instinct. Today the common word for it is conformism. It can be said that most men are not intelligent enough to pursue their own interests, not courageous enough to have self-esteem. It cannot be said that sociality means simple fraternity. Men have never loved their neighbors as themselves, still less all other men. Their natural loyalty to their own group has always tended to make them suspicious of outsiders, hostile to other groups. Societies have most clearly exhibited the selfishness and aggressiveness that have been attributed to the anti-social nature of man, and conflicts between them have been fiercer because their members have usually been willing to sacrifice their personal interests to the cause, even to die for the group.

Hence "realists" may still find sufficient propensity to evil, or, if they prefer, Original Sin. My point is merely that it is not realistic to describe man as an animal who has been driven into society in defiance of his natural instincts, and who can be held there only by force or through fear. The life of the lone wolf is no more natural to him than the life of the hermit. In the tensions of our own society, which has set up an ideal of individualism, encouraged competition in education and recreation as well as business, demanded an unprecedented extent of co-operation, achieved an unprecedented degree of organization, and provided an unprecedented wealth of opportunity for self-realization and for maladjustment, it is both more tempting and more misleading to assume an inveterate hostility between the individual and society. The rugged individualism that alarms some critics and the lack of individuality that depresses others are alike social products. Today, as in the past, society dominates the great majority of its members. From its domination arise the major issues of freedom.

Also beyond dispute, and a source of incessant dispute, are the powers of mind that most clearly distinguish man from all other animals. In physiological terms, he has by all odds the most complex, elaborate nervous system, centered in the brain, which gives him abilities different not only in degree but in kind from the intelligence displayed by other "higher" animals. Some animals can solve problems, and many—down to chickens, fish, and cockroaches—can learn from experience after a fashion; only man can consciously remember what he learns, conceptualize it, put it into words, teach it to his young. With his power of reasoning he has as distinctive capacities of imagination, sensibility, and insight. His consciousness is a stream of perceptions, intuitions, feelings, fantasies, impulses, thoughts unimaginably different from whatever goes on in an animal's mind. As Dewey observed, the idiomatic meanings of *mind* give a more comprehensive, just idea of its nature than do the formal definitions of logicians and most psychologists. I have states of mind, good and bad; I make up or change my mind; I keep things on it, and put it on matters; I may lose it, though without losing my consciousness or my nervous system; I may be of two minds or half a mind; I mind my step, mind my own business; I mind my children and make them mind me; I mind if I am deprived of my freedom. Ultimately *mind* involves the vague but real power of the "human spirit," which seeks the good, the true, and the beautiful, and inspires the exalted idea of soul. Immediately it also involves less agreeable possibilities. Because man can make conscious choices, he may make unintelligent, ridiculous, even fatal choices. No other animal is so stupid as a human fool.

Only with drastic qualifications, then, can man be defined as a "rational animal." His experience is much broader and richer, untidier and wilder, than a pure rationalist would have it. His basic impulses—to eat, to make love, to rest, or simply to go on living—are all non-rational; his behavior is often positively irrational, more "brutal" than the purely instinctive behavior of brutes. Still, this is to judge him by rational standards, and finally to emphasize his capacity for rational thought and behavior. The capacity is most apparent in the practical activities by which he has gained power over the natural environment, but it is also implicit in his co-operation with his fellows. In every known society he has recognized the principle of *ought* by assuming responsibilities, committing himself to duties at the expense of his own sweet pleasure. In every society he is *held* responsible, punished when he does what he ought not to do. In civilized societies those who insist on the basic irrationality of man still lay down the law for him and insist that he obey it, stay in his place. Such demands on him are grounds for the assumption that he ought to be treated as potentially a rational animal, not a brute. If thought does not make the whole dignity of man, as Pascal declared, his capacity for thought in the broadest sense remains the clearest index of his humanity, the basis of his claims to dignity and worth—and so to the right of freedom.

Together with his sociality, it has made him a culture-building animal. Whereas every generation of apes begins and ends where the last generation did, without benefit of the wisdom of their ancestors, the children of men begin by acquiring the knowledge, skills, and arts accumulated over the countless generations before them. With these they absorb the whole way of life of the fathers. And here the most pertinent fact is the most conspicuous one in an anthropological and historical view—the extraordinary diversity of the world's cultures. It makes plain what is never plain to men in any given society. Man lives primarily in a symbolical world, a world of his own creation. Always set in a natural environment, always compelled to deal with natural forces, he gets from his society all his ruling ideas about the nature of the world and how to deal with it. His basic "reality" is not physical but cultural, spiritual. He begins learning metaphysics in his cradle. If he becomes a professional metaphysician, he is more likely to lose sight of the cultural facts of life.

So we might pause to consider the familiar term *nature,* which is as ambiguous and confusing as any in the language. His mentors have often told man to live "in accordance with Nature," finding in Nature the source of his duties and more recently of his rights. So capitalized, the word means something like God and enjoins some ethical code, but it only veils the mystery of the nature and the will of God; what code it enjoins will depend upon the speaker and his culture. Another common meaning of *nature,* the unbaptized universe and everything in it, is no more helpful; in this sense nothing can be contrary to nature, whatever man chooses to do is a natural event in the universal show. In the more common sense of the external world, everything in the universe apart from man, *nature* becomes more misleading. It may now mean a bountiful provider, a haven from care, a playfield, a bloody battleground, a constant menace, an enemy of all man's works—a spectacle beautiful or grim, serene or wild, majestic or awful; but if the familiar counsel to "follow nature" means to follow instincts, live like other animals, it is positively inhuman so far as it is feasible at all. At best, the simple idea of going back to nature simply obscures the real problem, the ultimate concern of all philosophy and religion—the problem of what is the good life for man, a creature for whom all kinds of behavior, from loving to killing, are on the face of it "natural."

Immediately it obscures the basic fact that "human" nature is a second nature—largely made by man, not simply born in him. Whatever instincts he is born with may be cultivated, blended, modified, diverted, or suppressed in so many different ways that they appear to be bare potentialities, raw materials for the unconscious artistry of culture. The ruling drive in one society may be a matter of indifference to another, a positive abnormality to still another. Hence when men grew self-conscious and sophisticated enough to inquire into their nature, their culture suggested the answers; and the endless confusion began. In the Western world the answers grew more diverse as society grew more complex and unsettled, but the confusion was intensified by the nature of thinkers—their common craving for simplicity, the One instead of the Many. Bent on reducing the many apparent motives to a single ruling motive, they have variously defined it as self-interest, the will to power, sexual drive, the craving for freedom, the craving for security. Today many still overlook the plain implications of the diversity of human culture, the radically different ways of life that alike seem natural to men brought up in them. The most solemn injunctions about the needs of Man usually spring from the parochial needs of some contemporaries.

We can still make out basic uniformities, however, else we could not speak of *man* at all. Men everywhere have a common structure, common needs and desires, common capacities; everywhere they have to cope with the same exigencies of birth, growth, sex, toil, suffering, and death. Their common mortality is the strongest reminder that their common humanity is not a mere ideal, but a fact. Hence even the apparent artificialities of culture are to some extent natural outgrowths of common potentialities. A man might think it patently unnatural for women to paint their fingernails and toenails—were it not that women have always been doing such things, as far back as we can see; and men have seemed no less interested in improving on God's or nature's handiwork. The universal vanity involves the common possession of an aesthetic sense. The rise of civilization brought ways of life that would seem still more artificial, except that all along the most natural behavior for man was evidently not to follow nature but to master it, adapt it to his own purposes. Finally, in the Greek world, there emerged the ideal of culture in the high sense of the word, the conscious cultivation of human nature and its capacities for the pursuit of truth, goodness, and beauty. With this emerged the choicest and the most troublesome product of civilization—the self-conscious individual. The dignity of man, wrote G. H. Mead, consists in the fact that when he calls upon himself he finds himself at home.

In the Western world this fortunate caller has dared as never before, dared even to stand alone. He has made extreme claims for himself. He has demanded political freedom, to participate in the determination of the group purposes, the means to the common good; individual freedom within the state to carry out his private purposes, realize his own good; freedom against the state, to assure his inalienable rights. He has proclaimed the supreme value of personality, even when he no longer identifies it with an immortal soul. He has declared that the individual must be regarded as an end in himself—the state exists only to serve him.

He is therefore apt to forget that he is a parvenu in history. Whatever consciousness other animals may have is certainly not self-consciousness. If man in primitive societies ever thinks of calling upon himself, he seldom finds his *self;* he has little consciousness of individuality apart from his group, and less of rights against it. In most civilizations it never occurred to men to think of consciousness as intrinsically individual, or of individuality as the quintessence of human nature. Hence, too, this parvenu has been liable to extravagance. His rise in the world has inspired an atomic individualism that represents society as a kind of artificial bond, created by self-conscious individuals for the sake of enlightened self-interest, with the policeman on the corner to keep watch on the unenlightened; a rugged individualism that makes self-interest a moral principle, and tends to narrow and impoverish individuality by an exclusive devotion to economic ends; a romantic individualism, or cult of genius, that conceives individuality as the sum or essence of what distinguishes or separates a man from his fellows, excluding all that unites them. It becomes necessary to repeat the commonplace that man is a social animal. His very consciousness is a social product; he becomes aware of himself only through his relations with other selves. Likewise his individuality can be realized only in a society, and a rich one achieved only in a highly developed society. The gospel of individualism is itself a product of a free society.

Today, however, students of society are most likely to ignore the individual or to deny his importance. Anthropologists have generally treated him as a mere carrier of culture, which has its own laws and seems to carry on by itself. Historians concentrate on the deep, involuntary processes of social change, and in reacting against the Hero theories of history they often explicitly minimize the role of individuals. Sociologists likewise concentrate on impersonal processes that may appear to be automatic. Some have declared that the individual is only a cell in the social organism, and that as a creature having an independent reality he is a "discredited hypothesis"; more have buried him in statistical abstractions like the "average man"—a monster who has 2½ children. Many students of the life and work of even the great men of the past study them primarily as products of their age or examples of major tendencies. It appears that the deepest meaning of a play by Shakespeare or Racine must be the thought or feeling of most ordinary men of their time.

I therefore judge that what most needs to be stressed today is the reality and the unique importance of the individual. Physiologically, man is the most highly individualized of animals, and as he developed his latent powers of mind he would naturally become more so. Individual differences have made a great deal of difference, even if during most of his history man has put little stock in any except military prowess; for whatever progress he has made must ultimately be traced to them. Knowing nothing about the origins of culture, we can still be confident that it was a very gradual, unplanned growth, not the conscious creation of farsighted individuals; yet it did depend upon the discoveries and inventions of exceptional individuals. "Society" did not dream up the idea of pots and looms and wheels. With the rise of civilization came a massive growth that may look involuntary and certainly was beyond the understanding and control of the individual; yet it involved more conscious doing and making, in which gifted individuals had freer play for creative achievement. If society now made possible a Socrates, a Confucius, an Archimedes, a Christ, it still cannot claim full credit for their greatness—it produced chiefly ordinary men. And as we begin to trace the growth of freedom, it becomes more necessary to keep an eye on the individual. Whether or not we regard him as an end in himself, the freedom of a society is meaningful only as it is exercised by individuals, and can be observed only in their behavior.

A more debatable issue, however, is raised by the democratic tradition that has made so much of the individual and done so much for him. Eighteenth-century philosophers who helped to shape this tradition commonly assumed that man is a rational animal who has not only a natural right to freedom but a natural passion for it. History hardly supports this congenial idea: until recently the masses of men have not demanded such a right or displayed such a passion. History suggests rather that Dostoyevsky's Grand Inquisitor may have been right. For the great majority of man, he said, the freedom of choice offered by Christ is an intolerable burden; what they want and need first of all is bread, and then "miracle, mystery, and authority." Now psychologists and sociologists are asserting that the ruling passion of man is for security. Hitler may have been sincere when he proclaimed himself an emancipator: "Providence has ordained that I should be the greatest liberator of humanity. I am freeing man from the demands of a freedom and personal independence that only a few can sustain."

STUDY QUESTIONS

1. Muller says that man is an animal who resembles other animals in some ways and differs from them in others. What points of difference and resemblance does he mention?

2. What important point made by Susanne K. Langer in "Language and Thought" does Muller use as a part of his argument about the nature of man?

3. What relation does Muller see between culture and the concept that nature may be regarded as a guide to behavior?

4. What is Muller's view of the fatalism vs. heroism issue discussed in Schlesinger's "Decline of Heroes"?

5. At the end of this selection, Muller refers to the view that ordinary men do not want freedom and cannot exercise it satisfactorily. Discuss this question, being sure to begin with a good definition of "freedom."

6. Muller says that man is properly guided both by accumulated cultural ideas and by individualism. Are these contradictory? How can they be reconciled with each other?

PART FOUR

Popular

Culture

1. THE POPULAR MEDIA

British, French, and American Films*

Martha Wolfenstein and Nathan Leites

The dramatic productions of a particular culture at a particular time, or even over a considerable period, tend to exhibit a distinctive
plot configuration. This configuration gives the various individual dramas
the distinctive atmosphere which we can recognize as pervading them all.
Obviously a group of plots or even a single plot is exceedingly complex.
Nevertheless a certain basic plan may be discerned: we can see that one
pattern from among the range of dramatic alternatives has been chosen
for major emphasis.

Looking back over the films which we have been discussing, we shall
now indicate briefly the essential plot configuration which distinguishes
each of the three groups of films with which we have been concerned, the
British, the French, and the American.

The essential plot in British films is that of the conflict of forbidden
impulses with conscience. Either one of the contending forces may win out
and we may follow the guilt-ridden course of the wrong-doer or experience
the regrets of the lost opportunity virtuously renounced. In the happy
instance, wishes may coincide with the demands of virtue and a fatherly
fate will reward the good children. The world is presided over by authorities who are wise and good and against whom the wilful and unlucky
may contend. But the counterpart of these authorities is also implanted
in the individual soul; the evil-doer will be self-condemned as well as
pursued by the authorities.

British films evoke the feeling that danger lies in ourselves, especially

* From *Movies: A Psychological Study* by Martha Wolfenstein and
Nathan Leites. Copyright, 1950, by The Free Press. Reprinted by permission of The Free Press.

in our impulses of destructiveness. In a cautionary way they show what happens if these impulses break through, particularly where the weak become the victims. Thus they afford a catharsis at the same time that they demonstrate the value of defenses by showing the consequences of their giving way. The character who embodies dangerous impulses is apt to be a superior person, one who should be able to control his own destructiveness, and in whom it is all the more terrible to see it get out of hand. Violence is not simply a destructive force but a breaking both of the pattern within the individual personality and of the order which prevails in his world. The complete murderer is one who disputes the rule of just authorities, in his pride setting himself up as an arbiter of life and death, and doomed by his own struggle. While violence is on one side related to a whole social framework, it has also another side of intimacy and isolation. The act of violence is slowly prepared and may be preceded by special closeness between murderer and victim. Violence is thus often pervaded by the tenderness which in ordinary circumstances serves to ward it off.

Self-accusation is prominent in British films and may be evoked by wishes no less than by acts. Characters feel guilty when circumstances beyond their control produce fatalities coinciding with unconscious wishes. Lovers tempted to overstep lawful bounds draw back alarmed by guilty apprehensions. However, the pure in heart find that the authorities of this world and the next are their allies. The hero, temporarily distressed by a false charge, discovers that the police know all along that he is innocent and are quietly working side by side with him. The fine young couple who for the moment fear that fate has brought them together only to separate them learn that even death can be set aside so that they can be joined.

British films preserve, in a modern idiom (the peculiarities of which we shall not analyze here), many of the themes of Shakespearean drama. There are heroes who like Macbeth are carried away by criminal impulses and then punished; heroes who like Hamlet suffer pangs of conscience for crimes they did not commit. And there are young couples briefly and playfully threatened by the same fate which intended all along to wed them as Prospero did with his daughter and Ferdinand. The image of a perfect father, like Hamlet Sr., still presides over the scene, and constitutes the model for an exacting conscience.

In the major plot configuration of French films, human wishes are opposed by the nature of life itself. The main issue is not one of inner or outer conflicts in which we may win or lose, be virtuous or get penalized. It is a contest in which we all lose in the end and the problem is to learn to accept it. There are inevitable love disappointments, the world is not arranged to collaborate with our wishes, people grow older, lovers become fathers, the old must give way to the young, and eventually everyone dies. The desire for justice is ranged alongside other human wishes which are more likely than not to be frustrated. French films repeatedly present these aspects of life so that we may inure ourselves to them and master the pain they cause us. It is the Mithridates principle of taking a little poison every day so that by and by one becomes less vulnerable to it.

It is in keeping with this tendency that French films so often take as their central character an aging man. He is not the triumphant hero whom we wish to become nor the criminal hero whom we fear to become, but simply what we must become: old. In him we see concentrated disappointment, lost hopes, change, decline of physical powers, and imminent death. We can observe his sadly comic struggle against his fate as he refuses to realize that he is no longer eligible to be the lover of a young girl, or learn from him the compensations of later life as he renounces the role of lover for that of father. He helps to reconcile us both to our past and to our future. We see in him our own father no longer dominant and powerful but a sharer of our common human fate. He who was in possession of things which we as children were denied is now seen suffering disappointments more grevious than we suffered then. In making peace with him we also make peace with our own future.

The young hero no less than the aging one in French films is likely to be disappointed. We see him in his pursuit of a beloved woman about whom he gradually learns much that is contrary to his wishes. He is not spared the discovery that this woman is involved with another man, and we in following his fate may work through our own similar disillusionments. Knowledge which at first glance increases sorrow in the end mitigates the pain which, we see, could not be avoided.

We must learn that the world is not arranged to fulfil our demands for justice any more than to satisfy our longings for happiness. Human agencies of justice are obtuse and inefficient, and there are no divine ones. We are shown how the innocent are convicted, how the guilty are exonerated; they may even confess without being believed. Where justice is done, it is made clear that this is a happy accident. A clue uncovered by chance a moment earlier or later makes the difference between life and death for an innocent man. No one is watching over him, nor is he able to be master of his own fate. Things may turn out happily. The suicidal bullet misses, the brain tumor may be operable, the hostages facing execution may be rescued at the last moment, the aging couple may find an unexpected revival of pleasure in life. The pleasure, no less sweet for that, is tinged with sadness; we know it is only a reprieve.

The major plot configuration in American films contrasts with both the British and the French. Winning is terrifically important and always possible though it may be a tough fight. The conflict is not an internal one; it is not our own impulses which endanger us nor our own scruples that stand in our way. The hazards are all external, but they are not rooted in the nature of life itself. They are the hazards of a particular situation with which we find ourselves confronted. The hero is typically in a

strange town where there are apt to be dangerous men and women of ambiguous character and where the forces of law and order are not to be
relied on. If he sizes up the situation correctly, if he does not go off half-
cocked but is still able to beat the other fellow to the punch once he is
sure who the enemy is, if he relies on no one but himself, if he demands
sufficient evidence of virtue from the girl, he will emerge triumphant.
He will defeat the dangerous men, get the right girl, and show the authorities what's what.

When he is a child, he is the comic hero, showing off, blundering, cocky,
scared, called on to perform beyond his capacities, and pulling through by
surprising spurts of activity and with the help of favorable circumstances.
He is completely harmless, free from sexual or aggressive impulses, and
the world around him reflects his own innocuous character. Its threats are
playful and its reproaches ridiculous. When he is a man he is the melodrama hero and the world changes to reflect his changed potentialities;
it becomes dangerous and seriously accusing, and launches him on his
fighting career. The majority of the melodramas show him coming
through successfully. A minority reveal various perils which lie off the
main track; they are cautionary tales. The hero may succumb to his attacker; this is his bad dream. The men around him may be less dangerous
than he suspects. Under the delusion that he attacks in self-defense, he
may initiate hostilities; then he will lose. In this case he is crazy. Without being deluded to this extent, out of greed and overconfidence, he may
try to get away with murder; he commits the crime of which he is usually
only suspected and he has to pay for it. The girl may turn out to be worse
than he believed. He will have to go off without her; then he is lonely. He
may not be able to produce anyone on whom to pin the blame for his
crimes of which he is falsely accused; then he is a victim of circumstances.
If circumstances fail to collaborate with his need to blame someone else,
he may even end by blaming himself. These are the various hazards
which the usual melodrama hero safely passes on the way.

The fantasy which provides for defeating dangerous men, winning the
right girl, and coming out in the clear, is produced under the auspices of
two major mechanisms: projection and denial. Self-accusations are embodied in the blundering police and destructive impulses in the unpro-
voked attacker. The beloved woman seems to be involved with another
man but investigation ends in the gratifying demonstration that she never
loved anyone but the hero. The love disappointment to which the French
movie hero is repeatedly exposed is here denied.

The external world may be dangerous but manageable, or, at other
times, uncontrollable but gratifying. Where things seem to get out of
control the results turn out to be wish-fulfilling. The overturning automobile throws the girl into the hero's arms, the rocking boat tosses the
heroine's rival into the waves. The world that is uncontrollable but gratifying expresses an omnipotence fantasy while at the same time eliminating

guilt. As soon as an internal problem is replaced by an external one, we can see the promise of success. The hero suffering from kleptomania becomes involved in investigating the activities of a gang of thieves; the amnesiac hero pursues his memories only long enough to unearth clues of someone else's crime before he rises impatiently from the psychiatrist's couch to embark on a successful detective job.

The world, which is not effectively policed, does not need to be policed at all. The hero, the self-appointed investigator and agent of justice, is able to set things right independently. The world thus appears as a kind of workable anarchic arrangement where, although hostilities are far from eliminated, life need not be nasty, brutish, and short, at any rate not for anyone we care about. The unofficial supervisors of private morals, the comic onlookers, are just as superfluous as the police. No one has any intention of doing anything naughty; only the mistakenly suspicious onlooker fails to recognize the natural goodness of the clean-cut young people.

American film plots are pervaded by false appearances. In this shadowy but temporarily vivid guise, the content of what is projected and denied tends to reappear. It is in false appearances that the forbidden wishes are realized which the hero and heroine so rarely carry into action. In a false appearance the heroine is promiscuous, the hero is a murderer, the young couple carry on an illicit affair, two men friends share the favors of a woman. This device makes it possible for us to eat our cake and have it, since we can enjoy the suggested wish-fulfilments without empathic guilt; we know that the characters with whom we identify have not done anything. The contention of American films is that we should not feel guilty for mere wishes. The hero and heroine are threatened with penalties for the incriminating appearance but in the end are absolved. The misguided police or the foolish onlooker in comedies convey a self-accusation from which the hero and heroine struggle to dissociate themselves, a vestige of archaic conscience which is to be dispensed with.

What the plot unfolds is a process of proof. Something is undone rather than done: the false appearance is negated. The hero and heroine do not become committed to any irretrievable act whose consequences they must bear. Nor do they usually undergo any character transformation, ennoblement or degradation, gain or loss of hope, acceptance of a new role or the diminution and regrets of age. They succeed in proving what they were all along. They emerge from the shadow of the false appearance. What has changed is other people's impressions of them. In so far as the hero and heroine may be unsure of who or what they are except as they see themselves mirrored in the eyes of others, they have succeeded in establishing for themselves a desirable identity. In so far as they struggle against a projected archaic conscience that persecutes the wish as if it were the act, they win a victory for a more tolerant and discriminating morality.

STUDY QUESTIONS

1. This selection is taken from a point very near the end of an entire book in which the authors have developed their analysis of films. They are concerned here to draw broad general conclusions. How do they support their generalizations here? Could different generalizations be supported by a different selection of evidence? Do the authors' generalizations seem reasonably valid? Explain.

2. In what ways do the authors find foreign films more realistic and mature than American ones?

3. It is pointed out in this discussion that representatives of morality and law-enforcement agents have a different character in the films of the different countries. What are these differences?

4. Do you see any relation between the American pattern of life and the plot characteristics of American movies? What can American movie heroes do that seems unnatural or forbidden for the heroes of foreign films?

5. Do you consider these generalizations about movie plots largely correct or incorrect? Write a theme giving your opinion of one or all of them, basing your criticism, whether favorable or unfavorable, upon your own experience with movies.

6. Do the movies generally give a realistic or honest view of life? It is important, in discussing this subject to limit yourself to one or two aspects, such as the portrayal of love or old age or business or sports or family life.

The Gangster as Tragic Hero*

Robert Warshow

America, as a social and political organization, is committed to a cheerful view of life. It could not be otherwise. The sense of tragedy is a luxury of aristocratic societies, where the fate of the individual is not conceived of as having a direct and legitimate political importance, being determined by a fixed and supra-political—that is, non-controversial—moral order or fate. Modern equalitarian societies, however, whether democratic or authoritarian in their political forms, always base themselves on the claim that they are making life happier; the avowed function of the modern state, at least in its ultimate terms, is not only to regulate social relations, but also to determine the quality and the possibilities of human life in general. Happiness thus becomes the chief political issue—in a sense, the only political issue—and for that reason it can never be treated as an issue at all. If an American or a Russian is unhappy, it im-

* "The Gangster as Tragic Hero" by Robert Warshow, copyright, 1948, by *Partisan Review*. Reprinted by permission.

plies a certain reprobation of his society, and therefore, by a logic of which we can all recognize the necessity, it becomes an obligation of citizenship to be cheerful; if the authorities find it necessary, the citizen may even be compelled to make a public display of his cheerfulness on important occasions, just as he may be conscripted into the army in time of war.

Naturally, this civic responsibility rests most strongly upon the organs of mass culture. The individual citizen may still be permitted his private unhappiness so long as it does not take on political significance, the extent of this tolerance being determined by how large an area of private life the society can accommodate. But every production of mass culture is a public act and must conform with accepted notions of the public good. Nobody seriously questions the principle that it is the function of mass culture to maintain public morale, and certainly nobody in the mass audience objects to having his morale maintained.[1] At a time when the normal condition of the citizen is a state of anxiety, euphoria spreads over our culture like the broad smile of an idiot. In terms of attitudes towards life, there is very little difference between a "happy" movie like *Good News,* which ignores death and suffering, and a "sad" movie like *A Tree Grows in Brooklyn,* which uses death and suffering as incidents in the service of a higher optimism.

But, whatever its effectiveness as a source of consolation and a means of pressure for maintaining "positive" social attitudes, this optimism is fundamentally satisfying to no one, not even to those who would be most disoriented without its support. Even within the area of mass culture, there always exists a current of opposition, seeking to express by whatever means are available to it that sense of desperation and inevitable failure which optimism itself helps to create. Most often, this opposition is confined to rudimentary or semi-literate forms: in mob politics and journalism, for example, or in certain kinds of religious enthusiasm. When it does enter the field of art, it is likely to be disguised or attenuated: in an unspecific form of expression like jazz, in the basically harmless nihilism of the Marx Brothers, in the continually reasserted strain of homelessness that often seems to be the real meaning of the soap opera. The gangster film is remarkable in that it fills the need for disguise (though not sufficiently to avoid arousing uneasiness) without requiring any serious distortion. From its beginnings, it has been a consistent and astonishingly complete presentation of the modern sense of tragedy.[2]

[1] In her testimony before the House Committee on Un-American Activities, Mrs. Leila Rogers said that the movie *None But the Lonely Heart* was un-American because it was gloomy. Like so much else that was said during the unhappy investigation of Hollywood, this statement was at once stupid and illuminating. One knew immediately what Mrs. Rogers was talking about; she had simply been insensitive enough to carry her philistinism to its conclusion.

[2] Efforts have been made from time to time to bring the gangster film into

In its initial character, the gangster film is simply one example of the movies' constant tendency to create fixed dramatic patterns that can be repeated indefinitely with a reasonable expectation of profit. One gangster film follows another as one musical or one Western follows another. But this rigidity is not necessarily opposed to the requirements of art. There have been very successful types of art in the past which developed such specific and detailed conventions as almost to make individual examples of the type interchangeable. This is true, for example, of Elizabethan revenge tragedy and Restoration comedy.

For such a type to be successful means that its conventions have imposed themselves upon the general consciousness and become the accepted vehicles of a particular set of attitudes and a particular aesthetic effect. One goes to any individual example of the type with very definite expectations, and originality is to be welcomed only in the degree that it intensifies the expected experience without fundamentally altering it. Moreover, the relationship between the conventions which go to make up such a type and the real experience of its audience or the real facts of whatever situation it pretends to describe is of only secondary importance and does not determine its aesthetic force. It is only in an ultimate sense that the type appeals to its audience's experience of reality; much more immediately, it appeals to previous experience of the type itself: it creates its own field of reference.

Thus the importance of the gangster film, and the nature and intensity of its emotional and aesthetic impact, cannot be measured in terms of the place of the gangster himself or the importance of the problem of crime in American life. Those European movie-goers who think there is a gangster on every corner in New York are certainly deceived, but defenders of the "positive" side of American culture are equally deceived if they think it relevant to point out that most Americans have never seen a gangster. What matters is that the experience of the gangster *as an experience of art* is universal to Americans. There is almost nothing we understand better or react to more readily or with quicker intelligence. The Western film, though it seems never to diminish in popularity, is for most of us no more than the folklore of the past, familiar and understandable only because it has been repeated so often. The gangster film comes much closer. In ways that we do not easily or willingly define, the gangster speaks for us, expressing that part of the American psyche which rejects the qualities and the demands of modern life, which rejects "Americanism" itself.

The gangster is the man of the city, with the city's language and knowledge, with its queer and dishonest skills and its terrible daring, carrying his life in his hands like a placard, like a club. For everyone else, there is

---

line with the prevailing optimism and social constructiveness of our culture; *Kiss of Death* is a recent example. These efforts are usually unsuccessful; the reasons for their lack of success are interesting in themselves, but I shall not be able to discuss them here.

at least the theoretical possibility of another world—in that happier American culture which the gangster denies, the city does not really exist; it is only a more crowded and more brightly lit country—but for the gangster there is only the city; he must inhabit it in order to personify it: not the real city, but that dangerous and sad city of the imagination which is so much more important, which is the modern world. And the gangster—though there are real gangsters—is also, and primarily, a creature of the imagination. The real city, one might say, produces only criminals; the imaginary city produces the gangster: he is what we want to be and what we are afraid we may become.

Thrown into the crowd without background or advantages, with only those ambiguous skills which the rest of us—the real people of the real city—can only pretend to have, the gangster is required to make his way, to make his life and impose it on others. Usually, when we come upon him, he has already made his choice or the choice has already been made for him, it doesn't matter which: we are not permitted to ask whether at some point he could have chosen to be something else than what he is.

The gangster's activity is actually a form of rational enterprise, involving fairly definite goals and various techniques for achieving them. But this rationality is usually no more than a vague background; we know perhaps, that the gangster sells liquor or that he operates a numbers racket; often we are not given even that much information. So his activity becomes a kind of pure criminality: he *hurts* people. Certainly our response to the gangster film is most consistently and most universally a response to sadism; we gain the double satisfaction of participating vicariously in the gangster's sadism and then seeing it turned against the gangster himself.

But on another level the quality of irrational brutality and the quality of rational enterprise become one. Since we do not see the rational and routine aspects of the gangster's behavior, the practice of brutality—the quality of unmixed criminality—becomes the totality of his career. At the same time, we are always conscious that the whole meaning of this career is a drive for success: the typical gangster film presents a steady upward progress followed by a very precipitate fall. Thus brutality itself becomes at once the means to success and the content of success—a success that is defined in its most general terms, not as accomplishment or specific gain, but simply as the unlimited possibility of aggression. (In the same way, film presentations of businessmen tend to make it appear that they achieve their success by talking on the telephone and holding conferences and that success *is* talking on the telephone and holding conferences.)

From this point of view, the initial contact between the film and its audience is an agreed conception of human life: that man is a being with the possibilities of success or failure. This principle, too, belongs to the city; one must emerge from the crowd or else one is nothing. On that basis the necessity of the action is established, and it progresses by inalterable paths to the point where the gangster lies dead and the principle has been modified; there is really only one possibility—failure. The final meaning of the city is anonymity and death.

In the opening scene of *Scarface,* we are shown a successful man; we know he is successful because he has just given a party of opulent proportions and because he is called Big Louie. Through some monstrous lack of caution, he permits himself to be alone for a few moments. We understand from this immediately that he is about to be killed. No convention of the gangster film is more strongly established than this: it is dangerous to be alone. And yet the very conditions of success make it impossible not to be alone, for success is always the establishment of an *individual* preeminence that must be imposed on others, in whom it automatically arouses hatred; the successful man is an outlaw. The gangster's whole life is an effort to assert himself as an individual, to draw himself out of the crowd, and he always dies *because* he is an individual; the final bullet thrusts him back, makes him, after all, a failure. "Mother of God," says the dying Little Caesar, "is this the end of Rico?"—speaking of himself thus in the third person because what has been brought low is not the undifferentiated *man,* but the individual with a name, the gangster, the success; even to himself he is a creature of the imagination. (T. S. Eliot has pointed out that a number of Shakespeare's tragic heroes have this trick of looking at themselves dramatically; their true identity, the thing that is not destroyed when they die, is something outside themselves—not a man, but a style of life, a kind of meaning.)

At bottom, the gangster is doomed because he is under the obligation to succeed, not because the means he employs are unlawful. In the deeper layers of the modern consciousness, *all* means are unlawful, every attempt to succeed is an act of aggression, leaving one alone and guilty and defenseless among enemies; one is *punished* for success. This is our intolerable dilemma: that failure is a kind of death and success is evil and dangerous, is—ultimately—impossible. The effect of the gangster film is to embody this dilemma in the person of the gangster and resolve it by his death. The dilemma is resolved because it is *his* death, not ours. We are safe; for the moment, we can acquiesce in our failure, we can choose to fail.

STUDY QUESTIONS

1. What does Warshow think to be the relation of the gangster movie, which has considerable sadness in it, to the optimism that generally prevails in mass culture? Does his thesis seem reasonable to you? Why? Are other explanations possible? How do you think other standard types of movies or TV shows are related to our culture?

2. What does Warshow mean by saying that the gangster movie

"creates its own field of reference"? Is this true of any other art or medium of entertainment?

3. What difference is suggested by Warshow's careful use of the two words, "criminal" and "gangster"?

4. What, according to Warshow, is the "style of life" the movie gangster represents, even to himself?

5. Do you agree with Warshow that it is the function of the movie gangster to reflect our feelings of guilt and to enable us to satisfy the feeling that we should be punished for our successes? Or is it possible to apply a different interpretation to the plot of the gangster film? Write a theme explaining what emotions and attitudes you believe gangster films express.

6. Compare Warshow's conception of the tragic role of the movie gangster with Edith Hamilton's definition of tragedy.

*Epitaph for a Tough Guy**

Alistair Cooke

And just what was this new sort of hero, whose originality I have hinted at in a menacing phrase or two? Looked at after twenty years' familiarity, it is a surprise to see that he is a direct descendant of Sherlock Holmes, as indeed are most fictional private detectives invented since Conan Doyle cast the original mold: a depressed, eccentric bachelor of vast, odd knowledge, whose intelligence is poised over the plot like a dagger, which in the moment of resolution slices through the butter of the surrounding confusion. This is the elementary recipe for all the moderns, from Perry Mason to Philip Marlowe. Where Holmes knew the soil classification of the Home Counties, Bogart—sharing an unfriendly drink with Sidney Greenstreet—sees a ship slink by on the horizon and calls off the full-load displacement, overall length, gun caliber, muzzle velocity. Holmes possessed an uncanny sense of the whereabouts of distressed gentlewomen and had memorized the Paddington train schedules against the day of their rescue. Bogart knows all about hotels, from Yokohama to New York: the tactical geography of suites, connecting doors, and fire escapes, how to confuse the room clerk and evade the house dick, determine the clientele by a glance around the lobby, know who is up to no good and where she is likely to be.

The field maneuvers may be different from those in Holmes's day, and the villain is more socially mobile, but since Sir Arthur we have not changed the three essential ingredients of the private eye. He must be

* From *The Atlantic Monthly*, May, 1957. Reprinted by permission of *The Atlantic Monthly*

a bachelor, with the bachelor's harum-scarum availability at all hours. (William Powell's marriage to Myrna "Nora" Loy, a wistful concession to the family trade, fooled nobody). He must have an inconspicuous fund of curious knowledge, which in the end is always crucially relevant. He must pity the official guardians of the law.

Of course, the twentieth century has grafted some interesting personality changes on the original. Holmes was an eccentric in the Victorian sense, a man with queer hobbies—cocaine was lamentable but pardonably melodramatic—whose social code was essentially that of the ruling classes. He was, in a way, the avenging squire of the underworld ready to administer a horsewhipping to the outcasts who were never privileged by birth to receive it from their fathers. Bogart is a displaced person whose present respectability is uncertain, a classless but well-contained vagabond who is not going to be questioned about where he came from or where he is going. ("I came to Casablanca for the waters." "But there are no waters in Casablanca." "I was misinformed.")

As a Victorian bachelor-hero, Holmes must be presumed to be asexual. Bogart too is a lone wolf, but with a new and equal stress on the noun. His general view of women implies that he was brought up, sexually speaking, no earlier than the twenties. Hence he is unshockable and offhand, and, one gathers, a very devil with the women, who is saved from absurdity by never having time to prove it. ("Sorry, angel, I have a pressing date with a fat man.") Unlike Holmes, he cannot claim even the castle of a carefully cluttered set of rooms. He is always on the move, and his only domestic base is a fairly seedy hotel bedroom with an unmade bed (this is called audience identification, and to tell the truth is the sort of independent base of operations most college boys and many rueful husbands would like to have). Yet somehow, somewhere, in his baffling past he learned the habits of the *haut monde*. And his audience is constantly flattered by the revelation that a sudden call to dine with a jewel importer at the Ritz will find him shaved and natty and handling the right knives with easy boredom.

It is a gorgeous conception, fulfilling more fantasies in the male audience than a Freudian could shake a stick at, and it was given a very entertaining dry run in the appearances of Warren William as Perry Mason. But it was always thought of as B-film material until Bogart turned it into box office. The change may have been due in the first place to what Peter Ustinov has called his "enormous presence," the simple, inexplicable characteristic of natural stars: you cannot take your eyes off them. (No one in the history of the movies has made smoking a cigarette a more deadly and fascinating thing to watch.) It was also due to Bogart's graduation from mere gangster parts just when parliamentary Europe was caving in to gangsters on a grand scale. He is the first romantic hero who used the gangster's means to achieve our ends. And this character was suddenly very precious in the age of violence, for it satisfied a quiet, desperate need of the engulfed, ordinary citizen. When Hitler was acting out scripts more brutal and obscene than anything dreamed of by Chicago's North Side or the Warner Brothers, Bogart was the only possible antagonist likely to outwit him and survive. What was needed was no Ronald Colman, Leslie Howard, or other knight of the boudoir, but a conniver as subtle as Goebbels. Bogart was the very tough gent required, and to his glory he was always, in the end, on our side.

STUDY QUESTIONS

1. This brief selection is the central section from an essay of the same title in which Cooke describes and favorably evaluates the career and genuine contribution of Humphrey Bogart. Note and be prepared to discuss some of the differences in writing and purpose between this and the two preceding selections.

2. In what other ways besides his freedom does the character portrayed by Bogart offer his audience opportunities for "audience identification"?

3. In what way did the events of the time help Bogart become famous?

4. In what ways does the character portrayed by Bogart differ from other movie heroes? What can he do that other movie heroes never do? What sort of activities and ideas can he omit that would be required in another sort of hero? What conclusions do these observations suggest?

5. Write a theme describing the sort of character portrayed by another favorite movie star, telling why he appeals to (or is detested by) his audience.

6. Note that Alistair Cooke tries to give definite reasons for Bogart's popularity. Can the popularity of types of films and film personalities always be explained in this way? Write a theme giving definite reasons for the popularity of a particular type of movie, such as Westerns, family movies, science-fiction pictures or musicals, or a particular type of character, such as the earnest doctor, the hard-working girl singer, the tough outdoor man, or the poor little rich girl.

The Father on the Hearth*

Norman Podhoretz

At least fifty plays are produced on television every week. About a third of these are detective and mystery stories; another large slice is devoted to whimsical tales with surprise endings. But the re-

* From *Commentary*, 1953. Reprinted by permission of Norman Podhoretz.

mainder constitutes a genre peculiar to television. It has developed its own style, its own conventions, and to some extent its own subject matter.

These TV plays are theatrical rather than cinematic, taking their cue from Broadway, not Hollywood. Movie stars rarely appear in them, though prominent Broadway figures often do; the casts consist of extremely competent actors most of whom, I imagine, consider themselves theater people. The direction almost always betrays the influence of men like Kazan—which is to say that it tries to combine realism of surface with self-conscious, sometimes arty, arrangements, movement, and overtones. Both dialogue and acting are more sophisticated than is usual in the movies. In general the productions are on a surprisingly high level, considering the number of plays turned out every week.

The tendency is toward low-key drama, a kind of domestic realism whose effect derives from its accuracy in reflecting the ordinary man's conceptions of the world. The very style of the acting—always plausible, always controlled, never permitting itself the least intimation of hamminess, rarely even admitting that it is artifice rather than actual conversation—restricts the drama to that level of reality which is easily accessible to common sense. A whole play may be based on a very trivial incident, chosen because everyone in the audience will have experienced something similar. For example, a teenage boy takes the family car without his father's permission, gets involved in a minor accident, and doesn't come home until three in the morning. His parents wait up for him, anxiety-ridden, and when he finally returns, all is forgiven and the whole family goes to bed with the sense of having got through another crisis. This play is "true to life" in a way that popular culture seldom is: the audience has never had the stuff of its daily existence taken so seriously, and it responds with a new feeling of self-importance and dignity. Unlike the soap operas, which betray a masochistic relish in minor troubles, the point here is the relief people feel in being able to resume their usual routine: trouble teaches gratitude for the humdrum.

Depending for its effectiveness on its ability to remain content with the world perceived and comprehended by common sense, this kind of drama must resist appealing either to escapist fantasy or to the critical intelligence, never wandering above or below the staples of experience. Nowadays, to be sure, that can include a great deal of surprising matter. In a play about the relation between a mother and her son, suggestions of an Oedipus complex are offered in much the same way as characters appear wearing clothes: the writer, the director, the actors, take it completely for granted as an ordinary element in the family. It isn't a mysterious, sinister force (as it tends to be in the movies) but a tangible factor existing almost wholly on the surface and demanding to be observed. This means, of course, that it needn't have consequences; in this particular instance, it counted for nothing in the plot. That a son should be in love with his mother is an index of his normality, not of his monstrousness. This must imply, I suppose, that the audience has been trained to regard it thus, or is well on its way to doing so.

Life in these plays, then, is non-heroic: a world governed by common sense is a world where "everyone has his faults and his good points." No insuperable moral problems are recognized, for, in a universe ruled exclusively by forces visible to the common-sense eye, there can be no dilemma which resists the touch of good will and a spirit of compromise. Often a play will open with a situation in which right seems to conflict with right, but in the end someone is proved wrong or neurotic or misguided, and the difficulty immediately resolves *itself*. A common-sense ethos must always hack its way through to the simple truths which are supposed to lie buried beneath the ugly and delusory overgrowths of experience.

Though everyone in these plays has weaknesses as well as virtues, we find the weaknesses far less in evidence. If a man sins, he does so almost accidentally, for sin is something that happens to people, not something they do. They make errors of judgment all the time, but they generally know nothing of pure or gratuitous malice. Only their virtues are essential to them; their sins are somehow external, reefs against which they have blundered in the fog. (The TV crime plays, on the other hand, become a repository of much that is omitted from domestic drama: crime is a violation of common-sense living, and therefore results in the criminal's exclusion from the sphere in which all slips can be made good.)

One would expect that a world made by common sense, ruled by common sense, and upheld by common sense, would be a pleasant world to live in. In many ways it is. It produces people whose passions are under control, who are well-bred, well-mannered, open, friendly, helpful, and above all, reasonable. More than anything else, they want to get along, they will do nearly anything to keep the peace.

And yet the optimism we find here is gray rather than flaming; it is overcast with a sadness that seems a new element in American popular culture. There is a distinct feeling that life is tough even for those who aren't harassed by the landlord and the grocer; and there is a shade of disillusion over the discovery that human possibility is not infinite—reverberations of Korea are in the air. The mood is more sober than what used to be called American optimism, and, as we shall see, far more honest.

Before the dislocations caused by 3D, Hollywood had been gravitating in several full-dress productions toward a similar form of drama. . . . But the features characterizing the new genre—an insistent interest in domestic life, a *dramatis personae* entirely composed of ordinary people, a strict fidelity to the appearance of things, a quiet tone (everything is underplayed), a paucity of plot, and much discussion and debate—made it apparent that its real home was in television. Going to the movies is still more or less an occasion for most people, and an occasion demands something extraordinary. Even the size of the cinema screen insures that the movie world shall be larger than life (indeed, in answer to the small television screen, movie screens have become larger) ; perhaps for this reason, movies reproduced on television lose their bite. Watching television, on the other hand, has become an integral part of domestic routine, and the new genre serves an impulse to make the program a relevant and appropriate presence in the living room.

The living room, in fact, is the favorite setting of these plays, just as the favorite cast is a family. It is a middle-class family, neither unusually happy nor (as in the soap operas) continually besieged with trouble. Its most remarkable quality as a group is a negative one—fear is absent from the relations of its members and power thus becomes a corollary of love: it can only be had by free consent. The father guides and administers his household; he does not rule it. The plot always turns on some crisis that has suddenly developed, often in the family relations themselves: as in any family, its members are continually in the process of losing their illusions about one another, and the effort at readjustment is constant. Ultimately they emerge from their difficulties as more of a family, having restored a workable balance of power.

Almost always the father comes through as a sharper figure than the mother, who is supposed to have her being in and through her husband and children. A good woman is not so much *by* as *on* the side of her husband. If she asserts her personality too forcefully, we may be sure that calamity will result. Evil, when it makes one of its rare visits to these plays, is likely to come in the shape of a domineering wife or an overly possessive mother. As for the father, he is an earnest man, but his earnestness is mellow compared with the fierce unyielding grimness of his children or his wife's firm, uncritical loyalty to her feelings. Soft-spoken, controlled, never glamorous-looking, but always carrying himself with great dignity and self-assurance, he exhibits the palpable scars of a long combat with life. His humility, patience, and sadness are the products of many frustrations, and he is thus extremely skeptical of any comprehensive schemes or over-ambitious plans. Sometimes he is portrayed as a great disappointment to his children—for we live in an era where parents rather than children are perennially on trial—and in such cases the guilt and bitterness he feels are tempered by his pity for the son who will soon learn that all human beings are disappointing to those who make excessive demands on them.

We practically never see this new American father (as we used to in the movies and as we still do in television soap operas) involved in the big business deal, or embroiled in the problems of earning money: a comfortable income is taken for granted, while his career is merely a shadowy presence in the background. The great reality of his life, the sphere in which things happen to him, is his family. He carries his responsibilities willingly, without a sense of oppression, and the fact that they occupy him so fully, challenging all his resources of character and mind, never allowing him to get bored, is his most powerful proof to his son that the ordinary life is worth living. For this is the great lesson he is intent upon teaching. We find him telling his daughter that marriage, children, and love are far more important than fame and wealth; we find him insisting to his son that there is no disgrace in compromise. He represents reasonableness, tolerance, and good will: the image of American maturity.

Preserving the family from disruption is the role he is most often called upon to play. One species of disruption is conflict with his children. The conflict never takes the form of youth's rebellion against parental authority because the father's authority over his children is not given in the nature of things. Since he is a constitutional leader rather than an absolute monarch, his authority must constantly be reaffirmed at the polls. Nor can he assert it forcefully or arbitrarily: he must win the right to participate in his son's problems by making himself sufficiently attractive in the boy's eyes—good "public relations" is essential to his position. Interference with his son's private affairs being a matter of the greatest delicacy, he only presumes to speak in crucial matters. Otherwise he is there, looking on, setting an example, communicating through the silent power of his personality.

In an encounter with his children, he confronts them with a flexibility that often seems to be weakness but in reality turns out to be a wisdom based on the knowledge that human beings cannot afford to be too hard either on themselves or others. One play (already mentioned above) was about a young man of twenty who discovers his mother committing adultery while his father is away on a business trip. After wandering around the streets all night, the son staggers into his house, dishevelled, distraught, and looking a little drunk; to his amazement, he finds his father waiting for him. "Now, listen, son, I know everything; your mother wired me and I took the next plane back. She told me the whole story." [1] The boy covers his face with his hands, unable to speak. "What are you going to do?" asks his father. "What do you mean, what am *I* going to do? What are *you* going to do?" "Well, what do you expect me to do—leave your mother and break up our home because she made a mistake?" At this suggestion that his father wants to forget the whole thing, the boy stares at him incredulously; it's impossible to go on living with an immoral mother and a weak-kneed father. Patiently and sympathetically, the father persists in trying to convince his son that their family is too important to be destroyed by a mistake. His wife, he explains, is going through a difficult phase; her son is grown up, she has nothing left to do, she thinks she isn't needed. Now she's upstairs suffering more than her son would believe, terrified that he may turn away from her. "Our job is to help her, not to kill her. I've got to be more loving, you've got

---

[1] I quote from memory throughout this article.

to show that you understand her side of things. Will you do it?" And, of course, the play ends with the boy going upstairs to comfort his mother. This is an atmosphere in which adultery and betrayal breed not hatred, but new responsibility. Yet all this understanding disturbs one: is there no breaking point?

Occasionally there is, as when the father's worldliness becomes irrelevant (or worse) to his son's problems. A young man, caught violating the Honor System in his pre-graduation exams at college, is about to be expelled by a committee of his peers, when he offers to turn in the names of the others who had cheated with him. The list of names is confided to the chairman of the committee, a brilliant student who is planning to marry a sweet young classmate and to go into his father's business. On the list he finds his fiancée's name. Should he, before handing it in to the Dean, strike off her name? His father, guessing the boy's trouble, persuades him to do so: "You're going out into a tough world where nobody will care about you and your interests. You have to look out for yourself and the people you love. This is a small town, son; they never forget a scandal, they'll never let you forget that your wife was once expelled from college for cheating. Everybody cheats; the only difference between a respectable man and a cheater is that the cheater has been caught. Son, don't let your 'principles' destroy your happiness. Use your head, boy!" At first the boy takes this advice, but later, to the consternation of his father, confesses while delivering his valedictory address, and proclaims his own expulsion. The two young people leave the small university town together to begin a new life.

Though repudiated, the father in this play is not unsympathetically portrayed. He realizes that the Honor System places too great a burden on young people, and that there is something absurd—something that violates common sense—in allowing a trivial matter to ruin a life. He does not, as his own father might have done, advise his son to give up this girl who will disgrace him: the highest value is still preservation of the family, even if it hasn't quite been formed yet. And in this play the idea of family takes on a special significance. The world outside is assumed to be hostile (like the outraged student body demanding the expulsion of the cheaters), or, like the kindly Dean, helpless in the face of circumstances and the Rules. The world outside is mechanical, rigid, governed by cold standards of no one's making: even the Dean can't protect the students he would like to forgive. Within the family, however, a man has resources, for the family rests on love and reasonableness, and it is in the nature of love to persist despite circumstance, while reasonableness provides flexibility to liberate the spirit from the tyranny of Rules. A person is most a person to those who love him; otherwise he is judged and disposed of.

That understanding and flexibility should be the father's greatest qualities is not surprising. What does surprise us, however, is that he rarely feels ambition for his children, merely wishing them to lead normal, contented lives. The only ambitious father I remember seeing is the one in the play just discussed, and he is also the only father who comes off badly in the end—as if ambitiousness were an act of *hubris* to be avenged. The drive for extraordinary achievement has always been considered notoriously American. An identity is something that must be earned, not inherited, and once earned it remains precarious and must be vigilantly maintained: if you lose your money, you also lose your name. This compulsion to prove that we are "saved" is probably a consequence of being born into a Puritan culture—many marks of status in America are simply secularized versions of what once were the symptoms of grace.

We seem, however, under the influence of psychoanalysis, to have reached a point where the most important mark of status has become not money, power, or fame, but a reasonably happy family life. Play after play insists that everyone is saved, that all are granted grace if they are but willing to accept it: adjustment is supposed to be available to all.

The way to justify the space you take up in the world is—as one father puts it—not to be *somebody*, but just to *be*. An adaptation of Dos Passos' *The Big Money* is used as a vehicle for showing the disastrous consequences of the pursuit of wealth; a young boxer who had been a foundling realizes that he needn't be compulsive about becoming a champion in order to give his infant son a "name"; a great soprano feigns the loss of her voice because she has learned that happiness lies in raising children and being supported by a responsible husband; a distinguished (divorced) actress gives up her career because she falls in love with a man who teaches her that what she really wants is a husband and family; a potentially great pianist is forced to admit that he is incapable of performing on the concert stage, and finds that being released from an immature ambition allows him for the first time to feel content in his marriage.

A particularly interesting example is a play about a widower, father of a fifteen-year-old daughter, who falls in love with a formerly great concert pianist. We are given to understand that some sort of illness interrupted her career, but now she is working steadily to stage a comeback. The woman is in her thirties, completely dedicated to music, living in a room which is stuffed with busts of great composers and that suggests the atmosphere of a mausoleum. Pressured into a date with the widower by a friendly neighbor, she reveals herself as socially inept. Her behavior is awkward, she can't dance, and she commits the great crime of being a killjoy by leaving the country club at midnight. ("I'm so sorry to have ruined your evening," she apologizes pathetically. "I knew I shouldn't have come. I'm just no good at this sort of thing. And now I have to get some sleep, because I have a long day of practice ahead of me.") The widower was an extremely good representative of his type: equable, quiet, observant (the camera kept finding excuses for giving us close-ups of his intently serious eyes), sensible, understanding, and com-

pletely at his ease in the many different situations the play showed him
in. We soon discover that the widower's young daughter fancies herself
a pianist too. Against the tactful urging of her father, she breaks a date
for the junior prom in order to prepare for a high-school concert. Eventually, of course, the daughter and the ex-concert pianist become great
friends. Father is disturbed, but for the moment does nothing, allowing
her to study with the older woman. As soon as the high-school concert
is over, he intends to be firm. The night before the concert, however, he
is horrified to learn that great plans are being made for his daughter.
"She reminds me so much of what I was like at her age. And she has
talent. You can't stand in her way. I've sent for the Great Maestro to
hear her tomorrow night. He'll convince you." After the concert, the
Great Maestro tells his ex-pupil that her protégé is extremely talented,
but that she'll never be anything more than a competent performer: the
divine spark is missing. Father is pleased, but the woman refuses to
accept this judgment as final. "There are other teachers. We'll get them
to hear her. I *know* she has talent. She'll work hard, oh it will be very
hard, but she'll make it, I know she will." The father shakes his head
sadly. "Why did you stop giving concerts?" "Because I was ill." "No,
you weren't ill. I know because I looked up the reviews. They said you
had lost your genius, that you were a great child prodigy who never
developed." "No, no, it's not true!" "But it *is* true, my darling. Why can't
you face reality? Why won't you move out of this tomb and live?"
Through her tears she whimpers, "But don't you understand? I have to
be somebody." Then comes the clinching line of the play: "Why do you
have to be *somebody*? Why can't you just *be*?" And she collapses into
his arms. In the last act, the young girl tells her idol that she has to be
somebody, but the redeemed artist repeats father's epigram, adding that
"there are so many things in life for you. There's your first dance, and
the first time you fall in love, and marriage and children." The child
weeps hysterically and rushes out of the room, but father and stepmother-
to-be embrace. "Don't worry. She'll be all right now."

The play hardly entertains the suggestion that there are circumstances
in which a normal life is worth sacrificing, nor does the writer admit that
there may be more than one way of finding happiness, or that there may
be other forms of the good life which take place outside the family circle.
All this is typical of serious television drama. It would be a mistake,
however, to think that "conformity" is being urged, if we mean by that
imposing a specific model of behavior. On the assumption that everyone
really wants the same kind of things out of life, these plays argue, quite
plausibly, that only childishness or neurosis (both of which are characterized by the excessive demands they foster) will prevent people from
taking advantage of their inalienable right to pursue happiness. Nor is
there any uncertainty about the content of happiness; the only problem
is finding the surest, swiftest, and safest means to a predetermined end.

Yet, curiously enough, the most salient feature of this ethos remains its sadness. It presents itself as making a modest demand upon life, a demand so modest that life would be guilty of the cruelest perversity to deny it. Bearing in its countenance the lines and wrinkles of maturity, it is always opposed to the presumptuous, enthusiastic "idealism" of youth. Yet what could be more optimistic than the belief that contentment and security are within everyone's reach? When success is measured by money or fame, failure can be chalked up to bad luck; the whole man is rarely in the balance, for a certain distinction will be maintained between the private and public selves: the private self is there to fall back upon if the other turns out treacherous. But when success is conceived as an attribute of the personality rather than of the wallet, failure becomes the tenth circle of Hell. A new fortune can be made, but a man's personality is his essence—personality, in fact, is the modern word for soul—and if that proves befouled, then no good can come of it. In these plays personality itself figures as the goal of all striving; the object of ambition becomes not success but "successful living." The type of all failures is the neurotic, pictured writhing under his burdens like one of the damned; and appropriately so, for in this view of things, a failure of the personality is the last and most refined torture of the Devil. Perhaps some perception of this accounts for the resignation that overcomes the intrinsic cheeriness of the new ethos.

It would be foolish at this point to make any simple judgments of television drama as a whole. Its most notable achievements, I think, are the sharpness with which it has distinguished itself from the movies, the effort it has made to be honest, the success with which it has managed to be serious without being objectionably pretentious. Most important, perhaps, it gives pleasure as so many "serious" movies have failed to do —Hollywood's great fault is its inability to see any connection between "entertainment" and "significance." Apart from a few comic strips, television drama seems the only area of American popular culture that refuses to distinguish finally between the two. Because it isn't imitative, it gives a picture of American life whose accuracy may be difficult to measure but whose honesty is sometimes astonishing: there was a time when the play about the mother's adultery would have ended with the discovery that she hadn't really committed adultery at all.

It may be that this drama reflects the values and aspirations of the newly emerged middle class, now large enough to constitute a mass audience and powerful enough to set the stamp of its attitudes on an important segment of popular culture. Formed by psychoanalysis and nourished by the concepts of social work, this class shows a conspicuous distaste for violence and a remarkable lack of interest in the ungovernable passions of young love. It puts a very high value on the family, though not in order to retreat from the community. The family here is an expanding rather than a restrictive entity, the nucleus of community;

it comes to mean all decent, sensible, and understanding people, "people like us," people, that is, who act *as* people and not as "forces." The retreat to the home, then, means a retreat from "environment"—from the competitive world of business and politics, which menaces amiable human relations and does not yield easily to compromise and good will.

Finally, this drama has contributed a new figure to the popular imagination. Attractive and disturbing as he is, the father may turn out to be a summation of the postwar ethos. In his benign firmness, in his mature sobriety, in his sad but determined sense of responsibility, in his unceasing efforts to keep the peace, he can detect the traces of the contemporary political climate. He reflects the feeling that the only safe oasis in a dangerous, cold-war world is our own home, a home which, though it may once have been taken lightly, must now be preserved at all costs if the battle is not to be lost everywhere. And in the long series of plays which turn on a rediscovery of the father by his son, we find, perhaps, the mark of a generation which has moved out of rebellion and skepticism into a patient and humble acquiescence; and we may here discover the role the new middle class seems to have marked out for its own.

STUDY QUESTIONS

1. Why would not the father, as described in this article, qualify as a movie hero?
2. What are the elements of sadness in the basically optimistic picture of American life presented by the new TV drama?
3. In what ways are the TV dramas more realistic than the movies? Are there any ways in which they are less realistic?
4. Does this kind of drama make use of conventions peculiar to itself as Warshow has pointed out the gangster film does? Is it different in this respect from other dramatic and fictional media?
5. Do you agree with the author that this is a new kind of popular drama, which reflects changes in American life? Write a theme on this subject.
6. Following Podhoretz' method, analyze another staple TV product, such as the adventure story, the detective chase or the animal-hero story.

Popular Songs vs. The Facts of Life[1] *

S. I. Hayakawa

Because I have long been interested in jazz—its history, its implications, its present developments—I also listen to some extent to popular songs, which are, of course, far from being the same thing. My present subject is an attempt to examine, from a semantic point of view, the words of popular songs and jazz songs in order to discover their underlying assumptions, orientations, and implied attitudes.

First, let me clarify the distinction between popular songs and jazz. In "true" jazz, as the jazz connoisseur understands the term, the basic interest in the part of both musician and listener is in the music as music. Originality and inventiveness in improvisation are highly prized, as are the qualities of instrumentation and of rhythm. Popular music, on the other hand, stands in about the same relationship to jazz as the so-called "semi-classics" stand in relation to Bach, Beethoven, and Brahms. Just as the musical ideas of the classics are diluted, often to a point of insanity, in the "semi-classics," so are the ideas of jazz (and of semi-classics) diluted in popular music—diluted, sweetened, sentimentalized, and trivialized.

Now the contrast between the musical sincerity of jazz and the musical

[1] Originally presented at the Second Conference on General Semantics, held under the auspices of Washington University and the St. Louis Chapter of the International Society for General Semantics, at St. Louis, Missouri, June 12, 1954.

This paper was also presented before the Associated Students of San Francisco State College at Nourse Auditorium, San Francisco, July 8, 1954. On this occasion the lecture was illustrated by music performed by the Bob Scobey Frisco Jazz Band and Claire Austin. I wish to thank again, for their excellent and spirted contribution to the program, the performers of that evening: Bob Scobey (trumpet), Fred Higuera (drums), Dick Lammi (bass), Bill Napier (clarinet), Wally Rose (piano), Jack Buck (trombone), and Clancey Hayes (banjo and voice). Whatever was left unclear in the speech was made more than clear by the skilful interpretive singing of Mr. Hayes and the deeply felt blues-singing of Mrs. Austin.

The materials of this paper were again presented at the Folk and Jazz Festival at Music Inn, Lenox, Massachusetts, September 5, 1954. Music on this occasion was supplied by the Sammy Price Trio, with blues-singing by Jimmy Rushing and Myra Johnson. I am deeply indebted to these gifted performers for their help, and for their sympathetic understanding of the argument of this paper.

* Reprinted from *Etc.*, Vol. 12 (1955), pp. 83-95, by permission of the author and the publisher. (Copyright, 1955, by the International Society for General Semantics.)

slop of much of popular music is interestingly paralleled in the contrast between the literary sincerity of the words of blues songs (and the blues are the basic source of jazz inspiration) and the literary slop in the majority of popular songs. The words of true jazz songs, especially the Negro blues, tend to be unsentimental and realistic in their statements about life. (In saying "Negro blues," I should add that most of these are written by Negroes, but some have been written by whites under Negro inspiration.) The words of popular songs, on the other hand, largely (but not altogether) the product of white song-writers for predominantly white audiences, tend towards wishful thinking, dreamy and ineffectual nostalgia, unrealistic fantasy, self-pity, and sentimental clichés masquerading as emotion.

We have been taught—and rightly—to be more than cautious about making racial distinctions. Hence let me hasten to explain that the differences between (predominantly Negro) blues and (predominantly white) popular songs can, in my opinion, be satisfactorily accounted for without "racial" explanations. The blues arise from the experiences of a largely agricultural and working-class Negro minority with a social and cultural history different from that of the white majority. Furthermore, the blues—a folk music which underwent urbanization (in New Orleans, Chicago, New York, Memphis, Kansas City, and elsewhere)—developed in an economic or market situation different from that in which popular songs, aimed at mass markets through mass entertainment media, developed.[2] With these cultural and economic conditions in mind, let me restate the thesis of this paper, using this time the terminology of general semantics: The blues tend to be *extensionally* oriented, while popular songs tend to exhibit grave, even pathological *intensional* orientations.

Perhaps I can make my thesis come to life by discussing a specific area of emotion about which songs are written, namely, love in the light of what Wendell Johnson calls the IFD disease—the triple-threat semantic disorder of Idealization (the making of impossible and ideal demands upon life), which leads to Frustration (as the result of the demands not being met), which in turn leads to Demoralization (or Disorganization, or Despair).[3] What Johnson says in *People in Quandaries* is repeatedly illustrated in the attitudes toward love expressed in popular songs.

First, in looking forward to love, there is an enormous amount of unrealistic idealization—the creation in one's mind, as the object of love's search, a dream girl (or dream boy) the fleshly counterpart of which never existed on earth:

[2] I might add that I do not know enough about folk music among the whites (hillbilly music, cowboy songs, etc.) to be able to include these in my discussion. Hence in comparing folk blues with commercial popular songs, I am comparing two genres which are not strictly comparable.

[3] Wendell Johnson, *People in Quandaries* (New York, Harper, 1946), pp. 14-20.

Will I ever find the girl in my mind,
The girl who is my ideal? [4]

Every night I dream a little dream,
And of course Prince Charming is the theme,
The he for me . . .[5]

Next, of course, one meets a not-altogether-unattractive person of the other sex, and the psychological process called *projection* begins, in which one attributes to a real individual the sum-total of the imaginary perfections one has dreamed about:

I took one look at you,
That's all I meant to do,
And then my heart stood still . . .[6]

You were meant for me, and I was meant for you.
Nature fashioned you and when she was done,
You were all the sweet things rolled up in one . . .
I confess, the angels must have sent you,
And they meant you just for me.[7]

Wendell Johnson has commented frequently on what he calls a prevalent belief in magic.[8] Some of his clients in his speech clinic at the University of Iowa, he says, will do no drills, perform no exercises, read no books, carry out no recommendations; they simply seem to expect that now that they have come to THE right speech clinic their stuttering will somehow magically go away. The essence of magic is the belief that you don't have to do anything—the right magic makes all effort unnecessary.

Love is depicted in most popular songs as just this kind of magic. There is rarely an indication in the accounts of love-euphoria commonly to be found in these songs that, having found the dream-girl or dream-man, one's problems are just beginning. Rather it is explicitly stated that, having found one's ideal, all problems are solved:

We'll have a blue room, a new room, for two room,
Where every day's a holiday, because you're married
    to me . . .[9]

[4] "My Ideal," by Leo Robin, Richard Whiting, and Newell Chase. Copyright, 1930, by Famous Music Co.
[5] "The Man I Love," by George and Ira Gershwin. Copyright, 1924, by Harms, Inc.
[6] "My Heart Stood Still," by Lorenz Hart and Richard Rodgers. Copyright, 1927, by Harms, Inc.
[7] "You Were Meant for Me," with lyrics by Arthur Freed, melody by Nacio Herb Brown. Copyright, 1929, by Robbins Music Corp.
[8] For example, at a lecture at University College, University of Chicago, May 14, 1954, under the auspices of the Chicago Chapter of the International Society for General Semantics.
[9] "Blue Room," by Lorenz Hart and Richard Rodgers. Copyright, 1926, by Harms, Inc.

The "Blue Room" song hints at what other songs often state, namely, that not only are emotional problems (and apparently economic problems) automatically solved by finding "the sweetheart of all my dreams"; the housing problem is also solved:

> You'll find a smiling face, a fireplace, a cozy room,
> A little nest that's nestled where the roses bloom . . .[10]

> In a bungalow all covered with roses,
> I will settle down I vow,
> I'm looking at the world thru rose-colored glasses,
> And everything is rosy now.[11]

That, then, is the idealization. And students of general semantics know from reading Wendell Johnson what that leads to. The unrealistic expectations—for love is never expected to last for any shorter a period than "forever"—result inevitably in disappointment, disenchantment, frustration, and, most importantly, self-pity. Hence:

> I'm all alone every evening,
> All alone, feeling blue,
> Wondering where you are, and how you are,
> And if you are all alone too.[12]

What if it turns out that he wasn't all alone at all, but two-timing her? She complains bitterly:

> You were only fooling,
> While I was falling in love.[13]

> Little you care for the vows that you made,
> Little you care how much I have paid . . .[14]

But in spite of the disappointments he has caused, she still loves him:

> Yesterday's kisses are bringing me pain,
> Yesterday's sunshine has turned into rain,
> I'm alone because I love you,
> Love you with all my heart.[15]

[10] "My Blue Heaven," by George Whiting and Walter Donaldson. Copyright, 1927, by Leo Feist, Inc.
[11] "Looking at the World Thru Rose Colored Glasses," by Tommy Malie and Jimmy Steiger. Copyright, 1926, by Pickwick Music Corp.
[12] "All Alone," by Irving Berlin. Copyright, 1924, by Irving Berlin.
[13] "You Were Only Fooling," with words by Billy Faber and Fred Meadows, music by Larry Fotine. Copyright, 1948, by Shapiro, Bernstein & Co.
[14] "Somebody Else Is Taking My Place," by Dick Howard, Bob Ellsworth, and Russ Morgan. Copyright, 1937, by the Back Bay Music Co.—assigned to Shapiro, Bernstein & Co. Copyright, 1941, by Shapiro, Bernstein & Co.
[15] "I'm Alone Because I Love You," words and music by Joe Young. Copyright, 1930, by M. Witmark & Sons.

Am I blue, am I blue,
Ain't these tears in these eyes telling you? [16]

How can I go on living, now that we're apart? [17]

She admits vociferously, "I'm a fool to care," but she wallows never-theless in self-commiseration:

No day or night goes by,
That I don't have my cry . . . [18]

The next stage in the progress from disenchantment to demoralization and despair is, of course, another popular song theme, "I'm through with love, I'll never love again"—a theme which has such variants as these:

I'll never love again,
I'm so in love with you.
I'll never thrill again
To somebody new . . . [19]

And if I never fall in love again,
That's soon enough for me,
I'm gonna lock my heart and throw away the key.[20]

And what is the final stage? Students of general semantics are familiar enough with psychiatric concepts to know that when the world of reality proves unmanageable, a common practice is to retreat into a symbolic world, since symbols are more manageable and predictable than the extensional realities for which they stand. The psychiatric profession classifies this retreat as schizophrenia, but that does not prevent it from being the theme of a popular song:

I'm going to buy myself a paper doll to call my own,
A doll that other fellows cannot steal. . . .
When I come home at night she will be waiting,
She'll be the truest doll in all the world.
I'd rather have a paper doll to call my own
Than a fickle-minded real live girl.[21]

[16] "Am I Blue," by Grant Clarke and Harry Akst. Copyright, 1929, by M. Witmark & Sons.
[17] "Have You Ever Been Lonely?" with words by George Brown (Billy Hill) and music by Peter de Rose. Copyright, 1933, by Shapiro, Bernstein & Co., Inc.
[18] "I Need You Now," by Jimmy Crane and Al Jacobs. Copyright, 1953, by Miller Music Corp.
[19] "I'll Never Smile Again," with words and music by Ruth Lowe. Copyright, 1939, by Pickwick Music Corp.
[20] "I'm Gonna Lock My Heart," by Jimmy Eaton and Terry Shand. Copyright, 1938, by Shapiro, Bernstein & Co., Inc.
[21] "Paper Doll," by Johnny Black. Copyright, 1915, by E. B. Marks.

This, then, is the picture of love's unhappy progress, as presented by the song writers of the commercial song-publishing world. The unrealistic emotions and the bathos of popular songs have, of course, long been notorious. It may well be asked if songs can be otherwise and yet be popular.

In answer to this question, let me next present the problems of love as seen by the writers of blues songs, such as are the basis of jazz. The first thing to be noticed is that the object of love is not idealized, but is looked at fairly realistically. It is one thing to call a pretty girl an angel, but quite another to look at angels as they are seen in "Harlem Blues":

> Now you can have your Broadway, give me Lenox Avenue,
> Angels from the skies stroll Seventh, and for that thanks are due
> To Madam Walker's Beauty Shops and the Poro System too,
> That made them angels without any doubt.[22]

Shortcomings of character or appearance in the object of one's love are candidly acknowledged:

> The man I love's got lowdown ways for true,
> Well, I am hinkty and I'm lowdown too.[23]

> You're so mean and evil, you do things you ought not to do,
> But you've got my brand of honey, so I guess I'll have
>   to put up with you.[24]

In other words, there is no to-do made about looking and looking for an ideal girl or man—one adjusts oneself to the kind of women and men that actually exist. Refraining from "always chasing rainbows," the people depicted in the blues appear to save themselves a vast amount of emotional energy.

The loved one's imperfections, however, do not appear to stand in the way either of the intensity or durability of one's affections, as is indicated in this lament over a woman's death:

> I went down to St. James Infirmary,
> Heard my baby groan,
> I felt so broken-hearted,
> She used to be my own.

> I tried to keep from cryin'
> My heart felt just like lead,
> She was all I had to live for,
> I wish that it was me instead . . .

[22] "Harlem Blues," by W. C. Handy. Copyright, 1922, by W. C. Handy; copyright renewed. Included in *A Treasury of the Blues,* ed. W. C. Handy (New York: Simon and Schuster, 1949).

[23] "The Basement Blues," by W. C. Handy. Copyright, 1924, by Handy Bros. Music Co., Inc.

[24] "Goin' to Chicago Blues," by Jimmy Rushing and Count Basie. Copyright, 1941, by Bregman, Vocco and Conn, Inc.

Though she treated me mean and lowdown,
Somehow I didn't care.
My soul is sick and weary,
I hope we'll meet again up there.[25]

Furthermore, there is no magical attitude toward love indicated in the blues. Love means a mutual human relationship, and therefore there are duties and responsibilities, no less than there are rewards. In its crudest and most elementary statement, the duty is financial:

You want to be my man you got to give me $40 down,
If you don't be my man, your baby's gonna shake
    this town.[26]

You sittin' down wonderin' what it's all about,
If you ain't got no money, they will put you out,
Why don't you do right, like other men do?
Get out of here, and get me some money too.[27]

In general the duties described are those of living up to one's obligations as a mate, of providing that minimum of dependability that makes, as they say, a house a home:

Kind treatment make me love you, be mean and you'll drive me away,
You're gonna long for me baby, one of these old rainy days.
Yes, I love you, baby, but you don't treat me right,
Walk the streets all day, baby, and never come home at night.[28]

[25] "St. James Infirmary," by Joe Primrose. Copyright, 1930, by Gotham Music Co.

[26] "The Memphis Blues," by W. C. Handy. Copyright, 1912, by W. C. Handy. (Included in *A Treasury of the Blues*.) When the lecture on which this paper was based was delivered in San Francisco, it was extensively reported in the San Francisco *News*. In the correspondence columns of the *News* a few days later, there appeared a protest from a reader who remarked regarding my quotation of these lines, "It is good to know that our future teachers (at San Francisco State College) are acquiring moral and spiritual values by getting the good honest feel of the brothel." Mr. Ralph Gleason, writing in the musicians' magazine, *Downbeat*, and taking his interpretation of my lecture from the letter-writer in the *News*, worked himself up into quite a moralistic lather against what he imagined to be my recommendaton of love on a cash-down basis over white middle-class morality. I trust it is not necessary to explain to readers of *Etc.* that what I am doing here is attempting to draw a humorous contrast between love regarded as magic and love (including facsimiles thereof) regarded as involving mutual obligations. The statement that love involves obligations is not entirely absent, of course, from popular songs. A recent example is "Little Things Mean a Lot," by Edith Lindeman and Carl Stutz (New York: Leo Feist, 1954), which, as sung by Kitty Kallen, has recently enjoyed vast popularity.

[27] "Why Don't You Do Right?" by Joe McCoy. Copyright, 1942, by Mayfair Music Corp.

[28] "Blues in the Dark," by Jimmy Rushing and Count Basie. Copyright, 1943, by Bregman, Vocco and Conn, Inc.

And the famous blues singer, Bessie Smith, gives the following advice to girls—advice which is full of the sense of one's own responsibility in a love situation:

> So if your man is nice, take my advice,
> Hug him in the morning, kiss him every night,
> Give him plenty loving, treat him right,
> For a good man nowadays is hard to find.[29]

The physical basis of love is more candidly acknowledged in the blues than in most popular songs. I am indebted to Dr. Russell Meyers of the University of Iowa Hospitals for the following observation about Jelly Roll Morton's "Winin' Boy Blues," in which there occurs the line, "Pick it up and shake it, life's sweet stavin' chain." [30] Dr. Meyers equates this line to Herrick's "Gather ye rosebuds while ye may," translating thus: "A stavin' chain is the heavy chain used by loggers to bind together logs to be floated down river, so that it is metaphorically that which binds together, i.e., sexuality; the idea is, as in Herrick, that you shake it now, while you are still able."

Popular songs, to be sure, also refer to the physical basis of love, but usually in extremely abstract periphrasis, as in "All of me, why not take all of me?" In the blues, however, as in the Elizabethan lyric, the subject is treated metaphorically. The following is from a song made famous by Bessie Smith:

> You better get yourself to a blacksmith shop to get yourself overhauled,
> There ain't nothing about you to make a good woman bawl.
> Nobody wants a baby when a real man can be found,
> You been a good ole wagon, but you done broke down.[31]

So there are disappointments in love in the blues, no less than in popular songs. But the quality of disappointment is different. The inevitability of change in a changing world appears to be accepted. Conditions change, people change, and in spite of all one can do to preserve a valued relationship, failure may result:

> Folks I love my man, I kiss him morning, noon and night,
> I wash his clothes and keep him dry and try to treat him right.
> Now he's gone and left me, after all I've tried to do,
> The way he treat me, girls, he'll do the same thing to you.
> That's the reason I got those weeping willow blues.[32]

[29] "A Good Man Is Hard to Find," by Eddie Green. Copyright, 1917, by Mayfair Music Corp. This song is not of Negro composition and is not, strictly speaking, a blues. However, ever since its famous rendition by Bessie Smith (Columbia 14250-D), it has been part of the blues repertory.
[30] See General 4004-A, in the album *New Orleans Memories*, by Jelly Roll Morton.
[31] "You've Been a Good Ole Wagon" (Smith-Balcom), sung by Bessie Smith (Columbia 14079-D; re-issue, Columbia 35672).
[32] For this and several other quotations from blues songs in this paper, I am indebted to Professor John Ball of the Department of English, Miami

I've got a hard-working man,
The way he treats me I can't understand,
He works hard every day,
And on Sat'day he throws away his pay.
Now I don't want that man,
Because he's done gone cold in hand.

Now I've tried hard to treat him kind,
But it seems to me his love has gone blind,
The man I've got must have lost his mind,
The way he treats me I can't understand.
I'm gonna get myself another man,
Because the one I've got done gone cold in hand.[33]

The most vivid statement of a sudden change of situation, involving desertion and heartbreak, is made in "Young Woman's Blues," by Bessie Smith:

Woke up this morning when the chickens were crowin' for day,
Looked on the right side of my pillow, my man had gone away.
By the pillow he left a note,
Reading, "I'm sorry, Jane, you got my goat" ...

Her reaction to this blow, however, is not, as in popular songs, any giving away to self-pity. The song continues:

I'm a young woman, and I ain't done running round.[34]

In other words, she may be hurt, but she is far from demoralized. This refusal to be demoralized under conditions which in popular songs call for the utmost in wailing and self-commiseration is repeatedly to be found in the blues. Instead of the self-abasement that we find in the "kick-me-in-the-face-again-because-I-love-you" school of thought, the heartbroken men and women of the blues songs regroup their emotional forces and carry on without breakdown of morale. The end of a love relationship is by no means the end of life. As Pearl Bailey has sung:

Gonna truck downtown and spend my moo,
Get some short-vamp shoes and a new guy too ...
Cause I'm tired, mighty tired, of you.[35]

There is then, considerable tough-mindedness in the blues—a willingness, often absent in popular songs, to acknowledge the facts of life. Con-

---

University, Oxford, Ohio, who, as a student of jazz, has transcribed from his record collection the words of many blues songs, including many which have never appeared in print.

[33] "Cold in Hand Blues" (Gee-Longshaw), sung by Bessie Smith (Columbia 14064-D; re-issue, Columbia 35672).

[34] "Young Woman's Blues" (Bessie Smith), sung by Bessie Smith (Columbia 14179-D; re-issue, Columbia 35673).

[35] "Tired" (Roberts and Fisher), sung by Pearl Bailey (Columbia 36837).

sequently, one finds in the blues comments of many problems other than those of love, for example, the problem of urban congestion, as in "I'm going to move to the outskirts of town," or of alcoholism, as in the song, "Ignorant Oil." There is also much folk wisdom in the blues, as in "Nobody knows you when you're down and out," or in such observations as:

> Now if a woman gets the blues, Lawd, she hangs her head and cries,
> But if a man gets the blues, Lawd, he grabs a train and rides.[36]

I am often reminded by the words of blues songs of Kenneth Burke's famous description of poetry as "equipment for living." In the form in which they developed in Negro communities, the blues are equipment for living humble, laborious, and precarious lives of low social status or no status at all—nevertheless, they are valid equipment, in the sense that they are the opposite of escape literature. "Rock Pile Blues" states explicitly what the blues are for:

> My hammer's heavy, feels just like a ton of lead,
> If they keeps me slaving someone's gonna find me dead.
> Don't mind the rock pile, but the days are oh so long,
> Ain't no end of misery, that is why I sing this song.[37]

As a student of general semantics, I am concerned here with two functions which literary and poetic symbols perform with respect to our emotional life. First, by means of literary symbols we may be introduced vicariously to the emotions and situations which we have not yet had occasion to experience; in this sense, literature is preparation. Secondly, symbols enable us to organize the experiences we have had, make us aware of them, and therefore help us to come to terms with them; in this sense, literature is learning.

If our symbolic representations give a false or misleading impression of what life is likely to be, we are worse prepared for life than we would have been had we not been exposed to them at all. The frustration and demoralization of which Wendell Johnson writes are of necessity preceded by the expectations created by unrealistic idealizations. This is not to say, of course, that idealizations are in themselves unhealthy; they are a necessary and inescapable product of the human processes of abstraction and symbolization, and without idealizations we should be swine indeed. But there is a world of difference in the semantogenic effects of possible and impossible ideals. The ideals of love, as depicted in popular songs, are usually impossible ideals.

Hence the question arises: do popular songs, listened to, often memorized and sung in the course of adolescent and youthful courtship, make

---

[36] See note 32. Memo to Professor Ball: Where on earth did you find this, John?
[37] "Rock Pile Blues," by Spencer Williams. Copyright, 1925, by Lincoln Music Co. (Included in *A Treasury of the Blues*.)

the attainment of emotional maturity more difficult than it need be? It is almost impossible to resist having an opinion on this question, although it would be hard to substantiate one's opinion except on the basis of considerable experience in contact with the emotional problems of young people. Mr. Roy E. Dickerson, executive secretary of the Cincinnati Social Hygiene Society, who has had this experience, has offered the following comment on the thesis of this paper:

> In my judgment there is no doubt about the unfortunate influence of IFD upon the younger generation today. I detected it, I think, in even such a highly selected group as the delegates to the Seventh National Hi-Y-Tri-Hi-Y Congress held under the auspices of the National Council of YMCA's at Miami University recently. I had the pleasure of handling the group of the section of the Congress which gave attention to courtship and marriage. It was still necessary to debunk some super-romantic concepts.
>
> I am up to my eyes in marriage counseling. I feel that I am consulted again and again about ill-considered marriages based upon very superficial and inadequate ideas regarding the nature of love and how it is recognized.[38]

The existence of the blues, like the existence of occasional popular songs with love themes which do not exhibit the IFD pattern, demonstrates that it is at least possible for songs to be both reasonably healthy in psychological content and widely sung and enjoyed. But the blues cannot, of course, take over the entire domain of popular song because, as widely known as some of them have been, their chief appeal, for cultural reasons has been to Negro audiences—and even these audiences have been diminishing with the progressive advancement of Negroes and their assimilation of values and tastes in common with the white, middle-class majority. Furthermore, while there is lyricism to be found in blues tunes and their musical treatment, the words of blues songs are notoriously lacking in either lyricism or delicacy of sentiment—and it would seem that popular songs must, to some degree, supply the need for lyrical expression, especially about matters of love.

With all their limitations, however, the blues demonstrate that a popular art can function as "equipment for living." Cannot our poets and our song-writers try to do at least as much for our young people as Bessie Smith did for her audiences, namely, provide them with symbolic experiences which will help them understand, organize, and better cope with their problems? Or, if that is too much to ask (and perhaps it is, since Bessie Smith, was, in her own way, an authenic genius), can they not at least cease and desist from further spreading the all-too-prevalent IFD disease?

[38] From a personal letter dated July 13, 1954

STUDY QUESTIONS

1. How can the differences Hayakawa describes between the lyrics of jazz and popular songs be culturally explained?
2. Do you think the author may be exaggerating the importance of the words in songs of this kind?
3. This essay is particularly rich in examples. However, examples alone do not explain anything; they must be used as part of a discussion. Show how the author uses generalizations developed by authors (such as those about magic and the IFD disease) to explain his examples.
4. According to the literary standards mentioned here, which of the two types of songs described is more desirable?
5. Following the method of this essay, analyze the content of some other folk literature, such as traditional ballads, national anthems, soldiers' songs or college songs.
6. Discuss some song that is a favorite of yours. Has Hayakawa's essay changed your opinion of it? Has it perhaps explained why you find it pleasing?

Masterpieces as Cartoons*

Delmore Schwartz

Recently I have been trying hard to watch television and read comic books. I do not know whether this is an effort to keep in touch with the rest of the American population or an attempt to win the esteem of and keep up with my brother-in-law, aged twelve, who regards me as a hideous highbrow and thinks that I am probably a defrocked high school English teacher. The effort is, at any rate, one which permits me moments of self-congratulation. I feel that no one can say that I have not tried my best to keep open the lines of communication between myself and others, and to share the intellectual interests of the entire community.

The bottom of the pit has been reached, I think, in the cartoon books which are called *Classics Illustrated,* a series of picture-and-text versions of the masteprieces of literature. Seventy-eight of them have been published, but so far I have only been able to obtain six of them, and they have been so exciting and fascinating and distracting that I have only been able to read three of them with any care: Dostoevsky's *Crime and Punishment,* Shakespeare's *A Midsummer Night's Dream,* and *Gulliver's Travels.* The intention of the publishers and the editors of these illus-

* "Masterpieces as Cartoons" by Delmore Schwartz, copyright, 1952, by *Partisan Review.* Reprinted by permission of the *Partisan Review.*

trated classics are either good, or they feel guilty, or perhaps both, since at the end of *A Midsummer Night's Dream* there is a striking and entirely capitalized sentence: "NOW THAT YOU HAVE READ THE CLASSICS ILLUSTRATED EDITION, DON'T MISS THE ADDED ENJOYMENT OF READING THE ORIGINAL, OBTAINABLE AT YOUR SCHOOL OR PUBLIC LIBRARY." Notice how it is assumed that the reader has not read the original version of these works and it is taken for granted that he will not buy, he will only borrow, the original version from school or the public library. An interesting and significant fact to discover would be: just how many readers who first encounter Shakespeare, Dostoevsky, or Jonathan Swift in their comic strip garb are moved by this encounter to read the original. It would take a good detective or a good pollster to find out. When one feels optimistic, it seems possible that some quality of the masterpiece may bring some readers to the original; but when one feels pessimistic, one remembers an analogous phenomenon: even when a reader goes from James M. Cain to William Faulkner and James Joyce because they are all available in pocket book form for twenty-five cents, most readers who come to Faulkner and Joyce by means of pocket books do not know the difference between James M. Cain and James Joyce or Dashiel Hammett and William Faulkner; and some of the time they do not remember the names of the authors, no matter how many of their works they read.

The good intentions, or the guilty conscience, of the publishers of *Classics Illustrated* show clearly at the end of the cartoon version of *Crime and Punishment,* where again, as with Shakespeare, they write sentences of bold apology and excellent advice: "BECAUSE OF SPACE LIMITATIONS, WE REGRETFULLY OMITTED SOME OF THE ORIGINAL CHARACTERS AND SUB-PLOTS OF THIS BRILLIANTLY WRITTEN NOVEL. NEVERTHELESS, WE HAVE RETAINED ITS MAIN THEME AND MOOD. WE STRONGLY URGE YOU TO READ THE ORIGINAL." This explanation is more interesting and more inaccurate, the more one thinks about it and the more one remembers the novel which Dostoevsky wrote. For one of the characters who is omitted is Sonia, the heroine. She may have been omitted because of space limitations, but it is just as likely that her prostitution had something to do with her absence from the illustrated version. What remains after the deletion of some of the original characters and sub-plots is the thin line of a detective story in which a murderer is tracked down; as the publishers explain, at the end of the last slot in which Raskolnikov confesses his crime:

This then was the story of the intelligent young man who committed a premeditated "perfect crime." His conscience and the efforts of a brilliant police attorney brought about the dramatic confession and a just punishment. Raskolnikov was sentenced to serve a long term at hard labor in a Siberian prison.

Not much is left of the profound affirmation of Christianity with which the original work concludes, although there are cartoon book versions of the Old and New Testaments.

The miracle, or perhaps one should say the triumph of Dostoevsky's genius, is that despite all the cuts and mutilations of the original, there are gleams and glitters throughout the illustrated version of the psychological insight which Dostoevsky possessed to so powerful a degree and which made so stern a judge as Freud declare that only Shakespeare surpassed him as an author and as a literary psychologist. The brilliance and the originality of Dostoevsky's psychologizing comes through mainly in the exchanges between Raskolnikov and Porfiry the detective as the latter gradually traps the murderer into confessing his crime. There are also numerous moments in the illustrated edition which are unknowingly comic and probably the expression of deep unconscious attitudes upon the part of the illustrator and the editor. For example, Raskolnikov at times looks very much like a Russian delegate to the UN who is afraid that the NKVD is after him. At other times Raskolnikov has an unquestionable resemblance to Peter Lorre, the film star who has so often been a villain. At other moments the illustrations—but not the text—suggest a detestation of all intellectuals, not only Raskolnikov, and in general there is the sharp implication throughout that most Russians are either criminals or police agents, and all Russians are somehow fundamentally evil.

I tried to check on this impression which seemed possibly an overinterpretation by examining another cartoon series called *Crime Does NOT Pay* (an immortal aphorism which is not going to hold much weight when the readers and the children find out about Frank Costello); a series about true crimes in the United States. The results of the comparison are incontestable: American crimes and criminals do not resemble Russia's or Dostoevsky's in the least.

The illustrated "edition" of *A Midsummer Night's Dream* is much less of a distortion of the original work. There are none of the serious cuts and omissions which virtually reduce the cartoon version of *Crime and Punishment* to a trite detective story. And the reason is clear enough: Shakespeare's play was intended for an audience which was very much like the juvenile readers of *Classics Illustrated*, and *A Midsummer Night's Dream* is one of the most playful and child-like of plays. Nevertheless here too the medium of the cartoon tends to make this version misleading. For one thing, the title page presents the (juvenile) reader with boxed and oval portraits of four of the leading characters. Under them is a landscape—a lake, a grove of trees, a distant temple, and Puck flying through the air in front of an enormous rising moon—and at the foot of the page is a scroll-like band of words which announces the leading elements of the plot: "A dark forest . . . An angry fairy king . . . His mischievous messenger . . . A magic flower . . . Four thwarted lovers . . . And a troupe of wretched actors make a merry mix-up on a midsummer night . . . ," all of which is fair enough as a brief overture. The illustrated edition begins at the very beginning of the play (something which is certainly far from being the case in all cartoon versions of the classics) and it is at this point that the most important kind of distortion takes place. For, first, there is a slot which explains to the youthful reader the purpose of the scene: "In his palace, Theseus, Duke of Athens, and Hippolyta, Queen of the Amazons, discuss their coming wedding . . . ," an explanation which interferes with the natural dramatic unfolding, although the intention, I suppose, is to help the reader as much as possible and keep him from being in the least perplexed or from feeling that he has to make any serious exertion beyond keeping his eyes open.

Second, and more important by far, the opening speeches, which are in blank verse, are printed as if they were prose. This occurs from beginning to end. There is no conceivable way in which the juvenile reader can find out from the illustrated edition itself that he is reading poetry and not prose, although one would guess that some sense of the movement of language in blank verse rhythms certainly must impinge upon every reader. This failure to make it clear that the speeches are often poetry and not prose may not seem as serious, at first glance, as in actuality it is. For the speeches are bound to be read incorrectly; and worse still, when the juvenile reader does at some later date encounter poetry printed as poetry he is likely to be annoyed, if not irritated to the point where he refuses to read whatever is printed as poetry at all. His illustrated edition will have given him an easy and pleasant experience which becomes an obstacle in reading poetry straight, that is to say, as it was written and as it was meant to be read.

Perhaps it is not as important as I think it is that there should be a certain number of readers of poetry. But the fear that disturbs me can be exemplified by what occurred in a class of freshmen at one of the best universities in the world. The instructor, who was teaching English composition, asked the students to define blank verse. No student volunteered an answer. The instructor expressed his dismay and asked his class if they had not studied Shakespeare and other poets in high school. The students admitted that they had, and finally one student, perhaps feeling sympathy for the clearly distressed teacher, raised his hand and attempted a definition of blank verse: "Sir," he said, hesitantly, tentatively, and unsurely, "isn't blank verse something which looks like poetry, but is not poetry?" It turned out that the well-meaning student supposed that unless there were rhymes at the end of each line, he was not reading poetry. Now this class of students represented what was probably the most intensively and expensively educated young men in America. And as I have said, the incident and others like it occurred at one of the best schools in the world. If such a systematic misunderstanding of the nature of literature and poetry can exist among such young men, what, after all, can be expected of a population which first comes upon great literature in the guise of cartoon editions? One can well imagine a student insisting to his instructor that *A Midsummer Night's Dream* cannot be a play in blank verse, since the student has seen with his own eyes that it was printed as prose. And it is certainly not fanciful to suppose that the day is swiftly approaching when one human being says to another: "Have you read *Hamlet?*" and is answered: "No, but I seen the comic book edition."

Yet certainly there is a good side to everything, however infamous. There always is. And the good side to Shakespeare's plays as cartoon strips might be that some juvenile readers who are oppressed and biased by the way in which Shakespeare is for the most part taught in high schools all over America will now come upon Shakespeare first of all as a cartoon and see that he is really a great deal of fun, he is not a painful assignment in homework and a difficult, outmoded, canonized ancient author who wrote strange plays which provide the teachers of English with inexhaustible and eminently respectable reasons for boring their students. But there must be other and less misleading ways of demonstrating the pleasures of poetry to juvenile readers.

It is true that to encounter a literary masterpiece in a dramatic or cinematic form sometimes gives the reader, juvenile or adult, a new view and a new interest in the work. The French films of Dostoevsky's *The Idiot* and *Crime and Punishment* not only gave me a new and clarified understanding of both novels, but it seemed to me that the changes that were made in the original text were often improvements. The same was true of the German film version of *The Brothers Karamazov*, even though the character of Alyosha and the fable of the Grand Inquisitor were omitted, probably for theatrical reasons. And it is even more true that when a Shakespearean film is made well, as *A Midsummer Night's Dream* and *Henry V* were, there is a great gain for the common reader of Shakespeare who is used to reading him in a book rather than grasping his plays as visual experiences.

The fundamental question, whether it is a matter of the filmed Shakespeare or the cartoon book Shakespeare, seems to me to be: will the juvenile reader ever arrive at the point where he wants to see the original as it was intended to be, in its full actuality as a work? And the answer which suggests itself is a depressing one. If you get used to getting literature with illustrations—"visualized" is the phrase, I think—then you are likely to feel deprived when there are no illustrations and you have to do all the work yourself, depending upon the book itself. Moreover, the vice of having your visualizing done for you is all too likely to make you unused if not unwilling to read books which have no pictures in them. The Chinese proverb, "A picture is worth a thousand words," is often quoted by American advertisers. But the Chinese meant something very different from what the advertisers are trying to say. The Chinese meant that the visual experience of an object was more likely to give the full concreteness of that object than many of the words about it, which are for the most part abstract, generalized, colorless, and the like. The advertisers mean that human beings are more interested in looking at things (and find it easier) than in reading about them, so that the pictures in an ad are more efficacious in increasing sales than the words that accompany the pictures.

This fact is relevant to *Classics Illustrated* in the most direct way: the reader finds it easy and pleasant to look at words-with-pictures, he finds it more difficult and less pleasant to look at words which have no pictures to make them clear and visual. There is a tendency among some readers to read so much that their capacity to look at the visual world is spoiled. But far worse and far more prevalent is the tendency (of which masterpieces in cartoon form are an apt example) to read as little as possible and to prefer a thousand pictures to a single paragraph of intelligent reading matter. The over-all picture of the state of literacy was formulated two years ago by Gilbert Seldes in *The Great Audience,* a book which did not receive the attention it deserved: "In fourteen million homes equipped with radios, *no* magazines are read; families with television sets read fewer magazines than those who do not have them; half the adults in America never buy books." It is simple to transpose this statement to the great juvenile audience and to their reading of comic books and of the classics in cartoon form.

When we turn to the cartoon book version of *Gulliver's Travels,* other aspects of juvenile literacy (I was about to write, delinquency!) become clear. Of course *Gulliver's Travels* has been a children's classic for a long time as well as one of the greatest works of English literature for those who have reached the age of reason and consent. In the past, however, it is unquestionably true that the children's version of Swift's best work did not become a barrier to the interest of the same children in that work when they were old enough to want to enjoy the masterworks of their native language. The cartoon book version, unlike the older children's edition of *Gulliver's Travels,* goes much further in mutilation. At the end of the cartoon version, there is no plea by the publisher, as there was in *Crime and Punishment,* and in *A Midsummer Night's Dream,* telling the reader that he ought to read this work in its original form. There is, however, as in all the *Classics Illustrated,* a biography of the author. These biographies vary in inaccuracy, but they are all inaccurate to some degree. Swift's cartoon biography contains a number of trivial errors— such as the statement that he began to write in 1704—but the important distortion is a truth which is stated in such a way that it is likely to mislead and deceive anyone who wants to find out the truth and is limited in the resources and skills necessary to finding out what the truth is (as, obviously, most juvenile readers are, whether they are quiz kids or not).

The truth which is stated in such a way as to be entirely misleading is set forth in the cartoon biography of Swift as follows:

Gulliver's Travels was written by Swift as a savage commentary on the European world Swift knew, as a condemnation of the laws and customs of his own and other countries that led one of the characters in the story to describe the inhabitants of Europe as "the most pernicious race of little odious vermin that nature ever suffered to crawl upon the surface of the earth." In later years Swift's satire became more and more violently bitter, possibly the result of mental disease which, by 1736, caused him to become insane.

Whoever wrote the cartoon biography may not have a chance to read the cartoon version. For there is very little in the cartoon version to suggest that the original is a "savage commentary" in which human beings are condemned as "odious little vermin." Moreover, the cartoon biography suggests that Swift was commenting on the state of human nature in his own time, and not in all times and places which he knew about. There is also the suggestion that the bitterness and violence of his satire were probably due to the onset of mental disease. All of this apology is unnecessary, however, for the reader who only knows of Swift through the cartoon edition. And what the biography states is literally true, and as true, deceptive. Swift did suffer from mental disease, and the disappointment of his political ambition did inspire in part the savage indignation which makes *Gulliver's Travels* a masterpiece. But the juvenile reader has no need of reassurance as to the benign character of human nature and the one-sidedness of Swift's point of view. In the cartoon version Gulliver returns to England and we last see him as he stands at the wheel of the ship which is coming into an English harbor. The captain of the ship, who is standing next to him, says: "There she is! Good old Brittania!" and Gulliver expresses his own pleasure in returning to civilized Europe and merry England by saying: "I certainly am happy to be back . . . but it will take me weeks to get used to moving among people my own size!" He has had strange and interesting adventures and now he is delighted to be home.

Surely no explanation that Swift was a disappointed man of genius who concluded in insanity is necessary if all the reader has read is the cartoon edition. If he reads the original, he is certainly bound to be disturbed. For the original concludes in a way which is very different from *Classics Illustrated.* Gulliver explains to the "Courteous Readers," on the next to the last page, that having lived among horses and among human beings, he still prefers horses to human beings. When he has just come back to his own house in England, his wife's kiss makes him faint: "My Wife took me in her Arms, and kissed me; at which, having not been used to the touch of that odious Animal for so many years, I fell in a Swoon for almost an hour," and he feels disgusted with himself at the thought that he has become the father of human beings: the fact strikes him "with the utmost Shame, Confusion, and Horror." For the first year after his return to England "I could not endure my Wife or Children in my Presence, the Smell of them was intolerable." (I am quoting at length because anyone who has not read *Gulliver's Travels* recently will probably think any synopsis or paraphrase an exaggeration of Swift's satire.) As to the purpose of the work, Gulliver declares that "I write for the noblest End, to inform and instruct Mankind, over whom I may, without Breach of Modesty, pretend to some superiority, from the Advantages I received by conversing among the most accomplished Houyhnhnms. I write without any View toward Profit or Praise," which is to say that, having dwelt with horses, Gulliver feels superior to mankind and capable of instructing human beings in how to improve. At the very end, having been back among civilized human beings for five years, Gulliver declares that he is now able to sit at the same dinner table with his wife, although since the smell of any civilized being is still offensive to him, he has to keep applying rue, lavender, or tobacco to his nose. And he adds that he would be able to accept human nature as it is in most of its follies and vices except for one unbearable trait, the vice of pride, which causes more viciousness than any other human trait. It is the viciousness of pride and vanity which make civilized existence insupportable.

Clearly there is little likelihood that the juvenile reader of the cartoon version of *Gulliver's Travels* will be corrupted by Swift's cynicism and nihilism (which was inspired, we ought to remember, by an intense idealism and an intense purity as well as by the disappointment of ambition and the distortion of growing neurosis). But the important point here is not the juvenile reader himself or herself, but the adult publisher and editor who has exhibited a well-meaning solicitude for the juvenile reader's tender sensibility. For whoever is responsible for the cartoon version is very much aware of the true character of *Gulliver's Travels* and wishes to spare the feelings and the mind of the juvenile audience. But where does this solicitude stop?

I must turn to personal experience to show how far the solicitude and the censorship can go. When I taught English composition to freshmen and coeds ten years ago along with some twenty-five other instructors, a crisis occurred as a result of the modern novels which the students had been assigned to read. One of the coeds had been reading late at night at her English assignment, which was John Dos Passos' *U.S.A.* Dos Passos' savage indignation, which resembles Swift's, and his explicit account of the sexual experiences of his characters, terrified the young lady to the point where she had to waken her father (not her mother!) and tell him that she had been scared and shocked by her reading assignment in English. The unhappy father conferred with the head of the English staff, who in turn discussed the entire issue with the entire staff. The head of the staff was very much aware of both sides of the problem and he tried to be just to the interests and rights of his instructors as well as to the problems of adolescents who are in the first year of their undergraduate careers. But in such a situation, judiciousness and compromise can accomplish very little. Most of the instructors felt, whether rightly or wrongly, that they had been told not to assign Dos Passos, or Joyce, or Thomas Mann, or Proust, or Gide or Celine to their students. They felt that they probably would be fulfilling their duty as teachers of English composition and literature better if they went no further than such authors as Dickens, Thackeray, George Eliot, and George Meredith. Thomas Hardy was an ambiguous and questionable author, given the point of view which a shocked coed had brought to the fore, since *Jude the Obscure* and *Tess of the D'Urbervilles* were both books which might very well be shocking again as they had been when they first appeared (as a result of which scandal, the heartsick Hardy ceased to write novels).

The juvenile and adolescent reader certainly ought not to be scared and shocked. But he ought not to be cut off from the reality of great literature and of modern literature (the latter being, because of its contemporaneity, the best way of getting the ordinary adolescent reader interested in literature of any kind). And it is essential and necessary to remember that if a human being does not become interested in literature when he is an undergraduate, it is quite unlikely that he will become a devoted reader at any other time of life.

The teaching of English has a direct and continuous relationship to the kinds of books which juvenile, adolescent, and adult readers are likely to desire to read. The cartoon version of *Gulliver's Travels* suggests still another incident in the teaching of English literature. The text in this instance was Swift's *A Modest Proposal,* in which Swift proposes among other things that the economic problem of Ireland might be solved if the Irish bred children and then butchered them for food. In the seven years during which, at some point during the year, I had to assign this little classic of satire to freshman students, I naturally encountered a variety of impressions on their part. But the most frequent and representative comment was exemplified by a student of Armenian parents (he must have heard of the Turks) and a boy who was Irish (and who must have heard of the English in Ireland). Both students announced that Swift was "morbid." I was tempted to embark upon a self-indulgent excursion when I heard this comment and to say that I would not permit the greatest prose writer in English, except for Shakespeare, perhaps, to be called "morbid," and to recall to the students what they had heard about the Turks in Armenia, the English in Ireland, to say nothing of Buchenwald and Dachau. But I felt that the students would merely have concluded that I too was morbid. By questioning them with some degree of patience, I found out that after they had read comic books, listened to soap operas, and witnessed the sweetness and light of the motion pictures, they were inclined to regard anything which is serious satire as morbid sensationalism.

To return directly to the cartoon versions of the Classics: it is customary and habitual, when one has expressed the point of view I have suggested here, to be asked, *What is to be done?* I do not suffer from the delusion that I know what is to be done. But I confess that I sometimes entertain certain modest guesses, the practicality of which I cannot determine. The reading of comic books, and cartoon versions of the classics (and listening to the radio, looking at the motion pictures and listening and looking at television programs) cannot be stopped. Mass culture is here to stay: it is a major industry and a very profitable one, and one can no more banish it than one can banish the use of automobiles because thirty-four thousand people are killed by cars every year. And even if the reading of cartoon books might be stopped, it is probable the prohibition and censorship would have the usual boomerang effect.

What can be done, I think (or rather, I guess), is to set a good example, or perhaps I should say an example which is the least of all the possible evil examples, namely: each adult and literate human being who feels that literature is one of the necessary conditions of civilized existence can set the example of reading *both* the original classics and the cartoon versions. By doing both, he is keeping his hold on the literature at its best and at the same time he is remaining aware of the experience and thus the consciousness of any other reader: children, juveniles, adolescents, housewives, aged relatives, farmers, mechanics, taxi-drivers—in fact, everyone! For the products of mass culture preoccupy the minds of most human beings in America, whether they know it or not. And in setting the good or least evil example of maintaining his hold on great literature in the midst of forcing himself to be aware of the debased versions and mutilations and dilutions of it, he may make some other readers imitative enough to come or return to the classics in their full actuality. This proposal may seem very much like one of the labors of Hercules. But it is also a lot of fun, at least some of the time. Besides, Hercules was a hero, and as practically everyone knows, all human beings want to be heroic heroes and heroines, at least once in a while.

STUDY QUESTIONS

1. Is there anything fundamentally wrong about putting a profound and complicated work into such a medium as the comic-strip? Or is it possible to imagine a superior comic strip which does justice to the qualities of a great work, like the movie versions of Dostoevsky novels which, as Schwartz comments, were as good as or better than the originals?

2. Why does Schwartz feel that it is wrong to make things easy for the reader by means of pictures? Or that young readers should not be sheltered from the harsh realities some literature describes? Why does he feel it unlikely that the comic-book version of a classic will lead its readers to the original?

3. Why does Schwartz appear to be more concerned about the use of "masterpieces" as the subjects of cartoons than he would be if original scripts were used?

4. Select some short classic which has been published in comic-book form and compare the original in some detail with the comic-book version. Be prepared to explain to what extent your examination bears out or does not bear out Schwartz's conclusions.

5. Discuss some treatment of a classic in a popular culture medium such as TV or the movies. Were the original values retained? Did the interpretation do justice to the original? Was any improvement made?

6. There have always been objections to new forms of popular art. The stage, the movies and the novel were all criticized when they were new as vulgar and vulgarizing. Do you think that the criticism of the comics is a case of history repeating itself and that they will eventually come to occupy an accepted and valuable place in civilized life?

2. PERSPECTIVES ON POPULAR CULTURE

In What Spirit the Americans Cultivate the Arts*

Alexis de Tocqueville

It would be to waste the time of my readers and my own, if I strove to demonstrate how the general mediocrity of fortunes, the absence of superfluous wealth, the universal desire for comfort, and the constant efforts by which everyone attempts to procure it, make the taste for the useful predominate over the love of the beautiful in the heart of man. Democratic nations, among whom all these things exist, will therefore cultivate the arts which serve to render life easy, in preference to those whose object is to adorn it. They will habitually prefer the useful to the beautiful, and they will require that the beautiful should be useful.

But I propose to go further; and, after having pointed out this first feature, to sketch several others.

It commonly happens that, in the age of privilege, the practice of almost all the arts becomes a privilege, and that every profession is a separate domain into which it is not allowable for everyone to enter. Even when productive industry is free, the fixed character which belongs

* Reprinted from *Democracy in America* (1835). Adapted from the Henry Reeve translation.

to aristocratic nations gradually segregates all the persons who practice the same art till they form a distinct class, always composed of the same families, whose members are all known to each other, and among whom a public opinion of their own and a species of corporate pride soon spring up. In a class or guild of this kind each artisan has not only his fortune to make, but his reputation to preserve. He is not exclusively swayed by his own interest or even by that of his customer, but by that of the body to which he belongs; and the interest of that body is that each artisan should produce the best possible workmanship. In aristocratic ages the object of the arts is therefore to manufacture as well as possible, not with the greatest dispatch or at the lowest rate.

When, on the contrary, every profession is open to all, when a multitude of persons are constantly embracing and abandoning it, and when its several members are strangers, indifferent to, and because of their numbers hardly seen by, each other, the social tie is destroyed, and each workman, standing alone, endeavors simply to gain the most money at the least cost. The will of the customer is then his only limit. But at the same time a corresponding change takes place in the customer also. In countries in which riches, as well as power, are concentrated and retained in the hands of a few, the use of the greater part of this world's goods belongs to a small number of individuals, who are always the same. Necessity, public opinion, or moderate desires exclude all others from the enjoyment of them. As this aristocratic class remains fixed at the pinnacle of greatness on which it stands, without diminution or increase, it is always acted upon by the same wants and affected by them in the same manner. The men of whom it is composed naturally derive from their superior and hereditary position a taste for what is extremely well made and lasting. This affects the general way of thinking of the nation in relation to the arts. It often occurs, among such a people, that even the peasant will rather go without the objects he covets than procure them in a state of imperfection. In aristocracies, then, the handicraftsmen work for only a limited number of fastidious customers; the profit they hope to make depends principally on the perfection of their workmanship.

Such is no longer the case when, all privileges being abolished, ranks are intermingled and men are forever rising or sinking upon the social scale. Among a democratic people a number of citizens always exist whose patrimony is divided and decreasing. They have contracted, under more prosperous circumstances, certain wants, which remain after the means of satisfying such wants are gone; and they are anxiously looking out for some surreptitious method of providing for them. On the other hand, there are always in democracies a large number of men whose fortune is on the increase, but whose desires grow much faster than their fortunes, and who gloat upon the gifts of wealth in anticipation, long before they have means to obtain them. Such men are eager to find some short cut to these gratifications, already almost within their reach. From the combination of these two causes the result is that in democracies there is always a multitude of persons whose wants are above their means, and who are very willing to take up with imperfect satisfaction rather than abandon the object of their desires altogether.

The artisan readily understands these passions, for he himself partakes in them. In an aristocracy he would seek to sell his workmanship at a high price to the few; he now conceives that the more expeditious way of getting rich is to sell them at a low price to all. But there are only two ways of lowering the price of commodities. The first is to discover some better, shorter, and more ingenious method of producing them; the second is to manufacture a larger quantity of goods, nearly similar, but of less value. Among a democratic population all the intellectual faculties of the workman are directed to these two objects: he strives to invent methods which may enable him not only to work better, but quicker and cheaper; or, if he cannot succeed in that, to diminish the intrinsic quality of the thing he makes, without rendering it wholly unfit for the use for which it is intended. When none but the wealthy had watches, they were almost all very good ones; few are now made which are worth much, but everybody has one in his pocket. Thus the democratic principle not only tends to direct the human mind to the useful arts, but it induces the artisan to produce with great rapidity many imperfect commodities, and the consumer to content himself with these commodities.

Not that, in democracies, the arts are incapable, in case of need, of producing wonders. This may occasionally be the case, if customers appear who are ready to pay for time and trouble. In this rivalry of every kind of industry, in the midst of this immense competition and these countless experiments, some excellent workmen are formed who reach the utmost limits of their craft. But they rarely have an opportunity of showing what they can do; they are scrupulously sparing of their powers; they remain in a state of accomplished mediocrity, which judges itself, and though well able to shoot beyond the mark before it, aims only at what it hits. In aristocracies, on the contrary, workmen always do all they can; and when they stop, it is because they have reached the limit of their art.

When I arrive in a country where I find some of the finest productions of the arts, I learn from this fact nothing of the social condition or of the political constitution of the country. But if I perceive that the productions of the arts are generally of an inferior quality, very abundant, and very cheap, I am convinced that, among the people where this occurs, privilege is on the decline, and that ranks are beginning to intermingle and will soon be confounded together.

The handicraftsmen of democratic ages endeavor not only to bring their useful productions within the reach of the whole community, but strive to give to all their commodities attractive qualities that they do not in reality possess. In the confusion of all ranks, everyone hopes to appear what he is not, and makes great exertions to succeed in this object. This sentiment, indeed, which is but too natural to the heart of man, does not originate in the democratic principle; but that principle applies it to material objects. The hypocrisy of virtue is of every age, but the hypocrisy of luxury belongs more particularly to the ages of democracy.

To satisfy these new cravings of human vanity, the arts have recourse to every species of imposture; and these devices sometimes go so far as to defeat their own purpose. Imitation diamonds are now made which may be easily mistaken for real ones; as soon as the art of fabricating false diamonds shall become so perfect that they cannot be distinguished from real ones, it is probable that both will be abandoned, and become mere pebbles again.

This leads me to speak of those arts which are called, by way of distinction, the fine arts. I do not believe that it is a necessary effect of a democratic social condition and of democratic institutions to diminish the number of those who cultivate the fine arts; but these causes exert a powerful influence on the manner in which these arts are cultivated. Many of those who had already contracted a taste for the fine arts are impoverished; on the other hand, many of those who are not yet rich begin to conceive that taste, at least by imitation; the number of consumers increases, but opulent and fastidious consumers become more scarce. Something analogous to what I have already pointed out in the useful arts then takes place in the fine arts; the productions of artists are more numerous, but the merit of each production is diminished. No longer able to soar to what is great, they cultivate what is pretty and elegant, and appearance is more attended to than reality.

In aristocracies a few great pictures are produced; in democratic countries a vast number of insignificant ones. In the former, statues are raised of bronze; in the latter, they are modeled in plaster.

When I arrived for the first time at New York, by that part of the Atlantic Ocean which is called the East River, I was surprised to perceive along the shore, at some distance from the city, a number of little palaces of white marble, several of which were of classic architecture. When I went the next day to inspect more closely one which had particularly attracted my notice, I found that its walls were of whitewashed brick, and its columns of painted wood. All the edifices which I had admired the night before were of the same kind.

The social condition and the institutions of democracy impart, moreover, certain peculiar tendencies to all the imitative arts, which it is easy to point out. They frequently withdraw them from the delineation of the soul to fix them exclusively on that of the body, and they substitute the representation of motion and sensation for that of sentiment and thought; in a word, they put the Real in the place of the Ideal.

I doubt whether Raphael studied the minute intricacies of the mechanism of the human body as thoroughly as the draftsmen of our time. He did not attach the same importance as they do to rigorous accuracy on this point, because he aspired to surpass nature. He sought to make of man something which should be superior to man, and to embellish beauty itself. David and his scholars were, on the contrary, as good anatomists as they were painters. They wonderfully depicted the models which they had before their eyes, but they rarely imagined anything beyond them; they followed nature with fidelity, while Raphael sought for something better than nature. They have left us an exact portraiture of man, but he discloses in his work a glimpse of the Divinity.

This remark as to the manner of treating a subject is no less applicable to the choice of it. The painters of the Renaissance generally sought far above themselves, and away from their own time, for mighty subjects, which left to their imagination an unbounded range. Our painters often employ their talents in the exact imitation of the details of private life, which they have always before their eyes; and they are forever copying trivial objects, the originals of which are only too abundant in nature.

STUDY QUESTIONS

1. According to Tocqueville, what are the factors present in an aristocracy that encourage the artist to do his best? What factors in a democracy encourage him to compromise?

2. In what way does Tocqueville relate the demand for the kind of art that imitates the real thing to the social situation in a democracy?

3. Apply Tocqueville's observation about the tendency of artists in a democracy to produce much at the expense of quality to the popular literature found in magazines, newspapers and detective stories. Does his generalization hold true in the field of music or architecture?

4. Is Tocqueville's closing observation about the preference for dealing with the real rather than the ideal true in the light of present-day movies, novels and TV plays?

5. Is Tocqueville's generalization about the useful arts applicable today? Write a theme discussing this question. (Remember that in spite of his criticisms, he does admit that democracy can produce "wonders" in this field.)

6. Do you think Tocqueville has failed to mention some of the ways in which a democracy favors the production of excellent art? Write a theme defending democracy against his objections and showing how certain conditions present in a democracy work in the artist's favor.

Reflections on Mass Culture*

Ernest van den Haag

By and large, people seriously concerned with mass culture fall into three groups. There is first a nucleus of artists and literary men, supported by a few theoreticians. They feel isolated, alienated, submerged and pushed aside by mass culture; their hopes are dim and they detest it. The literati and the theoreticians are opposed by another group —the practical men, who have decided it is their duty to work for the mass media in spite of the opulent salaries pressed on them. Sedulously aided by academic fellow travelers, they resolutely defend popular culture and their own *sacrificium intellectus*.

The third and largest group stays squarely in the middle, although for motley reasons. Most sociologists are located here; they have been taught that to be anywhere else, particularly when cultural matters are involved, is unscientific. Besides, many of them lack the trained sensibility that would discriminate between, say, English prose and their own writing. Liberal philosophers, on the other hand, have investigated the impossibilities of justifying value judgments for so long that they regard anyone criticizing mass culture for moral or aesthetic reasons as bold but naïve. There is no evidence, they seem to say, for practically any view; hence, let's close our eyes and discuss methodology.

With all that, liberal philosophers seem to stress, somewhat unilaterally, the lack of evidence for negative views of mass culture. Perhaps they feel uneasy with rejections of mass culture because of political fears—misplaced ones, in my opinion. They seem unable to free themselves from the suspicion that a rejection of mass culture implies a rejection of the masses (although the contrary is no less logical) and is, therefore, antidemocratic. However, this is a *non sequitur*. One might think little of the cultural capacity of the masses but not therefore of their political capacity.[1] But even if one thinks little of their political competence, one might still feel that there is no reason why they should not suffer, benefit and possibly learn from its use (and no more is needed to argue for democracy). Finally, although one might be somewhat pes-

* Reprinted from *The American Scholar*, Volume 29, Number 2, Spring, 1960, © copyright 1960 by the United Chapters of Phi Beta Kappa. By permission of the publishers.
[1] Conversely, I have not found cultivated people to be politically very sagacious. (I'd prefer to entrust my political destiny to farmers or workers rather than to professors as a group.)

simistic about the masses, one might be even more so about the political capacity of restricted groups. At any rate, neither mass culture nor objections to it seem to promote specific political views: fascists and communists, as often as liberals, favor mass culture, although they occasionally borrow some phrases from its opponents.

Historians, who of all men might be expected to discern the uniqueness of mass culture, seldom do. When they pay heed to mass culture as a historical phenomenon, they seem to take the wrong cue. Thus, Stuart Hughes recently observed, in a perceptive paper, that "our students yawn over the classics" because they have "very little to do with their own lives." He implies that we might as well forget about the classics. This seems odd. Students have always yawned over the classics—only, in times past, teachers were not so sensitive to their own popularity rating nor so eager to entertain their students as to be willing to drop the classics. They dropped some yawning students instead and kept the interested ones. An immature mind cannot understand the classics; and it matures, in part, by learning to understand them—or, at least, to know them so that they may be understood later. Students brought up in an age of rapid technological change may be convinced that literature, like machinery, is subject to obsolescence—a conviction some teachers share or dare not oppose enough to crack the shell. Perhaps this is what makes the classics seem irrelevant.

Yet the classics, if truly classic, cannot be irrelevant, for they deal with subjects relevant to the universal human predicament in ways to be re-experienced perennially. Of course, it is possible that we have become irrelevant to the classics: if our lives have lost all meaning, then no literature worthy of that name can be meaningful to us. For it is the possible meaning of human life that classic literature explores; and we cannot be interested without any experience of meaning and style in our own lives. If we have no such experience, then entertainment bereft of meaning— diversion from boredom, time killing, mass culture—is all that remains. In this case, the relevant must become irrelevant, and only what is irrelevant to begin with can be absorbed. But I'm not yet willing to give up altogether. Under favorable conditions, the study of literature helps us see the possibilities of man's career on earth.

While some are ready to yield to those bored by high culture, others are convinced that the mass media can serve, indeed do serve, to bring high culture to the masses, and that in doing so they justify their existence or, at least, render an important service. Popular magazines may have authors such as Norman Vincent Peale, the argument goes, but don't they also publish an occasional uncensored article by Bertrand Russell? They do. However, a piece by a major philosopher does not make a philosophical magazine out of *Look*—it may make a popular journalist out of the philosopher. In the stream of, at best, diverting banalities, the worthwhile piece tends to disappear without impact. It may seduce a Russell to lower his standards and write more such pieces, becoming less worth while and more acceptable in the process. It won't lure *Look* readers into the *Principia Mathematica.* Mass culture can be decorated with high culture pieces without being otherwise changed.

Note further that Russell's opinions are not offered to *Look* readers because of their intrinsic merit; they are offered because they are *his* opinions. Russell is by now a public figure, which means that he can be published without being taken seriously. Had I written the same words, I could not have broken into *Look,* precisely because people might have taken the utterance seriously instead of gobbling it up with the rest of the fare, while captivated by the utterer's fame.

Not everybody defends the mass media as vehicles that bring elements of high culture to the masses. Some depict the culture of the masses, articulated by the mass media in their normal offerings, as superior to high culture to begin with. Thus, one of mass culture's most faithful admirers, Mr. Gilbert Seldes, recently explained that he thinks more highly of Charlie Chaplin than of Marcel Proust because the former has brought more happiness to more people than the latter. Now happiness is hard to measure, and I am not sure that it makes sense to compare the feeling of a person reading Proust to that of another seeing Chaplin. We may grant, however, that more persons have been amused and diverted by Chaplin than by Proust. Still more people are made happy or are diverted by whiskey, apple pie, penicillin, Marilyn Monroe or, perhaps, by a movie that Mr. Seldes and I might agree is thoroughly bad. In short, making people happy is a criterion only if that is what one sets out to do—and I doubt that this was Proust's purpose or the purpose of any serious writer. Surely more persons enjoy Rodgers and Hammerstein than Bach—more enjoy Liberace than Glen Gould. By definition, popular culture is enjoyed by more people than high culture. Mr. Seldes' view would sanction the elimination of art in favor of entertainment—high-class entertainment, at best.

And this is precisely what I am afraid of. Mass culture demands entertainment and so extravagantly rewards those who provide it with money, prestige and power that serious artists become isolated—and tempted. To be sure, such tendencies have always existed; but now they prevail. The strength of the offerings of mass culture, compared with those of art, has risen immensely, and the dividing line has been blurred.

The chances for the values of mass culture to be internalized in childhood also have greatly increased, so that what I have described as temptation is not felt to be such, but, on the contrary, as the due reward for well-directed, talented efforts. The view held by Mr. Seldes in all innocence is widely accepted by less articulate persons. It is a very basic American view, a naïvely pragmatic and philanthropic view that refuses to recognize what cannot be tangibly measured in terms at once hedonistic and altruistic.[2] The measurement for art thus becomes the number of people made happy—and as soon as this becomes the end of art, art ends.

The answer to those who oppose pessimistic views on mass culture lies here. They argue that there is no evidence that the masses are culturally worse off. (I suspect they are far from well off, but comparisons are nearly impossible.) As far as the elite is concerned, they ask what prevents it from being as creative as ever? Why can't it coexist with mass culture? Haven't there always been several coexisting levels of culture? Can't we have a pluralistic society?

This reasonable argument overlooks the historically most distinctive and important characteristic of mass culture: the dominant power of the mass of consumers over production, public opinion and prestige. The elite in the past was sufficiently isolated and protected from the masses (which, properly speaking, did not exist as such) to be able to cultivate its own garden. And the mass market (hardly in existence) had nothing much to offer. Further, power, income and prestige distribution being what they were, the masses had no desire to impinge on the culture of the elite; on the contrary, they made room for it. At any rate, if they had a wish to participate or encroach, they had no way of making their demands felt and of articulating them. (Even political revolutions, before Hitler, were led and inspired by members of the elite.) But this has changed. We all now cultivate cash crops in market gardens. Mass culture is manufactured according to the demands of the mass market. No *independent* elite culture is left, for mass culture is far too pervasive to permit it. Cultivated individuals and islands of high culture remain, of course. But they are interstitial and on the defensive even when admired and respected; indeed, then more than ever, for they easily may be "taken up" and typecast. The intellect when alive is not part of our social structure, nor does it have its own domicile.

A convinced egalitarian may ask, So what? No more elite, no more high culture; but the great majority of people—who never belonged— have what they wish. To be sure, most people never were, are not now, and are unlikely ever to be interested in high culture. Yet, it does not follow that high culture is unimportant. Its importance cannot be measured by the number of people to whom it is important. Political issues may be decided by majority vote (or, at least, by letting the majority choose who is to decide them). This is surely not a good way, but nevertheless, I think, the best available.

However, the analogy between political issues and cultural issues (or, for that matter, moral ones) is inappropriate. Political issues, by what-

---

[2] When the Puritan American heritage collided with the more hedonistic attitudes of later immigrants, an interesting fusion resulted. Pleasure, the Puritans implied, is bad; sacrifice, good. The immigrants wanted to pursue happiness. The resulting attitude is: the pleasure sacrificed and given to others is all right, as is the happiness shared and given. What is bad becomes good if it is not enjoyed by oneself but produced for others.

ever means they are decided, require collective action. Taxes cannot be levied only on those who feel they benefit proportionately from a pattern of public expenditure, or on individuals who are willing to vote for them. With art and literature it is otherwise, or it was. They could be cultivated by intellectual elites, without mass participation. This is becoming less possible every day. Mass culture threatens to decide cultural issues by a sort of universal suffrage. This is a threat to culture, not an occasion for rejoicing. For once cultural issues are regarded as indivisible, the majority view will prevail—and the majority prefers entertainment to art. Yet, unlike properly political matters, cultural ones do not require collective action, but rather that the mass of people and the law do not interfere. Culture cannot be created by political actions, although it can be destroyed by them. (The support of social groups is required, of course, but not that of society—or of masses—except inasmuch as it makes the existence of the social groups possible.) There would never have been any serious art, philosophy or literature if a majority vote had decided whether a given work was to be created and presented.

Yet, even if these things are important only to a few people, they are the best and most important people, the saving remnant. Actually, these things and these people are important even to those who ignorantly sneer at them. Such feelings as love; such experiences as wit, beauty or moral obligation; or styles of congress, housing and living—all, however degenerate they may become, are brought into existence and elaborated by artists and intellectuals. Without them, life is formless. With them, there is, at least, a paradigm. The most common of human experiences and the most trite still depend on artists and intellectuals to become fully conscious and articulate. Even the silliest entertainer and his public are part of, or are parasites of, a long line of creators of cultural expression—artists, philosophers, writers, composers, et cetera. For as Bernard Berenson suggested, "Popular art is always a derivation from professional individual art." Just as the technician depends on pure scientists he may never have heard of, so civilized nations in general depend on the creators of cultural expression—intellectuals and artists. The relation of the cultural elite to the masses may be compared to the relation of the saints and the cloistered to the faithful at large. Or, the cultural elite may be compared to the playwrights and the actors on stage, whose words, actions, costumes and settings are of significance to the spectators across the footlights, even though they are but spectators.

Although few people become outstanding mathematicians, scholars and artists, or understand what these are doing, society must permit those who cultivate such activities their separate existence or cease to be civilized. And the loss and degeneration of civilization injures everyone—the living and the unborn generations for whom we should hold in trust their rightful heritage. It is not enough, either, to permit some individual specialists to go their way. We need an intellectual and artistic elite (joined, of course, by merit) supported by a necessarily restricted and therefore discriminating public, both with reasonably continuous traditions. If this elite is not allowed autonomy and self-cultivation, if instead it is induced to follow mass tastes and to cater to them, there can be no cultural creation. We may parasitically ring a few changes on the culture of the past; we may find ways to entertain ourselves; but we won't have a style and an experience of our own.

I should not object to cultural pluralism—to mass culture coexisting with high culture—if it were possible. (Folk culture is long dead—although many people don't know a zombie when they see one.) A universally shared high culture is, of course, absurd and self-contradictory. This may sound snobbish, but I didn't make the world; I'm merely describing it. Talents as well as intelligence and sensitivity to various values are differentially distributed. We are lucky if 1 or 2 per cent of the population can be creative in any sense and 15 to 20 per cent can cultivate some sensibility. The remainder benefits indirectly.

The trouble with mass culture is that in various direct and indirect ways it tends to make the existence of high culture impossible. In our eagerness to open opportunity to everybody, we have greatly diminished the prizes available to anybody. Good wine is hard to cultivate when it is habitually diluted and we are brought up to be indiscriminate. We might do well to abandon the sterile and injurious attempts to "improve" mass culture, for its main effect is to debase high culture by "bringing it to the masses." What we must do is to bring some gifted people—not masses—to high culture. We must concentrate on finding ways to save and transmit high culture independently of the culture of mass society. My own view is pessimistic. I should like nothing better than to be proved wrong.

STUDY QUESTIONS

1. Van den Haag admits that popular magazines occasionally publish the work of serious and challenging writers, but he is unimpressed by this. What reasons does he give for not regarding it is an improvement in the level of mass culture?

2. The author makes a strong case in defense of the rights of minority preferences in cultural matters. Restate his views.

3. He rejects the creation of happiness as a criterion for evaluating art. What reasons does he or can he have for this?

4. Why is "pluralism" impossible in cultural matters? Why cannot the masses have their culture and the elite theirs?

5. Van den Haag does not systematically discriminate between "mass culture" and "high culture." Would it be possible to enumerate the contrasting qualities these two manifest in our own culture?

6. Do you think some examples, at least of mass culture, are defensible according to van den Haag's standards? He says that the invention of such things as styles, emotional experiences, and wit

justify a special position for high culture. Does mass culture do any of these things? Can you give some examples and show how they function?

Art and Democracy*

Lyman Bryson

It will help us to understand the problem of taste in a technological society, in a society where man is free and in possession of machinery for mass production and mass sales, to look at the older factors in the determination of taste, the aristocrats, the patronized artists, and the folk. But we are making an effort to deal with facts and not with sentimental memories. Most statements about the days "when there was a very high level of taste" are meaningless because one does not know what population was the repository of that fine taste.

The comparative statement is often made, for example, about books. There is supposed to have been a time when the "whole reading public" was excited about Macaulay's next volume. The inference is left that the generations have backslid. The whole reading public of Macaulay's time was a small, expensively educated part of the expensively maintained upper and upper middle class of a small country; what the farmer or the shopkeeper's assistant or the factory worker read, if he read anything, was not considered.

Today, men and women, and indeed adolescents, roughly comparable to these neglected ones, are part of the "whole reading public." It is evident that the same proportion of the larger group does not respond to the best that is now being written or to the best of the past. But whether or not the absolute number of persons who read a book of high quality in America now is a larger or smaller proportion of the total population than was the number that read a good book in England in the nineteenth century might be hard to determine. Our taste in reading for entertainment seems to have changed little.[1] It seems probable, judging from the figures on the printing of books, that the good nonfiction book of today gets a larger proportion of readers out of the whole population in either England or America, although a much smaller proportion of the general reading public, than it would have had a hundred years ago. None of this really makes a great deal of difference unless one believes that great books are

* From *The Next America* by Lyman Bryson. Copyright, 1952, by Harper and Brothers. Reprinted by permission.
[1] James D. Hart, *The Popular Book*. New York: Oxford University Press, 1950.

not now being written because there is no public for them. This is a not impressive kind of nostalgia.

There were three factors in the older situation: the aristocracy, the patronized artist, and the folk. What did each contribute and what did each enjoy? The aristocracy and its aesthetic camp followers did undoubtedly enjoy good things appreciatively and we can generously admit that a large number of them took full advantage of their training and their wealth. Some even sacrificed their comfort to their taste, as did Edward Fitzgerald, who was a great connoisseur and a great gentleman but a humble man. These real zealots of taste were few, of course, but probably roughly as numerous as their counterparts, the eccentrics, who took advantage of their social security to defy all taste.

The social role of the eccentric aristocrat, the man who would be a tramp if he were not endowed to be a gentleman, has never been well studied; it is not trivial. And it is possible that some mild eccentrics who happened also to be greatly gifted, as Walter Savage Landor was, for example, may contribute far more to the growth and variation of taste than is realized. The real eccentric aristocrat is often a moralist and even a reformer. Of Landor, Harriet Martineau said: "He was passionate and prejudiced, but usually in some great cause, and on the right side of it . . ." Wilfrid Scawen Blunt would be another good British example. The range of eccentrics, from rich rascals to eremites of good taste, is wide. It is, of course, also unpredictable, and the breeding and protection of all kinds of eccentrics is one of the prerogatives of an aristocracy that we, in our fashion, would give up. Leaving them aside, the steady educated taste of established families in most European countries has been a conservative but appreciative safeguard of good things. The real accumulation of culture has depended on it. The deviants and the scamps have had too much license behind their social protection but have done little harm. They are not the real price that is paid for the aristocratic system; they are only a minor cost.

The second factor in this older stock situation, to which some modern critics think they long to go back, was the patronage of new artists by the powerful and the wealthy. This does not include ordinary connoisseurship, which is patronage by merchants. Patronage of artists is now becoming, like so many other old cultural functions, the business of democratic government. In the past it has been a concomitant of power, whether governmental or feudal or merely personal. The Medicis, who spent so many millions in their job of being a prime factor in creating the greatest art period of modern times, were both bankers and tyrants. They can be seen as a kind of peak in the possible usefulness of deliberate bounty to creative brains.

If we should try to estimate the general run of patrons as factors in taste, we should have to be generous, I think, to countless men and women who took a decent respect for established art fashions to be a necessary part of their duty. They upheld the taste of their communities in art and music and letters in much the same spirit as nerved them to dispense justice and defend the peace. They seldom discovered or paid for the birth of new genius. In that they did no better, perhaps, than the boards of tax-supported museums today. The trouble with the really new in any art is that it offends taste and we are discussing taste, not creative greatness. There was a rough justice to taste in the patronage that privileged wealth and power could give.

These two factors in the older typical situations, aristocratic appreciation and patronage, did not in any way touch most of the people of the time. Matters of taste were the concern and pleasure of a small, fairly homogeneous social elite which was intelligent enough to be also an elite in refined judgment. The peasantry, the clerks, and the journeymen were not involved although the aesthetic aspects of their lives were marked by good taste, far more so probably than in the democratic present. It is that fact, in part, which accounts for the homesickness for a time of beauty that infects so many critics. Those who want to return to a culture of rigid class levels and those who, for aesthetic reasons, want to go back to the "folk," both argue that the old stratification was better because folk art is simple and substantial and pure. The question to be asked both of them is how much they would be willing to pay in other values, including the aesthetic, in order to get the old times back again. The fact is that the days of a powerful elite, moving circumspectly in the high levels of taste while the peasantry produces honest pots and fine embroidery, could not be recaptured, but that can be for the moment ignored since we are discussing comparative values, not possible reforms.

The folk art that is largely anonymous, conventional, and variant only in the handicraft of the single maker is often beautiful. It is almost never mean or vulgar. It was once worth having. What did it cost? The paradox is that it gave little play to the really creative impulses of the artist and his joy in it was that of the craftsman, which is admirable but different. It gave no scope to inventiveness or imagination. The folk artist created nothing; he made things. I have in several places in this book paid homage to the fine humanity of the craftsman; his use of skill with honesty and devotion is a great social contribution. But into the life of every man, the craftsman and all others, the good society would bring a chance at doing things not by the ancient designs, no matter how beautiful, but by his own invention, his own whim, his own self-developing experiments in freedom. Folk art is nearly always in good taste, not because the craftsman who makes it has creative taste but because he is bound to the old designs.

In all taste there is a dialectic effect; good taste means the standard arrived at in the past by thorough argument among those who are trying to find what is enduring and honest in experience. This dialectic has worked, through generations, in folk art and has produced its wonderful effect. But the folk artist is not, by reason of his craftsmanship, able to carry it on. If he does sometimes invent, that is because all men are artists when given a chance; he is all too likely to be afraid of his own inventions for fear of sacrilege. Folk art is good and its excellences are paid for by the tight restraint that a social system of the old type lays on the craftsman who makes it.

We can have a certainty of good taste if only the trained and sensitive have any freedom to choose; following them, the elites will make wise choices and the peasants will stay in their grooves. The cost of such a system, in so far as it works, is that it denies, to all but the few, any experience at all in aesthetic choice, in real aesthetic creation, in any inventive change. In the past this cost has been paid cheerfully enough, but by men and women who did not know what they were buying at what price.

In these days, and more in America than anywhere else, we have developed a new pattern. The uniformity ascribed to a machine age democracy is a myth, or a misstatement of culture patterns, but the vulgarity we are accused of is a fact. The rich vulgarity of the taste of the American people is the natural result of freedom for commonplace invention, for the small independence of choice in so many aspects of his life that an American enjoys. Instead of presenting to the eye of perspective a firm mosaic of rigid spot patterns, it presents a vast single pattern of dizzy variations. The aristocratic eccentric escaped being vulgar by being singular; there was only one of each kind at a time. The craftsman of folk art cannot show anything but dignity and good taste under the restraint of custom. The modern industrialized democrat shows all kinds of trivial inventions of his own and chooses freely in a wild profusion of the trivial, mass-produced inventions of others.

This kind of variation distresses the social aristocrat, as well as the aristocrat of taste, because it blurs hopelessly the distinctions of caste such as those that are publicly declared in dress. Even now, a peasant woman in her best costume on the streets of Paris is stigmatized for her class and identified for her province. But on Madison Avenue in New York, or Market Street in San Francisco, or anywhere else where this kind of culture has been established, the shopgirl at five o'clock comes into the street in a cheaper version of the same costume her lady customer just purchased. The clerk and the capitalist are hard to distinguish. This is true, of course, only if they want to be alike. In the older systems they could not be alike if they so desired. Now a man may, especially in summer, give a fair indication of his own estimate of his own position by the clothes he wears, the test being almost entirely one of quantity; but it is his own decision that he follows, not a sumptuary prescription of invariant costume or a class-imposed prohibition. He follows his bent.

Vulgarity is the result because vulgarity is the inventiveness of small or inexperienced or too numerous minds. The question that democracy poses is whether or not the restraint of peasant custom is better than the vulgarity of popular choice. To the fastidious onlooker the peasant's good taste is better, of course; there is never any doubt that restraint of those who differ from ourselves in standards of taste is pleasant to the fastidious. Is it better for the persons who must either wear the costumes and use the utensils of their ancestors or pick casually among the products of mass production? In one case, they use with indifferent habit the simple and beautiful things that ages have refined. In the other, they choose. The ease with which the shoddiest commercial gadgets invade a market of peasant buyers shows, first, how little attached they are by anything but habit to the fine old things and, second, how much pleasure they get out of choosing.

The act of choice, the experience of seeing several ways of expressing a need and considering them, and taking one that appeals to some trait of one's own character, is important even in trivial things. The fact that the choice when made will be the vagary of a passing momentary convention, rather than of an ancient one, does not matter. It will be a choice.

Do we dare affirm a hope that long practice in the freedom of small details of personal behavior will lead in the long run to something better than vulgarity? Not, I think, if by "something better" we continue to mean something stylized and localized like a peasant costume. Freedom of mass manufacture which leads to trivial but real differences in what is offered to the mass market, and to freedom for the customers to choose, will not lead to fixed styles. If the question is put in another way, can it get a more hopeful answer? Does industrial designing improve in time and do the customers respond to better ranges of choice? No one can offer anything but an impression on this, of course, but my impression is the hopeful one. The costumes of women in a modern American town today, compared with what their own peasant ancestors wore in Ireland or Poland or Sicily a few generations ago, will serve to give what reasons there are for optimism.

There is first the great gain in self-respect to women in all industrial societies that has come in the fact that their dress is no longer an enforced badge of status. There is also the fact that the present fashion is one of those waves of comparative good sense in which women's fashions are loose and free and healthy. Peasant clothing, in a variable climate, runs to caps and petticoats. But our present fashions run strongly to summer nakedness, and that brings up another aspect of this subject in which so many of the most important aspects of cultural democracy lie hidden in trivialities.

The worship of the sun, which is no doubt exaggerated as far as its hygienic value is concerned, the manners of the beach, and the fond romanticism of the middle-aged Midwesterners who have gone to Southern California and Florida, have all combined to make nakedness in public too common to be noticed, thus disappointing the pioneers. When a brilliantly colored and almost completely exposed young couple come into a roadside restaurant, one may frown in behalf of decorum but be persuaded into amused tolerance by the shapeliness and health of impersonally exhibited bodies. It is possible then to remember that we have talked for years about slavery to clothing, and the neglect of simple naturalness. An involuntary close association with a fat, middle-aged body of either sex, presented with equal assurance, is more disconcerting. One gets himself out of disdain then by hoping that a cult of nakedness may bring on a cult of health. It might even reform our laziness and gluttony until all bodies could be exposed without indecency or ugliness. What supports that hope? Not much perhaps. If there is to be freedom for people to be undressed, the only result one has any rational right to expect is the vulgar display of a good deal of ugliness. Most people are ugly just as most people are vulgar. We define ugliness and vulgarity, whether consciously or not, both in the same way. They are both failures to vary, in the direction of superiority, from the average.

The choice is philosophically simple: we can have men restrained from showing their commonness or we can see them as they are. I say philosophically because the practical choice is more complicated. In an industrial society, where material prosperity depends on inciting and satisfying an endless flood of small choices, difference in consuming interest between one man and another or, as is more common between a woman today and the same woman next week, is as essential to mass production as deeper differences are to democracy.

There are philosophers and poets of freedom who want freedom for all men, provided its beneficiaries express freedom in the way their patrons like. But here, again, we have to be realists and stand by our faith. This is the way men and women are; that is our realism. Freedom is the means by which they will be the best personalities they are capable of being; that is our faith. There is no contradiction between faith and realistic knowledge here but the compromises are seductive to most reformers because their love of mankind is poisoned with disdain.

Do we pay too great a price for freedom by losing little things that add up to good taste? The price paid by the older systems, all of them in fact that have been above savage manners, has been in a tolerance of eccentrics and bigots of judgment among the aristocrats, a sycophancy in the hope of survival among the artists, and a compulsory simplicity among the peasants. What we pay for our system is to tolerate a vast rich vulgarity that covers up the peripheral fossils of aristocracy and patronage still left.

What of the artists? There is a common myth that they have only succeeded in substituting fawning upon the crowd for the older need to flatter a lord. This has to be discussed elsewhere at greater length. I happen to believe that the artist is not damaged by living in our kind of society if he has the artist's real vocation of creative independence.

Moreover, we are a democracy. I am urging that we undertake to make ourselves into a true democracy of culture and of the spirit. The aim of a democracy of culture is to enrich the cultural experience of persons; it corresponds functionally to the political democracy whose end is the political experience of persons. A political democracy is successful not in terms of its political decisions but in the degree that it uses political experience to give every citizen the best chance to be his best self. A democracy of culture (using the word here, of course, in the narrower sense of the enduring things in any society that are sought for their own sake) must be measured by its success in giving its citizens the greatest chances to grow in their appreciation and, still more, in their creative capacities. We have to be brave enough to say, in the face of aesthetes and timid decorous critics, that justification of freedom of taste is not in what a free citizen chooses to wear, or how he builds his house, so much as in the reality of his freedom to follow his own taste whatever it is. The result in human experience is worth having now, and if it be true that taste grows by experience and by the dialectic of free social life, in the long run future taste will be better, also, for better reasons.

STUDY QUESTIONS

1. How does Bryson show that the formation of good taste in the general public is at odds with democratic principles? Do you agree with his argument?

2. In what way were artists better off under the old social situation described by Bryson?

3. What significance does Bryson attach to the fact that the social classes in a democracy are not distinguishable by their clothes?

4. Note that Bryson sees the vulgarity of popular culture as the result of the nature of the mass of people. Compare his cause-effect interpretation of the situation with that of Mills.

5. Write a theme explaining what Bryson means by "vulgarity" in popular art, giving examples from your own experience.

6. Social classes in modern America are much less clearly distinguished than they have been in other times and countries, but we are still aware of general differences among large groups of people depending, roughly, upon income, occupation, and education. Bryson has pointed out that clothes are not a good index to these differences. Does the same near-uniformity apply in other fields where taste plays a part? Have you noticed any correlation between particular entertainments (movies, the different kinds of music, libraries, museums) and "types" of people? If you have, you are in a position to write a theme supporting (or denying) the proposition that even in America taste is a matter of class, being sure to tell what you mean by "taste" and what you mean by "class."

Some Effects of Mass Media*

C. Wright Mills

Early observers believed that the increase in the range and volume of the formal means of communication would enlarge and animate the primary public. In such optimistic views—written before radio and television and movies—the formal media are understood as simply multiplying the scope and pace of personal discussion. Modern conditions, Charles Cooley wrote, "enlarge indefinitely the competition of ideas, and whatever has owed its persistence merely to lack of comparison is likely to go, for that which is really congenial to the choosing mind will be all the more cherished and increased." Still excited by the break-up of the conventional consensus of the local community, he saw the new means of communication as furthering the conversational dynamic of classic democracy, and with it the growth of rational and free individuality.

No one really knows all the functions of the mass media, for in their entirety these functions are probably so pervasive and so subtle that they cannot be caught by the means of social research now available. But we do now have reason to believe that these media have helped less to enlarge and animate the discussion of primary publics than to transform them into a set of media markets in mass-like society. I do not refer merely to the higher ratio of deliverers of opinion to receivers and to the decreased chance to answer back; nor do I refer merely to the violent banalization and stereotyping of our very sense organs in terms of which these media now compete for "attention." I have in mind a sort of psychological illiteracy that is facilitated by the media, and that is expressed in several ways:

I. Very little of what we think we know of the social realities of the world have we found out first-hand. Most of "the pictures in our heads" we have gained from these media—even to the point where we often do not really believe what we see before us until we read about it in the paper or hear about it on the radio. The media not only give us information; they guide our very experiences. Our standards of credulity, our standards of reality, tend to be set by these media rather than by our own fragmentary experience.

Accordingly, even if the individual has direct, personal experience of events, it is not really direct and primary: it is organized in stereotypes. It takes long and skillful training to so uproot such stereotypes that an

* From *The Power Elite* by C. Wright Mills. © 1956, by Oxford University Press, Inc. Reprinted by permission.

individual sees things freshly, in an unstereotyped manner. One might suppose, for example, that if all the people went through a depression they would all "experience it," and in terms of this experience, that they would all debunk or reject or at least refract what the media say about it. But experience of such a *structural* shift has to be organized and interpreted if it is to count in the making of opinion.

The kind of experience, in short, that might serve as a basis for resistance to mass media is not an experience of raw events, but the experience of meanings. The fleck of interpretation must be there in the experience if we are to use the word experience seriously. And the capacity for such experience is socially implanted. The individual does not trust his own experience, as I have said, until it is confirmed by others or by the media. Usually such direct exposure is not accepted if it disturbs loyalties and beliefs that the individual already holds. To be accepted, it must relieve or justify the feelings that often lie in the back of his mind as key features of his ideological loyalties.

Stereotypes of loyalty underlie beliefs and feelings about given symbols and emblems; they are the very ways in which men see the social world and in terms of which men make up their specific opinions and views of events. They are the results of previous experience, which affect present and future experience. It goes without saying that men are often unaware of these loyalties, that often they could not formulate them explicitly. Yet such general stereotypes make for the acceptance or the rejection of specific opinions not so much by the force of logical consistency as by their emotional affinity and by the way in which they relieve anxieties. To accept opinions in their terms is to gain the good solid feeling of being correct without having to think. When ideological stereotypes and specific opinions are linked in this way, there is a lowering of the kind of anxiety which arises when loyalty and belief are not in accord. Such ideologies lead to a willingness to accept a given line of belief; then there is no need, emotionally or rationally, to overcome resistance to given items in that line; cumulative selections of specific opinions and feelings become the pre-organized attitudes and emotions that shape the opinion-life of the person.

These deeper beliefs and feelings are a sort of lens through which men experience their worlds, they strongly condition acceptance or rejection of specific opinions, and they set men's orientation toward prevailing authorities. Three decades ago, Walter Lippmann saw such prior convictions as biases: they kept men from defining reality in an adequate way. They are still biases. But today they can often be seen as "good biases"; inadequate and misleading as they often are, they are less so than the crackpot realism of the higher authorities and opinion-makers. They are the lower common sense and as such a factor of resistance. But we must recognize, especially when the pace of change is so deep and fast, that common sense is more often common than sense. And, above all, we must recognize that "the common sense" of our children is going to be less the result of any firm social tradition than of the stereotypes carried by the mass media to which they are now so fully exposed. They are the first generation to be so exposed.

II. So long as the media are not entirely monopolized, the individual can play one media off against another; he can compare them, and hence resist what any one of them puts out. The more genuine competition there is among the media, the more resistance the individual might be able to command. But how much is this now the case? *Do* people compare reports on public events or policies, playing one medium's content off against another's?

The answer is: generally no, very few do: (1) We know that people tend strongly to select those media which carry contents with which they already agree. There is a kind of selection of new opinions on the basis of prior opinions. No one seems to search out such counter-statements as may be found in alternative media offerings. Given radio programs and magazines and newspapers often get a rather consistent public, and thus reinforce their messages in the minds of that public. (2) This idea of playing one medium off against another assumes that the media really have varying contents. It assumes genuine competition, which is not widely true. The media display an apparent variety and competition, but on closer view they seem to compete more in terms of variations on a few standardized themes than of clashing issues. The freedom to raise issues effectively seems more and more to be confined to those few interests that have ready and continual access to these media.

III. The media have not only filtered into our experience of external realities, they have also entered into our very experience of our own selves. They have provided us with new identities and new aspirations of what we should like to be, and what we should like to appear to be. They have provided in the models of conduct they hold out to us a new and larger and more flexible set of appraisals of our very selves. In terms of the modern theory of the self, we may say that the media bring the reader, listener, viewer into the sight of larger, higher reference groups—groups, real or imagined, up-close or vicarious, personally known or distractedly glimpsed—which are looking glasses for his self-image. They have multiplied the groups to which we look for confirmation of our self-image.

More than that: (1) the media tell the man in the mass who he is—they give him identity; (2) they tell him what he wants to be—they give him aspirations; (3) they tell him how to get that way—they give him technique; and (4) they tell him how to feel that he is that way even when he is not—they give him escape. The gaps between the identity and aspiration lead to technique and/or to escape. That is probably the basic psychological formula of the mass media today. But, as a formula, it is not attuned to the development of the human being. It is the formula of a pseudo-world which the media invent and sustain.

IV. As they now generally prevail, the mass media, especially television, often encroach upon the small-scale discussion, and destroy the chance for the reasonable and leisurely and human interchange of opinion. They are an important cause of the destruction of privacy in its full human meaning. That is an important reason why they not only fail as an educational force, but are a malign force: they do not articulate for the viewer or listener the broader sources of his private tensions and anxieties, his inarticulate resentments and half-formed hopes. They neither enable the individual to transcend his narrow milieu nor clarify its private meaning.

The media provide much information and news about what is happening in the world, but they do not often enable the listener or the viewer truly to connect his daily life with these larger realities. They do not connect the information they provide on public issues with the troubles felt by the individual. They do not increase rational insight into tensions, either those in the individual or those of the society which are reflected in the individual. On the contrary, they distract him and obscure his chance to understand himself or his world, by fastening his attention upon artificial frenzies that are resolved within the program framework, usually by violent action or by what is called humor. In short, for the viewer they are not really resolved at all. The chief distracting tension of the media is between the wanting and the not having of commodities or of women held to be good looking. There is almost always the general tone of animated distraction, of suspended agitation, but it is going nowhere and it has nowhere to go.

STUDY QUESTIONS

1. What are the four components of the "psychological illiteracy" that, according to Mills, is promoted by the mass media?

2. What values, actual or potential, does Mills recognize in the mass media? Why, if he recognizes these values, does he disapprove of the media?

3. Is Mills justified in expecting mass media to live up to such high standards? Can you find any evidence in his comments on television for saying that he is expecting too much? What would Mills say of Podhoretz' relatively favorable evalution of one kind of TV drama?

4. Mills sees a chain of relationships leading from the individual's experience to one's loyalties and beliefs to the mass media. Describe these connections.

5. Describe a book, movie or television show that portrays something or someone (a family, a businessman, soldiers, teen-agers, students) as "what we should like to be." Compare the portrayal with the actual reality as you have experienced it or know about it. Do you think the portrayal did harm or good or neither?

6. Write an essay doing the following: first, describe a book, movie or

television show that gives its audience the experience of "being correct without having to think." Tell what pre-formed attitude it exploited. Then, describe a statement you have found that seems intended to correct the reader's beliefs or to challenge him. These are usually easier to find in textbooks, serious magazines, and sometimes in newspaper editorials. Describe the attitude that it tries to attack or correct. Then conclude with some observation in which you compare these two examples.

The Great Stereopticon*

Richard Weaver

A great point is sometimes made of the fact that modern man no longer sees above his head a revolving dome with fixed stars and glimpses of the *primum mobile*. True enough, but he sees something similar when he looks at his daily newspaper. He sees the events of the day refracted through a medium which colors them as effectively as the cosmology of the medieval scientist determined his view of the starry heavens. The newspaper is a man-made cosmos of the world of events around us at the time. For the average reader it is a construct with a set of significances which he no more thinks of examining than did his pious forebear of the thirteenth century—whom he pities for sitting in medieval darkness—think of questioning the cosmology. This modern man, too, lives under a dome, whose theoretical aspect has been made to harmonize with a materialistic conception of the world. And he employs its conjunctions and oppositions to explain the occurrences of his time with all the confidence of the now supplanted disciple of astrology.

The Great Stereopticon, like most gadgets, has been progressively improved and added to until today it is a machine of three parts: the press, the motion picture, and the radio. Together they present a version of life quite as controlled as that taught by medieval religionists, though feeble in moral inspiration, as we shall see. . . .

If we are pleading for unity of mind and if we admit the necessity for some degree of subjective determination, it might appear that this machine, with its power to make the entire environment rhetorical, is a heaven-sent answer to our needs. We do not in the final reckoning desire uninterpreted data; it is precisely the interpretation which holds our interest. But the great fault is that data, as it passes through the machine, takes its significance from a sickly metaphysical dream. The ultimate source of evaluation ceases to be the dream of beauty and truth and becomes that of psychopathia, of fragmentation, of disharmony and nonbeing. The operators of the Stereopticon by their very selection of matter make horrifying assumptions about reality. For its audience that overarching dome becomes a sort of miasmic cloud, a breeder of strife and degradation and of the subhuman. What person taking the affirmative view of life can deny that the world served up daily by press, movie, and radio is a world of evil and negation? There is iron in our nature sufficient to withstand any fact that is present in a context of affirmation, but we cannot remain unaffected by the continued assertion of cynicism and brutality. Yet these are what the materialists in control of publicity give us.

The sickly metaphysical dream is not the creation solely of those who have cast restraint to the winds to seek profit in sensationalism. It is the work, too, of many who profess higher ideals but who cannot see where their assumptions lead. Fundamental to the dream, of course, is the dogma of progress, with its postulate of the endlessness of becoming. The habit of judging all things by their departure from the things of yesterday is reflected in most journalistic interpretation. Hence the restlessness and the criteria of magnitude and popularity. The fact that capitalism seems to flourish only by expansion is no doubt connected with this; but, whatever the cause may be, there is no law of perfection where there are no standards of measure. The touchstone of progress simply schools the millions in shallow evaluation.

Somewhere, moreover, the metaphysicians of publicity have absorbed the idea that the goal of life is happiness through comfort. It is a state of complacency supposed to ensue when the physical appetites have been well satisfied. Advertising fosters the concept, social democracy approves it, and the acceptance is so wide that it is virtually impossible today, except from the religious rostrum, to teach that life means discipline and sacrifice. It means, in the world picture of press agency, a job, domesticity, interest in some harmless diversion such as baseball and fishing, and a strong antipathy toward abstract ideas. This is the Philistine version of man in pursuit of happiness. Even Carlyle's doctrine of blessedness through work has overtones of strenuousness which are repugnant to the man of today. Because the journalist-philosophers evaluate the multifarious objects and events of the world by their appeal to the greatest possible number of this type, it is not to be expected that they will recommend the arduous road of spiritualization.

As for the latter, it cannot be said too emphatically that the operators of the Great Stereopticon have an interest in keeping people from breaking through to deeper significances. Not only is the philosopher a notoriously poor consumer; he is also an unsettling influence on societies careless of justice. That there are abysses of meaning beneath his daily routine, the common man occasionally suspects; to have him realize them in some apocalyptic revelation might well threaten the foundations of materialist civilization. It is no wonder that experienced employers advertise for workers who are married and sober, for the other type sometimes begins to wonder which is the *real* reality, and they cannot afford help which might behave as Santayana, when he reportedly deserted the Harvard lecture room at the voice of spring, or Sherwood Anderson, when he left without adieu the Ohio paint factory.

The speculations of journalism seldom go beyond the confines of business and propriety, and its oracles have been quick to assail those who come with disturbing notions—quick and unscrupulous, too, if they sense that the notions contain some necessary truth. In this they bear out the observation of Socrates that society does not mind an individual's being wise; only when he begins to make others wise does it become apprehensive. This is to say that they fear the spread of what has truth and reason on its side. Has any brilliant social critic of the last century received something better than a sneer from the pundits of journalism until his appreciation by the thoughtful forced a grudging recognition? A Nietzsche, a Kierkegaard, a Péguy, a Spengler—it is impossible for journalism to take these people seriously. The existence of the one threatens the existence of the other. The proprietors of the Stereopticon have a pretty clear idea of the level at which thinking is safe for the established order. They are protecting a materialist civilization growing more insecure and panicky as awareness filters through that it is over an abyss.

Thus, by insisting upon the dogma of progress, by picturing physical sufficiency as the goal of living, by insulating the mind against thoughts of an immanent reality, the Great Stereopticon keeps the ordinary citizen from perceiving "the vanity of his bookkeeping and the emptiness of his domestic felicities." It is the great projection machine of the bourgeois mentality, which we have already seen to be psychopathic in its alienation from reality.

It is curious to see how this mentality impresses those brought up under differing conditions. I recall with especial vividness a passage from Walter Hines Page's *The Autobiography of Nicholas Worth*. Page, who grew up in the Reconstruction South and later went North to school, had received his earliest impressions in a society where catastrophe and privation had laid bare some of the primal realities, including the existence of evil—a society, too, in which the "primitive infection" of the African race, to use a term employed by Jung, had developed in the white man some psychological cunning. It seemed to Page that his northern acquaintances had "minds of logical simplicity." [1] Such, I think, must be the feeling of anyone who comes out of a natural environment into one in which education, however lengthy and laborious, is based on bourgeois assumptions

---

[1] In his novel *The Bostonians,* which deserves to be better known, Henry James sends the "southern" type of mind into a northern environment, with consequences that corroborate Page's thesis.

about the real character of the world. It is a mind which learns to play with counters and arrives at answers which work—in a bourgeois environment. If we reverse this process and send the "mind of logical simplicity" into regions where mystery and contingency are recognized, we re-enact the plot of Conrad's *Lord Jim*. There is a world of terrifying reality to which the tidy moralities of an Anglican parsonage do not seem applicable.[2]

Seen from another point of view, the Great Stereopticon is a translation into actuality of Plato's celebrated figure of the cave. The defect of the prisoners, let us recall, is that they cannot perceive the truth. The wall before them, on which the shadows play, is the screen on which press, motion picture, and radio project their account of life. The chains which keep the prisoners from turning their heads are the physical monopoly which the engines of publicity naturally possess. And is it not pathetically true that these victims, with their limited vision, are "in the habit of conferring honors among themselves to those who are quickest to observe the passing shadows and to remark which of them went before and which followed after, and which were together"?

The result is that insulation by technology has made the task of disseminating wisdom more difficult since Plato's day. In Athenian sophistry and demagoguery Plato faced evils of the same kind, but they could not work behind such strategic entrenchment, and it was hardly as difficult for the wise man to make himself heard in centers of influence. Nothing is more natural than that, in an age dominated by materialism, authority should attach to those who possess. What chance today, to make the situation concrete, has a street-corner preacher, without means and without institutional sponsorship, in competition with the glib assertions of a radio oracle? The denizens of the cave have never been so firmly enchained as in this age, which uses liberty as a veritable incantation.

There are, it is true, certain hopeful signs of restiveness growing out of our condition. Most of us have observed among ordinary people a deep suspicion of propaganda since the first World War. The lesson of that disillusionment has lasted surprisingly. So intense has been this distrust that during the recent conflict the most authentic stories of outrages, documented and proved in every possible way, either were met with outright disbelief or were accepted gingerly and with reservations. The common man realizes that he has been misled and that there are those who would

[2] An anthropologist related to me that certain Negro tribes of West Africa have a symbol for the white man consisting of a figure seated on the deck of a steamer in a position of stiffest rigidity. The straight, uncompromising lines are the betrayal; the primitive artist has caught the white man's unnatural rigor, which contrasts, ominously for him, with the native's sinuous adaptation

A mind nurtured on press, motion picture, and radio cannot be otherwise in relation to the complexity of the world. Its instructors do not teach it to use the "proper reticences and proprieties" toward different things, and so its ideas may be comical simplifications.

mislead him again; but, lacking analytical power, he tends to group every instance of organized expression with propaganda. In times of peace, too, he has exhibited a certain hard-headed resistance to attempts to drive or cajole him. We have seen in this country politicians elected in the face of almost unanimous press opposition; we note oftentimes a cagey dismissal of the obvious falsification in advertising, and I have heard simple men remark that newspapers should not print items of a private and distressing nature such as we have classified as obscene.

In serious writing, too, there are some hopeful portents of change. It has been noted how modern poets have reacted against the debased coinage of cliché language; and indications appear in other types of literature that the middle-class world picture is being abandoned. Perhaps Arthur Koestler is right: as the bourgeois novel flickers out, an entirely new type of writer is destined to appear: "airmen, revolutionaries, adventurers, men who lead the dangerous life." Such, indeed, seem Silone, Saint-Exupéry, Hemingway. They will carry the gift for reflection into experiences of intense physical distress, and they will emerge with a more genuine contempt for materialist explanations than has been seen for centuries. When Saint-Exupéry, for example, declares that "the physical drama itself cannot touch us until someone points out its spiritual sense," he makes an affirmation of tragedy and significance. In a way, these men have the same recourse as medieval mystics, who, in suffering, caught the vision. And, since their faith has been tested by fire, they cannot be intimidated by those things which reduce the armchair philosopher to meekness. They have broken through the falsity and have returned to tell that the world is not at all what it has been made to seem—not after one has cut loose from security and comfort and achieved a kind of freedom far different from that promised by political liberals, who are themselves pushing slides into the Stereopticon. In reflecting on what is taught by extremities, one is reminded of Yeats's saying that saints and drunkards are never Whigs.

It will certainly have to be asked whether European fascism was not just this impulse vulgarized and perverted. The rebellion of youth, the repudiation of bourgeois complacency, the attempt to renew the sense of "holiness and heroism," appear the beginning of a revolt at least as deep-seated as that which made the French Revolution. The revolt was led by ignorant spirits who were impelled from behind by resentment and who, through their determination to invert the Christian ethic, made an unexampled fiasco. There is no reason to believe, however, that the deep dissatisfaction with the superficiality of Western life has been removed or even mitigated. And this is why we wonder how long the Stereopticon can preserve the inane world which the bourgeois finds congenial. It is, after all, only a mechanical means of unifying empirical communities.

In summary, the plea that the press, motion picture, and radio justify themselves by keeping people well informed turns out to be misleading. If one thinks merely of facts and of vivid sensations, the claim has some foundation, but if he thinks of encouragement to meditation, the contrary rather is true. For by keeping the time element continuously present—and one may recall Henry James's description of journalism as criticism of the moment at the moment—they discourage composition and so promote the fragmentation already reviewed. We have seen in other connections how specialization is hostile to all kinds of organization, whether that organization is expressed as image, as whole, or as generalization. In the last analysis this reveals itself as an attempt to prevent the simultaneous perception of successive events, which is the achievement of the philosopher. Materialism and success require the "decomposed eternity" of time for their operation, and this is why we have these hidden but persistent attacks on memory, which holds successive events in a single picture. The successive perception of successive events is empiricism; the simultaneous perception is idealism. Need we go further to account for the current dislike of long memories and for the hatred of the past?

Recurring to Plato's observation that a philosopher must have a good memory, let us inquire whether the continuous dissemination of news by the media under discussion does not produce the provincial in time. The constant stream of sensation, eulogized as lively propagation of what the public wants to hear, discourages the pulling-together of events from past time into a whole for contemplation. Thus, absence of reflection keeps the individual from being aware of his former selves, and it is highly questionable whether anyone can be a member of a metaphysical community who does not preserve such memory. Upon the presence of the past in the present depends all conduct directed by knowledge.

There can be little doubt that this condition of mind is a large factor in the low political morality of our age. Oswald Garrison Villard, a political journalist of the old school, who spent half a century crusading for standards of probity in public administration, once declared that he has never ceased to marvel at the shortness of the public's memory, at the rapidity with which it forgets episodes of scandal and incompetence. It sometimes appeared to him of little use to attack a party for its unethical conduct, for the voters would have no recollection of it. The glee with which the epithet "ancient history" is applied to what is out of sight is of course a part of this barbarous attitude. The man of culture finds the whole past relevant; the bourgeois and the barbarian find relevant only what has some pressing connection with their appetites. Those who remember alone have a sense of relatedness, but whoever has a sense of relatedness is in at least the first grade of philosophy. Henry Ford's statement that history is bunk is a perfectly proper observation for a bourgeois industrialist, and it was followed with equal propriety by another: "Creeds must go." Technology emancipates not only from memory but also from faith.

What human spirit, after reading a newspaper or attending a popular motion picture or listening to the farrago of nonsense on a radio program, has not found relief in fixing his gaze upon some characteristic bit of nature? It is escape from the sickly metaphysical dream. Out of the surfeit of falsity born of technology and commercialism we rejoice in returning to primary data and to assurance that the world is a world of enduring forms which in themselves are neither brutal nor sentimental.

STUDY QUESTIONS

1. In what way, according to Weaver, does the modern consciousness resemble the medieval one?

2. What two beliefs in particular does Weaver think are primarily responsible for the distortions of the mass media? What conditions of modern life are responsible for these distortions?

3. What specific points of disagreement exist between Weaver's views and Bryson's? Note that some of these disagreements relate to the underlying assumptions and are not openly stated.

4. This and the preceding four selections offer several perspectives on popular culture from different points of view. Which of them seems to you the most "objective" analysis? If you feel that any of the writers are biased, how would you describe their particular bias? Which writer seems to you to present the most optimistic analysis? Which the most pessimistic?

5. Do you agree with Weaver that the role of the press, movies and radio (and TV) is primarily one of evil and negation? If you do, explain what you mean, giving examples from your own experience. If you do not, defend at least one of these mass media against Weaver's charges.

6. Weaver blames two beliefs for the disorders he is describing, but he never tries to explain why these beliefs are wrong. Write a theme on one of them, either supporting Weaver's point of view or defending the belief against his criticisms.

PART FIVE

Knowledge
and Value

1. PHILOSOPHY AND KNOWLEDGE

Two Kinds of Knowledge*

William James

There are *two kinds of knowledge* broadly and practically distinguishable: we may call them respectively *knowledge of acquaintance* and *knowledge-about*. Most languages express the distinction; thus, γνῶναι, εἰδέναι; *noscere, scire; kennen, wissen; connaître, savoir*. I am acquainted with many people and things, which I know very little about, except their presence in the places where I have met them. I know the color blue when I see it, and the flavor of a pear when I taste it; I know an inch when I move my finger through it; a second of time, when I feel it pass; an effort of attention when I make it; a difference between two things when I notice it; but *about* the inner nature of these facts or what makes them what they are, I can say nothing at all. I cannot impart acquaintance with them to any one who has not already made it himself. I cannot *describe* them, make a blind man guess what blue is like, define to a child a syllogism, or tell a philosopher in just what respect distance is just what it is, and differs from other forms of relation. At most, I can say to my friends, Go to certain places and act in certain ways, and these objects will probably come. All the elementary natures of the world, its highest genera, the simple qualities of matter, and mind, together with the kinds of relation that subsist between them, must either not be known at all, or known in this dumb way of acquaintance without *knowledge-about*. In minds able to speak at all there is, it is true, *some* knowledge about everything. Things can at least be classed, and the times of their appearance told. But in general, the less we analyze a thing, and the

* From *Principles of Psychology*, 1890.

fewer of its relations we perceive, the less we know about it and the more our familiarity with it is of the acquaintance-type. The two kinds of knowledge are, therefore, as the human mind practically exerts them, relative terms. That is, the same thought of a thing may be called knowledge-about it in comparison with a simpler thought, or acquaintance with it in comparison with a thought of it that is more articulate and explicit still.

The grammatical sentence expresses this. Its "subject" stands for an object of acquaintance which, by the addition of the predicate, is to get something known about it. We may already know a good deal, when we hear the subject named—its name may have rich connotations. But, know we much or little then, we know more still when the sentence is done. We can relapse at will into a mere condition of acquaintance with an object by scattering our attention and staring at it in a vacuous trance-like way. We can ascend to knowledge *about* it by rallying our wits and proceeding to notice and analyze and think. What we are only acquainted with is only *present* to our minds; we *have* it, or the idea of it. But when we know about it, we do more than merely have it; we seem, as we think over its relations, to subject it to a sort of *treatment* and to *operate* upon it with our thought. The words *feeling* and *thought* give voice to the antithesis. Through feelings we become acquainted with things, but only by our thoughts do we know about them. Feelings are the term and starting point of cognition, thoughts the developed tree. The minimum of grammatical subject, of objective presence, of reality known about, the mere beginning of knowledge, must be named by the word that says the least. Such a word is the interjection, as *lo! there! ecco! voilà!* or the article or demonstrative pronoun introducing the sentence, as *the, it, that.* . . .

The mental states usually distinguished as feelings are the *emotions*, and the *sensations* we get from skin, muscle, viscus, eye, ear, nose, and palate. The "thoughts," as recognized in popular parlance, are the *conceptions* and *judgments*. . . . It may perhaps be well to notice now that our senses only give us acquaintance with facts of body, and that of the mental states of other persons we only have conceptual knowledge. Of our own past states of mind we take cognizance in a peculiar way. They are "objects of memory," and appear to us endowed with a sort of warmth and intimacy that makes the perception of them seem more like a process of sensation than like a thought.

STUDY QUESTIONS

1. Describe the distinction James makes between "knowledge of acquaintance" and "knowledge-about."
2. Is this a distinction of kind or merely of degree? Can one of these kinds of knowledge be converted into the other?
3. Since feeling is related to one kind of knowledge and judgment to

the other, are these two related to each other as the two kinds of knowledge are related? That is, if one kind of knowledge is a preliminary to the other kind, can the same be said of feeling and thought? Do any other relationships of this kind seem to obtain?

4. According to James, what expressive power lacking in an exclamation does a sentence have?

5. Describe two of your own areas of knowledge, one in which you have "knowledge of acquaintance," and one in which you have "knowledge about" something. How do you account for the different state of your knowledge in these two fields? Is it due to motivation? Environment? Or some other cause?

6. What relation do James' distinctions have to educational problems? In what ways can a teacher apply this information?

The Value of Philosophy*

Bertrand Russell

Having now come to the end of our brief and very incomplete review of the problems of philosophy, it will be well to consider, in conclusion, what is the value of philosophy and why it ought to be studied. It is the more necessary to consider this question, in view of the fact that many men, under the influence of science or of practical affairs, are inclined to doubt whether philosophy is anything better than innocent but useless trifling, hair-splitting distinctions, and controversies on matters concerning which knowledge is impossible.

This view of philosophy appears to result, partly from a wrong conception of the ends of life, partly from a wrong conception of the kind of goods which philosophy strives to achieve. Physical science, through the medium of inventions, is useful to innumerable people who are wholly ignorant of it; thus the study of physical science is to be recommended, not only, or primarily, because of the effect on the student, but rather because of the effect on mankind in general. This utility does not belong to philosophy. If the study of philosophy has any value at all for others than students of philosophy, it must be only indirectly, through its effects upon the lives of those who study it. It is in these effects, therefore, if anywhere, that the value of philosophy must be primarily sought.

But further, if we are not to fail in our endeavour to determine the value of philosophy, we must first free our minds from the prejudices of what are wrongly called "practical" men. The "practical" man, as this word is often used, is one who recognises only material needs, who realises that

* From *The Problems of Philosophy* by Bertrand Russell, by permission of the Oxford University Press.

men must have food for the body, but is oblivious of the necessity of providing food for the mind. If all men were well off, if poverty and disease had been reduced to their lowest possible point, there would still remain much to be done to produce a valuable society; and even in the existing world the goods of the mind are at least as important as the goods of the body. It is exclusively among the goods of the mind that the value of philosophy is to be found; and only those who are not indifferent to these goods can be persuaded that the study of philosophy is not a waste of time.

Philosophy, like all other studies, aims primarily at knowledge. The knowledge it aims at is the kind of knowledge which gives unity and system to the body of the sciences, and the kind which results from a critical examination of the grounds of our convictions, prejudices, and beliefs. But it cannot be maintained that philosophy has had any very great measure of success in its attempts to provide definite answers to its questions. If you ask a mathematician, a mineralogist, a historian, or any other man of learning, what definite body of truths has been ascertained by his science, his answer will last as long as you are willing to listen. But if you put the same question to a philosopher, he will, if he is candid, have to confess that his study has not achieved positive results such as have been achieved by other sciences. It is true that this is partly accounted for by the fact that, as soon as definite knowledge concerning any subject becomes possible, this subject ceases to be called philosophy, and becomes a separate science. The whole study of the heavens, which now belongs to astronomy, was once included in philosophy; Newton's great work was called "the mathematical principles of natural philosophy." Similarly, the study of the human mind, which was, until very lately, a part of philosophy, has now been separated from philosophy and has become the science of psychology. Thus, to a great extent, the uncertainty of philosophy is more apparent than real: those questions which are already capable of definite answers are placed in the sciences, while those only to which, at present, no definite answer can be given, remain to form the residue which is called philosophy.

This is, however, only a part of the truth concerning the uncertainty of philosophy. There are many questions—and among them those that are of the profoundest interest to our spiritual life—which, so far as we can see, must remain insoluble to the human intellect unless its powers become of quite a different order from what they are now. Has the universe any unity of plan or purpose, or is it a fortuitous concourse of atoms? Is consciousness a permanent part of the universe, giving hope of indefinite growth in wisdom, or is it a transitory accident on a small planet on which life must ultimately become impossible? Are good and evil of importance to the universe or only to man? Such questions are asked by philosophy, and variously answered by various philosophers. But it would seem that, whether answers be otherwise discoverable or not, the answers suggested by philosophy are none of them demonstrably true. Yet, however slight may be the hope of discovering an answer, it is part of the business of philosophy to continue the consideration of such questions, to make us aware of their importance, to examine all the approaches to them, and to keep alive that speculative interest in the universe which is apt to be killed by confining ourselves to definitely ascertainable knowledge.

Many philosophers, it is true, have held that philosophy could establish the truth of certain answers to such fundamental questions. They have supposed that what is of most importance in religious beliefs could be proved by strict demonstration to be true. In order to judge of such attempts, it is necessary to take a survey of human knowledge, and to form an opinion as to its methods and its limitations. On such a subject it would be unwise to pronounce dogmatically; but if the investigations of our previous chapters have not led us astray, we shall be compelled to renounce the hope of finding philosophical proofs of religious beliefs. We cannot, therefore, include as part of the value of philosophy any definite set of answers to such questions. Hence, once more, the value of philosophy must not depend upon any supposed body of definitely ascertainable knowledge to be acquired by those who study it.

The value of philosophy is, in fact, to be sought largely in its very uncertainty. The man who has no tincture of philosophy goes through life imprisoned in the prejudices derived from common sense, from the habitual beliefs of his age or his nation, and from convictions which have grown up in his mind without the co-operation or consent of his deliberate reason. To such a man the world tends to become definite, finite, obvious; common objects rouse no questions, and unfamiliar possibilities are contemptuously rejected. As soon as we begin to philosophise, on the contrary, we find, as we saw in our opening chapters, that even the most everyday things lead to problems to which only very incomplete answers can be given. Philosophy, though unable to tell us with certainty what is the true answer to the doubts which it raises, is able to suggest many possibilities which enlarge our thoughts and free them from the tyranny of custom. Thus, while diminishing our feeling of certainty as to what things are, it greatly increases our knowledge as to what they may be; it removes the somewhat arrogant dogmatism of those who have never travelled into the region of liberating doubt, and it keeps alive our sense of wonder by showing familiar things in an unfamiliar aspect.

Apart from its utility in showing unsuspected possibilities, philosophy has a value—perhaps its chief value—through the greatness of the objects which it contemplates, and the freedom from narrow and personal aims resulting from this contemplation. The life of the instinctive man is shut up within the circle of his private interests: family and friends may be included, but the outer world is not regarded except as it may help or hinder what comes within the circle of instinctive wishes. In such a life there is something feverish and confined, in comparison with which the philosophic life is calm and free. The private world of instinctive interests is a small one, set in the midst of a great and powerful world which must, sooner or later, lay our private world in ruins. Unless we can so enlarge our interests as to include the whole outer world, we remain like a garrison in a beleaguered fortress, knowing that the enemy prevents escape and that ultimate surrender is inevitable. In such a life there is no peace, but a constant strife between the insistence of desire and the powerlessness of will. In one way or another, if our life is to be great and free, we must escape this prison and this strife.

One way of escape is by philosophic contemplation. Philosophic contemplation does not, in its widest survey, divide the universe into two hostile camps—friends and foes, helpful and hostile, good and bad—it views the whole impartially. Philosophic contemplation, when it is unalloyed, does not aim at proving that the rest of the universe is akin to man. All acquisition of knowledge is an enlargement of the Self, but this enlargement is best attained when it is not directly sought. It is obtained when the desire for knowledge is alone operative, by a study which does not wish in advance that its objects should have this or that character, but adapts the Self to the characters which it finds in its objects. This enlargement of Self is not obtained when, taking the Self as it is, we try to show that the world is so similar to this Self that knowledge of it is possible without any admission of what seems alien. The desire to prove this is a form of self-assertion, and like all self-assertion, it is an obstacle to the growth of Self which it desires, and of which the Self knows that it is capable. Self-assertion, in philosophic speculation as elsewhere, views the world as a means to its own ends; thus it makes the world of less account than Self, and Self sets bounds to the greatness of its goods. In contemplation, on the contrary, we start from the not-Self, and through its greatness the boundaries of Self are enlarged; through the infinity of the universe the mind which contemplates it achieves some share in infinity.

For this reason greatness of soul is not fostered by those philosophies which assimilate the universe to Man. Knowledge is a form of union of Self and not-Self; like all union, it is impaired by dominion, and therefore by any attempt to force the universe into conformity with what we find in ourselves. There is a widespread philosophical tendency towards the view which tells us that man is the measure of all things, that truth is man-made, that space and time and the world of universals are properties of the mind, and that, if there be anything not created by the mind, it is unknowable and of no account for us. This view, if our previous discussions were correct, is untrue; but in addition to being untrue, it has the effect of robbing philosophic contemplation of all that gives it value, since it fetters contemplation to Self. What it calls knowledge is not a union with the not-Self, but a set of prejudices, habits, and desires, making an impenetrable veil between us and the world beyond. The man who finds pleasure in such a theory of knowledge is like the man who never leaves the domestic circle for fear his word might not be law.

The true philosophic contemplation, on the contrary, finds its satisfaction in every enlargement of the not-Self, in everything that magnifies the objects contemplated, and thereby the subject contemplating. Everything, in contemplation, that is personal or private, everything that depends upon habit, self-interest, or desire, distorts the object, and hence impairs the union which the intellect seeks. By thus making a barrier between subject and object, such personal and private things become a prison to the intellect. The free intellect will see as God might see, without a *here* and *now*, without hopes and fears, without the trammels of customary beliefs and traditional prejudices, calmly, dispassionately, in the sole and exclusive desire of knowledge—knowledge as impersonal, as purely contemplative, as it is possible for man to attain. Hence also the free intellect will value more the abstract and universal knowledge into which the accidents of private history do not enter, than the knowledge brought by the senses, and dependent, as such knowledge must be, upon an exclusive and personal point of view and a body whose sense-organs distort as much as they reveal.

The mind which has become accustomed to the freedom and impartiality of philosophic contemplation will preserve something of the same freedom and impartiality in the world of action and emotion. It will view its purposes and desires as parts of the whole, with the absence of insistence that results from seeing them as infinitesimal fragments in a world of which all the rest is unaffected by any one man's deeds. The impartiality which, in contemplation, is the unalloyed desire for truth, is the very same quality of mind which, in action, is justice, and in emotion is that universal love which can be given to all, and not only to those who are judged useful or admirable. Thus contemplation enlarges not only the objects of our thoughts, but also the objects of our actions and our affections: it makes us citizens of the universe, not only of one walled city at war with all the rest. In this citizenship of the universe consists man's true freedom, and his liberation from the thraldom of narrow hopes and fears.

Thus, to sum up our discussion of the value of philosophy: Philosophy is to be studied, not for the sake of any definite answers to its questions, since no definite answers can, as a rule, be known to be true, but rather for the sake of the questions themselves; because these questions enlarge our conception of what is possible, enrich our intellectual imagination, and diminish the dogmatic assurance which closes the mind against speculation; but above all because, through the greatness of the universe which philosophy contemplates, the mind is rendered great, and becomes capable of that union with the universe which constitutes its highest good.

1. Russell opens his discussion by admitting that philosophy does not have the "utility" of physical science and that it is not "practical" in the sense in which that term is frequently used. What does Russell gain by opening with these statements? What does he claim as the principal aim and value of philosophy?

2. How does Russell account for the fact that philosophy is so often unable to give definite answers to the problems it is concerned with? How does Russell show that the "uncertainty" characteristic of philosophy is an advantage?

3. Russell says that philosophy usually contemplates problems of great importance. Is there any relation, however, between philosophy and the trivial everyday problems people have to face?

4. What relation between the Self and the world does philosophy make possible?

5. Does Russell's explanation of the end and nature of philosophy have any bearing upon education? What would education based upon his principles be like?

6. Russell speaks, at the end of this selection, of the value of philosophy in diminishing "the dogmatic assurance which closes the mind against speculation." Note that Martin and several other writers in this anthology have been concerned in one way or another with the need for and the value of cultivating an open mind, of diminishing "dogmatic assurance." Name two or three such writers and summarize their particular concerns.

Then Why Not Every Man?*

Barrows Dunham

When the sun hangs lower than the lowest branches, the world, much wearied, slides out of its day-long rut, and people move by various paths to their release. It has been a hard day, stirred with the little excitements of failure or success: eight hours of one's life, spent (who knows how fruitfully?) in acquiring the means of working another eight.

The man in the street, who is often quoted and has never said a word, is at last—in the street.

He walks past the bank that has his money and keeps it safe from him by closing at three, past the shop windows whose reductions he can't afford, past the bootblack-hatcleaner who beautifies both extremities, past the bars where desperate men are drinking and the literary assassins lurk.

* From *Giants in Chains* by Barrows Dunham, by permission of Little, Brown & Company. Copyright, 1953, by Barrows Dunham.

He takes a bus or train or trolley, and, after a forgetful interval, he comes home.

And here, if not quite heaven, there is a haven: the loved, enduring sameness which all the motions of his life go to sustain, the immediate hearth of values, the rock and tower whence he looks out, protected, upon the world. He is always building it, in fancy and in fact. Looking backward, he can see the history of half-unnoticed change through which it has survived and even grown. Looking forward, he can hopefully guess the ampler wage, the more rewarded talent, which is to make all happiness secure. And beyond that, his own ultimate, the very alteration of his being—not storm or terror, he will wish, but a simple leaving off of light.

Doubtless he does not always range through all these notions. Yet in each opening of the door there are the inevitable questions: Are they at home? And well? And happy? If so, then life may wander as it will until another evening and the questions come again.

The man in the street, now the man at home—who is nearer than he to the subtle conflict of permanence and change? Who knows, more than he, what effort it takes to make possession last, to hold within the moving universe some firm abode? Surely he is shrewder than Parmenides, who thought that logic had abolished change; sturdier than Hume, who found in all the fabric of the world mere causeless series of sensations.

And now at home, he shuts the door upon the outer world but not upon philosophy. Seated at table and exercising his right to the day's secrets, he learns everything that happened, what it was and how it felt. Though the notion may not rise into full consciousness, his behavior suggests an understanding that events such as these are what the world is really made of—not the gossip of headlines nor the loud obscurities of commentators, but the effort of people like his wife and children to do what they think ought to be done at the moment they have to do it.

Now, this is a generalization to the effect that history is made by people. It is not particularly a favorite with historians or philosophers, who have their eyes (let us say) upon the splendors and lusts of kings. Nevertheless, it is simple, it is very arguable, and it is in all probability true. The man at home, if modesty did not so shroud him, might marvel how many learned errors he had escaped.

But his acumen is not yet exhausted. For I fancy that as he reads his evening paper, backwards, from the comics through murder, theft, fire, and divorce to the serried horrors of Page One, he rejects this item, accepts that, rather doubts the other, and in general wonders how much correspondence there may be between the story and the event. He began life, to be sure, believing what he was told; but he has learned that many things which are told are erroneous, and that one must do a little testing for oneself. One seldom, perhaps, fully develops the technique of inquiry. One does know, however, that contradictions within a story will destroy it, and that prejudice will tear it loose from the sustaining facts.

These are the rudiments, indeed the essentials, of a theory of knowledge —a theory, that is to say, which should be able to give us the talent of true belief. We all have some impression of what this theory contains, for the total lack of it would leave us helpless; and very probably we all feel that, however much we now know of it, there would be benefit in knowing more.

The man at home, soon to be the man in bed, has thus spent an entire evening without being released from philosophy. His last reflections are set by an item in the paper to the effect that a lecturer at the Good Feeling Club has exhorted the audience not to care for material well-being, which is equally attainable by rabbits and snakes. But, on this supposition, one has labored for inferior substance, and all the iterated tasks were frauds. Moreover, shall one conclude that, in this fragment of the universe, what one buys with so much toil has really lesser value, while pearls abound for simple taking? That would be a paradox indeed, to make faint sense of. And thus over the long day ethics slides her curtain, the first and deepening purple of the night.

PHILOSOPHY AS REFLECTION

Unless I have misconceived the habits of homes and of evenings, I am entitled to my conclusion that it is very natural for men to philosophize and that they do it oftener than they know. They do it, moreover, better than they know, just because they do it naturally. They are not asked to publish their findings, and hence are not tempted to the platitude and obscurity of official pronouncements. Nor do they dispense that purchasable comfort which sighs and lies and lets the misery last.

On the contrary, they are simply trying to make their lives intelligible, a process they began in their cradles. If they are amateurs rather than professionals, they are so in a profound sense, namely, that they love understanding. They practice philosophy in its ancient and traditional form, as reflection.

And what is it to reflect? It is to draw the scattered data of experience into various unities, to find the likenesses and contrasts, to catch the logic moving throughout change. A sunrise and a sunset make one day, and of such days a handful makes a life. Yet in these regularities, dull (it has sometimes seemed) as the ticking of a clock, lies the vast stretch of objects to be known.

The simplest facts are pregnant with philosophy. Men, it is obvious enough, are born of their own kind, are reared among men, and die among men. The relations thus instituted are somewhat shifting, somewhat insecure, and at their extremes rapturous or tragic. During a lifetime, every man stores up some knowledge of them and some theories about them. Thus, despite prejudice and naïveté, every man is, at least in rudiments, a social scientist.

Secondly, men are everywhere and always in some relation with the physical world, which is the source of food, clothing, shelter, and the innumerable other commodities they need. During a lifetime, they acquire knowledge and develop theories about this world also. They are, in rather more than rudiments, physical scientists.

Now, it happens that between these worlds, the physical and the social, there are many interactions. The technology of producing goods is mainly a problem in physical science, and the distribution of those goods is mainly a problem in social science. Nevertheless, the two profoundly influence each other. Failures in the scheme of distribution will thwart technology and sometimes bring it to a halt. On the other hand, a failure (and sometimes a great success) in technology will unsettle all social relations. A crisis in either world begets a crisis in the other; and the human race, now master of the atom, stands terrified, knowing that it could be affluent and happy, knowing also that it may perish altogether.

Since in man these two worlds meet with cordiality or with violence, it is clear that there is a kind of knowledge incorporating what is known about society and about physical nature, but larger, more nearly universal than these. It will consist of statements describing the whole complex of relations in which we stand, the welter (as it may appear) of happenings which surge around us, jostling, pushing, driving us upon our destiny. It will consist, further, of statements asserting what goals we seek or ought to seek. And lastly there will be statements composing the master plan by which we are to direct, so far as we may, the whole great process to our human goal.

This congeries of statements—this *system* of them, as we must hope it may become—is philosophy. Its single theme is Man and His Place in Nature. Around this theme are gathered the clusters of knowledge and theory called, in the darkened language of tradition, ontology, epistemology, and ethics. Which words, taken all together, are a deafening way of saying that before mankind attains its ultimate safety, we shall need to know what the world is, how it is known, and to what ends it ought to be controlled.

Generalizations must be large to encompass such subjects. Their very size invites abstractness, as if it were their fate to obscure the labors of lesser but more lively men. This notion is due in part to the fact that the first acknowledged philosophers were leisured aristocrats and the latest are university professors.

It is also due, I fancy, to a certain aloof exercise of philosophical techniques. The thinker, demonstrating his claim to be the "spectator of all time and all existence," abstracts some attribute from the mass and hangs it like a blanket across the stars. Or, preferring the little world to the great, he may show us infinity in the palm of his hand, where the touch is thrilling but the shape is odd.

Though I seem reproachful of these exercises, the truth is that I know them and love them well. They are the sinews of meditation and are no less active for being calm. Scientists, to be sure, have public motion, even hurly-burly, for they are to be found in laboratories, looking through microscopes and into test tubes, and handling with a fine boldness much combustible material. Philosophers are, by habit and by reputation, a much quieter breed. They will be found in armchairs, and, when they are not found in armchairs, they will be found in bed. But this only means that some generalizations can be formulated seated or prone, and perhaps must be formulated that way.

Such, we say, are the habits of philosophers; but I think there are familiar moments when the process shows itself in every life. The mood, which now and then descends, of "What is it all about? What am I doing here?" differs only in precision from Kant's celebrated questions, "What can I know? What ought I to do? What may I hope for?"

It is the genuinely philosophic moods, into which, as most people have it, float scraps of ill-digested sermons, pedagogic homilies, and calendar mottoes. But the authentic content is various insights which experience has suggested and a native intelligence has made shrewd. It is this that gives such pith and pregnancy to folk sayings and emboldens us to hope that the world, which plainly will not be saved by its scientists, will be saved by its people.

PHILOSOPHY AS GUIDE

"Saved by its people"—the phrase suggests that philosophy is more than reflection. For if its people are to save the world by means of some wisdom original with them, they will have to philosophize with a view to guiding their actions. Thus philosophy gives eyes to practice, and practice informs philosophy.

That philosophy is the guide of life is an old boast, not limited to philosophers. It is sententious enough to invite agreement, and it can be made by men whose lives are not conspicuously guided in this way. Yet a precept coined by the richest of Athenian intellects and sanctified by the sufferings of Spinoza will not be much tarnished by inferior use.

There is reason to think, for example, that the philosopher-kings, rather too aristocratically defined by Plato, are an ultimate historical necessity. They will be, not kings, but a commonwealth of knowledgeable persons accustomed to settling problems by general principles. They will appear in that not unimaginable epoch when human science, no longer spent upon fattening an elite, brings treasures to every door.

Meanwhile philosophy needs some effort to make its value known. Part of that value, I suppose, is already recognized in Horace's maxim,

> Aequam memento rebus in arduis
> Servare mentem.

But calm in perplexity and courage under loss are attributes mainly personal. Now that everyone knows how closely each life is linked with others, how impossible the chance of living to oneself, philosophy appears anew, as guide to social action.

For such a use its very substance fits it. That substance, which we have called "Man and His Place in Nature," is also the stuff of politics, for man's political behavior is simply his effort to determine, by conflict as by concord, what his place in nature shall be. To this great theme no science or combination of sciences is adequate, for their generalizations are too small. No art or combination of arts suffices, for their skills govern only segments of the whole. The talent for discussing (so far as may be) all things and all relations, the given and the desired, the means and the end, is philosophy's alone.

If philosophy could not claim leadership by right of content, it would nevertheless acquire it by surrender. The sciences have for many years been as explicit concerning what their content is *not* as concerning what it is. They say, for example, and quite falsely, that they have nothing to do with ethics. The natural sciences say that they have nothing to do with politics—an illusion which not even the hydrogen bomb seems able to explode. And the social sciences, in terror of harboring dangerous knowledge, are beginning to talk as if they had no knowledge at all.

History, however, will not leave undone what scientists are thus neglecting to do. Despite the undoubted possibility, it seems improbable that mankind will permit science to work universal destruction. In conquering at last these lethal uses, mankind will work out the theory and practice which can adapt science entirely to human welfare. The theory and practice thus attained will mark the passage from philosophy militant to philosophy triumphant. I do not suggest that professional philosophers as we now know them are likely to achieve all this, but I do say that it will be achieved and that the men who achieve it may be called philosophers.

STUDY QUESTIONS

1. Like Russell, Dunham is concerned with defining philosophy and assessing its place and value in our lives. But his approach is highly informal compared with that of Russell. Point out significant differences in sentence structure and in vocabulary in the two essays. What other devices does Dunham use to make his writing appealing to the lay reader?

2. What kind of reader might prefer Russell? Dunham? Is one of the selections "better" than the other? Is one more informative? More accurate?

3. Try to construct a definition of philosophy from Dunham's observations. What is the relation of philosophy to other fields of learning? How does Dunham think the invention of the H-bomb will affect the practice of philosophy?

4. Is the "reflection" which Dunham describes like or unlike the "reflective thinking" which Dewey defines in "What is Thinking"?

5. In a part of this piece, Dunham shows how philosophy enters into everyday life. Write a theme showing how some field of study in which you are interested is involved in ordinary daily experience. Good possibilities are history, economics, or any of the sciences, though nearly every subject you have studied is also a possibility.

6. What was your idea of philosophy prior to reading Russell and Dunham in these selections? Write a paper in which you define your previous conception of philosophy, and assess the contribution which these two selections have made to your understanding.

On Not Being A Philosopher*

Robert Lynd

Have you read Epictetus lately?" "No, not lately." "Oh, you ought to read him. Tommy's been reading him for the first time, and is fearfully excited." I caught this scrap of dialogue from the next table in the lounge of an hotel. I became interested, curious, for I had never read Epictetus, though I had often looked at his works on the shelf—perhaps I had even quoted him—and I wondered if here at last was the book of wisdom that I had been looking for at intervals ever since I was at school. Never have I lost my early faith that wisdom is to be found somewhere in a book—to be picked up as easily as a shell from the sand. I desire wisdom as keenly as Solomon did, but it must be wisdom that can be obtained with very little effort—wisdom that can be caught almost by infection. I have no time or energy for the laborious quest of philosophy. I wish the philosophers to perform the laborious quest and, at the end of it, to feed me with the fruits of their labours; just as I get eggs from the farmer, apples from the fruit-grower, medicine from the chemist, so do I expect the philosopher to provide me with wisdom at the cost of a few shillings. That is why at one time I read Emerson and, at another, Marcus Aurelius. To read them, I hoped, was to become wise by reading. But I did not become wise. I agreed with them while I read them, but, when I had finished reading, I was still much the same man that I had been before, incapable of concentrating on the things on which they said I should concentrate or of not being indifferent to the things to which they said I should not be indifferent. Still, I have never lost faith in books, believing that somewhere printed matter exists from which I shall be able to absorb philosophy and strength of character while smoking in an

---

* From *It's a Fine World* by Robert Lynd. Reprinted with the permission of Methuen and Co., Ltd., London.

armchair. It was in this mood that I took down Epictetus after hearing the conversation in the hotel lounge.

I read him, I confess, with considerable excitement. He is the kind of philosopher I like, not treating life as if at its finest it were an argument conducted in difficult jargon, but discussing, among other things, how men should behave in the affairs of ordinary life. Also, I agreed with nearly everything he said. Indifference to pain, death, poverty—yes, that is eminently desirable. Not to be troubled about anything over which one has no control, whether the oppression of tyrants or the peril of earthquakes—on the necessity of this also, Epictetus and I are as one. Yet, close as is the resemblance between our opinions, I could not help feeling, as I read, that Epictetus was wise in holding his opinions and that I, though holding the same opinions, was far from wise. For, indeed, though I held the same opinions for purposes of theory, I could not entertain them for a moment for purposes of conduct. Death, pain, and poverty are to me very real evils, except when I am in an armchair reading a book by a philosopher. If an earthquake happened while I was reading a book of philosophy, I should forget the book of philosophy and think only of the earthquake and how to avoid tumbling walls and chimneys. This, though I am the staunchest possible admirer of Socrates, Pliny, and people of that sort. Sound though I am as an armchair philosopher, at a crisis I find that both the spirit and the flesh are weak.

Even in the small things of life I cannot comfort myself like a philosopher of the school of Epictetus. Thus, for example, when he advises us how to "eat acceptably to the gods" and bids us to this end to be patient even under the most incompetent service at our meals, he commends a spiritual attitude of which my nature is incapable. "When you have asked for warm water," he says, "and the slave does not heed you; or if he does heed you but brings tepid water; or if he is not even to be found in the house, then to refrain from anger and not to explode, is not this acceptable to the gods? . . . Do you not remember over whom you rule—that they are kinsmen, that they are brothers by nature, and they are the offspring of Zeus?" That is all perfectly true, and I should like very much to be a man who could sit in a restaurant, smiling patiently and philosophically while the waiter brought all the wrong things or forgot to bring anything at all. But in point of fact bad waiting irritates me. I dislike having to ask three times for the wine-list. I am annoyed when, after a quarter of an hour's delay, I am told that there is no celery. It is true that I do not make a scene on such occasions. I have not enough courage for that. I am as sparing of objurgations as a philosopher, but I suspect that the scowling spirit within me must show itself in my features. Certainly, I do not think of telling myself: "This waiter is my kinsman; he is the offspring of Zeus." Besides, even if he were, why should the offspring of Zeus wait so badly? Epictetus never dined at the —— Restaurant. And yet his patience might have served him even there. If so, what a difference between Epictetus and me! And, if I cannot achieve his imperturbability in so small affairs as I have mentioned, what hope is there of my being able to play the philosopher in presence of tyrants and earthquakes?

Again, when Epictetus expresses his opinions on material possessions and counsels us to be so indifferent to them that we should not object to their being stolen, I agree with him in theory and yet in practice I know I should be unable to obey him. There is nothing more certain than that a man whose happiness depends on his possessions is not happy. I am sure a wise man can be happy on a pittance. Not that happiness should be the aim of life, according to Epictetus or myself. But Epictetus at least holds up an ideal of imperturbability, and he assures us that we shall achieve this if we care so little for material things that it does not matter to us whether somebody steals them or not. "Stop admiring your clothes," he bids us, "and you are not angry at the man who steals them." And he goes on persuasively concerning the thief: "*He* does not know wherein the true good of man consists, but fancies that it consists in having fine clothes, the very same fancy that you also entertain. Shall he not come, then, and carry them off?" Yes, logically I suppose he should, and yet I cannot feel so at the moment at which I find that a guest at a party has taken my new hat and left his old one in its place. It gives me no comfort to say to myself: "*He* does not know wherein the true good of man consists, but fancies that it consists in having my hat." Nor should I dream of attempting to console a guest at a party in my own house with such philosophy in similar circumstances. It is very irritating to lose a new hat. It is very irritating to lose anything at all, especially if one thinks it has been taken on purpose. I feel that I could imitate Epictetus if I lived in a world in which nothing happened. But in a world in which things disappear through loss, theft, and "pinching," and in which bad meals are served by bad waiters in many of the restaurants, and a thousand other disagreeable things happen, an ordinary man might as well set out to climb the Himalayas in walking shoes as attempt to live the life of a philosopher at all hours.

In spite of this, however, most of us cannot help believing that the philosophers were right—right when they proclaimed, amid all their differences, that most of the things we bother about are not worth bothering about. It is easier to believe that oneself is a fool than that Socrates was a fool, and yet, if he was not right, he must have been the greatest fool who ever lived. The truth is, nearly everybody is agreed that such men as Socrates and Epictetus were right in their indifference to external things. Even men earning £10,000 a year and working for more would admit this. Yet, while admitting it, most of us would be alarmed if one of our dearest friends began to put the philosophy of Epictetus into practice too literally. What we regard as wisdom in Epictetus we should look on as insanity in an acquaintance. Or, perhaps, not in an acquaintance, but at least in a near relation. I am sure that if I became as indifferent to money and comfort and all external things as Epictetus, and reasoned in his fashion with a happy smile about property and thieves, my relations would become more perturbed than if I became a successful company promoter with the most materialistic philosophy conceivable. Think, for example, of the reasoning of Epictetus over the thief who stole his iron lamp:

He bought a lamp for a very high price; for a lamp he became a thief, for a lamp he became faithless, for a lamp he became bestial. This is what seemed to him to be profitable!

The reasoning is sound, yet neither individually nor as a society do we live in that contempt of property on which it is based. A few saints do, but even they are at first a cause of great concern to their friends. When the world is normally cheerful and comfortable, we hold the paradoxical belief that the philosophers were wise men, but that we should be fools to imitate them. We are convinced that, while philosophers are worth reading, material things are worth bothering about. It is as though we enjoyed wisdom as a spectacle—a delightful spectacle on a stage which it would be unseemly for the audience to attempt to invade. Were the Greeks and the Romans made differently? Did the admirers of Socrates and Epictetus really attempt to become philosophers, or were they like ourselves, hopeful of achieving wisdom, not by practice but through a magic potion administered by a wiser man than they? To become wise without effort —by listening to a voice, by reading a book—it is at once the most exciting and the most soothing of dreams. In such a dream I took down Epictetus. And, behold, it was only a dream.

STUDY QUESTIONS

1. Russell, Dunham, and Lynd all discuss the value of philosophy, but each approaches the subject with quite different attitudes and purposes. How would you explain the difference, exactly? What is the relative "formality" of each selection? Is Lynd less "serious" than Russell or Dunham? To what extent is the meaning of each of the selections dependent upon the style of its writer?

2. The selection from Epictetus, "Stoicism," which is found in this book is a good example of his views. Do you think Lynd's reaction to them justified?

3. Exactly what conclusion is to be drawn from Lynd's observation that there are discrepancies between philosophy and actuality?

4. Lynd says that philosophy does not help him to accept the inefficiency of waiters and other trials. Does he offer any other solution for problems of this kind?

5. Compare Lynd's evaluation of philosophy with that of Russell in "The Value of Philosophy." Has Lynd mistaken the value of philosophic study? Explain your answer.

6. Write a theme describing an experience you have had in trying to apply an abstract principle or generalization to a particular situation.

The Allegory of the Cave*

Plato

And now, I said, let me show in a figure how far nature is enlightened or unenlightened:—Behold! human beings living in an underground den, which has a mouth open towards the light and reaching all along the den; here they have been from their childhood, and have their legs and necks chained so that they cannot move, and can only see before them, being prevented by the chains from turning round their heads. Above and behind them a fire is blazing at a distance, and between the fire and the prisoners there is a raised way; and you will see, if you look, a low wall built along the way, like the screen which marionette players have in front of them, over which they show the puppets.

I see.

And do you see, I said, men passing along the wall carrying all sorts of vessels, and statues and figures of animals made of wood and stone and various materials, which appear over the wall? Some of them are talking, others silent.

You have shown me a strange image, and they are strange prisoners.

Like ourselves, I replied; and they see only their own shadows, or the shadows of one another, which the fire throws on the opposite wall of the cave?

True, he said; how could they see anything but the shadows if they were never allowed to move their heads?

And of the objects which are being carried in like manner they would only see the shadows?

Yes, he said.

And if they were able to converse with one another, would they not suppose that they were naming what was actually before them?

Very true.

And suppose further that the prison had an echo which came from the other side, would they not be sure to fancy when one of the passers-by spoke that the voice which they heard came from the passing shadow?

No question, he replied.

To them, I said, the truth would be literally nothing but the shadows of the images.

* From *The Republic*, translated by Benjamin Jowett.

That is certain.

And now look again, and see what will naturally follow if the prisoners are released and disabused of their error. At first, when any of them is liberated and compelled suddenly to stand up and turn his neck round and walk and look towards the light, he will suffer sharp pains; the glare will distress him, and he will be unable to see the realities of which in his former state he had seen the shadows; and then conceive some one saying to him, that what he saw before was an illusion, but that now, when he is approaching nearer to being and his eye is turned towards more real existence, he has a clearer vision,—what will be his reply? And you may further imagine that his instructor is pointing to the objects as they pass and requiring him to name them,—will he not be perplexed? Will he not fancy that the shadows which he formerly saw are truer than the objects which are now shown to him?

Far truer.

And if he is compelled to look straight at the light, will he not have a pain in his eyes which will make him turn away to take refuge in the objects of vision which he can see, and which he will conceive to be in reality clearer than the things which are now being shown to him?

True, he said.

And suppose once more, that he is reluctantly dragged up a steep and rugged ascent, and held fast until he is forced into the presence of the sun himself, is he not likely to be pained and irritated? When he approaches the light his eyes will be dazzled, and he will not be able to see anything at all of what are now called realities.

Not all in a moment, he said.

He will require to grow accustomed to the sight of the upper world. And first he will see the shadows best, next the reflections of men and other objects in the water, and then the objects themselves; then he will gaze upon the light of the moon and the stars and the spangled heaven; and he will see the sky and the stars by night better than the sun or the light of the sun by day?

Certainly.

Last of all he will be able to see the sun, and not mere reflections of him in the water, but he will see him in his own proper place, and not in another; and he will contemplate him as he is.

Certainly.

He will then proceed to argue that this is he who gives the season and the years, and is the guardian of all that is in the visible world, and in a certain way the cause of all things which he and his fellows have been accustomed to behold?

Clearly, he said, he would first see the sun and then reason about him.

And when he remembered his old habitation, and the wisdom of the den and his fellow-prisoners, do you not suppose that he would felicitate himself on the change, and pity them?

Certainly, he would.

And if they were in the habit of conferring honours among themselves on those who were quickest to observe the passing shadows and to remark which of them went before, and which followed after, and which were together; and who were therefore best able to draw conclusions as to the future, do you think that he would care for such honours and glories, or envy the possessors of them? Would he not say with Homer,

> Better, to be the poor servant of a poor master,

and to endure anything, rather than think as they do and live after their manner?

Yes, he said, I think that he would rather suffer anything than entertain these false notions and live in this miserable manner.

Imagine once more, I said, such an one coming suddenly out of the sun to be replaced in his old situation; would he not be certain to have his eyes full of darkness?

To be sure, he said.

And if there were a contest, and he had to compete in measuring the shadows with the prisoners who had never moved out of the den, while his sight was still weak, and before his eyes had become steady (and the time which would be needed to acquire this new habit of sight might be very considerable) would he not be ridiculous? Men would say of him that up he went and down he came without his eyes; and that it was better not even to think of ascending; and if any one tried to loose another and lead him up to the light, let them only catch the offender, and they would put him to death.

No question, he said.

This entire allegory, I said, you may now append, dear Glaucon, to the previous argument; the prison-house is the world of sight, the light of the fire is the sun, and you will not misapprehend me if you interpret the journey upwards to be the ascent of the soul into the intellectual world according to my poor belief, which, at your desire, I have expressed—whether rightly or wrongly God knows. But, whether true or false, my opinion is that in the world of knowledge the idea of good appears last of all, and is seen only with an effort; and, when seen, is also inferred to be the universal author of all things beautiful and right, parent of light and of the lord of light in this visible world, and the immediate source of reason and truth in the intellectual; and that this is the power upon which he who would act rationally either in public or private life must have his eye fixed.

I agree, he said, as far as I am able to understand you.

Moreover, I said, you must not wonder that those who attain to this beatific vision are unwilling to descend to human affairs; for their souls are ever hastening into the upper world where they desire to dwell; which desire of theirs is very natural, if our allegory may be trusted.

Yes, very natural.

And is there anything surprising in one who passes from divine contemplations to the evil state of man, misbehaving himself in a ridiculous manner; if, while his eyes are blinking and before he has become accustomed to the surrounding darkness, he is compelled to fight in courts of law, or in other places, about the images or the shadows of images of justice, and is endeavouring to meet the conceptions of those who have never yet seen absolute justice?

Anything but surprising, he replied.

Any one who has common sense will remember that the bewilderments of the eyes are of two kinds, and arise from two causes, either from coming out of the light or from going into the light, which is true of the mind's eye, quite as much as of the bodily eye; and he who remembers this when he sees any one whose vision is perplexed and weak, will not be too ready to laugh; he will first ask whether that soul of man has come out of the brighter life, and is unable to see because unaccustomed to the dark, or having turned from darkness to the day is dazzled by excess of light. And he will count the one happy in his condition and state of being, and he will pity the other; or, if he have a mind to laugh at the soul which comes from below into the light, there will be more reason in this than in the laugh which greets him who returns from above out of the light into the den.

That, he said, is a very just distinction.

But then, if I am right, certain professors of education must be wrong when they say that they can put a knowledge into the soul which was not there before, like sight into blind eyes.

They undoubtedly say this, he replied.

Whereas, our argument shows that the power and capacity of learning exists in the soul already; and that just as the eye was unable to turn from darkness to light without the whole body, so too the instrument of knowledge can only by the movement of the whole soul be turned from the world of becoming into that of being, and learn by degrees to endure the sight of being, and of the brightest and best of being, or in other words, of the good.

STUDY QUESTIONS

1. In this allegory, what does the cave represent? The prison house? The outside sunshine? What advantage does Plato gain from representing his argument in concrete, figurative language instead of in more abstract terms?

2. What is symbolized by the pain experienced by the man who goes into the light for the first time?

3. What possibilities of mutual understanding existed between those who remained in the cave and those who were exiled from it?

4. Does Plato offer any definite evidence to support his contention

that it is better to know reality directly? Or is it supported in other ways?

5. What place in this allegory is occupied by the objects and institutions of everyday life that represent justice?

6. Since the prisoners of the cave can see only shadows, are not these shadows reality as far as they are concerned? Could they not continue to think and act as they did as long as none of them could see beyond the shadows?

Existentialism*

Jean-Paul Sartre

What is meant by the term *existentialism?*

Most people who use the word would be rather embarrassed if they had to explain it, since, now that the word is all the rage, even the work of a musician or painter is being called existentialist. . . . It seems that for want of an advance-guard doctrine analogous to surrealism, the kind of people who are eager for scandal and flurry turn to this philosophy which in other respects does not at all serve their purposes in this sphere.

Actually, it is the least scandalous, the most austere of doctrines. It is intended strictly for specialists and philosophers. Yet it can be defined easily. What complicates matters is that there are two kinds of existentialist; first, those who are Christian, among whom I would include Jaspers and Gabriel Marcel, both Catholic; and on the other hand the atheistic existentialists, among whom I class Heidegger, and then the French existentialists and myself. What they have in common is that they think that existence precedes essence, or, if you prefer, that subjectivity must be the starting point.

Just what does that mean? Let us consider some object that is manufactured, for example, a book or a paper-cutter: here is an object which has been made by an artisan whose inspiration came from a concept. He referred to the concept of what a paper-cutter is and likewise to a known method of production, which is part of the concept, something which is, by and large, a routine. Thus, the paper-cutter is at once an object produced in a certain way and, on the other hand, one having a specific use; and one can not postulate a man who produces a paper-cutter but does not know what it is used for. Therefore, let us say that, for the paper-cutter, essence—that is, the ensemble of both the production routines and the properties which enable it to be both produced and defined—precedes existence. Thus, the presence of the paper-cutter or book in front of me is

* From *Existentialism*. By permission of publishers, Philosophical Library.

determined. Therefore, we have here a technical view of the world whereby it can be said that production precedes existence.

When we conceive God as the Creator, He is generally thought of as a superior sort of artisan. Whatever doctrine we may be considering, whether one like that of Descartes or that of Leibnitz, we always grant that will more or less follows understanding or, at the very least, accompanies it, and that when God creates He knows exactly what He is creating. Thus, the concept of man in the mind of God is comparable to the concept of paper-cutter in the mind of the manufacturer, and, following certain techniques and a conception, God produces man, just as the artisan, following a definition and a technique, makes a paper-cutter. Thus, the individual man is the realisation of a certain concept in the divine intelligence.

In the eighteenth century, the atheism of the *philosophes* discarded the idea of God, but not so much for the notion that essence precedes existence. To a certain extent, this idea is found everywhere; we find it in Diderot, in Voltaire, and even in Kant. Man has a human nature; this human nature, which is the concept of the human, is found in all men, which means that each man is a particular example of a universal concept, man. In Kant, the result of this universality is that the wild-man, the natural man, as well as the bourgeois, are circumscribed by the same definition and have the same basic qualities. Thus, here too the essence of man precedes the historical existence that we find in nature.

Atheistic existentialism, which I represent, is more coherent. It states that if God does not exist, there is at least one being in whom existence precedes essence, a being who exists before he can be defined by any concept, and that this being is man, or, as Heidegger says, human reality. What is meant here by saying that existence precedes essence? It means that, first of all, man exists, turns up, appears on the scene, and, only afterwards, defines himself. If man, as the existentialist conceives him, is indefinable, it is because at first he is nothing. Only afterward will he be something, and he himself will have made what he will be. Thus, there is no human nature, since there is no God to conceive it. Not only is man what he conceives himself to be, but he is also only what he wills himself to be after this thrust toward existence.

Man is nothing else but what he makes of himself. Such is the first principle of existentialism. It is also what is called subjectivity, the name we are labeled with when charges are brought against us. But what do we mean by this, if not that man has a greater dignity than a stone or table? For we mean that man first exists, that is, that man first of all is the being who hurls himself toward a future and who is conscious of imagining himself as being in the future. Man is at the start a plan which is aware of itself, rather than a patch of moss, a piece of garbage, or a cauliflower; nothing exists prior to this plan; there is nothing in heaven; man will be what he will have planned to be. Not what he will want to be.

Because by the word "will" we generally mean a conscious decision, which is subsequent to what we have already made of ourselves. I may want to belong to a political party, write a book, get married; but all that is only a manifestation of an earlier, more spontaneous choice that is called "will." But if existence really does precede essence, man is responsible for what he is. Thus, existentialism's first move is to make every man aware of what he is and to make the full responsibility of his existence rest on him. And when we say that a man is responsible for himself, we do not only mean that he is responsible for his own individuality, but that he is responsible for all men.

The word subjectivism has two meanings, and our opponents play on the two. Subjectivism means, on the one hand, that an individual chooses and makes himself; and, on the other, that it is impossible for man to transcend human subjectivity. The second of these is the essential meaning of existentialism. When we say that man chooses his own self, we mean that every one of us does likewise; but we also mean by that that in making this choice he also chooses all men. In fact, in creating the man that we want to be, there is not a single one of our acts which does not at the same time create an image of man as we think he ought to be. To choose to be this or that is to affirm at the same time the value of what we choose, because we can never choose evil. We always choose the good, and nothing can be good for us without being good for all.

If, on the other hand, existence precedes essence, and if we grant that we exist and fashion our image at one and the same time, the image is valid for everybody and for our whole age. Thus, our responsibility is much greater than we might have supposed, because it involves all mankind. If I am a workingman and choose to join a Christian trade-union rather than be a communist, and if by being a member I want to show that the best thing for man is resignation, and that the kingdom of man is not of this world, I am not only involving my own case—I want to be resigned for everyone. As a result, my action has involved all humanity. To take a more individual matter, if I want to marry, to have children; even if this marriage depends solely on my own circumstances or passion or wish, I am involving all humanity in monogamy and not merely myself. Therefore, I am responsible for myself and for everyone else. I am creating a certain image of man of my own choosing. In choosing myself, I choose man.

This helps us understand what the actual content is of such rather grandiloquent words as anguish, forlorness, despair. As you will see, it's all quite simple.

First, what is meant by anguish? The existentialists say at once that man is anguish. What that means is this: the man who involves himself and who realizes that he is not only the person he chooses to be, but also a law-maker who is, at the same time, choosing all mankind as well as himself, can not help escape the feeling of his total and deep responsibility.

Of course, there are many people who are not anxious; but we claim that they are hiding their anxiety, that they are fleeing from it. Certainly, many people believe that when they do something, they themselves are the only ones involved, and when someone says to them, "What if everyone acted that way?" they shrug their shoulders and answer, "Everyone doesn't act that way." But really, one should always ask himself, "What would happen if everybody looked at things that way?" There is no escaping this disturbing thought except by a kind of double-dealing. A man who lies and makes excuses for himself by saying "not everbody does that," is someone with an uneasy conscience, because the act of lying implies that a universal value is conferred upon the lie.

Anguish is evident even when it conceals itself. This is the anguish that Kierkegaard called the anguish of Abraham. You know the story: an angel has ordered Abraham to sacrifice his son; if it really were an angel who has come and said, "You are Abraham, you shall sacrifice your son," everything would be all right. But everyone might first wonder, "Is it really an angel, and am I really Abraham? What proof do I have?" . . .

Now, I'm not being singled out as an Abraham, and yet at every moment I'm obliged to perform exemplary acts. For every man, everything happens as if all mankind had its eyes fixed on him and were guiding itself by what he does. And every man ought to say to himself, "Am I really the kind of man who has the right to act in such a way that humanity might guide itself by my actions?" And if he does not say that to himself, he is masking his anguish.

There is no question here of the kind of anguish which would lead to quietism, to inaction. It is a matter of a simple sort of anguish that anybody who has had responsibilities is familiar with. For example, when a military officer takes the responsibility for an attack and sends a certain number of men to death, he chooses to do so, and in the main he alone makes the choice. Doubtless, orders come from above, but they are too broad; he interprets them, and on this interpretation depend the lives of ten or fourteen or twenty men. In making a decision he can not help having a certain anguish. All leaders know this anguish. That doesn't keep them from acting; on the contrary, it is the very condition of their action. For it implies that they envisage a number of possibilities, and when they choose one, they realize that it has value only because it is chosen. We shall see that this kind of anguish, which is the kind that existentialism describes, is explained, in addition, by a direct responsibility to the other men whom it involves. It is not a curtain separating us from action, but is part of action itself.

When we speak of forlornness, a term Heidegger was fond of, we mean only that God does not exist and that we have to face all the consequences of this. The existentialist is strongly opposed to a certain kind of secular ethics which would like to abolish God with the least possible expense. About 1880, some French teachers tried to set up a secular ethics which went something like this: God is a useless and costly hypothesis; we are discarding it; but, meanwhile, in order for there to be an ethics, a society, a civilization, it is essential that certain values be taken seriously and that they be considered as having an *a priori* existence. It must be obligatory, *a priori*, to be honest, not to lie, not to beat your wife, to have children, etc., etc. So we're going to try a little device which will make it possible to show that values exist all the same, inscribed in a heaven of ideas, though otherwise God does not exist. In other words—and this, I believe, is the tendency of everything called reformism in France—nothing will be changed if God does not exist. We shall find ourselves with the same norms of honesty, progress, and humanism, and we shall have made of God an outdated hypothesis which will peacefully die off by itself.

The existentialist, on the contrary, thinks it very distressing that God does not exist, because all possibility of finding values in a heaven of ideas disappears along with Him; there can no longer be an *a priori* Good, since there is no infinite and perfect consciousness to think it. Nowhere is it written that Good exists, that we must be honest, that we must not lie; because the fact is we are on a plane where there are only men. Dostoievsky said, "If God didn't exist, everything would be possible." That is the very starting point of existentialism. Indeed, everything is permissible if God does not exist, and as a result man is forlorn, because neither within him nor without does he find anything to cling to. He can't start making excuses for himself.

If existence really does precede essence, there is no explaining things away by reference to a fixed and given human nature. In other words, there is no determinism, man is free, man is freedom. On the other hand, if God does not exist, we find no values or commands to turn to which legitimize our conduct. So, in the bright realm of values, we have no excuse behind us, no justification before us. We are alone, with no excuses.

That is the idea I shall try to convey when I say that man is condemned to be free. Condemned, because he did not create himself, yet, in other respects is free; because, once thrown into the world, he is responsible for everything he does. The existentialist does not believe in the power of passion. He will never agree that a sweeping passion is a ravaging torrent which fatally leads a man to certain acts and is therefore an excuse. He thinks that man is responsible for his passion.

The existentialist does not think that man is going to help himself by finding in the world some omen by which to orient himself. Because he thinks that man will interpret the omen to suit himself. Therefore, he thinks that man, with no support and no aid, is condemned every moment to invent man. Ponge, in a very fine article, has said, "Man is the future of man." That's exactly it. But if it is taken to mean that this future is recorded in heaven, that God sees it, then it is false, because it would really no longer be a future. If it is taken to mean that, whatever a man may be, there is a future to be forged, a virgin future before him, then this remark is sound. But then we are forlorn.

To give you an example which will enable you to understand forlornness better, I shall cite the case of one of my students who came to see me under the following circumstances: his father was on bad terms with his mother, and, moreover, was inclined to be a collaborationist; his older brother had been killed in the German offensive of 1940, and the young man, with somewhat immature but generous feelings, wanted to avenge him. His mother lived alone with him, very much upset by the half-treason of her husband and the death of her older son; the boy was her only consolation.

The boy was faced with the choice of leaving for England and joining the Free French Forces—that is, leaving his mother behind—or remaining with his mother and helping her to carry on. He was fully aware that the woman lived only for him and that his going-off—and perhaps his death—would plunge her into despair. He was also aware that every act that he did for his mother's sake was a sure thing, in the sense that it was helping her to carry on, whereas every effort he made toward going off and fighting was an uncertain move which might run aground and prove completely useless; for example, on his way to England he might, while passing through Spain, be detained indefinitely in a Spanish camp; he might reach England or Algiers and be stuck in an office at a desk job. As a result, he was faced with two very different kinds of action: one, concrete, immediate, but concerning only one individual; the other concerned an incomparably vaster group, a national collectivity, but for that very reason was dubious, and might be interrupted en route. And, at the same time, he was wavering between two kinds of ethics. On the one hand, an ethics of sympathy, of personal devotion; on the other, a broader ethics, but one whose efficacy was more dubious. He had to choose between the two.

Who would help him choose? Christian doctrine? No. Christian doctrine says, "Be charitable, love your neighbor, take the more rugged path, etc., etc." But which is the more rugged path? Whom should he love as a brother? The fighting man or his mother? Which does the greater good, the vague act of fighting in a group, or the concrete one of helping a particular human being to go on living? Who can decide *a priori?* Nobody. No book of ethics can tell him. The Kantian ethics says, "Never treat any person as a means, but as an end." Very well, if I stay with my mother, I'll treat her as an end and not as a means; but by virtue of this very fact, I'm running the risk of treating the people around me who are fighting, as means; and, conversely, if I go to join those who are fighting, I'll be treating them as an end, and, by doing that, I run the risk of treating my mother as a means.

If values are vague, and if they are always too broad for the concrete and specific case that we are considering, the only thing left for us is to trust our instincts. That's what this young man tried to do; and when I saw him, he said, "In the end, feeling is what counts. I ought to choose whichever pushes me in one direction. If I feel that I love my mother enough to sacrifice everything else for her—my desire for vengeance, for action, for adventure—then I'll stay with her. If, on the contrary, I feel that my love for my mother isn't enough, I'll leave."

But how is the value of a feeling determined? What gives his feeling for his mother value? Precisely the fact that he remained with her. I may say that I like so-and-so well enough to sacrifice a certain amount of money for him, but I may say so only if I've done it. I may say "I love my mother well enough to remain with her" if I have remained with her. The only way to determine the value of this affection is, precisely, to perform an act which confirms and defines it. But, since I require this affection to justify my act, I find myself caught in a vicious circle. . . .

As for despair, the term has a very simple meaning. It means that we shall confine ourselves to reckoning only with what depends upon our will, or on the ensemble of probabilities which make our action possible. When we want something, we always have to reckon with probabilities. I may be counting on the arrival of a friend. The friend is coming by rail or street-car; this supposes that the train will arrive on schedule, or that the street-car will not jump the track. I am left in the realm of possibility; but possibilities are to be reckoned with only to the point where my action comports with the ensemble of these possibilities, and no further. The moment the possibilities I am considering are not rigorously involved by my action, I ought to disengage myself from them, because no God, no scheme, can adapt the world and its possibilities to my will. When Descartes said, "Conquer yourself rather than the world," he meant essentially the same thing.

The Marxists to whom I have spoken reply, "You can rely on the support of others in your action, which obviously has certain limits because you're not going to live forever. That means: rely on both what others are doing elsewhere to help you, in China, in Russia, and what they will do later on, after your death, to carry on the action and lead it to its fulfillment, which will be the revolution. You may even *have* to rely upon that, otherwise you're immoral." I reply at once that I will always rely on fellow-fighters insofar as these comrades are involved with me in a common struggle, in the unity of a party or a group in which I can more or less make my weight felt; that is, one whose ranks I am in as a fighter and whose movements I am aware of at every moment. In such a situation, relying on the unity and will of the party is exactly like counting on the fact that the train will arrive on time or that the car won't jump the track. But, given that man is free and that there is no human nature for me to depend on, I can not count on men whom I do not know by relying on human goodness or man's concern for the good of society. I don't know what will become of the Russian revolution; I may make an example of it to the extent that at the present time it is apparent that the proletariat plays a part in Russia that it plays in no other nation. But I can't swear that this will inevitably lead to a triumph of the proletariat. I've got to limit myself to what I see.

Given that men are free, and that tomorrow they will freely decide what man will be, I can not be sure that, after my death, fellow-fighters will carry on my work to bring it to its maximum perfection. Tomorrow, after my death, some men may decide to set up Fascism, and the others may be cowardly and muddled enough to let them do it. Fascism will then be the human reality, so much the worse for us.

Actually, things will be as man will have decided they are to be. Does that mean that I should abandon myself to quietism? No. First, I should involve myself; then, act on the old saw, "Nothing ventured, nothing gained." Nor does it mean that I shouldn't belong to a party, but rather that I shall have no illusions and shall do what I can. For example, suppose I ask myself, "Will socialization, as such, ever come about?" I know nothing about it. All I know is that I'm going to do everything in my power to bring it about. Beyond that, I can't count on anything. Quietism is the attitude of people who say, "Let others do what I can't do." The doctrine I am presenting is the very opposite of quietism, since it declares, "There is no reality except in action." Moreover, it goes further, since it adds, "Man is nothing else than his plan; he exists only to the extent that he fulfills himself; he is therefore nothing else than the ensemble of his acts, nothing else than his life."

STUDY QUESTIONS

1. What is Sartre's purpose in this piece? To define *existentialism?* To persuade readers that existentialism is a truer or better view of man than other views? A combination of these? Explain your answer by reference to specific passages and details.

2. Can Sartre's view of human nature be reconciled with that given by Herbert J. Muller in "The Nature of Man"?

3. Dostoevski's remark, "If God didn't exist, everything would be possible," means that God is the only thing that prevents man from being free to commit immoral actions. Does Sartre, though he denies the existence of God, offer any substitute guardian for morality?

4. How does Sartre explain the doctrine that the individual has an ethical responsibility? Through what feelings does this responsibility manifest itself? Explain Sartre's recommendation for solving moral and ethical problems.

5. What is the essential difference between existentialism, as it is explained here, and traditional Christian beliefs?

6. Do you find any weaknesses in the system described by Sartre? Has he made any assumptions that require proof? Has he contradicted himself? Write a criticism of his statement or of some part of it.

2. THE VOICE OF SCIENCE

All Men Are Scientists*

Thomas Henry Huxley

Scientific investigation is not, as many people seem to suppose, some kind of modern black art. You might easily gather this impression from the manner in which many persons speak of scientific inquiry, or talk about inductive and deductive philosophy, or the principles of the "Baconian philosophy." I do protest that, of the vast number of cants in this world, there are none, to my mind, so contemptible as the pseudo-scientific cant which is talked about the "Baconian philosophy."

To hear people talk about the great Chancellor—and a very great man he certainly was,—you would think that it was he who had invented science, and that there was no such thing as sound reasoning before the time of Queen Elizabeth! Of course you say, that cannot possibly be true; you perceive, on a moment's reflection, that such an idea is absurdly wrong. . . .

The method of scientific investigation is nothing but the expression of the necessary mode of working of the human mind. It is simply the mode at which all phenomena are reasoned about, rendered precise and exact. There is no more difference, but there is just the same kind of difference, between the mental operations of a man of science and those of an ordinary person, as there is between the operations and methods of a baker or of a butcher weighing out his goods in common scales, and the operations of a chemist in performing a difficult and complex analysis by means of his balance and finely-graduated weights. It is not that the action of the scales in the one case, and the balance in the other, differ in the principles of their construction or manner of working; but the beam of one is set on an infinitely finer axis than the other, and of course turns by the addition of a much smaller weight.

You will understand this better, perhaps, if I give you some familiar example. You have all heard it repeated, I dare say, that men of science work by means of induction and deduction, and that by the help of these operations, they, in a sort of sense, wring from Nature certain other things, which are called natural laws, and causes, and that out of these, by some cunning skill of their own, they build up hypotheses and theories. And it is imagined by many, that the operations of the common

* From *Darwiniana*, 1893.

mind can be by no means compared with these processes, and that they have to be acquired by a sort of special apprenticeship to the craft. To hear all these large words, you would think that the mind of a man of science must be constituted differently from that of his fellow men; but if you will not be frightened by terms, you will discover that you are quite wrong, and that all these terrible apparatus are being used by yourselves every day and every hour of your lives.

There is a well-known incident in one of Molière's plays, where the author makes the hero express unbounded delight on being told that he had been talking prose during the whole of his life. In the same way, I trust, that you will take comfort, and be delighted with yourselves, on the discovery that you have been acting on the principles of inductive and deductive philosophy during the same period. Probably there is not one who has not in the course of the day had occasion to set in motion a complex train of reasoning, of the very same kind, though differing of course in degree, as that which a scientific man goes through in tracing the causes of natural phenomena.

A very trivial circumstance will serve to exemplify this. Suppose you go into a fruiterer's shop, wanting an apple,—you take up one, and, on biting it, you find it is sour; you look at it, and see that it is hard and green. You take up another one, and that too is hard, green, and sour. The shopman offers you a third; but, before biting it, you examine it, and find that it is hard and green, and you immediately say that you will not have it, as it must be sour, like those that you have already tried.

Nothing can be more simple than that, you think; but if you will take the trouble to analyse and trace out into its logical elements what has been done by the mind, you will be greatly surprised. In the first place, you have performed the operation of induction. You found that, in two experiences, hardness and greenness in apples went together with sourness. It was so in the first case, and it was confirmed by the second. True, it is a very small basis, but still it is enough to make an induction from; you generalize the facts, and you expect to find sourness in apples where you get hardness and greenness. You found upon that a general law, that all hard and green apples are sour; and that, so far as it goes, is a perfect induction. Well, having got your natural law in this way, when you are offered another apple which you find is hard and green, you say, "All hard and green apples are sour; this apple is hard and green, therefore this apple is sour." That train of reasoning is what logicians call a syllogism, and has all its various parts and terms—its major premiss, its minor premiss, and its conclusion. And, by the help of further reasoning, which, if drawn out, would have to be exhibited in two or three other syllogisms, you arrive at your final determination, "I will not have that apple." So that, you see, you have, in the first place, established a law by induction, and upon that you have founded a deduction, and reasoned out the special conclusion of the particular case. Well now, suppose, having got your law, that at some time afterwards, you are discussing the qualities of apples with a friend: you will say to him, "It is a very curious thing,—but I find that all hard and green apples are sour!" Your friends say to you, "But how do you know that?" You at once reply, "Oh, because I have tried them over and over again, and have always found them to be so." Well, if we were talking science instead of common sense, we should call that an experimental verification. And, if still opposed, you go further, and say, "I have heard from the people of Somersetshire and Devonshire, where a large number of apples are grown, that they have observed the same thing. It is also found to be the case in Normandy, and in North America. In short, I find it to be the universal experience of mankind wherever attention has been directed to the subject." Whereupon, your friend, unless he is a very unreasonable man, agrees with you, and is convinced that you are quite right in the conclusion you have drawn. He believes, although perhaps he does not know he believes it, that the more extensive verifications are,—that the more frequently experiments have been made, and results of the same kind arrived at,—that the more varied the conditions under which the same results are attained, the more certain is the ultimate conclusion, and he disputes the question no further. He sees that the experiment has been tried under all sorts of conditions, as to time, place, and people, with the same result; and he says with you, therefore, that the law you have laid down must be a good one, and he must believe it.

In science we do the same thing;—the philosopher exercises precisely the same faculties, though in a much more delicate manner. In scientific inquiry it becomes a matter of duty to expose a supposed law to every possible kind of verification, and to take care, moreover, that this is done intentionally, and not left to a mere accident, as in the case of the apples. And in science, as in common life, our confidence in a law is in exact proportion to the absence of variation in the result of our experimental verifications. For instance, if you let go your grasp of an article you may have in your hand, it will immediately fall to the ground. That is a very common verification of one of the best established laws of nature—that of gravitation. The method by which men of science establish the existence of that law is exactly the same as that by which we have established the trivial proposition about the sourness of hard and green apples. But we believe it in such an extensive, thorough, and unhesitating manner because the universal experience of mankind verifies it, and we can verify it ourselves at any time; and that is the strongest possible foundation on which any natural law can rest.

So much, then, by way of proof that the method of establishing laws in science is exactly the same as that pursued in common life. Let us now turn to another matter (though really it is but another phase of the same question), and that is, the method by which, from the relations of certain phenomena, we prove that some stand in the position of causes towards the others.

I want to put the case clearly before you, and I will therefore show you what I mean by another familiar example. I will suppose that one of you, on coming down in the morning to the parlour of your house, finds that a tea-pot and some spoons which had been left in the room on the previous evening are gone,—the window is open, and you observe the mark of a dirty hand on the window-frame, and perhaps, in addition to that, you notice the impress of a hob-nailed shoe on the gravel outside. All these phenomena have struck your attention instantly, and before two seconds have passed you say, "Oh, somebody has broken open the window, entered the room, and run off with the spoons and the tea-pot!" That speech is out of your mouth in a moment. And you will probably add, "I know there has; I am quite sure of it!" You mean to say exactly what you know; but in reality you are giving expression to what is, in all essential particulars, an hypothesis. You do not *know* it at all; it is nothing but an hypothesis rapidly framed in your mind. And it is an hypothesis founded on a long train of inductions and deductions.

What are those inductions and deductions, and how have you got at this hypothesis? You have observed, in the first place, that the window is open; but by a train of reasoning involving many inductions and deductions, you have probably arrived long before at the general law—and a very good one it is—that windows do not open of themselves; and you therefore conclude that something has opened the window. A second general law that you have arrived at in the same way is, that tea-pots and spoons do not go out of a window spontaneously, and you are satisfied that, as they are not now where you left them, they have been removed. In the third place, you look at the marks on the window-sill, and the shoe-marks outside, and you say that in all previous experience the former kind of mark has never been produced by anything else but the hand of a human being; and the same experience shows that no other animal but man at present wears shoes with hob-nails in them such as would produce the marks in the gravel. I do not know, even if we could discover any of those "missing links" that are talked about, that they would help us to any other conclusion! At any rate the law which states our present experience is strong enough for my present purpose. You next reach the conclusion, that as these kinds of marks have not been left by any other animals than men, or are liable to be formed in any other way than by a man's hand and shoe, the marks in question have been formed by a man in that way. You have, further, a general law, founded on observation and experience, and that, too, is, I am sorry to say, a very universal and unimpeachable one,—that some men are thieves; and you assume at once from all these premises—and that is what constitutes your hypothesis—that the man who made the marks outside and on the window-sill, opened the window, got into the room, and stole your tea-pot and spoons. You have now arrived at a *vera causa;*—you have assumed a cause which, it is plain, is competent to produce all the phenomena you have observed. You can explain all these phenomena only by the hypothesis of a thief. But that is a hypothetical conclusion, of the justice of which you have no absolute proof at all; it is only rendered highly probable by a series of inductive and deductive reasonings.

I suppose your first action, assuming that you are a man of ordinary common sense, and that you have established this hypothesis to your own satisfaction, will very likely be to go for the police, and set them on the track of the burglar, with the view to the recovery of your property. But just as you are starting with this object, some person comes in, and on learning what you are about, says, "My good friend, you are going on a great deal too fast. How do you know that the man who really made the marks took the spoons? It might have been a monkey that took them, and the man may have merely looked in afterward." You would probably reply, "Well, that is all very well, but you see it is contrary to all experience of the way tea-pots and spoons are abstracted; so that, at any rate, your hypothesis is less probable than mine." While you are talking the thing over in this way, another friend arrives. And he might say, "Oh, my dear sir, you are certainly going on a great deal too fast. You are most presumptuous. You admit that all these occurrences took place when you were fast asleep, at a time when you could not possibly have known anything about what was taking place. How do you know that the laws of nature are not suspended during the night? It may be that there has been some kind of supernatural interference in this case." In point of fact, he declares that your hypothesis is one of which you cannot at all demonstrate the truth and that you are by no means sure that the laws of nature are the same when you are asleep as when you are awake.

Well, now, you cannot at the moment answer that kind of reasoning. You feel that your worthy friend has you somewhat at a disadvantage. You will feel perfectly convinced in your own mind, however, that you are quite right, and you say to him, "My good friend, I can only be guided by the natural probabilities of the case, and if you will be kind enough to stand aside and permit me to pass, I will go and fetch the police." Well, we will suppose that your journey is successful, and that by good luck you meet with a policeman; that eventually the burglar is found with your property on his person, and the marks correspond to his hand and to his boots. Probably any jury would consider those facts a very good experimental verification of your hypothesis, touching the cause of the abnormal phenomena observed in your parlour, and would act accordingly.

Now, in this suppositious case, I have taken phenomena of a very common kind, in order that you might see what are the different steps in an ordinary process of reasoning, if you will only take the trouble to analyze it carefully. All the operations I have described, you will see, are involved in the mind of any man of sense in leading him to a conclusion as to the course he should take in order to make good a robbery and punish the offender. I say that you are led, in that case, to your conclusion by exactly the same train of reasoning as that which a man of science pursues when he is endeavouring to discover the origin and laws of the most occult phenomena. The process is, and always must be, the same; and precisely the same mode of reasoning was employed by Newton and Laplace in their endeavours to discover and define the causes of the movements of the heavenly bodies, as you, with your own common sense, would employ to detect a burglar. The only difference is, that the nature of the inquiry being more abstruse, every step has to be most carefully watched, so that there may not be a single crack or flaw in your hypothesis. A flaw or crack in many of the hypotheses of daily life may be of little or no moment as affecting the general correctness of the conclusions at which we may arrive; but, in a scientific inquiry, a fallacy, great or small, is always of importance, and is sure to be in the long run constantly productive of mischievous, if not fatal results.

Do not allow yourselves to be misled by the common notion that an hypothesis is untrustworthy simply because it is an hypothesis. It is often urged, in respect to some scientific conclusion, that, after all, it is only an hypothesis. But what more have we to guide us in nine-tenths of the most important affairs of daily life than hypotheses, and often very ill-based ones? So that in science, where the evidence of any hypothesis is subjected to the most rigid examination, we might rightly pursue the same course. You may have hypotheses and hypotheses. A man may say, if he likes, that the moon is made of green cheese: that is an hypothesis. But another man, who has devoted a great deal of time and attention to the subject, and availed himself of the most powerful telescopes and the results of observations of others, declares that in his opinion it is probably composed of materials very similar to those of which our own earth is made up: and that is also only an hypothesis. But I need not tell you that there is an enormous difference in the value of the two hypotheses. That one which is based on sound scientific knowledge is sure to have a corresponding value; and that which is a mere hasty random guess is likely to have little value. Every great step in our progress in discovering causes has been made in exactly the same way as that which I have detailed to you. A person observing the occurrence of certain facts and phenomena asks, naturally enough, what process, what kind of operation known to occur in Nature applied to the particular case, will unravel and explain the mystery? Hence you have the scientific hypothesis; and its value will be proportionate to the care and completeness with which its basis has been tested and verified. It is in these matters as in the commonest affairs of practical life: the guess of the fool will be folly, while the guess of the wise man will contain wisdom. In all cases, you see that the value of the result depends on the patience and faithfulness with which the investigator applies to his hypothesis every possible kind of verification. . . .

STUDY QUESTIONS

1. Into what two main parts does this explanation fall? What is the tone of the essay? What sort of an audience do you think it was addressed to? What devices does Huxley use to achieve clarity and the understanding of the reader?

2. Define "hypothesis" and "scientific law." What is the difference between a scientific law and a legislative law?

3. In the example of the missing spoons and teapot, is the friend who objects to the hypothesis proved wrong? What part is played by *absolute proof* in this and the other examples? Illustrate the difference between a trustworthy hypothesis and an untrustworthy one.

4. Summarize the steps in the scientific method as defined by Huxley. Do the examples of scientific thinking by Huxley reflect the procedure followed by Poincaré? Explain.

5. Write a theme describing an actual episode in which you unconsciously used the scientific method to arrive at a conclusion about something.

6. Note that Huxley insists that the scientific method, if properly followed, and verified under different conditions, produces results which must be accepted. Is Huxley making too strong a claim? Are there exceptions or qualifications that should be pointed out? Have there been any recent developments that might force Huxley to change his opinion? In discussing these points, consider the essays by Eddington, Cohen and Nagel, and Dubos.

Mathematical Creation*

Henri Poincaré

It is time to penetrate deeper and to see what goes on in the very soul of the mathematician. For this, I believe, I can do best by recalling memories of my own. But I shall limit myself to telling how I wrote my first memoir on Fuchsian functions. I beg the reader's pardon; I am about to use some technical expressions, but they need not frighten him, for he is not obliged to understand them. I shall say, for example, that I have found the demonstration of such a theorem under such circumstances. This theorem will have a barbarous name, unfamiliar to

---

*From *Foundations of Science,* Science Press, 1913. Reprinted by permission of Jaques Cattell.

many, but that is unimportant; what is of interest for the psychologist is not the theorem but the circumstances.

For fifteen days I strove to prove that there could not be any functions like those I have since called Fuchsian functions. I was then very ignorant; every day I seated myself at my work table, stayed an hour or two, tried a great number of combinations and reached no results. One evening, contrary to my custom, I drank black coffee and could not sleep. Ideas rose in crowds; I felt them collide until pairs interlocked, so to speak, making a stable combination. By the next morning I had established the existence of a class of Fuchsian functions, those which come from the hypergeometric series; I had only to write out the results, which took but a few hours.

Then I wanted to represent these functions by the quotient of two series; this idea was perfectly conscious and deliberate, the analogy with elliptic functions guided me. I asked myself what properties these series must have if they existed, and I succeeded without difficulty in forming the series I have called theta-Fuchsian.

Just at this time I left Caen, where I was then living, to go on a geologic excursion under the auspices of the school of mines. The changes of travel made me forget my mathematical work. Having reached Coutances, we entered an omnibus to go some place or other. At the moment when I put my foot on the step the idea came to me, without anything in my former thoughts seeming to have paved the way for it, that the transformations I had used to define the Fuchsian functions were identical with those of non-Euclidean geometry. I did not verify the idea; I should not have had time, as, upon taking my seat in the omnibus, I went on with a conversation already commenced, but I felt a perfect certainty. On my return to Caen, for conscience's sake I verified the result at my leisure.

Then I turned my attention to the study of some arithmetical questions apparently without much success and without a suspicion of any connection with my preceding researches. Disgusted with my failure, I went to spend a few days at the seaside, and thought of something else. One morning, walking on the bluff, the idea came to me, with just the same characteristics of brevity, suddenness and immediate certainty, that the arithmetic transformations of indeterminate ternary quadratic forms were identical with those of non-Euclidean geometry.

Returned to Caen, I meditated on this result and deduced the consequences. The example of quadratic forms showed me that there were Fuchsian groups other than those corresponding to the hypergeometric series; I saw that I could apply to them the theory of theta-Fuchsian series and that consequently there existed Fuchsian functions other than those from the hypergeometric series, the ones I then knew. Naturally I set myself to form all these functions. I made a systematic attack upon them and carried all the outworks, one after another. There was one however that still held out, whose fall would involve that of the whole place. But all my efforts only served at first the better to show me the difficulty, which indeed was something. All this work was perfectly conscious.

Thereupon I left for Mont-Valérien, where I was to go through my military service; so I was very differently occupied. One day, going along the street, the solution of the difficulty which had stopped me suddenly appeared to me. I did not try to go deep into it immediately, and only after my service did I again take up the question. I had all the elements and had only to arrange them and put them together. So I wrote out my final memoir at a single stroke and without difficulty.

I shall limit myself to this single example; it is useless to multiply them. In regard to my other researches I would have to say analogous things, and the observations of other mathematicians given in *L'Enseignement Mathématique* would only confirm them.

Most striking at first is this appearance of sudden illumination, a manifest sign of long, unconscious prior work. The rôle of this unconscious work in mathematical invention appears to me incontestable, and traces of it would be found in other cases where it is less evident. Often when one works at a hard question, nothing good is accomplished at the first attack. Then one takes a rest, longer or shorter, and sits down anew to the work. During the first half-hour, as before, nothing is found, and then all of a sudden the decisive idea presents itself to the mind. It might be said that the conscious work has been more fruitful because it has been interrupted and the rest has given back to the mind its force and freshness. But it is more probable that this rest has been filled out with unconscious work and that the result of this work has afterward revealed itself to the geometer just as in the cases I have cited; only the revelation instead of coming during a walk or a journey has happened during a period of conscious work, but independently of this work which plays at most a rôle of excitant, as if it were the goad stimulating the results already reached during rest, but remaining unconscious, to assume the conscious form.

There is another remark to be made about the conditions of this unconscious work: it is possible, and of a certainty it is only fruitful, if it is on the one hand preceded and on the other hand followed by a period of conscious work. These sudden inspirations (and the examples already cited sufficiently prove this) never happened except after some days of voluntary effort which has appeared absolutely fruitless and whence nothing good seems to have come, where the way taken seems totally astray. These efforts then have not been as sterile as one thinks; they have set agoing the unconscious machine and without them it would not have moved and would have produced nothing.

The need for the second period of conscious work, after the inspiration, is still easier to understand. It is necessary to put in shape the results of this inspiration, to deduce from them the immediate consequences, to arrange them, to word the demonstrations, but above all is verification necessary. I have spoken of the feeling of absolute certitude accompanying the inspiration; in the cases cited this feeling was no deceiver, nor is it usually. But do not think this is a rule without exception; often this feeling deceives us without being any the less vivid, and we only find it out when we seek to put on foot the demonstration.

STUDY QUESTIONS

1. Both Huxley and Poincaré presumably based their descriptions of the scientific method on personal experience. What part was played in Poincaré's thinking by the method which Huxley describes? Does Poincaré add elements not discussed by Huxley? Do you think there is a disagreement between them on the nature of the process? On the relative importance of certain aspects?

2. What part did personal or emotional factors seem to play in Poincaré's work? Did environment and daily activity seem to have any effect on it?

3. What is the essential difference between the kind of scientific work described here by Poincaré and that carried on by Ittelson and Kilpatrick in "Experiments in Perception"?

4. Would it be accurate to call Poincaré's insights "intuitions"? Would it be fair to attribute them to "imagination"? Are they essentially like or unlike the artist's imaginative ordering of experience?

5. Have you ever had a sudden and unaccountable flash of insight into a difficult problem? If so, write a theme describing your experience.

6. Poincaré does not explain the mental processes that led to the solutions of these problems, because they were unconscious and therefore unknown to him. Is there any explanation of them? Is there any reason why his answers came to him at times when he was least concerned with his problems?

The Nature of the Physical World*

Arthur S. Eddington

I have settled down to the task of writing these lectures and have drawn up my chairs to my two tables. Two tables! Yes; there are duplicates of every object about me—two tables, two chairs, two pens.

This is not a very profound beginning to a course which ought to reach

* From *The Nature of the Physical World* by Sir Arthur S. Eddington, by permission of the Cambridge University Press. Copyright, 1928, by Cambridge University Press.

transcendent levels of scientific philosophy. But we cannot touch bedrock immediately; we must scratch a bit of the surface of things first. And whenever I begin to scratch the first thing I strike is—my two tables.

One of them has been familiar to me from earliest years. It is a commonplace object of that environment which I call the world. How shall I describe it? It has extension; it is comparatively permanent; it is colored; above all it is substantial. By substantial I do not merely mean that it does not collapse when I lean upon it; I mean that it is constituted of "substance" and by that word I am trying to convey to you some conception of its intrinsic nature. It is a *thing;* not like space, which is a mere negation; nor like time, which is—Heaven knows what! But that will not help you to my meaning because it is the distinctive characteristic of a "thing" to have this substantiality, and I do not think substantiality can be described better than by saying that it is the kind of nature exemplified by an ordinary table. And so we go round in circles. After all if you are a plain common-sense man, not too much worried with scientific scruples, you will be confident that you understand the nature of an ordinary table. I have even heard of plain men who had the idea that they could better understand the mystery of their own nature if scientists would discover a way of explaining it in terms of the easily comprehensible nature of a table.

Table No. 2 is my scientific table. It is a more recent acquaintance and I do not feel so familiar with it. It does not belong to the world previously mentioned—that world which spontaneously appears around me when I open my eyes, though how much of it is objective and how much subjective I do not here consider. It is part of a world which in more devious ways has forced itself on my attention. My scientific table is mostly emptiness. Sparsely scattered in that emptiness are numerous electric charges rushing about with great speed; but their combined bulk amounts to less than a billionth of the bulk of the table itself. Notwithstanding its strange construction it turns out to be an entirely efficient table. It supports my writing paper as satisfactorily as table No. 1; for when I lay the paper on it the little electric particles with their headlong speed keep on hitting the underside, so that the paper is maintained in shuttlecock fashion at a nearly steady level. If I lean upon this table I shall not go through; or, to be strictly accurate, the chance of my scientific elbow going through my scientific table is so excessively small that it can be neglected in practical life. Reviewing their properties one by one, there seems to be nothing to choose between the two tables for ordinary purposes; but when abnormal circumstances befall, then my scientific table shows to advantage. If the house catches fire my scientific table will dissolve quite naturally into scientific smoke, whereas my familiar table undergoes a metamorphosis of its substantial nature which I can only regard as miraculous.

There is nothing substantial about my second table. It is nearly all empty space—space pervaded, it is true, by fields of force, but these are assigned to the category of "influences," not of "things." Even in the minute part which is not empty we must not transfer the old notion of substance. In dissecting matter into electric charges we have traveled far from that picture of it which first gave rise to the conception of substance, and the meaning of that conception—if it ever had any—has been lost by the way. The whole trend of modern scientific views is to break down the separate categories of "things," "influences," "forms," etc., and to substitute a common background of all experience. Whether we are studying a material object, a magnetic field, a geometrical figure, or a duration of time, our scientific information is summed up in measures; neither the apparatus of measurement nor the mode of using it suggests that there is anything essentially different in these problems. The measures themselves afford no ground for a classification by categories. We feel it necessary to concede some background to the measures—an external world; but the attributes of this world, except in so far as they are reflected in the measures, are outside scientific scrutiny. Science has at last revolted against attaching the exact knowledge contained in these measurements to a traditional picture-gallery of conceptions which convey no authentic information of the background and obtrude irrelevancies into the scheme of knowledge.

I will not here stress further the nonsubstantiality of electrons, since it is scarcely necessary to the present line of thought. Conceive them as substantially as you will, there is a vast difference between my scientific table with its substance (if any) thinly scattered in specks in a region mostly empty and the table of every day conception which we regard as the type of solid reality—an incarnate protest against Berkeleian subjectivism. It makes all the difference in the world whether the paper before me is poised as it were on a swarm of flies and sustained in shuttlecock fashion by a series of tiny blows from the swarm underneath, or whether it is supported because there is substance below it, it being the intrinsic nature of substance to occupy space to the exclusion of other substance; all the difference in conception at least, but no difference to my practical task of writing on the paper.

I need not tell you that modern physics has by delicate test and remorseless logic assured me that my second scientific table is the only one which is really there—wherever "there" may be. On the other hand I need not tell you that modern physics will never succeed in exorcising that first table—strange compound of external nature, mental imagery and inherited prejudice—which lies visible to my eyes and tangible to my grasp. We must bid good-bye to it for the present for we are about to turn from the familiar world to the scientific world revealed by physics. This is, or is intended to be, a wholly external world.

"You speak paradoxically of two worlds. Are they not really two aspects or two interpretations of one and the same world?"

Yes, no doubt they are ultimately to be identified after some fashion. But the process by which the external world of physics is transformed into a world of familiar acquaintance in human consciousness is outside the scope of physics. And so the world studied according to the methods of physics remains detached from the world familiar to consciousness, until after the physicist has finished his labors upon it. Provisionally, therefore, we regard the table which is the subject of physical research as altogether separate from the familiar table, without prejudging the question of their ultimate identification. It is true that the whole scientific inquiry starts from the familiar world and in the end it must return to the familiar world; but the part of the journey over which the physicist has charge is in foreign territory.

Until recently there was a much closer linkage; the physicist used to borrow the raw material of his world from the familiar world, but he does so no longer. His raw materials are aether, electrons, quanta, potentials, Hamiltonian functions, etc., and he is nowadays scrupulously careful to guard these from contamination by conceptions borrowed from the other world. There is a familiar table parallel to the scientific table, but there is no familiar electron, quantum or potential parallel to the scientific electron, quantrum or potential. We do not even desire to manufacture a familiar counterpart to these things or, as we should commonly say, to "explain" the electron. After the physicist has quite finished his world-building a linkage or identification is allowed; but premature attempts at linkage have been found to be entirely mischievous.

Science aims at constructing a world which shall be symbolic of the world of commonplace experience. It is not at all necessary that every individual symbol that is used should represent something in common experience or even something explicable in terms of common experience. The man in the street is always making this demand for concrete explanation of the things referred to in science; but of necessity he must be disappointed. It is like our experience in learning to read. That which is written in a book is symbolic of a story in real life. The whole intention of the book is that ultimately a reader will identify some symbol, say BREAD, with one of the conceptions of familiar life. But it is mischievous to attempt such identifications prematurely, before the letters are strung into words and the words into sentences. The symbol *A* is not the counterpart of anything in familiar life. To the child the letter *A* would seem horribly abstract; so we give him a familiar conception along with it. "*A* was an Archer who shot at a frog." This tides over his immediate difficulty; but he cannot make serious progress with word-building so long as Archers, Butchers, Captains dance round the letters. The letters are abstract, and sooner or later he has to realize it. In physics we have outgrown archer and apple-pie definitions of the fundamental symbols. To a request to explain what an electron really is supposed to be we can only answer, "It is part of the A B C of physics."

The external world of physics has thus become a world of shadows. In removing our illusions we have removed the substance for indeed we have seen that substance is one of the greatest of our illusions. Later perhaps we may inquire whether in our zeal to cut out all that is unreal we may not have used the knife too ruthlessly. Perhaps, indeed, reality is a child which cannot survive without its nurse illusion. But if so, that is of little concern to the scientist, who has good and sufficient reasons for pursuing his investigations in the world of shadows and is content to leave to the philosopher the determination of its exact status in regard to reality. In the world of physics we watch a shadowgraph performance of the drama of familiar life. The shadow of my elbow rests on the shadow table as the shadow ink flows over the shadow paper. It is all symbolic, and as a symbol the physicist leaves it. Then comes the alchemist Mind who transmutes the symbols. The sparsely spread nuclei of electric force become a tangible solid; their restless agitation becomes the warmth of summer; the octave of aethereal vibrations becomes a gorgeous rainbow. Nor does the alchemy stop here. In the transmuted world new significances arise which are scarcely to be traced in the world of symbols; so that it becomes a world of beauty and purpose—and, alas, suffering and evil.

The frank realization that physical science is concerned with a world of shadows is one of the most significant of recent advances. I do not mean that physicists are to any extent preoccupied with the philosophical implications of this. From their point of view it is not so much a withdrawal of untenable claims as an assertion of freedom for autonomous development. At the moment I am not insisting on the shadowy and symbolic character of the world of physics because of its bearing on philosophy, but because the aloofness from familiar conceptions will be apparent in the scientific theories I have to describe. If you are not prepared for this aloofness you are likely to be out of sympathy with modern scientific theories, and may even think them ridiculous—as, I daresay, many people do.

It is difficult to school ourselves to treat the physical world as purely symbolic. We are always relapsing and mixing with the symbols incongruous conceptions taken from the world of consciousness. Untaught by long experience we stretch a hand to grasp the shadow, instead of accepting its shadowy nature. Indeed, unless we confine ourselves altogether to mathematical symbolism it is hard to avoid dressing our symbols in deceitful clothing. When I think of an electron there rises to my mind a hard, red, tiny ball; the proton similarly is neutral gray. Of course the color is absurd—perhaps not more absurd than the rest of the conception—but I am incorrigible. I can well understand that the younger minds are finding these pictures too concrete and are striving to construct the world out of Hamiltonian functions and symbols so far removed from human preconception that they do not even obey the laws of orthodox arithmetic. For myself I find some difficulty in rising to that plane of thought; but I am convinced that it has got to come. . . .

STUDY QUESTIONS

1. Divide this selection into its main parts. What does Eddington accomplish by opening with the comparison of the two tables? Would his explanation have been clearer if he had outlined his abstract idea first and then used the example of the two tables as illustration?

2. What, exactly, does Eddington mean when he says that science aims at constructing a world which is "symbolic of the world of commonplace experience"? Does his comparison of this process with that of learning to read help us to understand his meaning here? Is it a good comparison? Why?

3. What effect does the description of the physical world given by Eddington have upon the possibility of defining such terms as *real* and *reality?*

4. In such a world as Eddington describes, what is the value of "common sense"? What does Eddington mean by suggesting that reality cannot survive without illusion? Is this "common sense"?

5. What comfort might a poet, philosopher, theologian, or other person occupied with a non-specific discipline take in Eddington's description of the natural world?

6. Write a vivid and clear account of some piece of scientific knowledge intended for readers to whom this knowledge is unfamiliar.

Experiments In Perception*

W. H. Ittelson and F. P. Kilpatrick

What is perception? How do we see what we feel, feel what we feel, hear what we hear? We act in terms of what we perceive; our acts lead to new perceptions; these lead to new acts, and so on in the incredibly complex process that constitutes life. Clearly, then, an understanding of the process by which man becomes aware of himself and his world is basic to any adequate understanding of human behavior. But the problem of explaining how and why we perceive in the way we do is one of the most controversial fields in psychology. We shall describe here some recent experimental work which sheds new light on the problem and points the way to a new theory of perception.

The fact that we see a chair and are then able to go to the place at

*Reprinted with permission from *Scientific American*, August, 1951, Vol. 185, No. 2.

which we localize it and rest our bodies on a substantial object does not seem particularly amazing or difficult to explain—until we try to explain it. If we accept the prevailing current view that we can never be aware of the world as such, but only of the nervous impulses arising from the impingement of physical forces on sensory receptors, we immediately face the necessity of explaining the correspondence between what we perceive and whatever it is that is there.

An extremely logical, unbeatable—and scientifically useless—answer is simply to say there is no real world, that everything exists in the mind alone. Another approach is to postulate the existence of an external world, to grant that there is some general correspondence between that world and what we perceive and to seek some understandable and useful explanation of why that should be. Most of the prominent theories about perception have grown out of the latter approach. These theories generally agree that even though much of the correspondence may be due to learning, at some basic level there exists an absolute correspondence between what is "out there" and what is in the "mind." But there is a great deal of disagreement concerning the level at which such innately determined correspondence occurs. At one extreme are theorists who believe that the correspondence occurs at the level of simple sensations, such as color, brightness, weight, hardness, and so on, and that out of these sensations are compounded more complex awarenesses, such as the recognition of a pencil or a book. At the other extreme are Gestalt psychologists who feel that complex perceptions such as the form of an object are the result of an inherent relationship between the properties of the thing perceived and the properties of the brain. All these schools seem to agree, however, that there is some perceptual level at which exists absolute objectivity; that is, a one-to-one correspondence between experience and reality.

This belief is basic to current thinking in many fields. It underlies most theorizing concerning the nature of science, including Percy W. Bridgman's attempt to reach final scientific objectivity in the "observable operation." In psychology one is hard put to find an approach to human behavior which departs from this basic premise. But it leads to dichotomies such as organism *v.* environment, subjective *v.* objective. Stimuli or stimulus patterns are treated as though they exist apart from the perceiving organism. Psychologists seek to find mechanical relationships or interactions between the organism and an "objectively defined" environment. They often rule out purposes and values as not belonging in a strictly scientific psychology.

The experiments to be described here arose from a widespread and growing feeling that such dichotomies are false, and that in practice it is impossible to leave values and purposes out of consideration in scientific observation. The experiments were designed to re-examine some of the basic ideas from which these problems stem.

During the past few years Adelbert Ames, Jr., of the Institute for Associated Research in Hanover, N. H., has designed some new ways of studying visual perception. They have resulted in a new conception of the nature of knowing and of observation. This theory neither denies the existence of objects nor proposes that they exist in a given form independently, that is, apart from the perceiving organism. Instead, it suggests that the world each of us knows is a world created in large measure from our experience in dealing with the environment.

Let us illustrate this in specific terms through some of the demonstrations. In one of them the subject sits in a dark room in which he can see only two star points of light. Both are equidistant from the observer, but one is brighter than the other. If the observer closes one eye and keeps his head still, the brighter point of light looks nearer than the dimmer one. Such apparent differences are related not only to brightness but also to direction from the observer. If two points of light of equal brightness are situated near the floor, one about a foot above the other, the upper one will generally be perceived as farther away than the lower one; if they are near the ceiling, the lower one will appear farther away.

A somewhat more complex experiment uses two partly inflated balloons illuminated from a concealed source. The balloons are in fixed positions about one foot apart. Their relative sizes can be varied by means of a lever control connected to a bellows; another level controls their relative brightness. When the size and brightness of both balloons are the same, an observer looking at them with one eye from 10 feet or more sees them as two glowing spheres at equal distances from him. If the brightnesses are left the same and the relative sizes are changed, the larger balloon appears to nearly all observers somewhat nearer. If the size lever is moved continuously, causing continuous variation in the relative size of the balloons, they appear to move dramatically back and forth through space, even when the observer watches with both eyes open. The result is similar when the sizes are kept equal and the relative brightness is varied.

With the same apparatus the effects of size and brightness may be combined so that they supplement or conflict with each other. When they supplement each other, the variation in apparent distance is much greater than when either size or brightness alone is varied. When they oppose each other, the variation is much less. Most people give more weight to relative size than to relative brightness in judging distance.

These phenomena cannot be explained by referring to "reality," because "reality" and perception do not correspond. They cannot be explained by reference to the pattern in the retina of the eye, because for any given retinal pattern there are an infinite number of brightness-size-distance combinations to which that pattern might be related. When faced with such a situation, in which an unlimited number of possibilities can be related to a given retinal pattern, the organism apparently calls

upon its previous experiences and assumes that what has been most probable in the past is most probable in the immediate occasion. When
presented with two star-points of different brightness, a person unconsciously "bets" or "assumes" that the two points, being similar, are probably identical (*i.e.,* of equal brightness), and therefore that the one which
seems brighter must be nearer. Similarly the observed facts in the case
of two star-points placed vertically one above the other suggest that when
we look down we assume, on the basis of past experience, that objects in
the lower part of the visual field are nearer than objects in the upper
part; when we look up, we assume the opposite to be true. An analogous
explanation can be made of the role of relative size as an indication of
relative distance.

Why do the differences in distance seem so much greater when the relative size of two objects is varied continuously than when the size difference is fixed? This phenomenon, too, apparently is based on experience.
It is a fairly common experience, though not usual, to find that two similar objects of different sizes are actually the same distance away from us.
But it is rare indeed to see two stationary objects at the same distance,
one growing larger and the other smaller; almost always in everyday life
when we see two identical or nearly identical objects change relative size
they are in motion in relation to each other. Hence under the experimental conditions we are much more likely to assume distance differences in
the objects of changing size than in those of fixed size.

Visual perception involves an impression not only of *where* an object
is but of *what* it is. From the demonstrations already described we may
guess that there is a very strong relationship between localization in
space ("thereness") and the assignment of objective properties ("that-
ness"). This relationship can be demonstrated by a cube experiment.

Two solid white cubes are suspended on wires that are painted black so
as to be invisible against a black background. One cube is about 3 feet
from the observer and the other about 12 feet. The observer's head is in
a headrest so positioned that the cubes are almost in line with each other
but he can see both, the nearer cube being slightly to the right. A tiny
metal shield is then placed a few inches in front of the left eye. It is just
big enough to cut off the view of the far cube from the left eye. The result is that the near cube is seen with both eyes and the far cube with just
the right eye. Under these conditions the observer can fix the position of
the near cube very well, because he has available all the cues that come
from the use of the two eyes. But in the case of the far cube seen with
only one eye, localization is much more difficult and uncertain.

Now since the two cubes are almost in line visually, a slight movement
of the head to the right will cause the inside vertical edges of the cubes to
coincide. Such coincidence of edge is strongly related to an assumption
of "togetherness." Hence when the subject moves his head in this way,
the uncertainly located distant cube appears to have moved forward to a

position even with the nearer cube. Under these conditions not only does the mislocated cube appear smaller, but it appears different in shape, that is, no longer cubical, even though the pattern cast by the cube on the retina of the eye has not changed at all.

The most reasonable explanation of these visual phenomena seems to be that an observer unconsciously relates to the stimulus pattern some sort of weighted average of the past consequences of acting with respect to that pattern. The particular perception "chosen" is the one that has the best predictive value, on the basis of previous experience, for action in carrying out the purposes of the organism. From this one may make two rather crucial deductions: 1) an unfamiliar external configuration which yields the same retinal pattern as one the observer is accustomed to deal with will be perceived as the familiar configuration; 2) when the observer acts on his interpretation of the unfamiliar configuration and finds that he is wrong, his perception will change even though the retinal pattern is unchanged.

Let us illustrate with some actual demonstrations. If an observer in a dark room looks with one eye at two lines of light which are at the same distance and elevation but of different lengths, the longer line will look nearer than the shorter one. Apparently he assumes that the lines are identical and translates the difference in length into a difference in position. If the observer takes a wand with a luminous tip and tries to touch first one line and then the other, he will be unable to do so at first. After repeated practice, however, he can learn to touch the two lines quickly and accurately. At this point he no longer sees the lines as at different distances; they now look, as they are, the same distance from him. He originally assumed that the two lines were the same length because that seemed the best bet under the circumstances. After he had tested this assumption by purposive action, he shifted to the assumption, less probable in terms of past experience but still possible, that the lines were at the same distance but of different lengths. As his assumption changed, perception did also.

There is another experiment that demonstrates these points even more convincingly. It uses a distorted room in which the floor slopes up to the right of the observer, the rear wall recedes from right to left and the windows are of different sizes and trapezoidal in shape. When the observer looks at this room with one eye from a certain point, the room appears completely normal, as if the floor were level, the rear wall at right angles to the line of sight and the windows rectangular and the same size. Presumably the observer chooses this particular appearance instead of some other because of the assumptions he brings to the occasion. If he now takes a long stick and tries to touch the various parts of the room, he will be unsuccessful, even though he has gone into the situation knowing the true shape of the room. With practice, however, he becomes more and more successful in touching what he wants to touch with the stick. More important, he sees the room more and more in its true shape, even though the stimulus pattern on his retina has remained unchanged.

By means of a piece of apparatus called the "rotating trapezoidal window" it has been possible to extend the investigation to complex perceptual situations involving movement. This device consists of a trapezoidal surface with panes cut in it and shadows painted on it to give the appearance of a window. It is mounted on a rod connected to a motor so that it rotates at a slow constant speed in an upright position about its own axis. When an observer views the rotating surface with one eye from about 10 feet or more or with both eyes from about 25 feet or more, he sees not a rotating trapezoid but an oscillating rectangle. Its speed of movement and its shape appear to vary markedly as it turns. If a small cube is attached by a short rod to the upper part of the short side of the trapezoid, it seems to become detached, sail freely around the front of the trapezoid and attach itself again as the apparatus rotates.

All these experiments, and many more that have been made, suggest strongly that perception is never a sure thing, never an absolute revelation of "what is." Rather, what we see is a prediction—our own personal construction designed to give the best possible bet for carrying out our purposes in action. We make these bets on the basis of our past experience. When we have a great deal of relevant and consistent experience to relate to stimulus patterns, the probability of success of our prediction (perception) as a guide to action is extremely high, and we tend to have a feeling of surety. When our experience is limited or inconsistent, the reverse holds true. According to the new theory of perception developed from the demonstrations we have described, perception is a functional affair based on action, experience and probability. The thing perceived is an inseparable part of the function of perceiving, which in turn includes all aspects of the total process of living. This view differs from the old rival theories: the thing perceived is neither just a figment of the mind nor an innately determined absolute revelation of a reality postulated to exist apart from the perceiving organism. Object and precept are part and parcel of the same thing.

This conclusion of course has far-reaching implications for many areas of study, for some assumption as to what perception is must underly any philosophy or comprehensive theory of psychology, or science or of knowledge in general. Although the particular investigations involved here are restricted to visual perception, this is only a vehicle which carries us into a basic inquiry of much wider significance.

STUDY QUESTIONS

1. What possible effects may the results of these experiments have upon philosophical questions? How do they affect the usual meaning of terms such as "accurate observation," "objectivity," "the external world"?

2. Do the experiments described here seek to reproduce the usual conditions? If not, what is their value?

3. Do these experiments show that perception depends entirely upon the sense and the stimuli they encounter? If not, what do they show?

4. What is the "basic inquiry of much wider significance" which is mentioned at the end of the article as the end to which these experiments will lead?

5. Observe carefully what Ittelson and Kilpatrick have done to make their account of rather complicated experiments clear and interesting. Then write a theme describing accurately and in detail an experiment you have seen or have carried out yourself, giving the conclusions you drew from it.

6. Do the conclusions arrived at here have any effect upon daily life and social affairs? Write a theme applying the principles suggested by these experiments to everyday situations and problems.

The Limits and Value of the Scientific Method*

Morris R. Cohen and Ernest Nagel

The desire for knowledge for its own sake is more widespread than is generally recognized by anti-intellectualists. It has its roots in the animal curiosity which shows itself in the cosmological questions of children and in the gossip of adults. No ulterior utilitarian motive makes people want to know about the private lives of their neighbors, the great, or the notorious. There is also a certain zest which makes people engage in various intellectual games or exercises in which one is required to find out something. But while the desire to know is wide, it is seldom strong enough to overcome the more powerful organic desires, and few indeed have both the inclination and the ability to face the arduous difficulties of scientific method in more than one special field. The desire to know is not often strong enough to sustain critical inquiry. Men generally are interested in the results, in the story or romance of science, not in the technical methods whereby these results are obtained and their truth continually is tested and qualified. Our first impulse is to accept the plausible as true and to reject the uncongenial as false. We have not the time, inclination, or energy to investigate everything. Indeed, the call to do so is often felt as irksome and joy-killing. And when we are asked to treat our cherished beliefs as mere hypotheses, we rebel as violently as when

* From *An Introduction to Logic and Scientific Method* by Morris R. Cohen and Ernest Nagel. Copyright, 1934, by Harcourt, Brace and World, Inc. Reprinted by permission of Harcourt, Brace and World, Inc.

those dear to us are insulted. This provides the ground for various movements that are hostile to rational scientific procedure (though their promoters do not often admit that it is science to which they are hostile).

Mystics, intuitionists, authoritarians, voluntarists, and fictionalists are all trying to undermine respect for the rational methods of science. These attacks have always met with wide acclaim and are bound to continue to do so, for they strike a responsive note in human nature. Unfortunately they do not offer any reliable alternative method for obtaining verifiable knowledge. The great French writer Pascal opposed to logic the spirit of subtlety or finesse (*esprit géometrique and esprit de finesse*) and urged that the heart has its reasons as well as the mind, reasons that cannot be accurately formulated but which subtle spirits apprehend none the less. Men as diverse as James Russell Lowell and George Santayana are agreed that:

> The soul is oracular still,

and

> It is wisdom to trust the heart . . .
> To trust the soul's invincible surmise.

Now it is true that in the absence of omniscience we must trust our soul's surmise; and great men are those whose surmises or intuitions are deep or penetrating. It is only by acting on our surmise that we can procure the evidence in its favor. But only havoc can result from confusing a surmise with a proposition for which there is already evidence. Are all the reasons of the heart sound? Do all oracles tell the truth? The sad history of human experience is distinctly discouraging to any such claim. Mystic intuition may give men absolute subjective certainty, but can give no proof that contrary intuitions are erroneous. It is obvious that when authorities conflict we must weigh the evidence in their favor logically if we are to make a rational choice. Certainly, when a truth is questioned it is no answer to say, "I am convinced," or, "I prefer to rely on this rather than on another authority." The view that physical science is no guide to proof, but is a mere fiction, fails to explain why it has enabled us to anticipate phenomena of nature and to control them. These attacks on scientific method receive a certain color of plausibility because of some indefensible claims made by uncritical enthusiasts. But it is of the essence of scientific method to limit its own pretension. Recognizing that we do not know everything, it does not claim the ability to solve all of our practical problems. It is an error to suppose, as is often done, that science denies the truth of all unverified propositions. For that which is unverified today may be verified tomorrow. We may get at truth by guessing or in other ways. Scientific method, however, is concerned with verification. Admittedly the wisdom of those engaged in this process has not been popularly ranked as high as that of the sage, the prophet, or the poet. Admittedly, also, we know of no way of supplying creative intelligence to those who lack it. Scientists, like all other human beings, may get into ruts and apply their techniques regardless of varying circumstances. There will always be formal procedures which are fruitless. Definitions and formal distinctions may be a sharpening of tools without the wit to use them properly, and statistical information may conform to the highest technical standards and yet be irrelevant and inconclusive. Nevertheless, scientific method is the only way to increase the general body of tested and verified truth and to eliminate arbitrary opinion. It is well to clarify our ideas by asking for the precise meaning of our words, and to try to check our favorite ideas by applying them to accurately formulated propositions.

In raising the question as to the social need for scientific method, it is well to recognize that the suspension of judgment which is essential to that method is difficult or impossible when we are pressed by the demands of immediate action. When my house is on fire, I must act quickly and promptly—I cannot stop to consider the possible causes, nor even to estimate the exact probabilities involved in the various alternative ways of reacting. For this reason, those who are bent upon some specific course of action often despise those devoted to reflection; and certain ultramodernists seem to argue as if the need for action guaranteed the truth of our decision. But the fact that I must either vote for candidate X or refrain from doing so does not of itself give me adequate knowledge. The frequency of our regrets makes this obvious. Wisely ordered society is therefore provided with means for deliberation and reflection *before* the pressure of action becomes irresistible. In order to assure the most thorough investigation, all possible views must be canvassed, and this means toleration of views that are *prima facie* most repugnant to us.

In general the chief social condition of scientific method is a widespread desire for truth that is strong enough to withstand the powerful forces which make us cling tenaciously to old views or else embrace every novelty because it is a change. Those who are engaged in scientific work need not only leisure for reflection and material for their experiments, but also a community that respects the pursuit of truth and allows freedom for the expression of intellectual doubt as to its most sacred or established institutions. Fear of offending established dogmas has been an obstacle to the growth of astronomy and geology and other physical sciences; and the fear of offending patriotic or respected sentiment is perhaps one of the strongest hindrances to scholarly history and social science. On the other hand, when a community indiscriminately acclaims every new doctrine the love of truth becomes subordinated to the desire for novel formulations.

On the whole it may be said that the safety of science depends on there being men who care more for the justice of their methods than for any results obtained by their use. For this reason it is unfortunate when scientific research in the social field is largely in the hands of those not in a favorable position to oppose established or popular opinion.

We may put it the other way by saying that the physical sciences can be more liberal because we are sure that foolish opinions will be readily eliminated by the shock of facts. In the social field, however, no one can tell what harm may come of foolish ideas before the foolishness is finally, if ever, demonstrated. None of the precautions of scientific method can prevent human life from being an adventure, and no scientific investigator knows whether he will reach his goal. But scientific method does enable large numbers to walk with surer step. By analyzing the possibilities of any step or plan, it becomes possible to anticipate the future and adjust ourselves to it in advance. Scientific method thus minimizes the shock of novelty and the uncertainty of life. It enables us to frame policies of action and of moral judgment fit for a wider outlook than those of immediate physical stimulus or organic response.

Scientific method is the only effective way of strengthening the love of truth. It develops the intellectual courage to face difficulties and to overcome illusions that are pleasant temporarily but destructive ultimately. It settles differences without any external force by appealing to our common rational nature. The way of science, even if it is up a steep mountain, is open to all. Hence while sectarian and partisan faiths are based on personal choice or temperament and divide men, scientific procedure unites men in something nobly devoid of all pettiness. Because it requires detachment, disinterestedness, it is the finest flower and test of a liberal civilization.

STUDY QUESTIONS

1. The authors do not exclude emotion from scientific inquiry, but they do limit it to particular areas. What emotions do they think proper to scientific inquiry? What emotions do they think dangerous to it?

2. To what extent do the authors agree with Marchette Chute in "Getting at the Truth" as to the place of emotions in objective inquiry?

3. How would you relate this essay to the principles stated in Huxley's "All Men Are Scientists"?

4. According to Cohen and Nagel, there is something (actually, two things) more important about the scientific method than the results it can give. What is it?

5. Do you think that Cohen and Nagel overrate the value of scientific method in the social field? If you do, explain why it is not well adapted to historical, social or political problems. Or, if you agree with them that it is an effective instrument in these fields, write a theme explaining your point of view.

6. Does this essay help to explain, clarify or compromise the supposed conflict between science and religion? Write a theme expressing your opinions on this highly controversial subject.

Utopias and Human Goals*

René Jules Dubos

Modern man believes that he has achieved almost complete mastery over the natural forces which molded his evolution in the past and that he can now control his own biological and cultural destiny. But this may be an illusion. Like all other living things, he is part of an immensely complex ecological system and is bound to all its components by innumerable links. Moreover, as we have seen, human life is affected not only by the environmental forces presently at work in nature but even more perhaps by the past.

Any attempt to shape the world and modify human personality in order to create a self-chosen pattern of life involves many unknown consequences. Human destiny is bound to remain a gamble, because at some unpredictable time and in some unforeseeable manner nature will strike back. The multiplicity of determinants which affect biological systems limits the power of the experimental method to predict their trends and behavior. Experimentation necessarily involves a choice in the factors brought to bear on the phenomena under study. Ideally, the experimenter works in a closed system, affected only by the determinants that he has introduced, under the conditions that he has selected. Naturally, however, events never occur in a closed system. They are determined and modified by circumstances and forces that cannot be foreseen, let alone controlled. In part this is because natural situations are so complex that no experimental study can ever encompass and reproduce all the relevant factors of the environment. Furthermore, human behavior is governed not only by biological necessities but also by the desire for change. When surfeited with honey man begins to loathe the taste of sweetness, and this desire for change per se introduces an inescapable component of unpredictability in his life.

It is the awareness of these complexities which accounts for the clumsiness of the scientific language used in reporting biological events. The scientist emphasizes *ad nauseam* that what he states is valid only "under conditions of the experiment." As if apologetically, he is wont to qualify any assertion or general statement with the remark, "All other things being equal—which they never are . . ." Because things are never the same, almost everyone admits that prediction is always risky in political and social fields. But it is not so generally recognized that the same limitations apply to other areas usually regarded as falling within the realm of the so-called exact sciences, for instance, the epidemiology of disease.

Many examples have been quoted in earlier chapters to illustrate the unexpected and far-reaching effects that accidental circumstances have exerted in the past on the welfare of man. The introduction of inexpensive cotton undergarments easy to launder and of transparent glass that brought light into the most humble dwelling, contributed more to the control of infection than did all drugs and medical practices. On the other hand, a change in fur fashion brought about a few years later an outbreak of pneumonic plague in Manchuria; the use of soft coal in English grates caused chimney sweeps to develop cancer; Roentgen's discovery endangered the lives of scientists and physicians exposed to X rays in the course of their professional activities. Likewise oil and rubber may in the future come to be regarded as having been the indirect causes of disease and death. In addition to the human beings killed or maimed in automobile accidents, many are likely to suffer, directly or indirectly, from the air pollution brought about by the widespread use of oil and rubber. Furthermore, neuroses peculiar to our time may someday be traced to the speed and power that rubber and oil have made possible, as well as to the frustrations caused by crowded city streets and highways.

Human goals, which condition social changes, profoundly affect the physical and mental well-being of man. And, unfortunately, the most worthwhile goals may have results as disastrous as those of the most despicable ambitions. Industrial imperialism was responsible for an enormous amount of misery among children during the early nineteenth century. But, as we have seen, the present philosophy to assure the survival of all children and to protect them from any traumatic experience also is likely to have unfortunate consequences by interfering with the normal play of adaptive processes.

Philosophical and social doctrines have been the most influential forces in changing the human ways of life during historical times. The high regard in which the human body was held by the Greco-Roman world certainly played a role in the development of hygiene and medicine during the classical times of Western civilization. In contrast, the emphasis on mystical values and on eternal life, the contempt for bodily functions, which characterized certain early phases of the Christian faith, probably led to the neglect of sanitary practices during medieval times—even though it did not necessarily decrease the enjoyment of sensual pleasures by normal men and women. Today, as in the past, the relation that man bears to his total environment is influenced by values of which he is not always aware. A civilization that devotes page after page of its popular magazines to portraying the rulers of the business world is bound to produce men very different from those taught to worship Confucian wisdom, Buddhic mysticism, or Blake's poems—even if that worship often does not go far beyond mere lip service. To feel at ease among the neon lights of Broadway demands a type of body and mind not conducive to happiness in the mists of a Taoist moonscape.

Technology is now displacing philosophical and religious values as the dominant force in shaping the world, and therefore in determining human fate. What man does today and will do tomorrow is determined to a large extent by the techniques that expert knowledge puts at his disposal, and his dreams for the future reflect the achievements and promises of the scientists. From them he has acquired the faith—or rather the illusion—that society can be planned in a manner that will assure plenty, health, and happiness for everyone and thus solve all the great problems of existence.

As modern technological innovations are the direct outcome of scientific research, scientists can no longer afford to stand aloof from social problems. Knowledge can grow without regard for ethical values, but the modern scientist cannot help becoming involved in ethics, since science can no longer be dissociated from the applications of science. In the past the social effects of science were slow in manifesting themselves. Today they are immediate and reach every aspect of the life of every man, for good and for evil. The scientist has convinced society that his efforts deserve to be generously supported because he has become one of its most effective servants. As a penalty for his dependence on public support and for the influence that he has gained he cannot escape being made responsible for his activities, even if their results are different from what he had hoped. In the present decade he has to deal with the consequences of the release of man-made radiations. He may soon acquire the knowledge that will permit him to control the behavior of people and the genetic endowment of children to be born, a power frightening in its unpredictable potentialities for evil.

To discover, to describe, to classify, to invent, has been the traditional task of the scientist until this century; on the whole a pleasant occupation amounting to a sophisticated hobby. This happy phase of social irresponsibility is now over and the scientist will be called to account for the long-term consequences of his acts. His dilemma is and will remain that he cannot predict these consequences because they depend on many factors outside his knowledge or at least beyond his control—in particular on the exercise of free will by men. The scientist must therefore avoid pride of intellect and guard himself against any illusion or pretense as to the extent and depth of what he knows. He must also develop an alertness to the unexpected, an awareness of the fact that many surprising effects are likely to result from even trivial disturbances of ecological equilibria. Fortunately, the scientific method is well suited for the cultivation of this alertness to the advent of the unpredictable. The scientist cannot predict the remote consequences of his activities, but he can often provide techniques for recognizing them early. One of the few encouraging indications that science has come of age is the fact that extensive studies on the potential danger of radiations were initiated as soon as it became apparent that the forces unleashed by knowledge of the atom would find a place in the technology of war and peace.

To become worthy of his power the scientist will need to develop enough wisdom and humane understanding to recognize that the acquisition of knowledge is intricately interwoven with the pursuit of goals. It has often been pointed out that the nineteenth-century slogan, "Survival of the fittest," begged the question because it did not state what fitness was for. Likewise it is not possible to plan man's future without deciding beforehand what he should be fitted for, in other words, what human destiny ought to be—a decision loaded with ethical values. What is new is not necessarily good, and all changes, even those apparently the most desirable, are always fraught with unpredictable consequences. The scientist must beware of having to admit, like Captain Ahab in Melville's *Moby Dick*, "All my means are sane; my motives and objects mad."

Health, Happiness, and Human Values

It is often suggested that a moratorium on science would give mankind the opportunity to search its soul and discover a solution to the problems that threaten its very survival. Although no one is naïve enough to hope that stopping the clock would bring about the solution of ancient human problems, many believe that a scientific status quo might prevent or retard the development of new threats. This static formula of survival is not new; indeed, it has been used with much biological success by social insects. Certain species of ants and termites had completed at least fifty million years ago the highly stratified and efficient type of colonial organization which they still exhibit. They have solved many of the problems which are the subject of endless discussions and conflicts in most human societies. Their queens, warriors, and workers all are produced as needed by genetic and physiological control; they have functions which are clearly defined and regulated in terms of the welfare of the colony as a whole. Even problems of eugenics have been solved in these insect societies by confining reproduction to a certain caste and promptly eliminating all abnormal and diseased individuals.

The very survival and wide distribution of highly organized insect societies which have not changed in fifty million years is evidence that living things can achieve a more or less stable equilibrium with their environment and that, beyond a certain degree of adaptation, change is no longer necessary for biological survival. It is conceivable, therefore, that human societies also could stop evolving and thus avoid the dangers inevitably associated with the adaptive problems bound to arise from any change. In fact, this has happened on several occasions in many parts of the world.

Before their contact with the white man the Eskimos, the Polynesian Islanders, and certain nomadic tribes had worked out stable societies with an acceptable degree of physical health and happiness. As pointed out by Arnold J. Toynbee, however, the human beings in all these societies were degraded by specialization and by limitation of their activities to a level far below that of the ideal all-round men evoked in Pericles' funeral speech. These "arrested" societies resembled in some respects the societies of bees and ants. Their stability may have resulted in the avoidance of many new adaptation problems but proved incompatible with the growth of their civilizations, indeed, with the very growth of man. It was the awareness of this limitation which had estranged D. H. Lawrence from the Polynesian Paradise:

There they are, these South Sea Islanders, beautiful big men with their golden limbs and their laughing, graceful laziness. . . . They are like children, they are generous: but they are more than this. They are far off, and in their eyes is an early darkness of the soft, uncreate past. . . . There is his woman, with her knotted hair and her dark, inchoate, slightly sardonic eyes. . . . She has soft warm flesh, like warm mud. Nearer the reptile, the Saurian age. . . .

Far be it from me to assume any "white" superiority. It seems to me, that in living so far, through all our bitter centuries of civilization, we have still been living onwards, forwards. . . . The past, the Golden Age of the past—what a nostalgia we all feel for it. Yet we don't want it when we get it. Try the South Seas.

The fact that, except for a few arrested societies, man has been living and struggling forward in a great life-development shows that utopias and all static formulas of society are out of tune with the human condition. It is the desire for change which has set man apart from the rest of the living world, by leading him to a life of adventure away from the environments to which he was biologically adapted, and it is this desire that will continue to generate the creative forces of his future. The Athenians symbolize for us the most brilliant achievement of mankind because, according to Thucydides, "They go on working away in hardship and danger all the days of their lives, seldom enjoying their possessions as they are always adding to them. They prefer hardship and activity to peace and quiet."

Once his essential biological needs are satisfied, man develops other urges which have little bearing on his survival as a species. When he no longer needs to struggle for his loaf of bread he is wont to crave an unessential savory, then to long for some artistic expression. When he has established all kinds of direct and indirect contacts with the surrounding world he begins to worry about the next television set and soon longs to explore the rest of the universe. Indeed, it is probably the most distinguishing aspect of human life that it converts essential biological urges and functions into activities which have lost their original significance and purpose. Eating habits are now determined by acquired tastes and by social conventions rather than by nutritional requirements. The acts of love are performed for pleasure rather than for reproduction. "If all our women were to become as beautiful as the Venus de' Medici," wrote Charles Darwin in Chapter XIX of *The Descent of Man and Selection in Relation to Sex,* "we should be for a time charmed; but we should soon wish for variety, and as soon as we had obtained variety, we should wish to see certain characteristics a little exaggerated." Thus, man desires change for change's sake, without regard to any biological need. This desire expresses itself in the most ordinary manifestations of life, like the choice of food, and in the most sophisticated occupations, like the various forms of art. It affects the newest technological developments, like the hoods of motorcars, as well as the most ancient occupations, like hunting. Now that highpower rifles are available, sportsmen are returning to the use of primitive weapons. In 1957 forty thousand adults registered for the right to hunt with bow and arrow in the state of Michigan alone.

It is important, indeed, that there be available opportunities for change, for when they are lacking man is apt to satisfy his thirst for change by acts of violence or destruction. Dostoevsky's sniveling hero in *Letters from the Underworld* could not find satisfaction in the order and comfort of the "Crystal Palace" world in which he lived; he chose an antisocial way of life because it was the one form of freedom of action still available to him. "Well, gentlemen, what about giving all this commonsense a mighty kick . . . simply to send all these logarithms to the devil so that we can again live according to our foolish will?" "Man only exists for the purpose of proving to himself that he is a man and not an organ-stop! He will prove it even if it means physical suffering, even if it means turning his back on civilization." Many forms of delinquency among our overfed teenagers probably come from their unspent creative energy.

Mankind behaves like the restless, sleepless traveler who turns in his berth to one side and then to the other, feeling better while changing position even though he knows that the change will not bring him lasting comfort. This restlessness is commonly identified with the concept of progress. In reality, however, the only certain fact is that human history is increasingly governed by the search for variety, at times for the sake of creation, more commonly just for recreation, but in any case unrelated to the forces which determine the evolution of biological traits. Progress means only movement without implying any clear statement of direction. At most it can be said that, despite so many disheartening setbacks, the activities of man seem to have on the whole a direction upward and forward which tends to better his life physically, intellectually, and morally.

The desire for progress may be nothing more than man's declaration of independence from the blind forces of nature. To paint the Last Supper, to write a poem, or to build an empire demands the expenditure of a form of energy and produces a type of result which does not have an obvious place in the natural order of things. In fact, as we have seen, certain of man's ideals and goals threaten to have consequences unfavorable for the human species. The cultivation of refined or esoteric tastes may interfere with the play of adaptive mechanisms and render man more vulnerable to some of his ancient plagues. The very mastery of nature may release dangers that cannot be controlled. Changes in the social order which increase the richness and variety of life can also, especially if too rapid, upset the ecological equilibria on which depends the continuation of the human species.

Awareness of dangers is not likely to deflect the course of mankind, for man does not live by bread alone. "All man wants," wrote Dostoevsky, "is an absolutely *free* choice, however dear that freedom may cost him and wherever it may lead him." True enough, most men run almost mechanically like clocks from their birth to their death, motivated only by their biological needs of the moment and by the desire to feel socially secure. But their very passivity makes them of little importance for social evolution. The aspect of human nature which is significant because unique is that certain men have goals which transcend biological purpose.

Among other living things, it is man's dignity to value certain ideals above comfort, and even above life. This human trait makes of medicine a philosophy that goes beyond exact medical sciences, because it must encompass not only man as a living machine but also the collective aspirations of mankind. A perfect policy of public health could be conceived for colonies of social ants or bees whose habits have become stabilized by instincts. Likewise it would be possible to devise for a herd of cows an ideal system of husbandry with the proper combination of stables and pastures. But, unless men become robots, no formula can ever give them permanently the health and happiness symbolized by the contented cow, nor can their societies achieve a structure that will last for millennia. As long as mankind is made up of independent individuals with free will, there cannot be any social status quo. Men will develop new urges, and these will give rise to new problems, which will require ever new solutions. Human life implies adventure, and there is no adventure without struggles and dangers.

Men naturally desire health and happiness. For some of them, however, perhaps for all, these words have implications that transcend ordinary biological concepts. The kind of health that men desire most is not necessarily a state in which they experience physical vigor and a sense of well-being, not even one giving them a long life. It is, instead, the condition best suited to reach goals that each individual formulates for himself. Usually these goals bear no relation to biological necessity; at times, indeed, they are antithetic to biological usefulness. More often than not the pursuit of health and happiness is guided by urges which are social rather than biological; urges which are so peculiar to men as to be meaningless for other living things because they are of no importance for the survival of the individual or of the species.

The satisfactions which men crave most, and the sufferings which scar their lives most deeply, have determinants which do not all reside in the flesh or in the reasonable faculties and are not completely accounted for by scientific laws.

"Reason," wrote Dostoevsky, "can only satisfy the reasoning ability of man, whereas volition is a manifestation of the whole of life. . . . Reason knows only what it has succeeded in getting to know . . . whereas human nature acts as a whole, with everything that is in it, consciously, and unconsciously, and though it may commit all sorts of absurdities, it persists." Exact sciences give correct answers to certain aspects of life problems, but very incomplete answers. It is important of course to count and measure what is countable and measurable, but the most precious values in human life are aspirations which laboratory experiments cannot yet reproduce. As Haeckel pointed out, Richtigkeit—correctness—is not sufficient to reach Wahrheit—the real truth.

Homo sapiens as a biological machine may not have changed much since Pleistocene times, but mankind has continued to evolve, developing a new kind of life almost transcendental to its earthly biological origin. It is a paradoxical attribute of many human beings that their behavior is often governed by criteria and desires that they value more than life itself. To comprehend the biology of mankind, the story of human evolution, it is helpful to remember Aristotle's saying: "The nature of man is not what he is born as, but what he is born for." Indeed, some men in all ages have been guided by the faith that "he who would save his life first must lose it." Alone among living things, men are willing to sacrifice the purely biological manifestation of their existence at the altar of a higher form of life—conceived in the soul rather than experienced in the flesh. Even the least religious of thinking men believes in the deep symbolism of what Paul wrote of human nature: "It is sown a natural body; it is raised a spiritual body. . . . The first man is of the earth, earthy: the second man is the Lord from heaven."

Because man is a spiritual body he is more concerned with a way of life than with his physical state. Balzac, on his deathbed, projected Herculean labors and pleaded with his physician to keep him alive six weeks longer in order that he might finish his work. "Six weeks with fever is an eternity. Hours are like days . . . and then the nights are not lost." Marcel Proust, also on the day before he died, wrote of those obligations of the artist which seem to be derived from some other world, "based on goodness, scrupulousness, sacrifice."

"Work is more important than life," Katherine Mansfield confided to the last pages of her *Journal*. Searching for a definition of health that would satisfy her body riddled with tuberculosis and also her tormented soul, she could only conclude: "By health, I mean the power to live a full, adult, living, breathing life in close contact with what I love—the earth and the wonders thereof—the sea—the sun. . . . *I want to be all that I am capable of becoming*, so that I may be . . . there's only one phrase that will do—*a child of the sun*."

The sun is not merely a source of warmth, of light, of food, of power. It is also the symbol of human aspirations. Like Icarus, who soaring upward to heaven plummeted to the sea and died when his waxen wings were melted by the sun, man deliberately exposes himself to dangers and even to destruction whenever he tries to escape from his biological and earthly bondage. Wherever he goes, whatever he undertakes, he will encounter new challenges and new threats to his welfare. Attempts at adaptation will demand efforts, and these efforts will often result in failure, partial or total, temporary or permanent. Disease will remain an inescapable manifestation of his struggles.

While it may be comforting to imagine a life free of stresses and strains in a carefree world, this will remain an idle dream. Man cannot hope to find another Paradise on earth, because paradise is a static concept while human life is a dynamic process. Man could escape danger only by renouncing adventure, by abandoning that which has given to the human condition its unique character and genius among the rest of living things. Since the days of the cave man, the earth has never been a Garden of Eden, but a Valley of Decision where resilience is essential to survival. The earth is not a resting place. Man has elected to fight, not necessarily for himself but for a process of emotional, intellectual, and ethical growth that goes on forever. To grow in the midst of dangers is the fate of the human race, because it is the law of the spirit.

STUDY QUESTIONS

1. What dangers and disadvantages of technological progress does Dubos describe?

2. Dubos, like Muller in "The Nature of Man" and Wheelwright in "The Meaning of Ethics," mentions a characteristic that differentiates man from other animals. What distinguishing characteristic does he choose?

3. According to Dubos, what responsibilities does the scientist have outside his own field? What criterion of maturity for science does Dubos mention?

4. What implications do Dubos' ideas have for such fields as city planning, transportation, public health and education?

5. Describe a historical or cultural situation you are familiar with

which shows men acting in opposition to their biological or rational interests, as Dubos says they often do.

6. Do you think Dubos' ideas contradict the familiar view that science should be objective and detached in its investigations?

3. MORAL LAW AND THE CONDUCT OF LIFE

*The Meaning of Ethics**

Philip Wheelwright

M an is the animal who can reflect. Like other animals, no doubt, he spends much of his time in merely reacting to the pressures and urgencies of his environment. But being a man he has moments also of conscious stock-taking, when he becomes aware not only of his world but of himself confronting his world, evaluating it, and making choices with regard to it. It is this ability to know himself and on the basis of self-knowledge to make evaluations and reflective choices that differentiates man from his subhuman cousins.

There are, as Aristotle has pointed out, two main ways in which man's power of reflection becomes active. They are called, in Aristotle's language, *theoretikos* and *praktikos* respectively; which is to say, thinking about what is actually the case and thinking about what had better be done. In English translation the words *contemplative* and *operative* probably come closest to Aristotle's intent. To think comparatively is to ask oneself what *is;* to think operatively is to ask oneself what to *do*. These are the two modes of serious, one might even say genuine thought —as distinguished from day dreams, emotional vaporizings, laryngeal chatter, and the repetition of clichés. To think seriously is to think either for the sake of knowing things as they are or for the sake of acting upon, and producing or helping to produce, things as they might be.

Although in practice the two types of thinking are much interrelated, it is operative thinking with which our present study is primarily concerned. Ethics, although it must be guided, limited, and qualified constantly by considerations of what is actually the case, is focused upon questions of what should be done. The converse, however, does not follow. Not all questions about what should be done are ethical questions. Much of our operative thinking is given to more immediate needs—to means whereby some given end can be achieved. A person who deliber-

* From *A Critical Introduction to Ethics*, 3rd ed., The Odyssey Press, Inc., 1959. Printed by permission of the publisher.

ates as to the most effective way of making money, or of passing a course, or of winning a battle, or of achieving popularity, is thinking operatively, but if that is as far as his planning goes it cannot be called ethical. Such deliberations about adapting means to an end would acquire an ethical character only if some thought were give to the nature and value of the end itself. Ethics cannot dispense with questions of means, but neither can it stop there.

Accordingly, ethics may be defined as that branch of philosophy which is the systematic study of reflective choice, of the standards of right and wrong by which it is to be guided, and of the goods toward which it may ultimately be directed. The relation between the parts of this definition, particularly between standards of right and wrong on the one hand and ultimately desirable goods on the other, will be an important part of the forthcoming study.

The soundest approach to ethical method is through reflection on our experience of moral situations which from time to time we have had occasion to face, or through an imagined confrontation of situations which others have faced and which we can thus make sympathetically real to ourselves. For instance:

Arthur Ames is a rising young district attorney engaged on his most important case. A prominent political boss has been murdered. Suspicion points at a certain ex-convict, known to have borne the politician a grudge. Aided by the newspapers, which have reported the murder in such a way as to persuade the public of the suspect's guilt, Ames feels certain that he can secure a conviction on the circumstantial evidence in his possession. If he succeeds in sending the man to the chair he will become a strong candidate for governor at the next election.

During the course of the trial, however, he accidentally stumbles on some fresh evidence, known only to himself and capable of being destroyed if he chooses, which appears to establish the ex-convict's innocence. If this new evidence were to be introduced at the trial an acquittal would be practically certain. What ought the District Attorney to do? Surrender the evidence to the defence, in order that, as a matter of fair play, the accused might be given every legitimate chance of establishing his innocence? But to do that will mean the loss of a case that has received enormous publicity; the District Attorney will lose the backing of the press; he will appear to have failed, and his political career may be blocked. In that event not only will he himself suffer disappointment, but his ample plans for bestowing comforts on his family and for giving his children the benefits of a superior education may have to be curtailed. On the other hand, ought he to be instrumental in sending a man to the chair for a crime that in all probability he did not commit? And yet the ex-convict is a bad lot; even if innocent in the present case he has doubtless committed many other crimes in which he has escaped detection. Is a fellow like that worth the sacrifice of one's career? Still, there is no proof that he has ever committed a crime punishable by death. Until a man has been proven guilty he must be regarded, by a sound principle of American legal theory, as innocent. To conceal and destroy the evidence, then, is not that tantamount to railroading an innocent man to the chair?

So the District Attorney reasons back and forth. He knows that it is a widespread custom for a district attorney to conceal evidence prejudicial to his side of the case. But is the custom, particularly when a human life is at stake, morally right? A district attorney is an agent of the government, and his chief aim in that capacity should be to present his accusations in such a way as to ensure for the accused, not condemnation but justice. The question, then, cannot be answered by appealing simply to law or to legal practice. It is a moral one: *What is Arthur Ames' duty? What ought he to do?*

Benjamin Bates has a friend who lies in a hospital, slowly dying of a painful and incurable disease. Although there is no hope of recovery, the disease sometimes permits its victim to linger on for many months, in even greater torment and with threatened loss of sanity. The dying man, apprised of the outcome and knowing that the hospital expenses are a severe drain on his family's limited resources, decides that death had better come at once. His physician, he knows, will not run the risk of providing him with the necessary drug. There is only his friend Bates to appeal to.

How shall Bates decide? Dare he be instrumental in hastening another's death? Has he a moral right to be accessory to the taking of a human life? Besides, suspicion would point his way, and his honorable motives would not avert a charge of murder. On the other hand, can he morally refuse to alleviate a friend's suffering and the financial distress of a family when the means of doing so are in his hands? And has he not an obligation to respect a friend's declared will in the matter? To acquiesce and to refuse seem both somehow in different ways wrong, yet one course or the other must be chosen. *What ought Bates to do? Which way does his duty lie?*

In the city occupied by Crampton College a strike is declared by employees of all the public-transit lines. Their wages have not been increased to meet the rising cost of living, and the justice of their grievance is rather widely admitted by neutral observers. The strike ties up business and causes much general inconvenience; except for the people who have cars of their own or can afford taxi fare, there is no way of getting from one part of the city to another. Labor being at this period scarce, an appeal is made by the mayor to college students to serve the community by acting in their spare time as motormen and drivers. The appeal is backed by a promise of lucrative wages and by the college administration's agreement to coöperate by permitting necessary absences from classes.

What ought the students of Crampton College to do? If they act as strike-breakers they aid in forcing the employees back to work on the corporation's own terms. Have they any right to interfere so drastically and one-sidedly in the lives and happiness of others? On the other hand, if they turn down the mayor's request the community will continue to suffer grave inconveniences until the fight is somehow settled. *What is the students' duty in the matter? What is the right course for them to follow?*

These three situations, although perhaps unusual in the severity of their challenge, offer examples of problems distinctively moral. When the act of moral deliberation implicit in each of them is fully carried out, certain characteristic phases can be discerned.

(i) *Examination and clarification of the alternatives.* What are the relevant possibilities of action in the situations confronting me? Am I clear about the nature of each? Have I clearly distinguished them from one another? And are they mutually exhaustive, or would a more attentive search reveal others? In the case of District Attorney Ames, for example, a third alternative might have been to make a private deal with the ex-convict by which, in exchange for his acquittal, the District Attorney would receive the profits from some lucrative racket of which the convict had control. No doubt to a reputable public servant this line of conduct would be too repugnant for consideration; it exemplifies, nevertheless, the ever-present logical possibility of going "between the horns" of the original dilemma.

(ii) *Rational elaboration of consequences.* The next step is to think out the probable consequences of each of the alternatives in question. As this step involves predictions about a hypothetical future, the conclusions can have, at most, a high degree of probability, never certainty. The degree of probability is heightened according as there is found some precedent in past experience for each of the proposed choices. Even if the present situation seems wholly new, analysis will always reveal *some* particulars for which analogies in past experience can be found or to which known laws of causal sequence are applicable. Such particulars will be dealt with partly by analogy (an act similar to the one now being deliberated about had on a previous occasion such and such consequences) and partly by the inductive-deductive method: appealing to general laws (deduction) which in turn have been built up as generalizations from observed particulars (induction). Mr. Ames, we may suppose, found the materials for this step in his professional knowledge of law and legal precedent, as well as in his more general knowledge of the policies of the press, the gullibility of its readers, and the high cost of domestic luxuries.

(iii) *Imaginative projection of the self into the predicted situation.* It is not enough to reason out the probable consequences of a choice. In a moral deliberation the chief interests involved are not scientific but human and practical. The only way to judge the comparative desirability of two possible futures is to live through them both in imagination. The third step, then, is to project oneself imaginatively into the future; i.e., establish a dramatic identification of the present self with the future self to which the now merely imagined experiences may become real. Few persons, unfortunately, are capable of an imaginative identification force-ful enough to give the claims of the future self an even break. Present goods loom larger than future goods, and goods in the immediate future than goods that are remote. The trained ethical thinker must have a sound *temporal perspective*, the acquisition of which is to be sought by a frequent, orderly, and detailed exercise of the imagination with respect to not yet actual situations.

(iv) *Imaginative identification of the self with the points of view of those persons whom the proposed act will most seriously affect.* Whatever decision I make here and now, if of any importance, is likely to have con-sequences, in varying degrees, for persons other than myself. An impor-tant part of a moral inquiry is to envisage the results of a proposed act as they will appear to those other persons affected by them. I must under-take, then, a dramatic identification of my own self with the selves of other persons. The possibility of doing this is evident from a consideration of how anyone's dramatic imagination works in the reading of a novel or the witnessing of a play. If the persons in the novel or play are dramati-cally convincing it is not because their characters and actions have been established by logical proof, but because they are presented so as to pro-voke in the reader an impulse to project himself into the world of the novel or play, to identify himself with this and that character in it, to share their feelings and moods, to get their slant on things.

In most persons, even very benevolent ones, the social consciousness works by fits and starts. To examine fairly the needs and claims of other selves is no less hard and is often harder than to perform a similar task with regard to one's own future self. Accordingly the ethical thinker must develop *social perspective*—that balanced appreciation of others' claims and needs which is the basis of justice.

In this fourth, as in the third step, the imaginative projection is to be carried out for each of the alternatives, according as their consequences shall have been predicted by Step ii.

(v) *Estimation and comparison of the values involved.* Implicit in the third and fourth steps is a recognition that certain values both positive and negative are latent in each of the hypothetical situations to which moral choice may lead. The values must be made explicit in order that they may be justly compared, for it is as a result of their comparison that a choice is to be made. To make values explicit is to give them a relatively abstract formulation; they still, however, derive concrete sig-nificance from their imagined exemplifications. District Attorney Ames, for example, might have envisaged his dilemma as a choice between family happiness and worldly success on the one hand as against professional honor on the other. Each of these is undoubtedly good, that is to say a value, but the values cannot be reduced to a common denominator. Family happiness enters as a factor into Benjamin Bates' dilemma no less than into that of Arthur Ames, but it stands to be affected in a different way and therefore, in spite of the identical words by which our linguistic poverty forces us to describe it, it does not mean the same thing. Family happiness may mean any number of things; so may success, and honor—although these different meanings have, of course, an intelligible bond of unity. Arthur Ames' task is to compare not just any family happiness with any professional honor but the particular exemplifications of each that enter into his problem. The comparison is not a simple calculation but an imaginative deliberation, in which the abstract values that serve as the logical ground of the comparison are continuous with, and interactive with, the concrete particulars that serve as its starting-point.

(vi) *Decision.* Comparison of the alternative future situations and the values embodied in each must terminate in a decision. Which of the possible situations do I deem is better to bring into existence? There are no rules for the making of this decision. I must simply decide as wisely and fairly and as relevantly to the total comparison as I can. Every moral decision is a risk, for the way in which a person decides is a factor in determining the kind of self he is going to become.

(vii) *Action.* The probable means of carrying out the decision have been established by Step ii. The wished-for object or situation is an end, certain specific means toward the fulfillment of which lie here and now within my power. These conditions supply the premises for an ethical syllogism. When a certain end, x, is recognized as the best of the available alternatives, and when the achievement of it is seen to be possible through a set of means a,b,c . . . which lie within my power, then whichever of the means a,b,c . . . is an action that can here and now be performed becomes at just this point my duty. If the deliberative process has been carried out forcefully and wisely it will have supplied a categorical answer to the question, What ought I to do?—even though the answer in some case may be, Do nothing.

Naturally, not all experiences of moral deliberation and choice reveal these seven phases in a distinct, clear-cut way. Nor is the order here given always the actual order. . . . The foregoing analysis does, however, throw some light on the nature of a moral problem. . . .

STUDY QUESTIONS

1. Wheelwright begins by identifying the characteristic that he thinks distinguishes men from other animals. How does this distinction compare with those made by Muller in "The Nature of Man"?

2. This analysis does not provide standards for solving moral problems. What does it do?

3. What methods other than the ones described here have been proposed for solving ethical problems? Can you think of any that you prefer to the one described?

4. What do the four dilemmas described by Wheelwright have in common? In what ways do they differ from each other?

5. Write a theme resolving one of the examples using the steps described in the latter part of the essay.

6. Compare Wheelwright's advice with the ideas of Westermarck's "Emotional Origin of Moral Judgments." Do you think Wheelwright makes sufficient allowances for emotional and traditional considerations?

The Emotional Origin of Moral Judgments*

Edward Westermarck

Society is the school in which men learn to distinguish between right and wrong. The headmaster is Custom, and the lessons are the same for all. The first moral judgments were pronounced by public opinion; public indignation and public approval are the prototypes of the moral emotions. As regards questions of morality, there was, in early society, practically no difference of opinion; hence a character of universality, or objectivity, was from the very beginning attached to all moral judgments. And when, with advancing civilization, this unanimity was to some extent disturbed by individuals venturing to dissent from the opinions of the majority, the disagreement was largely due to facts which in no way affected the moral principle, but had reference only to its application.

Most people follow a very simple method in judging of an act. Particular modes of conduct have their traditional labels, many of which are learnt with language itself; and the moral judgment commonly consists simply in labelling the act according to certain obvious characteristics which it presents in common with others belonging to the same group. But a conscientious and intelligent judge proceeds in a different manner. He carefully examines all the details connected with the act, the external and internal conditions under which it was performed, its consequences, its motives; and, since the moral estimate in a large measure depends upon the regard paid to these circumstances, his judgment may differ greatly from that of the man in the street, even though the moral standard which they apply be exactly the same. But to acquire a full insight into all the details which are apt to influence the moral value of an act

*From *The Origin and Development of the Moral Ideas* by Edward Westermarck. Reprinted by the kind permission of Hugo E. Pipping.

is in many cases anything but easy, and this naturally increases the disagreement. There is thus in every advanced society a diversity of opinion regarding the moral value of certain modes of conduct which results from circumstances of a purely intellectual character—from the knowledge or ignorance of positive facts,—and involves no discord in principle.

Now it has been assumed by the advocates of various ethical theories that all the differences of moral ideas originate in this way, and that there is some ultimate standard which must be recognised as authoritative by everybody who understands it rightly. According to Bentham, the rectitude of utilitarianism has been contested only by those who have not known their own meaning:

When a man attempts to combat the principle of utility . . . his arguments, if they prove anything, prove not that the principle is wrong, but that, according to the applications he supposes to be made of it, it is misapplied.

Mr. Spencer, to whom good conduct is that "which conduces to life in each and all," believes that he has the support of "the true moral consciousness," or "moral consciousness proper," which, whether in harmony or in conflict with the "pro-ethical" sentiment, is vaguely or distinctly recognised as the rightful ruler. Samuel Clarke, the intuitionist, again, is of opinion that if a man endowed with reason denies the eternal and necessary moral differences of things, it is the very same

. . . as if a man that has the use of his sight, should at the same time as he beholds the sun, deny that there is any such thing as light in the world; or as if a man that understands Geometry or Arithmetick, should deny the most obvious and known proportions of lines or numbers.

In short, all disagreement, as to questions of morals is attributed to ignorance or misunderstanding.

The influence of intellectual considerations upon moral judgments is certainly immense. We shall find that the evolution of the moral consciousness to a large extent consists in its development from the unreflecting to the reflecting, from the unenlightened to the enlightened. All higher emotions are determined by cognitions, they arise from "the presentation of determinate objective conditions"; and moral enlightenment implies a true and comprehensive presentation of those objective conditions by which the moral emotions, according to their very nature, are determined. Morality may thus in a much higher degree than, for instance, beauty be a subject of instruction and of profitable discussion, in which persuasion is carried by the representation of existing data. But although in this way many differences may be accorded, there are points in which unanimity cannot be reached even by the most accurate presentation of facts or the subtlest process of reasoning.

Whilst certain phenomena will almost of necessity arouse similar moral emotions in every mind which perceives them clearly, there are others with which the case is different. The emotional constitution of man does not present the same uniformity as the human intellect. Certain cognitions inspire fear in nearly every breast; but there are brave men and cowards in the world, independently of the accuracy with which they realise impending danger. Some cases of suffering can hardly fail to awaken compassion in the most pitiless heart; but the sympathetic dispositions of men vary greatly, both in regard to the beings with whose sufferings they are ready to sympathise, and with reference to the intensity of the emotion. The same holds good for the moral emotions. The existing diversity of opinion as to the rights of different classes of men and of the lower animals, which springs from emotional differences, may no doubt be modified by a clearer insight into certain facts, but no perfect agreement can be expected as long as the conditions under which the emotional dispositions are formed remain unchanged. Whilst an enlightened mind *must* recognise the complete or relative irresponsibility of an animal, a child, or a madman, and *must* be influenced in its moral judgment by the motives of an act—no intellectual enlightenment, no scrutiny of facts, can decide how far the interests of the lower animals should be regarded when conflicting with those of men, or how far a person is bound, or allowed, to promote the welfare of his nation, or his own welfare, at the cost of that of other nations or other individuals. Professor Sidgwick's well known moral axiom, "I ought not to prefer my own lesser good to the greater good of another," would, if explained to a Fuegian or a Hottentot, be regarded by him, not as self-evident, but as simply absurd; nor can it claim general acceptance even among ourselves. Who is that "Another" to whose greater good I ought not to prefer my own lesser good? A fellow-countryman, a savage, a criminal, a bird, a fish—all without distinction? It will, perhaps, be argued that on this, and on all other points of morals, there would be general agreement, if only the moral consciousness of men were sufficiently developed. But then, when speaking of a "sufficiently developed" moral consciousness (beyond insistence upon a full insight into the governing facts of each case), we practically mean nothing else than agreement with our own moral convictions. The expression is faulty and deceptive, because, if intended to mean anything more, it presupposes an objectivity of the moral judgments which they do not possess, and at the same time seems to be proving what it presupposes. We may speak of an intellect as sufficiently developed to grasp a certain truth, because truth is objective; but it is not proved to be objective by the fact that it is recognised as true by a "sufficiently developed" intellect. The objectivity of truth lies in the recognition of facts as true by all who understand them fully, whilst the appeal to a *sufficient* knowledge assumes their objectivity. To the verdict of a perfect intellect, that is, an intellect which knows everything existing, all would submit; but we can form no idea of a moral consciousness which could lay claim to a similar authority. **If** the believers in an all-good God, who has revealed his will to mankind, maintain that they in this revelation possess a perfect moral standard, and that, consequently, what is in accordance with such a standard must be objectively right, it may be asked what they mean by an "all-good" God. And in their attempt to answer this question, they would inevitably have to assume the objectivity they wanted to prove.

The error we commit by attributing objectivity to moral estimates becomes particularly conspicuous when we consider that these estimates have not only a certain quality, but a certain quantity. There are different degrees of badness and goodness, a duty may be more or less stringent, a merit may be smaller or greater. These quantitative differences are due to the emotional origin of all moral concepts. Emotions vary in intensity almost indefinitely, and the moral emotions form no exception to this rule. Indeed, it may be fairly doubted whether the same mode of conduct ever arouses exactly the same degree of indignation or approval in any two individuals. Many of these differences are of course too subtle to be manifested in the moral judgment; but very frequently the intensity of the emotion is indicated by special words, or by the way in which the judgment is pronounced. It should be noticed, however, that the quantity of the estimate expressed in a moral predicate is not identical with the intensity of the moral emotion which a certain mode of conduct arouses on a special occasion. We are liable to feel more indignant if an injury is committed before our eyes than if we read of it in a newspaper, and yet we admit that the degree of wrongness is in both cases the same. The quantity of moral estimates is determined by the intensity of the emotions which their objects tend to evoke under exactly similar external circumstances.

Beside the relative uniformity of moral opinions, there is another circumstance which tempts us to objectivise moral judgments, namely, the authority which, rightly or wrongly, is ascribed to moral rules. From our earliest childhood we are taught that certain acts *are* right and that others *are* wrong. Owing to their exceptional importance for human welfare, the facts of the moral consciousness are emphasized in a much higher degree than any other subjective facts. We are allowed to have our private opinions about the beauty of things, but we are not so readily allowed to have our private opinions about rights and wrongs. The moral rules which are prevalent in the society to which we belong are supported by appeals not only to human, but to divine, authority, and to call in question their validity is to rebel against religion as well as against public opinion. Thus the belief in a moral order of the world has taken hardly less firm hold of the human mind than the belief in a natural order of things. And the moral law has retained its authoritativeness even when the appeal to an external authority has been regarded as inadequate. It filled Kant with the same awe as the star-spangled firmament. According to Butler, conscience is "a faculty in kind and in nature supreme over all others, and which bears it own authority of being so." Its supremacy is said to be "felt and tacitly acknowledged by the worst no less than by the best of men." Adam Smith calls the moral faculties the "viceregents of God within us," who "never fail to punish the violation of them by the torments of inward shame and self-condemnation; and, on the contrary, always reward obedience with tranquility of mind, with contentment, and self-satisfaction." Even Hutcheson, who raises the question why the moral sense should not vary in different men as the palate does, considers it "to be naturally destined to command all the other powers."

Authority is an ambiguous word. It may indicate knowledge of truth, and it may indicate a rightful power to command obedience. The authoritativeness attributed to the moral law has often reference to both kinds of authority. The moral lawgiver lays down his rules in order that they be obeyed. But he is also believed to know what is right and wrong, and his commands are regarded as expressions of moral truths. As we have seen, however, this latter kind of authority involves a false assumption as to the nature of the moral predicates, and it cannot be justly inferred from the power to command. Again, if the notion of an external lawgiver be put aside, the moral law does not generally seem to possess supreme authority in either sense of the word. It does not command obedience in any exceptional degree; few laws are broken more frequently. Nor can the regard for it be called the mainspring of action; it is only one spring out of many, and variable like all others. In some instances it is the ruling power in a man's life, in others it is a voice calling in the desert; and the majority of people seem to be more afraid of the blame or ridicule of their fellowmen, or of the penalties with which the law threatens them, than of the "viceregents of God" in their own hearts. That mankind prefer the possession of virtue to all other enjoyments, and look upon vice as worse than any other misery, is unfortunately an imagination of some moralists who confound men as they are with men as they ought to be.

It is said that the authority of the moral law asserts itself every time the law is broken, that virtue bears in itself its own reward, and vice its own punishment. But, to be sure, conscience is a very unjust retributor. The more a person habituates himself to virtue the more he sharpens its sting, the deeper he sinks in vice the more he blunts it. Whilst the best men have the most sensitive consciences, the worst have hardly any consciences at all. It is argued that the habitual sinner has rid himself of remorse at a great cost; but it may be fairly doubted whether the loss is an adequate penalty for his wickedness. We are reminded that men are rewarded for good and punished for bad acts by the moral feelings of their neighbors. But public opinion and law judge of detected acts only. Their judgment is seldom based upon an exhaustive examination of the case. They often apply a standard which is itself open to criticism. And the feelings with which men regard their fellow-creatures, and which are some of the main sources of human happiness and suffering, have often very little to do with morality. A person is respected or praised, blamed or despised, on other grounds than his character. Nay the admiration which men feel for genius, courage, pluck, strength, or accidental success, is often superior in intensity to the admiration they feel for virtue.

In spite of all this however, the supreme authority assigned to the moral law is not altogether an illusion. It really exists in the minds of the best, and is nominally acknowledged by the many. By this I do not refer to the universal admission that the moral law, whether obeyed or not, ought under all circumstances to be obeyed; for this is the same as to say that what ought to be ought to be. But it is recognised, in theory at least, that morality, either alone or in connection with religion, possesses a higher value than anything else; that rightness and goodness are preferable to all other kinds of mental superiority, as well as of physical excellence. If this theory is not more commonly acted upon, that is due to its being, in most people, much less the outcome of their own feelings than of instruction from the outside. It is ultimately traceable to some great teacher whose own mind was ruled by the ideal of moral perfection, and whose words became sacred on account of his supreme wisdom, like Confucius or Buddha, or on religious grounds, like Jesus. The authority of the moral law is thus only an expression of a strongly developed, overruling moral consciousness. It can hardly, as Mr. Sidgwick maintains, be said to "depend upon" the conception of the objectivity of duty. On the contrary, it must be regarded as a cause of this conception—not only, as has already been pointed out, where it is traceable to some external authority, but where it results from the strength of the individual's own moral emotions. As clearness and distinctness of the conception of an object easily produces the belief in its truth, so the intensity of a moral emotion makes him who feels it disposed to objectivise the moral estimate to which it gives rise, in other words, to assign to it universal validity. The enthusiast is more likely than anybody else to regard his judgments as true, and so is the moral enthusiast with reference to his moral judgments. The intensity of his emotions makes him the victim of an illusion.

The presumed objectivity of moral judgments thus being a chimera, there can be no moral truth in the sense in which this term is generally understood. The ultimate reason for this is, that the moral concepts are based upon emotions, and that contents of an emotion fall entirely outside the category of truth. But it may be true or not that we have a certain emotion, it may be true or not that a given mode of conduct has a tendency to evoke in us moral indignation or moral approval. Hence a moral judgment is true or false according as its subject has or has not that tendency which the predicate attributes to it. If I say that it is wrong to resist evil, and yet resistance to evil has no tendency whatever to call forth in me an emotion of moral disapproval, then my judgment is false.

If there are no general moral truths, the object of scientific ethics cannot be to fix rules for human conduct, the aim of all science being the discovery of some truth. It has been said by Bentham and others that moral principles cannot be proved because they are first principles which are used to prove everything else. But the real reason for their being inaccessible to demonstration is that, owing to their very nature, they can never be true. If the word "Ethics," then, is to be used as the name for a science, the object of that science can only be to study the moral consciousness as a fact.

Ethical subjectivism is commonly held to be a dangerous doctrine, destructive to morality, opening the door to all sorts of libertinism. If that which appears to each man as right and good, stands for that which is right or good; if he is allowed to make his own law, or to make no law at all; then, it is said, everybody has the natural right to follow his caprice and inclinations, and to hinder him from doing so is an infringement on his rights, a constraint with which no one is bound to comply provided that he has the power to evade it. This inference was long ago drawn from the teaching of the Sophists, and it will no doubt be still repeated as an argument against any theorist who dares to assert that nothing can be said to be truly right or wrong.

To this argument may, first, be objected that a scientific theory is not invalidated by the mere fact that it is likely to cause mischief. The unfortunate circumstance that there do exist dangerous things in the world proves that something may be dangerous and yet true. Another question is whether any scientific truth really is mischievous on the whole, although it may cause much discomfort to certain people. I venture to believe that this, at any rate, is not the case with that form of ethical subjectivism which I am here advocating. The charge brought against the Sophists does not at all apply to it. I do not even subscribe to that beautiful modern sophism which admits every man's conscience to be an infallible guide. If we had to recognise, or rather if we did recognise, as right everything which is held to be right by anybody, savage or Christian, criminal or saint, morality would really suffer a serious loss. But we do not, and we cannot, do so. My moral judgments are my own judgments; they spring from my own moral consciousness; they judge of the conduct of other men not from their point of view but from mine, not with primary reference to their opinions about right and wrong, but with reference to my own. Most of us indeed admit that, when judging of an act, we also ought to take into consideration the moral conviction of the agent, and the agreement or disagreement between his doing and his idea of what he ought to do. But although we hold it to be wrong of a person to act against his conscience, we may at the same time blame him for having such a conscience as he has. Ethical subjectivism covers all such cases. It certainly does not allow everybody to follow his own inclinations; nor does it lend sanction to arbitrariness and caprice. Our moral consciousness belongs to our mental constitution, which we cannot change as we please. We approve and we disapprove because we cannot do otherwise. Can we help feeling pain when the fire burns us? Can we help sympathising with our friends? Are these phenomena less necessary or less powerful in their consequences, because they fall within the subjective sphere of experience? So, too, why should the moral law command less obedience because it forms part of our own nature?

Far from being a danger, ethical subjectivism seems to me more likely to be an acquisition for moral practice. Could it be brought home to people that there is no absolute standard in morality, they would perhaps be somewhat more tolerant in their judgments, and more apt to listen to the voice of reason. If the right has an objective existence, the moral consciousness has certainly been playing at blindman's buff ever since it was born, and will continue to do so until the extinction of the human race. But who does admit this? The popular mind is always inclined to believe that it possesses the knowledge of what *is* right and wrong, and to regard public opinion as the reliable guide of conduct. We have, indeed, no reason to regret that there are men who rebel against the established rules of morality; it is more deplorable that the rebels are so few, and that, consequently, the old rules change so slowly. Far above the vulgar idea that the right is a settled something to which everybody has to adjust his opinions, rises the conviction that it has its existence in each individual mind, capable of any expansion, proclaiming its own right to exist, and, if need be, venturing to make a stand against the whole world. Such a conviction makes for progress.

STUDY QUESTIONS

1. What evidence does Westermarck offer to show that moral attitudes are essentially emotional? Do you consider the evidence convincing? Has he overlooked evidence which would contradict his thesis?

2. How does he explain the fact that moral opinions are, as he observes, relatively uniform?

3. What are some of the reasons Westermarck gives for denying that such a concept as "moral truth," which implies an objective morality, can exist? Are his reasons persuasive?

4. What does Westermarck mean by the term "ethical subjectivism"? What advantages does he see in it?

5. Compare Westermarck's view of moral law with Wheelwright's. Which do you find more persuasive? To what extent is your decision here determined by your own preconceptions?

6. Do you agree with Westermarck that conscience is not a sufficient guide for morality? Illustrate your answer with examples drawn from your own experience.

Chronometricals and Horologicals*

Herman Melville

LECTURE FIRST, BY PLOTINUS PLINLIMMON

(Being not so much the Portal, as part of the temporary Scaffold to the Portal of this New Philosophy).

Few of us doubt, gentlemen, that human life on this earth is but a state of probation; which among other things implies, that here below, we mortals have only to do with things provisional. Accordingly, I hold that all our so-called wisdom is likewise but provisional.

"This preamble laid down, I begin.

"It seems to me, in my visions, that there is a certain most rare order of human souls, which if carefully carried in the body will almost always and everywhere give Heaven's own Truth, with some small grains of variance. For peculiarly coming from God, the sole source of that heavenly truth, and the great Greenwich hill and tower from which the universal meridians are far out into infinity reckoned; such souls seem as London sea-chronometers (*Greek*, time-namers) which as the London ship floats past Greenwich down the Thames, are accurately adjusted by Greenwich time, and if heedfully kept, we still give that same time, even though carried to the Azores. True, in nearly all cases of long, remote voyages—to China, say—chronometers of the best make, and the most carefully treated, will gradually more or less vary from Greenwich time, without the possibility of the error being corrected by direct comparison with their great standard; but skilful and devout observations of the stars by the sextant will serve materially to lessen such errors. And besides, there is such a thing as *rating* a chronometer; that is, having ascertained its degree of organic inaccuracy, however small, then in all subsequent chronometrical calculations, that ascertained loss or gain can be readily added or deducted, as the case may be. Then again, on these long voyages, the chronometer may be corrected by comparing it with the chronometer of some other ship at sea, more recently from home.

"Now in an artificial world like ours, the soul of man is further removed from its God and the Heavenly Truth, than the chronometer carried to China, is from Greenwich. And, as that chronometer, if at all accurate, will pronounce it to be 12 o'clock high-noon, when the China local watches say, perhaps, it is 12 o'clock midnight; so the chronometric

* From *Pierre, or the Ambiguities*, 1852.

soul, if in this world true to its great Greenwich in the other, will always, in its so-called intuitions of right and wrong, be contradicting the mere local standards and watchmaker's brains of this earth.

"Bacon's brains were mere watchmaker's brains; but Christ was a chronometer; and the most exquisitely adjusted and exact one, and the least affected by all terrestrial jarrings, of any that have ever come to us. And the reason why his teachings seemed folly to the Jews, was because he carried that Heaven's time in Jerusalem, while the Jews carried Jerusalem time there. Did he not expressly say—My wisdom (time) is not of this world? But whatever is really peculiar in the wisdom of Christ seems precisely the same folly to-day as it did 1850 years ago. Because, in all that interval his bequeathed chronometer has still preserved its original Heaven's time, and the general Jerusalem of this world has likewise carefully preserved its own.

"But though the chronometer carried from Greenwich to China, should truly exhibit in China what the time may be at Greenwich at any moment; yet, though thereby it must necessarily contradict China time, it does by no means thence follow, that with respect to China, the China watches are at all out of the way. Precisely the reverse. For the fact of that variance is a presumption that, with respect to China, the Chinese watches must be all right; and consequently as the China watches are right as to China, so the Greenwich chronometers must be wrong as to China. Besides, of what use to the Chinaman would a Greenwich chronometer, keeping Greenwich time, be? Were he thereby to regulate his daily actions, he would be guilty of all manner of absurdities:—going to bed at noon, say, when his neighbours would be sitting down to dinner. And thus, though the earthly wisdom of man be heavenly folly to God; so also, conversely, is the heavenly wisdom of God an earthly folly to man. Literally speaking, this is so. Nor does the God at the heavenly Greenwich expect common men to keep Greenwich wisdom in this remote Chinese world of ours; because such a thing were unprofitable for them here, and, indeed, a falsification of Himself, inasmuch as in that case, China time would be identical with Greenwich time, which would make Greenwich time wrong.

"But why then does God now and then send a heavenly chronometer (as a meteoric stone) into the world, uselessly as it would seem, to give the lie to all the world's time-keepers? Because He is unwilling to leave man without some occasional testimony to this:—that though man's Chinese notions of things may answer well enough here, they are by no means universally applicable, and that the central Greenwich in which he dwells goes by a somewhat different method from this world. And yet it follows not from this, that God's truth is one thing and man's truth another; but—as above hinted, and as will be further elucidated in subsequent lectures—by their very contradictions they are made to correspond.

"By inference it follows, also, that he who finding in himself a chrono-metrical soul, seeks practically to force that heavenly time upon the earth; in such an attempt he can never succeed, with an absolute and essential success. And as for himself, if he seek to regulate his own daily conduct by it, he will but array all men's earthly time-keepers against him, and thereby work himself woe and death. Both these things are plainly evinced in the character and fate of Christ, and the past and present condition of the religion he taught. But here one thing is to be especially observed. Though Christ encountered woe in both the precept and the practice of his chronometricals, yet did he remain throughout entirely without folly or sin. Whereas, almost invariably, with inferior beings, the absolute effort to live in this world according to the strict letter of the chronometricals is, somehow, apt to involve those inferior beings eventually in strange, *unique* follies and sins, unimagined before. It is the story of the Ephesian matron, allegorised.

"To any earnest man of insight, a faithful contemplation of these ideas concerning Chronometricals and Horologicals, will serve to render provisionally far less dark some few of the otherwise obscurest things which have hitherto tormented the honest-thinking men of all ages. What man who carries a heavenly soul in him, has not groaned to perceive, that unless he committed a sort of suicide as to the practical things of this world, he never can hope to regulate his earthly conduct by the same heavenly soul? And yet by an infallible instinct he knows, that that monitor cannot be wrong in itself.

"And where is the earnest and righteous philosopher, gentlemen, who looking right and left, and up and down, through all the ages of the world, the present included; where is there such an one who has not a thousand times been struck with a sort of infidel idea, that whatever other worlds God may be Lord of, he is not the Lord of this; for else this world would seem to give the lie to Him; so utterly repugnant seem its ways to the instinctively known ways of Heaven. But it is not, and cannot be so; nor will he who regards this chronometrical conceit aright, ever more be conscious of that horrible idea. For he will then see, or seem to see, that this world's seeming incompatibility with God, absolutely results from its meridional correspondence with Him.

"This chronometrical conceit does by no means involve the justification of all the acts which wicked men may perform. For in their wickedness downright wicked men sin as much against their own horologes, as against the heavenly chronometer. That this is so, their spontaneous liability to remorse does plainly evince. No, this conceit merely goes to show, that for the mass of men, the highest abstract heavenly righteousness is not only impossible, but would be entirely out of place, and positively wrong in a world like this. To turn the left cheek if the right be smitten, is chronometrical; hence, no average son of man ever did such a thing. To give *all* that thou hast to the poor, this too is chronometrical;

hence no average son of man ever did such a thing. Nevertheless, if a man gives with a certain self-considerate generosity to the poor; abstains from doing downright ill to any man; does his convenient best in a general way to do good to his whole race; takes watchful loving care of his wife and children, relatives, and friends; is perfectly tolerant to all other men's opinions, whatever they may be; is an honest dealer, an honest citizen, and all that; and more especially if he believes that there is a God for infidels, as well as for believers, and acts upon that belief; then, though such a man falls infinitely short of the chronometrical standard, though all his actions are entirely horologic;—yet such a man need never lastingly despond, because he is sometimes guilty of some minor offence:—hasty words, impulsively returning a blow, fits of domestic petulance, selfish enjoyment of a glass of wine while he knows there are those around him who lack a loaf of bread. I say he need never lastingly despond on account of his perpetual liability to these things; because *not* to do them, and their like, would be to be an angel, a chronometer; whereas, he is a man and a horologe.

"Yet does the horologe itself teach, that all liabilities to these things should be checked as much as possible, though it is certain they can never be utterly eradicated. They are only to be checked, then, because, if entirely unrestrained, they would finally run into utter selfishness and human demonism, which, as before hinted, are not by any means justified by the horologe.

"In short, this chronometrical and horological conceit, in sum, seems to teach this:—That in things terrestrial (horological) a man must not be governed by ideas celestial (chronometrical); that certain minor self-renunciations in this life his own mere instinct for his own everyday general well-being will teach him to make, but he must by no means make a complete unconditional sacrifice of himself in behalf of any other being, or any cause, or any conceit. (For, does aught else completely and unconditionally sacrifice itself for him? God's own sun does not abate one tittle of its heat in July, however you swoon with that heat in the sun. And if it *did* abate its heat on your behalf, then the wheat and the rye would not ripen; and so, for the incidental benefit of one, a whole population would suffer.)

"A virtuous expediency, then, seems the highest desirable or attainable earthly excellence for the mass of men, and is the only earthly excellence that their Creator intended for them. When they go to heaven, it will be quite another thing. There, they can freely turn the left cheek, because there the right cheek will never be smitten. There they can freely give all to the poor, for *there* there will be no poor to give to. A due appreciation of this matter will do good to man. For, hitherto, being authoritatively taught by his dogmatical teachers that he must, while on earth, aim at heaven, and attain it, too, in all his earthly acts, on pain of eternal wrath; and finding by experience that this is utterly impossible; in his

despair, he is too apt to run clean away into all manner of moral abandonment, self-deceit, and hypocrisy (cloaked, however, mostly under an
aspect of the most respectable devotion); or else he openly runs, like a
mad dog, into atheism. Whereas, let men be taught those Chronometricals and Horologicals, and while still retaining every common-sense in-
centive to whatever of virtue be practicable and desirable, and having
these incentives strengthened, too, by the consciousness of powers to
attain their mark; then there would be an end to that fatal despair of becoming at all good, which has too often proved the vice-producing result
in many minds of the undiluted chronometrical doctrines hitherto taught
to mankind. But if any man say, that such a doctrine as this I lay down
is false, is impious; I would charitably refer that man to the history of
Christendom for the last 1800 years; and ask him, whether, in spite of all
the maxims of Christ, that history is not just as full of blood, violence,
wrong, and iniquity of every kind, as any previous portion of the world's
history? Therefore, it follows, that so far as practical results are concerned—regarded in a purely earthly light—the only great original moral
doctrine of Christianity (*i.e.* the chronometrical gratuitous return of good
for evil, as distinguished from the horological forgiveness of injuries
taught by some of the Pagan philosophers), has been found (horo-
logically) a false one; because after 1800 years' inculcation from tens of
thousands of pulpits, it has proved entirely impracticable.

"I but lay down, then, what the best mortal men do daily practise; and
what all really wicked men are very far removed from. I present consolation to the earnest man, who, among all his human frailties, is still
agonisingly conscious of the beauty of chronometrical excellence. I hold
up a practicable virtue to the vicious; and interfere not with the eternal
truth, that, sooner or later, in all cases, downright vice is downright woe.

"Moreover: if——"

But here the pamphlet was torn, and came to a most untidy termina-
tion.

STUDY QUESTIONS

1. This selection from Melville's novel *Pierre, or The Ambiguities* is
   a "lecture" which Melville represents as written by a philosopher
   named Plotinus Plinlimmon. The lecture deals with one possible
   view of the paradox of Christian ideals in an unideal world. Explain the main symbols of Melville's allegory. That is, what does
   he mean by Greenwich time, China time, "chronometers" and
   "horologicals"?

2. Would Melville agree with Westermarck that concepts of morality
   are relative?

3. What policy does Melville recommend with regard to moral problems?

4. What is the tone of this discussion? Do you think it is appropriate? How does it help or hinder Melville in making his point?

5. Some may feel that Melville's analogy, in which time and the various ways it can be kept, stand for moral systems, is unfair and misleading. If that is your opinion, write a theme showing why Melville's analogy is faulty.

6. Write a theme giving some examples of the differences in moral ideas to which Melville is referring by his symbols, "China time" and "Greenwich time." What do you think is the significance of these differences?

The Practice of Stoicism*

Epictetus

Of all existing things some are in our power, and others are not in our power. In our power are thought, impulse, will to get and will to avoid, and, in a word, everything which is our own doing. Things not in our power include the body, property, reputation, office, and, in a word, everything which is not our own doing. Things in our power are by nature free, unhindered, untrammelled; things not in our power are weak, servile, subject to hindrance, dependent on others. Remember then that if you imagine that what is naturally slavish is free, and what is naturally another's is your own, you will be hampered, you will mourn, you will be put to confusion, you will blame gods and men; but if you think that only your own belongs to you, and that what is another's is indeed another's, no one will ever put compulsion or hindrance on you, you will blame none, you will accuse none, you will do nothing against your will, no one will harm you, you will have no enemy, for no harm can touch you.

Aiming then at these high matters, you must remember that to attain them requires more than ordinary effort; you will have to give up some things entirely, and put off others for the moment. And if you would have these also—office and wealth—it may be that you will fail to get them, just because your desire is set on the former, and you will certainly fail to attain those things which alone bring freedom and happiness.

Make it your study then to confront every harsh impression with the words, "You are but an impression, and not at all what you seem to be." Then test it by those rules that you possess; and first by this—the chief test of all—"Is it concerned with what is in our power or with what is not

* From Epictetus, *The Discourses and Manual*. Translated with Introduction and Notes by P. E. Matheson, Vol. II (Oxford: The Clarendon Press, 1916), pp. 213-219, 234.

in our power?" And if it is concerned with what is not in our power, be ready with the answer that it is nothing to you.

Remember that the will to get promises attainment of what you will, and the will to avoid promises escape from what you avoid; and he who fails to get what he wills is unfortunate, and he who does not escape what he wills to avoid is miserable. If then you try to avoid only what is unnatural in the region within your control, you will escape from all that you avoid; but if you try to avoid disease or death or poverty you will be miserable.

Therefore let your will to avoid have no concern with what is not in man's power; direct it only to things in man's power that are contrary to nature. But for the moment you must utterly remove the will to get; for if you will to get something not in man's power you are bound to be unfortunate; while none of the things in man's power that you could honourably will to get is yet within your reach. Impulse to act and not to act, these are your concern; yet exercise them gently and without strain, and provisionally.

When anything, from the meanest thing upwards, is attractive or serviceable or an object of affection, remember always to say to yourself, "What is its nature?" If you are fond of a jug, say you are fond of a jug; then you will not be disturbed if it be broken. If you kiss your child or your wife, say to yourself that you are kissing a human being, for then if death strikes it you will not be disturbed.

When you are about to take something in hand, remind yourself what manner of thing it is. If you are going to bathe put before your mind what happens in the bath—water pouring over some, others being jostled, some reviling, others stealing; and you will set to work more securely if you say to yourself at once: "I want to bathe, and I want to keep my will in harmony with nature," and so in each thing you do; for in this way, if anything turns up to hinder you in your bathing, you will be ready to say, "I did not want only to bathe, but to keep my will in harmony with nature, and I shall not so keep it, if I lose my temper at what happens."

What disturbs men's minds is not events but their judgements on events. For instance, death is nothing dreadful, or else Socrates would have thought it so. No, the only dreadful thing about it is men's judgement that it is dreadful. And so when we are hindered, or disturbed, or distressed, let us never lay the blame on others, but on ourselves, that is on our own judgements. To accuse others for one's own misfortunes is a sign of want of education; to accuse oneself shows that one's education has begun; to accuse neither oneself nor others shows that one's education is complete.

Be not elated at an excellence which is not your own. If the horse in his pride were to say, "I am handsome," we could bear with it. But when you say with pride, "I have a handsome horse," know that the good horse is the ground of your pride. You ask then what you can call your own. The answer is—the way you deal with your impressions. Therefore when you deal with your impressions in accord with nature, then you may be proud indeed, for your pride will be in a good which is your own.

When you are on a voyage, and your ship is at anchorage, and you disembark to get fresh water, you may pick up a small shellfish or a truffle by the way, but you must keep your attention fixed on the ship, and keep looking towards it constantly, to see if the Helmsman calls you; and if he does, you have to leave everything, or be bundled on board with your legs tied like a sheep. So it is in life. If you have a dear wife or child given you, they are like the shellfish or the truffle, they are very well in their way. Only, if the Helmsman call, run back to your ship, leave all else, and do not look behind you. And if you are old, never go far from the ship, so that when you are called you may not fail to appear.

Ask not that events should happen as you will, but let your will be that events should happen as they do, and you shall have peace.

Sickness is a hindrance to the body, but not to the will, unless the will consent. Lameness is a hindrance to the leg, but not to the will. Say this to yourself at each event that happens, for you shall find that though it hinders something else it will not hinder you.

When anything happens to you, always remember to turn to yourself and ask what faculty you have to deal with it. If you see a beautiful boy or a beautiful woman, you will find continence the faculty to exercise there; if trouble is laid on you, you will find endurance; if ribaldry, you will find patience. And if you train yourself in this habit your impressions will not carry you away.

Never say of anything, "I lost it," but say, "I gave it back." Has your child died? It was given back. Has your wife died? She was given back. Has your estate been taken from you? Was not this also given back? But you say, "He who took it from me is wicked." What does it matter to you through whom the Giver asked it back? As long as He gives it you, take care of it, but not as your own; treat it as passers-by treat an inn. . . .

Remember that you must behave in life as you would at a banquet. A dish is handed round and comes to you; put out your hand and take it politely. It passes you; do not stop it. It has not reached you; do not be impatient to get it, but wait till your turn comes. Bear yourself thus towards children, wife, office, wealth, and one day you will be worthy to banquet with the gods. But if when they are set before you, you do not take them but despise them, then you shall not only share the gods' banquet, but shall share their rule. For by so doing Diogenes and Heraclitus and men like them were called divine and deserved the name.

When you see a man shedding tears in sorrow for a child abroad or dead, or for loss of property, beware that you are not carried away by the impression that it is outward ills that make him miserable. Keep this thought by you: "What distresses him is not the event, for that does not distress another, but his judgement on the event." Therefore do not hesitate to sympathize with him so far as words go, and if it so chance, even to groan with him; but take heed that you do not also groan in your inner being.

Remember that you are an actor in a play, and the Playwright chooses the manner of it: if he wants it short, it is short; if long, it is long. If he wants you to act a poor man you must act the part with all your powers; and so if your part be a cripple or a magistrate or a plain man. For your business is to act the character that is given you and act it well; the choice of the cast is Another's.

On no occasion call yourself a philosopher, nor talk at large of your principles among the multitude, but act on your principles. For instance, at a banquet do not say how one ought to eat, but eat as you ought. Remember that Socrates had so completely got rid of the thought of display that when men came and wanted an introduction to philosophers he took them to be introduced; so patient of neglect was he. And if a discussion arise among the multitude on some principle, keep silent for the most part; for you are in great danger of blurting out some undigested thought. And when some one says to you, "You know nothing," and you do not let it provoke you, then know that you are really on the right road. For sheep do not bring grass to their shepherds and show them how much they have eaten, but they digest their fodder and then produce it in the form of wool and milk. Do the same yourself; instead of displaying your principles to the multitude, show them the results of the principles you have digested.

STUDY QUESTIONS

1. How well do Epictetus' ideas on self-control and the display of virtue through action correspond with ideas expressed by Sartre in "Existentialism"?

2. What part do awareness and forethought play in Epictetus' advice? Do you think he pays too little attention to emotions?

3. Explain the parable of the Helmsman and the ship. What sort of behavior is Epictetus advising here?
4. Would you call this philosophy basically optimistic or pessimistic?
5. Do you agree that "Sickness is a hindrance to the body, but not to the will . . ."? Is there such a thing as a sickness of the will? Explain this point.
6. Epictetus seems to assume that men can control their minds if they exercise enough self-control. What has modern psychology to add to this? Should Epictetus' principles be reformed in the light of what we know now about the human mind?

The Pleasure Principle*

John Stuart Mill

The creed which accepts as the foundation of morals *utility,* or the *greatest happiness principle,* holds that actions are right in proportion as they tend to promote happiness, wrong as they tend to produce the reverse of happiness. By "happiness" is intended pleasure, and the absence of pain; by "unhappiness," pain, and the privation of pleasure. To give a clear view of the moral standard set up by the theory, much more requires to be said; in particular, what things it includes in the ideas of pain and pleasure; and to what extent this is left an open question. But these supplementary explanations do not affect the theory of life on which this theory of morality is grounded—namely, that pleasure, and freedom from pain, are the only things desirable as ends; and that all desirable things (which are as numerous in the utilitarian as in any other scheme) are desirable either for the pleasure inherent in themselves, or as means to the promotion of pleasure and the prevention of pain.

Now such a theory of life excites in many minds, and among them in some of the most estimable in feeling and purpose, inveterate dislike. To suppose that life has (as they express it) no higher end than pleasure— no better and nobler object of desire and pursuit—they designate as utterly mean and groveling; as a doctrine worthy only of swine, to whom the followers of Epicurus were, at a very early period, contemptuously likened; and modern holders of the doctrine are occasionally made the subject of equally polite comparisons by its German, French, and English assailants.

When thus attacked, the Epicureans have always answered that it is not they but their accusers who represent human nature in a degrading light; since the accusation supposes human beings are to be capable of no

* From *Utilitarianism,* 1863.

pleasures except those of which swine are capable. If this supposition were true, the charge could not be gainsaid, but would then be no longer an imputation; for if the sources of pleasure were precisely the same to human beings and to swine, the rule of life which is good enough for the one would be good enough for the other. The comparison of the Epicurean life to that of beasts is felt as degrading, precisely because a beast's pleasures do not satisfy a human being's conceptions of happiness. Human beings have faculties more elevated than the animal appetites, and when once made conscious of them, do not regard anything as happiness which does not include their gratification. I do not, indeed, consider the Epicureans to have been by any means faultless in drawing out their scheme of consequences from the utilitarian principle. To do this in any sufficient manner, many Stoic, as well as Christian elements require to be included. But there is no known Epicurean theory of life which does not assign to the pleasures of the intellect, of the feelings and imagination, and of the moral sentiments, a much higher value as pleasures than to those of mere sensation. It must be admitted, however, that utilitarian writers in general have placed the superiority of mental over bodily pleasure chiefly in the greater permanency, safety, uncostliness, etc., of the former—that is, in their circumstantial advantages rather than in their intrinsic nature. And on all these points utilitarians have fully proved their case; but they might have taken the other, and, as it may be called, higher ground, with entire consistency. It is quite compatible with the principle of utility to recognize the fact, that some *kinds* of pleasure are more desirable and more valuable than others. It would be absurd that while, in estimating all other things, quality is considered as well as quantity, the estimation of pleasures should be supposed to depend on quantity alone.

If I am asked what I mean by difference of quality in pleasures, or what makes one pleasure more valuable than another merely as a pleasure, except its being greater in amount, there is but one possible answer. Of two pleasures, if there be one to which all or almost all who have experience of both give a decided preference, irrespective of any feeling of moral obligation to prefer it, that is the more desirable pleasure. If one of the two is, by those who are competently acquainted with both, placed so far above the other that they prefer it, even though knowing it to be attended with a greater amount of discontent, and would not resign it for any quantity of the other pleasure which their nature is capable of, we are justified in ascribing to the preferred enjoyment a superiority in quality, so far outweighing quantity as to render it, in comparison, of small account.

Now it is an unquestionable fact that those who are equally acquainted with, and equally capable of appreciating and enjoying both, do give a most marked preference to the manner of existence which employs their higher faculties. Few human creatures would consent to be changed into

any of the lower animals, for a promise of the fullest allowance of a
beast's pleasures; no intelligent human being would consent to be a fool,
no instructed person would be an ignoramus, no person of feeling and conscience would be selfish and base, even though they should be persuaded
that the fool, the dunce, or the rascal is better satisfied with his lot than
they are with theirs. They would not resign what they possess more than
he for the most complete satisfaction of all the desires which they have in
common with him. If they ever fancy they would, it is only in cases of
unhappiness so extreme, that to escape from it they would exchange their
lot for almost any other, however undesirable in their own eyes. A being
of higher faculties requires more to make him happy, is capable probably
of more acute suffering, and certainly accessible to it at more points, than
one of an inferior type; but in spite of these liabilities, he can never really
wish to sink into what he feels to be a lower grade of existence. We may
give what explanation we please of this unwillingness: we may attribute
it to pride, a name which is given indiscriminately to some of the most
and to some of the least estimable feelings of which mankind are capable; we may refer it to the love of liberty and personal independence, an
appeal to which was with the Stoics one of the most effective means for the
inculcation of it; to the love of power, or to the love of excitement, both of
which do really enter into and contribute to it: but its most appropriate
appellation is a sense of dignity, which all human beings possess in one
form or another; and in some, though by no means in exact, proportion to
their higher faculties, and which is so essential a part of the happiness of
those in whom it is strong, that nothing which conflicts with it could be,
otherwise than momentarily, an object of desire to them. Whoever supposes that this preference takes place at a sacrifice of happiness—that the
superior being, in anything like equal circumstances, is not happier than
the inferior—confounds the two very different ideas, of *happiness* and
content. It is indisputable that the being whose capacities of enjoyment
are low, has the greatest chance of having them fully satisfied; and a
highly endowed being will always feel that any happiness which he can
look for, as the world is constituted, is imperfect. But he can learn to bear
its imperfections, if they are at all bearable; and they will not make
him envy the being who is indeed unconscious of the imperfections, but
only because he feels not at all the good which those imperfections
qualify. It is better to be a human being dissatisfied than a pig satisfied;
better to be Socrates dissatisfied than a fool satisfied. And if the fool, or
the pig, are of a different opinion, it is because they only know their own
side of the question. The other party to the comparison knows both sides.

It may be objected that many who are capable of the higher pleasures,
occasionally, under the influence of temptation, postpone them to the
lower. But this is quite compatible with a full appreciation of the intrinsic superiority of the higher. Men often, from infirmity of character,
make their election for the nearer good, though they know it to be the less

valuable; and this no less when the choice is between two bodily pleasures, than when it is between bodily and mental. They pursue sensual indulgences to the injury of health, though perfectly aware that health is the greater good. It may be further objected that many who begin with youthful enthusiasm for everything noble, as they advance in years sink into indolence and selfishness. But I do not believe that those who undergo this very common change, voluntarily choose the lower description of pleasures in preference to the higher. I believe that before they devote themselves exclusively to the one, they have already become incapable of the other. Capacity for the nobler feelings is in most natures a very tender plant, easily killed, not only by hostile influences, but by mere want of sustenance; and in the majority of young persons it speedily dies away if the occupations to which their position in life has devoted them, and the society into which it has thrown them, are not favorable to keeping that higher capacity in exercise. Men lose their high aspirations as they lose their intellectual tastes, because they have not time or opportunity for indulging them; and they addict themselves to inferior pleasures not because they deliberately prefer them, but because they are either the only ones to which they have access or the only ones which they are any longer capable of enjoying. It may be questioned whether anyone who has remained equally susceptible to both classes of pleasures, ever knowingly and calmly preferred the lower; though many, in all ages, have broken down in an ineffectual attempt to combine both.

From this verdict of the only competent judges I apprehend there can be no appeal. On a question which is the best worth having of two pleasures, or which of two modes of existence is the most grateful to the feelings, apart from its moral attributes and from its consequences, the judgment of those who are qualified by knowledge of both, or, if they differ, that of the majority among them, must be admitted as final. And there need be the less hesitation to accept this judgment respecting the quality of pleasures, since there is no other tribunal to be referred to even on the question of quantity. What means are there of determining which is the acutest of two pains, or the intensest of two pleasurable sensations, except the general suffrage of those who are familiar with both? Neither pains nor pleasures are homogeneous, and pain is always heterogeneous with pleasure. What is there to decide whether a particular pleasure is worth purchasing at the cost of a particular pain, except the feelings and judgment of the experienced? When, therefore, those feelings and judgment declare the pleasures derived from the higher faculties to be preferable *in kind*, apart from the question of intensity, to those of which the animal nature, disjoined from the higher faculties, is susceptible, they are entitled on this subject to the same regard.

I have dwelt on this point, as being a necessary part of a perfectly just conception of utility, or happiness, considered as the directive rule of human conduct. But it is by no means an indispensable condition to the acceptance of the utilitarian standard; for that standard is not the agent's own greater happiness, but the greatest amount of happiness altogether; and if it may possibly be doubted whether a noble character is always the happier for its nobleness, there can be no doubt that it makes other people happier, and that the world in general is immensely a gainer by it. Utilitarianism, therefore, could only attain its end by the general cultivation of nobleness of character, even if each individual were only benefited by the nobleness of others, and his own, so far as happiness is concerned, were a sheer deduction from the benefit. But the bare enunciation of such an absurdity as this last renders refutation superfluous.

According to the "greatest happiness principle," as above explained, the ultimate end, with reference to and for the sake of which all other things are desirable (whether we are considering our own good or that of other people), is an existence exempt as far as possible from pain, and as rich as possible in enjoyments, both in point of quantity and quality; the test of quality, and the rule for measuring it against quantity, being the preference felt by those who in their opportunities of experience, to which must be added their habits of self-consciousness and self-observation, are best furnished with the means of comparison. This, being, according to the utilitarian opinion, the end of human action, is necessarily also the standard of morality; which may accordingly be defined, the rules and precepts for human conduct, by the observance of which an existence such as has been described might be, to the greatest extent possible, secured to all mankind; and not to them only, but, so far as the nature of things admits, to the whole sentient creation.

STUDY QUESTIONS

1. How does Mill answer the argument that his "greatest happiness principle" is degrading?
2. Are you satisfied with Mill's evidence that the pleasures of the intellect and sensibility are higher in quality than those of the body?
3. What distinction does Mill make between happiness and contentment?
4. How well do Mill's ideas correspond with those of Westermarck?
5. Do you agree with Mill that questions of right and wrong should be decided according to the amount of pleasure and pain that will result? Write a theme defending or attacking this principle.
6. Do you think Mill's principle would be desirable or workable on the practical level? Write a theme giving your opinion of it as the basis for a practical morality.

The Morality of Inertia*

Lionel Trilling

A theological seminary in New York planned a series of lectures on "The Literary Presentations of Great Moral Issues," and invited me to give one of the talks. Since I have a weakness for the general subject, I was disposed to accept the invitation. But I hesitated over the particular instance, for I was asked to discuss the moral issues in *Ethan Frome*. I had not read Edith Wharton's little novel in a good many years, and I remembered it with no pleasure or admiration. I recalled it as not at all the sort of book that deserved to stand in a list which included *The Brothers Karamazov* and *Billy Budd, Foretopman*. If it presented a moral issue at all, I could not bring to mind what that issue was. And so I postponed my acceptance of the invitation and made it conditional upon my being able to come to terms with the subject assigned to me.

Ethan Frome, when I read it again, turned out to be pretty much as I had recalled it, not a great book or even a fine book, but a factitious book, perhaps even a cruel book. I was puzzled to understand how it ever came to be put on the list, why anyone should want to have it discussed as an example of moral perception. Then I remembered its reputation, which, in America, is very considerable. It is sometimes spoken of as an American classic. It is often assigned to high-school and college students as a text for study.

But the high and solemn repute in which it stands is, I am sure, in large part a mere accident of American culture. *Ethan Frome* appeared in 1911, at a time when, to a degree that we can now only wonder at, American literature was committed to optimism, cheerfulness, and gentility. What William Dean Howells called the "smiling aspects of life" had an importance in the literature of America some fifty years ago which is unmatched in the literature of any other time and place. It was inevitable that those who were critical of the prevailing culture and who wished to foster in America higher and more serious literature should put a heavy stress upon the grimmer aspects of life, that they should equate the smiling aspects with falsehood, the grimmer aspects with truth. For these devoted people, sickened as they were by cheerfulness and hope, the word "stark" seemed to carry the highest possible praise a critical review or a blurb could bestow, with "relentless" and "inevitable" as its proper variants. *Ethan Frome* was admired because it was "stark"—its action, we note, takes place in the New England village of Starkville—and because the fate it describes is *relentless* and *inevitable*.

No one would wish to question any high valuation that may be given to the literary representation of unhappy events—except, perhaps, as the high valuation may be a mere cliché of an intellectual class, except as it is supposed to seem the hallmark of the superior sensibility and intelligence of that class. When it is only this, we have the right, and the duty, to look sniffishly at starkness, and relentlessness, and inevitability, to cock a skeptical eye at grimness. And I am quite unable to overcome my belief that *Ethan Frome* enjoys its high reputation because it still satisfies our modern snobbishness about tragedy and pain.

We can never speak of Edith Wharton without some degree of respect. She brought to her novels a strong if limited intelligence, notable powers of observation, and a genuine desire to tell the truth, a desire which in some part she satisfied. But she was a woman in whom we cannot fail to see a limitation of heart, and this limitation makes itself manifest as a literary and moral deficiency of her work, and of *Ethan Frome* especially. It appears in the deadness of her prose, and more flagrantly in the suffering of her characters. Whenever the characters of a story suffer, they do so at the behest of their author—the author is responsible for their suffering and must justify his cruelty by the seriousness of his moral intention. The author of *Ethan Frome*, it seemed to me as I read the book again to test my memory of it, could not lay claim to any such justification. Her intention in writing the story was not adequate to the dreadful fate she contrived for her characters. She indulges herself by what she contrives— she is, as the phrase goes, "merely literary." This is not to say that the merely literary intention does not make its very considerable effects. There is in *Ethan Frome* an image of life-in-death, of hell-on-earth, which is not easily forgotten: the crippled Ethan, and Zeena, his dreadful wife, and Matty, the once charming girl he had loved, now bedridden and querulous with pain, all living out their death in the kitchen of the desolate Frome farm—a perpetuity of suffering memorializes a moment of passion. It is terrible to contemplate, it is unforgettable, but the mind can do nothing with it, can only endure it.

My new reading of the book, then, did not lead me to suppose that it justified its reputation, but only confirmed my recollection that *Ethan Frome* was a dead book, the product of mere will, of the cold hard literary will. What is more, it seemed to me quite unavailable for any moral discourse. In the context of morality, there is nothing to say about *Ethan Frome*. It presents no moral issue at all.

For consider the story it tells. A young man of good and gentle character is the only son of a New England farm couple. He has some intellectual gifts and some desire to know the world, and for a year he is happy attending a technical school. But his father is incapacitated by a farm accident, and Ethan dutifully returns to manage the failing farm and sawmill. His father dies; his mother loses her mental faculties, and during her last illness she is nursed by a female relative whom young Ethan marries, for no other reason than that he is bemused by loneliness. The new wife, Zeena, immediately becomes a shrew, a harridan and a valetudinarian—she lives only to be ill. Because Zeena now must spare herself, the Fromes take into their home a gentle and charming young girl, a destitute cousin of the wife. Ethan and Matty fall in love, innocently but deeply. The wife, perceiving this, plans to send the girl away, her place to be taken by a servant whose wages the husband cannot possibly afford. In despair at the thought of separation Matty and Ethan attempt suicide. They mean to die by sledding down a steep hill and crashing into a great elm at the bottom. Their plan fails: both survive the crash, Ethan to be sorely crippled, Matty to be bedridden in perpetual pain. Now the wife Zeena surrenders her claim to a mysterious pathology and becomes the devoted nurse and jailer of the lovers. The terrible tableau to which I have referred is ready for inspection.

It seemed to me that it was quite impossible to talk about this story. This is not to say that the story is without interest as a story, but what interest it may have does not yield discourse, or at least not moral discourse.

But as I began to explain to the lecture committee why I could not accept the invitation to lecture about the book, it suddenly came over me how very strange a phenomenon the book made—how remarkable it was that a story should place before us the dreadful image of three ruined and tortured lives, showing how their ruin came about, and yet propose no moral issue of any kind. And if *issue* seems to imply something more precisely formulated than we have a right to demand of a story, then it seemed to me no less remarkable that the book had scarcely any moral reverberation, that strange and often beautiful sound we seem to hear generated in the air by a tale of suffering, a sound which is not always music, which does not always have a "meaning," but which yet entrances us, like the random notes of an Aeolian harp, or merely the sound of the wind in the chimney. The moral sound that *Ethan Frome* makes is a dull thud. And this seemed to me so remarkable, indeed, that in the very act of saying why I could not possibly discuss *Ethan Frome*, I found the reason why it must be discussed.

It is, as I have suggested, a very great fault in *Ethan Frome* that it presents no moral issue, sets off no moral reverberation. A certain propriety controls the literary representation of human suffering. This propriety dictates that the representation of pain may not be, as it were, gratuitous; it must not be an end in itself. The naked act of representing, or contemplating, human suffering is a self-indulgence, and it may be a cruelty. Between a tragedy and a spectacle in the Roman circus there is at least this much similarity, that the pleasure both afford derives from observing the pain of others. A tragedy is always on the verge of cruelty. What saves it from the actuality of cruelty is that it has an intention beyond itself. This intention may be so simple a one as that of getting us to do something practical about the cause of the suffering or to help actual sufferers, or at least to feel that we should; or it may lead us to look beyond apparent causes to those which the author wishes us to think of as more real, such as Fate, or the will of the gods, or the will of God; or it may challenge our fortitude or intelligence or piety.

A sense of the necessity of some such intention animates all considerations of the strange paradox of tragedy. Aristotle is concerned to solve the riddle of how the contemplation of human suffering can possibly be pleasurable, of why its pleasure is permissible. He wanted to know what literary conditions were needed to keep a tragedy from being a display of horror. Here it is well to remember that the Greeks were not so concerned as we have been led to believe to keep all dreadful things off the stage—in the presentation of Aristotle's favorite tragedy, the audience saw Jocasta hanging from a beam, it saw the representation of Oedipus's bloody eyesockets. And so Aristotle discovered, or pretended to discover, that tragedy did certain things to protect itself from being merely cruel. It chose, Aristotle said, a certain kind of hero; he was of a certain social and moral stature; he had a certain degree of possibility of free choice; he must justify his fate, or seem to justify it, by his moral condition, being neither wholly good nor wholly bad, having a particular fault that collaborates with destiny to bring about his ruin. The purpose of all these specifications for the tragic hero is to assure us that we observe something more than mere passivity when we witness the hero's suffering, that the suffering has, as we say, some meaning, some show of rationality.

Aristotle's theory of tragedy has had its way with the world to an extent which is perhaps out of proportion to its comprehensiveness and accuracy. Its success is largely due to its having dealt so openly with the paradox of tragedy. It serves to explain away any guilty feelings that we may have at deriving pleasure from suffering.

But at the same time that the world has accepted Aristotle's theory of tragedy, it has also been a little uneasy about some of its implications. The element of the theory that causes uneasiness in modern times is the matter of the stature of the hero. To a society based in egalitarian sentiments, the requirement that the hero be a man of rank seems to deny the presumed dignity of tragedy to men of lesser status. And to a culture which questions the freedom of the will, Aristotle's hero seems to be a little beside the point. Aristotle's prescription for the tragic hero is clearly connected with his definition, in his *Ethics*, of the nature of an ethical action. He tells us that a truly ethical action must be a free choice between two alternatives. This definition is then wonderfully complicated by a further requirement—that the moral man must be so trained in making the right choice that he makes it as a matter of habit, makes it, as it were, instinctively. Yet it *is* a choice, and reason plays a part in its making. But we, of course, don't give to reason the same place in the moral life that Aristotle gave it. And in general, over the last hundred and fifty years, dramatists and novelists have tried their hand at the representation of human suffering without the particular safeguards against cruelty which Aristotle perceived, or contrived. A very large part of the literature of Western Europe may be understood in terms of an attempt to invert or criticize the heroic prescription of the hero, by burlesque and comedy, or by the insistence on the common-place, the lowering of the hero's social status and the diminution of his power of reasoned choice. The work of Fielding may serve as an example of how the mind of Europe has been haunted by the great image of classical tragedy, and how it has tried to lay that famous ghost. When Fielding calls his hero Tom Jones, he means that his young man is not Orestes or Achilles; when he calls him a foundling, he is suggesting that Tom Jones is not, all appearances to the contrary notwithstanding, Oedipus.

Edith Wharton was following where others led. Her impulse in conceiving the story of Ethan Frome was not, however, that of moral experimentation. It was, as I have said, a purely literary impulse, in the bad sense of the word "literary." Her aim is not that of Wordsworth in any of his stories of the suffering poor, to require of us that we open our minds to a realization of the kinds of people whom suffering touches. Nor is it that of Flaubert in *Madame Bovary*, to wring from solid circumstances all the pity and terror of an ancient tragic fable. Nor is it that of Dickens or Zola, to shake us with the perception of social injustice, to instruct us in the true nature of social life and to dispose us to indignant opinion and action. These are not essentially literary intentions; they are moral intentions. But all that Edith Wharton has in mind is to achieve that grim tableau of which I have spoken, of pain and imprisonment, of life-in-death. About the events that lead up to this tableau, there is nothing she finds to say, nothing whatever. The best we can conclude of the meaning of her story is that it might perhaps be a subject of discourse in the context of rural sociology—it might be understood to exemplify the thesis that love and joy do not flourish on poverty-stricken New England farms. If we try to bring it into the context of morality, its meaning goes no further than certain cultural considerations—that is, to people who like their literature to show the "smiling aspects of life," it may be thought to say, "This is the aspect that life really has, as grim as this"; while to people who repudiate a literature that represents only the smiling aspects of life it says, "How intelligent and how brave you are to be able to understand that life is as grim as this." It is really not very much to say.

And yet there is in *Ethan Frome* an idea of considerable importance. It is there by reason of the author's deficiences, not by reason of her powers —because it suits Edith Wharton's rather dull intention to be content with telling a story about people who do not make moral decisions, whose fate cannot have moral reverberations. The idea is this: that moral inertia, the *not* making of moral decisions, constitutes a large part of the moral life of humanity.

This isn't an idea that literature likes to deal with. Literature is charmed by energy and dislikes inertia. It characteristically represents morality as positive action. The same is true of the moral philosophy of the West—has been true ever since Aristotle defined a truly moral act by its energy of reason, of choice. A later development of this tendency said that an act was really moral only if it went against the inclination of the person performing the act: the idea was parodied as saying that one could not possibly act morally to one's friends, only to one's enemies.

Yet the dull daily world sees something below this delightful preoccupation of literature and moral philosophy. It is aware of the morality of inertia, and of its function as a social base, as a social cement. It knows that duties are done for no other reason than that they are said to be duties; for no other reason, sometimes, than that the doer has not really been able to conceive of any other course, has, perhaps, been afraid to think of any other course. Hobbes said of the Capitol geese that saved Rome by their cackling that they were the salvation of the city, not because they were they but there. How often the moral act is performed not because we are we but because we are there! This is the morality of habit, or the morality of biology. This is Ethan Frome's morality, simple, unquestioning, passive, even masochistic. His duties as a son are discharged because he is a son; his duties as a husband are discharged because he is a husband. He does nothing by moral election. At one point in his story he is brought to moral crisis—he must choose between his habituated duty to his wife and his duty and inclination to the girl he loves. It is quite impossible for him to deal with the dilemma in the high way that literature and moral philosophy prescribe, by reason and choice. Choice is incompatible with his idea of his existence; he can only elect to die.

Literature, of course, is not wholly indifferent to what I have called the morality of habit and biology, the morality of inertia. But literature, when it deals with this morality, is tempted to qualify its dullness by endowing it with a certain high grace. There is never any real moral choice for the Félicité of Flaubert's story "A Simple Heart." She is all pious habit of virtue, and of blind, unthinking, unquestioning love. There are, of course, actually such people as Félicité, simple, good, loving—quite stupid in their love, not choosing where to bestow it. We meet such people frequently in literature, in the pages of Balzac, Dickens, Dostoievski, Joyce, Faulkner, Hemingway. They are of a quite different order of being from those who try the world with their passion and their reason; they are by way of being saints, of the less complicated kind. They do not really exemplify what I mean by the morality of inertia. Literature is uncomfortable in the representation of the morality of inertia or of biology, and overcomes its discomfort by representing it with the added grace of that extravagance which we denominate saintliness.

But the morality of inertia is to be found in very precise exemplification in one of Wordsworth's poems. Wordsworth is pre-eminent among the writers who experimented in the representation of new kinds and bases of moral action—he has a genius for imputing moral existence to people who, according to the classical morality, should have no moral life at all. And he has the courage to make this imputation without at the same time imputing the special grace and interest of saintliness. The poem I have in mind is ostensibly about a flower, but the transition from the symbol to the human fact is clearly, if awkwardly, made. The flower is a small celandine, and the poet observes that it has not, in the natural way of flowers, folded itself against rough weather:

> But lately, one rough day, this Flower I passed
> And recognized it, though in altered form,
> Now standing as an offering to the blast,
> And buffeted at will by rain and storm.

> I stopped, and said with inly-muttered voice,
> It doth not love the shower nor seek the cold;
> This neither is its courage nor its choice,
> But its necessity in being old.

Neither courage nor choice, but necessity: it cannot do otherwise. Yet it acts as if by courage and choice. This is the morality imposed by brute circumstance, by biology, by habit, by the unspoken social demand which we have not the strength to refuse, or, often, to imagine refusing. People are scarcely ever praised for living according to this morality—we do not suppose it to be a morality at all until we see it being broken.

This is morality as it is conceived by the great mass of people in the world. And with this conception of morality goes the almost entire negation of any connection between morality and destiny. A superstitious belief in retribution may play its part in the thought of simple people, but essentially they think of catastrophes as fortuitous, without explanation, without reason. They live in the moral universe of the Book of Job. In complex lives, morality does in some part determine destiny; in most lives it does not. Between the moral life of Ethan and Matty and their terrible fate we cannot make any reasonable connection. Only a moral judgment cruel to the point of insanity could speak of it as anything but accidental.

I have not spoken of the morality of inertia in order to praise it but only to recognize it, to suggest that when we keep our minds fixed on what the great invigorating books tell us about the moral life, we obscure the large bulking dull mass of moral fact. Morality is not only the high, torturing dilemmas of Ivan Karamazov and Captain Vere. It is also the deeds performed without thought, without choice, perhaps even without love, as Zeena Frome ministers to Ethan and Matty. The morality of inertia, of the dull unthinking round of duties, may, and often does, yield the immorality of inertia; the example that will most readily occur to us is that of the good simple people, so true to their family responsibilities, who gave no thought to the concentration camps in whose shadow they lived. No: the morality of inertia is not to be praised, but it must be recognized. And Edith Wharton's little novel must be recognized for bringing to our attention what we, and literature, so easily forget.

STUDY QUESTIONS

1. Exactly what is meant by "the morality of inertia"? How does it differ from the usual concept of morality? Why does *Ethan Frome* present "no moral issue at all"?

2. Is "the morality of inertia" really morality? Is it possible to conceive of morality in the absence of choice? Can a person be moral if his course of action is compulsory? In considering these questions, refer to Milton's views about the freedom to read in evil books as he expresses them in *Areopagitica*.

3. What reasons does Trilling give for the decline of tragedy in modern times?

4. What importance is attributed to the presence of a "moral issue" in a work of literatuure? What does Trilling mean when he says the "mind can do nothing with" the suffering depicted in *Ethan Frome?*

5. In what ways do some of the works mentioned by the author fulfill the requirement that they be concerned with a moral intention? What does Trilling mean when he speaks of a book as having or not having a "moral reverberation"?

6. Can you give some example from your experience of the kind of morality described by Trilling?

What I Believe*

E. M. Forster

I do not believe in belief. But this is an age of faith, in which one is surrounded by so many militant creeds that, in self-defense, one has to formulate a creed of one's own. Tolerance, good temper, and sympathy are no longer enough in a world which is rent by religious and

* From *Two Cheers for Democracy*, copyright 1938, 1939, 1947, 1949, 1951 by E. M. Forster. Reprinted by permission of Harcourt, Brace and Company, Inc. and Edward Arnold, Ltd.

racial persecution, in a world where ignorance rules, and science, which ought to have ruled, plays the subservient pimp. Tolerance, good temper, and sympathy—well, they are what matter really, and if the human race is not to collapse they must come to the front before long. But for the moment they don't seem enough; their action is no stronger than a flower battered beneath a military jack-boot. They want stiffening, even if the process coarsens them. Faith, to my mind, is a stiffening process, a sort of mental starch, which ought to be applied as sparingly as possible. I dislike the stuff. I do not believe in it, for its own sake, at all. My law-givers are Erasmus and Montaigne, not Moses and St. Paul. My temple stands not upon Mount Moriah but in that Elysian Field where even the immoral are admitted.

I have, however, to live in an Age of Faith—the sort of thing I used to hear praised and recommended when I was a boy. It is damned unpleasant, really. It is bloody in every sense of the word. And I have to keep my end up in it. Where do I start?

With personal relationships. Here is something comparatively solid in a world full of violence and cruelty. Not absolutely solid, for psychology has split and shattered the idea of a "person" and has shown that there is something incalculable in each of us, which may at any moment rise to the surface and destroy our normal balance. We don't know what we're like. We can't know what we're like. We can't know what other people are like. How then can we put any trust in personal relationships, or cling to them in the gathering political storm? In theory we can't. But in practice we can and do. For the purpose of living one has to assume that the personality is solid, and the "self" is an entity, and to ignore all contrary evidence. And since to ignore evidence is one of the characteristics of faith, I certainly can proclaim that I believe in personal relationships.

Starting from them, I get a little order into the contemporary chaos. One must be fond of people and trust them if one isn't to make a mess of life, and it is therefore essential that they shouldn't let one down. They often do. The moral of which is that I must, myself, be as reliable as possible, and this I try to be. But reliability isn't a matter of contract. It is a matter for the heart, which signs no documents. In other words, reliability is impossible unless there is a natural warmth. Most men possess this warmth, though they often have bad luck and get chilled. Personal relationships are despised today. They are regarded as bourgeois luxuries, as products of a time of fair weather which has now passed, and we are urged to get rid of them, and to dedicate ourselves to some movement or cause instead. I hate the idea of dying for a cause, and if I had to choose between betraying my country and betraying my friend, I hope I should have the guts to betray my country. Such a choice may scandalize the modern reader, and he may stretch out his patriotic hand to the telephone at once, and ring up the police. It wouldn't have shocked Dante, though. Dante placed Brutus and Cassius in the lowest circle of

Hell because they had chosen to betray their friend Julius Caesar, rather than their country, Rome.

This brings me along to democracy, "even Love, the Beloved Republic, which feeds upon Freedom and lives." Democracy isn't a beloved republic really, and never will be. But it is less hateful than other contemporary forms of government, and to that extent it deserves our support. It does start from the assumption that the individual is important, and that all types are needed to make a civilization. It doesn't divide its citizens into the bossers and the bossed, as an efficiency-regime tends to do. The people I admire most are those who are sensitive and want to create something or discover something, and don't see life in terms of power, and such people get more of a chance under a democracy than elsewhere. They found religions, great or small, or they produce literature and art, or they do disinterested scientific research, or they may be what are called "ordinary people," who are creative in their private lives, bring up their children decently, for instance, or help their neighbors. All these people need to express themselves, they can't do so unless society allows them liberty to do so, and the society which allows them most liberty is a democracy.

Democracy has another merit. It allows criticism, and if there isn't public criticism there are bound to be hushed-up scandals. That is why I believe in the press, despite all its lies and vulgarity, and why I believe in Parliament. The British Parliament is often sneered at because it's a talking-shop. Well, I believe in it *because* it is a talking-shop. I believe in the Private Member who makes himself a nuisance. He gets snubbed and is told that he is cranky or ill-informed, but he exposes abuses which would otherwise never have been mentioned, and very often an abuse gets put right just by being mentioned. Occasionally, too, in my country, a well-meaning public official loses his head in the cause of efficiency, and thinks himself God Almighty. Such officials are particularly frequent in the Home Office. Well, there will be questions about them in Parliament sooner or later, and then they'll have to mend their ways. Whether Parliament is either a representative body or an efficient one is very doubtful, but I value it because it criticizes and talks, and because its chatter gets widely reported.

So two cheers for democracy: one because it admits variety and one because it permits criticism. Two cheers are quite enough: there is no occasion to give three. Only Love, the Beloved Republic, deserves that.

What about force, though? While we are trying to be sensitive and advanced and affectionate and tolerant, an unpleasant question pops up; doesn't all society rest upon force? If a government can't count upon the police and the army how can it hope to rule? And if an individual gets knocked on the head or sent to a labor camp, of what significance are his opinions?

This dilemma doesn't worry me as much as it does some. I realize that all society rests upon force. But all the great creative actions, all the decent human relations, occur during the intervals when force has not managed to come to the front. These intervals are what matter. I want them to be as frequent and as lengthy as possible and I call them "civilization." Some people idealize force and pull it into the foreground and worship it, instead of keeping it in the background as long as possible. I think they make a mistake, and I think that their opposites, the mystics, err even more when they declare that force doesn't exist. I believe that it does exist, and that one of our jobs is to prevent it from getting out of its box. It gets out sooner or later, and then it destroys us and all the lovely things which we have made. But it isn't out all the time, for the fortunate reason that the strong are so stupid. Consider their conduct for a moment in the Niebelungs' Ring. The giants there have the gold, or in other words the guns; but they do nothing with it, they do not realize that they are all-powerful, with the result that the catastrophe is delayed and the castle of Valhalla, insecure but glorious, fronts the storms for generations. Fafnir, coiled round his hoard, grumbles and grunts; we can hear him under Europe today; the leaves of the wood already tremble, and the Bird calls its warnings uselessly. Fafnir will destroy us, but by a blessed dispensation he is stupid and slow, and creation goes on just outside the poisonous blast of his breath. The Nietzschean would hurry the monster up, the mystic would say he didn't exist, but Wotan, wiser than either, hastens to create warriors before doom declares itself. The Valkyries are symbols not only of courage but of intelligence; they represent the human spirit snatching its opportunity while the going is good, and one of them even finds time to love. Brunhilde's last song hymns the recurrence of love, and since it is the privilege of art to exaggerate, she goes even further and proclaims the love which is eternally triumphant and feeds upon Freedom, and lives.

So that is what I feel about force and violence. I look the other way until fate strikes me. Whether this is due to courage or to cowardice in my own case I cannot be sure. But I know that if men hadn't looked the other way in the past nothing of any value would survive. The people I respect most behave as if they were immortal and as if society were eternal. Both assumptions are false: both of them must be accepted as true if we are to go on eating and working and loving, and are to keep open a few breathing holes for the human spirit. No millennium seems likely to descend upon humanity; no better and stronger League of Nations will be instituted; no form of Christianity and no alternative to Christianity will bring peace to the world or integrity to the individual; no "change of heart" will occur. And yet we needn't despair, indeed we cannot despair; the evidence of history shows us that men have always insisted on behaving creatively under the shadow of the sword, and that we had better follow their example under the shadow of the airplanes.

There is of course hero worship, fervently recommended as a panacea in some quarters. But here we shall get no help. Hero worship is a dangerous vice, and one of the minor merits of a democracy is that it does not encourage it, or produce that unmanageable type of citizen known as the Great Man. It produces instead different kinds of small men, and that's a much finer achievement. But people who can't get interested in the variety of life and can't make up their own minds get discontented over this, and they long for a hero to bow down before and to follow blindly. It's significant that a hero is an integral part of the authoritarian stock-in-trade today. An efficiency-regime can't be run without a few heroes stuck about to carry off the dullness—much as plums have to be put into a bad pudding to make it palatable. One hero at the top and a smaller one each side of him is a favorite arrangement, and the timid and the bored are comforted by such a trinity and, bowing down, feel exalted by it.

No, I distrust Great Men. They produce a desert of uniformity around them and often a pool of blood, too, and I always feel a little man's pleasure when they come a cropper. I believe in aristocracy though—if that's the right word, and if a democrat may use it. Not an aristocracy of power, based upon rank and influence, but an aristocracy of the sensitive, the considerate, and the plucky. Its members are to be found in all nations and classes, and all through the ages, and there is a secret understanding between them when they meet. They represent the true human tradition, the one permanent victory of our queer race over cruelty and chaos. Thousands of them perish in obscurity; a few are great names. They are sensitive for others as well as for themselves, they are considerate without being fussy, their pluck is not swankiness but the power to endure, and they can take a joke. I give no examples—it is risky to do that—but the reader may as well consider whether this is the type of person he would like to meet and to be, and whether (going further with me) he would prefer that the type should *not* be an ascetic one. I'm against asceticism myself. I'm with the old Scotchman who wanted less chastity and more delicacy. I don't feel that my aristocrats are a real aristocracy if they thwart their bodies, since bodies are the instruments through which we register and enjoy the world. Still, I don't insist here. This isn't a major point. It's clearly possible to be sensitive, considerate, and plucky and yet be an ascetic too, and if anyone possesses the first three qualities, I'll let him in! On they go—an invincible army, yet not a victorious one. The aristocrats, the elect, the chosen, the best people—all the words that describe them are false, and all attempts to organize them fail. Again and again authority, seeing their value, has tried to net them and to utilize them as the Egyptian priesthood or the Christian church or the Chinese civil service or the Group Movement, or some other worthy stunt. But they slip through the net and are gone; when the door is shut they are no longer in the room; their temple, as one of them remarked, is the holiness of the heart's imagination, and their kingdom, though they never possess it, is the wide-open world.

With this type of person knocking about, and constantly crossing one's path if one has eyes to see or hands to feel, the experiment of earthly life cannot be dismissed as a failure. But it may well be hailed as a tragedy, the tragedy being that no device has been found by which these private decencies can be transferred to public affairs. As soon as people have power they go crooked and sometimes dotty, too, because the possession of power lifts them into a region where normal honesty never pays. For instance, the man who is selling newspapers outside the House of Parliament can safely leave his papers to go for a drink, and his cap beside them: anyone who takes a paper is sure to drop a copper into the cap. But the men who are inside the houses of Parliament—they can't trust one another like that; still less can the government they compose trust other governments. No caps upon the pavement here, but suspicion, treachery, and armaments. The more highly public life is organized the lower does its morality sink; the nations of today behave to each other worse than they ever did in the past; they cheat, rob, bully, and bluff, make war without notice, and kill as many women and children as possible; whereas primitive tribes were at all events restrained by taboos.

The Savior of the future—if ever he comes—will not preach a new gospel. He will merely utilize my aristocracy; he will make effective the good will and the good temper which are already existing. In other words he will introduce a new technique. In economics, we are told that if there was a new technique of distribution, there need be no poverty, and people would not starve in one place while crops were dug under in another. A similar change is needed in the sphere of morals and politics. The desire for it is by no means new; it was expressed, for example, in theological terms by Jacopone da Todi over six hundred years ago. "Ordina questo amore, O tu che mi ami," he said. ("O thou who lovest me, set this love in order.") His prayer was not granted and I do not myself believe that it ever will be, but here, and not through a change of heart, is our probable route. Not by becoming better, but by ordering and distributing his native goodness, will man shut up force into its box, and so gain time to explore the universe and to set his mark upon it worthily.

Such a change, claim the orthodox, can only be made by Christianity, and will be made by it in God's good time: man always has failed and always will fail to organize his own goodness, and it is presumptuous of him to try. This claim leaves me cold. I cannot believe that Christianity will ever cope with the present world-wide mess, and I think that such influence as it retains in modern society is due to its financial backing rather than to its spiritual appeal. It was a spiritual force once, but the indwelling spirit will have to be restated if it is to calm the waters again, and probably in a non-Christian form.

These are the reflections of an individualist and a liberal who has found his liberalism crumbling beneath him and at first felt ashamed. Then, looking around, he decided there was no special reason for shame, since other people, whatever they felt, were equally insecure. And as for individualism—there seems no way out of this, even if one wants to find one. The dictator-hero can grind down his citizens till they are all alike, but he can't melt them into a single man. He can order them to merge, he can incite them to mass-antics, but they are obliged to be born separately and to die separately and, owing to these unavoidable termini, will always be running off the totalitarian rails. The memory of birth and the expectation of death always lurk within the human being, making him separate from his fellows and consequently capable of intercourse with them. Naked I came into the world, naked I shall go out of it! And a very good thing, too, for it reminds me that I am naked under my shirt. Until psychologists and biologists have done much more tinkering than seems likely, the individual remains firm and each of us must consent to be one, and to make the best of the difficult job.

STUDY QUESTIONS

1. Note that in this statement of his beliefs Forster says almost nothing about the sort of questions that are generally considered religious. Yet he does express "faith," a belief in something unproveable, and, in fact, not likely to be true. Explain what this belief is.

2. What are the two reasons—the "Two Cheers for Democracy"— that Forster gives for approving of a democratic form of government? Explain the difference Forster sees in the idea of achievement as conceived by "the artist and the lover" and as conceived by the Great Man.

3. Underlying this discussion is the feeling that there are two opposing elements in life. What are they?

4. There is an easy, relaxed informality about Forster's writing. Can you detect what gives it this quality? Is it appropriate to his attitudes and beliefs? Explain.

5. What would a government be like in which Forster's "aristocracy" had the upper hand? Write a theme describing how such a government would operate.

6. Do you think Forster has given a full or fair treatment of Democracy, Great Men, or Christianity? Write a theme criticizing (or agreeing with) the opinions he has given on any one of these subjects.

4. RELIGIOUS BELIEF IN OUR TIME

Science, Religion, and Reality*

Lord Balfour

Let us then consider, in the first place, some points on which all men are agreed. No one practically doubts that the world in which we live possesses a certain kind and measure of regularity. Every expectation that we entertain, every action that we voluntarily perform, implies the belief. The most fantastic fairy tale requires it as a background; there are traces of it even in our dreams.

Again, we are all at one in treating with suspicion any statement which, in our judgment, is inconsistent with the "sort of way things happen" in the world as we conceive it. It seems to us more probable that this or that witness should be mistaken or mendacious, than that the wonders to which he testified should be true. If we have no antecedent ground for thinking him a liar, we probably accept his statements when he confines his narrative to the familiar or the commonplace; when he deals in marvels we begin to doubt; when his marvels become too marvelous we frankly disbelieve—though well aware (if we be men of sense) that what is exceedingly marvelous may nevertheless be true.

Such, roughly speaking, has been, and is, the general procedure of mankind. But evidently it is ill-suited to satisfy historians, philosophers, or men of science. It lacks precision. It rests on no clear principles. It depends too obviously on personal predilections. We seek a criterion of credibility more objective and more fundamental. We should like to know, for example, whether there is any sort of statement which, without being self-contradictory, may always be pronounced untrue.

This question will, to many high authorities, seem capable of the simplest answer. Unbroken experience (they will tell us) establishes the uniformity of Nature, and it is the uniformity of Nature which makes inferences from experience possible. Were this disturbed by miraculous occurrences the very foundations of science would be shaken. On broad general grounds therefore "miracles" must be treated in this scientific age as intrinsically incredible. They never have happened, and they never can happen. Many excellent people have indeed professed to see them, and we need not doubt their veracity. But illusion is easy, credulity is

* From *Science, Religion, and Reality*, ed. by Joseph Needham, 1925. Reprinted by permission of the Society for the Promotion of Christian Knowledge.

limitless, and there is nothing in their testimony which can absolve us from the plain duty of purifying or rejecting every narrative in which a taint of the "miraculous" can be detected.

In spite of its apparent precision all this is very loose talk, raising more questions than it answers.

What, for example, is meant by the uniformity of Nature? About the course of Nature we know little; yet surely we know enough to make us hesitate to call it uniform. Phase follows phase in a perpetual flow; but every phase is unique. Nature, as a whole, neither repeats itself, nor (according to science) can possibly repeat itself. Why, then, when we are considering it as a whole, should we describe it as uniform?

Perhaps it will be said that amidst all this infinite variety some fixed rules are always obeyed. Matter (for example) always gravitates to matter. Energy is never either created or destroyed. May we not—nay *must* we not—extend yet further this conception of unbroken regularity, and accept the view that nature, if not uniform as a whole, is nevertheless compounded of uniformities, of causal sequences, endlessly repeated, which collectively illustrate and embody the universal reign of unalterable law? Were any of these causal sequences to fail, we should no doubt be faced with a "miracle"; but such an event (it is urged) would violate all experience, and it need not be seriously considered.

Now this has always seemed to me a most unsatisfactory theory. It throws upon experience a load of responsibility which experience is quite unable to bear. No doubt, as I have already pointed out, the whole conduct of life depends upon our assuming, instinctively or otherwise, that the kind of thing which has happened once, will, under more or less similar circumstances, be likely to happen again. But this assumption, whether instinctive or reflective, whether wisely acted on or unwisely, supplies a very frail foundation for the speculative structure sometimes based upon it. Can it be denied, for example, that nature, uncritically observed, seems honeycombed with irregularities, that the wildest excesses of credulity may arise not from ignoring experience, but from refusing to correct it, that the most ruthless editing is required to force the uncensored messages we receive from the external world into the ideal mold which satisfies our individual convictions?

But what is this ideal mold? We sometimes talk as if by the help of Scientific Method or Inductive Logic we could map out all reality into a scheme of well-defined causes indissolubly connected with well-defined effects, together forming sequences whose recurrence in different combinations constitutes the changing pattern of the universe.

But can such hopes be realized? In the world of concrete fact nothing occurs through the action of a single cause, nor yet through the simple cooperation of many causes, each adding its own unqualified contribution to the total effect, as we picture horse helping horse to draw a loaded dray. Our world is a much more complicated affair. Sequences are never exactly repeated. Causes can never be completely isolated. Their operation is never unqualified. Fence round your laboratory experiments with what precautions you will, no two of them will ever be performed under exactly the same conditions. For the purpose in hand the differences may be negligible. With skilled observers they commonly are. But the differences exist, and they must certainly modify, however imperceptibly, the observed result.

It seems evident from considerations like these that no argument directly based on mere experience can be urged either for or against the possibility of "miracles." Common sense looks doubtfully upon anything out of the common; and science follows suit. But this is very different from the speculative assertion that, since "miracles" are a violation of natural law, their occurrence must be regarded as impossible. The intrusion of an unexpected and perhaps anomalous element into the company of more familiar factors in world development may excite suspicion, but it does not of necessity violate anything more important than our preconceived expectations.

I think it will be found that those who most vehemently reject this way of regarding the world are unconsciously moved not by their knowledge of scientific laws, but by preference for a particular scientific ideal. They are persuaded that if only we had the right kind of knowledge and adequate powers of calculation, we should be able to explain the whole contents of possible experience by applying mathematical methods to certain simple data. They refuse to believe that this calculable "Whole" can suffer interference at the hands of any incalculable power. They find no room in the close-knit tissue of the world process, as they conceive it, for any arbitrary element to find lodgment. They have a clear notion of what science ought to be, and that notion is incompatible with the "miraculous."

The conception of a material universe, overwhelming in its complexity and its splendor, yet potentially susceptible of complete explanation by the actions and the reactions of two very minute and simple kinds of electrical sub-atom, is, without doubt, extraordinarily fascinating. From the early days of scientific philosophy or (if you prefer it) of philosophical science, thinkers have been hungering after some form of all-embracing atomism. They have now apparently reached it (so far as matter is concerned) by the way of observation and experiment—truly a marvelous performance. Yet the very lucidity of the new conceptions helps to bring home to us their essential insufficiency as a theory of the universe. They may be capable of explaining the constitution and behavior of inanimate objects. They may go some (as yet unmeasured) distance towards explaining organic life. But they certainly cannot explain mind. No man really supposes that he personally is nothing more than a changing group of electrical charges, so distributed that their relative motions enable or compel them in their collective capacity to will, to hope, to love, to think, perhaps to discuss themselves as a physical multiplicity, certainly to treat themselves as a mental unity. No creed of this kind can ever be extracted by valid reasoning from the sort of data which the physics either of the present or the future can possibly supply.

The truth is that the immense advances which in modern times have been made by mechanical or quasi-mechanical explanations of the material world have somewhat upset the mental balance of many thoughtful persons who approach the problems of reality exclusively from the physical side. It is not that they formulate any excessive claims to knowledge. On the contrary, they often describe themselves as agnostics. Nevertheless they are apt unconsciously to assume that they already enjoy a good bird's-eye view of what reality *is*, combined with an unshaken assurance about what it is *not*. They tacitly suppose that every discovery, if genuine, will find its place within the framework of a perfected physics, and, if it does not, may be summarily dismissed as mere superstition.

After all, however, superstition may be negative as well as positive, and the excesses of unbelief may be as extravagant as those of belief. Doubtless the universe, as conceived by men more primitive than ourselves, was the obscure abode of strange deities. But what are we to say about a universe reduced without remainder to collection of electric charges radiating energy through a hypothetical ether? Thus to set limits to reality must always be the most hazardous of speculative adventures. To do so by eliminating the spiritual is not only hazardous but absurd. For if we are directly aware of anything, it is of ourselves as personal agents; if anything can be proved by direct experiment it is that we can, in however small a measure, vary the "natural" distribution of matter and energy. We can certainly act on our environment, and as certainly our action can never be adequately explained in terms of entities which neither think, nor feel, nor purpose, nor know. It constitutes a spiritual invasion of the physical world:—it is a miracle.

To me therefore it seems that in the present state of our knowledge or (if you prefer it) of our ignorance, we have no choice but to acquiesce provisionally in an unresolved dualism. Our experience has a double outlook. The first we may call material. It brings us face to face with such subjects as electricity, mass, motion, force, energy, and with such manifestations of energy as ethereal radiation. The second is spiritual. The first deals with objects which are measurable, calculable, capable (up to a point) of precise definition. The second deals with the immeasurable, the incalculable, the indefinable and (let me add) the all-important. The first touches the fundamentals of science; the second is intimately connected with religion. Yet different as they seem, both are real. They belong to the same universe; they influence each other; somewhere and somehow they must be in contact along a common frontier.

But where is that frontier to be drawn? And how are we to describe the relation between these co-terminous provinces of reality? This is perhaps a question for metaphysics rather than for religion or science; and some day, perhaps, metaphysics may provide us with a satisfying answer. In the meanwhile, I may conclude this Introduction at a less ambitious level—concerning myself rather with the relations between religion and science in the practice of life, than with any high problems of speculative philosophy.

I suggest then that in scientific research it is a wise procedure to press "mechanical" theories of the material world to their utmost limits. Were I, for example, a biologist I should endeavor to explain all the phenomena under investigation in terms of matter and motion. I should always be searching for what could be measured and calculated, however confident I might be that in some directions at least the hopeless limitations of such a view would very rapidly become apparent.

In the practice of life, on the other hand, and in the speculation of philosophy, we are free to move within wider horizons. In forming our estimate of the sort of beliefs which may properly be regarded as rationally acceptable, we ought not to be limited by mechanistic presuppositions, however useful these may be in our investigations of Nature. We are spiritual beings, and must take account of spiritual values. The story of man is something more than a mere continuation of the story of matter. It is different in kind. If we cannot calculate the flow of physical events, that is because our knowledge of natural processes is small, and our power of calculation feeble. If we cannot calculate the course of human history, that is because (among other reasons) it is inherently incalculable. No two specimens of humanity exactly resemble each other, or live in circumstances that are exactly comparable. The so-called "repetitions" of history are never more than vague resemblances. The science of history therefore, if there be one, is something quite different from (say) the science of physics. And this is true even when history is wholly divorced from religion. But when it is considered in a different setting, when man is regarded as a spiritual agent in a world under spiritual guidance, events of spiritual significance cannot be wholly judged by canons of criticism which seem sufficient for simpler cases. Unexampled invasions of the physical sphere by the spiritual are not indeed to be lightly believed. But they are certainly not to be rejected merely because historians cannot bring themselves to accept the "miraculous."

This point of view, for those who are prepared to take it, may help to eliminate some of the chief causes of conflict between science and religion. In times not far distant there were men devoted to religion who blundered ignorantly into science, and men devoted to science who meddled unadvisedly with religion. Theologians found their geology in Genesis; materialists supposed that reality could be identified with the mechanism of matters. Neither procedure is to be commended, nor is it by these paths that the unsolved riddle of the universe can best be approached. A science which declares itself incompatible with religion, a religion which deems itself a substitute for science, may indulge in controversies as interminable as they are barren. . . .

STUDY QUESTIONS

1. What, exactly, does Balfour mean when he says that "superstition may be negative as well as positive"? Do you find any example of superstition in this sense in your experience?

2. What does Balfour think of the regularity of nature revealed by science? Why, according to Balfour, is it wrong to deny the possibility of miracles? What does science often unjustifiably assume, in Balfour's opinion?

3. Is there any relation between Balfour's view of the "uniformity of nature" and the views of Krutch in "The Colloid and the Crystal"? To what extent are his views of the limits of science like or unlike those of Cohen and Nagel?

4. How well do Balfour's concepts of the relations between science and philosophy agree with Russell's views of the value and aims of philosophy?

5. What double outlook does Balfour recommend? Do you think his views of the relations between science and religion do in fact eliminate some of the "chief sources of conflict" between the two? Are the conflicts deeper than he acknowledges? Consider the following selection by Huxley in making your answer here.

6. Many think that our inability to predict events is a defect in our knowledge, rather than a result of the existence of incalculable factors, as Balfour believes. Which view do you consider correct? Would it be possible to increase our mastery of reality and to control it by increasing our knowledge? Or do we have to resign ourselves to limited knowledge?

Agnosticism and Christianity*

Thomas Henry Huxley

The present discussion has arisen out of the use, which has become general in the last few years, of the terms "Agnostic" and "Agnosticism."

The people who call themselves "Agnostics" have been charged with doing so because they have not the courage to declare themselves "Infidels." It has been insinuated that they have adopted a new name in order to escape the unpleasantness which attaches to their proper denomi-

* From *Essays on Some Controverted Subjects*, 1892.

nation. To this wholly erroneous imputation, I have replied by showing that the term "Agnostic" did, as a matter of fact, arise in a manner which negatives it; and my statement has not been, and cannot be refuted. Moreover, speaking for myself, and without impugning the right of any other person to use the term in another sense, I further say that Agnosticism is not properly described as a "negative" creed, nor indeed as a creed of any kind, except in so far as it expresses absolute faith in the validity of a principle which is as much ethical as intellectual. This principle may be stated in various ways, but they all amount to this: that it is wrong for a man to say that he is certain of the objective truth of any proposition unless he can produce evidence which logically justifies that certainty. This is what Agnosticism asserts; and, in my opinion, it is all that is essential to Agnosticism. That which Agnostics deny and repudiate, as immoral, is the contrary doctrine, that there are propositions which men ought to believe, without logically satisfactory evidence; and that reprobation ought to attach to the profession of disbelief in such inadequately supported propositions. The justification of the Agnostic principle lies in the success which follows upon its application, whether in the field of natural, or in that of civil, history; and in the fact that, so far as these topics are concerned, no sane man thinks of denying its validity.

Still speaking for myself, I add, that though Agnosticism is not, and cannot be, a creed, except in so far as its general principle is concerned; yet that the application of that principle results in the denial of, or the suspension of judgment concerning, a number of propositions respecting which our contemporary ecclesiastical "gnostics" profess entire certainty. And, in so far as these ecclesiastical persons can be justified in their old-established custom (which many nowadays think more honoured in the breach than the observance) of using opprobrious names to those who differ from them, I fully admit their right to call me and those who think with me "Infidels"; all I have ventured to urge is that they must not expect us to speak of ourselves by that title.

The extent of the region of the uncertain, the number of the problems the investigation of which ends in a verdict of not proven, will vary according to the knowledge and the intellectual habits of the individual Agnostic. I do not very much care to speak of anything as "unknowable." What I am sure about is that there are many topics about which I know nothing; and which, so far as I can see, are out of reach of my faculties. But whether these things are knowable by any one else is exactly one of those matters which is beyond my knowledge, though I may have a tolerably strong opinion as to the probabilities of the case. Relatively to myself, I am quite sure that the religion of uncertainty—the nebulous country in which words play the part of realities—is far more extensive than I could wish. Materialism and Idealism; Theism and Atheism; the doctrine of the soul and its mortality or immortality—appear in the history of philosophy like the shades of Scandinavian heroes, eternally slaying one another and eternally coming to life again in a metaphysical "Nifelheim." It is getting on for twenty-five centuries, at least, since mankind began seriously to give their minds to these topics. Generation after generation, philosophy has been doomed to roll the stone uphill; and, just as all the world swore it was at the top, down it has rolled to the bottom again. All this is written in innumerable books; and he who will toil through them will discover that the stone is just where it was when the work began. Hume saw this; Kant saw it; since their time, more and more eyes have been cleaned of the films which prevented them from seeing it; until now the weight and number of those who refuse to be the prey of verbal mystifications has begun to tell in practical life.

It was inevitable that a conflict should arise between Agnosticism and Theology; or rather, I ought to say, between Agnosticism and Ecclesiasticism. For Theology, the science, is one thing; and Ecclesiasticism, the championship of a foregone conclusion as to the truth of a particular form of Theology, is another. With scientific Theology, Agnosticism has no quarrel. On the contrary, the Agnostic, knowing too well the influence of prejudice and idiosyncrasy, even on those who desire most earnestly to be impartial, can wish for nothing more urgently than that the scientific theologian should not only be at perfect liberty to thresh out the matter in his own fashion; but that he should, if he can, find flaws in the Agnostic position; and, even if demonstration is not to be had, that he should put, in their full force, the grounds of the conclusions he thinks probable. The scientific theologian admits the agnostic principle, however widely his results may differ from those reached by the majority of Agnostics.

But, as between Agnosticism and Ecclesiasticism, or, as our neighbours across the Channel call it, Clericalism, there can be neither peace nor truce. The Cleric asserts that it is morally wrong not to believe certain propositions, whatever the results of a strict scientific investigation of the evidence of these propositions. He tells us that "religious error is, in itself, of an immoral nature." He declares that he has prejudged certain conclusions, and looks upon those who show cause for arrest of judgment as emissaries of Satan. It necessarily follows that, for him, the attainment of faith, not the ascertainment of truth, is the highest aim of mental life. And, on careful analysis of the nature of this faith, it will too often be found to be, not the mystic process of unity with the Divine, understood by the religious enthusiast; but that which the candid simplicity of a Sunday scholar once defined it to be. "Faith," said this unconscious plagiarist of Tertullian, "is the power of saying you believe things which are incredible."

Now I, and many other Agnostics, believe that faith, in this sense, is an abomination; and though we do not indulge in the luxury of self-righteousness so far as to call those who are not of our way of thinking hard names, we do feel that the disagreement between ourselves and those who hold this doctrine is even more moral than intellectual. It is desirable there should be an end of any mistakes on this topic. If our clerical opponents were clearly aware of the real state of the case, there would be an end of the curious delusion, which often appears between the lines of their writings, that those whom they are so fond of calling "Infidels" are people who not only ought to be, but in their hearts are, ashamed of themselves. It would be discourteous to do more than hint the antipodal opposition of this pleasant dream of theirs to facts.

The clerics and their lay allies commonly tell us, that if we refuse to admit that there is good ground for expressing definite convictions about certain topics, the bonds of human society will dissolve and mankind lapse into savagery. There are several answers to this assertion. One is that the bonds of human society were formed without the aid of their theology; and, in the opinion of not a few competent judges, have been weakened rather than strengthened by a good deal of it. Greek science, Greek art, the ethics of old Israel, the social organisation of old Rome, contrived to come into being, without the help of any one who believed in a single distinctive article of the simplest of the Christian creeds. The science, the art, the jurisprudence, the chief political and social theories, of the modern world have grown out of those of Greece and Rome—not by favour of, but in the teeth of, the fundamental teachings of early Christianity, to which science, art, and any serious occupation with the things of this world, were alike despicable.

Again, all that is best in the ethics of the modern world, in so far as it has not grown out of Greek thought, or Barbarian manhood, is the direct development of the ethics of old Israel. There is no code of legislation, ancient or modern, at once so just and so merciful, so tender to the weak and poor, as the Jewish law; and, if the Gospels are to be trusted, Jesus of Nazareth himself declared that he taught nothing but that which lay implicitly, or explicitly, in the religious and ethical system of his people.

"And the scribe said unto him, Of a truth, Teacher, thou hast well said that he is one; and there is none other but he and to love him with all the heart, and with all the understanding, and with all the strength, and to love his neighbour as himself, is much more than all the whole burnt offerings and sacrifices." (Mark xii: 32, 33.)

Here is the briefest of summaries of the teaching of the prophets of Israel of the eighth century; does the Teacher, whose doctrine is thus set forth in his presence, repudiate the exposition? Nay; we are told, on the contrary, that Jesus saw that he "answered discreetly," and replied, "Thou are not far from the kingdom of God."

So that I think that even if the creeds, from the so-called "Apostles" to the so-called "Athanasian," were swept into oblivion; and even if the human race should arrive at the conclusion that, whether a bishop washes a cup or leaves it unwashed, is not a matter of the least consequence, it will get on very well. The causes which have led to the development of morality in mankind, which have guided or impelled us all the way from the savage to the civilized state, will not cease to operate because a number of ecclesiastical hypotheses turn out to be baseless. And, even if the absurd notion that morality is more the child of speculation than of practical necessity and inherited instinct, had any foundation; if all the world is going to thieve, murder, and otherwise misconduct itself as soon as it discovers that certain portions of ancient history are mythical; what is the relevance of such arguments to any one who holds by the Agnostic principle?

Surely, the attempt to cast out Beelzebub by the aid of Beelzebub is a hopeful procedure as compared to that of preserving morality by the aid of immorality. For I suppose it is admitted that an Agnostic may be perfectly sincere, may be competent, and may have studied the question at issue with as much care as his clerical opponents. But, if the Agnostic really believes what he says, the "dreadful consequence" argufier (consistently, I admit, with his own principles) virtually asks him to abstain from telling the truth, or to say what he believes to be untrue, because of the supposed injurious consequences to morality. "Beloved brethren, that we may be spotlessly moral, before all things let us lie," is the sum total of many an exhortation addressed to the "Infidel." Now, as I have already pointed out, we cannot oblige our exhorters. We leave the practical application of the convenient doctrines of "Reserve" and "Non-natural interpretation" to those who invented them.

I trust that I have now made amends for any ambiguity, or want of fulness, in my previous exposition of that which I hold to be the essence of the Agnostic doctrine. Henceforward, I might hope to hear no more of the assertion that we are necessarily Materialists, Idealists, Atheists, Theists, or any other ists, if experience had led me to think that the proved falsity of a statement was any guarantee against its repetition. And those who appreciate the nature of our position will see, at once, that when Ecclesiasticism declares that we ought to believe this, that, and the other, and are very wicked if we don't, it is impossible for us to give any answer but this: We have not the slightest objection to believe anything you like, if you will give us good grounds for belief; but, if you cannot, we must respectfully refuse, even if that refusal should wreck morality and insure our own damnation several times over. We are quite content to leave that to the decision of the future. The course of the past has impressed us with the firm conviction that no good ever comes of falsehood, and we feel warranted in refusing even to experiment in that direction.

STUDY QUESTIONS

1. How does Huxley define "Agnosticism"? What misunderstanding about the beliefs of Agnostics does he attribute to his opponents?
2. What is the ecclesiastical argument which Huxley is attacking here? What evidence does Huxley offer to show that dogmatic religious belief is not essential to society?
3. What importance does Huxley attribute to faith and revelation as opposed to logic and evidence?
4. Do Huxley's opponents have the same concept of morality as he, or do they have a different one?
5. What is the principal purpose of Huxley in this selection? Does he intend primarily to clarify his beliefs? To defend and argue for his position? Point out details and phrases which support your answer.
6. Compare the views of Huxley and Lord Balfour, especially with regard to the unknown.

Knowledge and Faith*

John Henry Newman

People say to me that it is but a dream to suppose that Christianity should regain the organic power in human society which once it possessed. I cannot help that; I never said it could. I am not a politician; I am proposing no measures, but exposing a fallacy, and resisting a pretence. Let Benthamism reign if men have no aspirations; but do not tell them to be romantic, and then solace them with glory; do not attempt by philosophy what once was done by religion. The ascendancy of Faith may be impracticable, but the reign of Knowledge is incomprehensible. The problem for statesmen of this age is how to educate the masses, and literature and science cannot give the solution.

Not so deems Sir Robert Peel; his firm belief and hope is "that an increased sagacity will administer to an exalted faith; that it will make men not merely believe in the cold doctrines of Natural Religion, but that it will so prepare and temper the spirit and understanding, that they will be better qualified to comprehend the great scheme of human redemption." He certainly thinks that scientific pursuits have some considerable power of impressing religion upon the mind of the multitude. I think not, and will now say why.

Science gives us the grounds of premises from which religious truths are

* From *The Tamworth Reading Room,* 1841.

to be inferred; but it does not set about inferring them, much less does it reach the inference;—that is not its province. It brings before us phenomena, and it leaves us, if we will, to call them works of design, wisdom, or benevolence; and further still, if we will, to proceed to confess an Intelligent Creator. We have to take its facts, and to give them a meaning, and to draw our own conclusions from them. First comes Knowledge, then a view, then reasoning, and then belief. This is why Science has so little of a religious tendency; deductions have no power of persuasion. The heart is commonly reached, not through the reason, but through the imagination, by means of direct impressions, by the testimony of facts and events, by history, by description. Persons influence us, voices melt us, looks subdue us, deeds inflame us. Many a man will live and die upon a dogma: no man will be a martyr for a conclusion. A conclusion is but an opinion; it is not a thing which *is*, but which *we are "certain about"*; and it has often been observed, that we never say we are certain without implying that we doubt. To say that a thing *must* be, is to admit that it *may not* be. No one, I say, will die for his own calculations; he dies for realities. This is why a literary religion is so little to be depended upon; it looks well in fair weather, but its doctrines are opinions, and, when called to suffer for them, it slips them between its folios, or burns them at its hearth. And this again is the secret of the distrust and raillery with which moralists have been so commonly visited. They say and do not. Why? Because they are contemplating the fitness of things, and they live by the square, when they should be realizing their high maxims in the concrete. Now Sir Robert thinks better of natural history, chemistry, and astronomy, than of such ethics; but they too, what are they more than divinity *in posse?* He protests against "controversial divinity"; is *inferential* much better?

I have no confidence, then, in philosophers who cannot help being religious, and are Christians by implication. They sit at home, and reach forward to distances which astonish us; but they hit without grasping, and are sometimes as confident about shadows as about realities. They have worked out by a calculation the lie of a country which they never saw, and mapped it by means of a gazetteer; and like blind men, though they can put a stranger on his way, they cannot walk straight themselves, and do not feel it quite their business to walk at all.

Logic makes but a sorry rhetoric with the multitude; first shoot round corners, and you may not despair of converting by a syllogism. Tell men to gain notions of a Creator from His works, and, if they were to set about it (which nobody does), they would be jaded and wearied by the labyrinth they were tracing. Their minds would be gorged and surfeited by the logical operation. Logicians are more set upon concluding rightly, than on right conclusions. They cannot see the end for the process. Few men have that power of mind which may hold fast and firmly a variety of thoughts. We ridicule "men of one idea"; but a great many of us are born to be such, and we should be happier if we knew it. To most men argument makes the point in hand only more doubtful, and considerably less impressive. After all, man is *not* a reasoning animal; he is a seeing, feeling, contemplating, acting animal. He is influenced by what is direct and precise. It is very well to freshen our impressions and convictions from physics, but to create them we must go elsewhere. Sir Robert Peel "never can think it possible that a mind can be so constituted, that, after being familiarized with the wonderful discoveries which have been made in every part of experimental science, it can retire from such contemplations without more enlarged conceptions of God's providence, and a higher reverence for His name." If he speaks of religious minds, he perpetrates a truism; if of irreligious, he insinuates a paradox.

Life is not long enough for a religion of inferences; we shall never have done beginning, if we determine to begin with proof. We shall ever be laying our foundations; we shall turn theology into evidences, and divines into textuaries. We shall never get at our first principles. Resolve to believe nothing, and you must prove your proofs and analyze your elements, sinking further and further, and finding "in the lowest depths a lower deep," till you come to the broad bosom of skepticism. I would rather be bound to defend the reasonableness of assuming that Christianity is true, than to demonstrate a moral governance from the physical world. Life is for action. If we insist on proofs for everything, we shall never come to action: to act you must assume, and that assumption is faith.

Let no one suppose that in saying this I am maintaining that all proofs are equally difficult, and all propositions equally debatable. Some assumptions are greater than others, and some doctrines involve postulates larger than others, and more numerous. I only say that impressions lead to action, and that reasonings lead from it. Knowledge of premises, and inferences upon them,—this is not to *live*. It is very well as a matter of liberal curiosity and of philosophy to analyze our modes of thought; but let this come second, and when there is leisure for it, and then our examinations will in many ways even be subservient to action. But if we commence with scientific knowledge and argumentative proof, or lay any great stress upon it as the basis of personal Christianity, or attempt to make man moral and religious by Libraries and Museums, let us in consistency take chemists for our cooks, and mineralogists for our masons.

Now I wish to state all this as matter of fact, to be judged by the candid testimony of any persons whatever. Why we are so constituted that Faith, not Knowledge or Arguments, is our principle of action, is a question with which I have nothing to do; but I think it is a fact, and if it be such, we must resign ourselves to it as best we may, unless we take refuge in the intolerable paradox that the mass of men are created for nothing, and are meant to leave life as they entered it. So well has this practically been understood in all ages of the world, that no Religion has yet been a Religion of physics or of philosophy. It has ever been synonymous with Revelation. It never has been a deduction from what we know: it has ever been an assertion of what we are to believe. It has never lived in a conclusion; it has ever been a message, or a history, or a vision. No legislator or priest ever dreamed of educating our moral nature by science or by argument. There is no difference here between true religions and pretended. Moses was instructed, not to reason from the creation, but to work miracles. Christianity is a history, supernatural, and almost scenic: it tells us what its Author is, by telling us what He has done. . . .

When Sir Robert Peel assures us from the Town Hall at Tamworth that physical science must lead to religion, it is no bad compliment to him to say that he is unreal. He speaks of what he knows nothing about. To a religious man like him, Science has ever suggested religious thoughts; he colours the phenomena of physics with the hues of his own mind, and mistakes an interpretation for a deduction. "I am sanguine enough to believe," he says, "that that superior sagacity which is most conversant with the course and constitution of Nature will be first to turn a deaf ear to objections and presumptions against revealed religion, and to acknowledge the harmony of the Christian dispensation with all that reason, assisted by revelation, tells us of the course and constitution of Nature." Now, considering that we are all of us educated as Christians from infancy, it is not easy to decide at this day whether science creates faith, or only confirms it; but we have this remarkable fact in the history of heathen Greece against the former supposition, that her most eminent empirical philosophers were atheists, and that it was their atheism which was the cause of their eminence. "The natural philosophies of Democritus and others," says Lord Bacon, "*who allow no God or mind* in the frame of things, but attribute the structure of the universe to infinite essays and trials of nature, or what they call fate or fortune, and assigned the causes of particular things to the necessity of matter, *without any intermixture of final causes*, seems, as far as we can judge from the remains of their philosophy, *much more solid*, and to have *gone deeper into nature*, with regard to physical causes, than the philosophies of Aristotle or Plato: and this only because they *never meddled with final causes*, which the others were perpetually inculcating."

Lord Bacon gives us both the fact and the reason for it. Physical philosophers are ever inquiring *whence* things are, not *why*; referring them to nature, not to mind; and thus they tend to make a system a substitute for a God. Each pursuit or calling has its own dangers, and each numbers among its professors men who rise superior to them. As the soldier is tempted to dissipation, and the merchant to acquisitiveness, and the lawyer to the sophistical, and the statesman to the expedient, and the country clergyman to ease and comfort, yet there are good clergymen, statesmen, lawyers, merchants, and soldiers, notwithstanding; so there are religious experimentalists, though physics, taken by themselves, tend to infidelity; but to have recourse to physics to *make* men religious is like recommending a canonry as a cure for the gout, or giving a youngster a commission as a penance for irregularities.

The whole framework of Nature is confessedly a tissue of antecedents and consequences, we may refer all things forwards to design, or backwards on a physical cause. La Place is said to have considered he had a formula which solved all motions of the solar system; shall we say that those motions came from this formula or from a Divine Fiat? Shall we have recourse for our theory to physics or to theology? Shall we assume Matter and its necessary properties to be eternal, or Mind with its divine attributes? Does the sun shine to warm the earth, or is the earth warmed because the sun shines? The one hypothesis will solve the phenomena as well as the other. Say not it is but a puzzle in argument, and that no one ever felt it in fact. So far from it, I believe that the study of Nature, when religious feeling is away, leads the mind, rightly or wrongly, to acquiesce in the atheistic theory, as the simplest and easiest. It is but parallel to that tendency in anatomical studies, which no one will deny, to solve all the phenomena of the human frame into material elements and powers, and to dispense with the soul. To those who are conscious of matter, but not conscious of mind, it seems more rational to refer all things to one origin, such as they know, than to assume the existence of a second origin such as they know not. It is Religion, then, which suggests to Science its true conclusions; the facts come from Knowledge, but the principles come of Faith.

There are two ways, then, of reading Nature—as a machine and as a work. If we come to it with the assumption that it is a creation, we shall study it with awe; if assuming it to be a system, with mere curiosity. . . . The truth is that the system of Nature is just as much connected with religion, where minds are not religious, as a watch or a steam-carriage. The material world, indeed, is infinitely more wonderful than any human contrivance; but wonder is not religion, or we should be worshipping our railroads. What the physical creation presents to us in itself is a piece of machinery, and when men speak of a Divine Intelligence as its Author, this god of theirs is not the Living and True, unless the spring is the god of a watch, or steam the creator of the engine. Their idol, taken at advantage (though it is *not* an idol, for they do not worship it), is the animating principle of a vast and complicated system; it is subjected to laws, and it is connatural and co-extensive with matter. Well does Lord Brougham call it "the great architect of nature"; it is an instinct, or a soul of the world, or a vital power; it is not the Almighty God. . . .

I consider, then, that intrinsically excellent and noble as are scientific pursuits, and worthy of a place in a liberal education, and fruitful in temporal benefits to the community, still they are not, and cannot be, *the instrument* of an ethical training; that physics do not supply the basis, but only materials, for religious sentiment; that knowledge does but occupy, does not form, the mind; that apprehension of the unseen is the only known principle capable of subduing moral evil, educating the multitude, and organizing society; and that, whereas man is born for action, action flows not from inferences, but from impressions,—not from reasonings, but from Faith. . . .

STUDY QUESTIONS

1. What characteristic of human nature leads Newman to believe that religious belief performs a function which scientific belief cannot perform?
2. How do Newman and Huxley differ in their evaluation of logic and evidence?
3. What does Newman see as the proper relation between Knowledge and Religion? Would Balfour agree with Newman?
4. Who is the more democratic or the more concerned with humanity in general, Newman or Huxley?
5. Do you agree with Newman that reasoning and analysis lead away from action and serve merely to satisfy the curiosity?
6. Write a theme describing Newman's opinion of the limitation of science as a religious guide.

Man Against Darkness*

W. T. Stace

1

The Catholic bishops of America recently issued a statement in which they said that the chaotic and bewildered state of the modern world is due to man's loss of faith, his abandonment of God and religion. For my part I believe in no religion at all. Yet I entirely agree with the bishops. It is no doubt an oversimplification to speak of *the* cause of so complex a state of affairs as the tortured condition of the world today. Its causes are doubtless multitudinous. Yet allowing for some element of oversimplification, I say that the bishops' assertion is substantially true.

M. Jean-Paul Sartre, the French existentialist philosopher, labels himself an atheist. Yet his views seem to me plainly to support the statement of the bishops. So long as there was believed to be a God in the sky, he says, men could regard him as the source of their moral ideals. The uni-

* From *The Atlantic Monthly*, September, 1948. By permission of Walter T. Stace.

verse, created and governed by a fatherly God, was a friendly habitation for man. We could be sure that, however great the evil in the world, good in the end would triumph and the forces of evil would be routed. With the disappearance of God from the sky all this has changed. Since the world is not ruled by a spiritual being, but rather by blind forces, there cannot be any ideals, moral or otherwise, in the universe outside us. Our ideals, therefore, must proceed only from our own minds; they are our own inventions. Thus the world which surrounds us is nothing but an immense spiritual emptiness. It is a dead universe. We do not live in a universe which is on the side of our values. It is completely indifferent to them.

Years ago Mr. Bertrand Russell, in his essay *A Free Man's Worship*, said much the same thing.

Such in outline, but even more purposeless, more void of meaning, is the world which Science presents for our belief. Amid such a world, if anywhere, our ideals henceforward must find a home. . . . Blind to good and evil, reckless of destruction, omnipotent matter rolls on its relentless way; for man, condemned today to lose his dearest, tomorrow himself to pass through the gate of darkness, it remains only to cherish, ere yet the blow falls, the lofty thoughts that ennoble his little day; . . . to worship at the shrine his own hands have built; . . . to sustain alone, a weary but unyielding Atlas, the world that his own ideals have fashioned despite the trampling march of unconscious power.

It is true that Mr. Russell's personal attitude to the disappearance of religion is quite different from either that of M. Sartre or the bishops or myself. The bishops think it a calamity. So do I. M. Sartre finds it "very distressing." And he berates as shallow the attitude of those who think that without God the world can go on just the same as before, as if nothing had happened. This creates for mankind, he thinks, a terrible crisis. And in this I agree with him. Mr. Russell, on the other hand, seems to believe that religion has done more harm than good in the world, and that its disappearance will be a blessing. But his picture of the world, and of the modern mind, is the same as that of M. Sartre. He stresses the *purposelessness* of the universe, the facts that man's ideals are his own creations, that the universe outside nim in no way supports them, that man is alone and friendless in the world.

Mr. Russell notes that it is science which has produced this situation. There is no doubt that this is correct. But the way in which it has come about is not generally understood. There is a popular belief that some particular scientific discoveries or theories, such as the Darwinian theory of evolution, or the views of geologists about the age of the earth, or a series of such discoveries, have done the damage. It would be foolish to deny that these discoveries have had a great effect in undermining religious dogmas. But this account does not at all go to the root of the matter. Religion can probably outlive any scientific discoveries which could be made. It can accommodate itself to them. The root cause of the decay of faith has not been any particular discovery of science, but rather the general spirit of science and certain basic assumptions upon which modern science, from the seventeenth century onwards, has proceeded.

2

It was Galileo and Newton—notwithstanding that Newton himself was a deeply religious man—who destroyed the old comfortable picture of a friendly universe governed by spiritual values. And this was effected, not by Newton's discovery of the law of gravitation nor by any of Galileo's brilliant investigations, but by the general picture of the world which these men and others of their time made the basis of the science, not only of their own day, but of all succeeding generations down to the present. That is why the century immediately following Newton, the eighteenth century, was notoriously an age of religious skepticism. Skepticism did not have to wait for the discoveries of Darwin and the geologists in the nineteenth century. It flooded the world immediately after the age of the rise of science.

Neither the Copernican hypothesis nor any of Newton's or Galileo's particular discoveries were the real causes. Religious faith might well have accommodated itself to the new astronomy. The real turning point between the medieval age of faith and the modern age of unfaith came when the scientists of the seventeenth century turned their backs upon what used to be called "final causes." The final cause of a thing or event meant the purpose which it was supposed to serve in the universe, its cosmic purpose. What lay back of this was the presupposition that there is a cosmic order or plan and that everything which exists could in the last analysis be explained in terms of its place in this cosmic plan, that is, in terms of its purpose.

Plato and Aristotle believed this, and so did the whole medieval Christian world. For instance, if it were true that the sun and the moon were created and exist for the purpose of giving light to man, then this fact would explain why the sun and the moon exist. We might not be able to discover the purpose of everything, but everything must have a purpose. Belief in final causes thus amounted to a belief that the world is governed by purposes, presumably the purposes of some overruling mind. This belief was not the invention of Christianity. It was basic to the whole of Western civilization, whether in the ancient pagan world or in Christendom, from the time of Socrates to the rise of science in the seventeenth century.

The founders of modern science—for instance, Galileo, Kepler, and Newton—were mostly pious men who did not doubt God's purposes. Nevertheless they took the revolutionary step of consciously and deliberately expelling the idea of purpose as controlling nature from their new science of nature. They did this on the ground that inquiry into purposes is useless for what science aims at: namely, the prediction and control of events. To predict an eclipse, what you have to know is not its purpose but its causes. Hence science from the seventeenth century onwards became exclusively an inquiry into causes. The conception of purpose in the world was ignored and frowned on. This, though silent and almost unnoticed, was the greatest revolution in human history, far outweighing in importance any of the political revolutions whose thunder has reverberated through the world.

For it came about in this way that for the past three hundred years there has been growing up in men's minds, dominated as they are by science, a new imaginative picture of the world. The world, according to this new picture, is purposeless, senseless, meaningless. Nature is nothing but matter in motion. The motions of matter are governed, not by any purpose, but by blind forces and laws. Nature on this view, says Whitehead—to whose writings I am indebted in this part of my paper—is "merely the hurrying of material, endlessly, meaninglessly." You can draw a sharp line across the history of Europe dividing it into two epochs of very unequal length. The line passes through the lifetime of Galileo. European man before Galileo—whether ancient pagan or more recent Christian—thought of the world as controlled by plan and purpose. After Galileo European man thinks of it as utterly purposeless. This is the great revolution of which I spoke.

It is this which has killed religion. Religion could survive the discoveries that the sun, not the earth, is the center; that men are descended from simian ancestors; that the earth is hundreds of millions of years old. These discoveries may render out of date some of the details of older theological dogmas, may force their restatement in new intellectual frameworks. But they do not touch the essence of the religious vision itself, which is the faith that there is plan and purpose in the world, that the world is a moral order, that in the end all things are for the best. This faith may express itself through many different intellectual dogmas, those of Christianity, of Hinduism, of Islam. All and any of these intellectual dogmas may be destroyed without destroying the essential religious spirit. But that spirit cannot survive destruction of belief in a plan and purpose of the world, for that is the very heart of it. Religion can get on with any sort of astronomy, geology, biology, physics. But it cannot get on with a purposeless and meaningless universe.

If the scheme of things is purposeless and meaningless, then the life of man is purposeless and meaningless too. Everything is futile, all effort is in the end worthless. A man may, of course, still pursue disconnected ends, money, fame, art, science, and may gain pleasure from them. But his life is hollow at the center. Hence the dissatisfied, disillusioned, restless spirit of modern man.

The picture of a meaningless world, and a meaningless human life, is, I think, the basic theme of much modern art and literature. Certainly it is the basic theme of modern philosophy. According to the most characteristic philosophies of the modern period from Hume in the eighteenth century to the so-called positivists of today, the world is just what it is, and that is the end of all inquiry. There is no reason for its being what it is. Everything might just as well have been quite different, and there would have been no reason for that either. When you have stated what things are, what things the world contains, there is nothing more which could be said, even by an omniscient being. To ask any question about *why* things are thus, or what purpose their being so serves, is to ask a senseless question, because they serve no purpose at all. For instance, there is for modern philosophy no such thing as the ancient problem of evil. For this once famous question presupposes that pain and misery, though they seem so inexplicable and irrational to us, must ultimately subserve some rational purpose, must have their places in the cosmic plan. But this is nonsense. There is no such overruling rationality in the universe. Belief in the ultimate irrationality of everything is the quintessence of what is called the modern mind.

It is true that, parallel with these philosophies which are typical of the modern mind, preaching the meaninglessness of the world, there has run a line of idealistic philosophies whose contention is that the world is after all spiritual in nature and that moral ideals and values are inherent in its structure. But most of these idealisms were simply philosophical expressions of romanticism, which was itself no more than an unsuccessful counter-attack of the religious against the scientific view of things. They perished, along with romanticism in literature and art, about the beginning of the present century, though of course they still have a few adherents.

At the bottom these idealistic systems of thought were rationalizations of man's wishful thinking. They were born of the refusal of men to admit the cosmic darkness. They were comforting illusions within the warm glow of which the more tender-minded intellectuals sought to shelter themselves from the icy winds of the universe. They lasted a little while. But they are shattered now, and we return once more to the vision of a purposeless world.

3

Along with the ruin of the religious vision there went the ruin of moral principles and indeed of all values. If there is a cosmic purpose, if there is in the nature of things a drive towards goodness, then our moral systems will derive their validity from this. But if our moral rules do not proceed from something outside us in the nature of the universe—whether we say it is God or simply the universe itself—then they must be our own inventions. Thus it came to be believed that moral rules must be merely an expression of our own likes and dislikes. But likes and dislikes are notoriously variable. What pleases one man, people, or culture displeases another. Therefore morals are wholly relative.

This obvious conclusion from the idea of a purposeless world made its appearance in Europe immediately after the rise of science, for instance in the philosophy of Hobbes. Hobbes saw at once that if there is no purpose in the world there are no values either. "Good and evil," he writes, "are names that signify our appetites and aversions; which in different tempers, customs, and doctrines of men are different. . . . Every man calleth that which pleaseth him, good; and that which displeaseth him, evil."

This doctrine of the relativity of morals, though it has recently received an impetus from the studies of anthropologists, was thus really implicit in the whole scientific mentality. It is disastrous for morals because it destroys their entire traditional foundation. That is why philosophers who see the danger signals, from the time at least of Kant, have been trying to give to morals a new foundation, that is, a secular or nonreligious foundation. This attempt may very well be intellectually successful. Such a foundation, independent of the religious view of the world, might well be found. But the question is whether it can ever be a *practical* success, that is whether apart from its logical validity and its influence with intellectuals, it can ever replace among the masses of men the lost religious foundation. On that question hangs perhaps the future of civilization. But meanwhile disaster is overtaking us.

The widespread belief in "ethical relativity" among philosophers, psychologists, ethnologists, and sociologists is the theoretical counterpart of the repudiation of principle which we see all around us, especially in international affairs, the field in which morals have always had the weakest foothold. No one any longer effectively believes in moral principles except as the private prejudices either of individual men or of nations or cultures. This is the inevitable consequence of the doctrine of ethical relativity, which in turn is the inevitable consequence of believing in a purposeless world.

Another characteristic of our spiritual state is loss of belief in the freedom of the will. This also is a fruit of the scientific spirit, though not of any particular scientific discovery. Science has been built up on the basis of determinism, which is the belief that every event is completely determined by a chain of causes and is therefore theoretically predictable beforehand. It is true that recent physics seems to challenge this. But so far as its practical consequences are concerned, the damage has long ago been done. A man's actions, it was argued, are as much events in the natural world as is an eclipse of the sun. It follows that men's actions are as theoretically predictable as an eclipse. But if it is certain now that John Smith will murder Joseph Jones at 2.15 P.M. on January 1, 1963, what possible meaning can it have to say that when that time comes John

Smith will be *free* to choose whether he will commit the murder or not? And if he is not free, how can he be held responsible?

It is true that the whole of this argument can be shown by a competent philosopher to be a tissue of fallacies—or at least I claim that it can. But the point is that the analysis required to show this is much too subtle to be understood by the average entirely unphilosophical man. Because of this, the argument against free will is generally swallowed whole by the unphilosophical. Hence the thought that man is not free, that he is the helpless plaything of forces over which he has no control, has deeply penetrated the modern mind. We hear of economic determinism, cultural determinism, historical determinism. We are not responsible for what we do because our glands control us, or because we are the products of environment or heredity. Not moral self-control, but the doctor, the psychiatrist, the educationist, must save us from doing evil. Pills and injections in the future are to do what Christ and the prophets have failed to do. Of course I do not mean to deny that doctors and educationists can and must help. And I do not mean in any way to belittle their efforts. But I do wish to draw attention to the weakening of moral controls, the greater or less repudiation of personal responsibility which, in the popular thinking of the day, result from these tendencies of thought.

4

What, then, is to be done? Where are we to look for salvation from the evils of our time? All the remedies I have seen suggested so far are, in my opinion, useless. Let us look at some of them.

Philosophers and intellectuals generally can, I believe, genuinely do something to help. But it is extremely little. What philosophers can do is to show that neither the relativity of morals nor the denial of free will really follows from the grounds which have been supposed to support them. They can also try to discover a genuine secular basis for morals to replace the religious basis which has disappeared. Some of us are trying to do these things. But in the first place philosophers unfortunately are not agreed about these matters, and their disputes are utterly confusing to non-philosophers. And in the second place their influence is practically negligible because their analyses necessarily take place on a level on which the masses are totally unable to follow them.

The bishops, of course, propose as remedy a return to belief in God and in the doctrines of the Christian religion. Others think that a new religion is what is needed. Those who make these proposals fail to realize that the crisis in man's spiritual condition is something unique in history for which there is no sort of analogy in the past. They are thinking perhaps of the collapse of the ancient Greek and Roman religions. The vacuum then created was easily filled by Christianity, and it might have been filled by Mithraism if Christianity had not appeared. By analogy they think that

Christianity might now be replaced by a new religion, or even that Christianity itself, if revivified, might bring back health to men's lives.

But I believe that there is no analogy at all between our present state and that of the European peoples at the time of the fall of paganism. Men had at that time lost their belief only in particular dogmas, particular embodiments of the religious view of the world. It had no doubt become incredible that Zeus and the other gods were living on the top of Mount Olympus. You could go to the top and find no trace of them. But the imaginative picture of a world governed by purpose, a world driving towards the good—which is the inner spirit of religion—had at that time received no serious shock. It had merely to re-embody itself in new dogmas, those of Christianity or some other religion. Religion itself was not dead in the world, only a particular form of it.

But now the situation is quite different. It is not merely that particular dogmas, like that of the virgin birth, are unacceptable to the modern mind. That is true, but it constitutes a very superficial diagnosis of the present situation of religion. Modern skepticism is of a wholly different order from that of the intellectuals of the ancient world. It has attacked and destroyed not merely the outward forms of the religious spirit, its particularized dogmas, but the very essence of that spirit itself, belief in a meaningful and purposeful world. For the founding of a new religion a new Jesus Christ or Buddha would have to appear, in itself a most unlikely event and one for which in any case we cannot afford to sit and wait. But even if a new prophet and a new religion did appear, we may predict that they would fail in the modern world. No one for long would believe in them, for modern men have lost the vision, basic to all religion, of an ordered plan and purpose of the world. They have before their minds the picture of a purposeless universe, and such a world-picture must be fatal to any religion at all, not merely to Christianity.

We must not be misled by occasional appearances of a revival of the religious spirit. Men, we are told, in their disgust and disillusionment at the emptiness of their lives, are turning once more to religion, or are searching for a new message. It may be so. We must expect such wistful yearnings of the spirit. We must expect men to wish back again the light that is gone, and to try to bring it back. But however they may wish and try, the light will not shine again,—not at least in the civilization to which we belong.

Another remedy commonly proposed is that we should turn to science itself, or the scientific spirit, for our salvation. Mr. Russell and Professor Dewey both make this proposal, though in somewhat different ways. Professor Dewey seems to believe that discoveries in sociology, the application of scientific method to social and political problems, will rescue us. This seems to me to be utterly naïve. It is not likely that science, which is basically the cause of our spiritual troubles, is likely also to produce the cure for them. Also it lies in the nature of science that, though it can teach us the best means for achieving our ends, it can never tell us what ends to pursue. It cannot give us any ideals. And our trouble is about ideals and ends, not about the means for reaching them.

5

No civilization can live without ideals, or to put it in another way, without a firm faith in moral ideas. Our ideals and moral ideas have in the past been rooted in religion. But the religious basis of our ideals has been undermined, and the superstructure of ideals is plainly tottering. None of the commonly suggested remedies on examination seems likely to succeed. It would therefore look as if the early death of our civilization were inevitable.

Of course we know that it is perfectly possible for individual men, very highly educated men, philosophers, scientists, intellectuals in general, to live moral lives without any religious convictions. But the question is whether a whole civilization, a whole family of peoples, composed almost entirely of relatively uneducated men and women, can do this.

It follows, of course, that if we could make the vast majority of men as highly educated as the very few are now, we might save the situation. And we are already moving slowly in that direction through the techniques of mass education. But the critical question seems to concern the time-lag. Perhaps in a few hundred years most of the population will, at the present rate, be sufficiently highly educated and civilized to combine high ideals with an absence of religion. But long before we reach any such stage, the collapse of our civilization may have come about. How are we to live through the intervening period?

I am sure that the first thing we have to do is to face the truth, however bleak it may be, and then next we have to learn to live with it. Let me say a word about each of these two points. What I am urging as regards the first is complete honesty. Those who wish to resurrect Christian dogmas are not, of course, consciously dishonest But they have that kind of unconscious dishonesty which consists in lulling oneself with opiates and dreams. Those who talk of a new religion are merely hoping for a new opiate. Both alike refuse to face the truth that there is, in the universe outside man, no spirituality, no regard for values, no friend in the sky, no help or comfort for man of any sort. To be perfectly honest in the admission of this fact, not to seek shelter in new or old illusions, not to indulge in wishful dreams about this matter, this is the first thing we shall have to do.

I do not urge this course out of any special regard for the sanctity of truth in the abstract. It is not self-evident to me that truth is the supreme value to which all else must be sacrificed. Might not the discoverer of a truth which would be fatal to mankind be justified in suppressing it, even in teaching men a falsehood? Is truth more valuable than goodness and beauty and happiness? To think so is to invent yet another absolute, another religious delusion in which Truth with a capital T is substituted for God. The reason why we must now boldly and honestly face the truth that the universe is non-spiritual and indifferent to goodness, beauty, happiness, or truth is not that it would be wicked to suppress it, but simply that it is too late to do so, so that in the end we cannot do anything else but face it. Yet we stand on the brink, dreading the icy plunge. We need courage. We need honesty.

Now about the other point, the necessity of learning to live with the truth. This means learning to live virtuously and happily, or at least contentedly, without illusions. And this is going to be extremely difficult because what we have now begun dimly to perceive is that human life in the past, or at least human happiness, has almost wholly depended upon illusions. It has been said that man lives by truth, and that the truth will make us free. Nearly the opposite seems to me to be the case. Mankind has managed to live only by means of lies, and the truth may very well destroy us. If one were a Bergsonian one might believe that nature deliberately puts illusions into our souls in order to induce us to go on living.

The illusions by which men have lived seem to be of two kinds. First, there is what one may perhaps call the Great Illusion—I mean the religious illusion that the universe is moral and good, that it follows a wise and noble plan, that it is gradually generating some supreme value, that goodness is bound to triumph in it. Secondly, there is a whole host of minor illusions on which human happiness nourishes itself. How much of human happiness notoriously comes from the illusions of the lover about his beloved? Then again we work and strive because of the illusions connected with fame, glory, power, or money. Banners of all kinds, flags, emblems, insignia, ceremonials, and rituals are invariably symbols of some illusion or other. The British Empire, the connection between mother country and dominions, is partly kept going by illusions surrounding the notion of kingship. Or think of the vast amount of human happiness which is derived from the illusion of supposing that if some nonsense syllable, such as "sir" or "count" or "lord" is pronounced in conjunction with our names, we belong to a superior order of people.

There is plenty of evidence that human happiness is almost wholly based upon illusions of one kind or another. But the scientific spirit, or the spirit of truth, is the enemy of illusions and therefore the enemy of human happiness. That is why it is going to be so difficult to live with the truth.

There is no reason why we should have to give up the host of minor illusions which render life supportable. There is no reason why the lover should be scientific about the loved one. Even the illusions of fame and glory may persist. But without the Great Illusion, the illusion of a good, kindly, and purposeful universe, we shall *have* to learn to live. And to ask this is really no more than to ask that we become genuinely civilized beings and not merely sham civilized beings.

I can best explain the difference by a reminiscence. I remember a fellow student in my college days, an ardent Christian, who told me that if he did not believe in a future life, in heaven and hell, he would rape, murder, steal, and be a drunkard. That is what I call being a sham civilized being. On the other hand, not only could a Huxley, a John Stuart Mill, a David Hume, live great and fine lives without any religion, but a great many others of us, quite obscure persons, can at least live decent lives without it.

To be genuinely civilized means to be able to walk straightly and to live honorably without the props and crutches of one or another of the childish dreams which have so far supported men. That such a life is likely to be ecstatically happy I will not claim. But that it can be lived in quiet content, accepting resignedly what cannot be helped, not expecting the impossible, and thankful for small mercies, this I would maintain. That it will be difficult for men in general to learn this lesson I do not deny. But that it will be impossible I would not admit since so many have learned it already.

Man has not yet grown up. He is not adult. Like a child he cries for the moon and lives in a world of fantasies. And the race as a whole has perhaps reached the great crisis of its life. Can it grow up as a race in the same sense as individual men grow up? Can man put away childish things and adolescent dreams? Can he grasp the real world as it actually is, stark and bleak, without its romantic or religious halo, and still retain his ideals, striving for great ends and noble achievements? If he can, all may yet be well. If he cannot, he will probably sink back into savagery and brutality from which he came, taking a humble place once more among the lower animals.

STUDY QUESTIONS

1. In what way, according to Stace, did the development of science undermine religious belief? How did this lead to a destruction of moral values?

2. What does Stace see as the essential difference between the present situation in religion and that which obtained at the time of the decline of the pagan beliefs?

3. Although he feels that civilization can survive only if the mass of humanity is either religious or highly educated, Stace does not explain how an intense degree of education can become a substitute for religion. Can you explain this point?

4. Why does Stace think Truth is overrated? Are there any good arguments against his view?

5. Do you agree with Stace that religion has begun an inevitable decline? Write a theme in which you offer evidence for or against

his view, and follow this up by explaining what beliefs about the nature of the universe, the soul, immortality, the nature and existence of God, and the existence of evil underlie the condition you have described.

6. Discuss Stace's observation that ". . . human life in the past, or at least human happiness has almost wholly depended upon illusions."

The Justification of Belief*

Edwyn Bevan

You cannot, as some agnostics have supposed you can, keep simply to the ground of ascertained facts and make no leap off it into unprovable hypothesis. Supposing we were spectators only of reality, and not also makers of it, it might be possible to remain purely agnostic; but the moment you act, you have to be guided by some judgment of value, you have to take some realizable end as good, as something which ought to be or which satisfies desire. And the question what is good, what ought to be, depends very much on the question: What kind of universe is this, what is the Ground behind the phenomena? Reason, as inferring an unseen part of the world's design from parts of the design already known, can give you, as we have seen, no ground for a logically cogent inference from the world-design as a whole to what is behind and beyond it. Any hypothesis you adopt about the Ground of the world is a venture beyond experience, and yet the unarrestable advance of time pushes you, every moment of your conscious life, willy-nilly into action of some kind, and action necessarily presupposes some hypothesis regarding the Ground of the Universe. You are not securing yourself against the possibility of mistake if you decide to act on the hypothesis that there is no God, that the Ground of the Universe is wholly indifferent to the values which the spirit of man recognizes. You are acting just as much on an unproved hypothesis as the man who adjusts his action to belief that God is. And your action may turn out to have been defective because your hypothesis was wrong.

Of course it may be said that, quite apart from any hypothesis regarding the Ground of the Universe or the spiritual world, if one exists, around man on earth, there is a large measure of agreement among all men regarding what things are good, what are worthy ends of action. To take the proper steps to secure your health, to control your natural impulses according to some norm of conduct or other, to do whatever you can to

* From Edwyn Bevan, *Symbolism and Belief*. Reprinted by permission of George Allen & Unwin, Ltd., London, and of the Beacon Press, Boston.

secure for your neighbour, or for as many of your neighbours as your circumstances allow, an adequate share in the good things of life, to give your support to all movements for bringing about a happier state of the world, to pursue some particular activity which is of value to society, the increase of scientific knowledge by your specialist researches, the production of beautiful things in art or literature—all these kinds of action, it may be said, are recognized as good by everybody alike, by Christians and Jews and atheists, and the recognition furnishes a sufficient guide for life without dragging in any hypothesis about the Ground of the Universe.

Now it is of course true that the norm of conduct which determines the customs of people living in any society like ours is, for a good part of life, the same for everybody: even heroic actions outside the course of everyday routine may be recognized as good alike by a Christian and an atheist. Either of them might jump into the water at the risk of his own life to save someone from drowning. But it would be a perfunctory view to which the belief in God or in a spiritual world seemed to make no difference to conduct. In the first place, although a large number of actions would be recognized as good by Christians and atheists alike, critical problems of conduct very often arise in regard to which the decision what is good will differ very much according as you believe, or do not believe, in a spiritual Ground to the Universe and according to the idea you have of that Ground. There is no grosser confusion of thought than to say, for instance, that it does not make any practical difference whether there is, or is not, a future life, because it is nobler to act rightly without any prospect of satisfaction beyond death than to act rightly with such a prospect. What anyone uttering such a thought fails to see is that the rightness or goodness of an action is not something attached to that particular kind of action altogether apart from its connexion with the subsequent life of the agent, but in many cases essentially depends upon the anticipation to which it is adapted. If I am going on a long journey to-morrow it may be a reasonable action for me to spend a great part of to-day in packing my trunks: you cannot argue from that that it would be a much finer action if I were *not* going on a journey, and nevertheless spent a great part of to-day in packing my trunks. It is not a question of doing the same action, labelled "right" or "good," in the one case with a prospect of happy future consequences and in the other case without; it is that the question, What *is* right action? may depend on the future which is envisaged. As I have just admitted, there are a large number of actions which would be recognized as good whether there is a future life or not; it may be plausible (though I do not think true) in regard to these to say that belief in a future life makes no difference; but there are critical decisions when it actually determines a different course of action.

The difference which belief in a spiritual Ground to the Universe makes in conduct is not merely that in a certain number of cases a different form of action would follow according as you believe or do not believe; it is that even where the same form of action would be prescribed by the Christian norm and by atheist ethics, there would be a difference in the temper and mode of feeling accompanying the action, the inner spiritual background. And our actual value-judgment in regard to actions is determined more by their inner spiritual background than by what they are externally and formally. It must, one would think, act depressingly upon a man's moral energy, if he thinks that all his standards of what is good are simply modes of feeling which happen to have been developed in man, and that the great universe in which he lives is wholly indifferent to them. A man may determine indeed to adjust his own conduct to those values—to justice and honour and lovingkindness and truth and beauty—in the midst of a universe whose processes will sooner or later annihilate them all, make all things, in the eternal night wherein masses of matter will for ever rush through space without purpose, to be as if such values had never been, a man may follow the brief light of his candle during his days on earth by a defiant resolution. Stoical we must not call such an attitude, since for Stoicism it was an essential belief that the values recognized by man were derived from the Divine Wisdom which ruled the whole universe, the Wisdom of which the light in each man was a spark. It is an attitude which may have in it something of self-conscious defiance, the head "bloody but unbow'd" of a well-known poem.

But is it really to follow the nobler hypothesis about the universe? To be loyal to human values, as if they had an absolute claim upon one, while one attributes to the encompassing universe complete indifference to such values, may seem heroic, but, supposing the universe is not indifferent to such values, supposing its Ground is really Spirit whose character the values recognized by the human spirit reflect, will it ultimately seem to have been a fine thing to adopt the drearier hypothesis about the universe simply in order that you might follow goodness in spite of it? If that is a good reason for choosing the drearier hypothesis, why not go one better and choose the hypothesis that the universe is not merely indifferent, but is actually ruled by a malignant will, a will that loves what, according to man's system of values, is evil? To follow goodness then would be still more heroic. Just as now those who believe that God is good explain all the elements of evil in the universe as permitted by God because they subserve some ultimate good, or because a universe in which their occurrence is possible realizes a greater total good than a universe in which such evils were impossible, so you might then explain all the appearances of good in the world as ordained by the governing power to realize a completer evil, the idea of values put into the human spirit simply to delude and lead to a more exquisite misery in the end.

What would make everyone recoil from such an hypothesis as unthinkable? Not, I think, that a view of the world based on it was logically incoherent: I think you might invent one quite as logically coherent as the view that the Ground of the world is perfect goodness, for, after all, no one has succeeded in reconciling the goodness of God with the existence of evil in the world in a way which leaves no logical difficulty. What would make everyone recoil is, I think, partly the remains in men's subconsciousness of a very deep conviction that the world is reasonable in the sense that it *is* such as to promote value, at any rate the feeling that there is something in the nature of things to forbid such a hideous reversal of the order corresponding with value as a malignant Ground to the universe would be, and partly that to adopt a horrible hypothesis arbitrarily, when you are not forced to it by convincing evidence, simply in order to make your heroism shine out more signally on a blacker background, would seem to everyone absurd.

But if you adopt the hypothesis that the world surrounding man is indifferent to values you are in that case too adopting a dreary hypothesis without being forced to it by the evidence. You can no more prove that the world is indifferent to values than you can prove that behind it is a Power which cares for goodness: in the sense of a rational inference from a seen to an unseen part of the universe on the basis of the ascertained pattern, you cannot prove any hypothesis about that which is not a part of the pattern, but the Ground of it. You can only say: Some hypothesis regarding the Ground the necessity of action compels me to adopt: this is the one I choose to live by. If you determine to live by the faith that the Ground of the universe is Spirit, and that the values which man recognizes are the revelation of that Spirit's character, there is likely to be more buoyancy and drive in your fight for goodness and truth and beauty, in the world around you and in yourself, against all the things which militate for wrong and falsehood and ugliness. To feel that the battle for good is ultimately a losing one in an indifferent universe may make your battle, if you persist, the more admirable, but the confidence that the battle will be victorious in the long run, that you are fighting with the universe on your side, or rather that you are fighting on the side of God, may give a spiritual quality to your fight even more admirable than heroic despair. After all there will still be opportunities for heroism enough, if you seek them, in standing against the evil which seems, by all the appearances of the hour, to tower triumphant.

> To suffer woes which hope thinks infinite;
> To forgive wrongs darker than death or night;
> To defy power which seems omnipotent;
> To love and bear; to hope till hope creates
> From its own wreck the thing it contemplates;
> Neither to change, nor falter, nor repent;
> This, like thy glory, Titan, is to be
> Good, great and joyous, beautiful and free:
> This is alone Life, Joy, Empire and Victory!

It is true that the writer of those lines professed not to believe in a personal God; but Shelley's jubilant utterance was possible only because he did believe that the Ground of the Universe was spiritual in the sense of his hazy Platonism; Prometheus was to be ultimately *victorious*. We may question whether such a hope as Shelley entertained has any substance apart from belief in God. In any case, the fight for good, as Shelley saw it, was not a battle destined in the end to be a lost one in an indifferent universe. If you rule out the Christian confidence in the Power behind phenomena because it is nobler to fight without any supposition that you have the universe on the same side, then you must rule out Shelley's view of the heroic life too.

It is unquestionable that those human Figures who are generally recognized to be the most spiritually impressive, to begin with Jesus himself, do not show the heroism of despair, but a serenity of absolute confidence in the centre of their activity, a quiet and joy which is their commanding strength. Men have the option before them of two views of the ultimate ground of things, one that it is spiritual with a care for the values recognized by the human spirit, the other that it is some kind of physical law, or set of laws, wholly indifferent to values, whether it is in any sense like Mind or not; neither is a view of the universe capable of being demonstrated as a conclusive rational inference from phenomena; some men elect to choose the former hypothesis when they launch out into action, some elect to choose the latter. Why, it may be asked, without being shut up to it, should men choose the drearier hypothesis? One reason probably is that if you are going to take a hypothesis for action which goes beyond what can be rationally demonstrated, it seems less of a venture to suppose that behind physical law there is nothing but a blank than to suppose that there is something of so positive a character as God. To act on the hypothesis that the Ground of the Universe is God, when you have no conclusive proof that God exists, seems a more unwarrantable building on vain imagination than to act on the hypothesis of a blank when you have no conclusive proof of a blank. In the one case you fill the void with your fanciful idea of God; in the other case you simply leave a void. The negative hypothesis seems to be, as men say, the "safer" one.

I think that in this way of thought there is really a confusion between what holds good of a purely speculative problem, in which no question of action is involved, and what holds good of alternative hypotheses for action. In the case of a purely speculative problem, if no hypothesis is demonstrable, you can practise complete suspense of judgment. You can say that it is "safer" not to adopt any unproved supposition. The "danger" to be avoided—for the word "safer" of course points to some possible danger—is the danger of turning out to have been deceived. If you have withheld your belief from the unproved hypothesis you cannot turn out to have believed something untrue; you are uncommitted; you are in that respect safe.

But if you have to choose between two alternative hypotheses for action, you are no "safer" because the hypothesis you adopt is the negative one—because, that is to say, the existence of something being undemonstrated, you determine to disregard in action the possibility of its existing, to act as if it did not exist. Action commits you: suspense of judgment is no longer possible, or, rather, to suspend your judgment in theory is to commit yourself to the definitely negative judgment in practice. Thus it is just as possible for your action to turn out in the end to have been misdirected because it was based on the supposition that something did not exist which does exist, as for your action to turn out in the end to have been misdirected because it was based on the supposition that something existed which does not exist. If you have in practice to deal with a man and you have to act either on the hypothesis that he is trustworthy or on the hypothesis that he is not, you may, it is true, prove to have been deceived if you trust him and he turns out to be untrustworthy, but you may also prove to have made a mistake with unhappy consequences if you refuse to trust him and he turns out to be trustworthy. A man who has acted all his life on the hypothesis that the universe is governed by a good God may look foolish if it turns out that the universe outside man is wholly indifferent to values—though it may be asked to whom his foolishness will appear, since, on the atheistic hypothesis in its usual form, the ingenuous believer will cease altogether to exist at death, and by the time that the non-existence of God is demonstrated, it is likely that he will have been in his grave for a good many ages and long forgotten by everybody—but equally a man who has acted all his life on the supposition that there is no God will look foolish if in the end God confronts him. In action there is no possibility of "safety" in the sense of security from the danger of turning out in the end to have been mistaken. And act we all of us must, pushed by the onward unarrestable movement of time: as Pascal said, whether we like it or not, *"il faut parier."*

Perhaps however when people think that to disregard in action the supposition of God's existing is "safer," it is not that they fail to recognize a possibility of mistake either way; it is that it seems a worse mistake to adopt the optimistic hypothesis and prove in the end mistaken, than to adopt the pessimistic hypothesis and prove in the end mistaken. It is, in their view, the man who has thought too well of the universe who would appear the more foolish if he turned out wrong, not the man who has not thought well enough of the universe. Should we say, though, in regard to our human relations, that it is in all cases a greater evil to have trusted someone who was untrustworthy than not to have trusted someone who was trustworthy? Would not the pain of the man who has been taken in by a rogue be less bitter than the pain which a man who had failed to trust a friend would feel, when ocular proofs that the friend had been trustworthy came to light and he recognized the true application of the saying: "Blessed are they that have not seen and yet have believed"?

It has been contended throughout this discussion that neither the hypothesis that the Power behind the Universe is a spiritual Power which cares for values nor the hypothesis that the universe is indifferent to values can be demonstrated, that both the believer and the atheist or agnostic act upon an unproved hypothesis, make a leap beyond experience. But if the statement were left at that, it would be open to two definite misconstructions. One misconstruction would be taking it to mean that the man's choice of a hypothesis to live by is purely arbitrary, in the sense that he has no reason at all for choosing it. All that has been asserted is that neither hypothesis can be demonstrated with logical necessity, as a proposition in mathematics can be demonstrated, or as a rational inference, regarding the existence of something unseen, made from something known, on the basis of a knowledge of the pattern of the universe. But because the ground on which a man acts does not reach mathematical certainty, and does not have conclusiveness of the same kind as a rational inference based on knowledge of the pattern, that does not mean that the man acts without any ground at all. If there were nothing at all in the world we know by experience and trustworthy report to point to a spiritual Reality behind phenomena, to God and to the permanence of the soul, then to adopt quite arbitrarily the hypothesis that God is and that the soul is not involved in material decay, simply because we find it pleasant to believe these things, would hardly be the proper act of a reasonable creature. But, as a matter of fact, there are many manifestations of Spirit in the world we know which do point to Spirit as being the supreme Reality behind.

The idea of the world so presented is congenial to reason in the sense in which reason desiderates a worthy end for all events, whether human actions or the existence of the universe. The relation of the universe as a whole to its Ground would then be analogous to the relation between the activity of finite spirit and its spiritual ground in the world we know, whenever we call that activity reasonable; and, although it cannot be proved that this analogy holds, it certainly makes a universe which gives man a greater satisfaction to contemplate—gives this satisfaction to man not as a lover of pleasure or comfort, of whatever kind the pleasure or comfort may be, but to man, as a reasonable being, who desires the special satisfaction of finding in the universe a correspondence to his own recognition of values.

It has to be acknowledged that great tracts of the world seem to point the other way. Outside finite spirit and its activities the course of the world does seem wholly indifferent to values. Science does not regard such an explanation as Socrates wanted given of the processes of the natural world, such an explanation as he complains of Anaxagoras for not giving, that the reason why things take the course they do is in order to realize some demonstrable *good*—as coming within its sphere of interest at all. No doubt when Science gets to the treatment of living things, there is a way in which teleological explanation comes in, but living things occupy an infinitesimal space in the universe. In the measureless time before life appeared on our small planet, through the measureless time after life on our planet has been extinguished, we see material masses whirl in space without any consciousness for which values could subsist. Those men who adopt the hypothesis that Reality, outside the momentary flash of spirit on this planet, is indifferent to values, and that the appearance of spirit must somehow be explained as due merely to an odd accident in the working of regular, but purposeless, material laws, have also facts to go upon. What then it seems to come to is this: The world we know presents us with two regions of fact—that of inanimate nature, in which the universe appears wholly indifferent to values, and that of life, which reaches its culmination in the spirit of man, and shows a progressive apprehension of value as approximation is made in animal life to that culmination, the higher values being apprehended by the human spirit alone. You may take either of these regions of fact as the basis of your hypothesis regarding ultimate Reality.

The first region, that of inanimate nature, shows an immense preponderance of material extension over the other, the manifestations of life and spirit being confined, so far as observation has yet gone, to an infinitesimal point of space and span of time. On the other hand, spirit may be regarded as having a dignity which no possible extension of material masses can countervail—Pascal's *roseau pensant*, and Coventry Patmore's declaration that he is not intimidated by the astronomical figures indicating the size of the material universe, because their effect is only to "make dirt cheap." [1] Which of those regions of fact a man takes as being the key to Reality is a matter of personal choice, in which what is deepest in him expresses itself.

And here again the attitude of a man to the universe may find a kind of analogy in the attitude of a man to some one of his fellow-men. It may be that we have to judge of someone's character, whose conduct, in great tracts of it, is a matter of routine and gives no indication of what is really in the man, how much he cares for goodness and truth, whether he feels affection for us or not. But there have been brief moments in which that which was in the man flashed out, it seemed, in some act, in some look. It is open to us to take those moments as showing us what he really is, and in some cases a trust afterwards unshakable is based upon a few crucial moments when two spirits, we believe, touched each other—mo-

---

[1] Not greatly moved with awe am I
To learn that we may spy
Five thousand firmaments beyond our own.
The best that's known
Of the heavenly bodies does them credit small . . .
The Universe, outside our living Earth,
Was all conceiv'd in the Creator's mirth,
Forecasting at the time Man's spirit deep,
To make dirt cheap.
                                        (*Unknown Eros,* xviii.)

ments of revelation. Or we may take the apparent indifference of his conduct in its predominant tracts as showing us what he is and judge him by those. Those who believe the Reality behind phenomena to be Spirit, to be God, hold that we see the character of that Reality in the manifestations of the human spirit, and since we see those manifestations in a scale of worth, some higher than others—a more perfect goodness and loveliness of character, a more ardent loyalty to truth, a richer genius in apprehending beauty and making beautiful things—it is as they rise in the scale, as they are brighter and purer, that they are for us more perfect manifestations of the character of the Supreme Spirit. For Christians the human spirit reaches its highest possible point in Christ, and for that reason the Christian Church believes that in Christ may be seen that for which the whole universe has come into existence.

I say advisedly in this context Christ, and not Jesus, because the Christian view does not confine the life of Christ to the life of Jesus of Nazareth, but regards it as continued in the Christian society. The full range of the Spirit could not be shown in the circumstances and the years of the earthly life of Jesus, but it may be shown, according to Christian doctrine, in the world-wide Community, as ultimately made perfect, the glorified Community which will manifest, without any obscuration by sin or earthly infirmity, all the potentialities of the spirit of man, the full riches of the life of Christ for which it is the vehicle. This may be regarded as what the apostle meant when he said that the ultimate end to which the world-process moved was the summing up of all things in Christ.

I spoke just now of one misconception to be guarded against as being that the leap beyond experience was made, whether it was by the believer in God or by the disbeliever in God, from no ground of facts, and I have tried to explain how each of them bases his hypothesis on a certain part of the facts presented by the world we know, though on a different part. The other misconception may easily be suggested by the language hitherto used for short, about a man's "adopting" a hypothesis to live by. As a matter of psychological fact, it happens rarely, if ever, that a man comes to a consideration of the universe with a perfectly impartial mind and then calmly and deliberately adopts one of two or more possible hypotheses about it. In actual practice what I have called "adopting" a hypothesis could be more aptly described as adhering, after subsequent consideration, to a hypothesis which has come to rule a man's mind apart from any deliberate choice on his part. We might call it re-adopting a hypothesis. Any man who desires greatly to avoid believing things which are untrue, who wants to have some reason for his belief which he could present to another man, as a reason which all men thinking straight could find valid, will not rest simply in finding that a particular belief has laid hold of him. A man believes in God before he can say why he believes in God, but he will not go on believing in God if, being a rational man, he has brought the belief into connexion with other knowledge about the Universe and convinced himself that it is incompatible with some bit of Reality of which he is certain. If, however, after bringing his belief in God into connexion with other knowledge about the Universe, he finds the hold of the belief upon him unrelaxed, he will be able to point to grounds which seem to justify his belief. He will be able "to give a reason for the faith that is in him."

It is highly improbable that anyone who had no belief in God was ever led to believe in God by any of the standard "proofs" of God's existence —the ontological, cosmological, teleological proof. They were thought of by men who already believed in God as considerations harmonizing their belief, for themselves, and for others, with a general view of the universe. It is, of course, a dogma of the Roman Church that the existence of God can be demonstrated by rational inference from visible phenomena. But no Roman Catholic could take this to mean that it can be demonstrated by arguments which are sure to be recognized by all men of normal understanding as cogent, for it is a plain fact of the world that there are many men of normal understanding who do *not* recognize the arguments put forward as cogent. Nobody who believes the dogma could take it in any other sense than that the arguments *ought to be* recognized as cogent, that if people were perfectly rational they would recognize them as cogent. If you already believe in God, then you will see everything that exists as existing because of the one Will which called the world into being, and so the cosmological argument will indicate this rational agreement between your belief and your view of the universe: you will see the order of the universe as directed to realize value in a supreme degree, and so the teleological argument will indicate rational agreement between your belief and your view of the universe. It is only, I think, in the sense of giving rational comfort to people who already believe in God that the standard arguments can be regarded as demonstrating the existence of God. What actually causes anyone to believe in God is direct perception of the Divine.

STUDY QUESTIONS

1. Bevan says that a sense of the indifference of the universe "must . . . act depressingly upon a man's moral energy." How does this compare with the view of man in the universe expounded by Sartre in "Existentialism"?

2. What alternatives to religious belief does Bevan mention? Exactly what reasons does he give for rejecting the hypothesis that the universe is malignant?

3. Bevan admits that neither his point of view nor its opposite is subject to logical proof. What standard of judgment does he use?

4. In what ways do Bevan's views about evidence and faith agree with those of Newman in "Knowledge and Faith"?

5. How does Bevan attack the position taken by Huxley in "Agnosticism and Christianity," which holds that it is wrong to believe something unless one has evidence for it?
6. Identify the basic disagreement between Bevan and Stace, who discusses religious belief in "Man Against Darkness."

The Colloid and the Crystal*

Joseph Wood Krutch

The first real snow was soon followed by a second. Over the radio the weatherman talked lengthily about cold masses and warm masses, about what was moving out to sea and what wasn't. Did Benjamin Franklin, I wondered, know what he was starting when it first occurred to him to trace by correspondence the course of storms? From my stationary position the most reasonable explanation seemed to be simply that winter had not quite liked the looks of the landscape as she first made it up. She was changing her sheets.

Another forty-eight hours brought one of those nights ideal for frosting the panes. When I came down to breakfast, two of the windows were almost opaque and the others were etched with graceful, fernlike sprays of ice which looked rather like the impressions left in rocks by some of the antediluvian plants, and they were almost as beautiful as anything which the living can achieve. Nothing else which has never lived looks so much as though it were actually informed with life.

I resisted, I am proud to say, the almost universal impulse to scratch my initials into one of the surfaces. The effect, I knew, would not be an improvement. But so, of course, do those less virtuous than I. That indeed is precisely why they scratch. The impulse to mar and to destroy is as ancient and almost as nearly universal as the impulse to create. The one is an easier way than the other of demonstrating power. Why else should anyone not hungry prefer a dead rabbit to a live one? Not even those horrible Dutch painters of bloody still—or shall we say stilled?—lifes can have really believed that their subjects were more beautiful dead.

Indoors it so happened that a Christmas cactus had chosen this moment to bloom. Its lush blossoms, fuchsia-shaped but pure red rather than magenta, hung at the drooping ends of strange thick stems and outlined themselves in blood against the glistening background of the frosty

* From *The Best of Two Worlds* by Joseph Wood Krutch, copyright, 1950, by Joseph Wood Krutch. By permission of William Morrow & Co., Inc. (Copyright, 1950, by Street and Smith Publications, Inc., reprinted by permission of *Mademoiselle*.)

pane—jungle flower against frostflower; the warm beauty that breathes and lives and dies competing with the cold beauty that burgeons, not because it wants to, but merely because it is obeying the laws of physics which require that crystals shall take the shape they have always taken since the world began. The effect of red flower against white tracery was almost too theatrical, not quite in good taste perhaps. My eye recoiled in shock and sought through a clear area of the glass the more normal out-of-doors.

On the snow-capped summit of my bird-feeder a chickadee pecked at the new-fallen snow and swallowed a few of the flakes which serve him in lieu of the water he sometimes sadly lacks when there is nothing except ice too solid to be picked at. A downy woodpecker was hammering at a lump of suet and at the coconut full of peanut butter. One nuthatch was dining while the mate waited his—or was it her?—turn. The woodpecker announces the fact that he is a male by the bright red spot on the back of his neck, but to me, at least, the sexes of the nuthatch are indistinguishable. I shall never know whether it is the male or the female who eats first. And that is a pity. If I knew, I could say, like the Ugly Duchess, "and the moral of that is . . ."

But I soon realized that at the moment the frosted windows were what interested me most—especially the fact that there is no other natural phenomenon in which the lifeless mocks so closely the living. One might almost think that the frostflower had got the idea from the leaf and the branch if one did not know how inconceivably more ancient the first is. No wonder that enthusiastic biologists in the nineteenth century, anxious to conclude that there was no qualitative difference between life and chemical processes, tried to believe that the crystal furnished the link, that its growth was actually the same as the growth of a living organism. But excusable though the fancy was, no one, I think, believes anything of the sort today. Protoplasm is a colloid and the colloids are fundamentally different from the crystalline substances. Instead of crystallizing they jell, and life in its simplest known form is a shapeless blob of rebellious jelly rather than a crystal eternally obeying the most ancient law.

No man ever saw a dinosaur. The last of these giant reptiles was dead eons before the most dubious halfman surveyed the world about him. Not even the dinosaurs ever cast their dim eyes upon many of the still earlier creatures which preceded them. Life changes so rapidly that its later phases know nothing of those which preceded them. But the frostflower is older than the dinosaur, older than the protozoan, older no doubt than the enzyme or the ferment. Yet it is precisely what it has always been. Millions of years before there were any eyes to see it, millions of years before any life existed, it grew in its own special way, crystallized along its preordained lines of cleavage, stretched out its pseudo-branches and pseudo-leaves. It was beautiful before beauty itself existed.

We find it difficult to conceive a world except in terms of purpose, of will, or of intention. At the thought of the something without beginning and presumably without end, of something which is, nevertheless, regular though blind, and organized without any end in view, the mind reels. Constituted as we are it is easier to conceive how the slime floating upon the waters might become in time *homo sapiens* than it is to imagine how so complex a thing as a crystal could have always been and can always remain just what it is—complicated and perfect but without any meaning, even for itself. How can the lifeless even obey a law?

To a mathematical physicist I once confessed somewhat shamefacedly that I had never been able to understand how inanimate nature managed to follow so invariably and so promptly her own laws. If I flip a coin across a table, it will come to rest at a certain point. But before it stops at just that point, many factors must be taken into consideration. There is the question of the strength of the initial impulse, of the exact amount of resistance offered by the friction of that particular table top, and of the density of the air at the moment. It would take a physicist a long time to work out the problem and he could achieve only an approximation at that. Yet presumably the coin will stop exactly where it should. Some very rapid calculations have to be made before it can do so, and they are, presumably, always accurate.

And then, just as I was blushing at what I suppose he must regard as my folly, the mathematician came to my rescue by informing me that Laplace had been puzzled by exactly the same fact. "Nature laughs at the difficulties of integration," he remarked—and by "integration" he meant, of course, the mathematician's word for the process involved when a man solves one of the differential equations to which he has reduced the laws of motion.

When my Christmas cactus blooms so theatrically a few inches in front of the frost-covered pane, it also is obeying laws but obeying them much less rigidly and in a different way. It blooms at about Christmastime because it has got into the habit of doing so, because, one is tempted to say, it wants to. As a matter of fact it was, this year, not a Christmas cactus but a New Year's cactus, and because of this unpredictability I would like to call it "he," not "it." His flowers assume their accustomed shape and take on their accustomed color. But not as the frostflowers follow their predestined pattern. Like me, the cactus has a history which stretches back over a long past full of changes and developments. He has not always been merely obeying fixed laws. He has resisted and rebelled; he has attempted novelties, passed through many phases. Like all living things he has had a will of his own. He has made laws, not merely obeyed them.

"Life," so the platitudinarian is fond of saying, "is strange." But from our standpoint it is not really so strange as those things which have no life and yet nevertheless move in their predestined orbits and "act" though they do not "behave." At the very least one ought to say that if life is strange there is nothing about it more strange than the fact that it has its being in a universe so astonishingly shared on the one hand by "things" and on the other by "creatures," that man himself is both a "thing" which obeys the laws of chemistry or physics and a "creature" who to some extent defies them. No other contrast, certainly not the contrast between the human being and the animal, or the animal and the plant, or even the spirit and the body, is so tremendous as this contrast between what lives and what does not.

To think of the lifeless as merely inert, to make the contrast merely in terms of a negative, is to miss the real strangeness. Not the shapeless stone which seems to be merely waiting to be acted upon but the snowflake or the frostflower is the true representative of the lifeless universe as opposed to ours. They represent plainly, as the stone does not, the fixed and perfect system of organization which includes the sun and its planets, includes therefore this earth itself, but against which life has set up its seemingly puny opposition. Order and obedience are the primary characteristics of that which is not alive. The snowflake eternally obeys its one and only law: "Be thou six pointed"; the planets their one and only: "Travel thou in an ellipse." The astronomer can tell where the North Star will be ten thousand years hence; the botanist cannot tell where the dandelion will bloom tomorrow.

Life is rebellious and anarchial, always testing the supposed immutability of the rules which the nonliving changelessly accepts. Because the snowflake goes on doing as it was told, its story up to the end of time was finished when it first assumed the form which it has kept ever since. But the story of every living thing is still in the telling. It may hope and it may try. Moreover, though it may succeed or fail, it will certainly change. No form of frostflower ever became extinct. Such, if you like, is its glory. But such also is the fact which makes it alien. It may melt but it cannot die.

If I wanted to contemplate what is to me the deepest of all mysteries, I should choose as my object lesson a snowflake under a lens and an amoeba under the microscope. To a detached observer—if one can possibly imagine any observer who *could* be detached when faced with such an ultimate choice—the snowflake would certainly seem the "higher" of the two. Against its intricate glistening perfection one would have to place a shapeless, slightly turbid glob, perpetually oozing out in this direction or that but not suggesting so strongly as the snowflake does, intelligence and plan. Crystal and colloid, the chemist would call them, but what an inconceivable contrast those neutral terms imply! Like the star, the snowflake seems to declare the glory of God, while the promise of the amoeba, given only perhaps to itself, seems only contemptible. But its jelly holds, nevertheless, not only its promise but ours also, while the snowflake represents some achievement which we cannot possibly share. After the passage of billions of years, one can see and be aware of the other, but the relationship can never be reciprocal. Even after these billions of years no aggregate of colloids can be as beautiful as the crystal always was, but it can know, as the crystal cannot, what beauty is.

Even to admire too much or too exclusively the alien kind of beauty is dangerous. Much as I love and am moved by the grand inanimate forms of nature, I am always shocked and a little frightened by those of her professed lovers to whom landscape is the most important thing, and to whom landscape is merely a matter of forms and colors. If they see or are moved by an animal or flower, it is to them merely a matter of a picturesque completion and their fellow creatures are no more than decorative details. But without some continuous awareness of the two great realms of the inanimate and the animate there can be no love of nature as I understand it, and what is worse, there must be a sort of disloyalty to our cause, to us who are colloid, not crystal. The pantheist who feels the oneness of all living things, I can understand; perhaps indeed he and I are in essential agreement. But the ultimate All is not one thing, but two. And because the alien half is in its way as proud and confident and successful as our half, its fundamental difference may not be disregarded with impunity. Of us and all we stand for, the enemy is not so much death as the not-living, or rather that great system which succeeds without ever having had the need to be alive. The frostflower is not merely a wonder; it is also a threat and a warning. How admirable, it seems to say, not living can be! What triumphs mere immutable law can achieve!

Some of Charles Peirce's strange speculations about the possibility that "natural law" is not law at all but merely a set of habits fixed more firmly than any habits we know anything about in ourselves or in the animals suggest the possibility that the snowflake was not, after all, always inanimate, that it merely surrendered at some time impossibly remote the life which once achieved its perfect organization. Yet even if we can imagine such a thing to be true, it serves only to warn us all the more strongly against the possibility that what we call the living might in the end succumb also to the seduction of the immutably fixed.

No student of the anthill has ever failed to be astonished either into admiration or horror by what is sometimes called the perfection of its society. Though even the anthill can change its ways, though even ant individuals—ridiculous as the conjunction of the two words may seem—can sometimes make choices, the perfection of the techniques, the regularity of the habits almost suggests the possibility that the insect is on its way back to inanition, that, vast as the difference still is, an anthill crystallizes somewhat as a snowflake does. But not even the anthill, nothing else indeed in the whole known universe is so perfectly planned as one of these same snowflakes. Would, then, the ultimately planned society be, like the anthill, one in which no one makes plans, any more than a snowflake does? From the cradle in which it is not really born to the grave where it is only a little deader than it always was, the ant-citizen follows a plan to the making of which he no longer contributes anything.

Perhaps we men represent the ultimate to which the rebellion, begun so long ago in some amoeba-like jelly, can go. And perhaps the inanimate is beginning the slow process of subduing us again. Certainly the psychologist and the philosopher are tending more and more to think of us as creatures who obey laws rather than as creatures of will and responsibility. We are, they say, "conditioned" by this or by that. Even the greatest heroes are studied on the assumption that they can be "accounted for" by something outside themselves. They are, it is explained, "the product of forces." All the emphasis is placed, not upon that power to resist and rebel which we were once supposed to have, but upon the "influences" which "formed us." Men are made by society, not society by men. History as well as character "obeys laws." In their view, we crystallize in obedience to some dictate from without instead of moving in conformity with something within.

And so my eye goes questioningly back to the frosted pane. While I slept the graceful pseudo-fronds crept across the glass, assuming, as life itself does, an intricate organization. "Why live," they seem to say, "when we can be beautiful, complicated, and orderly without the uncertainty and effort required of a living thing? Once we were all that was. Perhaps some day we shall be all that is. Why not join us?"

Last summer no clod or no stone would have been heard if it had asked such a question. The hundreds of things which walked and sang, the millions which crawled and twined were all having their day. What was dead seemed to exist only in order that the living might live upon it. The plants were busy turning the inorganic into green life and the animals were busy turning that green into red. When we moved, we walked mostly upon grass. Our pre-eminence was unchallenged.

On this winter day nothing seems so successful as the frostflower. It thrives on the very thing which has driven some of us indoors or underground and which has been fatal to many. It is having now its hour of triumph, as we before had ours. Like the cactus flower itself, I am a hothouse plant. Even my cats gaze dreamily out of the window at a universe which is no longer theirs.

How are we to resist, if resist we can? This house into which I have withdrawn is merely an expedient and it serves only my mere physical existence. What mental or spiritual convictions, what will to maintain my own kind of existence can I assert? For me it is not enough merely to say, as I do say, that I shall resist the invitation to submerge myself into a crystalline society and to stop planning in order that I may be planned for. Neither is it enough to go further, as I do go, and to insist that the most important thing about a man is not that part of him which is "the product of forces" but that part, however small it may be, which enables him to become something other than what the most accomplished sociologist, working in conjunction with the most accomplished psychologist, could predict that he would be.

I need, so I am told, a faith, something outside myself to which I can be loyal. And with that I agree, in my own way. I am on what I call "our side," and I know, though vaguely, what I think that is. Wordsworth's God had his dwelling in the light of setting suns. But the God who dwells there seems to me most probably the God of the atom, the star, and the crystal. Mine, if I have one, reveals Himself in another class of phenomena. He makes the grass green and the blood red.

STUDY QUESTIONS

1. What is the basic principle of organization in this essay? In what ways do the opening three paragraphs suggest the central thesis? What purpose is served in the fifth paragraph by the details of the birds feeding?

2. Is the concluding contrast between "last summer" and "this winter day" suggestive of anything beyond the literal comparison? What? What other similar specific contrasts does Krutch employ in the essay? What do they contribute to the total effect of the essay?

3. Compare this essay in organization, style, and tone with those by Stace and Bevan.

4. What similarities and differences does Krutch perceive between living and non-living things? In what ways do the non-living seem superior? What feelings does the comparison arouse in the author? Why is the frostflower a "threat and a warning"?

5. What limitations of science are implicit in, Krutch's observations about the predictability of "rebellious and anarchial" life? What similarities and differences do you find between these implications and the ideas of Cohen and Nagel?

6. Write a theme in which you follow Krutch's method of evolving interesting generalizations and speculations from a familiar and everyday comparison.

PART SIX

On

Literature

1. THE NATURE OF LITERATURE

The Nature of the Arts*

Eric Newton

A postage stamp, the overture to "The Magic Flute," No. 7, Acacia Grove, Guerlain's latest perfume, Leonardo's "Last Supper," an innings by Don Bradman, Shakespeare's "Hamlet," a performance of "Sylphides," a dish of "homard à la cardinal," St. Paul's Cathedral, a Walt Disney cartoon—all these are (or can be) works of art.

There are other things that are not works of art. Niagara Falls is not a work of art, nor is the afterglow of the snows of Monte Rosa, nor the sound of breakers against a cliff, nor the dance executed by washing hanging on a clothes line in a stiff breeze, nor the scent of a pine wood on a summer day.

These two classes of phenomena are different in kind. The first are man-made and man-designed. They had to be conceived in the mind of a man (or group of men) and then made communicable to other men by the skill of the designer, working in some medium that could be perceived by the senses of other men—the eye, the ear, the nose, the palate.

The other set of phenomena—Niagara Falls, the sound of breakers and so on—are not man-made or man-designed. They may be equally beautiful or equally pleasurable. They may even be the result of design by God or the Laws of Nature or what you will, but they have not that double element in them of conception and parturition. They were not imagined first and then made manifest through the medium of visible materials, visible movements, audible sounds, perceptible smells.

Art has always fascinated the makers of definitions, and has always

---

*From *European Painting and Sculpture* by Eric Newton, by permission of Penguin Books, Ltd. Copyright, 1950, by Penguin Books, Ltd.

baffled them; the makers of definitions are never content to define what a thing *is*: they usually attempt to describe what it is *for*. And though I myself have no doubt at all about what art *is*, no sequence of words known to me will describe what art is *for*.

In trying to tell the story of art I shall therefore start with an initial advantage. I have no preconceived theories about the artist's purpose: therefore I have no prejudice against the artist who runs counter to such theories. If the artist tells me a story I shall exclaim "how interesting!"; if he wishes to overawe me with mystical conceptions of the Godhead I am ready to be impressed; if he wants to construct a purely formal pattern of line and colour or mass or sound, I will say "how beautiful!"; if he preaches I am ready to be converted; if he wants to be of use to me I shall say "thank you." Art has done all these things at various times in the history of civilization.

But if the story of art is to be told it is certainly necessary to know what art is, and if I define it briefly as a human conception made manifest by the use of a medium: and if I define good art (and no one wants to waste his time telling the story of bad art) as a noble (or arresting, or interesting, or valuable) conception made manifest by the skilful use of a medium, I can then have done with definitions and get on with the story. . . .

The artist, then, is a man of double activity. He has to have imagination and he has to have craftsmanship. He has to imagine (in his mind's eye, or his mind's ear, or his mind's nose) the thing he is going to make; and he must also have the power to translate the thing he has imagined into terms of his medium. Those are not separate activities. On the contrary, they affect one another in unpredictable and unanalysable ways, so that when an artist is at work he cannot possibly say at a given moment which part of himself he is using. Is the fact that he is working with a soft pencil on rough paper giving a breadth to Tintoretto's line, or had the image in his mind's eye already formed itself with that breadth of sweep? Did Mozart, in his mind's ear, conjure up a quality of sound that could be translated into music only by a certain combination of bassoons and strings? Or did his memory of that combination, heard perhaps by chance while an orchestra was tuning up, prompt him to make further experiments with it? No one can possibly answer these questions, since no one but Tintoretto himself knew the precise quality of the image in his mind's eye and no one but Mozart ever heard what was in Mozart's mind's ear. The work of art, the drawing or the overture, is all we have to judge by. We can only say, "this man *seems* to have found an adequate means of expression for the thing he had to say." A marriage has taken place between the visionary and the craftsman and one can judge of the success of the marriage only by examining the fruits of it—the work of art.

But this artistic activity—this making of drawings and overtures and books and postage stamps—is not a thing done just for the fun of doing it. No doubt it *is* fun to write a book or compose an overture, but no artist was ever content to have his fun and then throw the result of it away. The book has to be read, the overture performed, the ballet or picture seen. Art is a communication. Behind every work of art is the artist's appeal to his fellows, "Don't you see what I mean? Don't you see what I'm getting at?"

The story of art is therefore not merely the story of men who make things and of the kind of things they make. It is also the story of the relationship—the very complicated and always shifting relationship—between these men and their fellow men. It is a relationship full of contradictions and difficulties. For no workman can afford to produce unless he is paid to do so: therefore the artist has to have an employer. And no employer can afford to pay a workman unless he is producing something that he (the employer) needs. It follows, therefore, that (except in the rare case of artists of independent means) the artist's work of art is not merely the child of his own personal fancy, the thing he personally wants to communicate. It must also be something that his employer wants him to communicate to himself or to others. The work of art must be not only the result of an urge on the part of the producer, but also of a need on the part of the consumer. Here is a strange state of things indeed! For how can the consumer feel a need of something so personal and so (on the face of it) unnecessary as an artist's expression of his inner vision? And even supposing he does feel that need sufficiently strongly to induce him to pay an artist to produce a work of art, how is the artist going to reconcile his personal and private desire to communicate his own personal and private vision with his employer's or patron's specification of what he wants the artist to produce? In any other branch of human activity the question would not arise. No maker of chisels would say to his employer, "My whole nature rebels against the idea of making the kind of chisels you want. You wish me to make sharp chisels. I, on the other hand, can only express myself to the full by making blunt chisels. You want steel chisels; I, as a craftsman, feel irresistibly drawn to the use of lead as medium."

The more materially useful a man-made thing is, the more chance there is of complete agreement between artist and employer. But material usefulness is not the only kind of usefulness; there is such a thing as spiritual usefulness. To the maker of chisels the employer can justifiably say, "Make your chisels exactly thus," but to the maker of crucifixes he must say, "Let your crucifix conform to the minimum requirements of all crucifixes—a cross, a male human body, an impression of suffering, but also a sense of nobility. Beyond that I leave it to you. Add your own personal thoughts and feelings. Embody your own vision."

So long as the artist is an employed workman he must compromise, never losing touch with life and its requirements yet never sacrificing his own integrity in doing so. And that is almost always a good thing, for compromise of that kind is not a concession to a lower order of things. It is a dangerous holding of the balance between two sets of forces. The artist, like the maker of chisels, serves a master (Palestrina served the Pope, Shakespeare wrote his plays for a touring company), but in doing so he gives his master something he never bargained for. When Rembrandt painted the "Night Watch" he was ostensibly painting the portraits of a certain Captain Banning Cocq and the members of his shooting company. Presumably something corresponding to a group photograph of the school hockey team would have satisfied the club, but Rembrandt had things to say that had nothing to do with the likenesses of the captain and his friends—things about how light falls in dark places, and how it strikes hard here and gently caresses there—and he insisted on saying them. In doing so he began to lose sight of the original purpose of his picture. Banning Cocq and his friends became mere excuses for an essay in chiaroscuro. The club was offended; certain members of it complained that their faces had been plunged into semi-darkness; they were more interested in themselves than in chiaroscuro. We, on the other hand, are delighted. We have lost interest in seventeenth-century shooting clubs, but what Rembrandt has to say about the play of light on flesh is as fascinating today as it was in 1642. A similar controversy, it will be remembered, arose a few years ago in connection with the statue of Sir Douglas Haig in Whitehall. Michelangelo, faced with the same kind of criticism of his statues of Lorenzo and Giuliano de Medici, answered that in a thousand years' time nobody would know what the two Medicis were really like. Pope Clement VII, however, who ordered the statues, *did* know; he asked for portraits of two men and he was given symbols of mankind. Michelangelo was unwilling to make the compromise. We may be glad of his unwillingness, but his employer was anything but pleased.

This necessity of serving two masters has always been one of the artist's difficulties. He must deliver the goods he is asked for, and he must also be true to himself. And rightly so. Whenever either is sacrificed to the other the work of art suffers in quality. There are plenty of instances of both kinds of sacrifices in the art of to-day. There are commercial artists who produce flavourless trash in an attempt to give their employers what they want; and there are artists who, through lack of employers or through unwillingness to be employed, have nothing to serve but their own impulses, and whose work can only be described as psychological exhibitionism.

It is not by chance that the greatest periods of art have usually occurred when the artist was most firmly harnessed to a master or to a cause. Necessarily the pace of a man in harness is slower than that of a free man. He is less free to choose his own direction, but he has the satisfaction of knowing that he is an indispensable member of society—

or of a portion of society—and the further satisfaction of knowing that because society needs him, society will understand him—at any rate that portion of him that is in service. His double service gives him a double message and a double appeal. A Palestrina, left to himself, will merely further the cause of music: employed by the Pope, he also enriches the texture of Christian ritual and enlarges the meaning of Christianity.

The present-day cleavage of artists into two groups, those who are so enslaved to their employers that they "can't call their souls their own," and those unfettered spirits whose souls are so much their own that they are no use to anyone but themselves, is a comparatively new thing. It has led to the division of artists into two kinds known as "commercial" and "fine artists"—i.e., men who work only to please the man who pays them and men who have no one to please but themselves—though these latter always hope that they will happen to please someone else sufficiently to induce him to pay them enough to go on pleasing themselves without starving. Three-quarters of the films made, about a quarter of the books published, ninety per cent of the music composed are "commercial" in the true sense that they were created primarily in order to be turned into money. The bulk of the remainder, the "fine" works of art, are genuine attempts at self-expression without reference to the requirements of society. In some cases they succeed so well in impressing themselves on society that society begins to require them. In others they are so personal and so remote from average human experience that society, far from requiring them, complains of their uselessness, their unintelligibility, their divorce from "life." That complaint, so often heard nowadays, is not a criterion of the genuineness or sincerity of the works of art in question. It is an index of the unfamiliarity of the language in which those works of art are couched. For a personal vision demands a personal set of idioms to express it. Usually a generation or so must pass before those idioms become understood and accepted by the average man and pass into general currency. The time-lag between the appearance of an unfamiliar artistic message couched in an unfamiliar artistic idiom, and its acceptance by the average man can be reduced only when the artist can be harnessed to a cause that the average man understands. Giotto was as violent an innovator as Picasso, but as Giotto's innovations were harnessed to Christianity (while Picasso's are harnessed to nothing more stable than Picasso) the average contemporary of Giotto, shocked though he may have been by the new Giottesque idiom, felt that he could at least understand the cause that idiom served, and could dimly see how the new idiom somehow served the cause in a new and valuable way. Today the same phenomenon can be observed. The more the artist is willing to compromise between making what *he* wants (in Rembrandt's case, a study of light) and what his employer wants (in Banning Cocq's case, a set of recognizable portraits) the more immediately acceptable his work will be. A cubist whose picture conveys nothing but the cubiness of things in general is apt to leave the average man cold and puzzled. But a cubist who uses his cubism to advertise the merits of A's petrol or B's beer is understood at once. A cubized egg is, to the average man, simply a bad egg; but a cubized glass of beer grasped in a cubized hand is interesting and arresting. The one is merely an artist's visual adventure, the other is a voyage of discovery that carries the spectator along with it and deposits him surprisingly at his destination. Once the artist has harnessed himself to society, society at once begins to regard him as a workman performing a useful function and not as a playboy amusing himself in a vacuum.

In the same way a scientist's discovery that an electric current passed through metal coil will heat the metal leaves most people uninterested, but the man who uses that discovery to boil a kettle arouses an immediate interest.

This double function of the artist is the key to the story of art. Many learned books about art have been written which fail to tell the story because they lose sight of the perpetual adjustment that goes on in the artist between art-as-expression and art-as-service.

Meanwhile, before going on to examine the particular kinds of adjustments that take place when the artist happens to be a painter or a sculptor, one other thing must be said about the arts in general. A work of art may be an expression of the artist's inner vision, and it may also be a thing useful to society, but beyond both these it is a thing-in-itself. Apart from its function as a means of communion between one human being and another it exists in its own right. It consists of a series of sounds or words or movements or of a set of shapes made of pigment applied to canvas or of a set of masses carved out of stone or modelled out of clay. In a word, it has form; and it must obey the laws of form as dictated by whatever medium the artist uses. A sentence may embody an idea in the writer's mind, but it must also obey grammatical laws. A drawing may say what the draughtsman wanted it to say but it must also say it in the pencil's way. A statue may represent a man in a lounge suit, but, if it is made of stone, both flesh and cloth must be translated into terms of stone: stone must not be tortured into an imitation of flesh and cloth. Every medium has its own set of laws, and the work of art must obey them or perish. When the word is made flesh it ceases to have the qualities of word-ness. It must behave like flesh.

Moreover, the work of art is self-contained. A picture must have four edges, a play or piece of music must have a beginning and an end, whereas the experience it embodies has no edges, no beginning or end. It is just an indeterminate slice of an endless ebb and flow. But the work of art must be a thing that can be isolated from all surrounding things. A picture occupies a square yard of space, a symphony three-quarters of an hour of time, a play several cubic yards of space and a couple of hours of time. Having "edges," therefore, in space or time, it follows that it must also have a shape. E. M. Forster, in his remarkable essay on the novel, points out that Anatole France's "Thaïs" is shaped like an hour-glass. ("We do not see it as an hour-glass—that is the hard jargon of the lecture room—but if it was not for this hour-glass the story, the plot and the characters of Thaïs and Paphnuce would none of them exert their full force, they would none of them breathe as they do.") Percy Lubbock's "Roman Pictures" is shaped like a "grand chain." ("What is so good in 'Roman Pictures' is not the presence of the 'grand chain' pattern—anyone can organize a grand chain—but the suitability of the pattern to the author's mood.") Observe the word *pattern*. The arts are difficult things to write about because there is no adequate terminology that fits them all. "Pattern" is a word taken from graphic art, "rhythm" from music, "phrasing" from literature. But they all have their counterparts in one another and they have all been invented by people who want (as I do) to talk about the work of art as a thing-in-itself, a thing with form, as opposed to a thing with content. Pattern, for example, is visual rhythm; a set of relationships set up in the eye of the beholder. A drawing of a flower is just a drawing of a flower, a thing that imparts a certain amount of botanical information. But repeat that drawing three times side by side on a square of paper and you have a pattern. You have established a relationship between three things and not only between three things but also between them and the four edges of the paper, and that relationship can be pleasant or unpleasant without any reference to botany. As long as a work of art has a shape it must also have a pattern. Pattern is a subdivision of shape. The parts within the shape must be related to the shape and to one another.

The artist's feeling for form and shape has given birth, in all the arts, to a host of conventions that are on the face of them fantastic. Why should poets have invented a shape called the sonnet? Why should the ear have to be tickled with an elaborate system of rhymes? What is the virtue of fourteen iambic pentameters if thirteen or fifteen would equally well express the poet's thoughts? Why should Edward Lear, in recounting the brief but poignant story of the old man of Aosta, have decided to fit his story into the strange shape of a Limerick with its attendant pattern of lines—long, long, short, short, long—and its parallel pattern of rhymes—*a, a, b, b, a*? What gave birth to the Sonata form? One can only answer that deep down in mankind is a thirst for something we have agreed to call aesthetic pleasure, a thirst for order, harmony, balance, rhythm, pattern.

Each art has its own set of conventions, but this brief chapter is not the place to examine them in detail. . . . It is sufficient to remember that the artist, in the act of creation, is perpetually obsessed with this question of the form his work of art is taking. His picture is not merely a representation of an object, or an expression of his feeling about an object. It is a thing-in-itself, equally valid if it is turned upside down; equally valid if it is an inaccurate representation, or a representation of something that lies outside the spectator's experience (as, say, a picture of a snow scene would be to an inhabitant of the Sahara desert); a thing that justifies itself by its shape alone and the obedience of that shape to the laws of the medium in which it is made.

STUDY QUESTIONS

1. What, according to Newton, is the difference between pleasant things that are works of art and pleasant things that are not works of art? What are the three major considerations involved in the creation of a work of art that Newton discusses?

2. Do you see any danger in Newton's recommendation that the artist seek to make his work "acceptable" by working out a compromise between the demands of self-expression and the requirements of his public? What advantages does such a compromise have for the artist? For the public? What might the public lose?

3. What reasons does Newton give for saying that a work of art must have a "shape" or "pattern"? Compare the comments of Daiches in "The Literary Use of Language" in the first section of this anthology.

4. Newton's essay is, at least in part, a definition. What devices does he use to make clear exactly what he means by art? How is the selection organized? How does he develop it?

5. Do you agree with Newton that "double service" is a good requirement for an artist to have to meet? Or is something to be said for situations where only one type of service is necessary? Can you cite examples of artists who (a) would have done better with only one master to serve or (b) did good work because they had only a single aim?

6. Describe an episode involving some work of art—a book, a movie, a painting, a piece of music or an example of architecture—which reflected a disagreement between an artist and his public. Exactly what was the cause of the misunderstanding? How was it settled?

The Meaning of Appreciation*

Percy C. Buck

You will have noticed that in my previous lectures I have been at pains to make certain words, which we use loosely in conversation, carry a more definite meaning, believing as I do that shallow thinking is more often due to vagueness of terms than to incapacity of mind. I have tried to make you see that a critical mind is not one that adopts a rather

* From *The Scope of Music,* 1923. Reprinted by permission.

querulous and censorious attitude to everything presented to it, but that true criticism is, in the words of a recent writer, a hunt for buried treasure. And I have tried to show that the discriminating mind is not necessarily one provided with the most exact apparatus for classifying things, but that taste is the result of thought guiding feeling.

I now ask you to consider whether you really give the right meaning to the word appreciation, and I will begin by discussing imagination.

If a man is of a certain type of mind, if he is generally dreamy and unpractical, we are apt to label him imaginative. It does not much matter, so long as we understand one another, that we use words loosely in daily life. But when we are definitely inquiring into a branch of life where imagination assumes importance, it becomes imperative that the connotation of the word should be definite. And if you possess imagination, there are two types of it, either of which may be yours; but the two are so distinct, and in some ways so much in opposition, that I think no one can possess both in any full measure.

Imagination may be receptive or creative. If your type is receptive you will "follow" quickly. If I tell you the story of a railway accident you will see "in your mind's eye" the sudden catastrophe, the overturned carriages, and all the attendant confusion. You will probably even imagine the spot and the surrounding country so vividly that, if you are taken to the scene of the accident, you will say, "I hadn't thought of it as a bit like that." For the receptive imagination is primarily reconstructive, and deals with things that are concrete and particular; it is objective, and works by mental images.

All of us have this form of imagination in some degree, and most of us when young have it in a high state of perfection. Most children actually form mental images of the lions and tigers of the storyteller. All of us, however, listen with less concentration as we grow older, and the power of reconstruction dwindles from atrophy. You should all strive to keep it alive and develop it, in yourselves and especially in your children, for the value to you of any speech, any book, any piece of music depends on your power of holding it in your mind by giving it your concentrated attention. If one of my children is so absorbed in a book that he does not hear what I say to him, then I am delighted, for that is the way in which a book should be read; but I think a good many less sophisticated parents would be annoyed and blame the child.

Creative imagination is definitely constructive; it deals with general and abstract ideas and is subjective. It works through technique, because without the power of presentation in some medium the artist's idea remains for ever in his head. The early stages of everybody's artistic attempts are due to his receptive imagination. If you or I try for the first time to draw a man or write a tune we have to rely on our memory of men and tunes, and will really only be reproducing. But if either of us is endowed with the creative imagination, our pictures and our compositions will leave the ruts and gradually acquire a distinction, an "originality," which is due solely to our constructive as distinct from reconstructive powers. Consequently the more creative imagination we have the less we use the receptive, and indeed there is a danger of our losing it entirely. Few great creative artists have been good admirers of other people's work.

Now for appreciation. I will take for my text the remark made to me by a man to whom I was maintaining that mind had a part to play in enjoyment. He replied, "If I could appreciate anything as much as a dog does a bone, I should be happy." The question of "as much as" I shall deal with in my next lecture, and so will leave alone now. At the moment I want to claim that the various forms of appreciation can be graded, and that it is reasonable to say that one end of the scale is a lower type, qualitatively, than the other. Lecture VI will discuss the quantitative side.

Appreciation falls into three main groups. They are not, of course, watertight, for there is every conceivable step in a range which is continuous. But the three types will serve as landmarks.

1. *Crude Appreciation* is when we are concerned with almost pure sensation. The cat finds the sensation of warmth, when she sits by the fire, to be pleasant, and memory will suggest her making a habit of it. The child is pleased with the sound of the trumpet and wants the sensation to be repeated. But every experience in this opening stage is a result of simple sensation, and "liking" is a more appropriate term than "appreciating." If the latter word is to have any distinctive connotation to separate it from "liking" it must be through the addition of the intellectual process of comparison and appraisement. If I have only once in my life tasted an apple I may like it or dislike it, but I cannot "appreciate" it *qua* apple unless I have an apple-standard in my mind for comparison; though I may appreciate it *qua* food, if I find it nicer than other kinds of food. So I think it is not a quibble to say that the first time the cat sits by the fire she "likes" the warmth, and later on may or may not appreciate the experience according as she does, or does not, compare it with other experiences. Appreciation only begins when she says to herself, "This is a nicer fire than usual" or "This is better than being outside."

2. *Intelligent Appreciation* is established when the rudimentary intelligence hitherto scarcely brought into play has become the cardinal feature in the experience, as when a child listens to a story. It won't even "like" the story if it does not understand what happens; but having understood, it will compare the story with others, and its appreciation depends on its judgement. If you remember I am leaving aside entirely, for the moment, the comparison of the various *quantities* of enjoyment— the cat may, for all I know, enjoy the fire more than the child enjoys the story—I think you will admit that we may claim this "intelligent ap-

preciation" to be of a "higher" type than crude appreciation, and that the steps by which the one merges into the other are steps upward. They certainly seem to follow the laws of evolutionary progress, for they develop in an unbroken line, and always in the same direction as we grow from the simple sensational infant to the developed intellectual adult. And if you will admit that these steps are steps upward, and that "intelligent" is a higher form of appreciation than crude, you are admitting that the controlling factor, the element in appreciation that makes one form better than another, is judgement.

3.   Given, then, that we wish to increase our powers of appreciation, as distinct from the quantity of our enjoyment, we must set out to improve our powers of judgement and discrimination. And if we develop these to their limit we attain the third and final stage, the goal of all serious art-lovers, *Critical Appreciation.*

I think that all questions of this kind are made difficult for us because the circumstances of their discussion nearly always arouse the suspicion that some one is trying to "improve" us. However much we desire improvement in our inner soul, we resent the man who volunteers to undertake the job. So take a case, for your comfort, where you yourself are "top dog," and I think you will allow that the truth of what I have argued is obvious. Supposing some one told you that your errand boy, aged nine, appreciated as much as you do *Paradise Lost,* or the "Forty-eight," or some such miraculous testimony to the greatness of man. You resent, and this time quite rightly, the suggestion that mysteries which are only beginning to raise their veil for you, who have spent a lifetime at their shrine, are an open book to a child who has not lived long enough to have formed a standard of anything. He may enjoy the noble sounds, the rolling rhythms, the feeling of splendour and pageantry they evoke, and his enjoyment may be as great as you like; but as to appreciation, that, you will maintain, is not a gift of the senses but a reward of the mind.

True appreciation, then, is no isolated elementary thing, but a nexus. It is feeling combined with understanding, it is our verdict when the appeal to our feelings has been modified by our realization of value, it is "liking" corrected by judgement.

Should any one deny that "valuation" is a factor in appreciation, we come, of course, to a standstill. We use language in a different way. If he seriously maintains that a pig can appreciate port wine, we can only ask him what word he uses to express the fact that to a man one port is better than another. Once he admits the validity of the claim that "appraisement" is essential, he must allow the importance of the quality of judgement involved in valuation. It is not, as I explained when speaking *de gustibus,* a question of whether we can say the opinion of Mr. Jones on a glass of port is better than that of Mr. Brown, but whether the opinion of either of these gentlemen becomes more valuable as their judgement becomes riper by experience. So we come back to my original postulate that the better the understanding the greater the appreciation.

The corollary is simple. Improvement in taste means education in understanding. If you want your children to grow up to love great literature you must see to it that they acquire right standards of judgement. They may be by nature sensitive, even over-sensitive, to the emotional appeal of pictures or music or books, and they can only acquire discrimination by the education of their judgement. If we undertake the education our task lies in raising them from the mire of crude appreciation which is the common starting-point for all of us, and leaving them as near as we can to the goal where the power of critical appreciation makes life an inexhaustible well of joy. It is a road every one can travel, and all of us do travel some distance along it; for even the appreciation of a tale or a tune involves a rudimentary form of "intelligent appreciation." Only a fool will ever think the end of the road has been reached, for there is no end, and only conceit will allow any one to think he has gone as far as he might have gone. And the going a little farther, which is possible to all of us, will not only result in an increase of our own enjoyment of life, but will also prevent that atrophy of our power of enjoyment which, as Darwin so pathetically lamented, may make our later years emotionless and grey.

Hitherto, as you will have noticed, I have assumed in pleading the importance of the intellectual side in art that I was addressing people who wished to deny it. In general, especially when talking with young painters or poets or musicians, that assumption is necessary. But the danger that most people ignore or at all events never apprehend this truth, is scarcely greater than the converse danger that those earnest folk who have once realized it carry it to an extreme that defeats its purpose. There is some Puck-like gargoyle in the structure of the human mind that delights, when once it finds us taking a thing seriously, in making us suspect that any deviation from solemnity smacks of flippancy. We acquiesce in our sermons being long and austere, our leading articles being pompous and verbose, our art being pretentious and above our heads, until the acquiescence, if we are too intensely serious, becomes a demand. We like our medicines to be nasty.

There is more than a little danger, in this age of specialization, of those who take music seriously falling into this heresy and preaching the over-intellectualization of their art until the red blood has gone out of it. They forget that the appeal of music is to the feelings, and only to the feelings, and that the one function of the understanding is to act as the link, because there is no other possible link in existence. The intellectual factors in a work of art are only merits in so far as they are facilities in bridging the gulf to the feelings. The cleverness of a fugue, the structural complexity of a symphony, the masked unity of a set of variations, are only justifiable in so far as they help to establish the emotional connexion. It is true that we must not place the standard of intelligence on which the composer may count too low; it has been my main object to insist on our duty of educating this intelligence-link to its utmost limit. But it is equally true that it is easy and common to look on intellectualism in art as an end in itself. If you discuss a theatrical performance with an actor, a picture with an artist, a concert with a musician, another man's poem with a poet, I think you will in most cases be astonished at how much a thing which to you is a matter of feeling, is to them a matter of pure technique. I would remind you of what I said once before: we cannot "understand" art, because the part we understand is not art.

There is a *cliché* in common use, amongst people whose talk tends towards "journalese," which I should like you to examine and then dismiss from your vocabulary. An artist is often said to "construct a work of imagination." At best this is no more than a half-truth. The artist does, it is true, produce his work by the exercise of his creative imagination. His catharsis sets his creative powers to work, almost unconsciously, in that medium in which he has acquired technique. His function in life for you and me, however, is not to construct a work of imagination, but to make us do so. From the purely personal and selfish point of view, of course, the poet's work is ended when his poem is signed, sealed, and delivered. But our concern is with appreciation of the poem, and the function of the poem is to compel us to reconstruct in order that we may feel. It may be so overcharged with the sensuous element as compared with its grip on the understanding—like, for instance, some of Swinburne's poems—that we pronounce it, for our individual selves, a failure. Or it may—like Browning's *Sordello*—put so great a strain on our understanding that we cannot "reconstruct" anything at all, and our "feeling" is never called into play. Even the least competent judge of poetry has acquired some standard of judgement, however elementary, to which he will bring the poem for a verdict: a standard acquired from his experience of poems, however limited, which he uses to justify his verdicts even if it is too unorganized to be formulated.

If, then, you would "appreciate" anything, aim at the enlarging and defining of your standard of judgement. If you think when you listen— or, better still, think after you have listened—you will find inevitably that security of judgement arrives. It has arrived, I should think, to every one in the world in some branch of life. The most unmusical woman here probably feels certain as to the merits of pieces of needlework, and she knows that I, who am now in complete ignorance, would before long attain her certainty of judgement if I devoted time to the study of it. Gradually, but beyond doubt, it would "come." The reward is within the reach of every one who desires it, the danger being, indeed, that when it arrives we are apt to feel so self-satisfied that we progress no further. For we must always bear in mind that art is not stagnant, and that we are called on to recast and develop as art changes, recognizing that art is also testing us.

As an antidote to the danger of this self-satisfaction, let me tell you the story of the tourists in the gallery of masterpieces. After "doing" the gallery in half an hour they disdainfully remarked to the attendant, on leaving, that they did not think very much of his pictures. "Gentlemen," replied the attendant, "these pictures are not here for judgement; it is the spectators who are on their trial."

STUDY QUESTIONS

1. What two kinds of imagination does Buck recognize? Explain and illustrate each kind.
2. Buck notes three degrees of appreciation arranged on a scale from lower to higher. What are these three degrees of appreciation? What standard of measurement does he use? Do you find this an acceptable standard?
3. Buck observes that we cannot "understand" art. What does he mean by this observation? Do you agree with him? Support your answer with illustration from your own experience.
4. What place do experience and observation have in Buck's definition of appreciation?
5. In this selection Buck has defined "appreciation" by analyzing it and suggesting that the term really has various meanings. Could a different analysis have been made? Would there be any value in suggesting more than three kinds of appreciation? Choose some similar term and approach its definition by Buck's method.
6. Write an "appreciation" of some work of art that you have seen (or heard) recently, evaluating it by comparing it with other examples of this art and making clear what feelings it aroused in you.

Literature and the Adult Laity*

Robert B. Heilman

I think we may consider literature, in the words of a modern critic, a form of knowledge—a form available to human intelligence generally, granted any curiosity at all, and granted some areas of maturity. But literature, we may as well grant, is not altogether an easy form of knowledge, not least because its habits differ from those of organized knowledge as we usually think of it. Organized knowledge interprets chaotic experience by withdrawing from it, inspecting it from some prin-

* From *Pacific Spectator*, VI, Summer, 1952. Reprinted by permission of the *Pacific Spectator*, and of the author.

ciple of order, abstracting from it, and generalizing about it. It establishes totals, averages, tendencies, movements, behavior patterns, types, recurrencies, idealized and rationalized formulations. All these are removed from, set off against, the monstrous confusion of actual human existence, with its disorderly welter of innumerable diverse individual beings and events. Literature, however, falls somewhere between the disorder of existence and the rational order of sciences and philosophy: it works with individual beings and events, with the concrete rather than the abstract, with the unorganized immediacies of human experience; but at the same time it tries to transcend, and its ultimate quality is measured by its success in transcending, the immediate record of individuals, and to communicate truths of a general or multipersonal order. It atomizes only to generalize. It tries to be at once experience and knowledge, to imitate the many and the one, to swear by the unique and yet be true to the typical. It does not talk about youth as a generality, but it shows Tom Jones or Richard Feverel or Hamlet in action; it does not theoretically analyze the clash of ambition and the sense of order, but it shows Macbeth or Willie Stark in action; it does not issue warnings about pride, but it shows Oedipus or Lucifer or the Pardoner's three young enemies of death in action; it does not talk about the role of the Negro in Southern life, but it shows Dilsy and Nancy Mannigoe in action. But in every one of these actions of sharply defined individuals much is said that is more than individual history—much, that is, about youth and ambition and pride and the role of the Negro. Through the specific action of individuals we may know the type, or the idea, or the quality. But because we are so deeply immersed in the specific action and engaged with individuals, we do not always easily grasp the generality or the idea that is equally present—the artist's "knowledge," if we may so call it. Yet that idea or generality, that more-than-individual truth, is the ultimate reality of the work, and it is *that* that we must be concerned with. For that meaning, though it be formulated by the insight of a highly individualized artist, is embedded in the experience of human beings generally, and that is really what we have to talk to human beings about. To connect plot—a very specific thing—with meaning, which is general, is to connect the literary work—also a specific thing—with experience, which is general. Communication implies community. The artist can't write without it, and to interpret him may be defined as tying his work into the community, which is at once the source of his meaning and the audience to which he writes. It is asking the community to look at itself and its experience.

This makes four large assumptions: first, that the community exists (not a given local citizenry, but the human community generally); second, that it has enough experience to recognize meaningful experience; third, that it has enough maturity and curiosity to make possible a newer and sharper understanding of it: and fourth, that it will surrender to knowledge that is not statistically or clinically demonstrated but comes from special insight, is transmitted by the imagination, and derives its authority only from continuing persuasiveness. We must assume all that or do something else with our wares. But in relating literature to experience we must make doubly clear that we do not mean to traffic in elementary pleasures of recognition for the nearsighted imagination or to dish up "old truths," making literature into a kind of Old Faithful which every hour, more or less, gives the relaxed customer a nice warm shower of lazy truisms, well-worn sentiments, thought-saving reassurances, and vague emotions to go with his old house shoes and sedative contour chair —for instance, the beauty of being born, the difficulty of dying, the cheeriness of charity, the yeastiness of youth, and the oldness of old age; plus a lot of loose talk about the "unquenchable human spirit." This marshmallowy Christmas-carol sort of thing would be worse than nothing. W. H. Auden sums up the issue beautifully when he points out that it is a mediocre work which makes a reader say, "That's just how I feel," but a great one which makes him say, "I never realized before what I felt. From now on, thanks to this poem, I shall feel differently." If we can present works with this in mind, we will not fall into the extremes of either pedantry or schmaltz (which are, after all, distant cousins: pedantry is the schmaltz of the man of learning, and schmaltz is the pedantry of the man of feeling).

To set up the triangle, literature: experience: meaning, does not, of course, give us an immediate, easy way into any story, play, or poem. "Experience" and "meaning" are large affairs which for most of us need to be made manageable by special partition or formulation, by being "tabbed." In the twenty-five years since I was an undergraduate there have come into prominence five modes of literary interpretation, all of which are ways of making connections—connections between plot and meaning, that is to say, between literary work and human experience generally (what used to be rather sonorously called the "universal," which has now become almost as naughty a word as *absolute*). None of these is altogether new; some are quite old; but it is in recent years that they have attracted wide attention, become controversial, and generated a considerable body of literary criticism. All of these, I think, may have some utility for us who are trying to make some connection between literature and a more general public than we find in our classrooms. These five methods treat literature respectively as a part of the history of ideas, as an exemplification of Freudian psychology, as myth, as ritual, and as form. Each is a mode of generalizing—that is, of bridging the gap between the literary foreground, the mimesis of an individual act or feeling, and the realm of larger human significance.

The relationship of literature to the history of ideas is most fertile as an approach, I think, when the subject is the twentieth century. In one's own day, both the novel, say, and the ideas to which it is related have an appealing immediacy; surely there ought to be some ready-made interest in correspondences or resistances between our literary habits and positivism, pragmatism, secularism, individualism, Marxism, democracy, scientific advances, and so forth. Many such studies are completed or in progress, and can be made available to nonprofessionals. I'm not sure that the method is equally good for other periods, when it is likely to seem frigidly antiquarian. Sterne's use of Lockian psychology may not seem to shed much light on *Tristram Shandy;* as no more than a synthesis of Thomistic thought and medieval attitude, the *Divine Comedy* may seem thin and distant; to present Jane Austen as a belated neo-classicist in the midst of romanticism, or the Brontës as exemplifications of romantic temperament, is likely to reduce these writers to scholastic shadows. Our problem is to show, not their congruence of works with their times, but their transcendence of their times.

I use the term "Freudian method" to cover a vast realm of literary analysis, which includes the application not only of Freudian but of many varieties of post-Freudian concepts to literary concepts, to specific literary works, to the authors of works, and to the audiences at which the works are aimed. In one corner we find the works used largely as a source of inferences about writers as persons; here the study moves sharply toward psychology and biography, which are not our main concern. Another approach is to seek out what the work does for the writer (what Kenneth Burke calls "symbolic action"), as a clue to what it does for the reader. Here we are definitely on the way toward reading the work as meaning and experience. A very useful route toward the perception of relationships is the analysis of characters, situations, and images in terms of modern psychology; here we run immediately into the fact that in literature there is as much pre-Freud as post-Freud Freudianism—an exciting demonstration of the kind of continuity and uniformity of perception that argues the existence, on one plane at least, of the community which literature is written *from* and *to*. The dangers of literary Freudianism are an exclusion of other modes of meaning, an inflexible mechanical application; Francis Fergusson has shown, for instance, how much of *Hamlet* is simply not taken into account by the Freudian reading. Many works may be called Freudian, but few may be frozen into a formula.

In the study of literature as myth there should be real possibilities of bringing the work home to the general, nonprofessional reader, for the approach may be used without specific involvement in Jungian psychology or Cambridge anthropology. Here the basic assumption is that, in actuality, or in our imaginative grasp of actuality, certain types of character and situation tend to recur in quite different ages and conditions. These are "archetypes"; an archetypal work is "mythic." Not all works are mythic, by any means; but it is important to discern mythic elements when those are present. To see and appreciate the myth is to get hold of some share of larger reality. I should be inclined to argue that such diverse works as Richardson's *Pamela*, Austen's *Pride and Prejudice*, and Brontë's *Jane Eyre* are all versions of the Cinderella myth; to understand these works in this way is to see the relationship among them as individuals, to see the relationship between them as a group and a basic habit of the human mind, and, in the light of these relationships, to have a sounder perception of the variations among the three novels. Ibsen's *Master Builder* may be defined as a myth of the artist—a sort of generic account of a specialized type of human being. Thornton Wilder's *Skin of Our Teeth* is, like Joyce's *Finnegans Wake* and, more recently, Christopher Fry's *A Sleep of Prisoners,* an effort to get at a central mythic account of humankind—what some critics call *"the* Myth." Besides the basic type of character and situation which show their elemental quality by recurring everywhere from folk tale to sophisticated art, there is the single work which recurs, so to speak, by taking on a fresh aliveness in century after century. Surely the perennial fascination of *Oedipus* and *Hamlet* suggests that they are felt as mythic works—as having some archetypal human significance which the partial human being of each era feels as "whole" and endeavors to restate in such terms as his age has made available. These examples may suggest concretely how the mythic view of literature should provide a means of communicating with the general public—or what I have called the community. Myth conspicuously implies community—community which overrides both time and place.

Literature as ritual is a concept which has yet to be fully explored. In myth, man expresses the communal sense of reality by telling stories; in ritual, he expresses this sense by engaging in certain operations—that is, rites or ceremonials—of a public, repetitive kind. Ritual, therefore, is an important and identifiable aspect of community life, even where that life has become technically secular, so that the concept of ritual may provide a feasible way into the study of literature. "Rituality" is most clear at the historical level: the emergence of Greek drama from Dionysiac ritual and that of modern drama from Christian ritual are commonplaces. Epic and ballad seem to be rooted at least partly in social rituals. General participation—a work of ritual—is evident in all choral elements. How much unrecognized ritual survives in other literary forms? To what extent may characterization and thematic development have a ritual significance? How much of the literary appeal is directed to what we might call the "ritual sense"? These are questions for technical students. But we know that the ritual element survives strongly in the mature Greek tragedy of the fifth century. Recently it has been suggested that there is a considerable ritual element in Elizabethan tragedy. My colleague, Brents Stirling, has shown that an important element in the characterization of Brutus in *Julius Caesar* is his transformation, effected in dozens of lines, of assassination into the ritual of sacrifice. Edmund Wilson has convincingly argued that ritual murder was to be one of the dramatic strands in Dickens' unfinished *Edwin Drood*. Eliot's drama has a strong ritual element—conspicuously in the libation scenes in *The Cocktail Party*. Unless these few examples are entirely exceptional, as I do not believe they are, a wide access to literature should be provided by ritual—a mode of human conduct which has a very deep psychic grounding and a corresponding variety of manifestation.

The formalist approach to literature may seem least amenable for our purposes, since it is especially susceptible of specialized use—of leading to a contemplation of form for form's sake. But by formalist study I mean—and formalist critics usually mean—not form for form's sake but form for meaning's sake. Its basic assumption is that one doesn't know the meaning without knowing the form—that is to say, discerning the parts of the whole and understanding how they are related to one another in the communication of what the writer has to say. The more complex the work, the more subtle the formal ingredients and their mode of interplay, and the more exacting the interpretative problem. Ironically, this is most often true in lyric poetry, the one form of literary composition which it is physically possible to show on a television screen and thus have immediately present before whoever will read and listen. But the special understanding that can come only through form may be got more readily, at least at the start, through drama and even more through fiction, if only because the formal parts and their way of contributing to the total statement are more readily identifiable. For instance, in the third part of Charlotte Brontë's novel *Jane Eyre*, Jane, who has refused to become Rochester's mistress, refuses to marry the minister, St. John Rivers. Why introduce this affair? Just to mark time until Rochester becomes eligible through the death of his wife? Just to show that Jane loves Rochester? To serve such purposes would be a gross waste of space. Actually, when they are taken together, Jane's two refusals constitute a better definition of a love relationship than either does alone: one proposal is wrong because, although it has passion, the man is not free; the other is wrong because, although the man is free and suitable, there is a lack of passion. Or take *Pride and Prejudice:* surely it is doing something more than making the banal statement that we should not be proud and prejudiced. In looking for something beyond such a truism, we have to deal directly with the formal problem of the reason for the multiplicity of characters and plots which at first reading may make the work look formless and chaotic. What we then discover is that we have not one version, but many versions of pride in the book: we see pride as social snobbery and as arrogance, but we also see shyness and reserve taken for pride; further, we see pride as self-respect and as sense of responsibility; and still further, we see an absence of pride which is as bad as the worst vanity. Now this gives us a pretty rich and mature statement—but it is one we can reach only through a very careful consideration of form. Is not this the sort of meaning which we may suppose an adult lay audience capable of being interested in?

The methods of literary interpretation which I have sketched must, in critical practice, cross and recross; the present account has, for convenience' sake, taken on some of the excessive purity of the paradigm. The impure combinations of criticism-in-action have their own logic, for all methods are aimed at crossing the bridge from the highly concrete and individualized foreground of literature to the background of meaning and knowledge, or, if you prefer, simply awareness. This background, I have been suggesting, brings in the whole realm of human experience and our modes of understanding it. In this sense, literature is necessarily about and of the community, and our aim is to establish it in the community. This possibility we have founded on a single idea: that literature is a rich way of knowing human reality.

But it is no good to keep repeating even the best and most profound statement of what literature does. No amount of even philosophic praise of literature is worth much if people don't read it. People don't hit the sawdust trail because they are told that it is good for them—for their bodies, or minds, or souls. Literature cannot be prescribed or promoted or "sold." The impulse to read may be encouraged or strengthened—by such means, perhaps, as this paper suggests. But the world's best literary analysis is wasted on the man who hasn't read what is analyzed. The impulse itself, the impulse to read, lies deep in psychic forces as they are modified by a civilizational "style." When we consider the newsstands, the bookstores, and the lamentable state of twentieth-century drama, the impulse seems either sterile or perverted. Yet there is one ground for hope: the relatively mature public taste in music. Our musical sophistication is in shocking contrast to our literary naïveté. But there are definite lines of relationship between an adult enjoyment of music and an adult enjoyment of literature. At least one realm of adulthood is marked out. It may be possible to expand it.

STUDY QUESTIONS

1. What is the difference, according to Heilman, between the knowledge offered by literature and other kinds of knowledge?

2. What special conditions connected with literature enable the knowledge it communicates to compete with scientific and factual knowledge? Compare Heilman's suggestions about this with MacLeish's observations about the knowledge communicated by poetry.

3. List the five methods of criticism described here and develop a short, clear definition for each of them.

4. Do these methods of criticism enable one to judge the value or merit of a literary work? If not, what do they do?

5. Take a work you know which seems to have an element of myth, as

it is described by Heilman, and explain how the work corresponds
to the myth.

6. What definition of criticism is implied in this essay? Give the
evidence for your conclusion.

2. PROSE, POETRY, AND DRAMA

On Literary Taste*

Arnold Bennett

THE AIM

At the beginning a misconception must be removed from the
path. Many people, if not most, look on literary taste as an elegant accomplishment, by acquiring which they will complete themselves, and
make themselves finally fit as members of a correct society. They are
secretly ashamed of their ignorance of literature, in the same way as they
would be ashamed of their ignorance of etiquette at a high entertainment,
or of their inability to ride a horse if suddenly called upon to do so. There
are certain things that a man ought to know, or to know about, and literature is one of them: such is their idea. They have learnt to dress
themselves with propriety, and to behave with propriety on all occasions;
they are fairly "up" in the questions of the day; by industry and enterprise they are succeeding in their vocations; it behooves them, then, not
to forget that an acquaintance with literature is an indispensable part of
a self-respecting man's personal baggage. Painting doesn't matter; music
doesn't matter very much. But "everyone is supposed to know" about
literature. Then, literature is such a charming distraction! Literary taste
thus serves two purposes: as a certificate of correct culture and as a
private pastime. A young professor of mathematics, immense at mathematics and games, dangerous at chess, capable of Haydn on the violin,
once said to me, after listening to some chat on books, "Yes, I must take
up literature." As though saying: "I was rather forgetting literature.
However, I've polished off all these other things. I'll have a shy at
literature now."

This attitude, or any attitude which resembles it, is wrong. To him who
really comprehends what literature is, and what the function of literature

---

* From *Literary Taste* by Arnold Bennett. Copyright, 1927, by Doubleday and Co., Inc. Reprinted by permission of the publishers, the Trustee
for the Bennett Estate, and Jonathan Cape, Ltd.

is, this attitude is simply ludicrous. It is also fatal to the formation of literary taste. People who regard literary taste simply as an accomplishment, and literature simply as a distraction, will never truly succeed either in acquiring the accomplishment or in using it half-acquired as a distraction; though the one is the most perfect of distractions, and though the other is unsurpassed by any other accomplishment in elegance or in power to impress the universal snobbery of civilised mankind. Literature, instead of being an accessory, is the fundamental *sine qua non* of complete living. I am extremely anxious to avoid rhetorical exaggerations. I do not think I am guilty of one in asserting that he who has not been "presented to the freedom" of literature has not wakened up out of his prenatal sleep. He is merely not born. He can't see; he can't hear; he can't feel, in any full sense. He can only eat his dinner. What more than anything else annoys people who know the true function of literature, and have profited thereby, is the spectacle of so many thousands of individuals going about under the delusion that they are alive, when, as a fact, they are no nearer being alive than a bear in winter.

I will tell you what literature is! No—I only wish I could. But I can't. No one can. Gleams can be thrown on the secret, inklings given, but no more. I will try to give you an inkling. And, to do so, I will take you back into your own history, or forward into it. That evening when you went for a walk with your faithful friend, the friend from whom you hid nothing—or almost nothing . . . ! You were, in truth, somewhat inclined to hide from him the particular matter which monopolized your mind that evening, but somehow you contrived to get on to it, drawn by an overpowering fascination. And as your faithful friend was sympathetic and discreet, and flattered you by a respectful curiosity, you proceeded further and further into the said matter, growing more and more confidential, until at last you cried out, in a terrific whisper: "My boy, she is simply miraculous!" At that moment you were in the domain of literature.

Let me explain. Of course, in the ordinary acceptation of the word, she was not miraculous. Your faithful friend had never noticed that she was miraculous, nor had about forty thousand other fairly keen observers. She was just a girl. Troy had not been burnt for her. A girl cannot be called a miracle. If a girl is to be called a miracle, then you might call pretty nearly anything a miracle . . . That is just it: you might. You can. You ought. Amid all the miracles of the universe you had just wakened up to one. You were full of your discovery. You were under a divine impulse to impart that discovery. You had a strong sense of the marvelous beauty of something, and you had to share it. You were in a passion about something and you had to vent yourself on somebody. You were drawn towards the whole of the rest of the human race. Mark the effect of your mood and utterance on your faithful friend. He knew that she was not a miracle. No other person could have made him believe that she was a miracle. But you, by the force and sincerity of your own vision of her, and by the fervour of your desire to make him participate in your vision, did for quite a long time cause him to feel that he had been blind to the miracle of that girl.

You were producing literature. You were alive. Your eyes were unlidded, your ears were unstopped, to some part of the beauty and the strangeness of the world; and a strong instinct within you forced you to tell someone. It was not enough for you that you saw and heard. Others had to see and hear. Others had to be wakened up. And they were! It is quite possible—I am not quite sure—that your faithful friend the very next day, or the next month, looked at some other girl, and suddenly saw that she, too, was miraculous! The influence of literature!

The makers of literature are those who have seen and felt the miraculous interestingness of the universe. And the greatest makers of literature are those whose vision has been the widest, and whose feeling been the most intense. Your own fragment of insight was accidental, and perhaps temporary. *Their* lives are one long ecstasy of denying that the world is a dull place. Is it nothing to you to learn to understand that the world is not a dull place? Is it nothing to you to be led out of the tunnel on to the hillside, to have all your senses quickened, to be invigorated by the true savour of life, to feel your heart beating under that correct necktie of yours? These makers of literature render you their equals.

The aim of literary study is not to amuse the hours of leisure; it is to awake oneself, it is to be alive, to intensify one's capacity for pleasure, for sympathy, and for comprehension. It is not to affect one hour, but twenty-four hours. It is to change utterly one's relations with the world. An understanding appreciation of literature means an understanding appreciation of the world, and it means nothing else. Not isolated and unconnected parts of life, but all of life, brought together and correlated in a synthetic map! The spirit of literature is unifying; it joins the candle and the star, and by the magic of an image shows that the beauty of the greater is in the less. And, not content with the disclosure of beauty and the bringing together of all things whatever within its focus, it enforces a moral wisdom by the tracing everywhere of cause and effect. It consoles doubly—by the revelation of unsuspected loveliness, and by the proof that our lot is the common lot. It is the supreme cry of the discoverer, offering sympathy and asking for it in a single gesture. In attending a University Extension Lecture on the sources of Shakespeare's plots or in studying the researches of George Saintsbury into the origins of English prosody, or in weighing the evidence for and against the assertion that Rousseau was a scoundrel, one is apt to forget what literature really is and is for. It is well to remind ourselves that literature is first and last a means of life, and that the enterprise of forming one's literary taste is an enterprise of learning how best to use this means of life. People who don't want to live, people who would sooner hibernate than feel intensely, will be wise to eschew literature. They had better, to quote from the finest passage in a fine poem, "sit around and eat blackberries." The sight of a "common bush afire with God" might upset their nerves. . . .

WHERE TO BEGIN

I wish particularly that my readers should not be intimidated by the apparent vastness and complexity of this enterprise of forming the literary taste. It is not so vast nor so complex as it looks. There is no need whatever for the inexperienced enthusiast to confuse and frighten himself with thoughts of "literature in all its branches." Experts and pedagogues (chiefly pedagogues) have, for the purpose of convenience split literature up into divisions and sub-divisions—such as prose and poetry; or imaginative, philosophic, historical; or elegiac, heroic, lyric; or religious and profane, etc., *ad infinitum.* But the greater truth is that literature is all one—and indivisible. The idea of the unity of literature should be well planted and fostered in the head. All literature is the expression of feeling, of passion, of emotion, caused by a sensation of the interestingness of life. What drives an historian to write history? Nothing but the overwhelming impression made upon him by the survey of past times. He is forced into an attempt to reconstitute the picture for others. If hitherto you have failed to perceive that an historian is a being in strong emotion, trying to convey his emotion to others, read the passage in the *Memoirs* of Gibbon, in which he describes how he finished the *Decline and Fall.* You will probably never again look upon the *Decline and Fall* as a "dry" work.

What applies to history applies to the other "dry" branches. Even Johnson's Dictionary is packed with emotion. Read the last paragraph of the preface to it: "In this work, when it shall be found that much is omitted, let it not be forgotten that much likewise is performed . . . It may repress the triumph of malignant criticism to observe that if our language is not here fully displayed, I have only failed in an attempt which no human powers have hitherto completed . . ." And so on to the close "I have protracted my work till most of those whom I wish to please have sunk into the grave, and success and miscarriage are empty sounds: I therefore dismiss it with frigid tranquillity, having too little to fear or hope from censure or from praise." Yes, tranquillity; but not frigid! The whole passage, one of the finest in English prose, is marked by the heat of emotion. You may discover the same quality in such books as Spencer's *First Principles.* You may discover it everywhere in literature, from the cold fire of Pope's irony to the blasting temperature of Swinburne. Literature does not begin till emotion has begun.

There is even no essential, definable difference between those two great branches, prose and poetry. For prose may have rhythm. All that can be said is that verse will scan, while prose will not. The difference is purely formal. Very few poets have succeeded in being so poetical as Isaiah, Sir

Thomas Browne, and Ruskin have been in prose. It can only be stated that, as a rule, writers have shown an instinctive tendency to choose verse for the expression of the very highest emotion. The supreme literature is in verse, but the finest achievements in prose approach so nearly to the finest achievements in verse that it is ill work deciding between them. In the sense in which poetry is best understood, all literature is poetry—or is, at any rate, poetical in quality. Macaulay's ill-informed and unjust denunciations live because his genuine emotion made them into poetry, while his *Lays of Ancient Rome* are dead because they are not the expression of a genuine emotion. As the literary taste develops, this quality of emotion, restrained or loosed, will be more and more widely perceived at large in literature. It is the quality that must be looked for. It is the quality that unifies literature (and all the arts).

It is not merely useless, it is harmful, for you to map out literature into divisions and branches, with different laws, rules, or canons. The first thing is to obtain some possession of literature. When you have actually felt some of the emotion which great writers have striven to impart to you, and when your emotions become so numerous and puzzling that you feel the need of arranging them and calling them by names, then—and not before—you can begin to study what has been attempted in the way of classifying and ticketing literature. Manuals and treatises are excellent things in their kind, but they are simply dead weight at the start. You can only acquire really useful general ideas by first acquiring particular ideas, and putting those particular ideas together. You cannot make bricks without straw. Do not worry about literature in the abstract, about theories as to literature. Get at it. Get hold of literature in the concrete as a dog gets hold of a bone. If you ask me where you ought to begin, I shall gaze at you as I might gaze at the faithful animal if he inquired which end of the bone he ought to attack. It doesn't matter in the slightest degree where you begin. Begin wherever the fancy takes you to begin. Literature is a whole.

There is only one restriction for you. You must begin with an acknowledged classic; you must eschew modern works. The reason for this does not imply any depreciation of the present age at the expense of past ages. Indeed, it is important, if you wish ultimately to have a wide, catholic taste, to guard against the too common assumption that nothing modern will stand comparison with the classics. In every age there have been people to sigh: "Ah, yes. Fifty years ago we had a few great writers. But they are all dead, and no young ones are arising to take their place." This attitude of mind is deplorable, if not silly, and is a certain proof of narrow taste. It is a surety that in 1959 gloomy and egregious persons will be saying: "Ah, yes. At the beginning of the century there were great poets like Swinburne, Meredith, Francis Thompson, and Yeats. Great novelists like Hardy and Conrad. Great historians like Stubbs and Maitland, etc. etc. But they are all dead now, and whom have we to take their place?" It is not until an age has receded into history, and all its mediocrity has dropped away from it, that we can see it as it is—as a group of men of genius. We forget the immense amount of twaddle that the great epochs produced. The total amount of fine literature created in a given period of time differs from epoch to epoch, but it does not differ much. And we may be perfectly sure that our own age will make a favourable impression upon that excellent judge, posterity. Therefore, beware of disparaging the present in your own mind. While temporarily ignoring it, dwell upon the idea that its chaff contains about as much wheat as any similar quantity of chaff has contained wheat.

The reason why you must avoid modern works at the beginning is simply that you are not in a position to choose among modern works. Nobody at all is quite in a position to choose with certainty among modern works. To sift the wheat from the chaff is a process that takes an exceedingly long time. Modern works have to pass before the bar of the taste of successive generations. Whereas, with classics, which have been through the ordeal, almost the reverse is the case. *Your taste has to pass before the bar of the classics.* That is the point. If you differ with a classic, it is you who are wrong, and not the book. If you differ with a modern work, you may be wrong or you may be right, but no judge is authoritative enough to decide. Your taste is unformed. It needs guidance, and it needs authoritative guidance. Into the business of forming literary taste faith enters. You probably will not specially care for a particular classic at first. If you did care for it at first, your taste, so far as that classic is concerned, would be formed, and our hypothesis is that your taste is not formed. How are you to arrive at the stage of caring for it? Chiefly, of course, by examining it and honestly trying to understand it. But this process is materially helped by an act of faith, by the frame of mind which says: "I know on the highest authority that this thing is fine, that it is capable of giving me pleasure. Hence I am determined to find pleasure in it." Believe me that faith counts enormously in the development of that wide taste which is the instrument of wide pleasures. But it must be faith founded on unassailable authority.

STUDY QUESTIONS

1. To what extent, according to Bennett, is a knowledge of literature useful as a social accomplishment? Do you agree with his view? Does he seem to agree on this point with Rilke?

2. To what extent do Buck and Bennett agree about the place of emotion in art? What similar point do they make about established or classical works?

3. Bennett explains that literature is the result of a writer's impulse to express some intense feeling that is nearly inexpressible. Do you know some story or poem that seems to be the product of such an impulse?

4. Do Bennett's remarks about the formal study of literature help to explain the fact that people generally dislike the books they have to read in school?

5. Describe your experience in reading a book, play, or poem generally considered a classic, telling whether you passed or failed the test of good judgment mentioned by Bennett, and analyzing the situation.

6. Do you agree with Bennett that the right way for a beginner to approach the reading of a classic is with a feeling of faith in its greatness? Or is some other attitude more constructive?

Letters to a Young Poet*

Rainer Maria Rilke

You ask whether your verses are good. You ask me. You have asked others before. You send them to magazines. You compare them with other poems, and you are disturbed when certain editors reject your efforts. Now (since you have allowed me to advise you) I beg you to give up all that. You are looking outward, and that above all you should not do now. Nobody can counsel and help you, nobody. There is only one single way. Go into yourself. Search for the reason that bids you write; find out whether it is spreading out its roots in the deepest places of your heart, acknowledge to yourself whether you would have to die if it were denied you to write. This above all—ask yourself in the stillest hour of your night: *must* I write? Delve into yourself for a deep answer. And if this should be affirmative, if you may meet this earnest question with a strong and simple *"I must,"* then build your life according to this necessity; your life even into its most indifferent and slightest hour must be a sign of this urge and a testimony to it. Then draw near to Nature. Then try, like some first human being, to say what you see and experience and love and lose. Do not write love-poems; avoid at first those forms that are too facile and commonplace: they are the most difficult, for it takes a great, fully matured power to give something of your own where good and even excellent traditions come to mind in quantity. Therefore save yourself from these general themes and seek those which your own everyday life offers you; describe your sorrows and desires, passing thoughts and the belief in some sort of beauty—describe all these with loving, quiet, humble sincerity, and use, to express yourself, the things in your environment, the images from your dreams, and the objects of your memory. If your daily life seems poor, do not blame it; blame yourself, tell yourself that you are not poet enough to call forth its riches; for to the creator there is no poverty and no poor indifferent place. And even if you were in some prison the walls of which let none of the sounds of the world come to your senses—would you not then still have your childhood, that precious, kingly possession, that treasure-house of memories? Turn your attention thither. Try to raise the submerged sensations of that ample past; your personality will grow more firm, your solitude will widen and will become a dusky dwelling past which the noise of others goes by far away.—And if out of this turning inward, out of this absorption into your own world *verses* come, then it will not occur to you to ask anyone whether they are good *verses*. Nor will you try to interest magazines in your poems: for you will see in them your fond natural possession, a fragment and a voice of your life. A work of art is good if it has sprung from necessity. In this nature of its origin lies the judgment of it: there is no other. Therefore, my dear sir, I know no advice for you save this: to go into yourself and test the deeps in which your life takes rise; at its source you will find the answer to the question whether you *must* create. Accept it, just as it sounds, without inquiring into it. Perhaps it will turn out that you are called to be an artist. Then take that destiny upon yourself and bear it, its burden and its greatness, without ever asking what recompense might come from outside. For the creator must be a world for himself and find everything in himself and in Nature to whom he has attached himself.

But perhaps after this descent into yourself and into your inner solitude you will have to give up becoming a poet; (it is enough, as I have said, to feel that one could live without writing: then one must not attempt it at all). But even then this inward searching which I ask of you will not have been in vain. Your life will in any case find its own ways thence, and that they may be good, rich and wide I wish you more than I can say.

What more shall I say to you? Everything seems to me to have its just emphasis; and after all I do only want to advise you to keep growing quietly and seriously throughout your whole development; you cannot disturb it more rudely than by looking outward and expecting from outside replies to questions that only your inmost feeling in your most hushed hour can perhaps answer. . . .

Very dear Mr. Kappus: I have left a letter from you long unanswered, not that I have forgotten it—on the contrary: it was of the sort that one reads again, when one finds them among one's correspondence, and I recognized you in it as though you had been close at hand. It was the letter of May 2nd, and you surely remember it. When I read it, as now, in the great quiet of these distances, I am touched by your beautiful concern about life, more even than I had felt it in Paris, where everything resounds and dies away differently because of the too great noise that makes things vibrate. Here, where an immense country lies about me, over which the winds pass coming from the seas, here I feel that no human being anywhere can answer for you those questions and feelings that deep within them have a life of their own; for even the best err in words when they are meant to mean most delicate and almost inexpressible things. But I believe nevertheless that you will not have to remain without a solution if you will hold to objects that are similar to those from which my eyes now draw refreshment. If you will cling to Nature, to the simple in Nature, to the little things that hardly anyone sees, and that can so unexpectedly become big and beyond measuring; if you have this love of inconsiderable things and seek quite simply, as one who serves, to win the confidence of what seems poor: then everything will become easier, more coherent and somehow more conciliatory for you, not in your intellect, perhaps, which lags marveling behind, but in your inmost consciousness, waking and cognizance. You are so young, so before all beginning, and I want to beg you, as much as I can, dear sir, to be patient toward all that is unsolved in your heart and to try to love the *questions themselves* like locked rooms and like books that are written in a very foreign tongue. Do not now seek the answers, which cannot be given you because you would not be able to live them. And the point is, to live everything. *Live* the questions now. Perhaps you will then gradually, without noticing it, live along some distant day into the answer. Perhaps you do carry within yourself the possibility of shaping and forming as a particularly happy and pure way of living; train yourself to it—but take whatever comes with great trust, and if only it comes out of your own will, out of some need of your inmost being, take it upon yourself and hate nothing. Sex is difficult; yes. But they are difficult things with which we have been charged; almost everything serious is difficult, and everything is serious. If you only recognize this and manage, out of yourself, out of your *own* nature and ways, out of your *own* experience and childhood and strength to achieve a relation to sex wholly your own (*not* influenced by convention and custom), then you need no longer be afraid of losing yourself and becoming unworthy of your best possession.

Physical pleasure is a sensual experience no different from pure seeing or the pure sensation with which a fine fruit fills the tongue; it is a great unending experience, which is given us, a knowing of the world, the fullness and the glory of all knowing. And not our acceptance of it is bad; the bad thing is that most people misuse and squander this experience and apply it as a stimulant at the tired spots of their lives and as distraction instead of a rallying toward exalted moments. Men have made even eating into something else: want on the one hand, superfluity upon the other, have dimmed the distinctness of this need, and all the deep, simple necessities in which life renews itself have become similarly dulled. But the individual can clarify them for himself and live them clearly (and if not the individual, who is too dependent, then at least the solitary man). He can remember that all beauty in animals and plants is a quiet enduring form of love and longing, and he can see animals, as he sees plants, patiently and willingly uniting and increasing and growing, not out of physical delight, not out of physical suffering, but bowing to necessities that are greater than pleasure and pain and more powerful than will and withstanding. O that man might take this secret, of which the world is full even to its littlest things, more humbly to himself and bear it, endure it, more seriously and feel how terribly difficult it is, instead of taking it lightly. That he might be more reverent toward his fruitfulness, which is but *one,* whether it seems mental or physical; for intellectual creation too springs from the physical, is of one nature with it and only like a gentler, more ecstatic and more everlasting repetition of physical delight. "The thought of being creator, of procreating, of making" is nothing without its continuous great confirmation and realization in the world, nothing without the thousandfold concordance from things and animals—and enjoyment of it is so indescribably beautiful and rich only because it is full of inherited memories of the begetting and the bearing of millions. In one creative thought a thousand forgotten nights of love revive, filling it with sublimity and exaltation. . . .

Think, dear sir, of the world you carry within you, and call this thinking what you will; whether it be remembering your own childhood or yearning toward your own future—only be attentive to that which rises up in you and set it above everything that you observe about you. What goes on in your innermost being is worthy of your whole love; you must somehow keep working at it and not lose too much time and too much courage in clarifying your attitude toward people. Who tells you that you have one anyway?—I know, your profession is hard and full of contradiction of yourself, and I foresaw your complaint and knew that it would come. Now that it has come, I cannot comfort you, I can only advise you to consider whether all professions are not like that, full of demands, full of enmity against the individual, saturated as it were with the hatred of those who have found themselves mute and sullen in a humdrum duty. The situation in which you now have to live is no more heavily laden with conventions, prejudices and mistakes than all the other situations, and if there are some that feign a greater freedom, still there is none that is in itself broad and spacious and in contact with the big things of which real living consists. Only the individual who is solitary is like a thing placed under profound laws, and when he goes out into the morning that is just beginning, or looks out into the evening that is full of happening, and if he feels what is going on there, then all status drops from him as from a dead man, though he stands in the midst of sheer life. What you, dear Mr. Kappus, must now experience as an officer, you would have felt just the same in any of the established professions; yes, even if, outside of any position, you had merely sought some light and independent contact with society, this feeling of constraint would not have been spared you.—It is so everywhere; but that is no reason for fear or sorrow; if there is nothing in common between you and other people, try being close to things, they will not desert you; there are the nights still and the winds that go through the trees and across many lands; among things and with the animals everything is still full of happening, in which you may participate; and children are still the way you were as a child, sad like that and happy,—and if you think of your childhood you live among them again, among the solitary children, and the grownups are nothing, and their dignity has no value. . . .

I believe that almost all our sadnesses are moments of tension that we find paralyzing because we no longer hear our surprised feelings living. Because we are alone with the alien thing that has entered into our self; because everything intimate and accustomed is for an instant taken away; because we stand in the middle of a transition where we cannot remain standing. For this reason the sadness too passes: the new thing in us, the added thing, has entered into our heart, has gone into its inmost chamber and is not even there any more,—is already in our blood. And we do not learn what it was. We could easily be made to believe that nothing has happened, and yet we have changed, as a house changes into which a guest has entered. We cannot say who has come, perhaps we shall never know, but many signs indicate that the future enters into us in this way in order to transform itself in us long before it happens. And this is why it is so important to be lonely and attentive when one is sad: because the apparently uneventful and stark moment at which our future sets foot in us is so much closer to life than that other noisy and fortuitous point of time at which it happens to us as if from outside. The more still, more patient and more open we are when we are sad, so much the deeper and so much the more unswervingly does the new go into us, so much the better do we make it ours, so much the more will it be *our* destiny, and when on some later day it "happens" (that is, steps forth out of us to others), we shall feel in our inmost selves akin and near to it. And that is necessary. It is necessary—and toward this our development will move gradually—that nothing strange should befall us, but only that which has long belonged to us. We have already had to rethink so many of our concepts of motion, we will also gradually learn to realize that that which we call destiny goes forth from within people, not from without into them. Only because so many have not absorbed their destinies and transmuted them within themselves while they were living in them, have they not recognized what has gone forth out of them; it was so strange to them that, in their bewildered fright, they thought it must only just then have entered into them, for they swear never before to have found anything like it in themselves. As people were long mistaken about the motion of the sun, so they are even yet mistaken about the motion of that which is to come. The future stands firm, dear Mr. Kappus, but we move in infinite space. How should it not be difficult for us?

And to speak of solitude again, it becomes always clearer that this is at bottom not something that one can take or leave. We *are* solitary. We may delude ourselves and act as though this were not so. That is all. But how much better it is to realize that we are so, yes, even to begin by assuming it. We shall indeed turn dizzy then; for all points upon which our eye has been accustomed to rest are taken from us, there is nothing near any more and everything far is infinitely far. A person removed from his own room, almost without preparation and transition, and set upon the height of a great mountain range, would feel something of the sort: an unparalleled insecurity, an abandonment to something inexpressible would almost annihilate him. He would think himself falling or hurled out into space, or exploded into a thousand pieces: what a monstrous lie his brain would have to invent to catch up with and explain the state of his senses! So for him who becomes solitary all distances, all measures change; of these changes many take place suddenly, and then, as with the man on the mountaintop, extraordinary imaginings and singular sensations arise that seem to grow out beyond all bearing. But it is necessary for us to experience *that* too. We must assume our existence as *broadly* as we in any way can; everything, even the unheard-of, must be possible in it. That is at bottom the only courage that is demanded of us: to have courage for the most strange, the most singular and the most inexplicable that we may encounter. That mankind has in this sense been cowardly has done life endless harm; the experiences that are called "visions," the whole so-called "spirit-world," death, all those things that are so closely akin to us, have by daily parrying been so crowded out of life that the senses with which we could have grasped them are atrophied. To say nothing of God. But fear of the inexplicable has not alone impoverished the existence of the individual; the relationship between one human being and another has also been cramped by it, as though it had been lifted out of the riverbed of endless possibilities and set down in a fallow spot on the bank, to which nothing happens. For it is not inertia alone that is responsible for human relationships repeating themselves from case to case, indescribably monotonous and unrenewed; it is shyness before any sort of new, unforeseeable experience with which one does not think oneself able to cope. But only someone who is ready for everything, who excludes nothing, not even the most enigmatical, will live the relation to another as something alive and will himself draw exhaustively from his own existence. For if we think of this existence as a larger or smaller room, it appears evident that most people learn to know only a corner of their room, a place by the window, a strip of floor on which they walk up and down. Thus they have a certain security. And yet that dangerous insecurity is so much more human which drives the prisoners in Poe's stories to feel out the shapes of their horrible dungeons and not be strangers to the unspeakable terror of their abode. We, however, are not prisoners. No traps or snares are set about us, and there is nothing which should intimidate or worry us. We are set down in life as in the element to which we best correspond, and over and above this we have through thousands of years of accommodation become so like this life, that when we hold still we are, through a happy mimicry, scarcely to be distinguished from all that surrounds us. We have no reason to mistrust our world, for it is not against us. Has it terrors, they are *our* terrors; has it abysses, those abysses belong to us; are dangers at hand, we must try to love them. And if only we arrange our life according to that principle which counsels us that we must always hold to the difficult, then that which now still seems to us the most alien will become what we most trust and find most faithful. How should we be able to forget those ancient myths that are at the beginning of all peoples, the myths about dragons that at the last moment turn into princesses; perhaps all the dragons of our lives are princesses who are only waiting to see us once beautiful and brave. Perhaps everything terrible is in its deepest being something helpless that wants help from us. . . .

STUDY QUESTIONS

1. How does Rilke's advice to the young poet compare with Newton's attitude that it is up to the artist to reach a compromise with his public?

2. What does Rilke mean by his advice not to seek the answers to questions, but to "love" problems and "live" them? Of what value is this attitude to a poet or an artist?

3. To what aspects of life does Rilke call attention? How do you account for his omission of parts of life that are generally considered important, such as relationships with others, earning a living and being successful?

4. What is Rilke's philosophy of insecurity?

5. Write a theme summarizing the part of Rilke's ideas that seems most original to you, and tell whether or not this original idea seems to have any value for you.

6. Note that Rilke has assured the young poet that he himself is the best source of inspiration for his work and the best judge of it. Has Rilke omitted some of the important considerations an artist must face? Whether your answer to this question is positive or negative, write a theme expressing and explaining your opinion.

Why Do We Teach Poetry?*

Archibald MacLeish

There is something about the art of poetry which induces a defensive posture. Even in the old days when the primacy of poetry was no more challenged than the primacy of Heaven, which is now also challenged, the posture was habitual. If you published your reflections on the art in those days you called them a *Defense*. Today, when the queen of sciences is Science, you do not perhaps employ that term but you mean it. It is not that the gentlemen at the long table in the Faculty Club whose brains have been officially cleared to serve as depositories of scientific secrets of the eighth and thirteenth classes are patronizing in their manner. They are still gentlemen and therefore still modest no matter how great their distinction or how greatly certified. But one knows one's place. One knows that whereas the teachers of science meet to hear of new triumphs which the newspapers will proudly report, the teachers of poetry meet to ask old questions—which no one will report: such questions as, why teach poetry anyway in a time like this?

It is a relief in this general atmosphere to come upon someone who feels no defensiveness whatever: who is perfectly certain that poetry ought to be taught now as at any other time and who is perfectly certain also that he knows why. The paragon I have in mind is a young friend of mine, a devoted teacher, who was recently made headmaster of one of the leading American preparatory schools, and who has been taking stock, for some time past, of his curriculum and his faculty. Poetry, as he sees it, ought to be taught "as a most essential form of human expression as well as a carrier throughout the ages of some of the most important values in our heritage." What troubles him is that few teachers, at least in the schools he knows, seem to share his conviction. He is not too sure that teachers themselves have "an abiding and missionary faith in poetry" which would lead them to see it as a great clarifier—a "human language" capable of competing with the languages and mathematics and science.

But though teachers lack the necessary faith, the fault, as my young friend sees it, is not wholly theirs. The fault is the fault of modern criticism, which has turned poetry into something he calls "poetry itself"— meaning, I suppose, poetry for poetry's sake. "Poetry itself" turns out to be poetry with its meanings distilled away, and poetry with its meanings distilled away is difficult if not impossible to teach in a secondary

* From *The Atlantic Monthly*, March, 1956. Reprinted by the kind permission of the author.

school—at least *his* secondary school. The result is that secondary school teachers have gone back, as to the lesser of two evils, to those historical and anecdotal practices sanctified by American graduate schools in generations past. They teach "poets and not poetry." With the result that "students become acquainted with poets from Homer to MacLeish" (quite a distance no matter how you measure it!) "but the experience doesn't necessarily leave them with increased confidence in what poetry has to offer." I can well believe it.

The reason why modern criticism has this disastrous effect, the reason why it produces "an almost morbid apathy toward 'content' or 'statement of idea,'" is its excessive "preoccupation with aesthetic values." Modern criticism insists that poems are primarily works of art; and when you insist that poems are primarily works of art you cannot, in my friend's view, teach them as carriers "throughout the ages of some of the most important values in our heritage." What is important about Homer and Shakespeare and the authors of the Bible is that they were "realists with great vision . . . whose work contains immensely valuable constructions of the meaning of life"; and if you talk too much about them as artists, those constructions of the meaning of life get lost.

Now this, you will observe, is not merely another walloping of the old horse who was once called the New Criticism. It goes a great deal farther. It is a frontal attack upon a general position maintained by many who never accepted the New Criticism or even heard of it. It is an attack upon those who believe—as most poets, I think, have believed—that a poem *is* primarily a work of art and must be read as a work of art if it is to be read at all. It is a high-minded and disinterested attack delivered for the noblest of purposes, but an attack notwithstanding—and an effective one. What it contends is that an approach to poetry which insists that a poem is a work of art blocks off what the poem has to say, whereas what the poem has to say is the principal reason for teaching it. What the argument comes down to, in other words, is the proposition that it is a mistake, in teaching poetry, to insist that poetry is art, because, if you do so insist, you will not be able to bring your students to the meaning of the poem, the idea of the poem, what the poem has to tell them about man and world and life and death—and it is for these things the teaching of the poem is important.

Now, I can understand this argument and can respect the reasons for making it. Far too many of those who define poetry in exclusively artistic terms use their definition as a limiting and protective statement which relieves them of all obligation to drive the poem's meanings beyond the meanings of the poem: beyond the mere translation of the symbols and metaphors and the classical or other references—the whole apparatus of *explication du texte.* Far too many, indeed, of those who have to do with literature generally in our time, and particularly with modern literature, consider that meanings in any but a literary (which includes a Freudian) sense are not only outside, but beneath, their proper concern—that the intrusion of questions of morality and religion into the world of art is a kind of trespass and that works of literary art not only should but *can* be studied in a moral vacuum. Literature in the hands of such teachers is well on the way to becoming again that "terrible queen" which the men of the nineties raised above life and which Yeats, when he outgrew the men of the nineties, rejected.

But although I can understand this argument, and although I can respect its reasons, and although I believe it raises a true issue and an important issue, I cannot accept it; for it rests, or seems to me to rest, on two quite dubious assumptions. The first is the assumption, familiar in one form or another to all of us, that the "idea" of a work of art is somehow separable from the work of art itself. The most recent—and most egregious—expression of this persistent notion comes from a distinguished Dean of Humanities in a great institution of learning who is reported by the New York *Times* to have argued in a scholarly gathering that "the idea which the reader derives from Ernest Hemingway's *The Old Man and The Sea* comes after the reader has absorbed some 60,000 words. This takes at least an hour. . . . A similar understanding could come after a few minutes study of a painting by a skillful artist." Precisely, one imagines, as the Doré illustrations gave one the "idea" of the *Inferno* in a few easy looks!

2

It is the second assumption, however, which divides me most emphatically from my young friend. For the second assumption seems to be that *unless* idea and work of art are distinguished from each other in the teaching of a poem, the idea—and so the effectiveness of the teaching—will be lost. At this point my friend and I part company. I am ready, and more than ready, to agree that it is for the meanings of life that one reads (and teaches) poetry. But I am unable to see how there can be a distinction between a poem as a conveyer of such meanings and a poem as a work of art. In brief, the distinction between art and knowledge which is made throughout my friend's argument seems to me wholly without foundation. That it is a distinction almost universally recognized in our epoch I know well enough. Science makes it. Poetry makes it. And the world agrees with both. "Whatever can be *known*," says Bertrand Russell, "can be known by means of science." Poetry, say its professors, has no "messages" to deliver. And no one dissents from either. The exclusive proprietary right of science to know and to communicate knowledge is not only commonly recognized in our civilization: in a very real sense it is our civilization. For the characteristic of our civilization—that which distinguishes it from the civilizations which have preceded it—is the characteristic which knowledge-by-science has conferred upon it: its abstractness.

But though the agreement is general, the proposition is not one I can accept. I argue that the apologists for science are not justified in claiming, nor the apologists for poetry in admitting, the sole right of science to know. I insist that poetry is also capable of knowledge; that poetry, indeed, is capable of a kind of knowledge of which science is not capable; that it is capable of that knowledge *as poetry;* and that the teaching of poetry as poetry, the teaching of poem as work of art, is not only not incompatible with the teaching of poetry as knowledge but is, indeed, the only possible way of teaching poetry as knowledge.

To most of us, brought up as we have been in the world of abstractions which science has prepared for us, and in the kind of school which that world produces—schools in which almost all teaching is teaching of abstractions—the notion of poetry as knowledge, the notion of art as knowledge, is a fanciful notion. Knowledge by abstraction we understand. Science can abstract ideas about apple from apple. It can organize those ideas into knowledge about apple. It can then, by some means, introduce that knowledge into our heads—possibly because our heads are abstractions also. But poetry, we know, does not abstract. Poetry presents. Poetry presents the thing as the thing. And that it should be possible to *know* the thing *as the thing it is*—to *know* apple *as* apple—this we do not understand; this, the true child of the time will assure you, cannot be done. To the true child of abstraction you can't know apple as apple. You can't know tree as tree. You can't know man as man. All you can *know* is a world dissolved by analyzing intellect into abstraction—not a world composed by imaginative intellect into itself. And the result, for the generations of abstraction, is that neither poetry nor art can be a means to knowledge. To inspiration, yes; poetry can undoubtedly lead to that—whatever it is. To revelation, perhaps: there may certainly be moments of revelation in poetry. But to knowledge, no. The only connection between poetry and knowledge we can see is the burden of used abstractions—adages and old saws—which poetry, some poetry, seems to like to carry—adages most of which we knew before and some of which aren't even true.

But if all this is so, what then is the "experience of art"—the "experience of poetry"—which all of us who think about these things at all have known? What is the experience of *realization* which comes over us with those apples on a dish of Cézanne's or those three pine trees? What is the experience of realization which comes over us with Debussy's *Nuages?* What is the experience of realization which comes over us when Coleridge's robin sits and sings

> Betwixt the tufts of snow on the bare branch
> Of mossy apple-tree, while the nigh thatch
> Smokes in the sun thaw; . . .

or when his eave-drops fall

> Heard only in the trances of the blast,
> Or if the secret ministry of frost
> Shall hang them up in silent icicles,
> Quietly shining to the quiet Moon.

And if all this is so, why does one of the most effective of modern definitions of poetry (Arnold's in his letter to Maurice de Guérin) assign to that art the peculiar "power of so dealing with *things* as to awaken in us a wonderfully full, new and intimate sense of them and of our relation with them"?

The answer is, of course, that the children of abstraction are wrong—and are impoverished by their error, as our entire time is impoverished by it. They are wrong on both heads. They are wrong when they think they *can* know the world through its abstractions: nothing can be known through an abstraction but the abstraction itself. They are wrong also when they think they *cannot* know the world as the world: the whole achievement of art is a demonstration to the contrary. And the reason they are wrong on both heads is the reason given, quite unintentionally, by Matthew Arnold. They are wrong because they do not realize that all true knowledge is a matter of relation: that we *really* know a thing only when we are filled with "a wonderfully full, new and intimate sense of it" and, above all, of "our relation with" it. This sense—this *knowledge* in the truest meaning of the word knowledge—art can give but abstraction cannot.

There are as many proofs as there are successful works of art. Take, for obvious example, that unseen mysterious phenomenon, the wind. Take any attempt, by the familiar processes of abstraction, to "know" the wind. Put beside it those two familiar lines of George Meredith:—

> Mark where the pressing wind shoots javelin-like
> Its skeleton shadow on the broad-backd wave!

What will be the essential difference between the two? Will it not be that the first, the analytical, statement is or attempts to be a wholly objective statement made without reference to an observer (true everywhere and always), whereas an observer—*one's self* as observer!—is involved in the second? And will not the consequential difference be that a relation involving one's self is created by the second but not by the first? And will not the end difference be that the second, but not the first, will enable us to know the thing itself—to know what the thing is *like?*

It would be quite possible, I suppose, to semanticize this difference between knowledge by poetry and knowledge by abstraction out of existence by demonstrating that the word, know, is being used in two different senses in the two instances, but the triumph would be merely verbal, for the difference is real. It is indeed the realest of all differences, for what it touches is the means by which we come at reality. How are we to find the knowledge of reality in the world without, or in the shifting, flowing, fluid world within? Is all this a task for the techniques of abstraction—for science as it may be or as it is? Is it through abstraction alone that we are to find what is real in our experience of our lives—and so, conceivably, what is real in ourselves? Or do we need another and a different way of knowing—a way of knowing which will make that world out there, this world in here, available to us, not by translating them into something else—into abstractions of quantity and measure—but by bringing us ourselves to confront them as they are—man and tree face to face in the shock of recognition, man and love face to face?

The question, I beg you to see, is not what we *ought* to do. There is no ought. A man can "live" on abstractions all his life if he has the stomach for them, and many of us have—not the scientists only, but great numbers of the rest of us in this contemporary world, men whose days are a web of statistics, and names, and business deals, held together by the parentheses of a pair of commuting trains with three Martinis at the close. The question is not what we ought to do. The question is what we have the choice of doing—what alternatives are open to us. And it is here and in these terms that the issue presents itself to the teacher of poetry.

3

Colleges and universities do not exist to impose duties but to reveal choices. In a civilization like ours in which one choice has all but overwhelmed the other, a civilization dominated by abstraction, in which men are less and less able to deal with their experience of the world or of themselves unless experience and self have first been translated into abstract terms—a civilization like a foreign language—in such a civilization the need for an understanding of the alternative is urgent. What must be put before the generation of the young is the possibility of a knowledge of experience *as* experience, of self *as* self; and that possibility only the work of art, only the poem, can reveal. That it is so rarely, or so timidly, presented in our schools is one of the greatest failures of our educational system. Young men and young women graduate from American schools and colleges by the hundreds of thousands every year to whom science is the only road to knowledge, and to whom poetry is little more than a subdivision of something called "literature"—a kind of writing printed in columns instead of straight across the page and primarily intended to be deciphered by girls, who don't read it either.

This sort of thing has consequences. Abstractions are wonderfully clever tools for taking things apart and for arranging things in patterns but they are very little use in putting things together and no use at all when it comes to determining what things are *for*. Furthermore, abstractions have a limiting, a dehumanizing, a dehydrating effect on the relation to things of the man who must live with them. The result is that we are more and more left, in our scientific society, without the means of knowledge of ourselves as we truly are or of our experience as it actually is. We have the tools, all the tools—we are suffocating in tools—but we cannot find the actual wood to work or even the actual hand to work it. We begin with one abstraction (something we think of as ourselves) and a mess of other abstractions (standing for the world) and we arrange and rearrange the counters, but who we are and what we are doing we simply do not know—above all what we are doing. With the inevitable consequence that we do not know either what our purpose is or our end. So that when the latest discoveries of the cyclotron are reported we hail them with the cry that we will now be able to control nature better than ever before—but we never go on to say for what purpose, to what end, we will control her. To destroy a city? To remake a world?

It was something of this kind, I imagine, that Adlai Stevenson had in mind when he startled a Smith Commencement last spring by warning his newly graduated audience of prospective wives that the "typical Western man—or typical Western husband—operates well in the realm of means, as the Roman did before him. But outside his specialty, in the realm of ends he is apt to operate poorly or not at all. . . . The neglect of the cultivation of more mature values," Mr. Stevenson went on, "can only mean that his life, and the life of the society he determines, will lack valid purpose, however busy and even profitable it may be."

As he has so often done before, Mr. Stevenson there found words for an uneasiness which has been endemic but inarticulate in the American mind for many years—the sense that we are getting nowhere far too fast and that, if something doesn't happen soon, we may arrive. But when he came to spell out the causes for "the neglect of the cultivation of more mature values" Mr. Stevenson failed, or so it seems to me, to identify the actual villain. The contemporary environment in America, he told his young listeners, is "an environment in which 'facts,' the data of the senses, are glorified and value judgments are assigned inferior status as 'mere matters of opinion.' It is an environment in which art is often regarded as an adornment of civilization rather than a vital element of it, while philosophy is not only neglected but deemed faintly disreputable because 'it never gets you anywhere.'" It is true that philosophy is neglected, and even truer that art is regarded in this country generally as it seems to be regarded by the automobile manufacturers of Detroit: as so much enamel paint and chromium to be applied for allegedly decorative purposes to the outside of a car which would run better without it. But the explanation is not, I think, that we set facts—even facts in quotation marks—above values, or that we glorify the data of the senses, unless one means by that latter phrase not what the senses tell us of the world we live in but what the statistics that can be compiled out of the data of the senses would tell us if we were ever in touch with our senses.

In few civilizations have the senses been less alive than they are with us. Look at the cities we build and occupy—but look at them!—the houses we live in, the way we hold ourselves and move; listen to the speaking voices of the greater part of our women. And in no civilization, at least in recorded time, have human beings been farther from the *facts* if we mean by that word, facets of reality. Our indifference to ends is the result of our obsession with abstractions rather than facts: with the ideas of things rather than with things. For there can be no concern for ends without a hunger for reality. And there can be no hunger for reality without a sense of the real. And there can be no sense of the real in the world which abstraction creates, for abstraction is incapable of the real: it can neither lay hold of the real itself nor show us where to find it. It cannot, that is to say, create the *relation* between reality and ourselves which makes *knowledge* of reality possible, for neither reality nor ourselves exist in abstraction. Everything in the world of abstraction is object. And, as George Buttrick pointedly says, *we* are not objects: we are subjects.

4

But all this is a negative way of saying what a defender of poetry should not be afraid of saying positively. Let me say it. We have lost our concern with ends because we have lost our touch with reality and we have lost our touch with reality because we are estranged from the means to reality which is the poem—the work of art. To most members of our generation this would seem an extravagant statement but it is not extravagant in fact and would not have seemed so in another time. In ancient China the place of poetry in men's lives was assumed as matter of course; indeed, the polity was based on it. The three hundred and five odes or songs which make up the Song-word Scripture survived to the fourth century B.C., when Confucius is said to have collected them because they were part of the government records preserved in the Imperial Archive. For thousands of years the examinations for the Chinese civil service were examinations in poetry, and there is no record that the results were more disappointing to the throne than examinations of a different character might have been. Certainly there is no record that a Chinese civil servant ever attempted to deny an honor student in a military academy his commission in the imperial army *or* navy because he was friendly with his own mother! Idiocies which the study of science and of other abstractions in contemporary institutions of naval education in the United States seem to nourish were apparently cauterized from the mind by the reading of poems.

It was not for nothing that Confucius told his disciples that the three hundred and five songs of the Song-word Scripture could be boiled down to the commandment: "Have no twisty thoughts." You cannot have twisty thoughts if you are real and if you are thinking about real things. But if a mother is merely a biological event to you and if you yourself are merely a military event called an admiral, anything may happen: you may make your country ridiculous, humiliate a promising boy, and deprive the navy of a good officer, all in the twisted belief that you are being a wise man and a patriot.

One can see, not only in the three hundred and five songs, but in Chinese poetry of other periods, what Confucius meant. Consider two Chinese poems of the second century B.C. and the sixth of our era, both written by Emperors. The first is a poem of grief—of the sense of loss of someone loved: a poem therefore of that inward world of feeling, of emotion, which seems to us most nearly ourselves and which, because it is always in flux, always shifting and changing and flowing away, is, of all parts of our experience of our lives, most difficult to know. We cannot know it through science. We cannot know it by knowing things *about* it—even the shrewdest and most intelligent things, helpful though they may be to us in other ways. We cannot know it either by merely feeling it—by uttering its passing urgencies, crying out "I love" meaning "I think of myself as loving" or sobbing "I grieve" meaning "I think of myself as grieving." How then can we know it?

The Emperor Wu-ti wrote (this is Arthur Waley's beautiful translation) :—

> The sound of her silk skirt has stopped.
> On the marble pavement dust grows.
> Her empty room is cold and still.
> Fallen leaves are piled against the doors.
>
> Longing for that lovely lady
> How can I bring my aching heart to rest?

Four images, one of sound, two of sight, one of feeling, each like a note plucked on a stringed instrument. Then a question like the chord the four would make together. And all at once we *know*. We know this grief which no word could have described, which any abstraction the mind is capable of would have destroyed. But we know more than this grief: we know our own—or will when it shall visit us—and so know something of ourselves.

The second is a poem of that emotion, that feeling, which is even more difficult to know than grief itself. The second is a poem of delight: youth and delight—the morning of the world—the emotion, of all emotions, most difficult to stop, to hold, to see. "Joy whose hand is ever at his lips bidding adieu." How would you *know* delight in yourself and therefore yourself delighting? Will the psychiatrists tell you? Is there a definition somewhere in the folios of abstraction by which we attempt to live which will capture it for you? The Emperor Ch'ien Wen-ti (again Waley's translation) knew that there is only one mirror which will hold that vanishing smile: the mirror of art, the mirror of the poem:—

A beautiful place is the town of Lo-yang:
The big streets are full of spring light
The lads go driving out with harps in their hands:
The mulberry girls go out to the fields with their baskets
Golden whips glint at the horses' flanks,
Gauze sleeves brush the green boughs.
Racing dawn the carriages come home—
And the girls with their high baskets full of fruit.

In this world within, you see, this world which is ourselves, there is no possibility of knowing by abstracting the meaning out—or what we hope will be the meaning. There we must know things *as* themselves and it must be *we* who know them. Only art, only poetry, can bring about that confrontation, because only art, only poetry, can show us what we are and ourselves confronting it. To be ignorant of poetry is to be ignorant therefore of the one means of reaching the world of our experience of the world. And to be ignorant of *that* world is to be ignorant of who and what we are. And to be ignorant of who and what we are is to be incapable of reality no matter what tools we have, or what intelligence, or what skills. It is this incapacity, this impotence, which is the tragedy of the time we live in. We are spiritually impotent because we have cut ourselves off from the poem. And the crowning irony is that it is only in the poem that we can know how impotent we have become.

Why do we teach poetry in this scientific age? To present the great alternative not to science but to that knowledge by abstraction which science has imposed. And what is this great alternative? Not the "messages" of poems, their interpreted "meanings," for these are abstractions also—abstractions far inferior to those of science. Not the explications of poetic texts, for the explication of a poetic text which goes no farther ends only in abstraction.

No, the great alternative is the poem as itself, the poem as a poem, the poem as a work of art—which is to say, the poem in the context in which alone the work of art exists: the context of the world, of the man and of the thing, of the infinite relationship which is our lives. To present the great alternative is to present the poem not as a message in a bottle, and not as an object in an uninhabited landscape, but as an action in the world, an action in which we ourselves are actors and our lives are known.

STUDY QUESTIONS

1. To what characteristics of modern life does MacLeish attribute the distrust of poetry as a method of knowledge? Do you agree that there is such a distrust? Do you agree with MacLeish's analysis of its causes?

2. MacLeish says that poetry conveys knowledge by bringing the reader face to face with concrete reality. Is this how language is

usually used? What does MacLeish's point suggest about the difference between poetry and other uses of language?

3. In what way does MacLeish think a familiarity with poetry will help to ameliorate the present spiritual confusion?

4. Why does MacLeish think poetry better qualified than, for example, science or social science, as a medium of knowledge?

5. Try to explain to a friend who has read this essay and failed to understand it very well what MacLeish means by saying "we have lost our touch with reality." In order to do this you will have to explain the part played in this process by abstraction and "twisty thoughts."

6. Do you agree with MacLeish that poetry is *the* main way to satisfactory knowledge? If not, write a theme criticizing his opinion and pointing out alternatives.

*The New Compassion in the American Novel**
Edmund Fuller

Never a glycerin tear shed to the tune of "Hearts and Flowers" in a Victorian tear-jerker was so sloppy and false as is the weird sentimentality in some of the roughest and supposedly most "realistic" of modern novels. An inverted pathos has sprung up among what Maxwell Geismar has called "the brutes." For some years, authors, publishers and reviewers have kicked around the word *compassion* so loosely that its meaning may become corrupted and lost.

The present decline of compassion (which also is the decline of tragedy) began in an odd and relatively innocuous way. It started with the vogue of the lovable bums, and at first it was no worse than a foolish romanticizing of the scalawag: a beery, brass-rail sentimentality. This pattern was not completely new—we see a bit of it in all the classical picaros— but never had it been so elaborated as it began to be in the thirties. It had charm and appeal, at times, dealing good-naturedly with human foibles. It is possible to look affectionately upon such people, as with Wilkins Micawber, if you keep your head and don't elevate a mood into a philosophy.

Some writers, especially those talented men William Saroyan, in *The Time of Your Life,* and John Steinbeck, in several books from his early *Tortilla Flat* to his recent *Sweet Thursday,* developed the lovable bums into the fallacy of "the beautiful little people"—which almost always meant the shiftless, the drunk, the amoral and the wards of society. A

* This essay, from *Man in Modern Fiction,* by Edmund Fuller, originally appeared in the *American Scholar.* Copyright 1957 by Edmund Fuller. By permission of Random House, Inc.

corollary was implied: if you didn't love these characters, you were a self-righteous bigot, hard of heart by contrast to the author's compassion and love for the common clay of humanity. Conversely, these books imply another world of respectable and economically stable people who vaguely are not nice, not right, compared to the ineffable and intransigent "little people."

Yet some, though not all, of this stuff called itself "realistic." Its absurdities reached a point in Steinbeck's *The Wayward Bus,* which inspired John Mason Brown to one of the most searching remarks since the little boy said the emperor wasn't wearing any clothing: "If realism isn't real, then isn't it trash?"

A sinister twist came in the path some years ago, and abruptly this new soft streak lost its innocence. The lovable bum began to slip away, and in his place emerged the genial rapist, the jolly slasher, the fun-loving dope pusher. Now we see increasingly a technique of simple identification with the degraded which is miscalled compassion. It lacks the requisites for compassion as much as its subjects lack the requisites for tragedy.

What is compassion, anyhow? It means the sharing of a sorrow, a pity and sympathy, a desire to help—feeling another's pain or plight as if it were one's own, seeing "those in chains as bound with them." It applies to a man's moral as well as material or physical breakdown. In the moral realm it recognizes the sharing of all human guilt, the potentiality of evil in the most blameless, the element which the Christian calls original sin and the analyst calls the id. In the traditions of both tragic and pathetic literature there is an abundance of authentic compassion.

A large and generous view of life and a distinct standard of values are necessary to establish compassion. These need not, of course, be formulated, but at least you must be able to discriminate between a happy state and an unhappy one; you must be able to discern the difference between a man destroyed through his own fault and one destroyed through no fault of his own, with all the delicate gradations possible between. You must set a moral value on man's actions and circumstances. Compassion is not a suspension of judgment, it is a judgment tempered and chastened according to the facts under some definable theory of the human condition. Compassion is discernment of the gap between the man that is and the potential man that was.

The two old saws contain much of the truth about the compassionate view of life and, incidentally, remove its unavoidable judgments from any taint of smugness: "There but for the grace of God go I," and "To understand all is to forgive all." How these apply to the phony compassion in many current novels we shall see.

In the enthusiastic critical reception of *From Here to Eternity,* culminating in the National Book Award, the word *compassion* was sprayed all over the scene by the critical fraternity. The writing of James Jones may well have many admirable attributes, but I do not see wherein compassion is one of them.

Like all the other pseudo-tough writers engaged in this peculiar transposition of values, Mr. Jones is shamelessly and laughably sentimental. This is missed by some simply because he isn't sentimental about Mother or Dad or the Pure Girl or Jesus or Darling Babies. Instead, he is sentimental about incorrigible anti-social and criminal types and whores. He is said to be compassionate toward these—which is as you choose to think. Certainly, though, if you are *not* one of these you may expect short shrift from Mr. Jones, for he has precious little compassion for anyone else.

If you can wipe Mr. Jones's tears out of your eyes, you will see that the famous Private Robert E. Lee Prewitt is not a social being, nor are his buddies. Prewitt is not the most extreme of them, but he is the "hero." His type is a social hazard. Since many men have endured as much in the way of background experience as Prewitt did, he is no more the helpless creation of something outside him than anyone else. His character is partly, even largely, self-created, as is true, for practical purposes, of most of us.

But, says Compassionate Jones: Prewitt, Maggio, Stark and the others, drinking and whoring, knifing and slugging, rolling homosexuals, defying authority indiscriminately and eternally, are good, good people. All authority, all sobriety, all the rest of the world, are bad. He is vindictive against the socially adjusted or constructive. If you listen to him long you'll be ashamed to be sober and out of jail. This is not compassion; it is paranoia.

And this is why some of us regard *From Here to Eternity* not as a controlled work of art, but as a clinically interesting projection of personalities by a man endowed with genuine gifts for narrative and pictorial characterization. Whether we are right or wrong, the minority holding this opinion must state it, in the face of reviews, sales and awards.

The most interesting case I've seen since Jones is a first novel of some seasons ago by George Mandel, *Flee the Angry Strangers*. It made no special mark in hard covers, though circulated widely in paper reprint. I choose it as a peculiarly apt illustration of a tendency which can be demonstrated in variations in many novels. In it the false compassion takes the evermore common form of complete negation of values and denial of responsibility. The author's interpreter, in the book, looks on the world of dope addiction and shrugs away any helpful intervention on these grounds: "Who the hell am I to stop it? Who am I to decide about people? There's no harm in anything. You can't stop any of that. You have no right. Nobody has."

With this view, he concludes that all the fallen are the result of repressive nay-saying by the unfallen. (Why the unfallen didn't fall is never explained.) And again emerges the teary slobbering over the criminal and degraded, the refusal to assign any share of responsibility to them, and a vindictive lashing out against the rest of the world.

This particular "compassion" is the sentimental pretense that things are not what they are. Mr. Mandel's eighteen-year-old heroine, addicted to drugs, sexually delinquent, mother of an illegitimate child, finally has been put in an institution. Mr. Mandel supports her in the outraged lament, "My own mother put me there."

As this girl escapes, steps up the dope, takes on more men indiscriminately, and tries a little prostitution, she can still say, reproachfully, "You think I'm a tramp."

"Shucks, kid," is the general attitude of the new-compassion boys, "just going around and doing everything a tramp does, doesn't make a good, sweet, clean little kid like you a tramp."

In short, the new compassion is the denial that men and women are what their consistent, voluntary (and involuntary) patterns of action make them. The elements of true tragedy and compassion—the fall from a standard, responsibility however extenuated, repentance, and the struggle for rehabilitation—are not in this philosophy.

What is wrong with Mandel's approach to his delinquent heroine? He feels sorry for her—don't we all? Can he deny that she has become a tramp? Compassion is to see precisely what she is (which he evades), analyze how she got that way (which he distorts or oversimplifies), and seek for what can be done to rehabilitate her (which he refuses). This is the weakness of many such novels.

It is no casual matter that authors, publishers and reviewers should blandly accept such attitudes as compassion. It may be the most unwholesome and dangerous single symptom in modern literature, for as there is nothing more appealing than the cloak of compassion, there is nothing more treacherous when it is false. In literary art, this is the absolute end product of ethical relativism. No valid compassion can exist without a moral framework. The Greeks had such a framework. The Judaeo-Christian tradition has one. Only in recent years, and so far only in a handful of writers, especially in the French existentialist movement, has the moral framework quietly and completely dropped away. This new compassion is a danger to the art of writing, and a deadly one when it is accepted on its claims.

These writers are trapped in a terrible contradiction. Their form of compassion is not to blame, and they find that they cannot portray life at all without assigning blame. Therefore, since their concept of compassion will not permit them to blame anything upon the criminal, the degraded and the destroyed, they blame everything upon the noncriminal, the nondegraded and the undestroyed. It is a kind of counter-puritanism.

The irony is that these writers have no intermediate ground. Many so-called good people are responsible for the destruction of others. All of us are involved in the guilt of mankind. Throughout literature and life we see it. But you have to have a standard of values in order to see how corrupt, warped, misdirected values destroy themselves and others. That's the realm of tragedy, of individuality and subtlety. If you have no values, and see no values, you cannot distinguish the hypocrite from the virtuous man, the self-righteous man from the genuinely good, the Uriah Heep from the man of honest humility. The world contains them all, and more. Beginning by seeing only bad, the new compassion ends by inverting it to be a curious "good" to which normal life stands as a kind of "bad." "Evil, be thou my good": this is the key to our paranoid novelists.

The existentialists and those influenced by them, and many who unconsciously have been practicing existentialists without the fancy jargon, portray human depravity and degradation without comment, presumably as they see it. This is a kind of moral neutralism. It makes no judgment, on the grounds that there is no judgment. But these writers show phenomena without meaning. If we give depravity no significance we imply that it has no significance. Far from being neutral or unmoralistic or undogmatic, this is a highly partisan, positive philosophical position indeed.

The conflict between good and evil is a common thread running through all the great literature and drama of the world, from the Greeks to ourselves. The principle that conflict is at the heart of all dramatic action, when illustrated by concrete example, almost always turns up some aspect of the struggle between good and evil.

The idea that there is neither good nor evil—in any absolute moral or religious sense—is widespread in our times. There are various relativistic, behavioristic standards of ethics. If they even admit the distinction between good and evil they see it as a relative matter and not as the whirlwind of choices at the center of living. In any such state of mind, conflict can be only a petty matter at best, lacking true universality. The acts of the evildoer and of the virtuous man alike become dramatically neutralized. Imagine *Crime and Punishment* or *The Brothers Karamazov* if Dostoevsky had thought that the good and evil in those books were wholly a relative matter and had had no conviction about them.

You can't have a vital literature if you ignore or shun evil. What you get then is the goody-goody in the place of good, the world of Pollyanna. *Cry, the Beloved Country* is a great and dramatic novel because Alan Paton, in addition to his skill of workmanship, sees with clear eyes both good and evil, differentiates them, pitches them into conflict with each other, *and takes sides.* He sees that the native boy, Absalom Kumalo, who has murdered, cannot be judged justly without taking into account the environment that has partly shaped him. But he sees, too, that Absalom the individual, not society the abstraction, did the act and has responsibility. Mr. Paton understands mercy. He knows that this precious thing is not shown on sentimental impulse, but after searching examination of the realities of human action. Mercy follows a judgment; it does not precede it.

One of the novels of the talented Paul Bowles, *Let It Come Down*, is full of motion, full of sensational depravities, and is a crashing bore. For the book recognizes no good, admits no evil, and is coldly indifferent to the moral behavior of its characters. It is a long shrug. Such a view of life is nondramatic, negating the vital essence of drama.

Charles Jackson is a novelist unmistakably sensitive and gifted. His novels are terrifyingly preoccupied with modes of demoralization and collapse. They depict these faithfully, but take in no other aspects of life at all. He admires and partly emulates Dostoevsky, but he does not appear to realize that the difference between the dark tones of his own work and those in Dostoevsky's novels is precisely that Dostoevsky took sides. He was not neutral in the conflict between good and evil. The gulf fixed between Jackson and Dostoevsky is not one of literary craftsmanship but of moral sense.

Dostoevsky views Raskolnikov with compassion, for he sees and interprets for us the moral fallacy that entrapped Raskolnikov. If there were no such fallacy, if Dostoevsky had perceived no moral standard to be warped, Raskolnikov (whose name means "the dissenter") would have been a mere Russian Robert E. Lee Prewitt, and there would have been no tragedy. The great depth of *Crime and Punishment* (the very title states it) is that both Dostoevsky the author and Raskolnikov the created character are conscious of the moral dilemma.

Dreiser, in *An American Tragedy*, sees Clyde Griffiths with compassion because he shows us how the boy has been undermined by a shoddy set of material values and is poorly equipped to appraise them. Dreiser sees the good and evil in the American era he portrays; the social tragedy is that there are those like Clyde who can see them only dimly, if at all.

The original muckrakers portrayed horrors with a fierce indignation against the social injustice they saw as causative, if sometimes too simply. So it is in Upton Sinclair's *The Jungle*. But these men were reformers. Their eyes were fixed upon a good of which they saw men deprived, and which they were determined passionately to restore. In the writers we are discussing, the vision of the good is lost. They stare hypnotized upon the mess as if they conceived it to be the sole, or total, reality of life.

Many novelists of talent other than those named are more or less involved in the confusion of identification with compassion, in the process of representing a facet of life as if it were the whole and of presenting phenomena without the evaluation which the greatest of writers, and even the mere reformers, never have shrunk from offering. They feel that by detailing innumerable horrors without visible revulsion they are somehow demonstrating sympathy. They conceive their virtue as not casting stones at the sinner, but many cast stones in other directions, and some reverse the words of Jesus to say, in effect, "Neither do I condemn you—go and sin some more."

National Book Award juries have shown an affinity for new-compassion novels. In addition to *From Here to Eternity,* they have given the palm to *The Man With the Golden Arm* and Saul Bellow's *The Adventures of Augie March.* In Algren's skillful work, including the recent *A Walk on the Wild Side,* there may be sympathy, but it remains the one-sided sympathy of the new compassion. The promising talent of Norman Mailer has collapsed utterly into this genre in *Barbary Shore* and *The Deer Park.* Leonard Bishop's novels belong there, and Irving Shulman's at least lean that way. The total catalogue of writers and books within this category would be burdensome to compile.

Some borderline books of the kind we are discussing are no more than crying novels or—to be more blunt about a few—sniveling novels. A vast and blurred self-pity is appliquéd upon the fictional characters—as if to do this represented compassion in the author. In some cases it is simple transference of the author's own self-pity, as shown by the inability to see or move beyond it in portraying life. In some, the assiduous stockpiling of depravities has an unmistakable element of reveling, of wallowing, of bad-boy's glee. Many of these writers cry, "Look, Ma, I'm blaspheming."

There are merely fitful glimmerings of life and agitated motions in the books of such novelists. The vital questions which would bring them to profound life have been nullified. You cannot say of their attitude toward their characters, "To understand all is to forgive all." They see much but understand nothing. They do not understand all—they *devalue* all. They do not forgive anything. They say there is nothing to forgive. They take murder, rape, perversion and say, belligerently, "What's wrong with it?"

You cannot say of their characters, "There but for the grace of God go I," because you cannot find in their work any chain of moral cause and effect by which *you* could get from where *you* are to where their characters are (as you can in Dostoevsky and Paton). The placement of these characters in their situations is arbitrary and mechanical, as is the inversion of good and bad.

The iron of ironies is that these are not the most compassionate, but the most vindictive writers working today; not the most humble, but the most arrogant; not the binders of the wounds of their fallen brothers, but the destroyers of the social order. "Down! Down everybody!" they scream. "Down with us all!"

Dostoevsky anticipated this moral phenomenon as he did so many others. These paranoid novels are books that some of his brilliantly studied characters might have written. Ivan Karamazov said, "Everything is permitted," and Smerdyakov, acting accordingly, murdered. Raskolnikov saw moral law as inapplicable to some men, and acting accordingly, murdered. Ideas are more than abstractions, Dostoevsky shows us again and again. Ideas have consequences. God preserve us from the consequences of the ideas implicit in the novels of the new compassion.

STUDY QUESTIONS

1. Why does Fuller consider the compassion shown in the novels he is discussing to be "false"?

2. Do you know any recent American novels that this critic might find more satisfactory?

3. What does Fuller mean when he says that the novelist who writes of evil must "take sides"?

4. How does Fuller account for the origin of the "new compassion"?

5. Do you agree that showing phenomena in fiction without making judgments on them as the novelists criticized by Fuller do, constitutes a dangerous philosophy? Write a theme expressing your opinion on this point, using one or more recent American novels as evidence in your argument.

6. Would it be fair to say that Fuller's attack upon certain novelists here is really a defense of conventional moral or religious ideas? Is he resisting a revolution in morality? Does he fail to see constructive possibilities in the novels he is discusing?

The Timeless World of a Play*

Tennessee Williams

Carson McCullers concludes one of her lyric poems with the line: "Time, the endless idiot, runs screaming 'round the world." It is this continual rush of time, so violent that it appears to be screaming, that deprives our actual lives of so much dignity and meaning, and it is, perhaps more than anything else, the *arrest of time* which has taken place in a completed work of art that gives to certain plays their feeling of depth and significance. In the London notices of *Death of a Salesman* a certain notoriously skeptical critic made the remark that Willy Loman was the sort of man that almost any member of the audience would have kicked out of an office had he applied for a job or detained one for conversation about his troubles. The remark itself possibly holds some truth. But the implication that Willy Loman is consequently a character with whom we have no reason to concern ourselves in drama, reveals a strikingly false conception of what plays are. Contemplation is something that exists outside of time, and so is the tragic sense. Even in the actual world of commerce, there exists in some persons a sensibility to the unfortunate situations of others, a capacity for concern and compassion, surviving from a more tender period of life outside the present whirling wire-cage of business activity. Facing Willy Loman across an office desk, meeting his nervous glance and hearing his querulous voice, we would be very likely to glance at our wrist watch and our schedule of other appointments. We would not kick him out of the office, no, but we would certainly *ease* him out with more expedition than Willy had feebly hoped for. But suppose there had been no wrist watch or office clock and suppose there had *not* been the schedule of pressing appointments, and suppose that we were not actually facing Willy across a desk—and facing a person is *not* the best way to *see* him!—suppose, in other words, that the meeting with Willy Loman had somehow occurred in a world *outside* of time. Then I think we would receive him with concern and kindness and even with respect. If the world of a play did not offer us this occasion to view its characters under that special condition of a *world without time*, then, indeed, the characters and occurrences of drama would become equally pointless, equally trivial, as corresponding meetings and happenings in life.

The classic tragedies of Greece had tremendous nobility. The actors wore great masks, movements were formal, dance-like, and the speeches had an epic quality which doubtless were as removed from the normal conversation of their contemporary society as they seem today. Yet they did not seem false to the Greek audiences: the magnitude of the events and the passions aroused by them did not seem ridiculously out of proportion to common experience. And I wonder if this was not because the Greek audiences knew, instinctively or by training, that the created world of a play is removed from that element which makes people *little* and their emotions fairly inconsequential.

Great sculpture often follows the lines of the human body: yet the repose of great sculpture suddenly transmutes those human lines to something that has an absoluteness, a purity, a beauty, which would not be possible in a living mobile form.

A play may be violent, full of motion: yet it has that special kind of repose which allows contemplation and produces the climate in which tragic importance is a possible thing, provided that certain modern conditions are met.

In actual existence the moments of love are succeeded by the moments of satiety and sleep. The sincere remark is followed by a cynical distrust. Truth is fragmentary, at best: we love and betray each other not in quite the same breath but in two breaths that occur in fairly close sequence.

But the fact that passion occurred in *passing,* that it then declined into a more familiar sense of indifference, should not be regarded as proof of its inconsequence. And this is the very truth that drama wishes to bring us . . .

Whether or not we admit it to ourselves, we are all haunted by a truly awful sense of impermanence. I have always had a particularly keen sense of this at New York cocktail parties, and perhaps that is why I drink the martinis almost as fast as I can snatch them from the tray. This sense is the febrile thing that hangs in the air. Horror of insincerity, of *not meaning,* overhangs these affairs like the cloud of cigarette smoke and the hectic chatter. This horror is the only thing, almost, that is left unsaid at such functions. All social functions involving a group of people not intimately known to each other are always under this shadow. They are almost always (in an unconscious way) like that last dinner of the condemned: where steak or turkey, whatever the doomed man wants, is served in his cell as a mockingly cruel reminder of what the great-big-little-transitory world had to offer.

In a play, time is arrested in the sense of being confined. By a sort of legerdemain, events are made to remain *events,* rather than being reduced so quickly to mere *occurrences.* The audience can sit back in a comforting dusk to watch a world which is flooded with light and in which emotion and action have a dimension and dignity that they would likewise have in real existence, if only the shattering intrusion of time could be locked out.

About their lives people ought to remember that when they are finished, everything in them will be contained in a marvelous state of repose which is the same as that which they unconsciously admired in drama. The rush is temporary. The great and only possible dignity of man lies in his power deliberately to choose certain moral values by which to live as steadfastly as if he, too, like a character in a play, were immured against the corrupting rush of time. Snatching the eternal out of the desperately fleeting is the great magic trick of human existence. As far as we know, as far as there exists any kind of empiric evidence, there is no way to beat the game of *being* against *non-being,* in which non-being is the predestined victor on realistic levels.

Yet plays in the tragic tradition offer us a view of certain moral values in violent juxtaposition. Because we do not participate, except as spectators, we can view them clearly, within the limits of our emotional equipment. These people on the stage do not return our looks. We do not have to answer their questions nor make any sign of being in company with them, nor do we have to compete with their virtues nor resist their offenses. All at once, for this reason, we are able to *see* them! Our hearts are wrung by recognition and pity, so that the dusky shell of the auditorium where we are gathered anonymously together is flooded with an almost liquid warmth of unchecked human sympathies, relieved of self-consciousness, allowed to function . . .

Men pity and love each other more deeply than they permit themselves to know. The moment after the phone has been hung up, the hand reaches for a scratch pad and scrawls a notation: "Funeral Tuesday at five, Church of the Holy Redeemer, don't forget flowers." And the same hand is only a little shakier than usual as it reaches, some minutes later, for a highball glass that will pour a stupefaction over the kindled nerves. Fear and evasion are the two little beasts that chase each other's tails in the revolving wire-cage of our nervous world. They distract us from feeling too much about things. Time rushes toward us with its hospital tray of infinitely varied narcotics, even while it is preparing us for its inevitably fatal operation . . .

So successfully have we disguised from ourselves the intensity of our own feelings, the sensibility of our own hearts, that plays in the tragic tradition have begun to seem untrue. For a couple of hours we may surrender ourselves to a world of fiercely illuminated values in conflict, but when the stage is covered and the auditorium lighted, almost immediately there is a recoil of disbelief. "Well, well!" we say as we shuffle back up the aisle, while the play dwindles behind us with the sudden perspective of an early Chirico painting. By the time we have arrived at Sardi's, if not as soon as we passed beneath the marquee, we have convinced ourselves once more that life has as little resemblance to the curiously stirring and meaningful occurrences on the stage as a jingle has to an elegy of Rilke.

This modern condition of his theater audience is something that an author must know in advance. The diminishing influence of life's destroyer, time, must be somehow worked into the context of his play. Perhaps it is a certain foolery, a certain distortion toward the grotesque, which will solve the problem for him. Perhaps it is only restraint, putting a mute on the strings that would like to break all bounds. But almost surely, unless he contrives in some way to relate the dimensions of his tragedy to the dimensions of a world in which time is *included*—he will be left among his magnificent debris on a dark stage, muttering to himself: "Those fools . . ."

And if they could hear him above the clatter of tongues, glasses, chinaware and silver, they would give him this answer: "But you have shown us a world not ravaged by time. We admire your innocence. But we have seen our photographs, past and present. Yesterday evening we passed our first wife on the street. We smiled as we spoke but we didn't really see her! It's too bad, but we know what is true and not true, and at 3 a.m. your disgrace will be in print!"

STUDY QUESTIONS

1. What is the advantage of the "timelessness" that Williams sees as one of the qualities of the drama?

2. What is Williams' explanation for the decline of tragedy in the modern theater?

3. Explain Williams' point that, in spite of appearances, it is the rush of life that is an illusion and that seemingly impermanent passages in it are long-lasting. From this point of view does the distortion of time effected by drama seem more or less "true to life"?

4. According to Williams, what effect do the concerns of daily life have upon our ability to appreciate the worth and dignity of man?

5. What other methods are used by playwrights to heighten and fix the significance of fleeting experiences?

6. Write a theme describing a play you have seen in which some thought or experience of your own was given a fuller meaning than you realized it had.

The Idea of Tragedy*

Edith Hamilton

The great tragic artists of the world are four, and three of them are Greek. It is in tragedy that the pre-eminence of the Greeks can be seen most clearly. Except for Shakespeare, the great three, Æschylus, Sophocles, Euripides, stand alone. Tragedy is an achievement peculiarly Greek. They were the first to perceive it and they lifted it to its supreme height. Nor is it a matter that directly touches only the great artists who wrote tragedies; it concerns the entire people as well, who felt the appeal of the tragic to such a degree that they would gather thirty thousand strong to see a performance. In tragedy the Greek genius penetrated farthest and it is the revelation of what was most profound in them.

The special characteristic of the Greeks was their power to see the world clearly and at the same time as beautiful. Because they were able to do this, they produced art distinguished from all other art by an ab-

* From *The Great Age of Greek Literature* by Edith Hamilton. By permission of W. W. Norton and Company, Inc. Copyright 1943, by W. W. Norton and Company, Inc.

sence of struggle, marked by a calm and serenity which is theirs alone. There is, it seems to assure us, a region where beauty is truth, truth beauty. To it their artists would lead us, illumining life's dark confusions by gleams fitful indeed and wavering compared with the fixed light of religious faith, but by some magic of their own, satisfying, affording a vision of something inconclusive and yet of incalculable significance. Of all the great poets this is true, but truest of the tragic poets, for the reason that in them the power of poetry confronts the inexplicable.

Tragedy was a Greek creation because in Greece thought was free. Men were thinking more and more deeply about human life, and beginning to perceive more and more clearly that it was bound up with evil and that injustice was the nature of things. And then, one day, this knowledge of something irremediably wrong in the world came to a poet with his poet's power to see beauty in the truth of human life, and the first tragedy was written. As the author of a most distinguished book on the subject says: "The spirit of inquiry meets the spirit of poetry and tragedy is born." Make it concrete: early Greece with her godlike heroes and hero-gods fighting far on the ringing plains of windy Troy; with her lyric world, where every common thing is touched with beauty—her two-fold world of poetic creation. Then a new age dawns, not satisfied with beauty of song and story, an age that must try to know and explain. And for the first time tragedy appears. A poet of surpassing magnitude, not content with the old sacred conventions, and of a soul great enough to bear new and intolerable truth—that is Æschylus, the first writer of tragedy.

Tragedy belongs to the poets. Only they have "trod the sunlit heights and from life's dissonance struck one clear chord." None but a poet can write a tragedy. For tragedy is nothing less than pain transmuted into exaltation by the alchemy of poetry, and if poetry is true knowledge and the great poets guides safe to follow, this transmutation has arresting implications.

Pain changed into, or, let us say, charged with, exaltation. It would seem that tragedy is a strange matter. There is indeed none stranger. A tragedy shows us pain and gives us pleasure thereby. The greater the suffering depicted, the more terrible the events, the more intense our pleasure. The most monstrous and appalling deeds life can show are those the tragedian chooses, and by the spectacle he thus offers us, we are moved to a very passion of enjoyment. There is food for wonder here, not to be passed over, as the superficial have done, by pointing out that the Romans made a holiday of a gladiator's slaughter, and that even to-day fierce instincts, savage survivals, stir in the most civilized. Grant all that, and we are not a step advanced on the way to explaining the mystery of tragic pleasure. It has no kinship with cruelty or the lust for blood.

On this point it is illuminating to consider our everyday use of the words tragedy and tragic. Pain, sorrow, disaster, are always spoken of as depressing, as dragging down—the dark abyss of pain, a crushing sorrow, an overwhelming disaster. But speak of tragedy and extraordinarily the metaphor changes. Lift us to tragic heights, we say, and never anything else. The depths of pathos but never of tragedy. Always the height of tragedy. A word is no light matter. Words have with truth been called fossil poetry, each, that is, a symbol of a creative thought. The whole philosophy of human nature is implicit in human speech. It is a matter to pause over, that the instinct of mankind has perceived a difference, not of degree but of kind, between tragic pain and all other pain. There is something in tragedy which marks it off from other disaster so sharply that in our common speech we bear witness to the difference.

All those whose attention has been caught by the strange contradiction of pleasure through pain agree with this instinctive witness, and some of the most brilliant minds the world has known have concerned themselves with it. Tragic pleasure, they tell us, is in a class by itself. "Pity and awe," Aristotle called it, "and a sense of emotion purged and purified thereby." "Reconciliation," said Hegel, which we may understand in the sense of life's temporary dissonance resolved into eternal harmony. "Acceptance," said Schopenhauer, the temper of mind that says, "Thy will be done." "The reaffirmation of the will to live in the face of death," said Nietzsche, "and the joy of its inexhaustibility when so reaffirmed."

Pity, awe, reconciliation, exaltation—these are the elements that make up tragic pleasure. No play is a tragedy that does not call them forth. So the philosophers say, all in agreement with the common judgment of mankind, that tragedy is something above and beyond the dissonance of pain. But what it is that causes a play to call forth these feelings, what is the essential element in a tragedy, Hegel alone seeks to define. In a notable passage he says that the only tragic subject is a spiritual struggle in which each side has a claim upon our sympathy. But, as his critics have pointed out, he would thus exclude the tragedy of the suffering of the innocent, and a definition which does not include the death of Cordelia or of Deianira cannot be taken as final.

The suffering of the innocent, indeed, can itself be so differently treated as to necessitate completely different categories. In one of the greatest tragedies, the *Prometheus* of Æschylus, the main actor is an innocent sufferer, but, beyond this purely formal connection, that passionate rebel, defying God and all the powers of the universe, has no relationship whatever to the lovely, loving Cordelia. An inclusive definition of tragedy must cover cases as diverse in circumstance and in the character of the protagonist as the whole range of life and letters can afford it. It must include such opposites as Antigone, the high-souled maiden who goes with open eyes to her death rather than leave her brother's body unburied, and Macbeth, the ambition-mad, the murderer of his king and guest. These two plays, seemingly so totally unlike, call forth the same response. Tragic pleasure of the greatest intensity is caused by them both. They have something in common, but the philosophers do not tell us what it is. Their concern is with what a tragedy makes us feel, not with what makes a tragedy.

Only twice in literary history has there been a great period of tragedy, in the Athens of Pericles and in Elizabethan England. What these two periods had in common, two thousand years and more apart in time that they expressed themselves in the same fashion, may give us some hint of the nature of tragedy, for far from being periods of darkness and defeat, each was a time when life was seen exalted, a time of thrilling and unfathomable possibilities. They held their heads high, those men who conquered at Marathon and Salamis, and those who fought Spain and saw the Great Armada sink. The world was a place of wonder; mankind was beauteous; life was lived on the crest of the wave. More than all, the poignant joy of heroism had stirred men's hearts. Not stuff for tragedy, would you say? But on the crest of the wave one must feel either tragically or joyously; one cannot feel tamely. The temper of mind that sees tragedy in life has not for its opposite the temper that sees joy. The opposite pole to the tragic view of life is the sordid view. When humanity is seen as devoid of dignity and significance, trivial, mean, and sunk in dreary hopelessness, then the spirit of tragedy departs. "Sometime let gorgeous tragedy in sceptred pall come sweeping by." At the opposite pole stands Gorki with *The Lower Depths.*

Other poets may, the tragedian must, seek for the significance of life. An error strangely common is that this significance for tragic purposes depends, in some sort, upon outward circumstance, on

> pomp and feast and revelry,
> With mask, and antique pageantry—

Nothing of all that touches tragedy. The surface of life is comedy's concern; tragedy is indifferent to it. We do not, to be sure, go to Main Street or to Zenith for tragedy, but the reason has nothing to do with their dull familiarity. There is no reason inherent in the house itself why Babbitt's home in Zenith should not be the scene of a tragedy quite as well as the Castle of Elsinore. The only reason it is not is Babbitt himself. "That singular swing toward elevation" which Schopenhauer discerned in tragedy, does not take any of its impetus from outside things.

The dignity and the significance of human life—of these, and of these alone, tragedy will never let go. Without them there is no tragedy. To answer the question, what makes a tragedy, is to answer the question wherein lies the essential significance of life, what the dignity of humanity depends upon in the last analysis. Here the tragedians speak to us with no uncertain voice. The great tragedies themselves offer the solution to the problem they propound. It is by our power to suffer, above all, that we are of more value than the sparrows. Endow them with a greater or as great a potentiality of pain and our foremost place in the world would no longer be undisputed. Deep down, when we search out the reason for our conviction of the transcendent worth of each human being, we know that it is because of the possibility that each can suffer so terribly. What do outside trappings matter, Zenith or Elsinore? Tragedy's preoccupation is with suffering.

But, it is to be well noted, not with all suffering. There are degrees in our high estate of pain. It is not given to all to suffer alike. We differ in nothing more than in our power to feel. There are souls of little and of great degree, and upon that degree the dignity and significance of each life depend. There is no dignity like the dignity of a soul in agony.

> Here I and sorrows sit;
> Here is my throne, bid kings come bow to it.

Tragedy is enthroned, and to her realm those alone are admitted who belong to the only true aristocracy, that of all passionate souls. Tragedy's one essential is a soul that can feel greatly. Given such a one and any catastrophe may be tragic. But the earth may be removed and the mountains be carried into the midst of the sea, and if only the small and shallow are confounded, tragedy is absent.

One dark page of Roman history tells of a little seven-year-old girl, daughter of a man judged guilty of death and so herself condemned to die, and how she passed through the staring crowds sobbing and asking, "What has she done wrong? If they would tell her, she would never do it again"—and so on to the black prison and the executioner. That breaks the heart, but is not tragedy, it is pathos. No heights are there for the soul to mount to, but only the dark depths where there are tears for things. Undeserved suffering is not in itself tragic. Death is not tragic in itself, not the death of the beautiful and the young, the lovely and beloved. Death felt and suffered as Macbeth feels and suffers is tragic. Death felt as Lear feels Cordelia's death is tragic. Ophelia's death is not a tragedy. She being what she is, it could be so only if Hamlet's and Laertes' grief were tragic grief. The conflicting claims of the law of God and the law of man are not what make the tragedy of the *Antigone*. It is Antigone herself, so great, so tortured. Hamlet's hesitation to kill his uncle is not tragic. The tragedy is his power to feel. Change all the circumstances of the drama and Hamlet in the grip of any calamity would be tragic, just as Polonius would never be, however awful the catastrophe. The suffering of a soul that can suffer greatly—that and only that, is tragedy.

It follows, then, that tragedy has nothing to do with the distinction between Realism and Romanticism. The contrary has always been maintained. The Greeks went to the myths for their subjects, we are told, to insure remoteness from real life which does not admit of high tragedy. "Realism is the ruin of tragedy," says the latest writer on the subject. It is not true. If indeed Realism were conceived of as dealing only with the usual, tragedy would be ruled out, for the soul capable of a great passion is not usual. But if nothing human is alien to Realism, then tragedy is of her domain, for the unusual is as real as the usual. When the Moscow Art Players presented the *Brothers Karamazov* there was seen on the stage an absurd little man in dirty clothes who waved his arms about and shuffled and sobbed, the farthest possible remove from the traditional figures of tragedy, and yet tragedy was there in his person, stripped of her gorgeous pall, but sceptred truly, speaking the authentic voice of human agony in a struggle past the power of the human heart to bear. A drearier setting, a more typically realistic setting, it would be hard to find, but to see the play was to feel pity and awe before a man dignified by one thing only, made great by what he could suffer. Ibsen's plays are not tragedies. Whether Ibsen is a realist or not—the Realism of one generation is apt to be the Romanticism of the next—small souls are his dramatis personæ and his plays are dramas with an unhappy ending. The end of *Ghosts* leaves us with a sense of shuddering horror and cold anger against society where such things can be, and these are not tragic feelings.

The greatest realistic works of fiction have been written by the French and the Russians. To read one of the great Frenchmen's books is to feel mingled despair and loathing for mankind, so base, so trivial and so wretched. But to read a great Russian novel is to have an altogether different experience. The baseness, the beast in us, the misery of life, are there as plain to see as in the French book, but what we are left with is not despair and not loathing, but a sense of pity and wonder before mankind that can so suffer. The Russian sees life in that way because the Russian genius is primarily poetical; the French genius is not. *Anna Karénina* is a tragedy; *Madame Bovary* is not. Realism and Romanticism, or comparative degrees of Realism, have nothing to do with the matter. It is a case of the small soul against the great soul and the power of a writer whose special endowment is *"voir clair dans ce qui est"* against the intuition of a poet.

If the Greeks had left no tragedies behind for us, the highest reach of their power would be unknown. The three poets who were able to sound the depths of human agony were able also to recognize and reveal it as tragedy. The mystery of evil, they said, curtains that of which "every man whose soul is not a clod hath visions." Pain could exalt and in tragedy for a moment men could have sight of a meaning beyond their grasp. "Yet had God not turned us in his hand and cast to earth our greatness," Euripides makes the old Trojan queen say in her extremity, "we would have passed away giving nothing to men. They would have found no theme for song in us nor made great poems from our sorrows."

Why is the death of the ordinary man a wretched, chilling thing which we turn from, while the death of the hero, always tragic, warms us with a sense of quickened life? Answer this question and the enigma of tragic pleasure is solved. "Never let me hear that brave blood has been shed in vain," said Sir Walter Scott; "it sends an imperious challenge down through all the generations." So the end of a tragedy challenges us. The great soul in pain and in death transforms pain and death. Through it we catch a glimpse of the Stoic Emperor's Dear City of God, of a deeper and more ultimate reality than that in which our lives are lived.

STUDY QUESTIONS

1. Note that the author finds that the word "tragedy" is used in two ways, a common or familiar one and a more literary one. What is the distinction in meaning between these two uses?

2. Using the information provided in this essay, write an accurate one-sentence definition of the term "tragedy."

3. What is the philosophy of life upon which tragedy is based?

4. What methods does the author use for rejecting unsatisfactory definitions of tragedy and for arriving at a good one?

5. Take some novel or play with which you are familiar and write a theme telling why it is or is not a genuine tragedy.

6. Is our present civilization congenial to the expression of genuine tragic feeling as it is defined by Edith Hamilton? Since this is a rather abstract subject, you should be as explicit as possible in explaining your answer to this question.

Appendices

1. THE METHODS AND AIMS OF PROSE

THE METHODS OF PROSE

All writing is an attempt to make something clear to someone. The methods which the writers in this anthology use to attain this end are in one sense as numerous as the selections in the anthology, for the skillful writer is always trying to choose that combination of methods which will best communicate *his* unique material and ideas. In this sense, therefore, there are as many "methods of prose" as there are writers.

But in another sense all writing relies upon certain almost unavoidable means of organization and development. Modern and earlier rhetoricians have classified these methods of organization and development in many ways, and it may well be argued that the more conscious a writer becomes of the variety of techniques he can use, the easier will be his search for the forms most appropriate to any particular writing task he faces. The majority of elaborate classifications, however, derive from subdivision of five basic ways of organizing and developing our information, emotions, and ideas: development by analysis, classification, comparison and contrast, example or illustration, and by definition. A brief explanatory comment on each of these will be helpful as a guide to the use of the selected examples of each method which are listed below.

Analysis. We can clarify an action, the construction of a mechanism, our interpretation of a character or an experience, the steps in a process, or the structure of an idea by indicating to the reader its parts as we see them. By dividing the whole into segments and explaining in turn the nature of each segment, we explain the whole. An automatic toaster, thus, can be explained in part by noting that it has receptacles for the bread, a heating element, and a timing device controlling the length of time the bread is exposed to the heating element. Writing can be described as consisting of observing and collecting information, interpreting that information, and then recording it. The ends of education can be conceived as being liberal, vocational, or professional. And so on. In many ways expository writing, if not in fact all writing, depends upon the method of analysis, for although our observations, experiences, and concepts exist within our minds as total entities, the nature of language requires that our communication of them be spread out over time. If we are to be clear to our readers, this spread must almost inevitably be in some graspable segments of time, space, or logic into which we have analyzed our experience or ideas. It is for this reason, in part, that clear writing and clear thinking are virtually inseparable.

Classification. Classification may be thought of as a special kind of analysis, but it is profitably examined separately. Whenever we *sort* things into *groups,* as we might sort the apple harvest into large good apples, small good apples, and poor apples; or housing into low, middle, and upper income housing; or governments into dictatorships and democracies, we are *classifying.* All science, and all ordered knowledge for that matter, depends heavily upon the method of classification, for it is the method which allows us to group infinitely varying particulars under abstract headings so that we may see their similarities and thus retain them in our minds. A student asked to describe his professors is very likely to begin by suggesting that they fall generally into three groups: good, bad, and indifferent. A professor asked to define the C student may begin by suggesting that there is the C student who is average or mediocre in ability, and the C student who is able but lazy. In this anthology, John Dewey clarifies the nature of *thought* by suggesting different kinds or classes of thought; and Percy Buck clarifies the nature of *appreciation* by dividing appreciation into three different kinds.

Comparison and contrast. In our daily life, the value of experiences and relationships is frequently driven home to us by unexpectedly enforced comparisons, and previously unperceived aspects of things are frequently brought into focus when we are invited to put them beside others. Thus the living room which we had come to think of as cramped and shabby falls into a different perspective when something forces us to visit someone less fortunate; or the sister who seemed a quarrelsome competitor seems suddenly more like a genial companion after she has been away at camp for two weeks. The nature of poetry as a particular form of literature is clarified by the instructor who invites us to think of it in relation to fiction, history, and philosophy; or the special function of social science is defined more precisely when someone lines it up against natural science. In writing, we can capitalize upon this natural device for rendering experience sharper and ideas clearer. Thus, in this anthology Jesse Stuart intensifies our appreciation both of the child's sense of time as defined by daylight and dark and the winds of the four seasons, and the adult's time of man-made schedule by juxtaposing the two. By setting the colloid and the crystal against each other, Joseph Wood Krutch brings into focus the limitations of science when it is applied to animate things. And David Riesman explores the attitudes of his students toward their own civilization by encouraging them to compare American culture with the cultures of certain Indian tribes.

A special kind of comparison, *analogy,* is sometimes classified as a separate rhetorical method. This name is usually applied to an extended comparison and more frequently to a comparison in which something unfamiliar—and frequently abstract—is explained by comparing it to something familiar—and frequently concrete. Thus, in this anthology, Richard Weaver explains his concept of the effects of mass media upon contemporary culture by comparing the media to a "great stereopticon."

Example. A piece of writing is usually said to be developed or organized by example when a general statement is defined by citing a particular representative instance of a type or a particular application of a principle, or several such instances or applications. Thus, Podhoretz supports his general statements about contemporary television by describing particular TV dramas; and Wheelwright elaborates his idea of "ethics" by describing some crucial moral dilemmas. Although in rhetoric the term *example* is frequently reserved for the kind of development or organization just described, the method of making things clear by example is almost inseparable from clear and vivid writing. Whether the "examples" be the activities of the kitchen-maid and laborer with which Herbert Read gives substance to the "intense bustle" of the farm kitchen, the instances with which Ortega y Gasset supports his contention that modern man is "mass man," or the more extended illustrations which Podhoretz and Hayakawa use, the concreteness of specific instances is a large part of the life of writing.

Definition. The basic procedure of definition is to assign a thing to a class or genus, and then to set up differentiae which distinguish the thing defined from other members of its class. Since this is a specialized procedure, definition may usefully be considered as an independent method of organization. All definition, however, depends largely upon the basic principles of analysis and classification. And beyond *formal* or *logical definition,* all *extended definition,* concerned as it is to set unmistakably and unambiguously the bounds within which a writer wishes his reader to understand such words as "democracy," "thought," or "love," inevitably depends upon development by one of the methods outlined above. Thus, among the selections in this anthology, Bernard De Voto defines his concept of skill among mountain men by providing examples and illustrations, and John Dewey defines thought by classifying various kinds of thought.

It is worth noting that one of the principal objectives of the expository writer is to define the limits and precise meanings of abstract terms and concepts, as he understands them. Sound argument, clear understanding of explanations, and appreciation of evaluative judgments all rest largely upon agreement between writer and reader as to the meaning of the terms used. The mature and ethical writer usually intends less to argue for a particular meaning which he has assigned to a term than to clarify that meaning as he understands it, and is using it. By so doing he frequently provides his reader with new perspectives and insights, as do De Voto in defining "skill," Mill in defining "liberty," and Rossiter defining "conservatism."

It may not be amiss at the conclusion of this brief explanation of rhetorical methods to repeat the warning of the introductory generalization. No piece of writing which extends beyond a few hundred words will illustrate any of these techniques purely. To some extent, as we have noted, all writing depends upon the use of examples, it being difficult to develop a meaningful comparison or classification without resort to detail which always tends to grow into example or illustration. And comparison and classification, in their very nature, are particular varieties of the analysis which is always either explicit or implicit in a well ordered piece of writing.

In the following tables the editors have made no attempt to categorize every selection in the anthology. They have rather selected representative pieces which provide relatively clear-cut examples of each of the methods of prose outlined above.

Analysis

George Ruxton	"The Role of the Mountain Men"
Robert Sherwood	"A Speech Is Written"
Gilbert Highet	"The Gettysburg Address"
Wendell Johnson	"You Can't Write Writing"
Lionel Ruby	"Of Matters of Taste and Opinion"
Everett Dean Martin	"The Educational Value of Doubt"
Arthur M. Schlesinger, Jr.	"The Decline of Heroes"
Morris R. Cohen	"The Future of American Liberalism"
Alexis de Tocqueville	"In What Spirit the Americans Cultivate the Arts"
Morris R. Cohen and Ernest Nagel	"The Limits and Value of Scientific Method"
René-Jules Dubos	"Health, Happiness and Human Goals"
Edward Westermarck	"The Emotional Origin of Moral Judgments"
E. M. Forster	"What I Believe"
Edwyn Bevan	"The Justification of Belief"
Arnold Bennett	"On Literary Taste"

Classification

Newman and Genevieve Birk	"Persuasion and Logical Argument"
Martha Wolfenstein and Nathan Leites	"British, French and American Films"
Ernest van den Haag	"Reflections on Mass Culture"
C. Wright Mills	"Some Effects of Mass Media"
William James	"Two Kinds of Knowledge"

W. H. Ittelson and	
F. P. Kilpatrick	"Experiments in Perception"
Lord Balfour	"Science, Religion and Reality"
Eric Newton	"The Nature of the Arts"
Percy C. Buck	"The Meaning of Appreciation"

Comparison and Contrast

Jesse Stuart	"Child's Time and Clock Time"
David Daiches	"The Literary Use of Language"
Harold Whitehall	"Writing and Speech"
H. L. Mencken	"American Culture"
David Riesman	"Americans and Kwakiutls"
Edward Hallett Carr	"From Individualism to Mass Democracy"
José Ortega y Gasset	"The Mass Man"
Joseph Wood Krutch	"The Colloid and the Crystal"
Plato	"Allegory of the Cave"
Herman Melville	"Chronometricals and Horologicals"
John Henry Newman	"Knowledge and Faith"
Richard Weaver	"The Great Stereopticon"

Example

Graham Greene	"The Lost Childhood"
Marchette Chute	"Getting at the Truth"
Jacques Barzun	"The Teaching Process"
William H. Whyte, Jr.	"A Generation of Bureaucrats"
Bertrand Russell	"Fear of Public Opinion"
S. I. Hayakawa	"Popular Songs vs. The Facts of Life"
Delmore Schwartz	"Masterpieces as Cartoons"
Thomas Henry Huxley	"All Men are Scientists"
Henri Poincaré	"Mathematical Creation"

Definition

Bernard De Voto	"The Mountain Man"
Arthur Schopenhauer	"On Style"
John Dewey	"What Is Thinking?"
Edmund S. Morgan	"What Every Yale Freshman Should Know"
John Henry Newman	"Knowledge and Learning"
D. W. Brogan	"The New American"
Carl L. Becker	"The Ideal Democracy"
John Stuart Mill	From "On Liberty"
Clinton Rossiter	"The Conservative View of Man and Society"
Herbert J. Muller	"The Nature of Man"
Jean-Paul Sartre	"Existentialism"
Arthur S. Eddington	"The Nature of the Physical World"
Epictetus	"The Practice of Stoicism"
Edmund Fuller	"The New Compassion in the American Novel"

THE AIMS OF PROSE

Writing varies not only in its rhetorical methods but also in its aims, and the student can learn much from studying the ways in which experienced writers have gone about achieving their specific intentions. The main intentions of prose have dictated its division into four classical types of discourse—narration, description, exposition, and argument—and it would be possible to arrange all the selections in this anthology under those headings, the selections of Part One falling for the most part under the first two, and the bulk of the remainder falling under the last two. Since this text stresses the prose of exposition and argument, however, a grouping of selections which distinguishes more exact expository aims will be useful, and such an arrangement has been followed in the lists below.

It should be noted that, just as any analysis of the methods of prose shows few pure examples of one method, so an analysis of prose according to its aims will show that most pieces have a mixture of aims. Autobiographic narrative may be very heavily descriptive; a definition may seem at times to be persuading us to subscribe to its particular understanding of a term; or a reasoned argument may devote much time to explaining information upon which its conclusions are based. Hence some of the selections in the following list may appear under more than one heading, since they may be usefully examined as models of several kinds of writing. A brief description of each of the headings the editors have used will serve as a guide to the use of the selections as models for study.

Narration. Narration in the sense of a story or incident for its own sake has not been included in this collection of readings; but the opening section of the book has several examples of *autobiographical* writing, which is partly narrative and partly descriptive. A few narratives of varied purpose appear later in the anthology.

Description. The term *description* is traditionally used to mean *suggestive description,* which is concerned with conveying the qualities of a thing, the impression it has made on the writer's senses, as distinguished from *expository* and *technical description,* which are more objective. Suggestive description as an independent type of writing was considerably more common in the nineteenth century than in our time, and no pure examples of the form have been included in this collection, although Lafcadio Hearn's "Creole Carrier-Girl" and Robert Louis Stevenson's description of Monterey are close to it. But nearly all the autobiographical selections in Part One rely heavily upon this kind of description, as do most of the descriptions of places.

Exposition of process and technique. A good deal of our writing and reading is mainly informative, its intention being not to set limits, to convince us, or to evaluate something, but merely to explain how a thing is done, or how something came about. Most "how-to-do-it" books and most technical report writing today fall within this category. In this anthology, selections placed under this heading are both objective and subjective, many of the latter being interpretations of processes and techniques about which there may be wide differences of opinion.

Reasoned argument and persuasion. The intention of a goodly share of our writing and talking is essentially to convince someone that we are right, that our point of view is sound, or to persuade someone to act or believe in a certain way. In a time of conflicting political and philosophical beliefs we need both as readers and writers to be aware of the devices of argument and persuasion, and to be alert to the logic of a writer and the reliability of his evidence. A line is sometimes drawn between *reasoned argument* and *persuasion.* The term *argument* is then reserved for those attempts at persuasion which first carefully define their assumptions and then draw their conclusions logically from those assumptions. *Persuasion* connotes a heavier reliance upon the appeal of slanted evidence, loaded language, or unexamined analogy. In the hands of dictators, demagogues and other unscrupulous men the devices of persuasion can become deadly instruments, as is attested by the history of our century; but we should not forget that they can be equally forceful instruments for good. Since this anthology is concerned to present only mature and honest argument, there are no examples of what the editors would regard as dishonest persuasion.

Nonetheless, the reader will do well to be alert to such differences as those between John Stuart Mill's carefully reasoned definition of and argument for liberty, and Milton's impassioned plea; between the weighed evaluation of the scientific method presented by Cohen and Nagel, and the persuasiveness of Mencken and between the reasoned analysis of the effects of mass media by C. Wright Mills, and the loaded analogy upon which Richard Weaver builds his case against these same media in "The Great Stereopticon."

Evaluation. Much of the most valuable writing of all times is less concerned to inform or persuade us, than to weigh and evaluate. Because the respect for differences of view, and the relatively unbiased search for truth which this kind of writing embodies are qualities which have traditionally marked the liberally educated person, this kind of selection is heavily presented in this collection.

As with the representation of methods of prose, the editors have made no attempt in the following lists to classify every selection in the anthology, but rather have selected a representative cross-section of pieces illustrating the various types of writing defined above.

Autobiographical Narrative

Herbert Read	"The Vale and the Farm"
Dylan Thomas	"Reminiscences of Childhood"
Henry Adams	"A New England Boyhood"
H. L. Mencken	"I Discover *Huckleberry Finn*"
Graham Greene	"The Lost Childhood"

Description

Herbert Read	"The Vale and the Farm"
Dylan Thomas	"Reminiscences of Childhood"
Henry Adams	"A New England Boyhood"
Jesse Stuart	"Child's Time and Clock Time"
George Orwell	"Visiting a Coal Mine"
Lafcadio Hearn	"Creole Carrier-Girl"
Samuel Butler	"Dr. Skinner"
Mark Twain	"Steamboat Town"
E. B. White	"New York"
Robert Louis Stevenson	"The Old Pacific Capital"
Albert Camus	"The Wind at Djémila"

Exposition of Process and Technique

George Ruxton	"The Role of the Mountain Men"
Henry Nash Smith	"The Mountain Man as Western Hero: Kit Carson"
George Henry Lewes	"The Principle of Vision"
Marchette Chute	"Getting at the Truth"
David Daiches	"The Literary Use of Language"
Robert Sherwood	"A Speech Is Written"
Wendell Johnson	"You Can't Write Writing"
Susanne K. Langer	"Language and Thought"
John Dewey	"What is Thinking?"
Jacques Barzun	"The Teaching Process"
W. H. Ittelson and F. P. Kilpatrick	"Experiments in Perception"
Robert B. Heilman	"Literature and the Adult Laity"

Reasoned Argument

Everett Dean Martin	"The Educational Value of Doubt"
Edward Hallett Carr	"From Individualism to Mass Democracy"
Sidney Hook	"The Hero in Democracy"
Edward Westermarck	"The Emotional Origin of Moral Judgments"
Thomas Henry Huxley	"Agnosticism and Christianity"
John Henry Newman	"Knowledge and Faith"
C. Wright Mills	"Some Effects of Mass Media"
Archibald MacLeish	"Why Do We Teach Poetry?"

Persuasion

H. L. Mencken	"American Culture"
John Milton	From *"Areopagitica"*
Henry David Thoreau	From "Civil Disobedience"
José Ortega y Gasset	"The Mass Man"
Delmore Schwartz	"Masterpieces as Cartoons"
Richard Weaver	"The Great Stereopticon"

Evaluation

Morris Freedman	"Wonderful Town?"
Bertrand Russell	"Fear of Public Opinion"
José Ortega y Gasset	"The Mass Man"
Morris R. Cohen	"The Future of American Liberalism"
Herbert J. Muller	"The Nature of Man"
Robert Warshow	"The Gangster as Tragic Hero"
Norman Podhoretz	"The Father on the Hearth"
S. I. Hayakawa	"Popular Songs vs. the Facts of Life"
Alexis de Tocqueville	"In What Spirit the Americans Cultivate the Arts"
Ernest van den Haag	"Reflections on Mass Culture"
Lyman Bryson	"Art and Democracy"
Bertrand Russell	"The Value of Philosophy"
René-Jules Dubos	"Utopias and Human Goals"
E. M. Forster	"What I Believe"
W. T. Stace	"Man Against Darkness"
Percy C. Buck	"The Meaning of Appreciation"
Edmund Fuller	"The New Compassion in the American Novel"

2. BIOGRAPHICAL NOTES

HENRY ADAMS (1838–1918), descendant of two Presidents and son of a diplomat, studied at Harvard and spent many years in Europe as a young man. Later he became a Washington journalist, a magazine editor, and professor of history at Harvard. The author of a number of historical works, essays, and novels, he is best known for his autobiography, *The Education of Henry Adams* (1906).

ARTHUR JAMES BALFOUR (1848–1930), English Conservative politician and philosopher, was Prime Minister from 1902 to 1905. He wrote a number of books on economic and philosophic subjects.

JACQUES BARZUN (1907–   ) teaches history at Columbia University, where he is also Dean of the Graduate Faculty. Born in France, he came to America with his family in 1919 and studied at Columbia. His first books dealt with race, but he has since become well-known as a writer on a variety of subjects, including history, music, and literature. Among his books are *Darwin, Marx, Wagner* (1941) and *Berlioz and the Romantic Century* (1950).

MONROE BEARDSLEY (1915–   ), Professor of Philosophy at Swarthmore College, has also taught at Yale and Mount Holyoke. He has written on logic, language, and the problems of poetic expression.

CARL BECKER (1873–1945) taught history at Dartmouth College, the University of Kansas, and, from 1917 until his death, at Cornell University. Among recent historians, he was noted for his unusual clarity and ease of style. Among his best known works are *The Heavenly City of the Eighteenth Century Philosophers* (1932), *Every Man His Own Historian* (1935) and *Modern Democracy* (1941), the latter consisting of lectures delivered at the University of Virginia in 1940.

ARNOLD BENNETT (1867–1931), English novelist and playwright, began his career as a clerk in his father's law office. After a family disagreement, he went to London, where he supported himself for a time by hack journalism. In 1896 he gave up this employment to write. After earning money by reviews, stories, and articles, he sold a novel, and began his long career as a realistic novelist. Though he was more interested in making money than in producing art, Bennett produced many novels that are highly admired as examples of realistic fiction.

EDWYN BEVAN (1870–1943), English historian and philosopher, was born in London and educated at Oxford. He taught Hellenistic history and literature at King's College, London, from 1922 to 1933. After that he devoted himself to scholarship in the field of Hellenistic studies. Throughout his life, he was interested in religious problems, was an active Christian thinker, and wrote on this subject in his books, *Hellenism and Christianity* (1921) and *Christianity in a World at War* (1940).

NEWMAN P. BIRK (1906–   ) studied at Centre College, Kentucky; and at Tufts and Harvard Universities in Massachusetts. Since 1933 he has taught English at Tufts University, where he has been Director of Freshman English since 1940. He and his wife, Genevieve, are co-authors of a widely used freshman English text, *Understanding and Using English*.

MAX BLACK (1909–   ), Professor of Philosophy at Cornell University, is a specialist in the philosophy of language. Born in Baku, Russia, he studied at the Universities of Cambridge, Goettingen, and London, and came to the United States in 1940 to teach at the University of Illinois. He has been co-editor of the *Journal of Symbolic Logic* and the *Philosophy Review*.

DENIS WILLIAM BROGAN (1900–   ), British political scientist, is an authority on America and France. After spending two years at Harvard as a graduate student, he returned to England, where he taught at Oxford and Cambridge. He has written several books on American life and government.

LYMAN BRYSON (1888–   ), American educator, was born in Nebraska, attended the University of Michigan, and worked as a newspaper man in Omaha before coming to Columbia University as Professor of Education. He has been active in adult education, and is well known as director of the radio program "Invitation to Learning."

SIR PERCY CARTER BUCK (1871–1947) was an English musical scholar, composer, organist, and educationist noted for his careful scholarship, his skill as a contrapuntist, and his contributions to the teaching of music. After studying at the Guildhall School of Music and the Royal College of Music, he became successively organist at Worcester College, Oxford; Wells Cathedral; and Bristol Cathedral. From 1901 to 1927 he served as Director of Music at Harrow School, serving part of this time also as Professor of Music at the University of Dublin. In 1925 he became King Edward Professor of Music at the University of London, a position which he held until his retirement. He was knighted in 1935. He is the composer of a variety of music for strings, orchestra, and organ, and the author of numerous works on the method and history of music.

SAMUEL BUTLER (1835–1902), English novelist and satirist, was educated at Cambridge and went to New Zealand as a young man, where he made a comfortable fortune. He returned to England to pursue his interests, which included music and painting as well as writing. His first important book, *Erewhon* (1872), is a Utopian romance that satirizes European institutions. After writing it, Butler became interested in evolution and wrote a series of books taking issue with some of Darwin's theories. Butler also translated Homer, wrote some travel books, and a single novel, *The Way of All Flesh* (1903), which was not published until after his death, but is considered his greatest work.

ALBERT CAMUS (1913–1960) was born in Algeria and spent the early part of his life there. After working as a journalist in Algiers and Paris, he played an important part in the French Resistance and emerged after the war as one of France's leading philosophical writers. He has been editor of the periodical, *Combat,* and director of a publishing house. He is the author of many essays and some plays, but is best known for his novels, *The Stranger* (1946), *The Plague* (1948) and *The Fall* (1956). He won the Nobel Prize for Literature in 1957.

EDWARD H. CARR (1892–   ), British diplomat and political scientist, studied at Cambridge and worked in the foreign service for twenty years before becoming Professor of International Politics at the University of Wales. During World War II he returned to government service as director of the Ministry of Information. He has written numerous books about international affairs, is a specialist on Russia, and is working on a comprehensive *History of Soviet Russia.*

MARCHETTE CHUTE (1909–   ) was born in Minnesota and educated at the University of Minnesota. She is well known for her biographies of Chaucer, Shakespeare, and Ben Jonson.

MORRIS RAPHAEL COHEN (1880–1947), American philosopher and professor, spent most of his life as a student and Professor of Philosophy at the City College of New York. He also taught at the University of Chicago and many of the leading American universities and served as president of the American Philosophical Association.

ALISTAIR COOKE (1908–   ) is a journalist and television personality who was born in England, but came to America, first as a student, then as a correspondent for British newspapers, and has remained to become an American citizen. He was master of ceremonies of the television program "Omnibus" and has written a number of books on public figures, as well as *One Man's America* (1952), a book on the American scene.

DAVID DAICHES (1912–   ), English author and educator, was educated at the University of Edinburgh and at Balliol College, Oxford. After teaching for short periods in both of these universities, he taught in the United States, at the University of Chicago from 1937–1943, and at Cornell University from 1946 to 1951. In the intervening years he served in World War II with the British Information Services. Since

1951 he has been University Lecturer in English at Cambridge University. He is the author of several books of literary criticism, including *The Novel and the Modern World* (1939), *Virginia Woolf* (1942), *A Study of Literature* (1948) and *Critical Approaches to Literature* (1956). He is a contributor of poetry, essays, and articles to various periodicals.

BERNARD DE VOTO (1897–1956) was born in Utah, but spent most of his life in Cambridge, Massachusetts and New York City as a writer and critic. Primarily interested in American literature and civilization, he wrote books on these subjects, served as editor of the *Saturday Review,* and conducted the monthly Easy Chair column of *Harper's.*

JOHN DEWEY (1859–1952) has been an important influence in American education and philosophy. Born in Vermont, he taught philosophy at various midwestern universities before coming to Columbia University, where he stayed until his retirement. He wrote a number of books in the field of philosophy and education, including *School and Society* (1899), *Reconstruction in Philosophy* (1920), and *Art as Experience* (1934).

RENÉ-JULES DUBOS (1901–   ) is a bacteriologist who was born and educated in France, but moved to the United States to take his Ph.D. at Rutgers University in 1927, and to pursue a scientific career here. He has taught at various universities, has done research in public health, agronomy and other fields, and has been a professor at the Rockefeller Institute since 1957. In addition to considerable writing in his scientific field, he is the author of a biography of Louis Pasteur published in 1950.

BARROWS DUNHAM (1905–   ), for several years a Professor of Philosophy at Temple University, was born in New Jersey and studied at Princeton University. He has written on esthetics and social philosophy, his best-known book being *Man Against Myth.*

ARTHUR S. EDDINGTON (1882–1944), British astrophysicist, was for many years Professor of Astronomy at Cambridge and Director of the Cambridge Observatory. He lectured at many universities and wrote several books on relativity and astronomy, including *The Nature of the Physical World* (1928) and *The Expanding Universe* (1933).

EPICTETUS, the famous Stoic philosopher, was born in Phrygia about 60 A.D. He was one of the learned Greeks whom the Romans took as slaves to teach their children. After being given his freedom, he was banished from Rome and spent the rest of his life in Epirus, in northern Greece. Although he wrote nothing himself, his ideas have been recorded by his pupil, Arrian, in a work called "Enchiridion," or "Handbook."

ROBERT M. ESTRICH (1906–   ), a member of the Department of English at Ohio State University, took his graduate degrees there. A specialist in English philology, he is co-author, with Hans Sperber, of *Three Keys to Language* (1952).

EDWARD MORGAN FORSTER (1879–   ), English novelist, was educated at Cambridge and began to write short stories soon after his graduation. His best novel, *A Passage to India* (1924), was the result of his visits to India with a Cambridge teacher, G. Lowes Dickinson. In addition he has written essays, literary criticism, biography, and a travel book on Alexandria.

MORRIS FREEDMAN (1920–   ) is in the Department of English at the University of New Mexico. Born and educated in New York City, he took his Ph.D. at Columbia University in 1950. He has taught English at the City College of New York and served as an associate editor of *Commentary* magazine. He has written many articles on literature and other subjects and is the author of *Confessions of a Conformist* (1961).

EDMUND FULLER (1914–) is a teacher and critic who is on the faculty of Kent School in Connecticut. He has taught at Columbia University and is the author of many articles and reviews, as well as of a number of books including *George Bernard Shaw* (1950) and *Man in Modern Fiction* (1957).

ETIENNE GILSON (1884–), French student of philosophy, was born and educated in Paris, and has taught at Harvard and the University of Toronto, as well as universities in his own country. He is the author of a number of studies of medieval philosophy.

GRAHAM GREENE (1904–) is an English novelist who occasionally writes essays. He was educated at Oxford, worked as an editor of the London *Times,* served in Africa during World War II, and has been director of a publishing house. A well-known Roman Catholic convert, he writes novels on religious themes as well as suspense stories. His best-known serious novels are *The Power and the Glory* (1940), *The Heart of the Matter* (1948), and *The Quiet American* (1955).

EDITH HAMILTON (1869–), a specialist in Latin and Greek literature, founded the Bryn Mawr School in Baltimore, and was director of it for twenty years. She studied at Bryn Mawr College and at the Universities of Leipzig and Munich. After retiring from teaching she wrote *The Greek Way* (1930) and *The Roman Way* (1932), accurate accounts of ancient civilizations.

S. I. HAYAKAWA (1906–) was born in Canada and studied in Canada and the United States, where he took his Ph.D. at the University of Wisconsin in 1935. Originally a student of linguistics, he became interested in the field of general semantics, and wrote a highly successful popular treatment of the subject, *Language in Action* (1939). He has been editor of *ETC, a Review of General Semantics* since 1943 and has taught at the Illinois Institute of Technology, the University of Chicago, and San Francisco State College.

WILLIAM HAZLITT (1778–1830), English critic and essayist, earned his living by writing theater and art criticism for London periodicals and by giving lectures on art and literature. He had tried studying both theology and painting before he turned to writing. He is best known as a literary critic, and his writing is admired for its clear and vigorous style.

LAFCADIO HEARN (1950–1904) was born of mixed Greek and Irish parentage in Greece, was for a time a journalist in America, but eventually, after wide travels, became attracted by the culture of Japan, and settled down there to marry, become a citizen, and teach at the Imperial University of Tokyo. Hearn, one of the most exotic figures in American literature, transformed himself into a Japanese and is known as the leading interpreter of the culture of Japan.

ROBERT B. HEILMAN (1906–), who is head of the Department of English at the University of Washington, took his graduate degrees at Harvard and has taught English at a number of universities. He is the author and editor of numerous books and articles on English literature, including *America in English Fiction* (1937), *This Great Stage* (1948), and *Magic in the Web* (1956).

GILBERT HIGHET (1906–), born in Scotland, was educated at Glasgow University and Oxford University, in the latter of which he taught classics until 1938. Since that date he has been Professor of Greek and Latin at Columbia University. He is now an American citizen. Among his best-known recent books are *The Art of Teaching*

(1950), *The Classical Tradition* (1949), *Man's Unconquerable Mind* (1954) and *Talents and Geniuses* (1957). He is also well known for his radio book-talks, some of which have been published as *People, Places, and Books* (1953).

SIDNEY HOOK (1902–   ) is chairman of the Department of Philosophy at New York University. Born in New York City, he was a student of Morris R. Cohen and John Dewey. He has written a number of books on contemporary social and philosophical problems, contributes often to periodicals, and is a specialist in Marxism.

THOMAS HENRY HUXLEY (1825–1895) was a biologist by profession, but he is remembered today as a great English stylist and advocate of Darwin's theories in the evolution controversy. Huxley wrote some studies of marine zoology while on a four-year voyage on a naval vessel, and these made him famous. He served as Professor of Natural History at the Royal School of Mines and did much teaching in other institutions while writing on evolution and biology, contributing to periodicals, and taking a leading part in the controversy between scientific and religious interests that had been stirred up by Darwin's theories.

W. H. ITTLESON (1920–   ), Professor of Psychology at Brooklyn College, is co-author of *Perception: A Transactional Approach*. Educated at Columbia and Princeton, he served in the navy and taught psychology at Princeton from 1948 to 1955. He is resident consultant at the Veterans Hospital at East Orange, New Jersey.

WILLIAM JAMES (1842–1910), American psychologist and philosopher, took his M.D. at Harvard, and joined the faculty there as a teacher of physiology in 1872. During periods of illness James did much reading and writing, preparing himself for the more general problems of philosophy and psychology to which he turned after about 1877. He founded the first psychological laboratory in the United States and wrote a series of articles which later became his highly influential book, *The Principles of Psychology* (1890). James often travelled to Europe, was an active writer and lecturer, and made many contributions to psychology, one of the most famous being *The Varieties of Religious Experience* (1902).

WENDELL JOHNSON (1906–   ) is a specialist in speech pathology. He was educated at the University of Iowa and is now Director of the Speech Clinic there. He is an associate editor of *ETC.*, the journal of semantics, and has been president of the Speech and Hearing Association and the Society of General Semantics.

JOSEPH WOOD KRUTCH (1893–   ), American drama critic, essayist, and teacher, was born in Nashville, Tennessee, and educated at the University of Tennessee and Columbia, where he later became Brander Matthews Professor of Drama. He was drama critic of *The Nation* and one of the founders of the Literary Guild. His works include literary studies, nature writing, dramatic criticism, and discussions of moral and cultural problems. They include *Samuel Johnson* (1944), *The Modern Temper* (1929), and *The Measure of Man* (1955).

SUSANNE K. LANGER (1895–   ) studied at Radcliffe and the University of Vienna and taught philosophy at Radcliffe as well as at other colleges and universities before she went to her present post as professor of philosophy at Connecticut College. She is the author of *Philosophy in a New Key* and *Feeling and Form*.

GEORGE HENRY LEWES (1817–1878) was an English critic and philosophical writer, considerably influenced in his work by the French philosopher Auguste Comte. His connection with Marian Evans (George Eliot) was regarded by both partners as a marriage. He was the first editor of the *Fortnightly Review* (1865–66), and the author of a variety of books including the *Biographical History of Philosophy* (1845–

46), *Actors and the Art of Acting* (1875), and *Physical Basis of Mind* (1877). His *Life of Goethe* continues to have more than historical interest.

ROBERT LYND (1879–   ), English journalist, was born in Belfast, Northern Ireland, and came to London as a young man to work on newspapers as a dramatic critic, book reviewer, and writer of features. He joined the *Daily News* in 1908 and remained there as literary editor for the rest of his career. At the same time he wrote regularly for weekly magazines and established himself as a favorite columnist of the reading public. His essays have been collected in a number of volumes, and he has also written *The Art of Letters* (1920), and *Dr. Johnson and Company* (1927).

ARCHIBALD MACLEISH (1892–   ), American poet, went to Yale and Harvard Law Schools. He has served as an editor of *Fortune,* was Librarian of Congress, and worked as an Assistant Secretary of State. He is now Professor of Rhetoric at Harvard. He has written a number of volumes of verse including *Conquistador* (1930), which won the Pulitzer Prize, and he sometimes contributes essays to periodicals.

EVERETT DEAN MARTIN (1880–1941) was a Congregationalist minister and educator who taught social philosophy at the People's Institute of New York, where he became Director in 1922. He has written a number of books on social questions, including *The Meaning of a Liberal Education.*

HERMAN MELVILLE (1819–1891), the American novelist and author of *Moby Dick* (1851), spent his early years at sea working on merchant ships. In 1844 he left the sea, and began to write novels based on his experiences as a sailor. He had little recognition during his lifetime, and had to earn his living as a customs official, but is now considered one of the greatest American writers.

HENRY LOUIS MENCKEN (1880–1956) was a newspaper man whose active crusading in a number of social and literary causes made him a national figure. He wrote memoirs, literary studies, commentary on current affairs, and his own brand of philology, but is most famous for *The American Language,* which is both the best and the most entertaining work of scholarship in its field.

JOHN STUART MILL (1806–1873), English philosopher, economist, and politician, was a remarkable child prodigy who was educated by his father, James Mill. During most of his life he worked as an official of the East India Company. He served in Parliament from 1865 to 1868. Mill, one of the leading thinkers of his time, contributed articles to periodicals on such subjects as economics, social reform, the rights of women, and literature, and wrote a number of works on politics, logic, and economics that were of primary importance. His most popular books today are *On Liberty* (1859) and his *Autobiography* (1873).

C. WRIGHT MILLS (1916–   ) is Professor of Sociology at Columbia University. Educated at the Universities of Texas and Wisconsin, he has served as a consultant on labor and small business matters with the government.

JOHN MILTON (1607–1674) is best known as the great English poet, author of *Paradise Lost* (1667), but he was also a government official and vigorous controversialist on the side of civil liberties. Educated at Cambridge, he traveled in Italy and after the English revolution became an official in Cromwell's government. His *Areopagitica* (1644) is one of the classical defenses of freedom of the press.

EDMUND S. MORGAN (1916–   ), historian, was born in Minneapolis and took his degrees at Harvard. He has been acting dean of the graduate school at Brown University and has been professor of history at Yale since 1955. His research has been in the field of American history and he is author of *The Puritan Family* (1944),

Birth of the Republic (1956), and *The Puritan Dilemma* (1958), and is a member of the editorial board of the *Northeast Quarterly*.

HERBERT J. MULLER (1905–   ) teaches English at Purdue University. He was born in New York State, was educated at Cornell University, and has taught at the University of Istanbul. He is a literary critic who has also written a book on history, *The Uses of the Past* (1952).

ERNEST NAGEL (1901–   ) was born in Czechoslovakia, but came to the United States as a young man. He took degrees at the City College of New York and Columbia University and taught philosophy at both institutions. Among other research activities, he has been a Fellow of the Center for Advanced Study of the Behavioral Sciences. He has been editor of several learned journals and is the author of a number of books, including *Sovereign Reason* (1954) and with J. R. Neuman, *Logic Without Metaphysics* (1957).

JOHN HENRY NEWMAN (1801–1890), English author and churchman, was educated and taught at Oxford and was active as a reformer in the Anglican church until 1846 when he became a convert to Catholicism. He was for a time rector of the Catholic University in Dublin, and was made a Cardinal in 1875. Much of his writing resulted from the controversies in which he became involved, but he also wrote on educational theory, and produced some poetry. His most famous book is his autobiographical *Apologia Pro Vita Sua* (1864).

ERIC NEWTON (1893–   ), British art critic, was educated at the University of Manchester. After serving nearly four years in World War I, he returned to the family business in mosaic designing, from which he resigned in 1922 to devote his full time to art criticism. He has served as art critic of the Manchester *Guardian* and of the London *Sunday Times,* and currently writes for various British periodicals. He is known to American audiences by his frequent articles in the Sunday Art Section of the New York *Times,* and by his lecture tours of the United States and Canada. His best known books are his *Introduction to European Painting* (1949), *In My View* (1950), and *The Meaning of Beauty* (1950).

JOSE ORTEGA Y GASSET (1883–   ) is a leading Spanish philosopher. As a philosophy professor and periodical editor he fought against the Spanish monarchy, but when the Civil War broke out in Spain, he went into exile in France. After living and teaching in South America for many years, he returned to Spain in 1949. His best-known book is *The Revolt of the Masses* (1932).

GEORGE ORWELL (1903–1950) was the pen name of Eric Blair, whose *Animal Farm* (1946) and *Nineteen Eighty-Four* (1949) made him famous as a social prophet and satirist. After graduating from Eton College, Orwell spent five years in Burma as a policeman and then returned to England where, after a period spent doing odd jobs, he began to write articles, reviews, and then books. Always interested in social problems, Orwell at first specialized in clear and straightforward reporting designed to reveal little-known facts about the lives of working people.

PLATO (about 428–346 B.C.), the great Greek philosopher, was a student of Socrates, who is the leading speaker in his *Dialogues*. After Socrates was executed, Plato left Athens to travel, and then returned to found a school called the Academy. He has probably had more influence on thought than any other philosopher, and his work is also admired for its literary quality. *The Republic* is generally considered his greatest work.

NORMAN PODHORETZ (1929–   ), now associate editor of *Commentary,* was born in Brooklyn, New York, and educated at Columbia University and Cambridge University, England. In addition to his editorial work, Mr. Podhoretz has been a frequent reviewer and contributor of critical articles to such magazines as the *New Yorker,* the *New Leader, Midstream,* and others.

JULES HENRI POINCARÉ (1854–1912) was a French mathematician and theorist who taught at the University of Paris beginning in 1881. He made many important contributions to mathematical thought and to theoretical physics.

SIR HERBERT EDWARD READ (1893–　) was born in Yorkshire of a farming family. His writing career began with poetry and fiction about his experiences in World War I. He then turned to literary and art criticism, and held positions as a museum curator and university lecturer. He has written many books on art and literature as well as poetry and novels.

DAVID RIESMAN (1909–　) is professor of social science at the University of Chicago. He studied law at Harvard and taught law at the University of Buffalo and at Yale. He has been teaching social science at Chicago since 1949. He often contributes to periodicals and has written a number of books on the social sciences, the best known being *The Lonely Crowd.*

RAINER MARIA RILKE (1875–1926) was an Austrian poet born in Prague who studied philosophy and art at the Universities of Prague and Munich with only fair success. He published his first book of poems in 1894, traveled in various parts of Europe, served as secretary to the great sculptor, Rodin, and began to write his greatest poetry in the years 1906–1908. He was forced to leave Paris by World War I, and served for a time in the German army. His best-known group of poems is the "Duino Elegies."

CLINTON ROSSITER (1917–　) is professor of Government at Cornell University. He was educated at Cornell and Princeton and is a specialist in the problems of American government.

LIONEL RUBY (1899–　) is chairman of the Department of Philosophy at Roosevelt University. Born and educated in Chicago, he took his degrees at the University of Chicago and practiced law before becoming a faculty member, first at the University of Chicago and then at Indiana University. He has served with government bodies as an arbitrator in labor disputes; his specialty in philosophy, by contrast, is esthetics. He has written *Logic: An Introduction* (1950) and *The Art of Making Sense* (1954).

BERTRAND RUSSELL (1872–　), English essayist, philosopher, and mathematician, has made important contributions to mathematical theory, but is also the foremost living writer of the short essay. He won the Nobel Prize for literature in 1950. His book, *Principia Mathematica* (1913), written in collaboration with A. N. Whitehead, is a leading work in its field.

GEORGE RUXTON (1821–1848) was an English traveller who first came to North America as an officer in a British Army unit stationed in Canada. He soon resigned his commission to travel in the West, as well as in Africa and Mexico. He wrote two travel books, *Adventures in Mexico and the Rocky Mountains* (1847) and *Life in the Far West* (1849).

JEAN-PAUL SARTRE (1905–　), French philosopher, playwright and novelist, taught school and travelled before going to Germany to study with Husserl and Heidegger, two philosophers who influenced his later development. Returning to Paris as a teacher in 1935, he wrote critical essays on American and other literatures, and in 1938 published his novel, *Nausea.* During World War II he served in the army, was taken prisoner, and on his release, served in the resistance forces. His work includes plays such as *The Flies* (1943) and *No Exit* (1944), a philosophic treatise, *Being and Non-Being,* and many separate studies and articles. He was also the founder of the periodical, *Les Temps Modernes* in 1946.

ARTHUR M. SCHLESINGER, JR. (1917–   ) is a historian, born in Columbus, Ohio, whose father was a professor of American history at Harvard. After serving in the Office of War Information during World War II and doing intelligence work, he wrote *The Age of Jackson* (1945), which won the Pulitzer Prize for history. After returning to Harvard as associate professor of history, he took part in the founding of Americans for Democratic Action and wrote *The Vital Center* (1949). His current work is a series of volumes entitled *The Age of Roosevelt.*

ARTHUR SCHOPENHAUER (1788–1860), the great German philosopher, was a student of medicine and philosophy before he undertook his important work, *The World as Will and Idea* (1818), and became a lecturer on philosophy at the University of Berlin. His university career was unsuccessful and he left it to devote himself to his own writing. Generally known as a pessimist, he held that life was essentially painful, but that it could be relieved by such resources as art and music.

DELMORE SCHWARTZ (1914–   ) is an American poet and critic. Born in New York City and educated at various universities, he began literary work by writing translations and editing a little magazine. He has published several books of verse, often writes criticism for periodicals, and has taught English at Harvard.

ROBERT E. SHERWOOD (1896–   ) is a leading American playwright who has won the Pulitzer Prize three times. He was born in New Rochelle, New York, graduated from Harvard, and worked as a drama critic and editor of two periodicals. After the success of his first play, *The Road to Rome* (1927), he became prominent as a dramatist. He has been president of several theatrical organizations and has been active in national politics.

HENRY NASH SMITH (1906–   ), professor of English at the University of California, has taught at a number of universities as a specialist in American literature. Born in Texas, he took his graduate degrees at Harvard. He has edited a number of books relating to James Fenimore Cooper and Mark Twain and is the author of *Virgin Land: The American West as Symbol and Myth* (1950).

HANS SPERBER (1885–   ), professor of German at Ohio State University, was born in Vienna, took his Ph.D. there, and taught at Uppsala and Cologne before coming to this country. He is a specialist in German philology and co-author, with Robert M. Estrich, of *Three Keys to Language* (1952).

W. T. STACE (1886–   ) is an Englishman who is Professor of Philosophy at Princeton. He studied at universities in Scotland and Ireland and worked as a civil servant in Ceylon for twenty-two years. He has written on Greek philosophy and on the theories of morals and esthetics.

ROBERT LOUIS STEVENSON (1850–1894) studied engineering and law at the University of Edinburgh, but turned to writing, beginning as an author of travel books and a contributor of essays to periodicals. After falling in love, Stevenson followed his future wife, an American, to California, married her, and brought her back to England. His health soon forced him to leave England, and after living in various parts of the United States and Honolulu, he moved to Samoa, where he spent the rest of his life. Although he is most famous for such novels as *Treasure Island* (1883), and *The Strange Case of Dr. Jekyll and Mr. Hyde* (1886), he also wrote many fine essays and critical works.

JESSE STUART (1907–   ) was born on a remote Kentucky farm and went to a one-room school. He ran away from home as a boy and worked his way through school and Vanderbilt University. After graduating, he went back to farming, but continued to write poems which were eventually published as the volume *Man With a Bull-Tongue Plow* (1934). After his poems attracted attention, he began to write stories and novels, and his work often appeared in periodicals.

DYLAN THOMAS (1914–1953) was a Welsh poet who was a journalist for a time and worked for the British Broadcasting Corporation. He published his first book of poems at the age of nineteen. After his poetry had attracted wide attention, he began to give readings and lectures in America. In addition to his poetry, Thomas wrote short stories, essays, a movie-script, and a verse play.

HENRY DAVID THOREAU (1817–1862), American essayist and nature writer, is most famous for having left civilization to live alone in a cabin in the woods where he read, wrote, meditated, and provided for himself. He recorded this experience in his most famous book, *Walden* (1854). Thoreau was a great defender of freedom and individualism, and his essay *Civil Disobedience* (1849), has had world-wide influence.

ALEXIS DE TOCQUEVILLE (1805–1859) came to the United States as a young French magistrate to make a study of law enforcement agencies. The result of this trip was his book *Democracy in America* (1835), one of the great books in the social sciences and the most perceptive study of America ever written.

LIONEL TRILLING (1905–   ) is an American critic who teaches English at Columbia University. He was educated at Columbia, has contributed frequently to periodicals, and has written on Matthew Arnold and E. M. Forster. In addition, he is the author of a novel, *The Middle of the Journey* (1947), and some short stories.

MARK TWAIN (1835–1910) is the pen-name of Samuel Langhorne Clemens, the famous American humorist. Born in Missouri, Twain worked as a traveling printer and Mississippi River pilot in his youth, and went west as a prospector when the Civil War made traveling impossible. He began to write feature articles for the Virginia City *Enterprise,* then moved to San Francisco and continued to send correspondence to California papers as he traveled around the Pacific and the Mediterranean. After two years as editor of the Buffalo *Express,* Twain moved in 1871 to Hartford Connecticut, where he wrote most of his famous books, including *Tom Sawyer* (1876), and *Huckleberry Finn* (1884).

ERNEST VAN DEN HAAG (1914–   ) was born in the Hague, studied in France, Germany, and Italy and holds graduate degrees from Iowa and New York Universities. Widely known in America and Europe through his articles in the *Partisan Review,* the *British Journal of Sociology,* the *New Leader,* and similar publications, he is a lecturer at the new school for social research and since 1946 has taught at New York University, where he is an associate professor.

ROBERT WARSHOW (1917–1955), literary critic, graduated in 1937 from the University of Michigan where he edited *Contemporary,* a literary magazine. He wrote numerous reviews for such magazines as the *New Yorker,* the *New Leader, Commentary,* and the *Partisan Review,* and for the latter regularly wrote the "Film Chronicle" for several years. For a number of years prior to his death he was on the staff of *Commentary,* first as managing editor and later as associate editor.

RICHARD WEAVER (1910–   ), now an Associate Professor of English at the University of Chicago, was educated at the University of Kentucky, Vanderbilt, and Louisiana State, from the latter of which he received his Ph.D. in 1943. Prior to joining the faculty of the University of Chicago in 1944, he taught at various universities including Vanderbilt and Louisiana State. His special fields are the theory of rhetoric, American literature and culture, and problems of modern civilization. His best known books are *Ideas Have Consequences* and *The Ethics of Rhetoric*.

EDWARD WESTERMARCK (1862–1939) was a Finnish anthropologist who spent most of his life in England, first to gather material for his important work on marriage, and then as professor of sociology at the University of London, where he taught from 1907 to 1930. He wrote a number of scholarly works on morals, ethics and religion.

PHILIP WHEELWRIGHT (1901–   ), professor of philosophy at the University of California at Riverside, was born in New Jersey. He studied at the Union Theological Seminary and Princeton and has held teaching posts in many universities, including the chairmanship of the Department of Philosophy at Washington Square College. He was co-editor of the journal, *Symposium,* from 1930 to 1933. Among his publications are: *The Way of Philosophy* (1954) and *The Burning Fountain* (1954).

E. B. WHITE (1899–   ) is one of the most famous of contemporary American humorists. Born in Mount Vernon, New York, he graduated from Cornell University and worked as a reporter before joining the staff of *The New Yorker* magazine in the early twenties. He has since been one of the magazine's most active contributors, and his witty essays have been collected in a number of books including *The Second Tree from the Corner* (1953). His re-issue of William Strunk, Jr.'s *The Elements of Style* was extremely successful.

HAROLD WHITEHALL (1905–   ) was born and educated in England, but took his doctorate at the University of Iowa. He has taught linguistics at a number of colleges and universities, and is now chairman of the Department of Linguistics at the University of Indiana. He has written many works on language and served on the boards of some important reference works in the field of English.

W. H. WHYTE (1917–   ) was born in Pennsylvania and educated at Princeton. He was assistant managing editor of *Fortune* magazine and served as a captain in the Marine Corps. His books are *Is Anybody Listening?* (1952) and *The Organization Man* (1956).

TENNESSEE WILLIAMS (1914–   ) was born in Mississippi and took his B.A. at the University of Iowa. His plays, *A Streetcar Named Desire* (1947) and *Cat on a Hot Tin Roof* (1954), won Pulitzer Prizes. One of the most famous contemporary American authors, he has written many plays and two books, *27 Wagonsfull of Cotton* (1946) and *The Roman Spring of Mrs. Stone* (1950).

MARTHA WOLFENSTEIN (1911–   ), psychologist, was educated at Radcliffe, from which she received her A.B. in 1932, and her doctorate in 1939. From 1943 to 1950 she taught and did research at Hunter College and Columbia University. Since 1952 she has been a visiting professor at the College of the City of New York. Her special fields are clinical research and child psychology, culture, and personality.

Index